RESEARCHING THE FAR RIGHT

Researching the Far Right brings together researchers from across the humanities and social sciences to provide much needed discussion about the methodological, ethical, political, personal, practical and professional issues and challenges that arise when researching far right parties, their electoral support, and far right protest movements.

Drawing on original research focussing mainly on Europe and North America over the last 30 years, this volume explores in detail the opportunities and challenges associated with using ethnographic, interview-based, quantitative and online research methods to study the far right. These reflections are set within a wider discussion of the evolution of far right studies from a variety of disciplinary viewpoints within the humanities or the social sciences, tracing the key developments and debates that shape the field today.

This volume will be essential reading for students and scholars with an interest in understanding the many manifestations of the far right and cognate movements today. It also offers insight and reflection that are likely to be valuable for a wider range of students and scholars across the humanities and social sciences who are carrying out work of an ethically, politically, personally, practically and professionally challenging nature.

Stephen D. Ashe is a researcher working on racism, class, the far right, anti-racism and anti-fascism, institutional whiteness and racial inequality in higher education and workplace racism.

Joel Busher is an Associate Professor at the Centre for Trust, Peace and Social Relations (CTPSR), Coventry University, UK.

Graham Macklin is a Postdoctoral Fellow/Assistant Professor at the Center for Research on Extremism (C-REX), University of Oslo, Norway.

Aaron Winter is Senior Lecturer in Criminology at the University of East London, UK.

ROUTLEDGE STUDIES IN FASCISM AND THE FAR RIGHT

Series editors
Nigel Copsey, Teesside University, UK and Graham Macklin, Center for Research on Extremism (C-REX), University of Oslo, Norway.

This new book series focuses upon fascist, far right and right-wing politics primarily within a historical context but also drawing on insights from other disciplinary perspectives. Its scope also includes radical-right populism, cultural manifestations of the far right and points of convergence and exchange with the mainstream and traditional right.

Titles include:

Researching the Far Right
Theory, Method and Practice
Edited by Stephen D. Ashe, Joel Busher, Graham Macklin and Aaron Winter

The Rise of the Dutch New Right
An Intellectual History of the Rightward Shift in Dutch Politics
Merijn Oudenampsen

Anti-fascism in a Global Perspective
Transnational Networks, Exile Communities and Radical Internationalism
Edited by Kasper Braskén, Nigel Copsey and David Featherstone

British Fascism After the Holocaust
From the Birth of Denial to the Notting Hill Riots 1939–1958
Joe Mulhall

Fascism, Nazism and the Holocaust
Challenging Histories
Dan Stone

France's Purveyors of Hatred
Aspects of the French Extreme Right and its Influence, 1918–1945
Richard Griffiths

For more information about this series, please visit: www.routledge.com/Routledge-Studies-in-Fascism-and-the-Far-Right/book-series/FFR

RESEARCHING THE FAR RIGHT

Theory, Method and Practice

Edited by Stephen D. Ashe, Joel Busher,
Graham Macklin and Aaron Winter

Routledge
Taylor & Francis Group

LONDON AND NEW YORK

First published 2021
by Routledge
2 Park Square, Milton Park, Abingdon, Oxon OX14 4RN

and by Routledge
52 Vanderbilt Avenue, New York, NY 10017

Routledge is an imprint of the Taylor & Francis Group, an informa business

© 2021 selection and editorial matter, Stephen D. Ashe, Joel Busher, Graham Macklin and Aaron Winter; individual chapters, the contributors

British Library Cataloguing in Publication Data
A catalogue record for this book is available from the British Library

Library of Congress Cataloging-in-Publication Data
Names: Ashe, Stephen, editor. | Busher, Joel, editor. | Macklin, Graham, editor. | Winter, Aaron, editor.
Title: Researching the far right : theory, method and practice / edited by Stephen Ashe, Joel Busher, Graham Macklin, Aaron Winter.
Description: Abingdon, Oxon ; New York, NY : Routledge, 2020. | Series: Fascism and the far right | Includes bibliographical references and index.
Identifiers: LCCN 2020005127 (print) | LCCN 2020005128 (ebook) | ISBN 9781138219335 (hardback) | ISBN 9781138219342 (paperback) | ISBN 9781315304670 (ebook)
Subjects: LCSH: Right wing extremists–Research–Methodology. | Radicalism–Research–Methodology. | Social movements–Research– Methodology.
Classification: LCC HN49.R33 R473 2020 (print) | LCC HN49.R33 (ebook) | DDC 303.48/4–dc23
LC record available at https://lccn.loc.gov/2020005127
LC ebook record available at https://lccn.loc.gov/2020005128

ISBN: 9781138219335 (hbk)
ISBN: 9781138219342 (pbk)
ISBN: 9781315304670 (ebk)

Typeset in Bembo
by Taylor & Francis Books

CONTENTS

ILLUSTRATIONS

Figures

Tables

CONTRIBUTORS

Stephen D. Ashe is a researcher working on racism, class, the far right, anti-racism and anti-fascism, institutional whiteness and racial inequality in higher education and workplace racism. His recent publications include *Reframing the 'Left Behind': Race and Class in Post-Brexit Oldham* (co-authored with James Rhodes and Sivamohan Valluvan) and *Racism Ruins Lives: An Analysis of the 2016–2017 Trade Union Congress Racism at Work Survey* (co-authored with Magda Borkowska and James Nazroo). Stephen is currently working towards completing his monograph, *The Rise and Fall of the British National Party: A Sociological Perspective*, for the Routledge Studies in Fascism and the Far Right Series. He has published articles in *Ethnic and Racial Studies, Race & Class* and *Discover Society*.

Chip Berlet juggles being a journalist, scholarly researcher, and progressive movement activist. In the mid-1970s Berlet was recruited into the Public Eye Network, which was founded by a group of progressive investigative reporters, licensed private investigators, paralegal investigators, attorneys, and activists who shared information about political repression and right-wing movements. The network helped launch the *Public Eye Magazine*. Moving to Chicago in 1978 he and his spouse bought a house in a predominantly White working-class southwest-side neighborhood where a neonazi alliance with the Ku Klux Klan was fighting racial integration. They spent ten years working with the Southwest Community Congress battling White supremacist violence. In Chicago, Berlet was hired to work as a paralegal investigator on lawsuits against illegal government spying. From there he was hired in 1981 by professor Jean V. Hardisty as researcher at what became Political Research Associates where he worked for the next 30 years. PRA now publishes the *Public Eye Magazine*.

Kathleen Blee is Distinguished Professor of Sociology at the University of Pittsburgh, USA. She has published widely on US white supremacism, including the books *Understanding Racist Activism* (Routledge, 2017), *Inside Organized Racism* (2002); *Women of the Klan* (1991), and *Women of the Right*, coedited with Sandra Deutsch (2012).

Joel Busher is an Associate Professor at the Centre for Trust, Peace and Social Relations (CTPSR), Coventry University, UK. His primary research interests are in the social ecology of political violence; far right and anti-minority politics; and the enactment of counter-terrorism policy and its societal impacts. He has published extensively on these topics, and his book, *The Making of Anti-Muslim Protest: Grassroots Activism in the English Defence League* (Routledge), was awarded the British Sociological Association's Philip Abrams Memorial Prize. He is currently an associate editor at *Behavioral Sciences of Terrorism and Political Aggression*; a member of the editorial board of *Research in Social Movements, Conflicts and Change*; and a member of the editorial board for the McGill-Queen's University Press book series, 'Power, Protest and Resistance'.

Tereza Capelos is Senior Lecturer in Political Psychology at the University of Birmingham, UK and incoming Director of the Institute for Conflict Cooperation and Security (ICCS). Her research examines the psychological micro-foundations of political judgement and behaviour, focusing particularly on political emotions and motivational processes during international crises and tensions. Tereza is co-Convener of the Political Psychology Standing Group of the European Consortium for Political Research (ECPR), Co-Editor for the Palgrave Series in Political Psychology, past vice president of the International Society of Political Psychology (ISPP) and founder of the ISPP Summer Academy.

Nigel Copsey is Professor of Modern History at Teesside University, UK. His primary areas of research interest are fascism, neo-fascism and anti-fascism. Recent publications on fascism include *Cultures of Post-War British Fascism* (2015) (co-edited with John Richardson) and *'Tomorrow Belongs to Us': The British Far Right since 1967* (2018) (co-edited with Matthew Worley). He co-edits the Routledge Studies in Fascism and the Far Right series with Graham Macklin.

Guido Dijkstra received his bachelor degrees in Political Science and History at VU University Amsterdam and his master's degree in Political Science at the University of Amsterdam, the Netherlands. He is currently employed as an information specialist at the Christian University of Applied Sciences in Ede, the Netherlands. In this role he provides information services supporting research and education for both staff and students. He previously worked as a junior lecturer in research methodology at VU University Amsterdam. His primary research interests lie in the field of political sociology, political history and research methodology.

Betty A. Dobratz is Professor of Sociology at Iowa State University, USA. She received her PhD from the University of Wisconsin. She is first author of *White*

Power, White Pride! The White Separatist Movement in the U.S. and *Power, Politics, and Society* as well as numerous journal articles. Her research publications have focused on social inequality and political sociology including white power groups, Greek and American politics, and political graffiti in various nations. She has co-edited the *Journal of Political and Military Sociology, Research in Political Sociology*, and *The Sociological Quarterly*.

Katrine Fangen is a professor in sociology at the Department of Sociology and Human Geography, University of Oslo, Norway. Her magister thesis on anarchists, communists and neo-Nazis in Eastern Germany was based on half a year of fieldwork during the time of the reunification of the two German states (in 1990). Her prize awarded doctoral (Dr. Polit.)-thesis was based on fieldwork among Norwegian neo-Nazis (1993–1994), including life-story interviews and analyses of fanzines and other paraphernalia. Following her PhD she has worked as a migration researcher at FAFO social research institute, and thereafter as a post doc at the University of Oslo with a project on identity formations, citizenship and coping strategies among Norwegian-Somalis. Then she initiated and coordinated a 3-year EU funded international research project analysing the multidimensional processes of inclusion and exclusion among young adult immigrants and descendants in seven European countries. During recent years, her main research topics have been right-wing populism, anti-Islamism, and nationalism. Fangen has been the sole author and co-editor of several books in methodology, and has published a range of books and articles in the fields of far right studies, migration studies and youth research.

Vasiliki Georgiadou is a Professor of Political Science at the Department of Political Science and History, Panteion University, Greece. She studied Political Science in Athens and in Münster, Germany and she holds her PhD from the University of Münster. Her research interests focus on far right parties, populism, radicalism and political extremism. She is the director of the Centre for Political Research at the Panteion University and a member of the Editorial Board of *Science and Society: Journal of Political and Moral Theory*. She was Principal Investigator of the research programme "Examining xenophobia in Greece during the economic crisis: A computational perspective" (European Economic Area Financial Mechanism/EEA-Grants) (2015–2017). She is author (in German) of *Non-capitalist Aspects of Development in Greece in the 19th Century* (1991) and (in Greek) of *The Far Right and the Consequences of Consensus: Denmark, Norway, Netherlands, Switzerland, Austria, Germany* (Kastaniotis, 2008). Her articles appear, among others, in *Electoral Studies, Party Politics, International Journal of Politics, Culture and Society, Revue des Sciences Sociales, Zeitschrift für Politikwissenschaft, The Greek Journal of Political Science*.

Annett Graefe-Geusch is a PhD candidate in International Education at New York University (NYU), USA, and is currently writing her dissertation on diversity management in Berlin's ethics instruction focusing specifically on the treatment of minority religions from a teachers' perspective. Her interests include the intersections of migration, diversity and education, and school change driven by demographic variation.

Peter Hervik is a media anthropologist and migration studies scholar, who currently works as a Research Professor at the new Free University in Copenhagen, Denmark. He is the head of the team research project SERR (Study of Experiences and Reactions to Racialization in Denmark) (2015–2020). Originally trained at the University of Copenhagen, he also worked at the University of Oslo, Norway, Malmö University, Sweden, Aalborg University, Denmark and Hitotsubashi University, Japan. After anthropological dissertation fieldwork among the Yucatec Maya in Mexico, in the mid-1990s Hervik began studying the media coverage and popular understandings of ethnic and religious issues in Denmark and the other Nordic countries. Thus, his publication *The Annoying Difference. The Emergence of Danish Neonationalism, Neoracism, and Populism in the Post-1989 World.* (2011) follows the evolvement of neo-nationalism, neo-racism, the far right, populism and more in Denmark in a 20-year span. Other publications include: *Mayan Lives Within and Beyond Boundaries. Social Categories and Lived Identity in Yucatan* (1999); *Mediernes muslimer.* [Muslims of the Media] (2002); *Can Behaviour Be Controlled? Women in Post-Revolutionary Egypt* (with Mette Toft Nielsen) (2017); *Racialization, Racism and anti-Racism in the Nordic Countries* (editor). (2019).

Anders Ravik Jupskås is a senior researcher and deputy director at the Center for Research on Extremism (C-REX) at the University of Oslo, Norway. His research focuses on right-wing extremism, populism, political mobilization. He is currently part of a project on Far Right Politics Online and Societal Resilience (FREXO). He has published in *Scandinavian Political Studies, Swiss Political Science Review,* and authored several book chapters in recently published edited volumes on radical right parties in Europe.

Catarina Kinnvall is Professor at the Department of Political Science, Lund University, Sweden. She is the current Editor-in-Chief of the journal *Political Psychology* and the former vice president of the *International Society of Political Psychology,* as well as the co-editor for the Palgrave Series in Political Psychology. Her research interests involve political psychology, international relations and critical security studies, with a particular focus on gender, migration, radicalization and populism in Europe and South Asia.

Bert Klandermans is Professor in Applied Social Psychology at the Vrije Universiteit, Amsterdam, the Netherlands. He has published extensively on the social psychology of protest and social movement participation. He is the author of the now classic *Social Psychology of Protest* (1997). He is the editor and co-author (with Suzanne Staggenborg) of *Methods of Social Movement Research* (2002) and (with Nonna Mayer) of *Extreme Right Activists in Europe* (Routledge, 2006). With Conny Roggeband he edited the *Handbook of Social Movements Across Disciplines* (2007.

He is co-editor of the *Encyclopedia of Social Movements* and of *The Future of Social Movement Research Dynamics, Mechanisms, and Processes* (2013). He was the PI of large-scale comparative studies of contentious political action. In 2009 he received a royal decoration for his efforts to link science and society. In 2013 he received the Harold Lasswell Award of the International Society of Political Psychology for his lifelong contribution to political psychology. In 2014 he received the John D. McCarthy Award from Notre Dame University for his contribution to the study of social movements and collective action."

Ofra Klein is a PhD researcher at the European University Institute in Florence, Italy. She holds degrees in Sociology, Political Science, and Digital Humanities. She previously worked as a research assistant at VU University Amsterdam and the Berkman Klein Center for Internet and Society at Harvard University. Her research interests are in the field of online political mobilization.

Mehr Latif is a Post-doctoral Associate at the University of Pittsburgh, USA. She is currently contributing to research on white supremacist groups within the United States, including "Why White Supremacist Women Become Disillusioned, and Why They Leave," co-authored with Kathleen Blee, Matthew DeMichele, Pete Simi, and Shayna Alexander (*Sociological Quarterly*, 2019); "How Emotional Dynamics Maintain and Destroy White Supremacist Groups," coauthored with Kathleen Blee, Matthew DeMichele, and Pete Simi (*Humanities & Society*, 2018); and "Do White Supremacist Women Adopt Movement Archetypes of Mother, Whore, and Fighter?" coauthored with Kathleen Blee, Matthew DeMichele, and Pete Simi (*Studies in Conflict and Terrorism*, forthcoming).

Graham Macklin is a Postdoctoral Fellow/Assistant Professor at the Center for Research on Extremism (C-REX), University of Oslo, Norway. He has published extensively on extreme right-wing and anti-minority politics in Britain in both the inter-war and post-war periods. Major publications include *Very Deeply Dyed in the Black: Sir Oswald Mosley and the Resurrection of British Fascism after 1945* (2007) and *Failed Führers: A History of Britain's Extreme Right* (2020). His current work focusses on transnational right-wing networks, extreme right-wing terrorism and political violence. He co-edits the *Patterns of Prejudice, Fascism* and, with Nigel Copsey, the Routledge Studies in Fascism and the Far Right book series.

John Douglas Macready is a Professor of Philosophy at Collin College in Plano, TX, USA. His work focuses on critical issues in social and political philosophy with specific attention paid to the philosophy of human rights. He is the author of *Hannah Arendt and the Fragility of Human Dignity* (2018).

Geoff Manzi is a Professor of Philosophy and an Honors Faculty Fellow at Richland College in Dallas, TX, USA. He has previously taught at Loyola Marymount University, the University of Dallas, and North Lake College.

Nonna Mayer is Research Professor Emerita at CNRS affiliated to the Centre for European Studies and Comparative Politics of Sciences Po. She chaired the French Political Science Association from 2005 to 2016 and has been a member of the National Consultative Commission for Human Rights since 2015. Her main research topics are right-wing extremism, electoral behaviour, racism and anti-Semitism. Recent publications include: "The impact of gender on the Marine Le Pen vote," *Revue française de science politique, 67(6)*, 2017 (with A. Amengay and A. Durovic); "The Radical Right in France", in J. Rydgren (ed.), *The Oxford Handbook of the Radical Right*, (2018); "The political impact of social insecurity in France," *Partecipazione e conflitto*, 11(3), 2019; "The 'losers of automation': A reservoir of votes for the radical right?", *Research & Politics, 6(1)*, 2019 (with Z.J. Im, B. Palier, J. Rovny).

Pasko Kisić Merino holds an MSc degree in Global Studies from Lund University, Sweden, and his research is focused on the relationship between far-right mobilisation and discourses, social media massification, and radicalisation processes. He is the Editorial Manager for the journal *Political Psychology*, and has performed research on security, strategic planning, and socioeconomic development for Lund University, the UNDP, the United Nations Evaluation Group (UNEG), UNICEF, governmental agencies in Peru, as well as development organisations in Peru and Sweden.

Cynthia Miller-Idriss is Professor of Education and Sociology and Director of Research in the Center for University Excellence (CUE) at the American University in Washington, DC, USA, where she leads the Polarization and Extremism Research and Intervention Lab (PERIL). Dr. Miller-Idriss has spent over two decades researching far right youth culture and symbols, most recently through a focus on aesthetic mainstreaming and style. Her most recent books are *The Extreme Gone Mainstream: Commercialization and Far Right Youth Culture in Germany* (Princeton University Press, 2018) and *Hate in the Homeland: The New Spaces and Places of Far Right Extremism* (under contract). In addition to her academic work, Dr. Miller-Idriss writes frequently for mainstream audiences and appears regularly in the media as an expert source and political commentator.

Aurelien Mondon is a Senior Lecturer in politics at the University of Bath, UK. His research focuses predominantly on the impact of racism and populism on liberal democracies and the mainstreaming of far right politics through elite discourse. His first book, *The Mainstreaming of the Extreme Right in France and Australia: A Populist Hegemony?*, was published in 2013 and he recently co-edited *After Charlie Hebdo: Terror, Racism and Free Speech* published with Zed. His latest book, *Reactionary Democracy: How Racism and the Populist Far Right Became Mainstream*, co-written with Aaron Winter, was published by Verso in 2020.

Jasper Muis is employed as assistant professor at the Sociology Department of the VU University Amsterdam, the Netherlands. He graduated in Sociology at the

Radboud University Nijmegen, the Netherlands. His doctoral dissertation (cum laude) about the rise of right-wing populism in the Netherlands received the Research Prize of the Praemium Erasmianum Foundation. His primary research interests include the far right, protest behaviour, and research methodology.

Andreas Önnerfors is Associate Professor in the History of Sciences and Ideas at the University of Gothenburg, Sweden. Specializing in the intellectual history of the eighteenth-century, he has published widely on trans-cultural relations, press history and organized sociability, in particular freemasonry and other fraternal orders. He has recently developed a new research field in the study of the European New Right where he has focused on radicalization, in particular linguistic framings and the rela tionship between online- and offline-mobilization in Germany. Önnerfors frequently features in Swedish and European press and regularly writes columns for the Centre for Analysis of the Radical Right (UK). Since 2016, he has been a member of a European research group devoted to the study of conspiracy theories. Recent publications include *Freemasonry – A Very Short Introduction* (2017) and *Expressions of Radicalization: Global Politics, Processes and Practices*, together with Kristian Steiner (2018).

Barbara Perry is a Professor in the Faculty of Social Science and Humanities at Ontario Tech University, and the Director of the Centre on Hate, Bias and Extremism. She has written extensively on social justice generally, and hate crime specifically. She has also published in the area of Native American victimization and social control, including one book entitled *The Silent Victims: Native American Victims of Hate Crime*, and *Policing Race and Place in Indian Country: Over- and Under-enforcement*. She was the General Editor of a five volume set on hate crime (Praeger), and editor of *Volume 3: Victims of Hate Crime* of that set. Dr. Perry continues to work in the area of hate crime, and has made substantial contributions to the limited scholarship on hate crime in Canada, including work on anti-Muslim violence, hate crime against LGBTQ communities, the community impacts of hate crime, and right-wing extremism in Canada. She is regularly called upon by policy makers, practitioners, and local, national and international media as an expert on hate crime and right-wing extremism.

Vidhya Ramalingam has focused much of the past decade working to respond to far right extremism and terrorism. In 2010, she carried out fieldwork with far right movements in Sweden. Following the 22nd July 2011 attacks in Norway, she led the European Union's first inter-governmental initiative on far-right extremism, initiated by the Governments of Sweden, Norway, Denmark, Finland, and the Netherlands, and launched by the EU Commissioner for Home Affairs. She worked with hundreds of practitioners in 10 European countries to design policy, initiate projects, and build capacity to respond to far-right extremism. In 2015, Vidhya co-founded Moonshot CVE, an organisation that uses technology to disrupt and counter violent extremism globally. She directs overall strategy and oversees campaigns, software development, and digital projects in over 25 countries. She has held various roles including Commissioning Panellist for the UK Security and Intelligence agencies and Economic and

Social Research Council (ESRC), Research Associate at the School of Anthropology at the University of Oxford, and Board Member of Life After Hate. She was previously Senior Fellow on Far Right Extremism at the Institute for Strategic Dialogue (ISD), and Senior Research Fellow on Migration & Communities at the Institute for Public Policy Research (IPPR).

Jacob Aasland Ravndal is a Postdoctoral Fellow at the Center for Research on Extremism (C-REX) at the University of Oslo, Norway. Ravndal has published extensively on right-wing terrorism and militancy in Western Europe, with a particular focus on the Nordic countries. He has also developed the RTV dataset – an open access dataset documenting right-wing terrorism and violence in Western Europe since 1990. Ravndal's current research interests include the relationship between left- and right-wing militancy, terrorist tactics, and how ideas, emotions and relations shape violent extremist behaviour.

Peita L. Richards is a doctoral candidate at the Australian Graduate School of Policing and Security, Charles Sturt University, Australia. Her PhD portfolio applies social psychological theory to the understanding of online behaviours of the far right, predominantly in the United States. Peita holds a Bachelors degree in political science, history and psychological science, with a Masters in International Relations (Hons) majoring in international law and security. She is the recipient of the Australian Graduate Research Training Program scholarship for Higher Degree Research. Peita has previously received bursaries for new scholars in digital humanities, undergraduate and postgraduate travel scholarships. Peita's expertise focuses on the impact of social behaviour on policy, with an interest in online mediums in facilitating participation, the normalization of the far right, and factors influencing the intelligence and national security policy spheres.

Lamprini Rori is a Lecturer in Politics at the University of Exeter, UK. She has previously been a Leventis Fellow in Modern Greek Studies at Oxford University and a Marie Curie (Intra-European) Fellow at Bournemouth University. She holds a PhD in Political Science from Université Paris I, Panthéon-Sorbonne. Her thesis examined how the professionalization of political communication affected the organizational change of socialist parties in Europe and most particularly in France and Greece from mid-1970s to 2012. She is currently the Principal Investigator of the LSE grant 'Low-intensity violence in crisis-ridden Greece. Evidence from the radical right and the radical left', Early Career Fellow at the British School at Athens, Research Associate at SEESOX, and Media Officer of the Greek Politics Specialist Group of the PSA. Her research focuses on the far-right in Europe, radicalization, radicalism and political violence, the role of emotions in political behaviour, mass media effects, and the dynamics of political networks in social media. She has worked for research projects on political behaviour in crisis-ridden Greece and the Greek diaspora. Her publications appear, among others, in *West European Politics, Electoral Studies, Party Politics, Pôle Sud.*

Costas Roumanias is an assistant professor in Economics and Politics at the Department of International and European Studies, Athens University of Economics and Business, Greece. He holds a DPhil in Economics from the University of Oxford. His research interests involve areas of political economy, particularly games and empirics of elections, the far right and political extremism, applied auction theory and behavioral economics.

Ryan Scrivens is an Assistant Professor in the School of Criminal Justice at Michigan State University, USA. He is also a Research Fellow at the VOX-Pol Network of Excellence and a Research Associate at the International CyberCrime Research Centre at Simon Fraser University. Ryan conducts problem-oriented interdisciplinary research, with a focus on the local, national, and international threat of terrorism, violent extremism, and hatred as it evolves on- and offline. His primary research interests include terrorists' and extremists' use of the Internet, right-wing terrorism and extremism, combating violent extremism, hate crime, and computational social science. His research has been funded by Public Safety Canada, the Canadian Network for Research on Terrorism, Security and Society, and VOX-Pol. He has presented his findings before the Swedish Defence Research Agency in Stockholm, the Centre of Excellence for National Security in Singapore, and the United Nations in New York City and Vienna. His work has also been featured in over 100 new stories (television, radio, print) and covered by an array of national and international media sources. Ryan earned a PhD in criminology from Simon Fraser University in 2017.

Amy Fisher Smith is a licensed clinical psychologist and chair of the Department of Psychology at the University of Dallas. She has served on the executive committee of Division 24 of the American Psychological Association, *The Society for Theoretical and Philosophical Psychology* for more than a decade in various capacities, and currently serves on the editorial board of the Division 32 journal, *The Humanistic Psychologist.* Her research interests include Holocaust and Genocide studies and the psychology of terrorism and conflict, specifically deradicalization from extremist groups.

Charles R. Sullivan is Associate Professor of History at the University of Dallas, USA, and former chair of its Department of History. He is also Associate Professor in the Department of Human and Social Sciences and Director of Braniff Graduate School's Master in Leadership program. His most recent work has examined challenges in contemporary Holocaust education, the political philosophy of anti-totalitarianism in mid-twentieth-century Europe, the dynamics of Alt-Right movements in the Russian Federation, and processes of de-radicalization from far-right extremism.

John W.P. Veugelers is Assistant Professor of Sociology at the University of Toronto, Canada. A political sociologist, he has written widely on the far right, immigration politics, social movements, and voluntary associations in Canada,

France, and Italy. A recipient of awards for outstanding teaching at the University of Toronto, he has been a visiting professor at universities in Europe, Asia, and Africa, and a visiting fellow at the Camargo Foundation in Cassis, France. His articles have appeared in a range of scholarly journals (including *Ethnic and Racial Studies, International Sociology, British Journal of Sociology, Comparative European Politics, European Journal of Political Research, Current Sociology, Acta Sociologica*, and *West European Politics*) and he is the author of *Empire's Legacy: Roots of a Far-Right Affinity in Contemporary France* (2020).

Lisa K. Waldner is a Professor of Sociology and Associate Dean for the College of Arts and Sciences at the University of St. Thomas in St. Paul, Minnesota, USA. She received her PhD from Iowa State University. She has published on a variety of topics including intimate partner violence, sexual coercion, antigay hate crimes, political graffiti, and right-wing extremism. With Betty Dobratz she co-edited *The Sociological Quarterly* from 2012–2016; with both Betty Dobratz and Timothy Buzzell, she co-edited five volumes of *Research in Political Sociology* and authored *Power, Politics and Society,* second edition (2019).

Aaron Winter is Senior Lecturer in Criminology at the University of East London, UK. His research is on the far right, with a focus on racism, violence and mainstreaming. He is co-editor of *Discourses and Practices of Terrorism: Interrogating Terror* (Routledge 2010), *Reflectivity in Criminological Research: Experiences with the Powerful and Powerless* (2014) and *Historical Perspectives on Organised Crime and Terrorism* (Routledge 2018), and co-author with Aurelien Mondon, of *Reactionary Democracy: How Racism and the Populist Far Right Became Mainstream* (Verso 2020).

Ruth Wodak is Emerita Distinguished Professor of Discourse Analysis at Lancaster University, UK and of Applied Linguistics at Vienna University, Austria. She completed her PhD in 1974 and her habilitation in 1980, both at Vienna University. She has been the recipient of many awards, including the Wittgenstein Award for Elite Scholars (1996), the Grand Decoration of Honor in Silver for Services to the Republic of Austria (2011) and a Lifetime Achievement Award from the Austrian Ministry of Women (2018). She is a member of Academia Europaea and the British Academy of Social Sciences. Her research interests include critical discourse studies, language and politics (populism studies), identity politics and the politics of the past, gender studies, migration studies and the study of racism and antisemitism. Recent book publications include *Europe at the Crossroads* (2019, with P Bevelander); *The Handbook of Language and Politics* (2018, with B Forchtner); and *Politics of Fear. What Right-wing Populist Discourses Mean* (2015).

INTRODUCTION

Researching the far right

In recent years, concerns have intensified about the growing influence of the far right, whether at the ballot box or in terms of its wider cultural influence and the attendant threats to peace, societal cohesion and security. Europe has seen electoral gains for Jobbik and Fidesz in Hungary, Lega in Italy (whose leader, Matteo Salvini had served as both Italian Deputy Prime Minister of Italy and Minister of the Interior), Alternative für Deutschland in Germany, the National Rally (previously the Front National) in France, and Freiheitliche Partei Österreichs (FPÖ), founded by a former SS officer, in Austria, albeit some of these 'successes' have proved short-lived. In the USA, Donald Trump's candidacy and presidency has been characterized by dog whistling to the far right through anti-Muslim and anti-Mexican racist rhetoric, and a repeated failure to condemn hate speech and the actions of white nationalists, even attracting endorsements from former Klansman David Duke and Alt-Right figurehead Richard Spencer. Though the chapters in this volume are largely focused on Europe and North America it would be remiss not to highlight that in India, Hindu Nationalists further consolidated their power in 2019 as Narendra Damodardas Modi won a second term as president with a significantly larger majority; and far right nationalism has also made inroads in Latin America, most notably with the 2019 election of Jair Messias Bolsonaro as President of Brazil.

Meanwhile, away from the ballot box, far right inspired violence, aggression and intimidation has become an all too familiar feature of contemporary news bulletins. Less than a year after Trump became President, the 'Unite the Right Rally' in Charlottesville, Virginia, saw Neo-Nazi, Neo-Confederate, Identitarian and Klux Klan groups chant racist and antisemitic slogans while holding a torch light march which resulted in the death of Heather Heyer, an anti-fascist/anti-racist activist. Since Charlottesville, terrorist and other mass casualty attacks on racial and ethnic groups have occurred with increasing frequency. This has included Pittsburgh, Pennsylvania, on 28 October 2018, where eleven people were killed when a gunman opened fire on worshippers in the Tree of Life Synagogue; Christchurch, New Zealand, on 15 March 2019, where 51 people were killed and many more were wounded in attacks on the Al Noor Mosque and the Linwood Islamic Centre; and El Paso, on 3 August 2019, where 22 people were killed by a gunman targeting people who they identified as Hispanic. Such events appear to have confirmed the worst fears of many analysts (e.g. Ravndal, 2019) about the threat posed by global far right networks.

Not surprisingly, such developments have contributed to the emergence of a see-mingly 'insatiable demand' (Bale, 2012) from the public, the media, policy makers, and activists, for information and insight into the various forms of far right politics observable today. Academics and other researchers have been quick to respond to that demand. Much of this growing scholarship sets out to better understand the phenomenon in terms of the movements and parties themselves, and the ebb and flow of the fortunes of these political and social formations, whether from 'supply' or 'demand' side perspectives (see Part I). Today, there is a vast output of studies that examine far right social movements, political parties, voters, supporters, activists, 'scenes', 'milieus' and far right subcultural dynamics, not to mention far right vio-lence and terrorism. Alongside this, and sometimes intersecting with it, there has also emerged an important body of research that seeks to document and analyze the impacts of far right political formations and their ideas both on the various groups targeted by the far right and, more broadly, the threat it poses to the liberal post-war order, democracy, civil society and establishment parties.

Yet while there has been a substantial upsurge in empirical and theoretical research on the far right, there has been relatively little in the way of detailed dis-cussion about the *practice* of researching the far right: that is, about the methodo-logical, ethical, political, personal, practical and professional issues and challenges that arise from conducting research in this area. That is not of course to say that there has been a complete absence of such discussion. Researchers working on the far right have for a long time drawn on and contributed to the rich literature on doing research on 'sensitive topics' (Lee, 1993), on different types of 'unloved' groups (Fielding, 1993) and on the 'enemy' (Aho, 1994), as well as reflexive criminological research on 'criminals' and the 'the criminalized' (Lumsden and Winter, 2014). In 2007, Kathleen Blee assembled a range of papers for a special issue of the *Journal of Contemporary Ethnography* about conducting ethnographic research on the far right, a research strategy which at that time was considerably less widely used than it is today. The papers in that special issue not only inspired and provided valuable guidance for a new generation of ethnographic research on the far right, but also drew greater scholarly attention to issues such as the internal dynamics of far right organizations, the agency and motivations of far right activists, and the emotionality, culture and suspicion of outsiders that permeate such movements. The exploration of these issues has greatly enriched research on the far right during the last decade or so, generating valuable new insights about, for example, how far right organizations recruit members and generate support among the general public. More recently, Emanuele Toscano's (2019) edited collection on

Researching Far Right Movements has brought together the experiences and insights of scholars who have worked on far right and conservative movements in a number of countries, including Japan, Thailand, England, France, Italy, the United States and Turkey, using qualitative 'close-range' research methodologies to get 'up close' to the people who comprise these movements. The contributions to that volume encompass a range of issues such as researcher reflexivity and the ethical and political dilemmas that emerge when conducting research with those who assert ideas and values which differ from those of the researcher.

As the field expands however, and as the far right attracts the attention of scholars with an increasingly diverse range of disciplinary and methodological backgrounds, it is important that these conversations keep pace with and encompass the growing range of research perspectives and experiences within this field. This is partly about keeping pace with changes occurring within the far right itself, a point explored by several of the contributions to this volume. It is partly about helping researchers to identify and deploy the research strategies that will enable them to address the questions that they seek to answer, and about helping researchers working within different disciplinary or methodological traditions to engage in productive dialogue rather than, as sometimes happens, talking past one another. It is also about thinking seriously about and reflecting on issues related to researcher well-being and safety. There can be little doubt that researching the far right and similar groups can take an emotional toll on the researcher. As one recent report noted in relation to online research on the far right:

> The very nature of the work is itself a cognitive burden. Online extremism and media manipulation researchers spend their days sifting through hate-speech-ridden Reddit threads, dehumanizing YouTube videos, and toxic chat rooms where death threats and active harassment campaigns are par for the course. The deluge of hate and extremist content takes a toll on their mental health and leaves some with PTSD-like symptoms, much like those experienced by content moderators at Facebook, they say.
>
> *(Martineau, 2019)*

Researchers of the far right also often find themselves grappling, struggling even, with questions about whether their own research practices might even be fueling the very problems that they set out to understand and address. As James Aho reflected of his own research in the wake of the Oklahoma terrorist attack in April 1995, which killed 168 people:

> After the bombing, I began to have misgivings about my research, feeling that I was profiting from the misfortunes of others: g-men, the radicals themselves, and their wives and children. I came to believe that in a perverse way my fascination with political violence was adding to the seeming voracious appetite for it in the public. In other words, I felt like a hypocrite.
>
> *(Aho, 2016: 3)*

The aim of this volume then is to further widen and deepen these conversations about the politics, practice and ethics of researching the far right, bringing together the experiences and insights of scholars rooted in a range of different disciplinary and methodological traditions, and working across many different manifestations of the far right in a variety of national and transnational contexts.

The volume emerged from a series of conversations between the editors prior to sending out a call for papers in 2016. The bulk of the chapters presented are drawn from that call for papers, which attracted contributions from scholars working across several disciplines and exploring a broad range of methodological and ethical dilemmas facing researchers working at the cutting edge of research on far right politics in all of its various forms. The papers derived from the call were supplemented with invited contributions from prominent scholars in this field of study, who were asked to provide 'disciplinary overviews'. These set out how scholarship on the far right in their respective disciplines has developed and the ways in which scholars within their disciplines have sought to theorize and research the far right (see Part I). Each contributor was asked to reflect upon what they consider some of the most pressing theoretical and methodological problems that they have encountered whilst researching in the field. The result, we hope, will help to stimulate an ongoing dialogue between scholars from across a range of disciplines, methodological approaches and theoretical viewpoints as a means of advancing our collective research endeavour. We also hope that the volume will not only serve as a guide and reference point for scholars who might be new to this field, but also as a source of encouragement for such scholars who can draw succour from the fact that they are not alone as they wrestle with their various methodological and theoretical concerns and challenges.

This book: Scope and structure

Given our desire for this volume to engage and bring together perspectives across multiple disciplines and research traditions, we took a somewhat agnostic approach both towards how contributors interpreted the parameters of the 'far right', and to the use of other terms, such as 'extreme right' and 'radical right' within individual chapters, providing that contributors made clear how they are using the terms. This does raise challenges, most notably in relation to achieving a coherence of scope across the volume, with contributors deploying a range of more broad or narrow interpretations of 'the far right'. We took the position however that this enables the volume to better capture the often complex and somewhat fuzzy parameters of the field than would have been the case if we had adopted a more prescriptive approach. Such definitional debates are a core feature in the opening section of this volume.

Part I: Disciplinary overviews

The first section of this book brings together a series of disciplinary overviews. Each of these chapters explores the evolution of far right studies from a particular disciplinary viewpoint within the humanities or the social sciences, tracing the key developments and debates that have shaped the state of the field today.

Nonna Mayer provides an overview of how political scientists have defined, explained and operationalized the term far right, identifying a succession of key 'turning points' that have defined and redefined the field. She also explores the evolution and growth of the far right 'family' itself and considers the methodological challenges that this entails. **Nigel Copsey** maps historiographical interpretations of the far right between 1945 and the present, drawing attention to how the methodological insights offered by historians can assist scholars and students carrying out research in the present. Specifically, Copsey demonstrates how historical empirical inquiry, and the theoretical prism of fascism, has a significant role to play in helping contemporary far right scholars differentiate between organizational and ideological continuity, especially when it comes to the relationship between 'classic fascism' and the contemporary far right. **Kathleen Blee and Mehr Letif** then provide a survey of sociological research on the far right. As well as offering an overview of the theoretical and methodological perspectives that have shaped this field, they, like Mayer, also reflect on how the field itself is being shaped by the evolution of the far right. They note, for example, how new relationships between state and non-state actors, and new transnational constellations of actors, both demand scholarly attention and provide opportunities to elaborate on the interactions between micro-, meso- and macro-level processes relevant to the evolution of the far right. **Barbara Perry and Ryan Scrivens** discuss the specific contribution that criminologists have made to the field of far right studies. Drawing attention to the inherently interdisciplinary nature of criminology, Perry and Scrivens reflect on how criminologists situate analysis of right wing extremism within a wider set of understandings and insights about crime, criminality and the systems and procedures of criminal justice. Again, their discussion concludes with a series of observations about how the contemporary political context is affecting this field. Surveying the social and political psychology literatures, **Pasko Merino, Tereza Capelos and Catarina Kinnvall** then explore how our understandings and explanations of far right political parties or movements (i.e. the 'supply' side) and electoral behaviour (i.e. the 'demand' side) can and has been enhanced through analysis of the intersection of political developments and both individual and collective psychological experiences. Like Blee and Latif, they draw our attention to the relationship between micro- and macro-level processes by, for example, exploring how far right support may shape, and be shaped by, individual and collective psychology in societies characterized by 'extended' polarization, xenophobia and intolerance. And picking up a recurring theme, they also provide observations about how psychological analysis of the far right is today intersecting with analysis of other apparently cognate phenomena, such as populism, and extremist politics more broadly, including that which is propagated by groups such as Al Qaeda – or the so-called 'Islamic State'. Finally, in this section, **Peter Hervik** considers where anthropologists have, and have the potential to, contribute to research in this field. Central here, Hervik argues, is the way that 'good anthropology' scrutinizes key empirical and analytical concepts, engaging critically with the top-down analytical concepts that have to a large extent defined wider contemporary political and academic debate about phenomena such as 'the far right' and 'populism'. He also discusses two further contributions: the insights that anthropology offers with regard to how processes of racialization contribute to produce essentialist components of neo-national identity; and the methodological insights that can be derived from anthropological approaches to agency and researcher empathy.

Together, these chapters provide a helpful reminder, if one were needed, that while each of these disciplines makes specific contributions to the wider literature, the epistemological and theoretical boundaries between the various humanities and social science disciplines are not as clear cut as some would argue, or may have once been. Indeed, what is striking is the frequency with which the authors of these chapters reach across disciplinary boundaries and drawn insights and inspiration from scholars in other disciplines, whether in terms of theory, methods or practice. There can be little doubt that this inter-/ multi-disciplinarity reflects at least to some extent the intellectual debt owed by many contemporary scholars to explicitly inter-/multi-disciplinary studies that have shaped the field today, such as the Klandermans and Mayer's much-cited 2006 volume, *Extreme Right Activists in Europe*.

Part II: Quantitative and online research

Drawing across a range of disciplinary, inter- and multi-disciplinary perspectives, the second part comprises chapters that examine the use of quantitative approaches and online research to describe, analyze and interpret different dimensions of far right politics. The chapters in this part also highlight the strengths and limitations of such approaches.

Vasiliki Georgiadou, Lamprini Rori and Costas Roumanias explore the ways in which scholars of the far right estimate their share of electoral votes using election panel surveys. They draw particular attention to the methodological challenges associated with attempts to analyze the 'demand' for the far right, and suggest how alternate research strategies, including the use of panel selection-correction techniques, and the use of new multi-election datasets might enable researchers to address these challenges. **Jacob Aasland Ravndal and Anders Ravik Jupskås** examine the issues surrounding how researchers can accurately and effectively document and measure far right violence. As well as examining core definitional issues – such as how what constitutes far right violence can both overlap and be distinct from concepts such as hate crime and terrorism – Ravndal and Jupskås critically review the existing datasets that are commonly used to measure far right violence. While their assessment highlights the limitations of existing datasets, they also argue that moves towards crowd sourcing, international standardized police reporting and victimization surveys might serve to strengthen the existing evidence base. **Jasper Muis, Ofra Klein and Guido Dijkstra** then move the discussion onto some of the new opportunities and challenges for understanding far right discourses that are opening up with the advance of online methods. Focusing on Facebook and Twitter, they explore how content within these platforms can be used to analyze differences *between* and *within* far right parties and movements, particularly with regards to their framing of 'outgroups', and how far right leaders moderate their ideological standpoints once they have entered government. **Peita Richards'** chapter continues the focus on social media, but switches the analytical focus to questions of how social media analysis can be used to develop a more sophisticated understanding of individuals who are drawn to and associated with far right ideologies. In doing so, Richards elaborates on how new data posited in the public sphere via online platforms provide opportunities for qualitative and quantitative analyses of both content and behaviours. **Andreas Önnerfors'** chapter further illustrates this point, but also turns our attention to the challenges associated with capturing and theorizing the relationship between online and offline communication and socialization processes. Önnerfors does this through a case study that explores how PEGIDA and their allies on the far right of German politics have built popular support using stage-managed events that are recorded with the intention of being disseminated on the German online platform einprozent.de.

Section III: Interviewing the far right

The chapters in Part III consider issues relating to interview-based methods – a staple research strategy of much of the social and political sciences, but one that raises particular challenges for researchers of the far right.

In their chapter, **Amy Fisher Smith, Charles Sullivan, John Macready and Geoffrey Manzi** reflect on their experience of undertaking research with former far right extremists. As they observe, while the use of such methods are gaining in popularity, both in research on the far right and in cognate fields, such as research on terrorism, there is a need for greater attention to be paid to issues around methodological transparency, specification of methodological procedures, standardized reporting practices and developing a more refined understanding of the distinction and complementarities between qualitative and quantitative research traditions. They also reflect on issues of researcher bias, reflexivity, procedures for textual analysis and questions of interpretive validity. **Betty Dobratz and Lisa Waldner** build on the previous chapter. They explore a range of methodological issues that emerged during their decades-long research on the white power movement in the United States, during which they have combined interviews with observation-based methods. As in the previous chapter, they reflect on the relationship between qualitative and quantitative methods and the implications for interview-based research design. They also discuss questionnaire development, access issues, the dynamics of conducting face-to-face interviews, the role of emotions, establishing empathy and rapport, and the stigmatization of researchers of the white power movement. The chapter by **Bert Klandermans** provides further practical insight and advice about interviewing far right activists. Reflecting on his experience of conducting life history interviews as part of a cross-disciplinary, transnational comparative study of far right activism in five Western European countries, Klandermans offers guidance in relation to four key themes: asking questions about far right membership; issues of meaning and the rationalization of far right membership; questions of continuity in activism and membership over time; and the significance attributed to context and whether far right activist responses to the previous three themes vary from country to country. Cutting across this, Klandermans also emphasizes the advantages of asking 'what' rather than 'why' questions of interviewees.

Part IV: Ethnographic studies of the far right

The chapters in Part IV discuss ethnographic approaches to researching the far right. Picking up and continuing some of the conversations from the special issue of the *Journal of Contemporary Ethnography* referenced above, these chapters provide further reflection on ethical dilemmas that such research is likely to generate, and explore issues of access, negotiating the parameters of 'participation', and simultaneously managing relationships with activists, colleagues and the public authorities. They do so, however, in different national and local contexts, and from a range of quite different theoretical perspectives and personal positionalities.

Katrine Fangen looks back on her observational study of the Norwegian far right during the mid-1990s. Critically engaging with similar studies in the field, Fangen provides practical advice for far right researchers in relation to a number of issues, such as entering the research field and seeking access, as well as other ethical dilemmas associated with securing informed consent, maintaining anonymity and respecting participant integrity. In doing so, Fangen highlights the importance of openness, honesty and transparency when it comes to establishing rapport. Reflecting on her research on the Swedish Democrats between 2008 and 2011, **Vidhya Ramalingam** discusses both the unique opportunities afforded to her and the challenges she confronted as a female researcher of colour (ROC) working on the far right. She considers how the female ROC is required to adapt the framework of enquiry when researching and surrounded by 'unsympathetic research subjects', and also discusses how her ROC subject position shaped issues of access, personal safety and the emotional dynamics of participant observation and qualitative interviews. **Joel Busher** takes, as a starting point, one of the central ethical challenges for ethnographers working on the far right previously identified by Blee (2007): how to uphold the 'scholarly ethics of fairness' when researching and writing about a movement that the researcher considers distasteful and harmful. Busher describes how, in his research into activism in the English Defence League (EDL), he sought to address this through the adoption of a principle of 'non-dehumanization'. Tracing his own journey, he describes how this principle shaped decisions at design, fieldwork and writing up stages of the research. **Stephen Ashe** then charts his journey to what turned out to be an 18-month political ethnographic local case study on the electoral rise and fall of the British National Party

(BNP). Ashe provides an account of the twists, turns and ethical, political and practical dilemmas encountered. Throughout his chapter, Ashe pays particular attention to how questions of whiteness and class shaped both his research design and relationships in the field. He concludes by reflecting on some of the questions and criticisms he and other ethnographers have faced when disseminating their research.

Part V: The significance of place, culture and performance when researching the far right

As noted above, one of the key challengers for researchers of the far right is how to capture and analyze movements and cultures that are dynamic, multi-faceted and sometimes surprisingly diverse. The chapters in Part V all grapple with and offer strategies for responding to this challenge. In doing so, these chapters shed further light on questions of definition and categorization, method and scale, as well as turning attention to important issues such as how researchers can augment their understanding of the far right by paying more careful attention to crucial yet often overlooked elements of far right cultures such as place, consumption and the everyday practices through which far right discourse can become socially embedded.

John Veugelers' chapter provides us with a reminder that when it comes to understanding the far right, 'place matters'. Examining the importance of locality as a unit of analysis, and reflecting on his own work on the Front National in the Southern French city of Toulon, Veugelers focuses on the unique contribution that single-case studies can make to our understanding of the far right. He draws particular attention to the way that such research strategies can help to 'bridge' and integrate historical and other social scientific methods. **Cynthia Miller-Idriss and Annett Graefe-Geusch** discuss their research on the commercialization of far right youth culture in Germany, which combines interviews with analysis of a digitized archive of symbolic and commercial far right products. Their research leads them to two conclusions that might have profound implications for how we research the far right, particularly in relation to the iconography of such political and social formations: first, that holding on to fixed categories of far right membership can obscure important sources of information on the far right and mistakenly frame youths as having static identifications with certain ideological and political scenes; and second, that the integration of material culture into focused qualitative interviews can 'shift our understandings of what it means to be associated with or exposed to far right scenes and subcultures' by teasing out 'multiple layers of … affiliation'. **Ruth Wodak** then examines the merits and limitations of critical discourse studies, and discourse-historical approaches in particular, as strategies for analyzing and interpreting the far right. Grounding the discussion in the case study of the Austrian Freedom Party and their 'politics of denial' and use of the 'blame game', she considers how these approaches can assist our analysis of far right rhetoric and the micro-politics of such parties. Reflecting on her research experiences, she contends that if we are to understand both the resonance of far right messages and their electoral fortunes, it is imperative that we pay greater attention to 'everyday performances' which often transcend the analytical categories used by investigating the nature of far right ideology.

Section VI: The intersection of academic and activist positionalities and disseminating far right research

There are often important intersections and overlaps between research on the far right and efforts to counter, challenge and inhibit the growth or spread of such movements. This is perhaps not surprising. As Blee noted in the introduction to the special issue on ethnography and the far right, many scholars undertaking research on the far right are motivated to do so by their concerns about the impact that such movements have upon those targeted by its politics (as well as those drawn into such groups) and for society as a whole. Yet this intersection of research and activism can raise challenging questions for researchers about how they conduct their work. The two chapters that make up the sixth and final part in this collection provide reflections on negotiating researcher and activist positionalities, and on the challenges that come with, as well as some of consequences that emerge from, disseminating research on the far right.

Chip Berlet discusses the challenges that come with balancing a variety of different roles when working on the far right as a researcher committed to progressive social movements in the United States. In doing so, Berlet reflects on how he has managed to keep 'the archivists, journalist and scholar separate and ethical' over the course of 40 of research. Here Berlet outlines his work for the Public Eye Network, which monitors right-wing groups, studying neo-fascist and neo-Nazis, anti-racist research and organizing, being a journalist, a paralegal investigator and working for Political Research Associates, focusing on the organizing practices and ethical issues that this work entails. Berlet also discusses his work on the Christian Right and Gay Rights, being compelled to be an expert witness for the defense following the Oklahoma City bombing in 1995 and trying to work within the ethical parameters set by the American Sociology Association. **Aurelien Mondon and Aaron Winter** reflect on a number of challenges faced by far right researchers in the present context. Their chapter starts with an overview of the current landscape researchers are forced to navigate, with a particular focus on the media and the current hype around the topic and in the field. In response to the increasingly challenging environment that researchers face when presenting and disseminating research on the far right in media forums and to the wider public, they consider what they see as a variety of challenges, pitfalls and shortcomings that far right scholars ought to avoid and/or address: namely, issues of amplification; hype and legitimization; distraction and deflection; access, risk and representation; and 'bandwaggoning'. They conclude by setting out a number of questions which they have found important to consider and reflect upon in their own research and practice.

Concluding thoughts

This collection is not intended to be definitive, prescriptive or indeed the last word on the theory, method and practice of researching the far right. A single edited collection, no matter how ambitious, could not be expected to cover every single issue relating to the researching the far right. Indeed, the authors are conscious of a number of areas that are not covered in this volume – for instance a chapter on working with far right primary sources or researching the far right in a transnational context. Instead, what we have tried to do is to put together a volume which sparks further conversation, collaboration and debate about such issues more generally.

While the contributions to this volume highlight several areas of convergence between scholars working from within different disciplinary traditions (for instance, the fairly widespread embrace of theorizing the far right in terms of 'supply' and 'demand'), they also reveal important differences in terms of, for example, approaches to, and theorizations of, empathy, ethics and the politics of terminology. This volume also reveals variation in scholars' views about how they ought to respond to threats of far right violence directed either at themselves or others, and how researchers handle issues around potentially exaggerating or downplaying, normalizing or Othering both far right groups and those who participate in such groups. While some of these differences are informed by different disciplinary and research traditions, others are shaped by the researchers' political positionalities and by whether or not the researcher themselves would likely be constructed as 'Other' by the far right group that they study.

In light of the above, it seems appropriate to conclude by looking forward and drawing attention to three ways in which we hope the scholarship on the far right might develop over the years ahead. The first of these is that we hope that scholars researching the far right will, as they have done in recent years, continue to look outwards and engage with other subfields that may have much to offer in terms of enriching our understanding of the far right – today, more than ever, we cannot afford to retreat into our silos. One of the major innovations during the past decade or so has, for example, been a growing engagement with research on social movements. This has expanded the theoretical, conceptual analytical vocabulary of the wider field and provided a number of powerful conceptual tools for understanding the ebb and flow of far right politics at micro, meso and macro levels (Klandermans and Mayer, 2006; Caiani et al., 2012). So, what other subfields might research on the far right engage with? One obvious one would be the subfield on political violence, albeit there are a number of reasons why we might proceed with caution here (see Merino, Capelos and Kinnvall; Ravndal and Jupskås, all this volume). Others might include political and human geography, and it is also apparent that as the 'online' and 'offline' become increasingly interconnected and indistinguishable from one another it is clear that a constructive dialogue with Data Science will be of fundamental importance if researchers of the far right are to keep pace with the changing nature of such movements (see Muis, Klein and

Dijkstra; Richards; Önnersfors, all this volume). We believe that more could also be done to consider how postcolonial, decolonial and critical race theory can improve our understanding of the far right, both within Western and non-Western contexts (see Ashe, this volume), particularly as researchers begin to grapple with questions about the continuities and discontinuities between far right and nationalist politics in Western and non-Western contexts.

The second way in which we hope to see the scholarship on the far right evolve over the coming years would be for the field to be shaped by scholars from an increasingly diverse range of backgrounds, in terms of nationality, gender, ethnic and religious background. We very much acknowledge the irony of this point, given that the editorial team is comprised of four white men from the global north. There is an impressive literature on gender and sexuality in relation to the far right. Indeed, as this volume attests, women have played and continue to play a major role in shaping the field. It is important that women, researchers of colour and researchers from non-Western countries continue to have a growing presence within this field, and in doing so that the field incorporates different assumptions, perspectives, understandings and methodological and theoretical frames concerning the nature and impact of such politics. For example, the perspectives of scholars working and based in non-Western contexts experiencing forms of far right politics has the potential to generate important insights about the extent to which theories and concepts largely deployed and developed within Western contexts have wider applicability. In turn, this will enable critical reflection upon the theory, methods and practices that have come to characterize much of the scholarship on the far right in Europe and North America in particular. There are clearly challenges here. For example, it is likely that in many contexts researchers of colour will encounter greater barriers than white researchers when it comes to accessing members of far right formations (see Ashe; Dobratz and Waldner; Mondon and Winter; Ramalingam, all this volume). We believe, however, that such research has considerable potential to move the field forward.

Third, and finally, we hope that the growing number of research centres, departments and networks, book series and special issues devoted wholly or in part to advancing our understanding of the far right will dedicate greater time and space to questions relating to methods and the ethics, politics and practice of this research. More specifically, we hope that, as we have tried to do within this volume, these discussions of the methods, ethics, politics and practice of research on the far right will be inclusive discussions, characterized by a genuine will and desire on the part of researchers to enrich their ability to understand and interpret the far right by drawing across the full gamut of available methodologies and approaches. As far right politics continues to evolve, so too do the research methodologies and theoretical tools that individual researchers need in order to analyse and understand it. And given the breadth of scholarship currently being conducted into far right politics today, it is arguably beyond the resources of a single academic, or even any single centre or department, to stay abreast of even a portion of the published research or how their own particular specialism within the field relates to others. Yet achieving such inclusive discussions about research methods, ethics, politics and practice is not without its challenges. For example, at a time when academic research governance is increasingly subjected to the logics of market competition, researchers are often drawn into forms of territorialism and are likely to feel pushed to position themselves as a 'go-to' person on all things relating to the far right. Nonetheless, we must find a way to encourage a culture of collegiality, generosity, humility and mutual acknowledgement of expertise within the field. We would suggest that a good starting point for this would be for all of us to be as honest as possible about the limitations of our knowledge and about the fact that, while it is important that we take seriously and seek within our work to resolve the various political and ethical dilemmas discussed in this volume, the 'solutions' that we construct and find are unlikely ever to be easy or clear-cut, let alone 'perfect'.

References

Aho, J. 1994. *This Thing of Darkness: A Sociology of the Enemy*. Seattle, WA: University of Washington Press.

Aho, J. 2016. *Far-Right Fantasy: A Sociology of American Religion and Politics*. Abingdon: Routledge.

Bale, T. 2012. "Supplying the insatiable demand: Europe's populist radical right." *Government and Opposition*, 47(2), 256–274.

Caiani, M., D. della Porta, and C. Wagemann. 2012. *Mobilizing on the Extreme Right: Germany, Italy, and the United States*. London: Oxford University Press.

Fielding, N.G. 1993. "Mediating the message: Affinity and hostility in research on sensitive topics." In *Researching Sensitive Topics*, edited by C.M. Renzetti and R.M. Lee, 146–159. Newbury Park, CA: Sage.

Klandermans, B. and N. Mayer. (eds). 2006. *Extreme Right Activists in Europe: Through the Looking Glass*. Abingdon: Routledge.

Lee, R.M. 1993. *Doing Research on Sensitive Topics*. London: Sage.

Lumsden, K. and A. Winter. (eds). 2014. *Reflexivity in Criminological Research: Experiences with the Powerful and the Powerless*. London: Palgrave.

Martineau, P. 2019. "The existential crisis plaguing online extremism researchers." *Wired*, 5 February 2019. https://www.wired.com/story/existential-crisis-plaguing-online-extremism-researchers/ [accessed 5 February 2019].

Ravndal, J.A. 2019. "Right-wing terrorism and violence may actually have declined." *The Washington Post*. https://www.washingtonpost.com/politics/2019/04/02/is-right-wing-terrorism-violence-rise/?noredirect=on [accessed 5 April 2019].

Toscano, E. (ed.). 2019. *Researching Far Right Movements: Ethics, Methodologies and Qualitative Inquiries*. Abingdon: Routledge.

PART I
Disciplinary overviews

1

POLITICAL SCIENCE APPROACHES TO THE FAR RIGHT

Nonna Mayer

In June 1984, the French Front National (FN) led by Jean-Marie Le Pen drew an unexpected 10.9 per cent of the votes in the European elections.[1] His success marked the beginning of the so-called 'third wave' of right-wing extremism in Europe (Von Beyme, 1988: 11) which was the largest and the longest-lasting one since World War Two.[2] First understood through the prism of fascism, these parties soon appeared to be of a specific nature, and thus renamed 'post-fascist', 'post-industrial' or 'modern'. Nevertheless, these parties continue to be seen as posing a threat for democracy. The main challenge for political science research is to treat such parties with the kind of politically detached attitude, as well as the conceptual and methodological tools, applied to other parties. Rather than giving an exhaustive account of the proliferating literature that these parties sparked, this chapter focuses on key turning points in this area of research, showing how the change in definitions, explanations and operationalization of the far right followed the expansion and transformations of the party family itself, as well as discussing the methodological challenges that this involved. The conclusion explores new avenues for research.

Definitions: From extremism to populism

The question of how to define the parties composing the 'third wave' has been controversial. Right-wing extremism (RWE) was the first category to be used by political scientists. An overview of research in this field between 1980 and 1995 showed that there was a raging 'war of words', with no less than 28 competing definitions of RWE based on 58 distinctive ideological features (Mudde, 1996). Where some authors parsimoniously used a single criterion, such as 'anti-democratic', 'anti-immigrant' or 'exclusionist', others listed up to ten core features ranging from 'extreme nationalism' to 'cultural pessimism' (Falter and Schumann, 1988).[3]

Moreover, other scholars employed a combination of criteria. For example, Piero Ignazi's definition, one of the most used, combined a spatial dimension (i.e. perceived position of party on the left-/ right-wing scale), an ideological criterion (i.e. reference to fascism or not) and an attitudinal measure (i.e. pro- or anti-system; that is, pro- or anti-democracy), thus contrasting the 'old' type of extreme right party which had demonstrated a fascist imprint (e.g. National Democratic Party of Germany (NPD), German People's Union (DVU), Dutch Centre Party (CP'86) and British National Party (BNP) to a 'new' non-fascist type of party exuding more of a right-wing anti-system standpoint while delegitimizing the mainstream parties (e.g. French FN, German Republikaner, Dutch Centre Democrats (CD), Austrian Freedom Party (FPÖ) and the respective Danish and Norwegian Progress parties) (Ignazi, 1992). However, rarely were the categorizing criteria strictly defined, or were their respective weights assessed and any empirical validation provided.

The term 'radicalism' started to be used in the mid-1990s (see Merkl and Weinberg, 1993). Less stigmatizing and less connected to fascism and Nazism, this term quickly gained ground. In post-war Germany, extremism from the left and from the right were both considered to be antidemocratic and 'unconstitutional' by the Office for the Protection of the Constitution. This led to state surveillance and eventually a ban. Radicalism, or being 'in opposition to the principles of the Constitution', was seen as being the lesser evil and, therefore, not subject to such procedures. While in the United States the term 'radical right' was being used to refer to the 'pseudo-conservative' movements of the 1950s, such as the anti-communist McCarthyism crusade (Bell, 1963).

In France, Pierre-André Taguieff (1984) was the first to describe the ideology of the FN as 'national populist'. For Taguieff, it was the heir of both the ultra-nationalist and popular Boulangist movement of the end of the nineteenth century and the anti Dreyfus Leagues, thus demonstrating an ideological mix of nationalism, xenophobia, and demagogy in the name of 'the people'. In the English-speaking literature, Hans-Georg Betz labelled these 'third wave' parties 'radical right-wing populism' (Betz, 1994). For Betz, they differed from the extreme right because they did not reject the democratic rules of the game nor did they advocate violence. They also differed from the centre right parties because they were in favour of a radical transformation of the post-war social democrat consensus, mainly in relation to the welfare state and the acceptance of a multicultural society. These parties were populist in their political argumentation (i.e. showing faith in the common sense and moral superiority of the ordinary people while also offering simple solutions to complex problems) and in their political strategy (i.e. articulating a 'politics of resentment' in a bid to mobilize 'the people' against the political class and elites). Moreover, these parties exalted manual workers and small producers in opposition to non-productive workers described as being parasites and lazy. The term 'Radical Right Populism' was then redefined by Cas Mudde (2007) as a core ideology combining three components: nativism (i.e. a combination of nationalism and xenophobia), authoritarianism (i.e. belief in a strictly ordered society) and populism (i.e. position the pure people in opposition to corrupt elites).

Similar debates surround the varieties of radical/extreme/populist rights taking into account their respective ideological and programmatic diversity beyond just their focus on immigration. For instance, whereas Ignazi (1992) distinguished between old fascist and new anti-system extreme rights, Betz (1994) distinguished between national-populist and neoliberal populist parties, liberal on economic and cultural issues. At the same time, Husbands (1992) distinguished between populist-nationalist, neo-fascist, nationalist, traditional xenophobic and militant neo-Nazi extreme right parties, while Kitschelt and McGann (1995) distinguished between fascist, welfare chauvinist, right-wing authoritarian and populist anti-statist radical right parties.

The terms of radical/extreme/populist right can all be found in the existing literature. For example, in Mudde's (2017) edited collection on the contemporary Radical Right between 1988 and 2013, many of the authors disagree on which labels should be attributed to certain parties. However, the label 'populist radical right', as redefined by Mudde, is gradually starting to prevail. Indeed, a consensus is taking shape with regard to the necessity to adopt a wide and pragmatic definition of the Radical Right family's contours at large, including borderline cases which until now had been considered either too violent (i.e. the Greek Golden Dawn and the Hungarian Jobbik), or too mainstream (i.e. Norwegian Progress Party and the Swiss People's Party). For simplicity, the term Radical Right (RR) will be used in the remainder of this chapter.

Explanations: From demand-side to supply-side factors

Early studies of the aforementioned 'third wave', as well as the post-war neo-Nazi resurgences, were heavily inspired by interpretations of fascism and Nazism, thus stressing psychological or psycho-analytical factors. In their seminal study of the electoral rise of neo-Nazi parties in Germany during the mid-1960s, Erwin Scheuch and Hans-Dieter Klingemann referred to 'Right-Wing Extremism' as 'a normal pathological condition' of society that was likely to reappear periodically during times of social crisis and anomie. The potential supporters of these parties in the 1980s were thus described as authoritarian, ethnocentric, and more likely to be found among the less educated working class or the lower middle class (see Von Beyme, 1988; Merkl and Weinberg, 1993). Until now, innumerable surveys focus on the attitudes of RR voters, searching for xenophobia, nationalism, authoritarianism and political distrust as a precondition of their support for these parties.

Another block of theories focused on the correlation between these attitudes and macro-structural changes associated with processes of modernization. The 'third wave' of the RR was first attributed to the transition from industrial to 'post-industrial' societies. Ronald Inglehart (1977) argued that there was a 'silent revolution' at the heart of this process produced by the diffusion of post-materialist values which enhanced citizens' personal autonomy and tolerance. In fact, Ignazi (1992) described the rise of the RR as being a 'silent counter-revolution': that is, a reaction against these values. Indeed, while Inglehart had foreseen the resulting political changes on the left of the political spectrum, most notably the electoral rise of libertarian and green parties, he did not anticipate the neo-conservative backlash on the right. More specifically, Inglehart did not predict that social change could produce both libertarian and authoritarian-xenophobic values. In contrast, other authors focused on the political consequences of social change, noting that urbanization, social mobility, education, declining class and religion-based solidarities had produced a more fluid and atomized society, thus weakening old party loyalties, while favouring a 'politics of resentment' or 'anti-politics' that has proven fertile ground for the emergence of the RR (see Betz, 1994).

In the 1990s, globalization started to gain more attention. The increasing integration of markets in the world economy was seen as generating winners (i.e. who took economic advantage from globalization) and losers (i.e. those who felt threatened by globalization). Betz (1994) was one of the first to connect these changes with the electoral rise of RR parties during the mid-1980s. The opening of borders, the incoming flows of immigrants and economic competition from the low-wage countries of the global south, were perceived as threatening the jobs of the unskilled workers. Feeling ignored by the mainstream parties, they turned to the RR for protection. Later work subsequently differentiated between the so-called potential 'losers of economic globalization' (i.e. those more concerned with job insecurity and perceived competition from migrant workers) and the 'losers of cultural modernization' (i.e. those seeing multiculturalism, cosmopolitism and universalistic norms as a threat to their identity (see Bornschier and Kriesi, 2012).

Another factor put forward to explain support for the RR was the dualization of the labour market in capitalist societies. Since the 1970s, atypical forms of work arrangements had developed, increasing the divide between 'insiders' with high-wage protected jobs, and vulnerable 'outsiders', with unskilled, low-paid and fixed-term jobs (Emmenegger, Haüsermann, Palier, and Seeleib-Kaiser, 2012). This divide cuts through the old class lines, pitching outsiders against insiders, thus bringing the former to support either the extreme left or the extreme right or to abstain (Lindvall and Rueda, 2014; Rovny and Rovny, 2017). Moreover, Standing (2014) has conceptualized these outsiders as 'the precariat', a new 'dangerous' class in formation, who are:

> floating, rudderless and potentially angry, capable of veering to the extreme right or extreme left politically and backing populist demagoguery that plays on their fears or phobias.
>
> *(Standing, 2014: 4)*

The Great Recession of 2008 and the austerity policies that followed have sparked new interest in the political impact of the economy on support for the RR. It has been argued that popular discontent would lead to changes in voting patterns, thus breeding support for populist radical parties on both the right and the left, with voters punishing incumbent governments in line with the classical 'retrospective voting' logic, holding them responsible for the economic conditions prevailing in the period prior to elections (see Bartels and Bermeo, 2014; Kriesi and Pappas, 2015). Beyond the economic crisis, the appeal of the RR has been linked more deeply to the crisis of democratic politics in an age of globalization, austerity and rising inequalities. Peter Mair was the first to analyze citizens' growing disaffection towards political parties, as well as the tension between responsiveness (being reactive to citizens' demands) and responsibility (being accountable for their policy decisions), arguing that:

> In this way political parties become more like governors than representatives, at least within the mainstream or core of the party system. Representation itself either moves out of the electoral channel altogether or, when it remains within the electoral channel, becomes the primary preserve of so-called 'niche' or 'challenger' parties, which may downplay a governing ambition or which may lack a governing capacity.
>
> *(Mair, 2009: 6)*

The importance of the supply side

Structural changes do not mechanically foster support for RR. Moreover, holding anti-immigrant attitudes or economic grievances is not a sufficient explanation as to why some people vote for such parties. Indeed, Von Beyme argues that "xenophobia does not push the rigid nationalist potential into extremist parties if Chirac, Thatcher or Kohl offer an outlet for these feelings as part of the programme of their dominant, moderate, conservative parties" (1988: 15). It depends on how the mainstream parties react.

Kitschelt and McGann (1995) were among the first to bring the supply-side of politics back into the picture. Applying to the RR the model they had already applied to the emergence of the Green parties, they examined the electoral competition and the strategic interactions between political actors. For them, the structural and ideological changes affecting post-industrial societies offered a favourable 'political opportunity structure' (POS) to Right Authoritarian Politics.[4] In a competitive space defined by two dimensions, capitalist/socialist and authoritarian/libertarian orientations, the ideological convergence towards the centre of the moderate conservative right and social democratic left opened up political space for the RR. At the beginning of the 'third wave' period the 'winning formula' likely to maximize the RR's electoral gains appeared to be a combination of authoritarian (i.e. law and order) and capitalist (i.e. free market) appeals, the very strategy then implemented by the FN in France, the Vlaams Block (VB) in Belgium and the Danish Progress Party (DFK). Since the 1990s, the RR have developed other 'winning formulas'. The progress of European integration has resulted in the RR becoming the champions of anti-EU and anti-globalization stands, while also turning away from economic liberalism towards protectionism and welfare chauvinism (see Ivaldi, 2015).

Cas Mudde (2007) suggests that there are two kinds of supply factors: 'external' and 'internal'. The former refers to the elements of the POS which either create opportunities or constrain the RR's electoral fortunes. In contrast, the latter refers to the resources which the RR themselves develop such as leadership, party organization and funding, all of which are said to either enable or prevent the RR from benefitting from the POS and consolidating their political position (see Golder, 2016; Van der Brug, Fennema, and Tillie, 2005).

Hanspeter Kriesi and his colleagues (Kriesi et al., 2008; Bornschier, 2010) have also made an important contribution to this field of study, arguing that the contemporary processes of globalization/denationalization represent a 'critical juncture' which has produced new structural cleavages in Western Europe, as well as the emergence of a tripolar, and no more bipolar, party system. Increasing economic, cultural and political competition, these processes have created a political opportunity for RR parties to mobilize the 'losers of globalization' that strongly identify with the national community and feel threatened by the opening up of national borders. This cleavage Kriesi and his colleagues (2008) called 'integration' (in global society) versus 'demarcation' (of national community), a cleavage that has also been referred to as Green Alternative Libertarianism versus Traditional Authoritarian Nationalism, universalism versus particularism, cosmopolitism versus communitarianism, etc. Based on a content analysis of the written media outputs, their study provided an original cross-national comparative study of the electoral campaign strategies of the competing parties in Austria, Britain, France, Germany, the Netherlands and Switzerland (see Kriesi et al., 2008). Focusing on the specific institutional and electoral contexts in each country, they found that electoral success depended not only on the capacity of RR to adopt these anti-globalization 'demarcation' strategies, but also on the strategies adopted by mainstream parties (i.e. ideological convergence or polarization, cooperation with or stigmatization of RR parties).

There is now a considerably large body of literature which systematically explores the impact of supply-side factors. The literature has examined the impact of electoral systems (i.e. the role played by proportional or plurality systems and thresholds of eligibility) (see Norris, 2005); the nature of the party system and its degree of convergence or polarization (see Abedi, 2002); the specific resources available to RR parties (i.e. leadership, party size and structures); and RR strategies (i.e. radicalization, mainstreaming, alliances and conflict) (Art, 2011; Golder, 2016). Conversely, the existing literature in this area shows that how mainstream parties choose to respond is also important (Downs, 2001; Van Spanje, 2010), whether this be attempts to marginalize the RR through bans, establishing a 'cordon sanitaire', boycotting or anti-racist laws, or by responding to the RR by imitation or inclusion strategies such as electoral, parliamentary and governmental alliances. Studies have also shown that the role played by media can be important, particularly the way in which the media shape debate and 'discursive competition' in ways that either enhance or constrain the visibility and legitimacy of the RR claims (see Bos, Van Der Brug, and de Vreese, 2011; Ellinas, 2010; Aalberg et al., 2017). It has also been argued that the media are the 'missing link' between the attitudes of RR voters i.e. (anti-EU, anti-immigrant and/or anti-elite) and their actual votes for the RR, thus making particular issues salient and meaningful.

At first supply-side factors were added to demand-side factors when designing electoral surveys. Research then shifted away from voters to parties, and from

surveys to more qualitative approaches based on interviews and ethnographic observation. The first study of the motivations of French FN members was carried out by
the psychologist Birgitta Orfali (1990) at the end of the 1980s. The first large-scale
comparative study of RR activists, based on 157 interviews with members of RR
parties in five European countries, was conducted in 1997–1999 by a team of social
psychologists and political scientists (Klandermans and Mayer, 2005). Another large-
scale study based on fieldwork and interviews ($N = 140$) with RR activists from 20
parties in ten different countries is David Art's (2011). All of these studies underline
the normalcy of those who join RR parties, thus challenging the stereotypes of
violence and extremism that are typically attributed to neo-Nazi or neo-fascist
groups. These studies also stress the importance of party leadership and agency,
gender relations, the way in which the RR recruit and train the members, set up the
party structures and establish communication and alliance strategies.

Perspective on RR voters has also changed. For a long time, RR voters were
considered to be emotional, irrational and protest-led 'anti' voters without ideological convictions. In contrast, electoral support for the RR has gradually come to
be reinterpreted using rational choice theory. Van der Brug, Fennema, and Tillie
(2000), for example, have shown how the votes for the RR in Europe could be a
form of protest voting, demonstrating rejection of all other parties, while at the
same time being based on meaningful, substantive considerations, a combination of
ideological proximity with the mainstream right, and antagonistic attitudes towards
immigrants. This argument is also applicable to France, where strong anti-elite
sentiments underpin support for the FN. Yet the two main attitudinal predictors of
votes for Jean-Marie Le Pen and his daughter, Marie Le Pen, in presidential elections are self-placement on the left–right scale and feeling there are too many
immigrants (Mayer, 2015). Across Europe, polarization on the immigration issue
has been found to be a key driver of RR support (Ivarsflaten, 2008).

Another feature in the evolution of RR studies has been the shift away from
considering the RR as the dependent variable that required explaining towards
treating the RR as an independent variable (i.e. an explanatory factor). The focus
of research is also shifting towards the consequences of the electoral rise and insti-
tutionalization of RR parties, particularly their impact in terms of setting the
political agenda, and the policies of mainstream parties, especially mainstream
immigration policies (Van Spanje, 2010; Carvalho, 2013). Lastly, a whole new area
of research has recently opened up as these parties increasingly enter government
and, contrary to initial predictions, demonstrate a degree of longevity without
losing the support of either their voters and party members (Albertazzi and
McDonnell, 2015; Akkerman, de Lange, and Roodjuin, 2016).

Operationalization: Some methodological traps

Over the last 30 years the study of the RR's electoral base has become a 'minor
industry'. A mass of survey data is now available, ranging from commercial opinion
polls to national election studies and large comparative datasets such as the

Comparative Study of Electoral systems (CSES), the Word Values Survey (WVS), the European Values Study (EVS), the European Social Survey (ESS) and Eurobarometers. These datasets suggest that the RR vote tends to be predominantly male, uneducated and working class, regardless of the heterogeneity of parties which compose this political family. The greater reluctance of female voters to support the RR was noticed in the mid-1990s (see Betz, 1994) and a burgeoning literature seeks to explain it, drawing attention to the role played by the type of employment, religiosity, feminist values, conformity to social norms (see Harteveld and Ivarsflaten, 2018), in creating what has been referred to as the 'Radical Right Gender Gap' (Givens, 2004). There are large variations in the nature and scale of this gap from both country-to-country and from one election to another (see Immerzeel, Coffé and van der Lippe 2015; Harteveld et al., 2015; Spierings and Zaslove, 2015; Amengay, Durovic, and Mayer, 2018). Education is the other major predictor of support for the RR, because of the growing importance of 'cultural' issues like authority, immigration and national identity, developing at the expense of purely economic issues and cutting through class lines (Achterberg, Houtman, and Van der Waal, 2007). RR parties attract support from traditional class enemies, small shopkeepers as well as a growing portion of the manual blue-collar workers, who are predominantly men with low levels of formal education (Oesch, 2012).

However, the results of these studies based on survey data should be treated with a degree of caution (see Georgiadou, Rori and Roumanias, this volume). Survey samples traditionally underrepresent voters of low socioeconomic status, the most likely to support the RR. Interviewees tend to be reluctant to say they voted for such parties, seen as extremist. Comparative data are often based on cross-national surveys (such as the EVS, WVS, ESS, Eurobarometers) which are not electoral surveys and therefore collect voting intentions or past votes in national elections out of context. In addition to this, national subsamples of voters are usually small (i. e. $n = 1,000$ at the most). As a result, the datasets include very small numbers of self-reported RR voters, especially in mid-term elections with usually low rates of voter turnout. Re-analyzing the ESS data relating to 19 RR parties, Marc Hooghe and Tim Reeskens (2007) show convincingly that cross-national surveys are not the best way to study the extreme-right vote in Europe, on the grounds of both response and measurement bias, which in addition vary considerably from one country to another. Even a methodologically robust survey such as the ESS has its own limitations when it comes to comparing votes for the RR parties.

These biases encouraged a search for other sources of information than opinion polls. One possibility, drawing on a longstanding tradition of electoral geography developed by André Siegfried in France, is to use aggregate data (Bussi et al., 2016). However, this approach has its own limitations, namely the risk of 'ecological fallacy'.[5] Another alternative approach would be to adopt contextual and multilevel approaches, mixing individual and aggregate data in order to put voters back in their social and political environment (see Arzheimer, 2009; Werts, Scheepers, and Lubbers, 2013). The emergence of 'big data' has also revolutionized electoral studies on both a theoretical and a methodological level. For example, the multiple traces left by individuals on Google, social network platforms (i.e. Facebook and Twitter) and via their cell phones or other connected devices, bring a mass of information about their electoral preferences (see Richards, this volume).

The uptake of qualitative approaches has also become more common and has contributed to a better understanding of the RR by providing more detailed insights into the kinds of people who join RR parties. In doing so, such approaches have challenged the way in which RR activists have been understood in terms of marginality, pathology and the forms of violence associated with fascist and Nazi organizations. However, this type of in-depth research also faces epistemological and ethical problems. Some of these parties, especially the smaller less successful ones, are reluctant to open their doors to researchers. They often feel rejected, stigmatized and defensive because so many journalists attempted to infiltrate them. Other RR organizations have placed conditions on who the researcher is allowed to speak to and have even asked to be shown the results before they are published or to attend the researcher's PhD defence. Moreover, because academics tend to oppose the values held by the RR, they have shown a tendency to be reluctant to have direct contact with RR activists. The feedback of those who have chosen to conduct long-term immersion in RR parties, like Daniel Bizeul,[6] who observed a branch of the French FN over 2-year period, or Elisa Bellè, who carried out a 3-year study of the Italian Northern League, gives precious insight into the methodological difficulties encountered and the way to overcome them. For example, this includes criticism from relatives and colleagues (who question how researchers can spend time with such people). However, these methodological challenges can be turned into a resource, this leading to a reassessment of research ethics and value neutrality (see Bellè, 2016). There also is the difficulty in trying to remain neutral and controlling one's emotions when hearing racist, sexist or homophobic comments (especially when the researchers happens to be from an LGBT or ethnic minority background, or a feminist). There is also a question mark regarding the degree of intimacy to be allowed in the relationships between the researcher and the researched, particularly when it comes to striking a balance between distance and empathy. As the French radical left-wing journalist Anne Tristan sums it up in *Au Front* (1987: 22), based on covert observation inside a branch of the FN in Marseille: "the enemy is nice". There also is the fear of becoming impregnated with their ideology and stepping through the looking glass, as described by Daniel Bizeul who waited 3 years before writing his book, needing time to recover, de-impregnate himself and find good distance. There are several common criticisms of this type of ethnographic research; namely, that it is difficult to generalize from a single case study and the view that data collected during long-term immersion may not be reliable.

New avenues of research

The impact of religion on support for the RR has been for long understudied. First Christian religions were seen as antithetical to RR parties, whose ideology seemed at odds with the universalistic message of the Evangels, as well as the long-lasting links between the Church and with Christian democrat or conservative parties. Practising Christians appeared to be captive voters, vaccinated against the RR vote, even though some of these parties presented themselves as defenders of Christian identity and values. Indeed, there seems to be a *'religion gap'* in Europe, at least in the older established democracies (Montgomery and Winter, 2015). In France, for instance, one systematically found integration to Catholicism, measured by attendance to mass, to have a weak but significant negative impact on votes for the FN, even when controlling for age, gender, education and political orientation (Mayer, 2015).

The rise of Islamic fundamentalism, especially after 9/11, has triggered an anti-Muslim identitarian reaction inside the Christian electorate of Europe, making part of this demographic more receptive to the exclusionist messages of the RR. A recent study based on the 2008 EVS Survey confirms the existence of a negative link between religious practice and votes for the RR in seven of the countries studied. However, in three of the countries studied an interesting divide was found when taking into account not only church attendance but beliefs on a scale of fundamentalism which included belief in God, hell, sin, life after death and denial of the values underpinning other religions (see Immerzeel, Jaspers, and Lubbers, 2013). In Belgium, Norway and Switzerland, it was found that rigid 'orthodox believers', with high scores on the scale of fundamentalism, were more hostile towards immigrants and more likely to support the RR than 'non-orthodox believers' (with low scores). While in Austria, Finland and Italy, owing to the greater ideological proximity between RR and CD parties, one finds no such shift. Conversely, the RR are increasingly tempted to mobilize religion for their own end, not so much as a set of beliefs, but as an identity marker, tracing the border between 'them' and 'us' (Marzouki, McDonnell, and Roy, 2016). Meanwhile, more research on the relationship between minority religions and the RR is required as some RR parties are now actively targeting the support of Muslim and Jewish voters, considered as a symbolic catch by RR parties that are usually labelled as racist and anti-Semitic (Fourquet, 2015).

Another emerging line of research is the electoral impact of sexuality (for a detailed overview see Durand and Mayer, 2017). At a time where many RR parties present themselves as defenders of the rights of LGBT against an intolerant and violent Islam, and claim they defend 'sexual democracy', various forms of 'homonationalism' and 'sexual nationalism' are emerging, indicating a potential LGBT vote in favour of RR (on the Swedish and Norwegian RR, see Spierings and Laslove, 2015: 157; on the French case see Crépon, 2015).

Last, there is a fast growing body of research on RRs in Central-Eastern Europe (CEE). These parties and movements share many of the ideological viewpoints held by their Western counterparts, namely Euroscepticism, nativism, authoritarianism, populism (Mudde, 2007). Yet CEE RR parties have emerged in a very different context, where modernization was not linked to the passage from industrial to post-industrial societies, but from communism to post-communism and from state-controlled to free market economies, in nation-states with less solidified party systems and lacking a democratic culture. As noted by many authors (see Minkenberg, 2017; Pirro, 2015; Pytlas, 2016), the nature of these transitional processes is incomplete, and the process of nation building remains unfinished. The line between radical and mainstream parties in CEE is less clear and the left–right cleavage less suitable in this context. Also, post-communist RR parties appear less stable and more radical than in Western Europe. Therefore, it is impossible to apply without caution the theories and models developed by Western political science to the CEE context. Nevertheless, such comparisons are enlightening precisely because of these differences.

Drawing from a new party-election level dataset covering all post-communist countries over the 20 last years, Lenka Bustikova (2014) stresses the importance of relations between RR and non-proximate parties. Revisiting the 'silent counter-revolution' thesis (Ignazi, 1992), she shows that in the post-communist context, the RR have indeed benefited from a political backlash against policies put forward by ethno-liberal parties in favour of minorities. Drawing on European Social Survey (ESS) data from 2001 to 2008, Trevor Allen (2017) shows how post-communist RR voters share the same Eurosceptic and exclusionary populism than Western voters, but not exactly the same attitudes about religion, immigration, the economy and democracy. The data analysis shows that anti-immigrant sentiment is a weaker predictor of the RR vote than in the West, whereas Christian religiosity has a stronger impact in CEE, as do leftist attitudes concerning welfare and income redistribution. As for the functioning of democracy, negative judgments are both more frequent in the post-communist context, as well as being a stronger predictor of RR support.

Research carried out by Bartek Pytlas (2016) explores voter competition between what he calls 'near-radical right' mainstream parties[7] and the RR in Poland, Hungary and Slovakia, and the increasing discursive influence of the RR on the political debate despite their lack of electoral significance. Pytlas shows the central part played by the co-optation strategies adopted by mainstream parties who have adopted the policies and viewpoints of the RR in relation to issues such as collective identity, nationalizing politics and minority policies. Cultural issues appear more important than economic ones. RR parties appeal to what Pytlas has described as being 'axiological modernization losers', voters who feel their values and way of life threatened even more than their jobs. These voters can be seen as the Eastern equivalent of the Western 'cultural globalization losers' described by Bornschier and Kriesi (2012), more driven by cultural than economic insecurity. Last in Western and Eastern Europe as well, there is a debate about the efficiency of ideological co-optation or imitation of the RR by the mainstream parties. Some authors consider that this is as a way of deflating the RRs electoral progress (Meguid, 2008), whereas others argue that this legitimizes the RR positions and increases their electoral appeal (Arzheimer and Carter, 2006; Dahlström, and Sundell, 2012). Pytlas convincingly shows that it is not enough to consider 'which' issues are co-opted, we must consider 'how' certain issues are framed.

Over the last 30 years, European RR parties have turned from pariahs to threatening competitors for the mainstream political parties (Akkerman, de Lange, and Rooduijn, 2016). Not only are they gaining electoral support, they are entering coalition governments with increasing frequency, as in Austria, Slovakia, Bulgaria, Finland, Norway, Italy, and Switzerland. At the same time, Eastern Europe is becoming a political laboratory where 'near radical right' parties are in office, as is the case in Hungary and in Poland, and put into practice the very ideas of the RR, bending the existing laws and constitutions to their own advantage. Thus, a new field of research is opening up for political science, analyzing what RR anti-system parties can do to the political system, both from the inside and from the outside, as well as what kind of 'illiberal' democracy such parties are promoting (Müller, 2017).

Notes

1 At the request of 113 members of the European Parliament, and in spite of the fierce opposition from Jean-Marie Le Pen, a Committee of Inquiry was set up to examine 'the Rise of Fascism and Racism in Europe', chaired by the Greek MP Dimitrios Evrigenis, who authored the committee's final report which was published in 1985.
2 The first wave started in the immediate post War, notably in Germany with the political resurgence of Nazi parties. The second wave saw the rise of anti-statist and anti-tax protests, instigated by the small shopkeepers of Poujade movement in France in the mid-1950s and the Danish and Norwegian Progress parties during the 1970s.
3 "Extreme nationalism, ethnocentrism, anti-communism, anti-parliamentarism, anti-pluralism, militarism, law and order thinking, a demand for a strong political leader and/or executive, anti-Americanism and cultural pessimism" (Falter and Schumann, 1988: 101).
4 This term was introduced by Peter Einsiger in the 1970s, and experienced a new lease of life in the 1980s in the what was the growing field of research on social movements. It then referred to the specific configuration of resources, institutions and actors that facilitated or constrained the development of protest movements.
5 Name given by William Robinson (1950) to the error of inferring from a correlation observed at the level of groups that it applies at the level of the individuals (for instance the fact that areas with a high proportion of Black people also have a high proportion of illiterates does not mean that Blacks are more often illiterate).
6 See the summary of the articles and books in which he tells his experience and the methodological lessons he learned from it: https://www.cairn.info/publications-de-Bizeul-Daniel–17499.htm.
7 Ruling right wing parties with ideas close to the RR's such as Fidesz in Hungary or Law and Justice in Poland.

References

Aalberg, T., F. Esser, C. Reinemann, J. Stromback, and C.H. De Vreese. 2017. *Populist Political Communication in Europe*. Abingdon: Routledge.
Abedi, A. 2002. "Challenges to established parties: The effects of party system features on the electoral fortunes of anti-political-establishment parties." *European Journal of Political Research*, 41(4), 551–583.
Achterberg, P., D. Houtman, and J. Van der Waal. 2007. "Class is not dead – it has been buried alive: Class voting and cultural voting in postwar Western societies (1956–1990)." *Politics and Society*, 35(3), 403–426.

Akkerman, T., S.L. de Lange, and M. Rooduijn. 2016. *Radical Right-Wing Populist Parties in Western Europe: Into the Mainstream?* Abingdon: Routledge.

Albertazzi, D. and D. McDonnell. (eds). 2015. *Populists in Power.* Abingdon: Routledge.

Allen, T.J. 2017. "All in the party family? Comparing far right voters in Western and post-Communist Europe." *Party Politics,* 23(3), 274–285.

Amengay, A., A. Durovic, and N. Mayer. 2018. "L'impact du genre sur le vote Marine Le Pen." *Revue française de science politique,* 68(5), 1067–1087.

Art, D. 2011. *Inside the Radical Right. The Development of Anti-Immigrant Parties in Western Europe.* Cambridge: Cambridge University Press.

Arzheimer, K. 2009. "Contextual factors and the extreme right vote in Western Europe: 1980–2002." *American Journal of Political Science,* 53(2), 259–275.

Bartels, L. and N. Bermeo. 2014. *Mass Politics in Tough Times: Opinions, Votes and Protest in the Great Recession.* Oxford: Oxford University Press.

Bell, D. 1963. *The Radical Right. The New American Right, Expanded and Updated.* Garden City, NY: Doubleday.

Bellè, E. 2016. "Knowing as being. Knowing is being." *Anthropologie and développement,* 44, 79–100.

Betz, H.-G. 1994. *Radical Right-Wing Populism in Western Europe.* London: MacMillan.

Bornschier, S. 2010. *Cleavage Politics and the Populist Right. The New Cultural Conflict in Western Europe.* Philadelphia, PA: Temple University Press.

Bornschier, S. and H. Kriesi. 2012. "The populist right, the working class, and the changing face of class politics." In *Class Politics and the Radical Right,* edited by J. Rydgren, 10–29. Abingdon: Routledge.

Bos, L., W. van der Brug, and C. de Vreese. 2011. "How the media shape perceptions of right-wing populist leaders." *Political Communication,* 28(2), 182–206.

Bussi, M., C. Le Digol, and C. Voilliot. (eds). 2016. *Le Tableau politique de la France de l'Ouest d'André Siegfried. 100 ans après. Héritages et postérités.* Rennes: Presses Universitaires de Rennes.

Bustikova, L. 2014. "Revenge of the radical right." *Comparative Political Studies,* 47(12), 1738–1765.

Carvalho, J. 2013. *Impact of Extreme Right Parties on Immigration Policy. Comparing Britain, France and Italy.* Abingdon: Routledge.

Crépon, S. 2015. "La politique des mœurs au Front national." In *Les faux semblants du Front national. Sociologie d'un parti politique,* edited by S. Crépon, A. Dézé and N. Mayer, 185–206. Paris: Presses de Sciences Po.

Dahlström, C. and A. Sundell. 2012. "A losing gamble: How mainstream parties facilitate anti-immigrant party success." *Electoral Studies,* 31(2), 353–363.

Downs, W. 2001. "Pariahs in their midst: Belgian and Norwegian parties react to extremist threats." *West European Politics,* 24(3), 23–42.

Durand, M. and N. Mayer. 2017. "Genre, sexualité et vote." In *Analyses électorales,* edited by Y. Déloye and N. Mayer, 265–317. Brussels: Bruylant.

Ellinas, A.A. 2010. *The Media and the Far Right in Western Europe: Playing the Nationalist Card.* New York, NY: Cambridge University Press.

Emmenegger, P., S. Häusermann, B. Palier, and M. Seeleib-Kaiser. (eds). 2012. *The Age of Dualization. The Changing Face of Inequality in Deindustrializing Societies.* Oxford and New York, NY: Oxford University Press.

Falter, J.W. and S. Schumann. 1988. "Affinity towards right-wing extremism in Western Europe." In *Right-Wing Extremism in Western Europe,* edited by L. Von Beyme, 96–110. London: Frank Cass.

Fourquet, J. 2015. "Le vote Front National dans les électorats musulman et juif." In *Les faux semblants du Front national. Sociologie d'un parti politique*, edited by A. Dézé, S. Crépon, and N. Mayer, 375–394. Paris: Presses de Sciences Po.

Givens, T.E. 2004. "The radical right gender gap." *Comparative Political Studies*, 37(1), 30–54.

Golder, M. 2016. "Far right parties in Europe." *Annual Review of Political Science*, 19, 477–497.

Harteveld, E., W. Van Der Brug, S. Dahlberg, and A. Kokkonen. 2015. "The gender gap in populist radical-right voting: Examining the demand side in Western and Eastern Europe." *Patterns of Prejudice*, 49(1–2), 103–134.

Harteveld, E. and E. Ivarsflaten. 2018. "Why women avoid the radical right: Internalized norms and party reputations." *British Journal of Political Science*, 48(2), 369–384.

Hooghe, M. and T. Reeskens. 2007. "Are cross-national surveys the best way to study the extreme-right vote in Europe?" *Patterns of Prejudice*, 41(2), 177–196.

Husbands, C. 1992. "The other face of 1992: The extreme-right explosion in Western Europe." *Parliamentary Affairs*, 45(3), 267–284.

Ignazi, P. 1992. "The silent counter revolution." *European Journal of Political Research*, 22(1), 3–34.

Inglehart, R. 1977. *The Silent Revolution. Changing Values and Political Styles Among Western Publics*. Princeton, NJ: Princeton University Press.

Immerzeel, T., E. Jaspers, and M. Lubbers. 2013. "Religion as catalyst or restraint of radical right voting?" *West European Politics*, 36(5), 946–968.

Immerzeel, T., H. Coffé, and T. van der Lippe. 2015. "Explaining the gender gap in radical right voting: A cross-national investigation in 12 Western European countries." *Comparative European Politics*, 13(2), 263–286.

Ivaldi, G. 2015. "Du néolibéralisme au social-populisme ? La transformation du programme économique du Front National (1986-2012)". In *Les faux-semblants du Front national*, edited by S. Crépon, A. Dézé, and N. Mayer, 161–184. Paris: Presses de Sciences Po.

Ivarsflaten, E. 2008. "What unites right-wing populists in Western Europe? Re-examining grievance mobilization models in seven successful cases." *Comparative Political Studies*, 41(1), 3–23.

Kitschelt, H. and A.J. McGann. 1995. *The Radical Right in Western Europe. A Comparative Analysis*. Ann Arbor, MI: University of Michigan Press.

Klandermans, B. and N. Mayer. (eds). 2005. *Extreme Right Activists in Europe: Through the Magnifying Glass*. London and New York, NY: Routledge.

Kriesi, H., E. Grande, R. Lachat, M. Dolezal, S. Bornschier, and T. Frey. 2008. *West European Politics in the Age of Globalization*. Cambridge: Cambridge University Press.

Kriesi, H. and T.S. Pappas. 2015. "Populism and crisis: A fuzzy relationship." In *European Populism in the Shadow of the Great Recession*, edited by H. Kriesi and T.K. Pappas, 303–325. Colchester: ECPR Press.

Lindvall, J. and D. Rueda. 2014. "The insider–outsider dilemma." *British Journal of Political Science*, 44(2), 460–475.

Mair, P. 2009. *Representative versus Responsible Government*. MPIfG Working Paper, 09/8. Cologne: Max Planck Institute for the Study of Societies..

Marzouki, N., D. McDonnell, and O. Roy. 2016. *Saving the People. How Populists Hijack Religion*. London: Hurst.

Mayer, N. 2015. "The closing of the radical right gender gap in France?" *French Politics*, 13(4), 391–414.

Meguid, B. 2008. *Party Competition Between Unequals: Strategies and Electoral Fortunes in Western Europe*. Cambridge: Cambridge University Press.

Merkl, P.H. and L. Weinberg. (eds). 1993. *Encounters with the Contemporary Radical Right.* Boulder, CO: Westview Press.

Minkenberg, M. 2017. *The Radical Right in Eastern Europe. Democracy Under Siege?* Basingstoke: Palgrave McMillan.

Montgomery, K.A. and R. Winter. 2015. "Explaining the religion gap in support for radical right parties in Europe." *Politics and Religion*, 8(2), 379–414.

Mudde, C. 1996. "The war of words: Defining the extreme right party family." *West European Politics*, 19(2), 225–248.

Mudde, C. 2007. *Populist Radical Right Parties in Europe.* Cambridge: Cambridge University Press.

Mudde, C. 2017. *The Populist Radical Right: A Reader.* Abingdon: Routledge.

Müller, H.W. 2017. *What is Populism?*Philadelphia, PA: University of Pennsylvania Press.

Norris, P. 2005. *Radical Right: Voters and Parties in the Electoral Market.* Cambridge: Cambridge University Press.

Oesch, D. 2012. "The class basis of the cleavage between the new left and the radical right: An analysis for Austria, Denmark, Norway and Switzerland." In *Class Politics and the Radical Right*, edited by J. Rydgren, 31–52. Abingdon: Routledge.

Orfali, B. 1990. *L'adhésion au Front national. De la minorité active au mouvement social.* Paris: Kimé.

Pirro, A.L.P. 2015. *The Populist Radical Right in Central and Eastern Europe: Ideology, Impact, and Electoral Performance.* Abingdon: Routledge.

Pytlas, B. 2016. *Radical Right Parties in Central and Eastern Europe: Mainstream Party Competition and Electoral Fortune.* Abingdon: Routledge.

Robinson, W. 1950. "Ecological correlations and the behavior of individuals." *American Sociological Review*, 15(3), 351–357.

Rovny, A. and J. Rovny. 2017. "Outsiders at the ballot box: Operationalizations and political consequences of the insider-outsider dualism." *Socioeconomic Review*, 15(1), 161–185.

Spierings, N. and A. Zaslove. 2015. "Gendering the vote for populist radical-right parties." *Patterns of Prejudice*, 49(1–2), 135-162.

Standing, G. 2014. *The Precariat. The New Dangerous Class.* London: Bloomsbury Academic.

Taguieff, P.-A. 1984. "La rhétorique du national populisme. Les règles élémentaires de la propagande xénophobe." *Mots*, 9(1), 113–139.

Tristan, A. 1987. *Au Front.* Paris: Gallimard.

Van der Brug, W., M. Fennema, and J.N. Tillie. 2005. "Why some anti-immigrant parties fail and others succeed: A two-step model of aggregate electoral support." *Comparative Political Studies*, 38(5), 537–571.

Van der Brug, W., M. Fennema, and J.N. Tillie. 2000. "Anti-immigrant parties in Europe: Ideological or protest vote?" *European Journal of Political Research*, 37(1), 77–102.

Van Spanje, J. 2010. "Contagious parties: Anti-immigration parties and their impact on other parties' immigration stances in contemporary Western Europe." *Party Politics*, 16(5), 563–586.

Von Beyme, K. 1988. *Right-Wing Extremism in Western Europe.* London: Frank Cass.

Werts, H., P. Scheepers, and M. Lubbers. 2013. "Euro-scepticism and radical right-wing voting in Europe, 2002–2008: Social cleavages, socio-political attitudes and contextual characteristics determining voting for the radical right." *European Union Politics*, 14(2), 183–205.

2

HISTORIANS AND THE CONTEMPORARY FAR RIGHT

To bring (or not to bring) the past into the present?

Nigel Copsey

Some years before historians were invited to pass judgement on whether Donald Trump had the makings of a 'fascist', I recall that in June 2009, following the British National Party's capture of two seats in the European Parliament, the *Guardian* newspaper asked several leading historians whether 'fascism is on the march again'? (*The Guardian*, 9 June 2009). Michael Burleigh was at once dismissive and refused to draw 'stupid historical analogies'; Richard Overy could see no evidence of a 'revolutionary movement asserting a violent imperialism and promising a new social order'. For Overy, 'Fascism with a capital F was a phenomenon of the 20s and 30s'. Fascism belonged to 'then' and the contemporary far right belongs to 'now'. 'We live in a very different world', Burleigh had remarked somewhat tersely, 'and these parties organize themselves in a very different way. Hitler didn't Twitter'.

Is searching for a fascism in today's far right akin to a fool's errand, searching for something that isn't there? Or if there is a fascism in the 'here and now', does it merely linger on as some nostalgic, historical residuum – sometimes nasty, but otherwise just frankly odd? When the eccentric, uniformed leader of the 'New British Union' promised to promote the eternal values of Oswald Mosley, and barked 'Hail Britannia!', is this the reality of today's 'fascism' – the Alice-in-Wonderland world of the political crank and misfit?

By way of contrast, of course, the parties of the contemporary (non-fascist) far right represent a much more serious proposition altogether. Reflecting the seriousness of this populist *zeitgeist*, political scientist Cas Mudde opined over a decade ago that 'no party family has been studied as intensely as the populist radical right' (Mudde, 2007: 2). A decade on, and Mudde had crunched the numbers. At least from the early 1990s onwards, 'more articles and books have been written on far-right parties than on all other party families *combined*' (Mudde, 2017: 2, emphasis as original). And thanks to the hard work of present-minded political scientists we now have recourse to a new vocabulary for understanding and conceptualizing this contemporary far right. But this is not the place to dwell on the lexicon. The relative merits or demerits of terms such as 'radical right-wing populism', 'neo-populism', 'national populism', and the rest can be put to one side. The important point to make here is that all these terms share one thing in common: they establish ontological distance between the contemporary far right and 'classic' or 'historic' fascism. Whilst this is important, for we surely need to acknowledge difference and novelty, methodological approaches of this kind carry with them a serious disadvantage. The problem is that political scientists have been cutting threads connecting the past to the present (see Copsey, 2013; 2018).

Of course, some (traditionalist) historians still insist that historians should play no part whatsoever in studying the present (for if we do, we might be tempted to *manufacture* continuity). This hits on a valid point for like political scientists, we too can be labelled *presentists*. But if we abstain from the 'here and now', we can very quickly succumb to *historicism* (whereby *definitional* importance is assigned to specific historical contexts). And, what is more, historical specificity is a problem which weighs especially heavily on fascism. Fascism's deep historical imprint, its appalling outcomes, compels many of my colleagues to speak only of fascism in the past tense. David D. Roberts aptly described this as the 'unbearable weight of historical fascism' (see Roberts, 2016). 'The whole package' Roberts put it simply, 'ended in 1945' (2016: 289). Undoubtedly, this epochal-approach to fascism remains ever popular (as my introductory comments testify). Yet not all historians view their subject from such time-constrained positions. For some of us, fascism in the twenty-first century – in this 'post-fascist' era – is not phenomenologically dead.

In this chapter I will chart the evolution of historiographical interpretations of the contemporary far right (by contemporary I mean post-1945 through to the present day). In what ways have these historical interpretations developed, and what methodological insights might they offer students of the far right today? Some important points need to be made at the outset. The first is that since the principal *historical* exemplar of the far right is fascism, historians have typically approached the far right through fascism. Second, the study of fascism as a *particular* historical phenomenon did not really get under way until the 1960s. There were a number of reasons for this slow start. One was the dominance of the 'totalitarian' paradigm which twinned fascism with communism. But there were other reasons too. As Eugen Weber (1964: 9) explained, both Fascist and National Socialist movements

> expressed themselves in actions and statements which repelled serious scholars as they repelled any humane person; both movements were defeated in circumstances which make an unprejudiced approach difficult; and both movements, once defeated, were temporarily dismissed as having no further immediate significance, except of a purely historical order – and that could wait.

This brings me to my third point. Temporal distance between events and their analysis meant that when this early historical literature reflected upon developments on the far right after 1945, it did so only very fleetingly.

Beyond the totalitarian monolith

For two decades after the Second World War, under the 'totalitarian' monolith, the subject of fascism had shared an 'essential identity' with communism (Kitchen, 1976: 25–35). By the 1960s, however, as historian Gilbert Allardyce (1971: 18), observed, 'the world that had inspired the theory of totalitarianism was passing into history'. Allardyce saw that:

> With the early 1960s there was a developing inclination to consider the cold war was over and the West had passed through an extreme political crisis which had originated with the rise of fascism in the interwar years and climaxed with the death of Stalin in 1953. A new sense of historical periodization was emerging, an awareness that sometime in the 1950s the world had entered a new situation, and that we no longer lived in the era of depression, the fascist dictators, and the Stalinist purges.

This meant that historians were now at liberty to render their own 'independent' understanding of fascism – an understanding of fascism disentangled from the broader Cold War theory of 'totalitarianism'.

Ernst Nolte was one of the first historians to do so. Nolte's hugely influential *Der Faschismus in Seiner Epoche*, originally published in 1963, and translated into English in 1965 as *The Three Faces of Fascism*, approached fascism as *characteristic* of a specific era, 1919–1945:

> Even though fascism existed after 1945 and has continued to exist since that time, and even though it is still capable of arousing bitter conflicts, it cannot be said to have real significance as far as the image of the era is concerned unless the term be stripped almost entirely of its traditional connotation. Thus, the very subject of this study precludes any reference to events of the present day.
> *(Nolte, 1966: 4)*

For Nolte, whilst strictly-speaking man had not yet 'finally crossed the border into a postfascist era' (1966: 454), his reading proposed that fascism no longer possessed epoch-making characteristics. So why apply the concept of fascism to the far right after 1945 when fascism was more or less hermetically sealed within its own era between the wars?

If the starting point for this 'Age of Fascism' remained the subject of some debate – 1919, 1922, or 1933 – the end-point was not. Reflecting on the place of fascism in European history, Allardyce had written that 'Fascism had raged and stormed as though it would transform an entire continent, and then there was nothing left, neither loyalties, passions, nor beliefs' (1971: 3). After the global conflagration of 1939–45, fascism had burnt itself out, or more accurately, its enemies had doused the flames. Whatever, fascism was now phenomenologically 'dead'. Important implications for the historian followed because 'when fascism is dead', as Hugh Trevor-Roper (1968: 28) urged, the historian's role is not to oppose 'fascism' (in the present) but to understand it (in the past).

As these early historians of generic fascism understood it, the relationship between fascism and the *crisis* conditions of the turbulent age that had given rise to it was unequivocal. So much so that in a review article in the *Historical Journal* from 1968 Michael Hurst had commented that fascists,

> saw themselves in a vast national crisis and gained strength when large sections of their fellow countrymen came to share both their sense of urgency and radical response to it. To this extent, then, Fascism can well be termed the politics of crisis.
>
> *(1968: 169)*

The French neo-fascist writer Maurice Bardèche agreed. For him, fascism was 'impossible to define outside periods of crisis' (cited in C. Seton-Watson, 1968). Remove that crisis – the *specific* historical conjuncture – and it becomes understandable why there is no longer any fascism, and why the potential for any revival would seem extremely remote. Hence, for Francis Carsten, in *The Rise of Fascism*, originally published in 1967,

> The whole atmosphere in the Europe of the 1960s is so vastly different from that of the 1920s – the atmosphere of semi-religious frenzy, of fear and hatred, of violence and pogroms, of political murder and punitive expeditions – that the chances of a true Fascist revival seem rather small.
>
> *(1970: 237)*

Admittedly, some historians cast their net wider. John Weiss, in *The Fascist Tradition* (1967: 129) suspected that 'the greatest potential for fascism lies not in the liberal West, but rather in the dialectical polarities even now increasing in non-Western or underdeveloped societies'. Oxford University's Paul Hayes would similarly reflect in *Fascism*, published in 1973, that 'it seems to me that fascism is not a dead ideology, it still has political potential, particularly in non-European areas of the world' (1973: 224). The shifting foci from the land of fascism's birth to the Third World would gather some momentum during the 1970s, principally through the endeavours of scholars such as A. James Gregor and his acolytes (e.g., Joes, 1978). The effect of such departures, however, was to further limit the possibilities that Europe's contemporary far right might be usefully understood in terms of fascism. Gregor, for example, was more interested in Asian (Mao) and Caribbean (Castro) 'variants'. And when it came to Europe his attention lay not with the likes of the NPD – the *Nationaldemokratische Partei Deutschlands* but with left-wing student radicals, '*links-faschismus*', in the (polemical) words of German sociologist Jürgen Habermas (Gregor, 1974).

In 1975 as Ernst Nolte perused developments in recent scholarship in *Reappraisals of Fascism*, a volume edited by Yale Professor of History, Henry A. Turner, he still gave little encouragement to those who might have thought that a re-appearance of fascism lay within the realms of possibility. Nolte merely restated that the whole point behind his *Three Faces of Fascism* was 'To grasp the *historical* essence of fascism' (Nolte, 1975: 30, emphasis as original). At the same time, controversial Italian historian, Renzo De Felice, in *Intervista sul fascismo*, a best-selling paperback published in Italy in 1975, and subsequently translated into English, insisted that in terms of making reference to contemporary developments, the term fascism should be abandoned. For De Felice, 'fascism' described a moment in the *Italian* past – 'fascism is a historical fact and has to do with a precise period' (1976: 97). 'I am very insistent', De Felice wrote, 'that fascism is a phenomenon that must be rigidly limited, otherwise we shall not understand anything. It must be limited chronologically, between the two world wars' (1976: 89).

Even so, De Felice was more generous than Nolte. For he conceded that there was a neo-fascism in post-war Italy. The Cold War had created space for a 'revival of anticommunism of the classic type' (1976: 100) and this could take nostalgic neo-fascist form. But with the exception of youthful elements, these neo-fascists were a dying breed. More serious, De Felice thought, was an extra-parliamentary 'right-wing radicalism', which De Felice characterized as *neo-Nazism* (not neo-fascism). According to De Felice (1976: 103), there was 'a profound difference between fascism and Nazism, and even more between fascism and the neo-Nazism of the present'. Historical fascism as a mass-movement, he maintained, was revolutionary and optimistic. In Nazism, however, there was no idea of progress, 'if anything there is one of tradition, of race' (1976: 103). Hence, present-day *neo-Nazism*, is pessimistic and here, De Felice thought, 'we are no longer in the field of political thought but of fanaticism, which is an end in itself' (1976: 104).

De Felice incurred the wrath of Italian Marxist scholars who decried him for 'rehabilitating' fascism (De Felice had argued that fascism sprang from the revolutionary soil of 1789). Nolte, too, had inveighed against Marxist historians for insisting that 'fascism is nothing more than the nakedly exposed inner nature of capitalism: domination, force, exploitation, repression' (1975: 36). For where capitalism survives so too must fascism (even if in latent form). And so, it followed that for Marxist historians fascism did remain a possibility after 1945. When it came to fascism, Marxists told us, keep careful watch, remain eternally vigilant. 'Thus, the danger of fascism is still with us', Martin Kitchen warned in *Fascism* (1976: 91).

To his credit Kitchen was one of the first historians to make an open call for a new theory of neo-fascism, which 'would take the essential features of the fascism of the past, examine how these factors are likely to have changed, and see under what socio-economic crisis situations in contemporary advanced capitalism such drastic measures are likely to be employed' (1976; 91). Writing in 1979, Paul Hayes similarly called on scholars, for the sake of clarity, 'to describe any modern possibilities as "neo-fascist". This would then permit the acceptance of a variation of criteria from the model of the inter-war years without totally invalidating the notion of comparability' (1979: 10). But if Hayes detected neo-fascist potential in the underdeveloped world, Kitchen's primary interest lay with the new fascism in late-capitalist Western Europe which was 'bound to adapt itself to a new situation. This is already apparent in the fascistic movements such as the N.P.D. in Germany, the M.S.I. in Italy or the National Front in Britain' (1976: 90). Nevertheless, Kitchen's Marxist-inspired analysis would fall on some stony ground (the word 'fascism' all too readily bandied about by the left simply as a term of political abuse).

Tellingly, Walter Laqueur's edited volume, *Fascism: A Reader's Guide*, originally published in 1976, and which A. James Gregor described 'as surely one of the best single collections given over to a discussion of generic fascism'[1] had said next to nothing about neo-fascism. Juan Linz, in the conclusion to his expansive comparative chapter, had praised Gregor for isolating fascism's ideological formulations in 'many contemporary movements and regimes, sometimes where we would least expect it' (1991: 104). Three years later, in the conclusion to *International Fascism: New Thoughts and New Approaches*, an edited volume by the distinguished historian George Mosse, Hugh-Seton Watson would lament on the continued use of the word 'fascism' to describe contemporary movements and regimes:

> Neither this article nor this book will be able to prevent such use and abuse of the word in the future; yet it would certainly help clarity of historical and political thought if it could be discarded except in relation to a specific past era.
>
> *(1979: 371)*

Gilbert Allardyce ventured further. In what would later come across as a wanton act of historical vandalism, his 1979 article in the *American Historical Review* deflated 'fascism' to the point of declaring that it was not a generic concept at all, and its use should be strictly limited to Mussolini's Fascism (with a capital 'F'). So, come 1980 and little had changed. Thus, in *Fascism: Comparison and Definition*, US historian Stanley Payne felt no need to sail against the winds of historical orthodoxy. For Payne, 'As the two most assiduous students of fascism, Ernst Nolte and Renzo De Felice, have insisted, it was an historical phenomenon primarily limited to Europe during the era of the two world wars' (1980: 176).

In a recent review of the scholarship of far-right parties since 1945, Cas Mudde (2017: 3) suggested that we might differentiate between three distinct waves of scholarship:

> The first wave lasted roughly from 1945 till 1980, was mostly historical and descriptive, and focused on the historical continuity between the pre-war and post-war periods. The vast majority of the (relatively few) scholars were historians, experts of historical fascism, who studied the postwar populist radical right under the headings of "extreme right" and "neo-fascism".

The reality is rather different to what Mudde suggests (the references that Mudde cites are to *journalists* not historians, and to the work of an associate professor of political science).[2] Alas, any prospective student of the history of neo-fascism in Western Europe in this 'first wave' would have garnered little methodological insight from historians of 'classic' or 'historical' fascism.

Lifting the conceptual fog

The 1980s were hardly better. Rather than a historian of generic fascism, it was the 'terrorologist' Paul Wilkinson who penned *The New Fascists*, originally published in 1981, and later revised in 1983. Wilkinson's lively book had surveyed the resurgence of the far right from the 1970s through to the 1980s. For Wilkinson (1983: 8) it was 'a cardinal error to assume that fascist doctrines and movements are historical phenomena limited to a particular historical period or to specific countries'. Yet at the same time, Noël O'Sullivan's *Fascism*, published in 1983, remained silent on contemporary developments. O'Sullivan, an Oakeshottian conservative political theorist, revealed his true disciplinary colours when alighting on the significance of *novelty*:

> the common parentage does not mean that the children themselves can be properly described as fascist, neo-fascist, or quasi-fascist. To use the word fascist in this way is not only a piece of intellectual confusion, it is also to risk fixing one's eyes so firmly upon the past that the distinctive features of the new activist siblings are never noticed.
>
> *(1983: 190)*

This is not to say that for historians of generic fascism, there were no new departures. Significantly, one book, listed by *Le Monde* as one of the most important published in France during the 1980s, did push at the boundaries of periodization. Yet Israeli historian Zeev Sternhell's *Ni droite ni gauche. L'Idéologie fasciste en France* (1983), translated into English as *Neither Right nor Left: Fascist Ideology in France* (1996), went backwards, not forwards: 'Fascism belonged not just to the interwar period but to the whole period of history that began with the modernization of the European continent at the end of the nineteenth century' (1996: 29).

It was 1991 before at long last, a historian, Roger Griffin, offered an original schematic account of post-war fascism. For Griffin, writing in *The Nature of Fascism*, the 'fascist era' did not 'conveniently' end in 1945 and he stressed fascism's protean quality, its 'almost Darwinian capacity for adaption to its environment' (1991: 146). Griffin divided post-war fascism into three schematic categories: (a) 'Nostalgic Fascism/Neo-Nazism' (basic world-view of inter-war movements with some adaptations); (b) 'Mimetic Fascism/Neo-Nazism' (non-cosmetic Nazism); and (c) 'Neo-fascism'. Whilst the first two of his categories were a little clumsy – *two* categories for neo-Nazism[3] – his third category, neo-fascism, captured those organizations that either introduced original themes into major inter-war permutations, or rejected inter-war permutations altogether. For Griffin, the prefix 'neo' meant 'offering something new with respect to inter-war phenomena' – in other words 'neo-fascism' was a designation of *novelty* with respect to 'classic' fascism (1991: 167). Nonetheless, neo-fascists still retained *continuity* with inter-war fascism. Significantly, the (ineliminable) core of revolutionary ultra-nationalist rebirth – theorized by Griffin in terms of an abstract Weberian 'ideal-type' – remained present even though fascism was constantly evolving not only in terms of ideological content but also in terms of organizational complexity.

Stanley Payne, whom Roger Griffin described as 'the doyen of fascist studies', would also turn his attention to neo-fascism in the epilogue to his formidable *A History of Fascism, 1914–45*, published in 1995. Payne applied the same tripartite taxonomy for pre-1945 as for after, distinguishing between a (neo) fascist right, a radical right, and a moderate authoritarian right. For Payne, the

> true neofascist organizations, as distinct from the right radical political parties, propound much the same vitalist, nonrationalist, and violent creeds as their ideological forebears – often to an exaggerated extent – and in some cases advocate even more revolutionary social and economic changes, but this only further ensures their total marginalization.
>
> *(1996: 498).*

Payne's argument was that specific historical fascism could never be re-created and whilst fascism did exist beyond 1945 (as neo-fascism), it presented as a very marginal, historically insignificant, and disappearing cultural residue. For students of the contemporary far right there was, therefore, little point in trying to conceptualize neo-fascism because it was almost like classifying 'obscure Amazonian languages rapidly undergoing extinction' (Payne, 1993: 75).

Meanwhile, Walter Laqueur in his *Fascism: Past, Present and Future* (1996) was still wrestling with the methodological problem of *novelty* versus *continuity*. 'Neo makes it clear that it is not identical with historical fascism, but *fascist* is the stronger part of the definition' (1996: 7, emphasis as original):

> Fascism conjures up visions of hundreds of thousands of brown and black shirts marching in the streets of Europe, of civil violence and aggressive war, of terror and relentless propaganda, of millions of victims. This, of course, is no longer true with regard to the postwar period, certainly not with regard to the 1990s.
>
> *(1996: 7)*

Nonetheless, Laqueur elected to retain use of the term 'neo-fascism'. Invoking the sort of biological metaphor that Roger Griffin would appreciate – Griffin would liken post-war fascism to hydra-headed 'slime mould' – Laqueur proposed that, 'If microbes and pests have become resistant to the magic bullets and the miracle pesticides of the 1940s and 1950s, fascism has used evolutionary techniques to adjust itself to new conditions and outwit humans' (1996: 235). In other words, fascism *adapts* but it can of course adapt into something else if the 'ineliminable' core is removed.

Where change appears so significant that the terms fascism or neo-fascism no longer seem appropriate, we might decide on applying the term *post-fascism* instead. Laqueur had deemed it useful in capturing ultra-nationalist or religious fundamentalist 'fascistlike' movements outside Western Europe (1996: 147–215). But he left the term undefined. Over 20 years on, and in formulating their response to our populist *zeitgeist*, some historians are now *conceptualizing* post-fascism. One recent example is Federico Finchelstein. In his *From Fascism to Populism in History* (2017), populism (which he understands as an authoritarian form of democracy) is 'both genetically and historically linked to fascism' (2017: 251). In 1945, writes Finchelstein, emerging from defeat, fascism *became* populism in history, the historical moment when fascism was reconstituted as populism – a 'postfascism for democratic times' (2017: 251). Elsewhere, in Enzo Traverso's *The New Faces of Fascism* (2019), our present historical moment is conceptualized as a transitional moment of *post-fascism*. Post-fascism, Traverso says, should be 'distinguished from neofascism, that is, the attempt to perpetuate and regenerate an old fascism' (2019: 6). According to Traverso, applying the term 'post-fascism' locates today's post-millennial radical-right populists 'in an historical sequence implying both continuity and transformation; it certainly does not answer all the questions that have been opened up, but it does emphasize the reality of change' (2019: 4). For Traverso (2019: 186) then, 'the emergence of postfascism looks like a profound shift: the radical right is no longer represented by ultra-nationalists marching in uniform through the streets of European capitals'. However, as Roger Griffin recognized (see Griffin, 2007: ix), the issue here is that historians (like Traverso and Finchelstein) are simply falling into the trap of assuming that inter-war traits, such as uniforms, mass-mobilization, and the cult of violence are *definitional* of fascism.

Returning to the 1990s, as Roger Griffin set about disseminating his 'ideal-type' theory with missionary zeal, several younger historians of the contemporary far right, myself included, found heuristic value in Griffin's methodological approach. I recall being a doctoral student at the time: on reading *The Nature of Fascism*, the conceptual fog lifted. But if contributing to conceptual fog dispersal was one thing, self-proclaiming the emergence of a 'new consensus' in fascist studies was quite another (see Griffin, 1998). Unsurprisingly, therefore, Griffin soon found himself at the centre of a lively (and sometimes acerbic) international debate.

Setting aside the sometimes frosty reception from other disciplines to Griffin's lucubrations, the reception from fellow *historians* was not always so warm either. Why was this? Methodologically, as the historian Philip Morgan (2006: 158) explained, 'ideal-type' abstractions do not sit comfortably with most historians. These abstractions can be, by their very nature static, and therefore *atemporal* and *ahistorical*. As Finchelstein (2017: 1) put it, 'Ideal types ignore chronology and the centrality of historical processes'. What's more, such methodological abstractions run counter to the exacting empirical instincts of most historical researchers. Let me explain: *pure-types* do not correspond exactly to the messy empirical reality. They are *subjective* constructs – the researcher selects a limited number of essential traits (the 'fascist minimum') in order to render the generic phenomenon intelligible. For Robert Paxton (1998), the key methodological problem with this abstracted 'fascist minimum' is its fixed essence. This encourages historians to reify that 'essence'. As a consequence, historians can all too easily fall into the trap of 'essentialism', whereby the essence becomes the explanation (see also Passmore, 2006: 169).

Thus, in *The Anatomy of Fascism* (2004) Paxton proposed an alternative historical methodology. The best way to understand fascism, maintained Paxton, is to approach its 'historical trajectory as a series of processes working themselves out over time, instead of as the expression of some fixed essence' (2004: 15). The latter, for Paxton, is 'a bit like observing Madame Tussaud's waxworks instead of living people, or birds mounted in a glass case instead of alive in their habitat' (2004: 15). Paxton acknowledged that fascism continued to exist after 1945 (typically at the level of his first stage – the founding stage). So, does this mean that Europe's radical-right populists might be considered a form of 'updated fascism'? Paxton was of two minds. His definition of fascism, which talked about a 'mass party of committed nationalist militants' pursuing 'with redemptive violence and without ethical or legal restraints goals of internal cleansing and external expansion' would suggest not (see Paxton, 2004: 218). On later reflection, and when pushed further, he acknowledged that 'Some elements are missing in the post-war European versions: aggressive expansionism and the glorification of war; anti-market economic nostrums such as autarky and corporatism; sweeping constitutional revisionism' (2010: 562). And yet, he had 'no major objection to calling the more extreme forms of post-war European xenophobia and nationalism neo-fascist' (2010: 563).

But it is not just in the most extreme forms of the contemporary far right where we find this (neo) fascism. If we only look for it at the furthest reaches of the far-right spectrum, we miss where it can, and does, shade into radical-right populism. Elsewhere I have emphasized how radical right-wing populism has grown in sophistication largely due to the influence of European New Right (ENR) neo-fascist theorists, particularly with regard to the adoption of ethno-pluralist discourse. More recently, the influence of the ENR has traversed the Atlantic, finding expression in 'identitarian' ideas propounded by the 'Alt-Right' (Lyons, 2017). Moreover, with regard to organizational histories, I have also spoken of the many instances where the new radical right and more extremist groups interact (see Copsey, 2013; 2018). Significantly, by adopting similar methodological approaches, which do recognize that the history of neo-fascism is also bound up with the history of radical right-wing populism, historians can now extend their analytical reach into transnational arenas. Andrea Mammone's (2015) and Matteo Albanese and Pablo del Hierro's (2016) recent studies of transnational neo-fascist networks are both fine examples of this type of work.

Conclusion: Let's not state the (bleedin') obvious

In the end, of course, 'The test is pragmatic: does viewing some novel political formation in terms of "fascism" help us to understand it?' (see Roberts, 2016: 262). Like Griffin, my answer is yes. But I need to qualify this: in retaining the concept of fascism I am not denying that post-war forms do differ from their predecessors. I also accept (obviously) that fascism is not the historical force that it was between the two world wars although that does not mean that it is now entirely devoid of historical significance. Indeed, we would be wise not to close down the potential for fascism in the 'here and now'. The 'fascism-producing' crisis of the 1930s is clearly not being replicated, but the nature of the present 'crisis' (of mass migration; of the vulnerability of national space in the era of competitive globalization; of populist resentment towards traditional political elites) is undoubtedly offering deeper traction to what historian Geoff Eley refers to as the politics of 'right-wing contention' – blurring the boundaries between 'previously isolable groupings of the far right and mainstream conservativisms' (2015: 109). Nonetheless, today's radical right-wing populism can, and should be, differentiated from fascism or neo-fascism. Payne (2006: 177) warned that expanding the candidates for the concept of neo-fascism comes at the 'cost of unacceptable conflation and dilution. Ideal types are useless without certain boundaries'. Payne was right: let's be careful to retain conceptual boundaries.

Yet to insist upon some epochal break in the lines of continuity between 'classic' fascism and the contemporary far right is also a mistake. In so doing, historians cede space to those who insist that post-war variants are something *essentially* different. As we have seen, political scientists are not the only ones that cut the threads connecting the past to the present – regrettably, many historians have been (and continue to be) guilty of this too. In true 'Noltean' fashion, David D. Roberts declared that fascism was 'finite, epochal, in that as it happened, it came to an end' (2016: 290). But when it comes to methodological approaches to the contemporary far right, we really should be bringing fascism's past into the present. The comments of Jeffrey M. Bale (2006: 293) seem to me to be particularly appropriate in these circumstances:

> It frankly baffles me that so many experts on classic fascism continue to argue for, if not insist upon, the strictly "epochal" nature of fascism [...] a stance which implicitly suggests that distinctive political phenomena cease to exist as soon as they lose their overriding political importance or that they are somehow frozen in time and incapable of assuming new forms in response to changing historical circumstances [...] If by claiming that the "fascist epoch" is over these scholars simply mean that fascism is no longer of central importance as a political movement in Europe, they would simply be stating the obvious.

Notes

1 See review by Gregor in *Americal Political Science Review*, vol. 72, no. 4, December 1978, p. 1474.

2   Cas Mudde cites, as examples of the work of 'historians', Kurt Tauber's monumental *Beyond Eagle and Swastika* (Middlestown, CT: Wesleyan College, 1967), but Tauber was an associate professor in political science. Mudde also cites Dennis Eisenberg's 1967 book, *The Re-emergence of Fascism* (London: Macgibbon and Kee), but Eisenberg was an Israeli journalist. A further citation is to Angelo Del Boca and Mario Giovana's book, *Fascism Today* (London: Heinemann, 1970), a survey by two Italian journalists, which the historian Gerhard L. Weinberg would lambast as 'pseudo-history', see *Political Science Quarterly*, vol. 86, no. 4 (1971), pp. 665–67.

3   For a recent (Griffinesque) working definition of neo-Nazism, see Paul Jackson, *Colin Jordan and Britain's Neo-Nazi Movement: Hitler's Echo* (London: Bloomsbury, 2017).

References

Albanese, M. and P. del Hierro. 2016. *Transnational Fascism in the Twentieth Century: Spain, Italy and the Global Neo-Fascist Network*. London: Bloomsbury.

Allardyce, G. (ed.). 1971. *The Place of Fascism in European History*. Upper Saddle River, NJ: Prentice-Hall, Inc.

Allarydce, G. 1979. "What fascism is not: Thoughts on the deflation of a concept." *American Historical Review*, 84(2), 367–388.

Bale, J.M. 2006. "(Still) more on fascist and neo-fascist ideology and 'groupuscularity'." In *Fascism Past and Present, West and East*, edited by R. Griffin, W. Loh and A. Umland, 292–299. Stuttgart: Ibidem Verlag.

Carsten, F.L. 1970. *The Rise of Fascism*. London: Methuen & Co Ltd.

Copsey, N. 2013. "'Fascism… but with an open mind': Reflections on the Contemporary Far Right in (Western) Europe." *Fascism: Journal of Comparative Fascist Studies*, 2(1), 1–17.

Copsey, N. 2018. "The Radical Right and Fascism." In *The Oxford Handbook of the Radical Right*, edited by J. Rydgren, Oxford: Oxford University Press.

De Felice, R. 1976. *Fascism: An Informal Introduction to its Theory and Practice*. New Brunswick, NJ: Transaction Publishers.

Eley, G. 2015. "Fascism then and now." In *The Politics of the Right, Socialist Register 2016*, edited by L. Panitch and G. Albo, 91–117. Pontypool: Merlin Press.

Finchelstein, F. 2017. *From Fascism to Populism in History*. Oakland, CA: University of California Press.

Gregor, A.J. 1974. *The Fascist Persuasion*. Princeton, NJ: Princeton University Press.

Griffin, R. 1991. *The Nature of Fascism*. London: Pinter.

Griffin, R. (ed.). 1998. *International Fascism: Theories, Causes and the New Consensus*. London: Arnold.

Griffin, R. 2007. "Foreword" to T. Bar-On, *Where Have All the Fascists Gone?*Aldershot, Hants: Ashgate.

Hayes, P. 1973. *Fascism*. London: George Allen & Unwin.

Hayes, P. 1979. "Fascism and the contemporary world." *Patterns of Prejudice*, 13(2–3), 9–12.

Hurst, M. 1968. "What is fascism?" *Historical Journal*, 11(1), 165–185.

Joes, A.J. 1978. *Fascism in the Contemporary World: Ideology, Evolution, Resurgence*. Boulder, CO: Westview Press.

Kitchen, M. 1976. *Fascism*. London: Macmillan.

Laqueur, W. 1996. *Fascism: Past, Present and Future*. Oxford: Oxford University Press.

Linz, J.L. 1991. "Some notes toward a comparative study of fascism in sociological historical perspective." In *Fascism: A Readers Guide*, edited by W. Laqueur, 3–121. Aldershot, Hants: Scholar Press.

Lyons, M.N. 2017. *Ctrl-Alt-Delete: The Origins and Ideology of the Alternative Right*. New York, NY: Political Research Associates.

Mammone, A. 2015. *Transnational Neofascism in France and Italy*. Cambridge: Cambridge University Press.

Morgan, P. 2006. "Recognising the enemy." In *Fascism Past and Present, West and East*, edited by R. Griffin, W. Loh and A. Umland, 156–160. Stuttgart: Ibidem Verlag.

Mudde, C. 2007. *Populist Radical Right Parties in Europe*. Cambridge: Cambridge University Press.

Mudde, C. 2017. *The Populist Radical Right: A Reader*. Abingdon: Routledge.

Nolte, E. 1966. *Three Faces of Fascism*. New York, NY: Holt, Rinehart and Winston.

Nolte, E. 1975. "The problem of fascism in recent scholarship." In *Reappraisals of Fascism*, edited by H.A. Turner, 26–42. New York, NY: New Viewpoints.

O'Sullivan, N. 1983. *Fascism*. London: J M Dent.

Passmore, K. 2006. "Generic fascism and the historians." In *Fascism Past and Present, West and East*, edited by R. Griffin, W. Loh and A. Umland, 168–274. Stuttgart: Ibidem Verlag.

Paxton, R. 1998. "The five stages of fascism." *The Journal of Modern History*, 70(1), 1–23.

Paxton, R. 2004. *The Anatomy of Fascism*. New York, NY: Alfred A. Knopf.

Paxton, R. 2010. "Comparisons and definitions." In *The Oxford Handbook of Fascism*, edited by R. Bosworth, 547–565. Oxford: Oxford University Press.

Payne, S.G. 1993. "Historic fascism and neo-fascism." *European History Quarterly*, 23, 69–75.

Payne, S.G. 1995. *A History of Fascism, 1914–45*. London: UCL Press.

Payne, S.G. 2006. "Commentary on Roger Griffin's 'Fascism's new faces'." In *Fascism Past and Present, West and East*, edited by R. Griffin, W. Loh and A. Umland, 175–178. Stuttgart: Ibidem Verlag.

Roberts, D.D. 2016. *Fascist Interactions: Proposals for a New Approach to Fascism and Its Era, 1919–1945*. New York, NY: Berghahn Books.

Trevor-Roper, H. 1968. "The phenomenon of fascism." In *European Fascism*, edited by S.J. Woolf, 18–38. London: Weidenfeld & Nicolson.

Seton-Watson, H. 1968. "Fascism in contemporary Europe." In *European Fascism*, edited by S.J. Woolf, 337–353. London: Weidenfeld & Nicolson.

Seton-Watson, H. 1979. "The age of fascism and its legacy." In *International Fascism: New Thoughts and New Approaches*, edited by G.L. Mosse, 357–376. London: SAGE Publications.

Sternhell, Z. 1996. *Neither Right nor Left: Fascist Ideology in France*. Princeton, NJ: Princeton University Press.

Traverso, E. 2019. *The New Faces of Fascism: Populism and the Far Right*. London: Verso.

Weber, E. 1964. *Varieties of Fascism: Doctrines of Revolution in the Twentieth Century*. New York, NY: Van Rostrand Reinhold Co.

Weiss, J. 1967. *The Fascist Tradition: Radical Right-Wing Extremism in Modern Europe*. New York, NY: Harper & Row.

Wilkinson, P. 1983. *The New Fascists*. London: Pan Books.

3

SOCIOLOGICAL SURVEY OF THE FAR RIGHT

Kathleen Blee and Mehr Latif

Cases from the United States and Europe have informed much of the sociological research on the far right. In these contexts, scholars have defined the far right by rejection of the state and the democratic process as well as adherence to a virulently racist, xenophobic ideology, or, especially for modern European political parties and the Trump presidency in the USA, by ethno-nationalist populism. Such politics exist in the form of political parties, social movements, and right-wing subcultures; often, these forms overlap (Rosenthal and Trost 2012; Skocpol and Williamson 2012). Outside of Western industrial societies, the right-left continuum is often not as relevant, and the far right is defined by factors that include the politics of exclusion and use of violent tactics (Fallon and Moreau 2012). By focusing on these varied contexts and institutional forms, sociological studies have identified an array of state and non-state actors that comprise the far right and influence each other.

In this chapter, we examine the evolution of what is considered the far right in the field of sociology, relevant theoretical frameworks, emerging empirical evidence, and methodological issues. We also discuss how an interdisciplinary lens can open up new areas of research, especially through its ability to link macro and micro evidence, map contemporary and historical transnational networks in the far right, and examine membership of these networks on cognitive, emotional, and social levels.

Theories and types of research

Sociologists have studied the full range of far right organizations, from individuals engaged in right-wing extremism primarily by reading websites or commenting on internet discussion sites to informal and formal groups, networks, movements, formal organizations, and electoral parties (Hirsch-Hoefler and Mudde 2013;

Klandermans and Mayer 2006a, 2006b; Köttig, Bitzan, and Petö 2017; Rydgren 2007; Virchow 2017). In recent years, the theoretical lenses used in these studies have mirrored broader conceptual turns in the discipline (Blee 2017b), with greater attention to interpretative, cultural, and interactional aspects of right-wing extremism complementing traditional emphases on far-right structures, resources, and political opportunities. This essay examines the advantages and limitations of this literature for a broad understanding of the nature and trajectory of far right politics across the globe.

Much sociological research can be categorized into one or more focus areas, although many studies work within more than one area.

Movement-focused studies examine how people are mobilized by or exit from far right efforts; how right-wing extremism evolves over time and the actors involved; the relationships between leaders and rank-and-file members; and the ways in which the far right frames issues for its adherents and outside audiences (e.g., McVeigh 2009). This research tradition has been particularly valuable for bringing the insights of social movement analysis into the study of right-wing, fascist, and racist movements, although the predominance of analysis of progressive politics within social movement studies may reduce attention to issues of terrorism, internal brutality, and criminality that are central to many far right movements (Blee 2017b).

Context-focused studies analyze the external conditions under which right-wing extremism emerges and collapses; the relationships among far right movements and parties and the larger society and national state; and how far right networks at the regional, national, and global levels affect the strength and direction of specific right-wing efforts (e.g., Cunningham 2012). This literature has been significant in developing more precise comparisons of far right movements over time and across countries and regions, although such studies face serious challenges in collecting and assessing data that are comparable historically and nationally.

Culture/identity-focused studies explore the factors that create allegiance to and solidarity within far right parties and movements, including extremist rituals and musical performances; clothing, gestures, and bodily markings that signify far right beliefs; the cultivation of collective emotion and collective identity; and how individuals negotiate stigmatized and subcultural far right identities (e.g., Latif et al. 2018; Simi and Futrell 2010; Macklin 2013). Such research has been highly productive for understanding the micro-level dynamics of mobilization and allegiance to far right movements, although studies have focused more intensively on how people enter and stay in right-wing politics rather than how they leave (Simi, Blee, DeMichele, and Windisch 2017).

Outcomes-focused studies consider strategies and tactics associated with far right politics, as well as the consequences of right-wing extremism such as increases in racist and xenophobia attitudes and violence in the population, as along with rightist drifts in mainstream parties (e.g., Laryš and Mareš 2011). Precise measures of outcomes are difficult, but recent advances in contextual analysis have made it possible to trace the effects of far right activity long after extremist movements have collapsed (McVeigh and Cunningham 2012).

Member/constituent-focused studies examine the characteristics of those who join, support, or benefit from far right politics, often with particular attention to issues of gender, religion, social class, regional and national origin, and age/generation, as well as how the social characteristics of far rightists differ among movements and parties (e.g., Blee 2002; Simi, Blee, DeMichele, and Windisch 2017). This research has been important in identifying the broad reach of many far right movements, although estimates of the composition of far right support are more robust for political parties than for social movements of the right.

Ideology-focused studies analyze the discourses, rhetorics, and beliefs associated with the far right, especially those of anti-Semitism, Islamophobia, racism, sexism and misogyny, homophobia, nationalism, xenophobia, fascism, and militarism (e.g., Barkun 1997). Such research has yielded essential insights into the dynamic nature of far right ideology, which can blend ideas from a variety of movements and national contexts; its major challenge is differentiating between ideological frames that far right movements adopt for an external audience (including messages meant to terrorize its enemies) and the ideological commitments of its members and participants (Blee 2002).

How scholarship responded to changes in the far right

The far right has undergone substantial changes in recent decades, pushing sociologists to develop new conceptual tools and research strategies. The recent emergence of powerful far right political parties and authoritarian, ethno-nationalist, and right-wing populist electoral politics in many nations of Europe, including Austria, England, France, Germany, Greece, Hungary, Italy, Poland, Slovakia, Sweden, and The Netherlands, as well as Russia and the United States, has attracted considerable research. Many of these studies are focused on single countries, but comparison across national borders and efforts to trace transnational and global flows and networks are becoming more common (Klandermans and Mayer 2006a; Köttig, Bitzan, and Petö 2017).

Sociological studies have highlighted the ideological shifts and contradictions within modern far right politics, exemplified by the efforts of far right politicians such as Marine Le Pen of the French National Front and Norbert Hofer of the Austrian Freedom Party to publicly distance themselves from their party's earlier roots in anti-Semitic and World War II-era Nazi ideologies. At the same time, these parties embrace virulently anti-immigrant and anti-Muslim agendas, exploiting skepticism of the European Union and manipulating public fear of loss of national identity to restrict and racialize the definition of who belongs in a nation (Mudde 2010; Rydgren 2007; Pavan and Caiani 2017; Yuval-Davis 2006). Particularly interesting are studies of how far right parties attract supporters by embracing issues that are traditionally antithetical to right-wing politics such as gay/lesbian/bisexual/transgender rights, women's issues, critique of neoliberal economics, support for Jews and Sikhs, or policies of the welfare state (Ashe 2015; Busher 2016; Copsey and Macklin 2013; Köttig, Bitzan, and Petö 2017; Mayer 2015; Spierings and Zaslove 2015; Spierings, Lubbers, and Zaslove 2017).

Sociological studies also examine support for the far right and populist ethno-nationalism, especially its roots in widespread racist, Islamophobic, and xenophobic attitudes. This research examines the relationship between voting and affiliating with ethno-nationalist politics and social categories, especially those of gender and social class, as well as the ability of far right parties and movements to create, and benefit from, new political alliances that cut across traditional voting blocs (Betz 1994; Bonikowski and DiMaggio 2016). In addition, such studies explore how political polarization is spurred by residential segregation, social and cultural insularity, and media fragmentation (Baldassarri and Gelman 2008; McCright and Dunlap 2011; Mouw and Sobel 2001).

There also is a large body of sociological research on the non-electoral far right, especially movements of right-wing extremism that deploy tactics ranging from violence and terrorism to ideological messages spread across media outlets. For example, studies of the anti-Semitic, racist, homophobic, and anti-immigrant Ku Klux Klan in the USA have examined the conditions under which Klans arise or collapse, as well as their mobilizing strategies, use of emotion and ritual, ideological development, and outcomes (Blee 2017b; Blee et al. 2017, 2002; Cunningham 2012; McVeigh 2009). Other studies focus on more loosely organized far right movements such as neo-Nazi skinheads or Christian Identity sects, with particular focus on how they are fueled by social ties of friendship and comradeship, cultural practices such as music shows, clothing, hairstyles, and tattooing, and expressions of collective emotion (Barkun 1997; Blee 2002; Miller-Idriss 2017a, 2017b; Pilkington 2010; Simi and Futrell 2010; Windisch et al. 2018). Sociological studies also have examined the social processes by which far right identities become salient; as, for example, former military personnel become attracted to right-wing extremism when they lose identities such as of a warrior that were established during time in the armed services (Simi, Bubolz, and Hardman 2013).

Sociological work has just begun on more recent dissolution of far right politics into loosely connected networks, individuals who participate in right-wing extremism solely through digital communication such as internet forums or social media platforms, and lone wolf operators who commit acts of violence and terrorism on behalf of a far right agenda but do not participate in organized extremist groups (Simon 2013; also see essays by Önnerfors and Muis and Dijkstra in this volume). Research is just beginning on the digitally-propelled political phenomenon commonly referred to as the 'alt-right,' which gained sudden prominence with the ascendancy of one its most visible promoters, the former head of Breitbart News, into a position as advisor to US president Donald Trump. Such studies require a different conceptual approach than that used for social movements or parties. For example, identifying and measuring far right networks and interactions in digital spaces requires replacing current definitions of activism and activists that are based on group membership, voting, or attendance at events with new definitions that are more appropriate to the activities of and notions of belonging to far right activism in an on-line environment (Diani and McAdam 2003; Earl 2013; McInerney 2016: Polletta 2016; see Daniels 2018).

Empirical challenges and innovations

Sociological studies of the far right successfully employ methodologies that range from statistical analysis of quantitative data to narrative, discursive, thematic, and processual analysis of qualitative data. Across this methodological range, most researchers of the far right confront similar thorny issues of access, validity, and ethics.

Access

Representative sample surveys, a staple of most sociological research, are commonly used to understand public support for the candidates and parties of the far right and have been particularly useful in identifying the attitudinal and ideological basis of far right voting (Mayer 2013; Mieriņa and Koroļeva 2015). In contrast, representative samples are rarely possible for studies of non-electoral far right movements in which the identities of participants are so hidden that it is impossible to generate a list (sampling frame) from which to select a sample (Berezin 2007; Busher 2016; Pilkington 2010, 2016; Simi and Futrell 2009, 2010; Watters and Biernacki 1989). Snowball sampling is a common alternative in such situations, but the secrecy of far right movements makes it difficult to know to what extent snowball networks capture the range of the underlying population. Studies by the first author have addressed this problem in two ways. The first is to create a sampling frame of far right groups and draw purposive samples of groups and members. Blee's (2002) study of women in organized racism in the USA began with a year-long search for racist groups. From the resulting list of groups, Blee first selected groups that varied by type (e.g., neo-Nazi, Klan) and location in the country, and then selected members within these groups who varied by age and position within the group (leader, member). A second strategy is to use knowledgeable informants to establish a multi-start snowball sample. A study of exit from far right movements (Simi, Blee, DeMichele, and Windisch 2017) engaged members from Life After Hate, an organization that aids those who seek to leave US far right groups, to identify former racist activists who varied on a number of characteristics to be interviewed and to connect the researchers to networks of former white supremacists. The increasing importance of digital communications in disseminating far right ideas and creating networks of adherents presents new difficulties but also opportunities for researchers. It can be challenging to identify individual motivations and recruitment patterns in far rightist movements that operate largely through the internet or social media, but such movements can also generate substantial real-time data on the spread of extremist ideologies across space, population subgroups, and social institutions.

Much sociological research on the far right uses secondary data, that is, data collected by someone other than the researcher, so issues of access depend on how the data were collected originally (see the essay by Richards in this volume). Perhaps least problematic are data on voting for far right parties which are generally gathered from voting tallies or surveys of a representative set of voters (Lubbers and Scheepers 2001). Important data are also generated by anti-extremist, anti-racist, and anti-fascist advocacy organizations such as the US-based Southern Poverty Law Center, British *Searchlight*, or Anti-Defamation League, which collect information from their affiliates and supporters as well as from other sources. Although the political stances of such organizations may shape the data they receive, these groups can have remarkable access into the far right through their networks of informants and observers. Newspaper accounts and police or government investigatory reports provide a different insight into difficult-to-access far right events and activities. Data gathered from newspaper accounts and state agencies often are subject to biases of interpretation and are subject to decisions on what is recorded and preserved about events and people (Cunningham 2012; Giugni, Koopmans, Passy, and Statham 2005). These biases are likely to be particularly strong for highly-marginalized subjects such as far right extremists.

The devolution of far right movements into tiny, insular groups, thinly-connected networks, and decentralized but linked internet-based operators (misleadingly cast as 'lone wolves') has substantially increased the challenges of access for scholars. Even when far rightists can be located, it can be difficult to persuade them to participate in research studies. Right-wing extremists are notoriously suspicious that scholars will depict them negatively, sometimes even suspecting them to be agents of the police or anti-racist activists (but see Fielding 2015; Linden and Klandermans 2007). As a result, they often do not answer questions fully or to allow researchers unrestricted access to their events. Moreover, access to the far right is substantially complicated by the violence (both actual and physical) that surrounds these groups and their often-volatile members, so field researchers need to balance their desire for extensive data against the danger that such research can pose (Blee 1998; Lee-Treweek and Linkogle 2000).

Validity

All sociological researchers are concerned about the validity of their findings, but such concerns are especially pertinent in studies of the far right in which artifice and deception are part of the fabric of social and political life. This dilemma is manifest in a variety of ways. For one, the penchant for secrecy in the far right means that members who can be identified and are willing to participate in a study may be those with the least access to information as more central members endeavor to remain out of the public eye. Moreover, the ever-present threat of violence toward researchers, together with the suspicion and hostility of far rightists toward scholars makes it difficult to establish the prolonged and trusting relationships that constitute a basis for securing valid information in qualitative research. Finally, and rarely discussed in sociological research, the world of the far right is likely rife with police and anti-racist informants whose identities are rarely disclosed even in retrospect. There is a considerable scholarship on the distorting effect of police informants on the political direction of social movements (Greer 1995; Marx 1974), but virtually no attention to the effects on research when some information is likely provided by movement infiltrators.

A strategy that has proven helpful in the study of highly duplicitous persons and groups is using multiple sources from different vantage points, for example by comparing the accounts of far right rallies in their publications with accounts in mainstream newspapers and police reports. As important is balancing information collected through interviews with information gathered through observation, which allows verbal claims to be assessed against action and interaction that unfolds within the sight of the researcher (Blee 2017a; Ezekiel 1996; Jerolmack and Khan 2014).

Relying on data provided by far right groups or members themselves, in the form of websites, social media postings, speeches, and propaganda (e.g., Daniels 2009a), can create serious problems of validity. Such issues of validity are increased when these movements operate through the internet and social media, as it is difficult to assess the credibility of information garnered from digital postings. Indeed, there is rarely any way to confirm even the most basic aspects of the identities used by on-line far rightists, including their purported gender and nationality. In fact, it may be impossible to determine whether postings are computer-generated rather than being the product, and a reflection of the ideas, of an actual person (see, Daniels 2009b; Siapera and Veikou 2016; Zukowski 2011).

Ethical issues

Virtually all scholars of the far right explicitly reject its political claims and agendas. Very few have personal experience with, or personal contacts into, the far right, certainly in comparison to scholars of progressive politics. Thus, scholars of the far right are distanced from, and generally disdain the subject they study, in sharp contrast to the connection and appreciation that characterize the scholar–subject relationship in sociological research on progressive politics.

The acute separation of scholars from the far right creates difficult ethical issues in this research. One is the problem of assessing the researcher's ethical obligation, if any, to a far right focused on bolstering racial, religious, and national inequalities by spreading falsehoods such as that people of color are morally deficient, that Muslims are terrorists, and that the World War II holocaust of European Jewry is a myth created to bolster the state of Israel. Scholars generally try to avoid harming those they study by, for example, honoring commitments to keep information confidential or preserve the anonymity of informants. But in the case of the far right, the researcher's ethical concern not to harm an individual research subject chafes against a broader social ethic to promote social justice and social truth by combatting the ideas and mobilizing efforts of the far right. A second ethical concern is that studying the far right inherently brings publicity to its ideas and organizations, a problem that can be alleviated, but not resolved, by focusing on the structure of the far right rather than the details of members' beliefs. Finally, scholars of the contemporary far right are confronted with the need to assess the extent that they are willing to provide information to or work with state surveillance and police investigatory agents or advocacy groups to dismantle far right groups or prosecute its members (see Plemmons and Barker 2016; Schmidt and Sharkey 2011).

Future directions

Five avenues of research show particular promise for future sociological work on the far right by taking advantage of new conceptual frameworks, analytic techniques, and sources or scales of data. The first avenue of new research emerges from recent sociological theories of causation and timing. In contrast to traditional sociological models that assess cause and effect by examining the relationships between originating states (such as childhood abuse) and culminating states (such as membership in a far right movement), these more processual models pay attention to dynamic chains of causation that create trajectories in social life (Abbott 1997; Hemmingby and Bjørgo 2015; Blee 2013; Haydu 2010). Such models are able to trace variations in the evolving attachment of people to far right politics or changes in far right groups over time as well as to identify significant turning points and triggering events that propel, unravel, or stall far right efforts (Blee 2010; Goodwin 2006). For example, life history interviews can be used to trace the cumulative effects of violent actions or clandestinity on the cohesion of far right movements, or how the causal impact of factors such as social relationships, gender, economic vulnerability, or mental health problems on far right allegiance can operate under some conditions and not under others (della Porta 2013; Fangen 1999, 1988; Simi, Blee, and DeMichele 2015; Zwerman, Steinhoff, and della Porta 2000).

A second promising direction takes advantage of new methodological techniques in computational linguistics, network analysis, terrorism studies, and computing and internet sciences to mine, manage, and analyze big data on the far right, such as Twitter feeds, internet searches, or videos from surveillance cameras (Jackson 2011; Tinati, Halfrod, Carr, and Pope 2014). Such approaches can trace the leakage of far right ideologies into mainstream media and politics and vice versa, the diffusion of ideas or strategies across groups and national borders, or the effects of recruiting messages on mobilization and online socialization processes (Bail 2014).

A third avenue, borrowing from new theories and methods in visual, performance, and symbolic analysis, studies the cultural rituals and corresponding emotional appeals that underlie much of modern far right politics (Miller-Idriss 2017b; Sehgal 2007; Virchow 2007). This approach can take advantage of the rapidly proliferating system of symbols and memes that have become recruiting icons and cultural touchstones for an international far right, as in Cynthia Miller-Idriss's (2014; 2017b) discussion of how right-wing sentiments are signaled by wearing certain clothing such as the German brand Thor Steinar. Further, as Anikó Félix (2015) emphasizes, far right groups such as those in Hungary are situated within a wider ethnocentric subculture organized around food, literature, and culture that helps far right ideas resonate with the wider community. Virág Molnár (2016) also illustrates how non-state actors operating in a variety of cultural, economic, political, and social fields such as book and paraphernalia stores, rock bands, and informal credit lenders have contributed to normalizing ethno-nationalist symbols and slogans on both cognitive and social levels.

Fourth, the increasing availability of data presents an important opportunity for comparative interdisciplinary research that can elucidate how the agenda and strategies adopted by the far right are shaped through their interaction with global networks. This approach might be particularly useful for understanding how far right groups operate in a transnational public sphere (Castells 2008; Kaldor 2004; Pavan and Caiani 2017; Schaffar 2016; Wodak, Angouri, and Georgakopoulou 2014). For example, Clifford Bob (2012) describes how gun activists in Brazil reached out to the National Rifle Association (NRA), both members of an international network, when they needed help in organizing against a referendum to ban firearms in 2003. In Margaret Power's (2015) study of how anticommunist ideas and strategies connected conservative women in Brazil, Chile, and the United States, she both underscores the existence of transnational historical networks and highlights the multi-directional flow of ideas, such as how women from Brazil and Chile served as a role models for conservative women in the United States. These examples show the value of examining how the strategies of national far right movements are shaped and proliferate through global networks as well as the connections between the increasing diversity of actors operating on the far right.

A fifth important direction is research that links macro-level (e.g., voting patterns), meso-level (e.g., interactions between parties and movements and local groups), and micro-level (e.g., political identity) data and analytic strategies. For example, following Ferruh Yilmaz's (2012) insight that a wide range of political actors, including right and left wing parties in Europe, have contributed to the frame of immigrants as the ontological other and thus not part of the traditional social contract, scholars could examine how voting and national identities and definitions of belonging are shaped by how far right parties frame issues and influence mainstream politics (Karapin 2002). In addition, in her study of skinheads in Russia, Hilary Pilkington (2010) brings together public poll data that underscore increasing ethno-xenophobia in Russia with an analysis of particular groups and the proliferation of racist language to explain how racial intolerance manifests in people's everyday lives.

Focusing on the increasing institutional links between state and non-state actors could also provide evidence on the role of local groups in shaping far right affiliation and voting. For instance, while scholars dispute the division of labor between skinheads and nationalist parties in Russia today, there is evidence that right-wing parties have financed and politically supported skinhead groups, and, in fact, that the state itself directly and indirectly legitimates the actions of a wide range of actors involved in far right groups and movements, including unorganized individuals, gangs, youth groups, and the paramilitary (Laryš and Mareš 2011; Pilkington 2010). Anikó Félix (2015) also finds that far right parties and right-wing movements in eastern Europe reinforce each other. For instance, she discusses how the

Golden Dawn comprises non-state actors, such as charitable divisions and groups that perform cultural outreach. The organizing efforts of such groups, including food or blood donations for individuals who can prove their Greek identity, contribute to a frame of 'us versus them,' reinforcing the xenophobic agenda of the party. With its winner-take-all electoral system, the United States tends to be dominated by two parties that position themselves to appeal to the broadest range of voters. In this electoral landscape far right and other extremist politics rarely can win national or even state-level elections and, as a result, such politics are generally expressed in the form of social movements rather than electoral parties. The recent campaign and election of Republican Party nominee Donald Trump to the US presidency, however, has realigned far right politics in the USA, as far right ideas and spokespersons have found unusual acceptance within the executive branch and the Republican Party. Whether this alignment will survive over time and beyond the Trump presidency is difficult to predict, but the Trump presidency has created a unique moment to study the far right's influence on electoral politics and political behavior more broadly.

The evolution and proliferation of actors working on the far right is increasingly a global phenomenon. Understanding how these actors, ranging from formal parties, non-state actors, and others that work within both formal and informal spaces, are organized, support each other, and shape the identities and behaviors of their members presents a critical opportunity for interdisciplinary work. The extensive data on voting behavior and party organization coupled with sociology's focus on framing, mobilization, and organizational and wider societal sub-cultures can help to elucidate why such groups have resonance in varying contexts, including within the United States and Europe as well as more broadly.

References

Abbott, Andrew. 1997. "On the Concept of Turning Point." *Comparative Social Research*, 16: 89–109.

Ashe, Stephen. 2015. "The Rise of UKIP: Challenges for Anti-Racism." In Omar Khan and Kjartan Sveinsson (eds), *Race and Elections* (pp. 15–17). London: Runnymede Press. http://www.runnymedetrust.org/uploads/RaceandElectionsFINAL_interactive.pdf#page=17 (accessed 23 March 2017).

Bail, Christopher. 2014. *Terrified: How Anti-Muslim Fringe Organizations Became Mainstream.* Princeton, NJ: Princeton University Press.

Baldassarri, Delia and Andrew Gelman. 2008. "Partisans Without Constraint: Political Polarization and Trends in American Public Opinion." *American Journal of Sociology*, 114(2): 408–446.

Barkun, Michael. 1997. *Religion and the Racist Right: The Origins of the Christian Identity Movement.* Chapel Hill, NC: University of North Carolina Press.

Berezin, Mabel. 2007. "Revisiting the French National Front: The Ontology of a Political Mood." *Journal of Contemporary Ethnography*, 36(2): 129–146.

Betz, Hans-Georg. 1994. *Radical Right-Wing Populism in Western Europe.* London: Macmillan.

Blee, Kathleen. 1998. "White-Knuckle Research: Emotional Dynamics in Fieldwork with Racist Activists." *Qualitative Sociology*, 21(4): 381–399.

Blee, Kathleen. 2002. *Inside Organized Racism: Women in the Hate Movement.* Berkeley, CA: University of California Press.

Blee, Kathleen. 2010. "Trajectories of Action and Belief in U.S. Organized Racism." In Assaad E. Azzi, Xenia Chryssochoou, Bert Klandermans, and Bernd Simon (eds), *Identity and Participation in Culturally Diverse Societies: A Multidisciplinary Perspective* (pp. 239–255). London: Blackwell.

Blee, Kathleen. 2013. "How Options Disappear: Causality and Emergence in Grassroots Activist Groups." *American Journal of Sociology*, 119(3): 655–681.

Blee, Kathleen. 2017a. "How Field Relationships Shape Theorizing." *Sociological Methods and Research.* https://doi.org/10.1177/0049124117701482.

Blee, Kathleen. 2017b. "How the Study of White Supremacism is Helped and Hindered by Social Movement Research." *Mobilization: An International Journal*, 22(1): 1–15.

Blee, Kathleen, Matthew DeMichele, Pete Simi, and Mehr Latif. 2017. "How Racial Violence is Provoked and Channeled." *Socio*, 9: 257–276.

Bob, Clifford. 2012. *The Global Right Wing and the Clash of World Politics.* New York, NY: Cambridge University Press.

Bonikowski, Bart and Paul DiMaggio. 2016. "Varieties of American Popular Nationalism." *American Sociological Review*, 81(5): 949–980.

Busher, Joel. 2016. *The Making of Anti-Muslim Protest: Grassroots Activism in the English Defence League.* London: Routledge.

Castells, Manuel. 2008. "The New Public Sphere: Global Civil Society, Communication Networks, and Global Governance." *The Annals of the American Academy of Political and Social Science*, 616(1): 78–93.

Copsey, Nigel and Graham Macklin. (eds). 2013. *British National Party: Contemporary Perspectives.* London: Routledge.

Cunningham, David. 2012. *Klansville, U.S.A.: The Rise and Fall of the Civil Rights-Era Ku Klux Klan.* New York, NY: Oxford University Press.

Daniels, Jessie. 2009a. *Cyber Racism: White Supremacy Online and the New Attack on Civil Rights.* Lanham, MD: Rowman & Littlefield.

Daniels, Jessie. 2009b. "Cloaked Websites: Propaganda, Cyber-Racism, and Epistemology in the Digital Era." *New Media and Society*, 11(5): 659–683.

Daniels, Jessie. 2018. "The Algorithmic Rise of the Alt-Right." *Contexts*, 17(1): 60–65.

della Porta, Donatella. 2013. *Clandestine Political Violence.* New York, NY: Cambridge University Press.

Diani, Mario and Doug McAdam. 2003. *Social Movements and Networks: Relational Approaches to Collective Action.* New York, NY: Oxford University Press.

Earl, Jennifer. 2013. "Studying Online Activism: The Effects of Sampling Design on Findings." *Mobilization: An International Quarterly*, 18(4): 389–406.

Ezekiel, Raphael. 1996. *The Racist Mind: Portraits of American Neo-Nazis and Klansmen.* New York, NY: Penguin.

Fallon, Kathleen and Julie Moreau. 2012. "Righting Africa? Contextualizing Notions of Women's Right-Wing Activism in Sub-Saharan Africa." In K. Blee and S. Deutsch (eds), *Women of the Right: Comparisons and Interplay Across Borders* (pp. 68–80). State College, PA: Pennsylvania State University Press.

Fangen, Katrina. 1998. "Living Out Our Ethnic Instincts: Ideological Beliefs among Right-Wing Activists in Norway." In Jeffrey Kaplan and Tore Bjørgo (eds), *Nation and Race: The Developing Euro-American Racist Subculture* (pp. 202–230). Boston, MA: Northeastern University Press.

Fangen, Katrina. 1999. "On the Margins of Life: Life Stories of Radical Nationalists." *Acta Sociologica* 42: 357–373.

Félix, Aniko. 2015. "Old Missions in New Clothes: The Reproduction of the Nation as Women's. Main Role Perceived by Female Supporters of Golden Dawn and Jobbik." *Intersections: East. European Journal of Society and Politics* 1(1): 166–182.

Fielding, Nigel. 2015. *The National Front*. London: Routledge.

Giugni, Marco, Ruud Koopmans, Florence Passy, and Paul Statham. 2005. "Institutional and Discursive Opportunities for Extreme Right Mobilization in Five Countries." *Mobilization*, 10(1): 145–162.

Goodwin, Matthew J. 2006. "The Rise and Faults of the Internalist Perspective in Extreme Right Studies." *Representation*, 42(4): 347–364.

Greer, Steven. 1995. "Towards a Sociological Model of the Police Informant." *British Journal of Sociology*, 46(3): 509–527.

Haydu, Jeffrey. 2010. "Reversals of Fortune: Path Dependency, Problem Solving, and Temporal Cases." *Theory and Society*, 39(1): 25–48.

Hemmingby, Cato and Tore Bjørgo. 2015. *The Dynamics of a Terrorist Targeting Process: Anders B. Breivik and the 22 July Attacks in Norway*. London: Palgrave Macmillan.

Hirsch-Hoefler, Sivan and Cas Mudde. 2013. "Right-Wing Movements." In *The Wiley-Blackwell Encyclopedia of Social and Political Movements 3* (pp. 1116–1126). Hoboken, NJ: Wiley.

Jackson, Paul. 2011. "The English Defence League: Anti-Muslim Politics On Line." In Paul Jackson and G. Gable (eds), *Far-Right.Com: Nationalist Extremism on the Internet* (pp. 7–19). Northampton: Searchlight Magazine and the Radicalism and New Media Research Group.

Jerolmack, Colin and Shamus Khan. 2014. "Talk is Cheap: Ethnography and the Attitudinal Fallacy." *Sociological Methods & Research*, 43(2): 178–209.

Kaldor, Mary. 2004. "Nationalism and Globalisation." *Nations and Nationalism*, 10(1–2): 161–177.

Karapin, Roger. 2002. "Far-Right Parties and the Construction of Immigration Issues in Germany." In Martin Schain, Aristide Zolberg, and Patrick Hossay (eds), *Shadows over Europe: The Development and Impact of the Extreme Right in Western Europe* (pp. 187–219). New York, NY: Springer.

Klandermans, Bert and Nonna Mayer. 2006a. *Extreme Right Activists in Europe: Through the Magnifying Glass*. London: Routledge.

Klandermans Bert and Nonna Mayer. 2006b. "Right-Wing Extremism as a Social Movement." In Bert Klandermans and Nonna Mayer (eds), *Extreme Right Activists in Europe: Through the Magnifying Glass* (pp. 3–15). London: Routledge.

Köttig, Michaela, Renate Bitzan, and Andrea Petö. (eds). 2017. *Gender and Far Right Politics in Europe*. Cham, Switzerland: Palgrave Macmillan.

Laryš, Martin and Miroslav Mareš. 2011. "Right-Wing Extremist Violence in the Russian Federation." *Europe-Asia Studies*, 63(1):129–154.

Latif, Mehr, Kathleen Blee, Matthew DeMichele, and Pete Simi. 2018. "How Emotional Dynamics Maintain and Destroy White Supremacist Groups." *Humanity & Society*, 42(4): 480–501.

Lee-Treweek, G. and S. Linkogle. 2000. *Danger in the Field: Risk and Ethics in Social Research*. New York, NY: Psychology Press.

Linden, Annette and Bert Klandermans. 2007. "Revolutionaries, Wanderers, Converts, and Compliants: Life Histories of Extreme Right Activists." *Journal of Contemporary Ethnography*, 36(2): 184–201.

Lubbers, Marcel, and Peer Scheepers. 2001. "Explaining the Trend in Extreme Right-Wing Voting: Germany 1989–1998." *European Sociological Review*, 17(4): 431–449.

Macklin, Graham. 2013. "'Onward Blackshirts!' Music and the British Union of Fascists." *Patterns of Prejudice*, 47(4–5): 430–457.

Marx, Gary T. 1974. "Thoughts on a Neglected Category of Social Movement Participant: The Agent Provocateur and the Informant." *American Journal of Sociology*, 80(2): 402–442.

Mayer, Nonna. 2013. "From Jean-Marie to Marine Le Pen: Electoral Change on the Far Right." *Parliamentary Affairs*, 66: 160–178.

Mayer, Nonna. 2015. "The Closing of the Radical Right Gender Gap in France?" *French Politics*, 13(4): 391–414.

McCright, Aaron M. and Riley E. Dunlap. 2011. "The Politicization of Climate Change and Polarization in the American Public's Views of Global Warming, 2001–2010 ." *The Sociological Quarterly*, 52: 155–194.

McInerney, Paul-Brian. 2016. "@ctivism 2.0: An Attempt at Making Sense of the New Social Media Landscape #DigitallyEnabledSocialChange." *Mobilizing Ideas*. https://mobi lizingideas.wordpress.com/2016/11/28/ctivism-2-0-an-attempt-at-making-sense-of-the-new-social-media-landscape-digitallyenabledsocialchange/ (accessed 12 March 2017).

McVeigh, Rory. 2009. *The Rise of the Ku Klux Klan: Right-Wing Movements and National Politics*. Minneapolis, MN: University of Minnesota Press.

McVeigh, Rory and David Cunningham. 2012. "Enduring Consequences of Right-Wing Extremism: Klan Mobilization and Homicides in Southern Counties." *Social Forces*, 90(3): 843–862.

Mieriņa, Inta and Ilze Koroļeva. 2015. "Support for Far Right Ideology and Anti-Migrant Attitudes Among Youth in Europe: A Comparative Analysis." *The Sociological Review*, 63(S2): 183–205.

Miller-Idriss, Cynthia. 2017a. "Soldier, Sailor, Rebel, Rule-Breaker: Masculinity and the Body in the German Far Right." *Gender and Education*, 29(2): 195–215.

Miller-Idriss, Cynthia. 2017b. *The Extreme Gone Mainstream: Commercialization and Far Right Youth Culture in Germany*. Princeton, NJ: Princeton University Press.

Miller-Idriss, Cynthia. 2014. "Marketing National Pride: Commercialization and the Extreme Right in Germany." In Gavin Brent Sullivan (ed.), *Understanding Collective Pride and Group Identity: New Directions in Emotion Theory* (pp. 149–160). New York, NY: Routledge.

Molnár, Virág. 2016. "Civil Society, Radicalism and the Rediscovery of Mythic National-ism." *Nations and Nationalism*, 22(1): 165–185.

Mouw, Ted and Michael E. Sobel. 2001. "Culture Wars and Opinion Polarization: The Case of Abortion." *American Journal of Sociology*, 106(4): 913–943.

Mudde, Cas. 2010. "The Populist Radical Right: A Pathological Normalcy." *West European Politics* 33(6): 1167–1186.

Pavan, Elena and Manuela Caiani. 2017. "'Not in My Europe': Extreme Right Online Networks and Their Contestation of EU Legitimacy." In Manuela Caiani and Simona Guerra (eds), *Euroscepticism, Democracy and the Media: Communicating Europe, Contesting Europe* (pp. 169–193). London: Palgrave Macmillan UK.

Pilkington, Hilary. 2016. *Loud and Proud: Passion and Politics in the English Defence League*. Manchester: Manchester University Press.

Pilkington, Hilary. 2010. "'Skinhead is a Movement of Action': Ideology and Political Action." In Hilary Pilkington, Al'bina Garifzianova, and Elana Omel'chenko (eds), *Russia's Skinheads: Exploring and Rethinking Subcultural Lives* (pp. 99–120). New York, NY: Routledge.

Plemmons, Dena and Alex W.Barker (eds). 2016. *Anthropological Ethics in Context*. London: Routledge.

Polletta, Francesca. 2016. "Social Movements in an Age of Participation." *Mobilization: An International Quarterly*, 21(4): 485–497.

Power, Margaret. 2015. "Who But a Woman? The Transnational Diffusion of Anti-Communism Among Conservative Women in Brazil, Chile and the United States During the Cold War." *Journal of Latin American Studies*, 47(1): 93–119.

Rosenthal, Lawrence and Christine Trost. 2012. *Steep: The Precipitous Rise of the Tea Party*. Berkeley, CA: University of California Press.

Rydgren, Jens. 2007. "The Sociology of the Radical Right." *Annual Review of Sociology*, 33: 241–262.

Schmidt, Christopher W. and Rachel A. Lockhard Sharkey. 2011. "Ethical and Political Ramifications of Reporting/Non-Reporting of Native American Ritualized Violence." In Richard J. Chacon and Rubén G. Mendoza (eds), *The Ethics of Anthropology and Amerindian Research: Reporting on Environmental Degradation and Warfare* (pp. 27–36). London: Springer.

Siapera, E. and M. Veikou. 2016. "The Digital Golden Dawn: Emergence of a Nationalist-Racist Digital Mainstream." In A. Karatzogianni, D. Nguyen, and E. Serafinelli (eds), *The Digital Transformation of the Public Sphere* (pp. 35–59). London: Palgrave Macmillan.

Schaffar, Wolfram. 2016. *Social Media-Based Far Right Movements in Thailand*. Oral presentation at the Third ISA Forum of Sociology, 10–14 July 2016. https://isaconf.confex.com/isaconf/forum2016/webprogram/Paper77840.html

Sehgal, Meera. 2007. "Manufacturing a Feminized Siege Mentality: Hindu Nationalist Paramilitary Camps for Women in India." *Journal of Contemporary Ethnography*, 36(2): 165–183.

Simi, Pete and Robert Futrell. 2009. "Negotiating White Power Activist Stigma." *Social Problems*, 56(1): 89–110.

Simi, Pete and Robert Futrell. 2010. *American Swastika: Inside the White Power Movement's Hidden Spaces of Hate*. Lanham, MD: Rowman & Littlefield.

Simi, Pete, Kathleen Blee, and Matthew DeMichele. 2015. "Does Mental Health Influence Entry into Violent Extremism and Domestic Hate Groups?" *Clinical Psychiatric News*, July 18. http://www.clinicalpsychiatrynews.com/?id=2407&tx_ttnews[tt_news]=419129&cHash=cf0655974318667e26b7cb8dc47cdd8a (accessed 1 September 2016).

Simi, Pete, Kathleen Blee, Matthew DeMichele, and Steven Windisch. 2017. "Addicted to Hate: Identity Residual Among Former White Supremacists." *American Sociological Review*, 82(6): 1167–1187.

Simi, Pete, Bryan F. Bubolz, and Ann Hardman. 2013. "Military Experience, Identity Discrepancies, and Far Right Terrorism: An Exploratory Analysis." *Studies in Conflict & Terrorism*, 36(8): 654–671.

Simon, Jeffrey D. 2013. *Lone Wolf Terrorism: Understanding the Growing Threat*. Amherst, MA: Prometheus Books.

Skocpol, Theda and Vanessa Williamson. 2012. *The Tea Party and the Remaking of Republican Conservatism*. New York, NY: Oxford University Press.

Spierings, Niels and Andrej Zaslove. 2015. "Gendering the Vote for Populist Radical-Right Parties." *Patterns of Prejudice*, 49(1–2): 135–162.

Spierings, Niels, Marcel Lubbers, and Andrej Zaslove. 2017. "'Sexually Modern Nativist Voters': Do They Exist and Do They Vote for the Populist Radical Right?" *Gender and Education*, 29(2): 216–237.

Tinati, Ramine, Susan Halford, Leslie Carr, and Catherine Pope. 2014. "Big Data: Methodological Challenges and Approaches for Sociological Analysis." *Sociology*, 48(4): 663–681.

Virchow, Fabian. 2007. "Performance, Emotion, and Ideology: On the Creation of 'Collectives of Emotion' and Worldview in the Contemporary German Far Right." *Journal of Contemporary Ethnography*, 36(2): 147–164.

Virchow, Fabian. 2017. "Post-Fascist Right-Wing Social Movements." In Stefan Berger and Holger Nehring (eds), *The History of Social Movements in Global Perspective* (pp. 619–646). London: Palgrave Macmillan.

Watters, John K. and Patrick Biernacki. 1989. "Targeted Sampling: Options for the Study of Hidden Populations." *Social Problems*, 36(4): 416–430.

Windisch, Steve, Pete Simi, Kathleen Blee, and Matthew DeMichele. 2018. "Understanding the Micro-Situational Dynamics of White Supremacist Violence in the United States." *Perspectives on Terrorism*, 12(6): 23–37.

Wodak, Ruth, Jo Angouri, and Alexandra Georgakopoulou. 2014. "Small Stories Transposition and Social Media: A Micro-Perspective on the 'Greek Crisis'." *Discourse & Society*, 25(4): 519–539.

Yılmaz, Ferruh. 2012. "Right-Wing Hegemony and Immigration: How the Populist Far-Right Achieved Hegemony Through the Immigration Debate in Europe." *Current Sociology*, 60(3): 368–381.

Yuval-Davis, Nira. 2006. "Belonging and the Politics of Belonging." *Patterns of Prejudice*, 40(3): 197–214.

Zwerman, Gilda, Patricia Steinhoff, and Donatella della Porta. 2000. "Disappearing Social Movements: Clandestinity in the Cycle of New Left Protest in the US, Japan, Germany, and Italy." *Mobilization: An International Quarterly*, 5(1): 85–104.

Zukowski, Kassandra. 2011. *The Tea Party Movement: Grassroots Advocacy at its Finest, or Highly-Disguised Astroturfing?* Unpublished dissertation, Arizona State University, Tempe, AZ.

4

RIGHT THINKING

Criminologists on right-wing extremism

Barbara Perry and Ryan Scrivens

It has become a truism for many in the west that 'the world changed' on September 11, 2001 when jets flew into the Twin Towers in New York City and the Pentagon in Washington DC. But the same refrain has been widely heard in the wake of Donald Trump's upset electoral victory on November 8, 2016. If the former drew attention to the threat of Islamist inspired violence, the latter served as a flashpoint for the mobilization of right-wing extremism (RWE). Trump's call to "Make America Great Again" has been read by many as "Make America White Again." His appeal to white nationalism seems to have emboldened and empowered adherents of RWE, as evidenced in myriad ways: blatant hate speech and hate crimes; increased 'chatter' on white power forums; and increased visibility of 'alt-right' commentators. There can be no better time to take stock of how we, as academics, account for the discourses and actions associated with RWE.

In the introduction to a special edition of *Terrorism and Political Violence* devoted to criminological approaches to the study of terrorism, Freilich and LaFree (2015) made the claim that terrorism had not captured the imagination of criminologists. To some degree, this is probably an apt assessment. While the September 11 attacks in the USA resulted in unprecedented scholarly attention to Islamist terrorism, in particular, much of the work has come from disciplines such as international relations, political science, security studies, even history. Criminology has lagged behind. However, the one area within the broader field where criminologists do have a lengthy history of engagement is with respect to RWE. Indeed, since at least the 1970s, 'hate groups' have attracted considerable attention within the discipline. My goal in this chapter is to trace some of the more contemporary contours of scholarship around RWE, beginning with an assessment of where the boundaries of criminology lie, in terms of the discipline generally and extremism specifically. I then turn to a consideration of the dominant theoretical and methodological currents that inform our understanding of RWE, followed by a brief sketch of some of the prevailing substantive themes characterizing criminologists' work on on the theme.

Just criminology? The inter-disciplinarity of RWE studies

When I was invited to contribute a chapter to this volume, I was asked to sketch out how criminology had approached the study of RWE. As someone who identifies as a criminologist, I thought this would be relatively straightforward. However, as I began to review my archive of literature on RWE, I soon recognized that this would pose a greater challenge than anticipated. It was exceedingly difficult to winnow out the 'criminological' materials. Unlike most other disciplines, criminology is in fact the spawn of multiple disciplines. While the core focus is of course 'crime,' how this specific field of interest is understood varies across the discipline, borrowing both methodology and theory from such diverse areas as sociology, psychology, economics, history, law, communications, and political science. Thirty years ago, Paul Rock (1986) characterized the discipline as a "rendezvous" or "meeting place" for academics traveling to the same destination – crime – via very different routes. This has long been held to be the strength of the field – because criminology is multi/inter-disciplinary, it is able to draw on the 'best practices' from other areas in examining crime and justice concerns.

It is because of the hybrid nature of the discipline that we found ourselves confronted by the dilemma of how to narrow the scope of my assessment. We draw on scholarship from sociology, history, political science, law and philosophy, *inter alia*. What work, then, falls squarely within the albeit permeable boundaries of criminology? We found Weinberg's (2013) distinction between right-wing populists and right-wing revolutionaries – 'hate groups' – to be a useful one in this context. Work that focuses largely on the 'political' arm likely falls outside the gambit of criminology; that which focuses on the criminal, often violent activities of the 'shock troops' of the movement would sit more comfortably within the discipline.

Oddly, it seems that criminologists focusing on RWE struggle to find a place within criminology. Very little such scholarship appears in criminology journals. For example, a quick search for articles in what are arguably three of the 'top' criminology journals – *Criminology, British Journal of Criminology*, and *Justice Quarterly* – yielded only one paper explicitly focused on RWE (Treadwell and Garland, 2011). Work with a focus on the far-right is more likely to appear in terrorism studies (e.g., *Studies in Conflict and Terrorism*), cultural studies (e.g., *Journal of Intercultural Studies*), communications (e.g., *Critical Discourse Studies*), as examples. For all of these reasons, I apologize to my colleagues if, in what follows, we are treading on their disciplinary toes.

Conceptual divergences

As in all disciplines, the first point of contention in discussions around far-right extremism revolves around defining RWE. The challenge is a reflection of the heterogeneity of the groups in question. There are some threads that may be more likely than others to cut across ideological positions, but these are few. Nonetheless, there has been no shortage of attempts to define what is meant by 'right-wing' extremism. A US team of scholars has adopted a broadly descriptive conceptualization of the term:

> They are fiercely nationalistic (as opposed to universal and international in orientation), anti-global, suspicious of centralized federal authority, and reverent of individual liberty (especially their right to own guns, be free of taxes), and they believe in conspiracy theories that involve a grave threat to national sovereignty and/or personal liberty, that one's personal and/or national "way of life" is under attack and is either already lost or that the threat is imminent (sometimes such beliefs are amorphous and vague, but for some the threat is from a specific ethnic, racial, or religious group), and in the need to be prepared for an attack by participating in paramilitary preparations and training, and survivalism.
>
> *(Adamczyk, Gruenewald, Chermak, and Freilich, 2014: 327)*

This is perhaps an apt characterization of the RWE movement in the USA, but may not be as useful in other contexts. There is much less emphasis in Canada and Europe on gun rights, or survivalism, for example. Other observers have identified key pillars of RWE that likely have more resonance beyond the USA. Jamin (2013) suggests that the core tenets are:

(a)   The valorizing of inequality and hierarchy, especially along racial/ethnic lines;
(b)   Ethnic nationalism linked to a mono-racial community;
(c)   Radical means to achieve aims and defend the 'imagined' community.

With these frameworks in mind, Perry and Scrivens (2015) suggest that RWE is a loose movement, characterized by a racially, ethnically and sexually defined nationalism. This nationalism is often framed in terms of white power, and is grounded in xenophobic and exclusionary understandings of the perceived threats posed by such groups as non-Whites, Jews, immigrants, homosexuals and feminists, although the targets of enmity vary across groups. As a pawn of the Jews, the state is perceived to be an illegitimate power serving the interests of all but the white man. To this end, extremists are willing to assume both an offensive and defensive stance in the interests of 'preserving' their heritage and their 'homeland.'

What is especially disappointing is the trend whereby – as in the broader field of hate crime – criminological scholarship on RWE has tended to be largely atheoretical, especially in the USA where the tyranny of positivism prevails. Data are drawn from 'official' statistics and subjected to regression analyses with no framework to guide the selection of variables; descriptive accounts of RWE websites are offered; white power music is assessed with no reference to the conceptual tools that shape those assessments. These approaches may provide some awareness of RWE sentiment and activity, but they do not take us very far in terms of a deeper understanding of how or why the identified patterns emerge.

Nonetheless, there have been some useful attempts to apply criminological theory to RWE. Strain theory has proven popular among criminologists (Blazak, 2001; Wooden and Blazak, 1995). Those drawn to hate groups, it is argued, are responding to, on the one hand, their perceived loss of access to economic opportunity, and on the other, their belief that minority groups (racialized communities, LGBTQ communities and women, especially) are by contrast undeservedly privileged across all sectors of society. Consequently, they retreat into an alternative cultural milieu. Mark Hamm (1993; 2007) integrates traditional criminological theories to account for Skinheads specifically, and terrorism more broadly. In his seminal work on American Skinheads, Hamm (1993) collapses strain/anomic, neo-Marxist and differential association theories to unpack how disenfranchised youth might be socialized into a rebellious subculture. More recently, he has argued that social learning theory can account for the ways in which terrorists – including members of RWE groups – learn how to exploit opportunities for engaging in criminal activities via awareness of the routine activities (RAT) of security and intelligence personnel (Hamm, 2007). So, too, have Parkin and Freihlich (2015) tested RAT in the context of RWE, observing that both opportunity and proximity, for example, play a role in fostering violence by adherents.

The most exciting theoretical threads that have emerged of late, however, tend to be grounded in identity-based theories and social movement theory. The former class of scholarship grounds analyses in the precept that engagement in RWE activism is a means by which to 'do difference,' and especially to construct particular kinds of identities. For some, this involves considering the ways in which RWE adherents are engaged in constructing forms of hegemonic whiteness (Hughey, 2010; Simi, Futrell, and Bubolz, 2016), or hegemonic masculinities (Ferber, 2009; Treadwell and Garland, 2011), or both (Perry and Scrivens, 2016a; 2016b). Whichever the case, RWE groups are seen as locales in which white men are able to carve out places in which to exercise and in fact enhance – often through violence – power and privilege. As an offshoot, scholars like Kathleen Blee (2002) use a similar racialized and gendered lens to understand the role of women in such movements. In essence, scholarship in this vein stresses how "racist, reactionary and essentialist ideologies are used to demarcate inter-racial boundaries, and performances of white racial identity that fail to meet those ideals are marginalized and stigmatized" (Hughey, 2010: 1289).

Identity perspectives are closely linked to, if not explicitly derived from, social movement approaches. Of particular interest here are analyses that consider how RWE adherents are actively constructing not just individual but collective identities (Bowman-Grieve, 2009; Futrell and Simi, 2004; Oaten, 2014; Perry and Scrivens, 2016a; 2016b). The collective identity at issue here – the universal white man – is one such illustration of a "process that allows a disparate group of individuals to voice grievances and pursue a collective goal under the guise of a 'unified empirical actor'" (Adams and Roscignio, 2005: 760). Efforts to frame RWE groups within the social movement literature are rapidly emerging. Interestingly, scholars working in this area recognize the tendency to focus on progressive political movements, rather than on reactionary and regressive actors like right-wing extremists (e.g., Langman, 2005). Nonetheless, the theoretical frame allows the space to acknowledge oppositional groups (Adams and Roscigno, 2005; Tanner and Campana, 2014). Writing of the Quebec Skinhead community that was the focus of their study, Tanner and Campana (2014: 35) concluded that they could, in fact, be identified as such an oppositional movement by virtue of the fact that they "consciously and strategically adopt a marginalized position within society, following and defending alternative rules and norms."

Approaching right-wing extremism/ists

In a meta-analysis of scholarship on RWE, Gruenewald, Freilich and Chermak (2009) observed that there had been relatively few projects that engaged directly with adherents. As several of the chapters in this volume make clear, there are considerable challenges to studying RWE activists. Not least of these is access. The suggestion is that members of hate groups are largely clandestine, often paranoid, and for these reasons unwilling to expose themselves even to academic scrutiny (Blee and Creasap, 2010; Gruenewald et al., 2009). Yet several long-term ethnographies have illustrated that building rapport and thus trust is possible (Hamm, 1993; Simi and Futrell, 2015). However, the ability to build the needed relationships may well be constrained by the identity(ies) of the researcher. Simi and Futrell (2015) report that Simi was allowed access to their Aryan Nations group only on the condition that he was white. Even when groups invite academics into their midst, direct communication with far right adherents may also pose some risk to researchers (Blee and Creasap, 2010).

These challenges have not stymied all qualitative research. Hamm's (1993) *American Skinheads* was an early example of the depth of insight that could be gleaned from talking to adherents – in that case, yielding 36 extended interviews. Treadwell and Garland's (2011) ethnography of English Defence League adherents is another interesting case. Their very informal observations and interviews occurred 'where they lived,' that is, at demonstrations, and in local pubs, workplaces, homes, neighborhoods. Perhaps because they were approached on their own turf, participants seemed to be very forthcoming about their worldviews and their propensity for violence. A final example is Simi and Futrell's (2015) study of Aryan groups in the USA, which spanned the years 1996 to 2014, consisting of interviews, participant observation and content analysis of relevant websites. Like Treadwell and Garland (2011), they engaged with activists in their homes, favorite local hang-outs, white power events, even Bible studies.

There are two particular approaches that have seen remarkable advances in recent years. The first is the creation of terrorism databases that have collated extensive data on domestic and international terrorist activities. Among the most far-reaching of such databases are the RAND Database of Worldwide Terrorism Incidents (RDWTI; est. circa 1980); the Global Terrorism Database (GTD; est. 2001); the Worldwide Incidents Tracking System (WITS; est. 2004), and the United States Extremist Crime Database (ECDB; est. 2007). Because most of these databases include international data on diverse forms of terrorism – Islamist, right-wing, left-wing, environmental, etc. – they enable comparative analyses across nations, and across categories of terrorism and extremism. There have been a number of recent studies that have taken full advantage of these databases to enhance understanding of domestic RWE in the United States. The ECDB has been an especially fruitful foundation for scholarly work on far-right extremism (Chermak and Gruenewald, 2015). For instance, Gruenewald (2011) made use of the ECDB to explore differences between RWE homicides and other homicides. The database also framed Adamczyk et al.'s (2014) analysis of the links between hate groups and ideologically motivated extremist violence. And it has enabled insights into 'lone wolf' right-wing violence (Greunewald et al., 2013).

The second methodological approach that is beginning to provide remarkable insights into RWE activism is that grounded in 'big data.' The number of RWE and related websites has grown so dramatically in recent years that traditional methods of manually mining websites is no longer sufficient (Bouchard et al., 2014; Chau and Xu, 2007). This is particularly the case with respect to efforts to examine networks among RWE activists. Consequently, researchers in the field are increasingly developing models of machine-learning that allow them to extract not just content (Frank et al., 2015) but also sentiment/intensity of rhetoric (Mei and Frank, 2015; Figea et al., 2016), networks (Burris et al., 2000; O'Callaghan et al., 2012; Wong et al., 2015) and actor primacy (Scrivens et al., 2017). The Terrorism and Extremism Network Extractor (TENE), for example, is a custom-written computer program that was designed to capture vast amounts of data online according to user-specified conditions (Bouchard et al., 2014). The information drawn is then analyzed according to established rules, resulting in details about content and linkages within and between websites (Bouchard et al., 2014; Frank et al., 2015). Analyses grounded in these automated processes hold great promise for a much richer and deeper understanding of RWE networking and recruiting.

What's hot? Emerging topics

There are myriad strands of substantive analyses of RWE within criminology. Among them: the links between terrorism and hate crime (Deloughery, King, and Asal, 2012; Mills et al., 2015), and related to this the notion of 'cumulative extremism' (Bartlett and Birdwell, 2013; Busher and Macklin, 2015); RWE ideologies (Oaten, 2014; Pollard, 2016; Schafer et al., 2014); classes of violence associated with RWE (Berube and Campana, 2015; Mulholland, 2013; Petrou and Kandylis, 2016); and comparative/international analyses (Mammone, Godin, and Jenkins, 2013). I will, however, restrict my comments to four central foci: RWE use of media/social media; lone actors; the contexts of the rise of RWE; and responding to RWE.

Historically, hate groups recruited members or spread their message of intolerance through word of mouth, or through traditional media. However, by the early twenty-first century, engagement was largely transferred to the digital world. Indeed, the hate movement has been blessed with a valuable gift in the form of the Internet. Since the birth of the Internet in the 1990s, radical right groups have used it as an alternative form of media, both to publicize messages of hate and recruit and connect with like-minded others within and beyond domestic borders (Anahita, 2006; Chau and Xu, 2007; Wojcieszak, 2010).

Scholars have devoted considerable attention in recent years to the white power movement's growing presence on the Web. Analyses of how RWE use the Internet to recruit and sustain members have generally focused on the content featured on websites (e.g., Borgeson and Valeri, 2005; Bostdorf, 2004; Perry and Olsson, 2009) and web-forums (e.g., Anahita, 2006; Bowman-Grieve, 2009; Wojcieszak, 2010). We have also seen a handful on studies on how members of the radical Right use social media outlets, such as *Twitter* (Berger and Strathearn, 2013; Graham, 2016), blogs (e.g., Chau and Xu, 2007) and online newsgroups (e.g., Campbell, 2006).

An emerging strength of this focus on online hate is the recognition that digital media allow for dialogue and the *exchange* of ideas. Websites are not restricted to the provision of 'information' and literature; on the contrary, they enable participatory interaction and a shared construction of identity. The "virtual public sphere" that characterizes the Internet invites active participation whereby collectives "attempt to interpret and understand crises, injustice, and adversities, and to envision alternatives and map strategies" (Langman, 2005: 54). Importantly, the Internet also allows this shared project to cross the global rather than simply the local or national landscape. There have been some attempts to assess this trend at the global level (e.g., Caiani and Kröll, 2014; Grumke, 2013).

Ready accessibility to far right media has also meant that those without formal affiliation with a hate group can also draw on their discourse. Consequently, there is growing interest in the notion of the 'lone wolf' or 'lone actor.' Hoffman (2003) observes that there is an apparent increase in the tendency for individuals loosely or in fact not at all connected with formal organized groups to engage in extremist violence. Similarly, the *Toronto Star* (2015) reported on internal Canadian Security and Intelligence Service documents that suggested that RWE lone wolves represented a more pressing threat than did Islamic radicals in Canada. However, we are only just beginning to come to terms with the nature and potential of these extremists. There is considerable debate as to how closely these actors are allied with organized groups (Gruenewald, Chermak, and Freilich, 2013). Moreover, the breadth of the notion of 'lone' actor is debatable, as some would argue that the trio suspected of a Halifax mall shooting plot in Canada in 2015, for example, might loosely be described as a small 'pack' of lone wolves (Hoffman, 2003).

Mares and Stojar (2016) offer a comprehensive assessment of far-right lone actors globally, concluding that there is likely no profile that fits all such actors. Inspired by, sometimes loosely affiliated with organized hate groups, most of the actors identified seemed dissatisfied by the lack of action and impact of formal parts of the 'movement,' and thus enacted 'propaganda by the deed' in an effort to make a loud and clear statement. In the American context, Timothy McVeigh's 1995 Oklahoma City bombing was long held to represent the epitome of lone actor right-wing terrorism (Bates, 2012; Simon, 2013; Simi, 2010a). In more recent years, Anders Breivik has become the 'poster child' for RWE lone actors and has garnered considerable scholarly attention (Borchgrevink, 2013; Hemmingby and Bjørgo, 2015). Breivik's case has been used to highlight the challenges in predicting and defending against lone actor terrorism (Appleton, 2014; Bakker and De Graaf, 2011; Pantucci, 2011), as well as the intensity of the risk posed by right-wing lone actors relative to other ideological classes (Appleton, 2014; Gruenewald et al., 2013). Interestingly, Breivik has been linked not only to the extreme right-wing, but also to the mainstreaming of right-wing populism (Bangstad and Chapple, 2014; Michael, 2012).

The blurring of mainstream and extreme sentiment has perhaps made the challenge of responding to RWE a difficult one. Nonetheless, Dechesne (2011: 287) succinctly observes that "Deradicalization is hot." Across disciplines, within and outside the academy, in the media and among politicians, countering violent extremism (CVE) strategies are indeed 'hot.' An entire industry has sprung up around the project of challenging extremism on the ground and online. Scholars such as Bjørgo and Horgan (2009), Neumann (2013) and Schmid (2013), for example, draw our attention to factors that account for radicalization to extremism, and by extension, are ripe for targeting for counter-radicalization.

It is challenging to summarize the CVE literature. Both scholarly and policy approaches are varied and wide-ranging, including consideration of legislative measures, surveillance and monitoring, prevention, deterrence, deradicalization, and building community resilience, to name a few. Many criminologists are critical of securitized and/or criminal justice responses to extremism, largely because, while neutral on the face of it, they have largely been used to contain Muslims (Ahmed, 2014; Parmar, 2011). The legal label of 'terrorist' is far less likely to be applied to RWE (Perry and Scrivens, 2020; Simi, 2010b). From a law enforcement perspective, the activity of the far-right has not typically been monitored or taken seriously. Perry and Scrivens (2015) found that there is a tendency for officials to deny or trivialize the presence and threat of RWE. Moreover, the use of punitive measures to respond to extremist threats are often thought to be counter-productive, in that they have the potential to exacerbate hostility (Dechesne, 2011; McCauley, 2006).

In the best of all worlds, prevention initiatives would prevail, such that individuals are not motivated to enter the movement. A collection of essays edited by Rieker, Glaser and Schuster (2006) offers myriad analyses of preventative initiatives across Europe. Some of these are grounded in broad educative and policy approaches to enhancing practices of inclusivity and equity (Carlsson, 2006). Several highlight the development of countervailing discourses and social forces at the national level, recognizing that the hostility that shapes RWE is often grounded in normative discourses of hate and exclusion (Rieker, 2006; Dacombe and Sallah, 2006).

European countries, especially, have invested a significant amount of resources into counter-narrative initiatives, such as EXIT programs in Germany and Sweden, offering violent extremists a means of disengagement (Bjørgo and Horgan, 2009; Ramalingam and Tuck, 2014). According to Ramalingam and Tuck (2014), these strategies target three processes: group dissolution, disengagement, and deradicalization. We have seen, in recent years, case studies and life histories of individuals exiting from RWE groups, whether through formal or informal means (Bubolz and Simi, 2015; Gadd, 2006; Horgan et al., 2016). However, there is also considerable criticism of 'deradicalization' initiatives. Dechesne (2011), for instance, argues that many such programs often change only behavior without necessarily shifting adherents' 'worldviews,' leaving them at risk of lapsing back into the movement (see also Bubolz and Simi, 2015).

Finally, given that the Internet is such a crucial site of RWE activity, engagement and identity building, it is no surprise that there is considerable emphasis on strategies by which to counter online extremism. Western nations have struggled with the legal regulation of cyberhate and extremism online. In many cases, existing legislation has been invoked, as in the case of defamation laws, incitement to hatred policies, and human rights legislation. Bailey (2006) urges the innovative application of intellectual property law, libel law, and even the filing of union grievances in work places that are exposed to online hate. However, the law is not the only – or perhaps even the most effective – weapon available to counter cyberhate. There is growing interest in 'alternative' and 'counter' narratives in addressing terrorism generally and RWE specifically (Briggs and Feve, 2013). The former might be understood as an attempt to "Undercut violent extremist narratives by focusing on what we are 'for' rather than 'against'," while the latter represent efforts to "Directly deconstruct, discredit and demystify violent extremist messaging" (Briggs and Feve, 2013; see also Davies et al., 2016; Voogt, 2017; Williams and Burnap, 2015). These approaches often intersect with those emphasizing critical digital literacy borrowed from education and pedagogy studies (Ranieri et al., 2016; Williams and Pearson, 2016). However, criminologists will have to exploit their field's inherently interdisciplinary nature to take advantage of the insights offered in these other areas.

Indeed, as a general rule, as criminologists, we must continue to borrow from and collaborate with our colleagues in other fields. Recent patterns of escalation in RWE activity highlight the myriad social forces that enable such growth. It is an embedded response to diverse transformations in the economy, globalization, demographics, human mobility, and political discourse, to name a few. The foundations of RWE are multi-dimensional. So, too, must our approaches to understanding and countering the phenomenon be grounded in multi-dimensional, hence multi-disciplinary thinking.

I would like to end where I began, that is, with a consideration of how Trump's election victory in the USA, Brexit in the UK, the rise of Marine Le Pen in France and of right-wing populism generally in Europe will no doubt shape RWE and thus relevant scholarship in the coming years. We have already seen dramatic growth in RWE membership, visibility and activism across Europe and North America. The divisive and exclusionary rhetoric that has accompanied these campaigns has galvanized white supremacist ideologies, identities, movements and practices. This volume will no doubt provide many of the disciplinary and methodological tools that will allow scholars to confront the growing threat of RWE across the West.

References

Adamczyk, A., J. Gruenewald, and S. Chermak. 2014. "The Relationship Between Hate Groups and Far-Right Ideological Violence." *Journal of Contemporary Criminal Justice*, 30(3), 310–332.

Adams, J. and V. Roscigno. 2005. "White Supremacists, Oppositional Culture and the World Wide Web." *Social Forces*, 84(2), 759–778.

Ahmed, S. 2015. "The 'Emotionalization of the "War on Terror"': Counter-Terrorism, Fear, Risk, Insecurity and Helplessness." *Criminology & Criminal Justice*, 15(5), 545–560.

Anahita, S. 2006. "Blogging the Borders: Virtual Skinheads, Hypermasculinity, and Heteronormativity." *Journal of Political and Military Sociology*, 32(1), 143–164.

Appleton, C. 2014. "Lone Wolf Terrorism in Norway." *The International Journal of Human Rights*, 18(2), 127–142.

Bailey, J. 2006. "Strategic Alliances: The Inter-Related Roles of Citizens, Industry and Government in Combating Internet Hate." *Canadian Issues*, Spring, 56–59.

Bakker, E. and B. De Graaf. 2011. "Preventing Lone Wolf Terrorism: Some CT Approaches Addressed." *Perspectives on Terrorism*, 5(5–6).

Bangstad, S. and L. Chapple. 2014. *Anders Breivik and the Rise of Islamophobia*. London: Zed Books.

Bartlett, J. and J. Birdwell. 2013. *Cumulative Radicalisation Between the Far-Right and Islamist Groups in the UK: A Review of Evidence*. London: Demos.

Bates, R. 2012. "Dancing with Wolves: Today's Lone Wolf Terrorists." *Journal of Public and Professional Sociology*, 4(1), 1–14.

Berger, J.M. and B. Strathearn. 2013. *Who Matters Online: Measuring Influence, Evaluating Content and Countering Violent Extremism in Online Social Networks*. Developments in Radicalisation and Political Violence, The International Centre for the Study of Radicalisation and Political Violence, March 2013.

Berube, M. and A. Campana. 2015. "Hate-Motivated Violence: Ideologies and Acts by Right Extremists in Canada." *Criminologie*, 48(1), 215–234.

Bjørgo, T. and J. Horgan. (eds). 2009. *Leaving Terrorism Behind: Individual and Collective Disengagement*. London: Routledge.

Blazak, R. 2001. "White Boys to Terrorist Men: Target Recruitment of Nazi Skinheads." *American Behavioral Scientist*, 44(6), 982–1000.

Blee, K. 2002. "The Gendered Organization of Hate: Women in the U.S. Ku Klux Klan." In *Right-Wing Women: From Conservatives to Extremists Around the World*, edited by P. Bacchetta and M. Power, 101–114. London: Routledge.

Blee, K. and K.A. Creasap. 2010. "Conservative and Right-wing Movements." *Annual Review of Sociology*, 36, 269–286.

Borchgrevink, A. 2013. *A Norwegian Tragedy: Anders Behring Breivik and the Massacre on Utøya*, trans. Guy Puzey. Malden, MA: Polity.

Borgeson, K. and R. Valeri. 2005. "Identifying the Face of Hate." *Journal of Applied Sociology*, 22(1), 91–104.

Bostdorf, D.M. 2004. "The Internet Rhetoric of the Ku Klux Klan: A Case Study in Web Site Community Building Run Amok." *Communication Studies*, 55(2), 340–361.

Bouchard, M., K. Joffres, and R. Frank. 2014. "Preliminary Analytical Considerations in Designing a Terrorism and Extremism Online Network Extractor." *Computational Models of Complex Systems, Intelligent Systems Reference Library*, 53, 171–184.

Bowman-Grieve, L. 2009. "Exploring 'Stormfront:' A Virtual Community of the Radical Right." *Studies in Conflict & Terrorism*, 32 (11), 989–1007.

Briggs, R. and S. Feve. 2013. *Review of Programs to Counter Narratives of Violent Extremism*. London: Institute for Strategic Dialogue.

Bubolz, B. and P. Simi. 2015. "Leaving the World of Hate: Life-Course Transitions and Self-Change." *American Behavioral Scientist*, 59(12), 1588–1608.

Burris, V., E. Smith, and A. Strahm. 2000. "White Supremacist Networks on the Internet." *Sociological Focus*, 33(2), 215–235.

Busher, J. and G. Macklin. 2015. "Interpreting 'Cumulative Extremism': Six Proposals for Enhancing Conceptual Clarity." *Terrorism and Political Violence*, 27(5), 884–905.

Caiani, M. and P. Kröll. 2015. "The Transnationalization of the Extreme Right and the Use of the Internet." *International Journal of Comparative and Applied Criminal Justice*, 39(4), 331–351.

Campbell, A. 2006. "The Search for Authenticity: An Exploration of an Online Skinhead Newsgroup." *New Media Society*, 8(2), 269–294.

Carlsson, Y. 2006. "Violent Right-Wing Extremism in Norway: Community Based Prevention and Intervention." In *Prevention of Right-Wing Extremism, Xenophobia and Racism in European Perspective*, edited by P. Rieker, M. Glaser, and S. Schuster, 12–29. Halle, Germany: Center for the Prevention of Right-Wing Extremism and Xenophobia.

Chau, M. and J. Xu. 2007. "Mining Communities and Their Relationships in Blogs: A Study of Online Hate Groups." *International Journal of Human Computer Studies*, 65(1), 57–70.

Chermak, S. and J. Gruenewald. 2015. "Laying a Foundation for the Criminological Examination of Right-Wing, Left-Wing, and Al Qaeda-Inspired Extremism in the United States." *Terrorism and Political Violence*, 27, 133–159.

Dacombe, R. and M. Sallah. 2006. "Racism and Young People in the United Kingdom." In *Prevention of Right-Wing Extremism, Xenophobia and Racism in European Perspective*, edited by P. Rieker, M. Glaser, and S. Schuster, 79–95. Halle, Germany: Center for the Prevention of Right-Wing Extremism and Xenophobia.

Davies, G., C. Neudecker, M. Ouellet, M. Bouchard, and B. Ducol. 2016. "Toward a Framework Understanding of Online Programs for Countering Violent Extremism." *Journal for Deradicalization*, 6, 51–86.

Dechesne, M. 2011. "Deradicalization: Not Soft, but Strategic." *Crime, Law and Social Change*, 55, 287–292.

Deloughery, K., R. King, and V. Asal. 2012. "Close Cousins of Distant Relatives? The Relationship Between Terrorism and Hate Crime." *Crime and Delinquency*, 58(5), 663–688.

Ferber, A.L. 2009. "Gender, Privilege, and the Politics of Hate." In *Hate Crimes: Hate Crime Offenders* (Vol. 3), edited by B. Perry and R. Blazak, 69–84. Westport CT: Greenwood Publishing.

Figea, L., L. Kaati, and R. Scrivens. 2016. "Measuring Online Affects in a White Supremacy Forum." In *Proceedings of the 2016 IEEE International Conference on Intelligence and Security Informatics* (ISI).

Frank, R., M. Bouchard, G. Davies, and J. Mei. 2015. "Spreading the Message Digitally: A Look into Extremist Content on the Internet." In *Cybercrime Risks and Responses: Eastern and Western Perspectives*, edited by R.G. Smith, R.C.-C. Cheung, and L.Y.-C. Lau, 130–145. London: Palgrave Macmillan.

Freilich, J. and G. LaFree. 2015. "Criminology Theory and Terrorism: Introduction to the Special Issue." *Terrorism and Political Violence*, 27, 1–8.

Futrell, R. and P. Simi. 2004. "Free Spaces, Collective Identity, and the Persistence of U.S. White Power Activism." *Social Problems*, 51, 16–42.

Gadd, D. 2006. "The Role of Recognition in the Desistance Process: A Case Analysis of a Former Far-Right Activist." *Theoretical Criminology*, 10, 179–202.

Graham, R. 2016. "Inter-Ideological Mingling: White Extremist Ideology Entering the Mainstream on Twitter." *Sociological Spectrum*, 36(1), 24–36.

Gruenewald, J. 2011. "A Comparative Examination of Homicides Perpetrated by Far-Right Extremists." *Homicide Studies*, 15(2), 177–203.

Gruenewald, J., S. Chermak, and J. Freilich. 2013. "Far-Right Lone Wolf Homicides in the United States." *Studies in Conflict & Terrorism*, 36(12), 1005–1024.

Grumke, T. 2013. "Globalized Anti-Globalists: The Ideological Basis of the Internationalization of Right-Wing Extremism." In *Right-Wing Radicalism Today: Perspectives from Europe and the US*, edited by S. Von Mering and T. W. McCarty, 13–22. London: Routledge.

Hamm, M. 2007. *Terrorism as Crime*. New York, NY: New York University Press.

Hamm, M. 1993. *American Skinheads: The Criminology and Control of Hate Crime*. Westport CT: Praeger.

Hemmingby, C. and T. Bjørgo. 2015. *The Dynamics of a Terrorist Targeting Process: Anders B. Breivik and the 22 July Attacks in Norway*. Springer.

Hoffman, B. 2003. "Al Qaeda, Trends in Terrorism, and Future Potentialities: An Assessment." *Studies in Conflict & Terrorism*, 26(6), 429–442.

Horgan, J., M.B. Altier, N. Shortland, and M. Taylor. 2016. "Walking Away: The Disengagement and De-Radicalization of a Violent Right-Wing Extremist." *Behavioral Sciences of Terrorism and Political Aggression*, 9(2), 1–15.

Hughey, M.W. 2010. "The (Dis) Similarities of White Racial Identities: The Conceptual Framework of 'Hegemonic Whiteness'." *Ethnic and Racial Studies*, 33(8), 1289–1309.

Jamin, J. 2013. "Two Different Realities: Notes on Populism and the Extreme Right." In *Varieties of Right Wing Extremism in Europe*, edited by A. Mammone, E. Godin, and B. Jenkins, 38–52. Abingdon: Routledge.

Langman, L. 2005. "From Virtual Public Spheres to Global Justice: A Critical Theory of Internetworked Social Movements." *Sociological Theory*, 23(1), 42–74.

McCauley, C. 2006. "Jujitsu Politics: Terrorism and Response to Terrorism." In *Collateral Damage: The Psychological Consequences of America's War on Terrorism*, edited by P.R. Kimmel and C.E. Stout, 45–65. Westport, CT: Praeger.

Mei, J. and R. Frank. 2015. "Sentiment Crawling: Extremist Content Collection through a Sentiment Analysis Guided Web-Crawler." In *Proceedings of the International Symposium on Foundations of Open Source Intelligence and Security Informatics* (FOSINT).

Mammone, A., E. Godin, and B. Jenkins. (eds). 2013. *Varieties of Right-wing Extremism in Europe*. Abingdon: Routledge.

Mares, M. and R. Stojar. 2016. "Extreme Right Perpetrators." In *Understanding Lone Actor Terrorism: Past Experience, Future Outlook, and Response Strategies*, edited by M. Fredholm, 66–86. Abingdon: Routledge.

Michael, G. 2012. *Lone Wolf Terror and the Rise of Leaderless Resistance*. Nashville, TN: Vanderbilt University Press.

Mills, C., J. Freilich, and S. Chermak. 2017. "Extreme Hatred: Revisiting the Hate Crime and Terrorism Relationship to Determine Whether They Are 'Close Cousins' or 'Distant Relatives'." *Crime and Delinquency*, 63(19), 1191–1223.

Mulholland, S. 2013. "White Supremacist Groups and Hate Crime." *Public Choice*, 157(1–2), 91–113.

Neumann, P. 2013. "Options and Strategies for Countering Online Radicalization in the United States." *Studies in Conflict and Terrorism*, 36, 431–459.

Oaten, A. 2014. "The Cult Of The Victim: An Analysis of the Collective Identity of the English Defence League." *Patterns of Prejudice*, 48(4), 331–349.

O'Callaghan, D., D. Greene, M. Conway, J. Carthy, and P. Cunningham. 2012. "An Analysis of Interactions within and Between Extreme Right Communities in Social Media". 3rd International Workshop on Mining Ubiquitous and Social Environments (MUSE).

Pantucci, R. 2011. "What Have We Learned About Lone Wolves From Anders Behring Breivik?" *Perspectives on Terrorism*, 5(5–6).

Parkin, W.S. and J.D. Freilich. 2015. "Routine Activities and Right-Wing Extremists: An Empirical Comparison of the Victims of Ideologically Motivated and Non-Ideologically Motivated Homicides Committed by American Far-Rightists." *Terrorism and Political Violence*, 27(1), 182–203.

Parmar, A. 2011. "Stop and Search in London: Counter-terrorist or Counter-productive?" *Policing and Society*, 21(4), 369–382.

Perry, B. and P. Olsson. 2009. "Cyberhate: The Globalization of Hate." *Information and Communications Technology Law*, 18(2), 185–199.

Perry, B. and R. Scrivens. 2015. *Right-Wing Extremism in Canada: An Environmental Scan*. Ottawa: Public Safety Canada.

Perry, B. and R. Scrivens. 2016a. "White Pride Worldwide: Constructing Global Identities Online." In *The Globalization of Hate: Internationalizing Hate Crime?*, edited by J. Schweppe and M. Walters, 65–78. London: Oxford University Press.

Perry, B. and R. Scrivens. 2016b. "Uneasy Alliances: A Look at the Right-Wing Extremist Movement in Canada." *Studies in Conflict and Terrorism*, 39(9), 819–841.

Perry, B. and R. Scrivens. 2020. "Who's a Terrorist? What's Terrorism? Comparative Media Representations of Lone-Actor Violence in Canada." In *Canada Among Nations: Terrorism and Counterterrorism in Canada*, edited by J. Littlewood, L. Dawson, and S. Thompson, 242–264. Toronto, ON: University of Toronto Press.

Petrou, M. and G. Kandylis. 2016. "Violence and Extreme-right Activism: The Neo-Nazi Golden Dawn in a Greek Rural Community." *Journal of Intercultural Studies*, 37(6), 589–604.

Pollard, J. 2016 "Skinhead Culture: The Ideologies, Mythologies, Religions and Conspiracy Theories of Racist Skinheads." *Patterns of Prejudice*, 50(4–5), 398–419.

Ramalingam, V. and H. Tuck. 2014. *The Need for Exit Programmes: Why Deradicalisation and Disengagement Matters in the UK's Approach to Far-Right Violence*. London: Institute of Strategic Dialogue.

Ranieri, M., F. Fabbro, and P. De Theux. 2016. "Exploring the Potential of Media Literacy Education to Question Discrimination and Promote Civic Participation." In *Populism, Media and Education. Challenging Discrimination in Contemporary Digital Societies*, edited by M. Ranieri, 44–63. New York, NY: Routledge.

Rieker, P. 2006. "Juvenile Right-Wing Extremism and Xenophobia in Germany: Research and Prevention." In *Prevention of Right-Wing Extremism, Xenophobia and Racism in European Perspective*, edited by P. Rieker, M. Glaser, and S. Schuster, 67–78. Halle, Germany: Center for the Prevention of Right-Wing Extremism and Xenophobia.

Rieker, P., M. Glaser, and S. Schuster. (eds). 2006. *Prevention of Right-Wing Extremism, Xenophobia and Racism in European Perspective*. Halle, Germany: Center for the Prevention of Right-Wing Extremism and Xenophobia.

Rock, P. 1986. *A View from the Shadows*. Oxford: Clarendon.

Schafer, J., C. Mullins, and S. Box. 2014. "Awakenings: The Emergence of White Supremacist Ideologies." *Deviant Behavior*, 35 (3), 173–196.

Schmid, A. 2013. *Radicalisation, De-Radicalisation, Counter-Radicalisation: A Conceptual Discussion and Literature Review*. The Hague: International Centre for Counter-Terrorism.

Scrivens, R., G. Davies, and R. Frank. 2018. "Searching for Signs of Extremism on the Web: An Introduction to Sentiment-based Identification of Radical Authors." *Behavioral Sciences of Terrorism and Political Aggression*, 10(1), 39–59.

Simi, P. 2010a. "What is Lone Wolf Terrorism? A Research Note." In *Terrorism Research and Analysis Project (TRAP): A Collection of Research Ideas, Thoughts, and Perspectives*, Volume I, edited by A. J. Bringuel, 311–340. Washington, DC: Government Printing Office.

Simi, P. 2010b. "Why Study White Supremacist Terror? A Research Note." *Deviant Behavior*, 31, 251–273.

Simi, P. and R. Futrell. 2015. *American Swastika: Inside the White Power Movement's Hidden Spaces of Hate*. Lanham, MD: Rowman & Littlefield.

Simi, P., R. Futrell, and B.F. Bubolz. 2016. "Parenting as Activism: Identity Alignment and Activist Persistence in the White Power Movement." *The Sociological Quarterly*, 57(3), 491–519.

Simon, J.D. 2013. *Lone Wolf Terrorism: Understanding the Growing Threat*. Amherst, NY: Prometheus Books.

Tanner, S. and Campana, A. 2014. *The Process of Radicalization: Right-Wing Skinheads in Quebec*. Vancouver: Canadian Network for Research on Terrorism, Security and Society. No. 7–14.

Toronto Star. 2015. "Terrorism Threat Runs Broad 'Gamut'." March 15, p.1.

Treadwell, J. and J. Garland. 2011. "Masculinity, Marginalization and Violence: A Case Study of the English Defence League." *British Journal of Criminology*, 51(4), 621–634.

Voogt, S. 2017. "Countering Far-right Recruitment Online: CAPE's Practitioner Experience." *Journal of Policing, Intelligence and Counter Terrorism*, 12(1), 34–46.

Weinberg, L. 2013. "Violence by the Far Right: The American Experience." In *Extreme Right-Wing Political Violence and Terrorism*, edited by M. Taylor, P.M. Currie and D. Holbrook, 15–30. London: Bloomsbury.

Williams, M.L. and P. Burnap. 2015. "Combating Cyber-hate on Social Media Through Counter-speech". Paper presented at the Symposium on Anti-Muslim Hate Crime, University of Cambridge, Cambridge, UK, 16 June 2015.

Williams, M. L. and O. Pearson. 2016. *Hate Crime and Bullying in the Age of Social Media*. Conference Report, University of Cardiff.

Wooden, W.S. and R. Blazak. 1995. *Renegade Kids, Suburban Outlaws: From Youth Culture to Delinquency*. Belmont, CA: Wadsworth.

Wojcieszak, M. 2010. "'Don't Talk to Me': Effects of Ideological Homogenous Online Groups and Politically Dissimilar Offline Ties on Extremism." *New Media & Society*, 12(4), 637–655.

Wong, M.A., R. Frank, and R. Allsup. 2015. "The Supremacy of Online White Supremacists – An Analysis of Online Discussions by White Supremacists." *Information & Communications Technology Law*, 24(1), 41–73.

5

GETTING INSIDE 'THE HEAD' OF THE FAR RIGHT

Psychological responses to the socio-political context

Pasko Kisić Merino, Tereza Capelos and Catarina Kinnvall

Can we get inside the head of the Far Right? This chapter seeks to understand the psychological processes that explain the rise of the Far Right in Europe and discusses how political developments shape our individual, social and collective psychological experiences. The Far Right is a very heavily studied 'family' of political parties (Ellinas, 2010: 4; Mudde, 2017: 4). We complement party and electoral behavior research by highlighting the underlying psychological and structural dynamics that explain far right[1] preferences and behaviors among followers and leaders. The electoral success of far right parties across Europe that often promote Euro-sceptic and populist narratives is testament to their ability to mobilize constituencies against a number of socio-economic threats and vulnerable groups (e.g. ethnic minorities and immigrants), other European countries, and EU institutions. Versions of cultural and gendered nationalism underpin such mobilization, characterized by xenophobia, anti-Semitism, Islamophobia and violence. Simultaneously, both new and old democracies witness an upsurge of far right movements and groups set on filling a political space across Europe, appealing to a population in search of solutions to an ever-changing political and economic landscape. What are the psychological mechanisms that explain engagement with the Far Right? Do the political preferences of far right support affect the psychological experiences of individuals and societies amidst extended polarization, xenophobia and intolerance?

We review areas of psychological inquiry that complement non-psychological accounts of socio-political conditions (rise in relative deprivation, economic frustrations, rise in migration, and challenges of globalization and EU integration). We discuss 'who engages with the Far Right', focusing on the personality and qualities of far right followers and leaders, ideological orientations, values, emotions, group identification, social identity, psychoanalytical approaches, political participation and engagement.

The rise of the Far Right is a global phenomenon, which spans across continents and cultures like the USA, Russia, Turkey, Brazil and India. We focus on Europe because the rhetoric of the Far Right has not only been directed against immigrant others, but also against national establishments and the European Union (EU). Three major developments have contributed to the emergence of the Far Right in Europe: the austerity measures after the euro crisis of 2010; the so-called 'migration crisis' of 2015–2016; and the latest confrontations with 'illiberal' governments in Hungary, Poland, and now Italy accused of undermining the legal system.

In relation to these developments, we discuss the psychological dynamics of far right politics alongside phenomena like populism, extreme politics and extreme Islamism. More often than not, the Far Right is discussed focusing on populism and in isolation from other studies of radical mobilization, grievances, discrimination and insecurity. Here Ignazi (2003) outlines five features that correspond with current populist politics: nationalism and nativism, racism, xenophobia, new forms of democratic governance, and appeals for a strong state – and leader. Although research on populism is important for understanding the psychological dynamics of the Far Right, research on other forms of extremism and radicalism, such as extreme Islamism, terrorism, and radicalization, can offer valuable insights into the gradual processes of psychological transformation of beliefs and actions of movements and groups of the Far Right.

This requires methodological triangulation and empirical focus on discourses, narratives and practices that obstruct and facilitate the growth of the Far Right as part of a complex set of political phenomena. As Mudde (2017: 432) argued, the radicalization of the mainstream is often left out of the analysis and little attention is paid to the transition moment itself when mainstream actors and processes move to the right. In our closing section we address academics, practitioners and policy makers who seek to promote deliberative democratic engagement, equality, justice-inclusive values for trust-building, cohesion, inclusion and peaceful practices.

The psychology of the Far Right: Individual and group-based processes and dynamics

Who is the far right supporter?

The growing electoral success of far right parties across Europe has urged political and social psychologists to ask whether certain voter types are attracted to authoritarian narratives of anti-immigration, anti-EU, and xenophobia, looking at personal and psychological factors instead of socio-economic or educational factors. Inspired by the seminal sociological work of Adorno et al. (1950) on the authoritarian personality, studies borrow the concept of the 'Big Five' personality traits from psychology (Goldberg, 1993) and examine whether there is a character structure for the far right supporter. These models use qualities such as openness to experience, extraversion, conscientiousness, agreeableness and emotional instability to predict support for far right or populist parties and leaders (Bakker et al., 2016). The findings are mixed and vary across countries and contexts, suggesting that measures of personality cannot on their own predict far right political preferences (Aichholzer and Zandonella, 2016). An additional complication is that traits are *unobserved* character qualities measured by approximation relying on behavioral indicators (Allport, 1961). What is measured is a consistent pattern between political and nonpolitical behaviors, rather than a direct measure of an individual's personality (Capelos and Katsanidou, 2018).

Borrowing from models of attitudinal orientations such as right wing authoritarianism and social dominance (Altemeyer, 1981), some studies predict support for the Far Right on the basis of the cognitive motivational goals of individuals, seen as *sources of our personality* (Jost et al., 2009). The submissive, aggressive and conventionalist motivations of right wing authoritarians and the competitive motivations of individuals with social dominance orientation are associated with perceptions of social threat and political distrust, prejudice and feelings of insecurity (Hibbing et al., 2014), which in turn predict far right support (Aichholzer and Zandonella, 2016). These models show that voters support parties that appear to match their goals, suggesting that the far right voter can be mobilized to act on certain ideological preferences, but do not explain when these considerations are salient during certain times but dormant in other times.

Studies on *core* (or basic) *values*, particularly the enduring beliefs connected to desirable goals about preserving social arrangements that give certainty to life, protecting oneself against threats and risks, and abiding by tradition offer an alternative approach to explaining support for extreme politics (Capelos et al., 2017). Conformity and opposition to new experiences constitute the foundation of reactionary orientations, a complex cluster of core desires and resentful affect that explains anti-immigration and anti-EU preferences (Capelos and Katsanidou, 2018). Core values represent what individuals consider important in life. They are lasting orientations that reflect motivations like self-direction, stimulation, hedonism, achievement, power, security, conformity, tradition, benevolence and universalism. Values exist in hierarchical structures, and span across two dimensions: openness to change vs. to conservation, and self-transcendence vs. self-enhancement. They represent guiding principles in individuals' lives, and thus differ from attitudes which are evaluations of objects, beliefs which are ideas about how things are, norms which lay out rules and standards, and traits which describe what people are like (Schwartz, 2012). Values underlie attitudes, and because they refer to lasting priorities, aspirations and wishes, they are useful concepts when we seek to understand consistent patterns of social and political preferences. In addition, because they are less rigid than personality traits, they allow us to examine when and how these priorities change slowly over time according to individual experiences, societal and political conditions (Rokeach, 1973).

Core values also provide a stable and flexible basis for understanding variations in *political values* (such as moral traditionalism, ethnocentrism, economic security, law and order) between individuals and also within the same individual over time (Ciuk and Jacoby, 2015). There is an ongoing debate on whether economic *or* cultural political values are driving far right support: is it the rise in post-materialist values that has generated a counter-revolution, a backlash amongst those who did not share the left ideology? Or is it the rise in immigration and financial insecurities brought by globalization which drive right wing reactions? (Norris and Inglehart, 2019). The studies that diagnose the rise of the 'reactionary right' do not engage with the psychological properties of reaction, often equating it with far-right politics. It is worth scrutinizing the psychological mechanism of reactionism. Is it an exclusive property of the Far Right? Or is it a characteristic of extreme politics and radicalization processes more generally as well as of terrorist violence (Capelos and Demertzis, 2018; Lilla, 2016)?

Political affect is important for understanding far-right and ultra-conservative politics. Lipset (1960) identified anxieties instrumental for the rise of fascist parties, and Betz (2018) discussed the mobilization of resentment and hatred by far right parties. Rico et al. (2017) showed that angry voters choose anti-establishment populist parties, Vasilopoulou and Wagner (2017) identified links between anger and support for leaving the EU, and Vasilopoulou et al. (2018) found anger to drive support for the Far Right in France. It is not puzzling that in times of crisis individuals harbor negative emotions like anger, but also feelings of loss, grievance, anxiety, and uncertainty. Affective experiences are fluid, ever-evolving, and significantly richer than discrete emotions. Although it is certainly challenging to capture blends of anger, anxiety, envy, shame, feelings of loss, and nostalgic accounts of pride, resentful and *ressentimentful* affect,[2] our empirical models should expand beyond anger and fear, and focus on how complex affective structures fuel the psychological mechanisms that drives far-right support (Kenny, 2017; Capelos and Demertzis, 2018).

Citizens are often unaware of the processes that drive their decision-making. Bos et al. (2018) show that unconscious thoughts and emotions towards salient issues and outgroups mediate and predict support for far-right parties. Van Hauwaert and van Kessel (2017) find that individuals with populist attitudes support populist political parties even if they betray their own best policy interests (e.g. owners of small businesses voting for Brexit even if they will be hurt in the short, medium, and long term). Schmuck and Matthes (2018), focusing on Austria, find that anti-Islamic far right religious advertisements change viewers' implicit attitudes and they in turn mediate the formation of explicit attitudes against Muslims, thus affecting voting preferences.

Leaders and followers of the Far Right: Holding a far right identity

Studying far right leadership is important because far right leaders promote narratives and discourses that often increase intolerance and diminish the possibility of a broader political community. Art (2011) examined the attitudes, skills and experiences of far right party candidates in 11 western European countries and concluded that there is not one prototypical leader type. Because leaders require followers, some studies focus on supporters' perceptions of far right leaders and particularly their psychological appeal and charisma (McDonnell, 2016), especially for those disconnected from mainstream politics.

Leadership and identity formation are intertwined. Different individuals, when coming together as group members to support a leader, share a consensual social identity; and leaders construct and frame shared notions of identity. In other words, identity is important for understanding leadership, and the very possibility of leadership depends upon the existence or creation of a shared group identity, language, and influence tactics (Haslam et al., 2010). Identity construction and identity mobilization are parts of the attraction of far right rhetoric. Social identity theory (SIT; Tajfel, 1982) and its derivative, self-categorization theory (SCT; Hogg and Abrams, 1988; Turner et al., 1994), explain the psychological dynamics behind individuals' and groups' attraction to the Far Right. Groups provide self-esteem and individuals seek to improve the status of their ingroup in relation to the outgroup (Billig and Tajfel, 1973). SCT emphasizes that individuals see themselves as members of social groups when group membership maximizes the similarities between oneself and other group members, and increases differences with other groups (Huddy, 2001). A number of studies show that far right leaders use populist narratives that render three social categories salient: those at the top (malicious elite), those at the bottom (immigrants, asylum seekers), and those in between (the virtuous people) (Mols and Jetten, 2016; Steffens et al., 2018). Successful far right leaders unite strange bedfellows and instil a sense of togetherness and common fate among groups of individuals whose interests are not necessarily aligned (Haslam et al., 2010: 290).

However, we should not ignore the subjective process of why individuals are attracted to the Far Right and the role of others within this process. Without theories of ideology, culture, and discourse we cannot explain why some make sacrifices for the group whereas others stay marginally involved. There is also a difference between belonging to a group and internalizing its meaning (Huddy, 2001). This refers to the distinction between belonging to a common category by sharing certain characteristics obvious to the outsider, and group membership that is meaningful for the actual definition of oneself and one's identity (see discussion in Huddy, 2001). With its strong focus on categorization as a constant cognitive aim, SCT may find it difficult to explain subjective interpretations of what different group memberships mean for the individual. This, in turn, is likely to affect its explanatory power for understanding how previously harmless others may suddenly become reconstructed into the stranger-enemy (Kinnvall, 2004). Here psychoanalysis offers explanations of how the Far Right appeals to self-notions of belonging in relation to the stranger-other.

Psychoanalytical readings of the Far Right

Psychoanalytical accounts of identity and identity conflict emphasize the understanding of present actions in light of the past and the future while also providing explicit accounts of the emotional aspects of these processes (Craib, 1989; Kristeva, 1991; Volkan, 1988). Proceeding from object relations theory and Lacanian analysis, respectively, Volkan and Kristeva highlight the search for stable, clearly defined boundaries in the formation of self. Kristeva suggests that the antidote to xenophobia, racism, and the marginalization of others is to recognize the foreigner within ourselves. The 'other' exists in our minds through imagination even when he or she is not physically present. The existence of anti-Semitism in Poland despite the small numbers of Jews is suggestive of this power of imagination. Similarly, anti-immigrant feelings are sometimes stronger in places with few or no immigrants than in places that have experienced large immigration (Kinnvall, 2004). Recent studies (Kinnvall, 2018; Browning, 2018; Eberle, 2019; Ejdus, 2017) use Lacanian analysis to understand the power of imagination, myth and fantasy in relation to ontological insecurity among far right leaders and followers, and the emotional appeal of far right rhetoric and discourse in times of uncertainty.

Securitization is a key political process in the containment of anxiety and the production of ontological security (Rumelili, 2015), leading to an emphasis on the 'securitization of subjectivity' which refers to attempts made to intensify the search for one stable identity in order to reduce ontological insecurity and existential anxiety (Kinnvall, 2004). Moving away from Giddens' (1991) 'security of being', towards a 'security of becoming', the ontological insecurities people experience require a "leap in faith" (Cash, 2017) towards an imagined secure future that can relieve the individual from their present predicament (Kinnvall, 2018). For Eberle (2019: 246), to "filter away anxiety, we construct fantasies that promise a resolution, or at least an 'occlusion', of this 'original deadlock' … of the absence of a stable, unique and complete identity". A Lacanian approach means to accept the fragile nature of a constant 'becoming' – of learning to live with a constitutive lack. In the language of the Far Right, the fantasies of the past conjure up images of a country free from migration and untouched by global forces. It entails a *fantasmatic* (fictional) narrative of past greatness that is transmitted to new generations in search of answers to their own anxieties, while it simultaneously points to those who have taken this 'greatness' away (the establishment/immigrants) (Kinnvall, 2018). Using the discourse of 'stranger-danger', Ahmed highlights how the enforcement of boundaries takes shape between bodies that belong and bodies that are the 'origin of danger' (Ahmed, 2014: 4), where 'strangers' are already recognized as not belonging, as being 'out of place'.

Gender and far right masculinity

The rationalization, internalization, and normalization of extremist behavior exemplifies the sequence by which individuals join and remain in far right groups (Doosje et al., 2016). This sequence creates a sense of unity around gender as a basic identity, and several scholars have established the large gender gap between men and women supporting the Far Right (Givens, 2004; Mudde, 2017). Far right groups are particularly skilled at picking up the feelings of alienation, inadequacy, and overall disempowerment from young white men, and repackaging these feelings into a collective ethos and a sense of ontological purpose (Kinnvall, 2015; Mattheis, 2018). Far right groups usually take advantage of sub-cultural networks as breeding grounds for toxic masculinities and political extremism, such as football hooliganism, to attain new recruits (Veugelers and Menard, 2018). These sub-cultural milieus are spaces in which masculine symbology is explored and reinforced due to the influence of far right imagery on ideas of 'power', 'rebellion', and 'hegemony' in an otherwise hostile social environment (Miller-Idriss, 2017). The constant reinforcement of this imagery and discourse also determines how female members join and remain in these groups, and recruit other women. Women adapt their speech and discourse to the myths and symbology of far right value systems, by which (i) women are essentially complementary to men in their social performativity; (ii) women are caregivers and ideologically-fused mothers; and (iii) (white) women are entirely protected by (white) men, and "Western civilization" is the ultimate "romantic gesture to white women" (Mattheis, 2018: 156).

In far right politics the attachment to a justifying ideology (religion, nation) and its myths and symbols (cultural memorialization), provides a sense of belonging, rewards personal and social ties, and increases status and self-esteem, while also offering a sense of risk, excitement and danger and fulfilling a desire for vengeance. Thus it contributes to specific masculine attachments that provide bonds and comradeship and an emotional pull to act in the face of injustice (Kinnvall, 2018). It is worth exploring this 'masculinization' (Scrinzi, 2017) of nationalist discourse in the study of the Far Right: it has a particular appeal for disaffected males joining the Far Right in search of a place of belonging, exploring their own cultural identity through collective memorialization, narratives, myths or spaces.

Kimmel refers to this socio-psychological state as 'aggrieved entitlement' to explain a "gendered sense of entitlement thwarted by larger economic and political shifts, their ambitions choked, their masculinity lost" (2018: 1). We need, a "gendered political psychology of extremism" which highlights

> that the men who join do experience the need for camaraderie and community; the threats to a solid, grounded identity; the desire for a life of meaning and purpose; and the inability to achieving that life as specifically gendered feelings, urges, and emotions.
>
> (Kimmel, 2018: 9)

He points to downsizing, outsourcing, and economic displacement, phenomena that work in gendered ways to make young men feel emasculated in a structural and personal sense. Their own histories of isolation and exclusion work with structural forces to reclaim their manhood and restore their sense of entitlement. It is worth exploring these links for the Far Right: whether joining or sympathizing becomes a way to prove one's masculinity. Herein lies a sense of victimhood in which these men become convinced that somebody else is responsible for their emasculation (the establishment, the EU, immigrants), which is then turned into a righteous political rage against what they see as a politically correct multicultural society (Kimmel, 2018). Media discourse is crucial for understanding the stories, symbols and myths that combine into these imaginary others with online activism.

Media use and online activism

Media discourse and socio-political studies devote significant attention to the role of the media in the growth of the Far Right (Ellinas, 2010; Wodak, 2013). Far right parties are skilful in media use and their leaders are tasked with "rallying people around simplified social identities" (Kinnvall and Nesbitt-Larking, 2011: 60), through intensive media use (Wodak, 2013: 27). Online activism and street-level politics are linked to processes of joining, remaining, and exiting radical political groups. Online activism affects intrapersonal, interpersonal, intragroup and intergroup dynamics in contexts of high political polarization (Brady et al., 2017; Fullam, 2017). Through the constant and decentralized use of imagery that essentializes diverse sociocultural conflicts (Doerr, 2017), the Far Right and other radical groups use social media to diminish the distance between political leaders and individuals. For instance, Doerr (2017) cites the case of the Swiss People's Party (SVP), who made a multi-lingual visual representation of their xenophobic agenda via the 'black sheep' poster (representing an essentialized vision of immigrants as criminals who needed to be 'kicked out' of Switzerland) for the 2007 parliamentary elections. Partly due to the simplified visual style and the efficient multi-lingual approach, this xenophobic poster drew enormous international attention from fellow far right parties across Europe, who imitated their visual and communicative style (Doerr, 2017: 5–6).

In these spaces, strongly emotional language is used to cement a sense of collectiveness and belonging (Koehler, 2014) and to desensitize the members of the in-group with regards to the 'target' subject of the extremist discourse. The dual process of belonging-building and desensitization is achieved through the exploitation of 'outrage inducing content' (Crockett, 2017) or 'moralized content' (Brady et al., 2017), which becomes increasingly efficient as more individuals politically engage in online spaces. The spread of political ideas and beliefs through social media ('moral contagion') depends on the diffusion of 'moralized emotion' within common sociopolitical groups (ibid.).

While online activism becomes a universal type of political engagement, street-level politics – e.g. marches, protests, demonstrations – compose a manifestation of political will that transcends political agendas and discourses, while also shedding light on identity formation processes (Klandermans, 2014; Simões and Campos, 2016). From a psychoanalytic perspective, street-level political mobilization stems from a 'quest' for the formation of individual and collective identities and socio-political recognition (Rogers and Zevnik, 2017), as well as being a political tool or platform for challenging authorities (van Stekelenburg and Klandermans, 2018). Far right movements and parties are skilled at catching the emotions related to this quest for recognition and reinserting them into their discourse, reinforcing the self-perceived identities of the protestors (ibid.), especially when political activism becomes part of one's own lifestyle, moral and social commitments (Fernandes-Jesus et al., 2018). The identification with such collective identities determines the possibility of them being politicized and publicly expressed: "Politicization of collective identity takes place when grievances are turned into claims and citizens begin to campaign and mobilize to win support for their cause. In the process of politicization, the social environment changes into allies and opponents" (Klandermans, 2014: 20).

The level of moral conviction associated with specific outgroups, social issues, and political contexts also explains acceptance or involvement in violent solutions to ongoing conflicts at the street level (Skitka and Morgan, 2014). Effective displays of symbolic and real violence by far right movements can result in a fast-paced dual-process of identity and bordering formation: towards the ingroup, and against outgroups and society in general (Caiani et al., 2012: 209).

Stages of engagement in radical spaces

Social and political psychology have extensively studied the mobilization of radical groups and parties – or, rather, the *stages* of engagement into radical groups and politics. Emotions related to unmet psychological and social needs play a substantial role in how individuals join and remain in far right groups (Bos et al., 2018). Youth in particular decide to search, join and encroach in far right groups and parties (Jasko et al., 2017) to satisfy emotional needs related to traumatic experiences, and socioeconomic detachment (Aichholzer and Zandonella, 2016; Miller-Idriss, 2018) unmet in familial, friendship, and community circles (Mattson and Johansson, 2018). This emotional encroachment process strengthens the influence of radical discourses within these groups, as radical thoughts and actions shared and perpetrated by radical peers further sustain the feeling of camaraderie and belonging (Jasko et al., 2017).

Desiring, seeking, and finding a sense of community and belonging to a cause, ideology, or worldview are also strong factors concerning both joining and remaining in far right groups and parties (Aichholzer and Zandonella, 2016; Miller-Idriss, 2018). Through face-to-face and online interactions, these groups provide spaces and platforms in which new and veteran members feel secure, recognized, and validated in their radical thoughts and actions (Mattson and Johansson, 2018; Simões and Campos, 2016). This level of perceived internal support and mutual validation (Jasko et al., 2017) severely contrasts with the confrontational environments experienced at family and society levels, which makes both new and veteran recruits further isolated (Koehler, 2014).

This level of isolation has been linked to the pervasive effects of structural conditions and perceptions of critical sociocultural contexts experienced by far right activists. Cultural environments that tolerate, normalize, or even support radical and violent attitudes and behavior, such as schools, friend groups, and families, determine whether individuals join far right groups or parties (Mattson and Johansson, 2018; Miller-Idriss, 2018). These environments are formed by perceived 'critical' contexts, such as immigration and asylum seeker 'crises', and as the consequences of medium and long-term socioeconomic marginalization, deprivation, and distress (Caiani et al., 2012).

Joining and remaining in far right groups are also mediated by the tension between exposure to violence and the rise of social anxiety. Stemming from critical economic and political periods (Mattson and Johansson, 2018) and personalized readings of past events, such anxiety affects how political violence is rationalized in the context of belonging to far right groups. While numerous far right groups refrain from resorting to openly violent means and discourses to portray a 'clean' and 'modern' image (Mudde, 2017), this gradual rationalization and internalization of a constant 'threat' status (Aichholzer and Zandonella, 2016) further compel individuals to remain in extremist groups and 'double-down' on the use of violent means when their peers also fall into this mutually-reassuring dynamic (Jasko et al., 2017).

The psychological dimension of the stages of exiting a radical group and de-radicalization – processes that usually do not happen simultaneously (Mattson and Johansson, 2018) – have also been addressed by several authors (Bubolz and Simi, 2015; Doosje et al., 2016; Jasko et al., 2017; Mattson and Johansson, 2018). Bubolz and Simi (2015) argue that de-radicalization of white supremacists in the USA often occurs at an individual level through self-reflection by managing expectations of ingroup belonging over time, and at a group level via significant livelihood experiences like incarceration. According to Doosje et al. (2016), white suprema-cists begin reflecting and doubting their standing and actions once their 'shield of resilience' – the psychological defence mechanisms which make individuals "less likely to be persuaded by anti-radical messages from outside their group" – starts to shatter (Doosje et al., 2016: 82). Due to major emotional life events unlinked to the far right group (such as childbirth, forming of families, marriages), the breakage of this 'shield' becomes evident as individuals gradually stop engaging in violent action while still sponsoring far right views or ideologies, to eventually fully decreasing their commitment to the group or cause. Contact with non-violent circles of friends and family members can also reduce the chances of commitment to enacting violent political action (Jasko et al., 2017). These 'challenges' to the social frustrations, anger, and anxieties can eventually become detrimental to maintaining individuals committed to a far right cause (Jasko et al., 2017). At the same time, the process of exiting any radical group is affected by the constant role changes that members experience, since not all are involved in openly violent endeavours. Other conditioning factors include disillusionment with the far right leadership, emotional exhaustion, and intra-group conflict due to decreasing com-mitment and opposing micro-views on society (Doosje et al., 2016).

Learning from research on the political psychology of extremism and terrorism

The Far Right has been examined alongside populism, nationalism, Islamophobia, anti-Semitism, fascism, Euroscepticism and extremism (see Rydgren, 2018). The strong focus on populist politics in western democracies tends to overlook much work on extremism in general, and extreme Islamism in particular, as well as studies on radicalization and terrorism. This is not to downplay the emergence of a number of recent studies on how the Far Right and extreme Islamism feed into one another in patterns of 'cumulative extremism' and 'reciprocal radicalization' (Bjørgo, 2009; Busher and Macklin, 2015), but it is to argue that most often these literatures have developed in isolation of one another. Studies on extremism and extremist Islamism often proceed from a socio-psychological examination of how and why individuals engage in radical and extremist actions and reactions. Much of this research is located in political psychology, peace and conflict studies, and studies of terrorism, rather than in the study of populism, social movements or party politics. In this section we draw these links and provide some theoretical and empirical examples of how research on the political psychology of extremism offers valuable insights for the study of the Far Right.

Specific insights from the study of extremism and radical Islam

In the study of extremism, think tanks and law enforcement agencies often see religious ideology, especially Islam, as the most significant factor, despite relying on data from small samples and a handful of case studies (Sageman, 2004; Wiktor-owicz, 2005). Some terrorism studies have warned against such essentialist understandings of religious discourse and ideology (see e.g. Horgan, 2008) and we caution against similar practices in the study of the Far Right, which would render comparison and generalization problematic (see e.g. della Porta, 2009). Studies which lack a non-violent Muslim or non-religious control group cannot assess whether the socio-psychological process by which individuals become active in extremist Islamist or other extreme groups is indeed different from non-violent or non-religious individuals, even if their ideology differs (e.g. see Bartlett and Miller, 2012).

To understand why people join or sympathize with the Far Right, we should also move beyond the narrow focus on 'vulnerable' young people prevalent in much radicalization research (Bartlett et al., 2012; Kimmel, 2018). Recent reports on violent extremism show a large number of push and pull factors (Kundnani, 2015; Mattson and Johansson, 2018; Schmid, 2013; Vidino and Brandon, 2012). The same is true for factors that impact on de-radicalization and disengagement. The study of the Far Right gains from focusing on political affectivity (hope, anger, fear, shame, distress, resentment, envy), perceptions of efficacy, and instrumental values to bring about change, to understand how ordinary citizens engage, disengage, oppose or show dormant support for a wide range of behaviors (Capelos et al., 2017).

To further understand the attractions of the Far Right, we need to consider how graduate processes of psychological transformation occur. Research on extremist Islamism and radicalization pay attention to the beliefs and actions of oppositional groups, the extremist societal milieu, and the radicalization of public opinion to understand extremism, radicalization, and self-radicalization. Research on the Far Right could similarly interrogate how people join or feel attracted to this movement. As Blee (2007: 120) argues: "a more complete understanding of the occurrence of far-right movements also requires attention to issues of micro-mobilization, especially why people are attracted to such groups". This requires knowing more about central actors involved in recruitment and socialization, those who are its 'moving spirits' (Klandermans and Mayer, 2005), and who provide answers to the challenges faced by modern democracies. Far right parties (and movements) are different from traditional ideologically driven parties as they frame themselves as 'catch-all-parties', claiming to represent the 'whole people' rather than catering to various interests and values (Müller, 2016). But this does not prevent them from entering into coalitions or tempering their claims to represent the people; they also act as meeting spaces for the 'disaffected', as a magnet for the 'dispossessed', and as an 'amplifier' of grievances (for example Nigel Farage and UKIP in the UK and Victor Orban and his Fidesz party in Hungary).

Drawing from literature on extremism, a number of contextual drivers of radicalization are often noted. These refer to factors like the deprivation, poor integration, and the segregation and enclavization in which isolated groups lead parallel lives (Cantle, 2002; Kinnvall and Nesbitt-Larking, 2011). They also often involve socio-economic and political grievances, such as unemployment, perceived 'threats' of immigration, alienation and distance from mainstream society, all of which are said to accentuate the search for social bonds and networks (Mudde and Kaltwasser, 2017). This research does not explain, however, how far right attitudes, emotions, and behavior also manifest themselves among parts of the majority populations (as witnessed in growing anti-EU, anti-globalization sentiments, racism, xenophobia, anti-Semitism and hate-crimes), and how the reaction to societal factors is embedded within larger narratives and counter-narratives of belonging. Contemporary research on migration, citizenship, and the emergence of extremist groups shows that groups, institutions and states in Europe and elsewhere become increasingly concerned with defining and closing down community and national boundaries in response to actual or perceived threats against what they see as 'their' culture, religion and tradition (Kinnvall, 2015; Kinnvall and Nesbitt-Larking, 2011).

In addition to leadership and political organizations, social spaces or locales like schools, prisons, transnational networks, and social media are key battlegrounds for political extremism. Studies in Northern Ireland show, for instance, how prison experiences increased extremism, and how they affected the reintegration of former combatants after the Good Friday Agreement (Ferguson, 2010; Rolston, 2007). Hence, the turn towards an extremist organization may be a simpler form of (often gendered) resistance to a crowded, confined environment or the need to build opportunistic alliances between inmates (Silke, 2008). Such dynamics are worth exploring in the case of the Far Right. More research is needed on whether the process of far right politics and extremism in prisons is the same as in the community, as well as the scale of extremism within prisons and their gendered effects.

Studies on extremism and radicalization have also looked at transnational networks and how they deal with former recruits or returnees. Most cases concentrate on extreme Islamist recruitment, while comparatively less attention is paid to investigating the role of transnational networks for far right politics (see Caiani, 2013; Doerr, 2017; Macklin, 2013; Macklin and Virchow, 2016; Mammone et al., 2012), which often share some characteristics in the processes of recruitment strategies (Doosje et al., 2016). Similarly, there is a tendency to equal certain social spaces, such as mosques, with extremism. However, as Bigo et al. (2014) have argued, young individuals are often recruited in mundane settings such as cafes, gyms, or football clubs, in closed environments such as prisons, and through participation in political parties and various anti-establishment movements.

Conclusion: Towards an integrative model of researching the Far Right

Following this detailed account of the field, we think research on the Far Right benefits from employing mixed methods to study the individual and collective side of far right politics and the populist appeal of these movements and parties. We find it essential (a) to consider the interplay between factors and mechanisms at the individual, collective and contextual level; (b) to analyze the Far Right and the possibilities for democratic engagement in their psychological, discursive, political, and legal dimensions; and (c) to make use of complementary methodological tools that allow for a comparative investigation. These include definitions and studies of the Far Right that account for religious, nationalist and gendered contestations. This mixed-methods framework also has a normative purpose: to provide a deeper understanding of how far right politics can be countered, how individuals and groups can be disengaged, and how democratic engagement can be encouraged.

The study of the Far Right is, we argue, incomplete without the examination of adequate policy responses. Existing policy frameworks have proven ineffective at both the nation state level and the EU level: immigration policies do not allow for a proper integration of migrants despite the various models adopted (more assimilationist policies have not been more effective than more multicultural); asylum policies do not meet the needs of a better life for third country nationals (Kinnvall and Nesbitt-Larking, 2011); economic policies fail to create enough work opportunities for young people among both majority and minority populations; state welfare policies are unable to secure adequate levels of protection and equal chances to individuals (European Youth Forum, 2011). The financial, health, and economic crises constrain the economic and political reach of these measurements, and their acceptance within societies. In addition, pandemics pose new challenges of cooperation among states; they require policy coordination and exacerbate existing inequalities and marginalization.

Future studies should focus on the detection and examination of discourses, narratives, practices and policies that are less conducive to or constrain far right politics. This includes the role of leadership, social networks and group-identification, the role of social media as conveyors of counter-narratives and alternative forms of belonging, the effects of different policies and legal frameworks, and the role of wider socioeconomic welfare policies targeting discrimination and inequalities. This would allow for informed suggestions for a (national, European and global) legal framework conducive to democratic engagement and disengagement from far right orientations.

We close with acknowledging the collective responsibility of the academic, political and practitioner communities for proactive and impactful knowledge building, dissemination and communication. The academic research community *can and should* deliver knowledge that effectively transforms or reverses far right discourses, narratives and practices, with the aim to affect the wider socioeconomic and legal policies that target discrimination and inequalities, thereby strengthening democratic practices. We can only secure impact to knowledge, by investing and communicating knowledge on best practice, founded on conceptually sound, methodologically diverse, and ethically grounded scholarship.

Notes

1 We introduce **the Far Right** as a category, but we refer to **far right** (lower case) policies, leaders, approaches, when it is not about the group but about the ideological orientation.
2 See Capelos and Demertzis (2018) for a discussion of resentment as moral indignation versus *ressentiment* as compensatory emotion of the powerless that expedites transvaluation so that the person can stand and handle her or his frustrations.

References

Adorno, T.W., E. Frenkel-Brunswik, D.J. Levinson, and R.N. Sanford. 1950. *The Authoritarian Personality*. New York, NY: Harper.
Ahmed, S. 2014. *The Cultural Politics of Emotion* (2nd edition). Edinburgh: Edinburgh University Press.
Aichholzer, J. and M. Zandonella. 2016. "Psychological bases of support for radical right parties." *Personality and Individual Differences*, 96, 185–190.
Allport, G.W. 1961. *Pattern and Growth in Personality*. Oxford: Holt, Reinhart & Winston.
Altemeyer, R.A. 1981. *Right-Wing Authoritarianism*. Winnipeg, MN: University of Manitoba Press.
Art, D. 2011. *Inside the Radical Right: The Development of Anti-Immigrant Parties in Western Europe*. New York, NY: Cambridge University Press.
Bakker, B.N., M. Rooduijn, and G. Schumacher. 2016. "The psychological roots of populist voting: Evidence from the United States, the Netherlands and Germany." *European Journal of Political Research*, 55(2), 302–320.
Bartlett, J., J. Birdwell, and M. Littler. 2012. *The New Face of Digital Populism*. Working Paper. London: Demos.
Bartlett, J. and C. Miller. 2012. "The edge of violence: Towards telling the difference between violent and non-violent radicalization." *Terrorism and Political Violence*, 24(1), 1–21.
Betz, H.-G. 2018. "The radical right and populism." In *The Oxford Handbook of the Radical Right*, edited by J. Rydgren, 139–164. New York, NY: Oxford University Press.
Bigo, D., L. Bonelli, E.-P. Guittet, and F. Ragazzi. 2014. *Preventing and Countering Youth Radicalisation in the EU*. Study for the LIBE Committee No. PE 509.977. http://www.europarl.europa.eu/thinktank/en/document.html?reference=IPOL-LIBE_ET(2014)509977

Billig, M. and H. Tajfel. 1973. "Social categorization and similarity in intergroup beha-viour." *European Journal of Social Psychology*, 3(1), 27–52.

Bjørgo, T. 2009. "Processes of disengagement from violent groups of the extreme right." In *Leaving Terrorism Behind: Individual and Collective Disengagement*, edited by T. Bjørgo and J. Horgan, 30–48. New York, NY: Routledge.

Blee, K.M. 2007. "Ethnographies of the Far Right." *Journal of Contemporary Ethnography*, 36(2), 119–128.

Bos, L., P. Sheets, and H.G. Boomgaarden. 2018. "The role of implicit attitudes in populist radical-right support." *Political Psychology*, 39(1), 69–87.

Brady, W., J.A. Wills, J. Jost, J. Tucker, and J. Van Bavel. 2017. "Emotion shapes the dif-fusion of moralized content in social networks." *Proceedings of the National Academy of Sciences*, 114, 1–6.

Browning, C.S. 2018. "Brexit, existential anxiety and ontological (in)security." *European Security*, 27(3), 336–355.

Bubolz, B.F. and P. Simi. 2015. "Leaving the world of hate: Life-course transitions and self-change." *American Behavioral Scientist*, 59(12), 1588–1608.

Busher, J. and G. Macklin. 2015. "Interpreting 'cumulative extremism': Six proposals for enhancing conceptual clarity." *Terrorism and Political Violence*, 27(5), 884–905.

Caiani, M. 2013. *"A transnational extreme right? New right-wing tactics and the use of the internet."* Paper presented at the Paper presented at the SISP Conference 2013, Florence.

Caiani, M., D. della Porta, and C. Wagemann. 2012. *Mobilizing on the Extreme Right: Germany, Italy, and the United States*. Oxford and New York, NY: Oxford University Press.

Cantle, T. 2002. *Community Cohesion. A Report by the Independent Review Team*. Independent Review. Retrieved from Home Office UK website: http://tedcantle.co.uk/pdf/comm unitycohesion%20cantlereport.pdf

Capelos, T. and N. Demertzis. 2018. "Political action and resentful affectivity in critical times." *Humanity & Society*, 42(4), 410–433.

Capelos, T. and A. Katsanidou. 2018. "Reactionary politics: Explaining the psychological roots of anti preferences in European integration and immigration debates." *Political Psychology*, 39(6), 1271–1288.

Capelos, T., A. Katsanidou, and N. Demertzis. 2017. "Back to black: Values, ideology and the black box of political radicalization." *Επιστήμη Και Κοινωνία: Επιθεώρηση Πολιτικής Και Ηθικής Θεωρίας*, 35, 35–68.

Cash, J. 2017. "The dilemmas of ontological insecurity in a postcolonising Northern Ire-land." *Postcolonial Studies*, 20(3), 387–410.

Ciuk, D.J. and W.G. Jacoby. 2015. "Checking for systematic value preferences using the method of triads." *Political Psychology*, 36(6), 709–728.

Craib, I. 1989. *Psychoanalysis and Social Theory*. London: Harvester Wheatsheaf.

Crockett, M.J. 2017. "Moral outrage in the digital age." *Nature Human Behaviour*, 1, 769–771.

della Porta, D. 2009. *Social Movement Studies and Political Violence*. Aarhus: Centre for Studies in Islamism and Radicalisation, Aarhus University.

Doerr, N. 2017. "Bridging language barriers, bonding against immigrants: A visual case study of transnational network publics created by far-right activists in Europe." *Discourse & Society*, 28(1), 3–23.

Doosje, B., F.M. Moghaddam, A.W. Kruglanski, A. de Wolf, L. Mann, and A.R. Feddes. 2016. "Terrorism, radicalization and de-radicalization." *Current Opinion in Psychology*, 11, 79–84.

Eberle, J. 2019. "Narrative, desire, ontological security, transgression: Fantasy as a factor in international politics." *Journal of International Relations and Development*, 22(1), 243–268.

Ejdus, F. 2017. "'Not a heap of stones': Material environments and ontological security in international relations." *Cambridge Review of International Affairs*, 30(1), 23–43.

Ellinas, A. 2010. *The Media and the Far Right in Western Europe: Playing the Nationalist Card.* New York, NY: Cambridge University Press.

European Youth Forum. 2011. *Annual Report 2011.* Brussels: European Youth Forum.

Ferguson, N. 2010. "Disarmament, demobilization, reinsertion and reintegration: The Northern Ireland experience." In *Post Conflict Reconstruction*, edited by N. Ferguson, 151–164. Newcastle: Cambridge Scholars Publishing.

Fernandes-Jesus, M., M.L. Lima, and J.-M. Sabucedo. 2018. "Changing identities to change the world: Identity motives in lifestyle politics and its link to collective action." *Political Psychology*, 39(5), 1031–1047.

Fullam, J. 2017. "Becoming a youth activist in the internet age: A case study on social media activism and identity development." *International Journal of Qualitative Studies in Education*, 30(4), 406–422.

Giddens, A. 1991. *Modernity and Self-identity: Self and Society in the Late Modern Age.* Cambridge: Polity.

Givens, T.E. 2004. "The radical right gender gap." *Comparative Political Studies*, 37(1), 30–54.

Goldberg, L.R. 1993. "The structure of phenotypic personality traits." *American Psychologist*, 48(1), 26–34.

Haslam, S.A., S.D. Reicher, and M.J. Platow. 2010. *The New Psychology of Leadership: Identity, Influence and Power.* Hove, UK and New York, NY: Psychology Press.

Hibbing, J.R., K.B. Smith, and J.R. Alford. 2014. "Differences in negativity bias underlie variations in political ideology." *The Behavioral and Brain Sciences*, 37(3), 297–307.

Hogg, M.A. and D. Abrams. 1988. *Social identifications: A social psychology of intergroup relations and group processes.* Florence, KY: Taylor & Francis/Routledge.

Horgan, J. 2008. "From profiles to pathways and roots to routes: Perspectives from psychology on radicalization into terrorism." *The Annals of the American Academy of Political and Social Science*, 618, 80–94.

Huddy, L. 2001. "From social to political identity: A critical examination of social identity theory." *Political Psychology*, 22(1), 127–156.

Ignazi, P. 1992. "The silent counter-revolution." *European Journal of Political Research*, 22(1), 3–34.

Ignazi, P. 2003. *Extreme Right Parties in Western Europe.* New York, NY: Oxford University Press.

Jasko, K., G. LaFree, and A. Kruglanski. 2017. "Quest for significance and violent extremism: The case of domestic radicalization." *Political Psychology*, 38(5), 815–831.

Jost, J.T., C.M. Federico, and J.L. Napier. 2009. "Political ideology: Its structure, functions, and elective affinities." *Annual Review of Psychology*, 60(1), 307–337.

Kenny, M. 2017. "Back to the populist future? Understanding nostalgia in contemporary ideological discourse." *Journal of Political Ideologies*, 22(3), 256–273.

Kimmel, M. 2018. *Healing from Hate: How Young Men Get Into – and Out of – Violent Extremism* (1st edition). Oakland, CA: University of California Press.

Kinnvall, C. 2004. "Globalization and religious nationalism: Self, identity, and the search for ontological security." *Political Psychology*, 25(5), 741–767.

Kinnvall, C. 2015. "Borders and fear: Insecurity, gender and the far right in Europe." *Journal of Contemporary European Studies*, 23(4), 514–529.

Kinnvall, C. 2018. "Ontological insecurities and postcolonial imaginaries: The emotional appeal of populism." *Humanity & Society*, 42(4), 523–543.

Kinnvall, C. and P.W. Nesbitt-Larking. 2011. *The Political Psychology of Globalization: Muslims in the West.* Oxford and New York, NY: Oxford University Press.

Klandermans, P.G. 2014. "Identity politics and politicized identities: Identity processes and the dynamics of protest." *Political Psychology*, 35(1), 1–22.

Klandermans, P. and N. Mayer. 2005. *Extreme Right Activists in Europe: Through the Magnifying Glass*. Abingdon: Routledge.

Koehler, D. 2014. "The radical online: Individual radicalization processes and the role of the internet." *Journal for Deradicalization*, Winter No. 1, 116–134.

Kristeva, J. 1991. *Strangers to Ourselves* (L.S. Roudiez, trans.). New York, NY: Columbia University Press.

Kundnani, A. 2015. *A Decade Lost: Rethinking Radicalisation and Extremism*. London: Claystone.

Lilla, M. 2016. "The shipwrecked mind: On political reaction." In *New York Review Books*. New York, NY: New York Review of Books.

Lipset, S.M. 1960. *Political Man: The Social Bases of Politics*. Garden City, NY: Doubleday.

Macklin, G. 2013. "Transnational networking on the far right: The case of Britain and Germany." *West European Politics*, 36(1), 176–198.

Macklin, G., and F. Virchow. (eds). 2016. *Transnational Extreme Right Networks*. Abingdon: Routledge.

Mammone, A., E. Godin, and B. Jenkins. (eds). 2012. *Mapping the Extreme Right in Contemporary Europe: From Local to Transnational*. Abingdon: Routledge.

Mattheis, A. 2018. "Shieldmaidens of whiteness: (Alt) maternalism and women recruiting for the far/alt-right." *Journal for Deradicalization*, Winter No. 17, 128–162.

Mattson, C. and T. Johansson. 2018. "Becoming, belonging and leaving – exit processes among young neo-Nazis in Sweden." *Journal for Deradicalization*, Fall No. 16, 33–69.

McDonnell, D. 2016. "Populist leaders and coterie charisma." *Political Studies*, 64(3), 719–733.

Miller-Idriss, C. 2017. "Soldier, sailor, rebel, rule-breaker: Masculinity and the body in the German far right." *Gender and Education*, 29(2), 199–215.

Miller-Idriss, C. 2018. "Youth and the Radical Right." In *The Oxford Handbook of the Radical Right*, edited by J. Rydgren, 498–521. New York, NY: Oxford University Press.

Mols, F. and J. Jetten. 2016. "Explaining the appeal of populist right-wing parties in times of economic prosperity." *Political Psychology*, 37(2), 275–292.

Mudde, C. 2017. *The Populist Radical Right: A Reader*. Abingdon, Oxon and New York, NY: Taylor & Francis.

Mudde, C. and C.R. Kaltwasser. 2017. *Populism: A Very Short Introduction*. Very Short Introductions.Oxford and New York, NY: Oxford University Press.

Müller, J.-W. 2016. *What Is Populism?*Philadelphia, PA: University of Pennsylvania Press.

Norris, P. and R. Inglehart. 2019. *Cultural Backlash: Trump, Brexit, and Authoritarian Populism*. Cambridge: Cambridge University Press.

Rico, G., M. Guinjoan, and E. Anduiza. 2017. "The emotional underpinnings of populism: How anger and fear affect populist attitudes." *Swiss Political Science Review*, 23(4), 444–461.

Rogers, J. B. and A. Zevnik. 2017. "The symptoms of the political unconscious: Introduction to the special issue." *Political Psychology*, 38(4), 581–589.

Rokeach, M. 1973. "The nature of human values." In *The Nature of Human Values*. New York, NY: Free Press.

Rolston, B. 2007. "Demobilization and reintegration of ex-combatants: The Irish case in international perspective." *Social & Legal Studies*, 16(2), 259–280.

Rumelili, B. 2015. *Conflict Resolution and Ontological Security: Peace Anxieties*. New York, NY: Routledge.

Rydgren, J. (ed.). 2018. *The Oxford Handbook of the Radical Right*. New York, NY: Oxford University Press.

Sageman, M. 2004. *Understanding Terror Networks*. Philadelphia, PA: University of Pennsylvania Press.

Schmid, A.P. 2013. *Radicalisation, De-Radicalisation, Counter-Radicalisation: A Conceptual Discussion and Literature Review*. The Hague: The International Centre for Counter-Terrorism.

Schmuck, D. and J. Matthes. 2018. "Voting 'against Islamization'? How anti-Islamic right-wing, populist political campaign ads influence explicit and implicit attitudes toward Muslims as well as voting preferences." *Political Psychology*. https://doi.org/10.1111/pops.12557

Schwartz, S.H. 2012. "An overview of the Schwartz Theory of Basic Values." *Online Readings in Psychology and Culture*, 2(1), 3–20.

Scrinzi, F. 2017. "A 'new' National Front? Gender, religion, secularism and the French populist radical right." In *Gender and Far Right Politics in Europe*, edited by M. Köttig, R. Bitzan, and A. Petö, 127–140. London: Palgrave.

Silke, A. 2008. "Holy warriors: Exploring the psychological processes of Jihadi radicalization." *European Journal of Criminology*, 5(1), 99–123.

Simões, J.A. and R. Campos. 2016. "Youth, social movements and protest digital networks in a time of crisis." *Juventude, Movimentos Sociais e Redes Digitais de Protesto Em Época de Crise*, 13(38), 126–145.

Skitka, L.J. and G.S. Morgan. 2014. "The social and political implications of moral conviction." *Political Psychology*, 35(S1), 95–110.

Steffens, N.K., S.A. Haslam, J. Jetten, and F. Mols. 2018. "Our followers are lions, theirs are sheep: How social identity shapes theories about followership and social influence." *Political Psychology*, 39(1), 23–42.

Tajfel, H. 1982. "Social psychology of intergroup relations." *Annual Review of Psychology*, 33(1), 1–39.

Turner, J.C., P.J. Oakes, S.A. Haslam, and C. McGarty. 1994. "Self and collective: Cognition and social context." *Personality and Social Psychology Bulletin*, 20(5), 454–463.

Van Hauwaert, S.M. and S. Van Kessel. 2017. "Beyond protest and discontent: A cross-national analysis of the effect of populist attitudes and issue positions on populist party support." *European Journal of Political Research*, 57(1), 68–92.

van Stekelenburg, J. and B. Klandermans. 2018. "In politics we trust…or not? Trusting and distrusting demonstrators compared." *Political Psychology*, 39(4), 775–792.

Vasilopoulos, P., G.E. Marcus, N.A. Valentino, and M. Foucault. 2018. "Fear, anger, and voting for the far right: Evidence from the November 13, 2015 Paris terror attacks." *Political Psychology*. https://doi.org/10.1111/pops.12513

Vasilopoulou, S. and M. Wagner. 2017. "Fear, anger and enthusiasm about the European Union: Effects of emotional reactions on public preferences towards European integration." *European Union Politics*, 18(3), 382–405.

Veugelers, J. and G. Menard. 2018. "The non-party sector of the radical right." In *The Oxford Handbook of the Radical Right*, edited by J. Rydgren, 412–438. New York, NY: Oxford University Press.

Vidino, L. and J. Brandon. 2012. *Countering Radicalization in Europe*. Policy Report. London: The International Centre for the Study of Radicalisation and Political Violence (ICSR).

Volkan, V.D. 1988. *The Need to Have Enemies & Allies: From Clinical Practice to International Relationships*. Northvale, NJ: Jason Aronson, Inc.

Wiktorowicz, Q. 2005. *Radical Islam Rising: Muslim Extremism in the West*. Lanham, MD: Rowman & Littlefield Publishers, Inc.

Wodak, R. 2013. "'Anything goes!' – The Haiderization of Europe." In *Right-wing Populism in Europe: Politics and Discourse*, edited by R. Wodak, M. Khosravinik, and B. Mral, 23–37. London: Bloomsbury.

6

NEO-NATIONALISM AND FAR RIGHT STUDIES

Anthropological perspectives

Peter Hervik

From an anthropological perspective, scholarly work on the far right in Europe suffers on at least two accounts. Any time issues of populism, nationalism, and far right are reduced to an issue of political parties, who qualify as a far right party, anthropologists like myself feel perplexed. Not least since this focus comes from the structure of political science studies that prioritizes a top-down, political party focus over the phenomenon itself. The second point springs from this observation. From a classic anthropological methods principle, you should be careful not to impose your categories upon your field-site or phenomenon under study. Thus, as Janet Carsten (1995) convinced us, you do not study kinship by asking people for specific kinship categories as your starting point. You try to follow different forms of relatedness and then 'discover' the categories in play. This principle is challenged when violent events are categorized as 'terrorism' from the outset and provides a formidable view of how hegemonic understandings operate (Hervik, 2017).

School shootings and other mass killings are often mistakenly first represented as "terror", "terror-like" or "cannot be said to be terror" committed by people of Muslim background. However, against this common belief, killings by right wing activists in Norway, Sweden, Germany, and Russia have outnumbered those associated with Islamist terror (Jåsund and Topdahl, 2017; C-REX, 2016). At the same time, radical right wing violence, often meant to threaten but not kill, has risen dramatically (Jåsund and Topdahl, 2017). These two factual statements help bring attention to the double standards of news media coverage and political rhetoric, where spectacular violence and massacres are labelled and perceived along neo-nationalist, racial, and "left–right" lines.

Within anthropology, and science more broadly, the struggle is ongoing to properly conceptualize and understand the current trend that the right and far right embrace the idea that immigration threatens the nation's cultural homogeneity and the politics of fear that accompany it. Anthropologists have attempted to understand this trend as neo-nationalism (Gingrich and Banks, 2006), nationalist populism (Gullestad, 2006a; Kalb and Halmai, 2011), and "paranoid nationalism" (Hage, 2003), with an embedded naturalization of xenophobia and "cultural differences" (Stolcke, 1995; Hervik, 2011. At the same time, the political communication industry is furthering this process by "dumbing down" conversations and interviews to reach the maximum number of voters and media customers. Since Habermas wrote famously about the public sphere, it has "degenerated in industrialized mass-welfare democracies through processes of commoditization, monopolization, and competition among private interests over state-directed resource allocation" (Cody, 2011: 39). What this adds up to – and this volume bears witness to – is an insistence that neo-nationalism cannot be studied separately from neo-racism, processes of racialization, anti-elitism, anti-intellectualism, anti-multiculturalism, anti-feminism and a host of other things.

While observing the drastic changes around the turn of the millennium, European anthropologists began to show explicit interest in studying both political party and majority constructions of reinvigorated nationalism with its racial implications. With a special issue of a journal on racism (Ethnos, 2004) and an edited volume on neo-nationalism (Gingrich, 2004; Gingrich and Banks, 2006), neo-nationalism and neo-racism emerged as analytical concepts that sought to capture a trans-national and drastic global increase in anti-migration sentiments and practices springing from them.

In this chapter, I will emphasize three perspectives anthropology can offer to the study of neo-nationalism and far right studies in the era of global populism, the explosion of neo-nationalism, and the hostile, racialized reactions to migrants and refugees.

First of all, good anthropology will scrutinize key empirical and analytical concepts relevant for the ethnographic analysis of fieldwork material among, in this case, people who can be said to belong to the far right. When anthropologists began turning attention more generally to the world they inhabited, not least in the 1990s (Hervik, 2004), they would, so to speak, return from social spaces in faraway places, where they could never take the social space for granted, but had to learn everything from scratch. Once researching at home, they knew that their own familiarity and vocabulary had to be scrutinized for hidden meanings and assumptions. James Clifford formulated this process as making the familiar surreal, just like they were making the surreal familiar in faraway places (Clifford, 1988). In particular, I will deal with the taken-for-granted word "right" as in "far right", and approach it for its shadow meanings and accidental baggage. Then, I will turn to "neo-nationalism" itself. Its meanings and its short history.

The second perception anthropology can offer in studying neo-nationalism and the far right is how, since the millennium, racialization has emerged to become the lens through which Western societies view Muslim populations (as well as so-called "non-Westerners" and other Others). Racialization is embedded in the anti-Muslim, anti-Migration and anti-refugee, anti-foreigner nexus of thinking, and as such, one of the most important features tied to neo-nationalism. Racialization consists of social and psychological processes of exclusion that occur along racial, cultural, national, social, and class lines, while agents of this practice rely on a fixed, essentialist concept of identity that sees certain people as foreigners with unbridgeable differences and thereby legitimizing austerity measures and sanctions.

Third, and lastly, one of anthropology's potential and general contributions is to apply its ethnographic methodology and way of thinking to a personalized, or person-centric, understanding of actors within the far right and neo-nationalist movement. This third anthropological perspective evolves from asking the polemic question: to what extent can we empathize with the "devoted agents" including people at the far right? (Atran, 2016). As such, empathy can be an important contribution from anthropology, and may emerge as the ability to provide insightful personalized understandings of "ordinary" extremist sympathizers. Empathy is a buzz word that is popular and misunderstood, though; for instance, in mistaking the Siberian hunter's moose call (in order to kill the moose) as empathy (Bubandt and Willerslev, 2015) (more on this later). When historians and political scientists in quiet moments say we need anthropological methods to tell us what motivates people across demographic divides to vote for the radical right populists, or to join extremist groups, empathy is a key word that emerges despite the dangers and accidental luggage that comes with it.

If researchers reach through the fog of the discourse of moralization and regard their agents as rational, fellow human beings with concerns and worries within a society where an extreme style of language and confrontational way of thinking has become "the new normal," then we could get to know "the beast", so to speak, from the inside. William Westermeyer did this in his ethnographic study of the local chapters of the Tea Party Movement in the United States. His work revealed that members did not see themselves as "racists" in the sense of being motivated by hatred towards blacks; but on the contrary, they see oppression as the racial differences created by the government and liberals. They insisted that they are not "racists" but patriots, or simply "telling the truth" (Westermeyer, 2018).

Conceptual perspectives

"Right–left" and "Neo-nationalism"

A scrutiny of current categories is always part of an anthropological perspective with a depth of thick description (Geertz, 1973) or thick contextualization (Ortner, 1995). The meaning and use of terms such as "far right", "extreme right", "populism", "nationalist populism", "global populism", "neo-nationalism", "left", "liberal" and "Non-Westerner" reveal they are ubiquitous, opaque, and contain hidden asymmetries and contradictions. Moreover, they all more or less need to be suspended during experience-near, ethnographic fieldwork, so they do not "contaminate" what shared social practice and interviewing may bring.

The right–left division is not a relationship of equals. Mark Sedgwick finds no real difference between the terms "far" and "extreme" right. The one important difference, he argues, is between "extreme" and "radical". The "radical" right (and left) consist of people who are ready to use violence (Sedgwick, 2010). However, this distinction is more blurred than Sedgwick indicates, since violence comes in both direct and indirect, symbolic and cultural forms. Accordingly, the verbal radicalism and securitization of language of populists can be seen as forms of symbolic violence that often precede physical violence (Betz in Mondon, 2013).

The use of the qualifier "right" as in "far right", "radical-right", "right-wing", and "alt-right" suggests its categorical opposite; yet, this opposition is deceiving. The opposition embraced by the "right" can be regarded either as a construction within itself or as an attempt to represent a category of "real" people. Today, opposition to "left-wingers", "liberals", "liberal media", "Marxism", and "cultural Marxists" can be found in rhetoric, articulated ideologies, systems of beliefs, and in practice. However, the left is not what it used to be. Politically, labor parties throughout Europe are in serious decline and under re-construction to reappear in a reduced version as value-oriented parties often with nationalist undertones (Kalb and Haimai, 2011). The celebration of authoritarian values in light of external threats, whether phrased as globalization, migration, nationalism of other states, or climate change, presents situations of crisis, or states of exception, where the language of securitization and threat call for strong, authoritarian-oriented leadership to enter with promises of solving the problems, whether these are national, family, or masculine values. Dressed up in populist clothes, such dominant discourse requires a contestable set of opponents for bonding purposes (Hervik, 2011). Accordingly, the right has constructed a targetable "left" while the remaining, self-identifying left is busy trying to jump on the idea of tough talk on migration.

A further conceptual complication to the category "far right" and "radical-right" is the so-called "mainstreaming of the radical right". While there is no doubt that extremist views have become mainstream (Hervik and Berg, 2007; Feischmidt and Hervik, 2015; Mondon, 2013), there is little discussion of the process of becoming dominant and hegemonic. "Far", "extreme" and "radical" are concepts left at the periphery, but mainstreaming will inevitably "naturalize" extreme speech, extreme policies and practices. "New restrictions" become the "new normal". Similarly, when far right parties adhere to older social democratic welfare values and hardline nationalists on the other, they are still extremists, I would argue.

It should be added, that these binary divisions, left and right, the West vs. Islam (Huntington, 1993, 1996; Lewis, 1990), Good vs. Bad Muslim (Mamdani, 2002) are deceiving, yet in spite of their different meanings still dovetail with the structure of the news media and the media's need for simplification to reach the largest audience possible (Peterson, 2007). The political "dumbing down" follows the same trajectory (Williams, 2014).

As part of his study of French and Australian "far right", Aurelien Mondon suggested the usages of "far right" and the "left" could be boiled down to "equality" and "inequality", respectively. He found that the right was preoccupied with "inequality" and its opposition whereas "the left" was concerned about ideas of equality and solidarity (Mondon, 2013). This inequality assumed by the far right can take various forms such as "nationality, race, ethnic group and/or religious denomination", and lead, in turn, to the use of "nationalism, xenophobia, racisms and ethnocentrism" as political tools (Carter, in Mondon, 2013). Yet, far right does not simply pro-actively promote inequality, but inequality is an outcome of a strong construction of and reaction to the left, and more broadly, to the Enlightenment (ibid.). But these -isms are not defining characteristics. They are "mere manifestations of the principle of fundamental human inequality, which lies at the heart of right-wing extremism" (Mondon, 2013: 18) and its racialized inferiorization of non-Western migrants.

The conceptual discussion has left us with a traditional right–left division that is outdated, misleading, and with an asymmetric relation of power. As Mondon has argued, the most fundamental difference between the sides is the opposition of the right to any issue associated with claims and demands for equality. In the absence of a clear vision and some plan of action to follow, the far right as well as neo-nationalism is devoted to an anti-equality discourse and practice. The far right builds on an idea of incompatibility between "our" and "their" values. In this optic, any initiative that seeks to "ignore" this maxim can be accused of ignorantly introducing equality.

The emergence of the study of neo-nationalism

Michael Billig's *Banal Nationalism* (1995) has become a classic within studies of nationalism. Through a critique of earlier theories, he emphasized the importance of understanding the everyday evocations of the national order. While he found that this order tended to relegate nationalism to the periphery's separatist rebellions against the nation-state system and to "forget" its presence in the everyday, he emphasized omnipresence and priming of the national order in everyday discourse and practice of established nation-states. This "banal nationalism" is everything but banal and could easily be mobilized to wars, for instance, in faraway places like the Falkland Islands and Iraq. A key point in Billig's book is that the "banal nationalism" is what feeds the "hot" nationalism; what we today roughly would call "neo-nationalism." That is to say, neo-nationalism and neo-racism make sense with reference to the taken-for-grantedness of the nation as the dominant accepted form of community and point of reference. The glue that holds this together is not some age-old primordial condition, but it is the product of the age of modern nation-state. And it does so through concepts such as "national security", "national interests", "national values", and a specific logic of the "nation-in-danger".

One of the first and biggest boosts for the use of "neo-nationalism" came with Andre Gingrich and Marcus Banks' (2006) edited volume, which came out of an almost week-long seminar held in early 2002. Neo-nationalism is a term used in short for "nationalism under new circumstances", particularly the post 1989-world and set within established nation-states. In 2004, similar issues had already been discussed at the meetings of EASA (European Association of Social Anthropologists) in 2000 and published by Ethnos (2004), with Gingrich (2004), Gullestad

(2004) and Hervik (2004) being part of both events. The issues focused on racism that anthropologists observed in their country of origin when politicians and media saw possibilities in organizing voters and readers around strong reactions to the increased number of refugees and co-citizens with diverse immigrant backgrounds (Hervik, 2011).

The growth of pro-nation, anti-migrant sentiments and practices could be found particularly in Europe's smallest and most affluent countries (Banks and Gingrich, 2006). Forces within these countries, including media, politicians, and scholars, began to claim that immigration would threaten the cultural fabric of their nation. A discourse of the emergent threat emerged, the likes of which had never been seen before. Gingrich noted that the common response from most of these early European neo-nationalists was a narrow law and order practice that offered authoritarian values with a strengthening of national, family and male values (Gingrich, 2006a, 2006b).

These associations were linked to notions of home community, homeland nation, danger, alertness, commitment, and bravery. Gullestad found a neo-nationalism more narrowly focusing on "neo-ethnification of national identity", in which she observed a reinforcement of ideas about "family life, kinship, ancestry and descent" (2006a, 2006b). This development occurred, she argued, along with the collapse of the neighbourhood that had been the site of primary social relations and now shifted to the national level instead (Gullestad, 2006b). Gingrich wrote about reactions to "illegal immigrants" nearly 20 years ago; neo-nationalists today also focus on the flow of migrants and refugees in general. Yet, after more than 20 years, neo-nationalists still highlight the "threat to cultural homogeneity" migrants and refugees pose to "our values". "Our" values, as Billig reminds us, refers to the "nation" as "our" place in the world, where we make the decisions.

Inspired partly by Robert Miles and Etienne Balibar, I emphasize that neo-nationalism and neo-racism are part of the same project of inclusion and exclusion in an analysis of Danish media coverage and interviews in the late 1990s (Hervik, 2011). The nation as imagined community (Anderson, 1991) is the shared belief that some people are part of the imagination of the nation, and some people are not. And since the division tends to fall along racial and cultural lines, neo-nationalism and neo-racism are part of the same ideology and exclusionary rhetoric (Hervik, 2011).

Dan Kalb and Gábor Halmai (2011) tie the emergence of neo-nationalism to the social and structural changes related to neoliberal globalization with its decline of blue-collar work in Europe leading to "a displacement of experiences of dispossession and disenfranchisement onto the imagined nation as a community of fate, crafted by the new political entrepreneur generation's protest votes against neoliberal rule" (Kalb and Halmai, 2011: 2–3). Along similar lines, Ghassan Hage (2003), finds "paranoid nationalism" as a negative reaction to the capitalism's decline of hope.

None of these authors is explicit about situating these trends idiosyncratically on the "far right" side of the traditional political spectrum. They do identify that the Austrian Freedom Party, the Danish People's Party, and the Progressive Party in

Norway belong to the same family of "radical" or "radical right wing" parties, but they also recognize that these parties are only some of the reactions the mega-events and political changes defining the so called post-1989 world. Populism can indeed not to be reduced to single political parties.

Racialization

Today, racialization is seen as a medium for race-thinking or racial reasoning that is a better way than race and racism to emphasize how people are put into racial categories. In this way, racialization is more basic and a condition for racism but not directly reducible to racism. Thus, the second anthropological perspective, racialization, must begin by asking questions such as who racializes whom? In what context? And which categories and words co-occur? (Hervik, 2004, 2011).

The discourses and practices of racialization, racialized integration, and radicalization coupled with "the War on Terror" are issues that have brought Muslims to the forefront of negative public attention. One of the effects is that racialization is now directed at entire communities of people associated with Muslims, Islam, or "Muslim culture" as well as "parallel societies" and "non-Western" migrants that as "a whole way of life" becomes explanations for peoples' beliefs and social actions (Hervik, 2014; Kundnani, 2015). Moreover, with the dominance of racialization of "Muslims", "Whites" or "Danes", the principles of fixing group identities spreads from "Muslims" to "foreignness;" to transracially and transnationally adopted Danish Danes (Myong 2009; Hübinette and Tigervall, 2009); East-Europeans and Jews (Sacks, 1996); and children of mixed marriages (Törngren, 2019). The emergence of racializing categories appears as "bilingual students", which is a euphemism in schools for students with visible minority backgrounds (Gilliam, 2006; Andreassen, 2005). In public debates, categories such as "non-Western" migrants, "immigrants", "integration", and "ethnic minorities" have come to denote "racialized" or "cultural" others (Hervik, 2011; Andreassen, 2007; Gullestad, 2006b) who are prototypically perceived as Arab, Muslim, and from the Middle East.

Frantz Fanon is often regarded as having pioneered the work on "racialization of thought", which took place when colonialism erased differences among and within Africans and blacks in place of racial categories such as "Negro" (Miles, 1989). In this way, both "whites" and "blacks" are caught up in racialization and racisms (Gullestad, 2004). Marcus Banks made the argument that neo-nationalism is not "just" racism (Banks and Gingrich, 2006). Yet, even though he was partly right, today we can see a re-conceptualization of racism. Racialization studies have moved away from being synonymous with racism; the idea of a single monolithic racism and the approach to different forms of discrimination are studied as "distinct silos" (Goldberg, 1990; Meer, 2012: 2) or single-axis explanations that only focus on race but leave aside the intersections of race with gender or class (Crenshaw, 1991) or nationalism (Hervik, 2011, 2019; Miles, 1993).

The first point provided by evoking racialization as a key concept is that we are better equipped to grasp the essentialization of racial identity across the political spectrum. Racialization comes in the everyday forms of interaction. It comes out particularly strong in connection with the enforcement of national values and out-right warfare, although racialization also pops up separately from neo-nationalism. While the idea of the *nation in danger* is the underlying engine behind racialization of "Danes" and visible "non-Danes", then whiteness as a racialized dimension of nationalism has become more and more pronounced (Hervik, 2018b).

Racialization is thought to co-exist with other forms off subordination as approaches to intersectionality have demonstrated. Yet, intersectionality studies never seem to fully give in to a person-centric perspective that captures what motivates agents. In the present case, the question of what motivates people to engage themselves in neo-nationalist and neo-racist activities including violence and hate crimes must be examined. Therefore, we turn to anthropological efforts to understand "devoted agents" through an empathy perspective – as a way of thinking in a personalized, or person-centric, understanding of actors (and within the far right).

Empathizing with "devoted agents'

Empathy has long been a cornerstone of anthropological fieldwork practice that may be useful for understanding morally devoted agents from within. Empathy is the third anthropological perspective presented here in an attempt to understand the current trend that the right and far right embrace the idea that immigration threatens the nation's cultural homogeneity and the politics of fear that accompany it. Before this perspective can be applied the concept must be discussed critically for its accidental baggage. Current use of the term ranges from the ability to distinguish self from the "other" to more scholarly definitions of understanding another person's first-person subjective experience while upholding a self and other distinction that fosters a true and accurate emphatic understanding (Hollan and Throop, 2008: 291–392). Empathy is popularly contrasted with sympathy. Empathy is a positively laden emotion and strategy to pursue because it holds recognition, mutuality, reciprocity, and attempts to bring a non-hierarchical form of genuine dialogue. Sympathy is the caring and feeling of pity or sorrow for those who suffer. Sympathy does not include sharing distress and therefore easily leads to victimization.

The theorizing of empathy has a history that goes back at least as far as George Herbert Mead and his ideas and practices of "taking the role of the other". According to Mead, only by perceiving one's own behaviour from the standpoint of other persons does identity and consciousness properly evolve (Mead, 1934). In other words, the recognition, the misrecognition, or absence heavily influences our identity (Taylor, 1994; Honneth, 1995). For many years, Clifford Geertz's strong work impeded the study of empathy:

> We cannot live other people's lives, and it is a piece of bad faith to try. We can but listen to what, in words, in images, in actions they say about their lives. As Victor Turner … argued, it is with expressions – representations,

objectifications, discourses, performances, whatever – that we traffic … .
Whatever sense we have of how things stand with someone's inner life, we
gain it through their expressions, not through some magical intrusion into
their consciousness.

(Geertz, 1986: 373)

Geertz warned us that the assumptions about empathy to reach people's inner lives
were faulty and merely the projection of one's own thought into the other.
Recently, Douglas Hollan has reminded us that empathy, in contrast to psychological projection, implicates the emotional and imaginative capacities of the people
we are attempting to understand as well as our own (Hollan, 2008). When we seek
to understand another person's first-person subjective experience, we must uphold
a self and other distinction to foster an accurate emphatic understanding (ibid.)

Anthropologists have argued that empathy is paradigmatic and good, while lack
of empathy is simply bad. Norwegian anthropologist, Anne Sigfrid Grønseth, has
written extensively about empathy in relation to her ethnographic fieldwork with
Tamils in the remotest area of Northern Norway. Grønseth sees empathy as a
psychological transcendence of self in shared practical activity (Grønseth, 2010),
embracing the willingness to engage one's self in the life of others. Empathy and
mutuality are keys to overcome social and cultural differences, including times of
friction and conflict. It is the appreciation of individual experiences that cultural
differences can be transcended and makes reciprocity and mutuality possible
(Grønseth, 2010). While Grønseth's embrace of empathy goes to those whom she
works closest with, whom she likes the most, and who provides a formidable ethnography, she isn't concerned with the new Russian employees, a shop owner, or
the health care workers who often make the lives of the Tamil residents difficult.
Does that mean empathy is reserved for the ones we like?

Some anthropologists have embraced empathy in an attempt to cash in on the
hot currency of the term. While not using empathy to approach what seems to be
"the disliked", Nils Bubandt and Rane Willerslev (2015) recently argued for
attention to the dark side of empathy. Instead of mutual understanding, empathy is
much about deception, the aggressive intent, profound in nature, and seizing
empathy for the purpose of deception and even killing. They use two illustrative
incidents from Siberia and Indonesia of "tactical empathy" of which only the first is
relevant here. A male Siberian Yukaghir hunter uses his (empathic) knowledge of
the female moose and disguises himself to imitate a moose and catch its curiosity.
Once the female moose approaches the hunter, he kills it. Moreover, it is for the
better since the moose associates a spiritual being engaged in a predatory act against
the human hunter, like accepting seduction for the purpose of acquiring a spouse
(Bubandt and Willerslev, 2015). According to Michael Jackson, entering the world
of another can be achieved mimetically:

Attempting to go native by decking oneself out in the costume of the other
can only end in parody. Unlike imitation, analogy does not eclipse self in an

attempt to become other. Its strategy is, by contrast, to have recourse to common images – such as the metaphors of paths or bridges – that are already part of the discursive repertoire of human relationships.

(1998: 97)

Upon closer look, Bubandt and Willerslev are hardly talking about empathy. Empathy for a quick kill, or seduction, dismantles the empathy itself, and even, according to the authors, disregards the "accuracy" of the empathic insight (Bubandt and Willerslev, 2015).

In addition, the authors fail to include themselves in the emphatic relationship, giving rise to the risk Geertz warned about, namely, psychological projection, which is no less problematic as both authors as fieldworkers remain in the periphery as observers of the hunter and observer of a relationship he is not himself part of. On the other hand, even though it does not follow from the two incidents they set out to analyze in order to bring out the "dark side of empathy", the authors make an important point. Can a person literally enact empathy for the intention of killing, whether literally or metaphorically, as in seduction?

Students of uncompromised violence seem to agree that motivation to extreme violence against unknown civilians does not spring so much from ideological doctrine as from different deontic (duty-based) acts (see Devji, 2005; Bjørgo and Horgan, 2009; Atran, 2016; Blee and Creasap, 2010; Christensen, 2015). In Atran's words, "devoted agents" are defined as the following:

People will become willing to protect morally important or sacred values through costly sacrifice and extreme actions, even being willing to kill and die, particularly when such values are embedded in or fused with group identity, becoming intrinsic to "Who I am" and "Who We are".

(Atran, 2016: 192)

Atran analyzes how marginalized youth in transitional states of life are the targets of, and volunteers, to become devoted agents. He argues that ideas of small groups, sacred values, and identity fusion are more applicable to any "devoted agent" acting out of a sense of moral duty (see also Devji, 2005). I believe anti-migrant, neo-nationalists can be approached as devoted agents determined to defend the secular nation as a sacred value and at any cost, although the degree of commitment varies.

In his methodological observations and in reference to the study of Austrian Freedom Party supporters, Andre Gingrich maintains that it may be "impossible for the ethnographer to identify with the people he works with in any positive way" (2006b). Subscribing to an "agree to disagree" strategy allows them "to put some skeptical distance between ethnographer and 'natives'" (ibid.). More broadly, "there are some topics on which the ethnographer cannot possibly agree, for basic professional reasoning, anthropologists value cultural diversity, while nationalists embrace some ideal of cultural homogeneity" (Gingrich, 2006b: 209). Traditionally, anthropologists have helped give voice to muted groups through commitment and advocacy, but Gingrich, as I read him, finds empathizing with people who are openly racist impossible (2004: 161), and in this way he agrees with Grønseth.

In Bubandt and Willerslev's account, it is unclear what the motivation is for stressing how empathy, deception, and killing can be misconstrued. In Gingrich's reasoning, it is equally unclear why it is so important to convey to "the disliked" that he disagrees with the "native". Anthony Wallace reminded us a long time ago that "much of social life goes on without intimate knowledge of others' motives and intentions – through habit, routine, common expectation, and widely shared rules of social engagement and etiquette" (Wallace cit. in Hollan and Throop, 2008: 385–386), so how do we know beforehand that we disagree, or assume there may be a "kill" being unfolded in the name of empathy? Entering the field and suspending judgments and disagreements temporarily has always been a methodological lead in my own practice. Not least of which is following a quest for genuine and naturalized conversations to engage with adversaries with dignity (Gullestad, 2006b). Gullestad discusses a power that starts, "Racist I accept you", which exaggerates the need for hatred to such an extent that it loses any realism (Gullestad, 2004: 180). Jackson also sees ethnographic empathy as more than a reciprocity and exchange of agreements:

> It is a mode of embodied, intersubjective negotiated understanding that comes of coexistence and coordination in common tasks; it is not a form of knowledge consolidated in precepts and enshrined in dogma.
>
> *(1998: 97)*

Let me illustrate. As part of our research on racialization and social media, we set out to interview Ann. Ann is an important figure in the history of the involvement of the so-called Islam-critical network in Denmark that goes back to the early 2000s. As we discussed how to approach the interviews in our research project on social media activism, we did not choose the Gingrich option, "agree to disagree". But more generally and following an empathy track, we decided that the right thing to do, and the only thing to do, was to approach her with a genuine interest in understanding Ann's worries, concerns, reflections, motivations and so on for her engagement and motivation. Ann was open to talking and explaining her beliefs and activities:

> I have been … well, I do not think it is too much to say: desperate. In despair of what I see is happening to my country. I love Denmark, and right now my country is being undermined by an inward migration of people that for the most part do not fit in our culture. It is that simple.
>
> *(Ann, Adult Education Teacher, 64).*

Originally, her moral outrage was evoked when, in the capacity of board member in various associations, she was approached by an anthropologist. Ann was told that a new report about young immigrants' understanding of their view on gender and sexuality had been produced, but was now being withheld. It was "as if" someone was intentionally preventing the truth from coming out. This moral outrage pushed her into collaboration and networking that eventually became known as the Islam-critical network and a new political party to the far right. Ann conveys her experiences and tells us about how sees migration. This is not an object relevant for the researcher to disagree with.

Now, one of the important points coming out of the talks with Ann and others has been raised by the late reading of Bubandt and Willerslev's piece. Do I go into talks with Ann in order to "seduce" and "empathize tactically", only to "kill" her? The answer is no. However, I did discover, or perhaps rediscover, something in my former publications. Hollan and Throop wrote the "Anthropology of Empathy" as one of the more comprehensive anthropological treatments of the topic. It seems to me that their treatment of the phenomenon of empathy, the actual experiences of other people, while maintaining their own, misses the idea or value of empathy as a condition of life. Or, to put it differently, one could argue that if empathy is evoked as a means to gain something, then it hardly qualifies as empathy, if empathy is stretched to its fullest meaning. Empathy – as a condition of life – approaches the stranger as a person and not a category.

Concluding remarks

Without reducing anthropology's contribution to the study of neo-nationalism and the far right to the "usual" sustained ethnographic fieldwork and everything included, anthropology's ethnographic practice still carries tremendous value. In this chapter I suggested three perspectives that I found significant as anthropological contributions to the study of the far right and neo-nationalism in the mid to late 2010s. The critical scrutiny of concepts such as "far right", "neo-nationalism", and the nature of the "right–left" division, illustrate the necessity to continuously challenge the concepts we use in everyday talk as well as in academic practice. The second perspective is racialization (which is a concept that cannot be reduced to the right or left) that opens up for the inclusion of co-existing forms of subordination. Such co-existence is part of the re-conceptualization of racism. The third perspective comes from asking whether you can empathize for the "kill", which I argue is a false one. With the critical adjustment of empathy as a guiding principle for anthropological fieldwork and in-depth interviewing, this could be a key to entering a genuine dialogue while still maintaining one's own view of the world.

At a general level, it seems, that neo-nationalism is still inseparable from neo-racism, much like I analyzed in earlier research (Hervik, 2004, 2011), but today racialization and neo-racism are more entrenched in the white hegemonic majority than before (Hervik, 2019). This majority attracts new individuals and groups from where moral outrage can become spurs to increased antagonism and direct violence (Hervik, 2018a). The issues of masculinity and gender within neo-nationalism, rightly emphasized by Gingrich (2006b), are characteristics of the far right, however the increased support of austerity measures and sanctions can hardly be explained by the return of white masculine values. The election of Donald Trump for president both testifies to a media savvy, rich businessman and the majority segment of votes being white women, who find Trump's sexism appalling but identity politics towards foreigners more important (Harris-Perry, 2016). Similarly, Kalb and Halmai are surely right in the importance of the decline of the labour movements following structural transformations that take blue-collar jobs away from Europe. However, these structural changes can hardly explain the scope, agency, and activism of the far right, which is now becoming mainstreamed as the "new normal". Fear of downward mobility is a contributing factor, but it is not a constitutive one.

Because a reconceptualization of racialization is necessary, anthropology's contribution, I argue, is to insist on including the study of actual social practices and personalized approaches to actors situated in a larger context. This endeavour depends on a revision of empathy as a condition for fieldwork and human relations. Empathy-based ethnographic fieldwork has been carried out under difficult circumstances that include violent street gangs, irregular migrants, prisoners, Satanists, military personnel, supporters of genital mutilation, infanticide, and so on. Now, the task is to turn to people, who are categorized by many progressive people as "far right" and "extremists", and you consider antagonists, into parts of your ethnographic fieldwork that includes temporarily suspending judgement and morality, even if it borders on threats of violence, involves statements about superior morality and the consumption of the most controversial memes and emblems.

References

Anderson, B. 1991[1983]. *Imagined Communities: Reflections on the Origin and Spread of Nationalism*. Revised edition. London: Verso.

Andreassen, R. 2005. "The Mass Media's Construction of Gender, Race, Sexuality and Nationality: An. Analysis of the Danish News Media's Communication about Visible Minorities from 1971 to 2004." Unpublished Ph.D. dissertation, Department of History, University of Toronto.

Andreassen, R. 2007. *Der er et yndigt land. Medier, minoriteter og danskhed*. Copenhagen: Tiderne Skifter.

Atran, S. 2016. "The Devoted Actor. Unconditional Commitment and Intractable Conflict across Cultures." *Current Anthropology*, 57(S13), 192–203.

Banks, M. 2006. "Performing 'Neo-Nationalism': Some Methodological Notes." In *Neo-Nationalism in Europe and Beyond: Perspectives from Social Anthropology*, edited by A. Gingrich and M. Banks, 1–28. New York and London: Berghahn Books.

Banks, M. and A. Gingrich. 2006. "Neo-Nationalism in Europe and Beyond." In *Neo-Nationalism in Europe and Beyond: Perspectives from Social Anthropology*, edited by A. Gingrich and M. Banks, 1–28. New York, NY and London: Berghahn Books.

Billig, M. 1995. *Banal Nationalism*. London: Sage Publications.

Bjørgo, T. and J. Horgan. (eds). 2009. *Leaving Terrorism Behind. Individual and Collective Disengagement*. New York, NY: Routledge.

Bubandt, N. and R. Willerslev. 2015. "The Dark Side of Empathy: Mimesis, Deception, and the Magic of Alterity." *Comparative Studies in Society and History*, 57(1), 5–35.

Blee K.M. and K.A. Creasap. 2010. "Conservative and Right-Wing Movements." *Annual Review of Sociology*, 36(1), 269–286.

Carsten, J. 1995. "The Substance of Kinship and the Heat of the Hearth: Feeding, Personhood, and Relatedness among Malays in Pulau Langkawi." *American Ethnologist*, 22(2), 223–241.

Christensen, T.W. 2015. *A Question of Participation – Disengagement from the Extremist Right. A Case Study from Sweden*. PhD thesis. Roskilde: Roskilde University.

Clifford, J. 1988. *The Predicament of Culture*. Cambridge, MA: Harvard University Press.

Cody, F. 2011. "Publics and Politics." *Annual Review of Anthropology*, 40, 37–52.

Crenshaw, K.W. 1991. "Mapping the Margins: Intersectionality, Identity Politics, and Violence against Women of Color." *Stanford Law Review*, 43(6), 1241–1299.

C-REX: Center for Research on Extremism2016 "RTV Dataset on Right-wing Terrorism and Violence in Western Europe." http://www.sv.uio.no/c-rex/english/news-and-events/news/2016/rtv-dataset.html

Devji, F. 2005. *Landscapes of the Jihad*. Ithaca, NY: Cornell University Press.

*Ethnos*2004. *Journal of Anthropology Museum of Etnography*, 69(2), Theme issue "The New Racism in Europe", edited by P. Hervik.

Feischmidt, M. and P. Hervik. 2015. "Mainstreaming the Extreme: Intersecting Challenges from the Far Right in Europe." *Intersections. East European Journal of Society and Politics*, 1, 3–17.

Geertz, C. 1973. "Thick Description. Towards an Interpretive Theory of Culture." In *The Interpretation of Cultures: Selected Essays by Clifford Geertz*, by C. Geertz, 3–30. New York, NY: Basic Books.

Geertz, C. 1986. "Making Experiences, Authoring Selves." In *The Anthropology of Experience*, edited by V.W. Turner and E.M. Bruner, 373–380. Urbana, IL: University of Illinois Press.

Gilliam, L. 2006. *De Umulige Børn og Det Ordentlige Menneske. Et studie af identiet, ballade og muslimske fællesskaber blandt etniske minoritetsbørn i en dansk folkeskole*. PhD dissertation, The Danish University of Education, Copenhagen.

Gingrich, A. 2004. "Concepts of Race Vanishing, Movements of Racism rising? Global Issues and Austrian Ethnography." *Ethnos*, 69(2), 156–176.

Gingrich, A. 2006a. "Nation, Status and Gender in Trouble? Exploring Some Contexts and Characteristics of Neo-Nationalism in Western Europe." In *Neo-Nationalism in Europe and Beyond: Perspectives from Social Anthropology*, edited by A. Gingrich and M. Banks, 29–49. New York, NY and London: Berghahn Books.

Gingrich, A. 2006b. "Neo-Nationalism and the Reconfiguration of Europe." *Social Anthropology*, 14(2), 195–217.

Gingrich, A. and M. Banks. (eds). 2006. *Neo-Nationalism in Europe and Beyond: Perspectives from Social Anthropology*. New York, NY and London: Berghahn Books.

Goldberg, D.T. (ed.). 1990. *The Anatomy of Racism*. Minneapolis, MN: University of Minnesota Press.

Grønseth, A.S. 2010. "Sharing Experiences with Tamil Refugees in Northern Norway." In *Mutuality and Empathy: Self and Other in the Ethnographic Encounter*, edited by A.S. Grønseth and D.L. Davis, 143–161. Wantage, UK: Sean Kingston Publishing.

Gullestad, M. 2004. "Blind Slaves of our Prejudices: Debating 'Culture' and 'Race' in Norway." *Ethnos*, 69(2), 177–203.

Gullestad, M. 2006a. "Imagined Kinship: The Role of Descent in the Rearticulation of Norwegian Ethno-Nationalism." In *Neo-Nationalism in Europe and Beyond: Perspectives from*

Social Anthropology, edited by A. Gingrich and M. Banks, 69–91. New York, NY and London: Berghahn Books.

Gullestad, M. 2006b. *Plausible Prejudice*. Oslo: Universitetsforlaget.

Hage, G. 2003. *Against Paranoid Nationalism: Searching for hope in a Shrinking Society*. Sydney: Pluto Press.

Harris-Perry, M. 2016. "What Just Happened? Making Sense of the Election and Social Policy Priorities in the Post-Obama Era." Keynote address, 115th Meeting of the American Anthropological Association, 16–20 November, Minneapolis.

Hervik, P. 2004. "The Danish Cultural World of Unbridgeable Differences." *Ethnos*, 69(2), 247–267.

Hervik, P. 2011. *The Annoying Difference. The Emergence of Danish Neonationalism, Neoracism, and Populism in the Post-1989 World*. New York, NY and Oxford: Berghahn Books.

Hervik, P. 2014. "Cultural War of Values: The Proliferation of Moral Identities in the Danish Public Sphere." In *Becoming Minority: How Discourses and Policies Produce Minorities in Europe and India*, edited by J. Tripathy and S. Padmanabhan, 154–173. New Delhi: Sage Publications, India.

Hervik, P. 2017. "Ten Years After the Danish Muhammad Cartoon News Stories: Terror and Radicalization as Predictable Media Events." *Television and Social Media*, 19(2), 146–154.

Hervik, P. 2018a. "Afterword." Special issue: "Moral Outrage as a Mobilizing Force to Action." *Conflict and Society*, September 2018.

Hervik, P. 2018b. "Refiguring the Public, Political and Personal in Current Danish Exclusionary Reasoning." In *Political Sentiments and Social Movements: The Person in Politics and Culture*, edited by C. Strauss and J. Friedman, 91–117. New York, NY: Palgrave Macmillan.

Hervik, P. 2019. "Racialization in the Nordic countries: An introduction." In *Racialization in the Nordic Countries*, edited by P. Hervik, 3–37. New York, NY: Palgrave Macmillan.

Hervik, P. and C. Berg. 2007. "Denmark: A Political Struggle in Danish Journalism." In *Reading the Mohammed Cartoons Controversy. An International Analysis of Press Discourses on Free Speech and Political Spin*, edited by R. Kunelius, E. Eide, O. Hahn and R. Schroeder, 25–39. Working Papers in International Journalism. Bochum and Freiberg: Projekt Verlag GbR.

Hollan, D. 2008. "Being There: On the Imaginative Aspects of Understanding Others and Being Understood." *Ethos*, 36(4), 475–489.

Hollan, D. and C. Throop. 2008. "Whatever Happened to Empathy? Introduction." *Ethos*, 36(4), 385–401.

Honneth, A. 1995. *The Struggle for Recognition. The Moral Grammar of Social Conflicts*. Cambridge, MA: MIT Press.

Hübinette, T. and C. Tigervall. 2009. "To be Non-White in a Colour-Blind Society: Conversations with Adoptees and Adoptive Parents in Sweden on Everyday Racism." *Journal of Intercultural Studies*, 30(4), 335–355.

Huntington, S. 1993. "The Clash of Civilizations?" *Foreign Affairs*, 72(3), 22–49.

Huntington, S. 1996. *The Clash of Civilizations and the Remaking of World Order*. New York, NY: Simon & Schuster.

Jackson, M. 1998. *Mimima Ethnographica. Intersubjectivity and the Anthropological Project*. Chicago, IL and London: The University of Chicago Press.

Jåsund, C.B. and R.C. Topdahl. 2017. "Mer Højreekstrem Vold enn før." *NRK Rogaland*. https://www.nrk.no/rogaland/_-mer-hoyreekstrem-vold-enn-for-1.13303686

Kalb, D., and G. Halmai. (eds). 2011. *Headlines of Nation, Subtexts of Class. Working Class Populism and the Return of the Repressed in Neoliberal Europe*. Oxford: Berghahn Books.

Kundnani, A. 2015. *The Muslims are Coming! Islamophobia, Extremism, and the Domestic War on Terror.* London and New York, NY: Verso

Lewis, B. 1990. "The Roots of Muslim Rage." *Atlantic Monthly,* 266(3), 47–60.

Mamdani, M. 2002. "Good Muslim, Bad Muslim; A Political Perspective on Culture and Terrorism." *American Anthropologist,* 104(3), 766–775.

Mead, G.H. 1934. *Mind, Self, and Society,* Charles W. Morris (ed.). Chicago, IL: University of Chicago Press.

Meer, N. 2012. "Racialization and Religion: Race, culture and Difference in the Study of Antisemitism and Islamophobia." *Ethnic and Racial Studies,* 36(3), 385–398.

Miles, R. 1989. *Racism.* London: Routledge.

Miles, R. 1993. *Racism After "Race Relations."* London: Routledge.

Mondon, A. 2013. *The Mainstreaming of the Extreme Right in France and Australia. A Populist Hegemony?*Farnham, UK: Ashgate.

Myong, L. 2009. *Adopteret – fortællinger om transnational og racialiseret tilblivelse.* PhD dissertation, Department of Learning, Aarhus University.

Ortner, S. 1995. "Resistance and the Problem of Ethnographic Refusal. In Recapturing Anthropology." In *Working in the Present,* edited by R.G. Fox, 163–190. Santa Fe, NM: School of American Research Press.

Peterson, M.A. 2007. "Making Global News: 'Freedom of speech' and 'Muslim rage' in U. S. journalism." *Contemporary Islam,* 1, 247–264.

Sacks, K.B. 1996. "How Did Jews Become White Folks?" In *Race,* edited by S. Gregory and R. Sanjek, 78–102. New York, NY and London: Routledge.

Sedgwick, M. 2010. "The Concept of Radicalization as a Source of Confusion." *Terrorism and Political Violence,* 22, 479–494.

Stolcke, V. 1995. "Talking Culture: New Boundaries, New Rhetorics of Exclusion in Europe." *Current Anthropology,* 36(1), 1–24.

Taylor, C. 1994. *Multiculturalism. Examining the Politics of Recognition.* Princeton, NJ: Princeton University Press.

Törngren, S.O. 2019. "Justification and Rationalization of Attitudes Toward Interracial Relationships in Color-Blind Sweden." In *Racialization, Racism and anti-Racism in the Nordic Countries,* edited by P. Hervik. New York, NY: Palgrave Macmillan.

Wallace, A.F.C. 1961. *Culture and Personality.* New York, NY: Random House.

Westermeyer, B. 2018. "Progressives' Plantation: Race, Resentment and Cultural Citizenship Among North Carolina Tea Party Activists." In *Political Sentiments and Social Movements: The Person in Politics and Culture,* edited by C. Strauss and J. Friedman. New York, NY: Palgrave Macmillan.

Williams, R. 2014. "Anti-Intellectualism and the 'Dumbing Down' of America." *Psychology Today.* https://www.psychologytoday.com/blog/wired-success/201407/anti-intellectualism-and-the-dumbing-down-america

PART II

Quantitative approaches and online research

7

ESTIMATING THE FAR RIGHT VOTE WITH AGGREGATE DATA

Vasiliki Georgiadou, Lamprini Rori and Costas Roumanias

As the European far right (FR) vote shares continue to rise for a third decade in a row, accurate estimation of the factors that drive this increase is pivotal to our understanding of the economic, socio-cultural or political mechanics which underlie this process. The need has become more urgent in light of the recent generalized electoral successes of populist radical right (PRR) parties in Europe. The PRR has moved from the fringes of European politics to the foreground, often setting the agenda and narrative of modern elections, thus, pressuring mainstream parties to move to the right. In the relatively brief time span of our sample (2000–2014), the European FR has witnessed its average vote share almost tripling from below 5 per cent in 1999 to 14.39 per cent in 2014. Electoral success of FR parties can no longer be considered a localized phenomenon arising under particular circumstances in selected regions or countries. Their success in "first" and "second" order elections renders the FR a European phenomenon that should merit global attention alongside case studies.

This chapter revisits the discussion on the determinants of the FR vote in the light of methodological choices made for its estimation. In particular, we examine the theoretical hypotheses underlying alternative explanations and methodologies and their implications with respect to interpreting the results derived by different econometric models: using selection correction procedures in the place of the current standard in the literature, Tobit models,[1] might have several advantages. Conditions under which the two methodologies might be employed are explored.

Methodologically, a fundamental issue for cross-national studies is the selection of countries or elections that should be included in the analysis. Some authors have included only countries and/or elections in which FR parties have contested.[2] Jackman and Volpert (1996) first pointed out that this can produce biased estimations. The issue has since been addressed by use of Tobit models (Swank and Betz, 2003; Golder, 2003; Jesuit et al., 2009), designed to deal with censored data.

Censoring implies that when support for the FR drops below a critical level, no parties compete, so the FR vote shares are missing. This essentially amounts to saying that *demand drives supply*. Tobit models replace the missing values with zero values and treat these zero values as censored. In order to do so, one has to be very explicit about the assumptions underlying the use of censored data techniques to correct for missing values.

Coffé, Heyndels and Vermeir (2007) used a type II Tobit model for the estimation of the Vlaams Blok vote in the 1999 municipal election in Flanders. This introduced for the first time a selection-correction procedure à la Heckman (1979) in the estimation of the FR vote. We argue that Coffé et al.'s (2007) method constitutes a more general approach to modelling the FR vote, particularly in comparative aggregate studies, since it allows joint estimation of factors that affect the demand side (vote) and the supply side (party contestation) of the FR. We derive explicit theoretical conditions under which different methodologies might be used.

Explanations for the electoral fortunes of the FR parties concentrate on demand-side and supply-side factors (Golder, 2003; Mudde, 2007). Demand-side factors reflect different sets of far-reaching transformations, such as changes in citizens' economic status and socio-cultural identity; determinants of the supply side are related to the organizational structure and the ideology of the FR parties as well as the country's political opportunity structure (institutional make-up, party antagonism, etc.). Demand-side and supply-side factors can be linked to each other (Rydgren, 2007). Only when the supply side (contesting parties) exists, can demand (vote shares) be observed. However, we argue that the supply side needs not necessarily be driven by demand or indeed by the same determinants that affect demand. When supply – determined by a variety of socio-economic, institutional or organizational factors, which could in principle differ from the factors that determine demand – is present, demand can be observed in elections. However, when no FR parties compete, we are unable to observe demand for FR, even if there is a latent support for the FR and demand might have been expressed had a FR party participated in the electoral race.

From an econometrics point of view, this process is a case of incidental truncation and to address it one has to view the issue of existence of FR parties separately from the expression of electoral support for them.[3] This approach might have several advantages: it does not equate missing observations with zero values and offers a more intuitive explanation for the cause of missing values – it is a case of sample selection. To correct it, the supply- and the demand-side determinants of FR politics and success should be *decoupled*. Hence, a second substantive contribution to the demand-side and supply-side relationship involves the separation of the effect of important supply-side covariates on the demand side. In other words, factors that facilitate the participation of FR parties in elections might reduce their vote share.[4]

From a policy point of view, decoupling the effects on the supply side from the effects on the demand side can offer new insight into the mechanics of FR politics.

Factors that induce FR parties to contest in elections might affect the political demand for them negatively. Identifying the effects on the supply and demand sides separately may have important policy implications. Controlling the appearance of FR parties might require different tools than reducing their electoral appeal in regions where they contest. Hence, reducing extremist appeal in countries such as Ireland or Luxembourg with no FR present may require use of different instruments than controlling the rise of right-wing radicalism in countries with well-established FR parties.

We compare classical Tobit (type I) models to Coffé et al.'s (2007) methodology and extend it by using panel data estimators for both the classical Tobit models and selection correction models. We illustrate the different estimation methodologies in a regional sample of legislative and European parliament elections.

Our analysis contributes to the literature by clarifying the theoretical and methodological preconditions underlying different estimation choices, proposes the use of panel data estimators that best fit comparative databases of European elections for the estimation of the FR vote, and suggests that different estimators might best suit different electoral environments or research questions.

What drives the FR vote? Theory and data

Research for the determinants of the FR vote can be schematically divided into two distinct categories: individual characteristics or factors that affect voters at a micro level and structural conditions linking socio-economic factors to the FR vote at a macro or meso level of aggregation (Arzheimer, 2018).

The FR vote has been associated with three kinds of individual-level characteristics: demographic characteristics, citizens' attitudes, and socio-economic conditions, such as unemployment at an individual level or crime rates in one's area (Arzheimer, 2009; Lubbers, Gijsberts and Scheepers, 2002; Veugelers and Chiarini, 2002; Arzheimer and Carter, 2006; Arzheimer, 2009). Individual-level determinants can lead to a causal interpretation, or at least, they reveal a predisposition to vote for FR parties. Focus on socio-economic contextual factors that can be used instrumentally to control voting merits separate attention.

A number of factors that might act on an aggregate level have been proposed as possible determinants of the FR vote. They may act on a macro (e.g. national) or on a meso level (e.g. regional, district etc.). From a demand-side perspective, those factors could reflect the effect of economic and cultural changes (Inglehart and Norris, 2016):

- *Economic crises*. Deterioration of economic conditions has often been cited as a main trigger of electoral turn towards the FR. Recent research has established a link between financial crises and extreme left-wing and right-wing voting (Funke, Schularick and Trebesch, 2016). Almost all applied research on economic crises focuses on unemployment; however, its conclusions are often conflicting. For example, some authors (Jackman and Volpert, 1996; Falk and

Zweimüller, 2005; Lubbers, Gijsberts and Scheepers, 2002; Arzheimer, 2009) found that the FR vote increases with unemployment, whereas others rejected the link between tightening conditions in the labour market and FR party success (Knigge, 1998; Golder, 2003; Arzheimer and Carter, 2006; Coffé et al., 2007). It is also argued that unemployment has a negative impact on the vote share of FR parties or that a positive relationship between unemployment and crime reinforce the electoral demand for the FR (Falk and Zweimüller, 2005; Falk et al., 2011).

- *Immigration and ethnic backlash.* It has been argued that the rise of the FR might be a reaction to a perceived cultural threat posed by the increased inflow of immigrants (Husbands, 2002; Fennema 1997). As with unemployment, there is no consensus on the effect of immigration on the FR vote. By using individual (Lubbers, Gijsberts and Scheepers, 2002; Quillian, 1995; Arzheimer, 2009; Arzheimer and Carter, 2006) or aggregate data (Jackman and Volpert, 1996; Knigge, 1998), some researchers found a positive link between immigration and the FR vote, whereas other authors (Dülmer and Klein, 2005; Evans and Need, 2002) find no correlation or even a negative relationship between immigration and FR parties' electoral success. Most recent data (Inglehart and Norris, 2016) show that cultural factors are more consistent predictors for the rising electoral support for FR parties.

This chapter places itself within the economic crisis/cultural backlash strand of the literature, using a meso-level analysis with regional data. It considers a variety of economic and immigration indices while controlling for political institutions without modelling them explicitly, as these remain constant within the time span of the sample and cannot be identified within panel framework.[5] We use the database of Georgiadou et al. (2018) and a number of different estimators to illustrate the repercussions of our theoretical discussion for the estimation of the European FR vote.

The European FR: Methodological issues and estimation strategy

In examining the economic factors that affect the FR vote, two main methodological issues have to be addressed: unobserved heterogeneity between regions that might correlate with the explanatory variables, and selection bias.

Heterogeneity between regions might be present both between and within countries. This is a cause of concern as a number of cultural, anthropological, religious, political or historical elements likely to be correlated with the explanatory variables can possibly affect the FR vote. Voigtlander and Voth (2012) show that violent pogroms against Jews following the Black Death in fourteenth-century Europe can predict the Nazi vote, deportations and violence against Jews six centuries later, suggesting that there are latent historical or cultural forces affecting the support for FR. These forces might be persisting, despite being dormant for centuries.

Literature on FR has dealt with the problem in two ways: with country dummies[6] that capture unconditional fixed effects (Knigge, 1998; Golder, 2003; Jackman and Volpert, 1996) or by including proxies for key political variables (Golder, 2003; Jackman and Volpert, 1996). Although including additional controls for political rules that might affect the FR vote helps control for some of the omitted variable bias, all possible sources of heterogeneity cannot be accounted for. Country dummies can estimate country effects; however, caution is needed when introducing dummies in nonlinear model as this might bias the estimations.[7] To estimate Tobit models of the European FR, we use Honoré's (1992) panel Tobit estimator that is suitable for controlling for regional fixed effects without being susceptible to the incidental parameters problem.

Sample selection problems arise from the fact that we only observe support for FR parties in regions where such parties contest. Analyzing only countries with FR might yield biased estimations due to selection bias. Since Jackman and Volpert (1996), selection issues in the literature have been almost invariably addressed by means of Tobit models. To get a clearer idea of what different estimation techniques estimate, consider the following simple model of supply and demand for FR parties.

A simple model of supply and demand for the FR

To estimate the effect of the covariates of interest on the vote shares of FR parties, we need existence of a supply side (contesting parties) and data on the demand side (vote shares) where supply exists. Figure 7.1 presents the selection process and illustrates the two sides of FR politics. Suppose for simplicity that unemployment is the only determinant affecting the FR vote. The bottom graph depicts the supply side. It graphs the probability that a FR party contests as a function of the unemployment rate. So, for example, when the unemployment rate is 12 per cent, there is a 50 per cent probability that a FR party will contest.

The upper graph of Figure 7.1 plots the voters' demand curve (intended vote share) DD as a function of the unemployment rate. Curve DD depicts the demand that we *would* observe if FR parties *contested* in all elections. Clearly, DD is not observable in elections where no FR parties contest. What we do observe on average, however, is the dashed curve DS. This is derived as follows: at say 12 per cent unemployment rate, the probability that a FR party contests is 0.5, as is indicated by the bottom graph. At that rate of unemployment, the upper graph gives us the *true* demand for FR; that is the vote share that we would observe conditional on the fact that a FR party exists VS_1, and the *observed* average vote share $VS_2 = \frac{1}{2} VS_1$. Similarly, if the unemployment rate is 25 per cent, we observe the demand for FR with probability 72 per cent, so the average observed vote share DS is closer, on average, to the *true* demand curve DD.

Hence DS represents the *equilibrium* vote shares; that is, it corresponds to the demand for FR *weighing* for the probability that such demand is given an opportunity to express itself by existence of a supply side. Data on all European elections

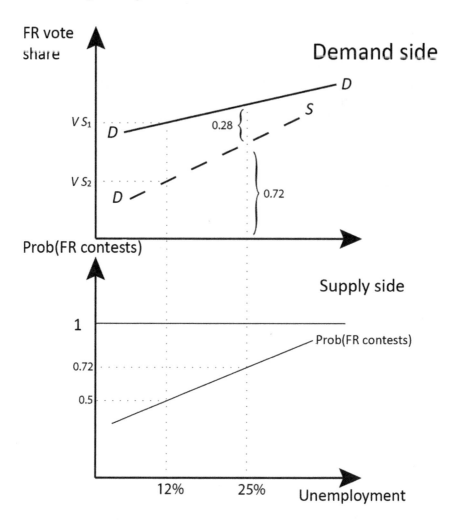

FIGURE 7.1 Supply, demand and equilibrium vote shares
Notes: The graph depicts the interaction of the supply and demand sides for the FR. The bottom graph plots the probability that a FR party contests as function of a determinant, say unemployment. The upper graph plots the true demand for the far right *DD* that we would observe *conditional that a far right party contests*, and the *actual equilibrium observed demand DS*, that is the true demand weighted by the probability that a far right party contests.

(both ones in which FR parties contest and ones in countries where they don't) correspond to the dotted equilibrium curve *DS*. Simple ordinary least squares (OLS) or fixed effects regressions on the selected sample fail to estimate the demand for FR (*DD*) consistently, however pooling all European elections (including zero values for regions where no parties contest) together is far from uninformative as it estimates the equilibrium FR vote *DS*. Excluding countries with zero FR of course fails to estimate *DS* as it excludes elections in which no FR parties contest and it also fails to estimate the true demand *DD* as the estimation is subject to selection bias. Hence, in the current analysis, no elections will be excluded on the basis of failing to observe FR parties contesting.

FR and sample selection

The most common way of dealing with zero values[8] is to interpret the observed zeroes as censoring and proceed with estimating a Tobit model. Although not explicitly mentioned, this methodology implies the following assumption:

Assumption 1. *The data generating process for the FR vote share is given by:*

$$VS_E = max(\widehat{VS}_E, y) \tag{1}$$

$$y = \beta_0 + X\beta + u, u|X \sim Normal(0, \sigma^2) \tag{2}$$

where *y* is a latent normal variable the value of which determines whether the FR vote share is observed: when *y* is greater than $\widehat{VS}_E$, it coincides with the FR vote share VS_E. Otherwise, the FR vote share will be equal to $\widehat{VS}_E$. *X* is a vector of demand-side controls. In equation (2), the interpretation of *y* would be latent (possibly unobserved) support for FR parties. Latent support for the FR is a linear function of *X*. Equation (1) implies that when the latent support exceeds a minimum level of support $\widehat{VS}_E$ necessary to induce participation of FR parties in the race, then the observed FR vote shares VS_E coincide with the latent support $\widehat{VS}_E$, it cannot be observed and we observe zero values instead. For this to be the case, a number of implicit assumptions should hold:

A1. Censoring depends on the (latent) dependent variable (support for FR). This amounts to saying that *demand drives supply*: parties contest (*y* is not censored) only if the support is above $\widehat{VS}_E$.
A2. $\widehat{VS}_E$ is the level of left censoring: the support threshold needed to be reached in order for a party to contest.
A3. $\widehat{VS}_E$ should be lower than the minimum observed vote share. Otherwise we would observe $\widehat{VS}_E$ rather than the minimum.
A4. There should be a mass of censored values $\widehat{VS}_E$. Since we typically observe a mass of zeroes, $\widehat{VS}_E$ must be practically indistinguishable from zero.
A5. The linear relationship between the dependent variable and the covariates is the same for both the censored and the uncensored data and given by (2).

It is clear that use of Tobit models exerts a heavy toll in terms of severity of assumptions needed to justify it. If we are satisfied from both a theoretical (assumptions A1–A2) and an empirical (assumptions A3–A5) standpoint that these are reasonable, we should employ a Tobit model. Even then, it is difficult to ascribe any intuitive meaning to y, particularly when it assumes negative values.

A competing interpretation of the selection procedure offers a more general and intuitive interpretation of sample selection.

Assumption 2. *The data generating process for the FR vote share is given by:*

$$s = 1(Z\gamma + v \geq 0) \tag{3}$$

$$VS_E = s[\beta_0 + X\beta + u], \text{ with } E(u|X) = 0 \tag{4}$$

The vote share for the FR parties, VS_E is given by (4) and is a linear function of a vector X of covariates. The observance of (positive) VS_E depends on the outcome of s, which is specified in (3) and indicates the existence of FR parties in the region at the time of the election. The appearance of FR parties depends on a number of factors Z, which in principle might include some or all of Xs and other variables that might affect the creation of FR parties. The function $1()$ is an indicator function taking the value 1 when the condition mentioned as its argument is satisfied and 0 otherwise. This is a clear case of incidental truncation, where the observance of a variable of interest (VS_E) depends upon the outcome of another variable s (formation of FR parties).

Equation (4) essentially captures the *demand* side for FR as expressed by voters in ballots as a function of the socio-economic environment and corresponds to the *DD* curve in the upper graph of Figure 7.1. Equation (3) refers to the process leading to participation of FR parties in elections (*supply* side) and corresponds to the bottom graph of Figure 7.1. Whereas X, Z and s are always observed, VS_E is only observed when $s = 1$. The process described corresponds to Heckman's (1979) sample selection. Finally, note that if s depended on the outcome of VS_E, we would fall within the traditional Tobit framework. If X was not observed when VS_E was zero, we would fall within the truncated Tobit framework.

Heckman (1979) shows that the sample selection can be corrected by his celebrated two-step estimator. Estimating (3) and (4) to correct for selection has advantages: it allows separation of the selection stage (3) from the population model (4). Most importantly, the first step estimation of the selection process (estimation of (3)), allows identification of the factors that favour the creation of FR parties and is informative about the supply side of FR. The second step estimation (estimating (4)), identifies the economic determinants of the FR vote. So, we allow a particular economic indicator to favour, say, the appearance of FR parties but not the support for them.

In the estimation of the FR vote that follows, all different approaches to estimating the FR vote will be tried. A fixed effects estimation for the whole sample will estimate the equilibrium FR vote *DS*. To estimate the demand for FR *DD*, we will operate under both Assumption 1 and Assumption 2 and compare the estimates of the effects of various socio-economic variables obtained under the two competing methodologies.

Estimating the European FR: An illustration

We next illustrate different estimation approaches for the regional FR vote share in Europe between 2001 and 2014. We use data from Georgiadou et al. (2018) to compare the estimation of the equilibrium FR vote (dashed line *DS* in Figure 7.1) with the demand (solid *DD* line) and supply (probability in the bottom graph of Figure 7.1) of the FR vote. Table 7.1 reports the results of our estimations.

Column (1) reports the results of a simple baseline OLS estimation. Column (2) controls for time-invariant unobserved heterogeneity at the NUTS 2 level using linear fixed effects. This essentially estimates the equilibrium FR vote (dashed line *DS*). Column (3) attempts to estimate the demand for FR (solid line *DD*) under the assumption that demand drives supply, by means of a panel Tobit estimator. Column (4) estimates both demand and supply of FR using a Heckit estimator. Heckman's estimator corrects for sample selection by including the inverse Mills ratio $\Lambda(Zit\gamma)$ on the right-hand side (for more details see Wooldridge (2010)). So, in our case, we would estimate

$$VSit = Xit\beta + di + \Lambda(Zit\gamma) + \varepsilon it \qquad (8)$$

In (8), the FR vote share of region i at time t (*VSit*) is a linear function of a number of explanatory variables (**X**) and time-invariant regional characteristics (fixed effects) di. To correct for sample selection, Heckman (1979) adds the inverse Mills ratio, $\Lambda(Zit\gamma)$.

This however, would require knowledge of the individual fixed effects di. To eliminate fixed effects, we proceed by differencing (8) to obtain:

$$\Delta VS_{it} = \Delta X_{it}\beta + \Lambda(Z_it\gamma) - \Lambda(Z_{i(t-1)}\gamma) + u_it \qquad (9)$$

where $u_{it} = \Delta\varepsilon_{it} = \varepsilon_{it} - \varepsilon_{i(t-1)}$. Equation (9) is simply equation (8) in first differences. Estimating (9) we obtain estimates of the vector of coefficients β, controlling for fixed effects.[9] This is of particular interest as it decouples the effects of key covariates on the probability that we observe FR supply from their effects on demand.

Read vertically, column (4) of Table 7.1 informs us of the factors associated with the supply (column 4a) or demand (column 4b) of FR. So that for example the probability that a FR party contests in a particular European region is positively associated with GDP per habitant, between regions inequality, property rents, less corrupt countries or business freedom, but negatively associated with regional immigration, effective tax rates, wage shares, growth or investment freedom. On the other hand, the demand for FR is positively associated with high unemployment, GDP per capita and the wage share over primary income, but negatively associated with income inequality between NUTS 3 regions and growth.

TABLE 7.1 Selection-correction in the estimation of the FR

Dependent variable: FR vote share	(1) OLS	(2) FE	(3) Panel Tobit Honoré (1992)	(4) Heckit		(5) Wooldridge (1995) 2nd stage
				a Selection	*b* 2nd Stage	
Unemployment rate$_{t-1}$	0.300**	1.456***	2.447***	−2.610	0.513***	0.431***
	(0.147)	(0.195)	(0.265)	(3.068)	(0.150)	(0.165)
Immigration$_{t-1}$	−0.250	0.299	1.530**	−13.604***	0.165	−0.153
	(0.215)	(0.513)	(0.695)	(3.108)	(0.774)	(0.315)
GDP PPS per capita$_{t-1}$	−0.001	0.036***	0.056***	0.339**	0.045**	−0.007
	(0.009)	(0.012)	(0.015)	(0.142)	(0.021)	(0.010)
Tax rate$_{t-1}$	0.180**	0.231**	0.326**	−3.238***	−0.172	0.242**
	(0.079)	(0.103)	(0.130)	(1.200)	(0.172)	(0.083)
Between regions inequality$_{t-1}$	−0.037	−0.751***	−0.903**	5.956***	−0.989***	−0.105*
	(0.054)	(0.266)	(0.390)	(1.573)	(0.316)	(0.057)
Wage share$_{t-1}$	−0.049	0.439***	0.534***	−3.766**	0.262*	−0.033
	(0.046)	(0.115)	(0.134)	(1.472)	(0.143)	(0.047)
Growth Dummy$_{t-1}$	−0.231***	−0.164***	−0.159**	−4.052*	−0.150***	−0.198**
	(0.083)	(0.059)	(0.073)	(2.149)	(0.054)	(0.085)
Rise in unemployment Dummy$_{t-1}$	−0.012	−0.016	−0.022	0.212	0.032	−0.004
	(0.060)	(0.048)	(0.065)	(1.766)	(0.047)	(0.069)

Dependent variable: FR vote share	*(1)* OLS	*(2)* FE	*(3)* Panel Tobit Honoré (1992)	*(4)* Heckit		*(5)* Wooldridge (1995) 2nd stage
				Selection *a*	2nd Stage *b*	
Parliamentary election Dummy$_{t-1}$	0.002	0.001	0.001	−0.232	−0.010★★	0.002
	(0.003)	(0.002)	(0.003)	(0.166)	(0.004)	(0.004)
log(population)				−0.333		
				(0.222)		
Land area				−0.200★★★		
				(0.061)		
Life expectancy$_{t-1}$				−0.819		
				(0.599)		
Property rents$_{t-1}$				0.056★★		
				(0.026)		
Investment freedom$_{t-1}$				−0.035★★★		
				(0.008)		
Freedom from corruption$_{t-1}$				0.039★★★		
				(0.009)		
Business freedom$_{t-1}$				0.028★★★		
				(0.011)		

TABLE 7.1 (continued)

	(1)	(2)	(3)	(4)		(5)
				Heckit		Wooldridge (1995)
			Panel Tobit			2nd stage
Dependent variable: FR vote share	OLS	FE	Honoré (1992)	a	b	
				Selection	2nd Stage	
Mills Ratio ($\Delta\Lambda(\mathbf{Z}_{it})$)					0.075★★	
					(0.030)	
Constant	0.106★★★	−0.327★★★		13.513★★	0.006	0.107★★★
	(0.038)	(0.089)		(5.960)	(0.004)	(0.039)
Observations	812	812	812	735	565	750
Adjusted R–squared	0.029	0.172			0.059	0.042
Region FE	yes	yes	yes	no	yes	Yes
time effects	No	no	no	no	no	No
Number of nuts_2		229				

Source: Authors' calculations based on electoral, OECD, Eurostat and Manifesto Project data.

Notes: The table reports the results of FE, panel Tobit and selection correction estimations of the FR vote. Columns (1) and (2) report the results of linear OLS and FE estimations. Column (3) uses Honoré's (1992) panel Tobit estimator. Columns (4) and (5) use Heckman's (1979) and Wooldridge's (1995) selection correction estimators as described in the text. Standard errors are given in parentheses below the coefficients. For column (5) standard errors were bootstrapped as suggested by Wooldridge (2010). ★, ★★, and ★★★ denote statistical significance at the 10%, 5%, and 1% level of significance, respectively.

Read horizontally, columns 4a and 4b demonstrate that a specific socio-economic trigger might affect the two sides of FR politics in different ways. So that, for example the wage share is negatively related to the probability that at least a FR party competes in the election, but positively related to the demand for FR by the voters. Similarly, immigration affects negatively the formation/participation of FR parties, but is not shown to have an effect on the demand side.

Finally, column (5) uses an alternative panel selection correction estimator by Wooldridge (1995). Note that, with few exceptions, the estimation of the demand side does not differ substantially from the panel selection-correction estimator based on differences. We do not report the estimation of the supply side (selection) for the Wooldridge (1995) estimator, because the selection stage is estimated separately for each year and inverse Mills ratios are obtained for each estimation and included as covariates in the second stage regression for the relevant years. Table 7.2 repeats all estimations, controlling for year fixed effects.

We close the presentation of our results with a graphical illustration of the estimations obtained for both the supply and demand sides. Figure 7.2 plots our estimations of the effect of unemployment on the supply side (bottom graph) and the demand side (upper graph) on the European FR vote. The bottom graph plots the predicted probability that at least one FR party competes in the election as function of unemployment (all other covariates are held at their means). The upper graph is a scatter plot of the European FR as a function of unemployment with the fitted lines of our different estimators with year effects (presented in Table 7.2). The black solid line plots a fit for the fixed effect estimator. Honoré's (1992) estimation is depicted by the green dashed line. Note that compared with the fixed effect estimator, the Tobit estimator gives a higher effect for the demand side. Both selection correction estimators, that is Wooldridge (1995) (long-dashed magenta line) and Heckman (1979) (long-dashed and dotted brown line) estimators give similar magnitudes for the effect of unemployment, which are lower than the effect estimated by simple linear fixed effects.

With respect to unemployment, the two panel selection-correction estimators give a consistent story: the effect of unemployment is positive but lower than the one obtained by simple fixed effects. If theory gives us good reason to expect that the assumptions implied by the Tobit model, particularly that demand drives the supply of FR politics, then the Tobit estimator implies that the effect of unemployment is higher than simple fixed effects would suggest. If there are other possible factors that might affect the appearance of FR parties, our selection correction estimations would suggest that the effect of unemployment is positive but smaller in magnitude than that implied by simple fixed effects.

Discussion and conclusions

We investigated the main determinants of the European FR vote using a regional-level database on national and European parliament elections. Our purpose was to explore theoretical issues related to the rising support of FR parties, as well as

TABLE 7.2 Section-correction in the estimation of the FR vote controlling for year effects

Dependent variable: FR vote share	(1) OLS-TE	(2) FE-TE	(3) Panel Tobit Honoré (1992) – TE	(4) Heckit-TE		(5) Wooldridge (1995) – TE
				Selection	2nd Stage	
Unemployment rate$_{t-1}$	0.271*	1.245***	2.295***	4.423	0.303**	0.421***
	(0.140)	(0.186)	(0.317)	(3.353)	(0.144)	(0.163)
Immigration$_{t-1}$	−0.188	0.245	1.053	−13.953***	0.618	−0.086
	(0.228)	(0.452)	(0.727)	(3.129)	(0.697)	(0.320)
GDP PPS per capita$_{t-1}$	0.008	−0.009	0.023	0.229	0.061***	−0.013
	(0.010)	(0.014)	(0.023)	(0.151)	(0.022)	(0.011)
Tax rate$_{t-1}$	0.267***	0.343***	0.454***	−1.604	−0.066	0.308***
	(0.085)	(0.129)	(0.139)	(1.289)	(0.157)	(0.094)
Between regions inequality$_{t-1}$	−0.025	−0.727***	−0.868**	4.692***	−0.773***	−0.087
	(0.054)	(0.249)	(0.366)	(1.674)	(0.276)	(0.056)
Wage share$_{t-1}$	−0.010	0.332***	0.428***	−6.481***	0.449***	0.022
	(0.046)	(0.112)	(0.149)	(2.061)	(0.128)	(0.048)
Growth Dummy$_{t-1}$	−0.168*	0.061	0.057	−0.988	−0.207***	−0.149
	(0.100)	(0.061)	(0.067)	(2.682)	(0.058)	(0.102)
Rise in unemployment Dummy$_{t-1}$	−0.019	0.002	−0.004	2.932	−0.017	−0.055
	(0.065)	(0.049)	(0.065)	(2.113)	(0.047)	(0.074)
Parliamentary election Dummy$_t$	−0.007	−0.005	−0.001	−0.810*	−0.004	−0.068

−1

Dependent variable: FR vote share	(1) OLS-TE	(2) FE-TE	(3) Panel Tobit Honoré (1992) – TE	(4) Heckit-TE Selection	(4) Heckit-TE 2nd Stage	(5) Wooldridge (1995) – TE
	(0.008)	(0.008)	(0.005)	(0.446)	(0.007)	(0.008)
log(population)				−0.385		
				(0.256)		
Land area				−0.192★★		
				(0.066)		
Life expectancy$_{t-1}$				−0.970		
				(0.701)		
Property rents$_{t-1}$				0.074★★★		
				(0.027)		
Investment freedom$_{t-1}$				−0.044★★★		
				(0.011)		
Freedom from corruption$_{t-1}$				0.063★★★		
				(0.012)		
Business freedom$_{t-1}$				−0.007		
				(0.019)		
Mills Ratio ($\Delta\Lambda(\mathbf{Z}_{it}\gamma)$)				0.029		
				(0.028)		

TABLE 7.2 (*continued*)

Dependent variable: FR vote share	(1) OLS-TE	(2) FE-TE	(3) Panel Tobit Honoré (1992) – TE	(4) Heckit-TE Selection	(4) Heckit-TE 2nd Stage	(5) Wooldridge (1995) – TE
Constant	0.120***	−0.160		17.548**	−0.036**	0.149***
	(0.039)	(0.097)		(7.408)	(0.014)	(0.041)
Observations	812	812	812	714	542	750
Adjusted R-squared	0.087	0.320			0.258	0.110
Region FE	yes	yes	Yes	no	Yes	yes
time effects	yes	yes	Yes	yes	Yes	yes
Number of nuts_2		229				

Source: Authors' calculations based on electoral, OECD, Eurostat and Manifesto Project data.

Notes: The table reports the results of FE, panel Tobit and selection correction estimations of the FR vote, controlling for year fixed effects. Columns (1) and (2) report the results of linear OLS and FE estimations. Column (3) uses Honoré's (1992) panel Tobit estimator. Columns (4) and (5) use Heckman's (1979) and Wooldridge's (1995) selection correction estimators as described in the text. Standard errors are given in parentheses below the coefficients. For the Wooldridge (1995) estimator, bootstrapped standard errors are reported. *, **, and *** denote statistical significance at the 10%, 5% and 1% level of significance, respectively.

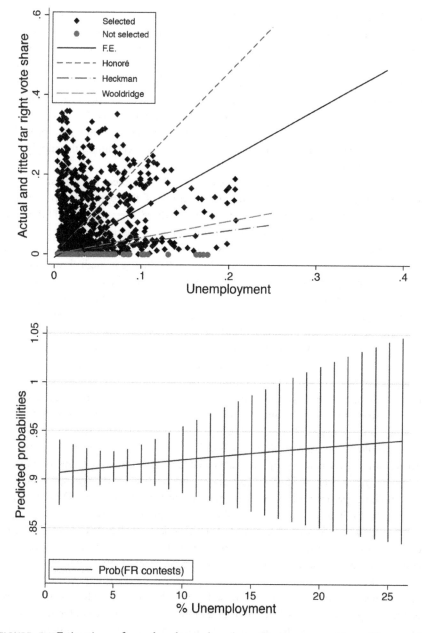

FIGURE 7.2 Estimation of supply, demand and equilibrium vote shares. The graph depicts our estimations of effects of unemployment the supply side (bottom) and demand side (top) of the European FR. The bottom figure plots the estimated effect of unemployment on the probability that FR contests in the election with 95% confidence intervals. The upper graph is a scatterplot of our data (both censored and uncensored) and the fitted values of the different estimators discussed in the text.

methodological implications of unobserved heterogeneity and selection bias. The usual way of addressing selection bias, that is by using Tobit models for censored data, is not the only or indeed the best way to correct for selection. The problem of not observing support even when it exists due to lack of supply-side FR politics might well be a problem of selection that needs selection-correction techniques rather than a problem of censoring. Using two such methods, the one introduced by Heckman's (1979) seminal paper and one after Wooldridge (1995) to correct for selection bias, apart from helping obtain more general estimates also provided valuable information on the determinants of the FR by decoupling the supply side from the demand for FR.

The economic and social conditions examined do not affect the two sides symmetrically. Factors that might inhibit the creation of FR parties (supply) might boost their electoral support (demand) in areas where these contest. This might have interesting policy implications. For example, consider the link between regional inequality and voting for the FR. The implications for policies that reduce between-regions inequality are far from obvious. Reducing it might lower support for the FR in regions where FR parties compete, but might induce higher participation of FR parties in elections. Similarly, increasing the wage share of primary income might reduce participation of the FR parties in elections but might boost their vote in regions with established FR. The instrument chosen has to be tailored to the target at hand. The methodological contribution has substantive consequences depending which side of FR politics one might wish to affect. For example, cordon sanitaire strategies implied by mainstream parties vis-à-vis the FR component of the party system aim to isolate the later. Even if the supply side is affected, since the cordon sanitaire limits the FR parties' ability to attract party members and activists (Golder, 2003), this does not mean that demand for these parties would be negatively affected unless they are "consistently ostracized" by the mainstream parties (van Spanje and de Graaf, 2018). Instead of being ostracized, FR parties have been attributed exaggerated significance mainly by mass media or other political parties with respect to their political or electoral rise (Mondon and Glynos, 2016). This increases both visibility and support for FR parties.

Although the analysis is suggestive of a potential causal pathway between past socio-economic grievances and levels of support for the FR, the revealed relation between several measures of economic performance and support for the FR can only be the starting point for further enquiries. For one thing, the underlying mechanisms that transform say increased unemployment to FR votes, are not readily interpretable at this level of aggregation. To make further inferences about the demography of the FR, use of individual data can offer fresh insight. Establishing the results with individual-level data will enhance our understanding of who exactly votes for the FR in high unemployment or tax-laden regions.

Applying selection correction methods to estimate vote shares need not be confined to the economic determinants of the FR vote. Subject to availability, the effect of political, historical, social or cultural variables can be examined. Distinguishing between factors affecting the demand side and ones affecting the supply side while controlling for electoral heterogeneity can only open the door to more promising, interesting and rich future research.

Notes

1 The Tobit model is a statistical model describing the relation between a limited dependent variable (y), and the explanatory variables (X). The dependent variable (y) in Tobit models is typically zero for a non-trivial fraction of the population and is continually distributed over positive values for the rest of the population.
2 Indicatively Knigge (1998) considers support in FR only in six countries with established FR presence; Lubbers, Gijsberts and Scheepers (2002) include in their sample only countries where FR parties exist; van der Brug, Fennema and Tillie (2005), Koopmans (1996), Veugelers and Magnan (2005) also select countries where the FR competes. Individual-level analysis is not in principle immune to the problem as it often only focuses on individuals in selected countries where FR exists without controlling for individual behaviour in countries in which the FR vote is not observed (see for example Arzheimer and Carter, 2006).
3 The problem was first identified and addressed in Heckman (1979). Correctly identifying and addressing sample selection is of fundamental importance in empirical work. Since then, a number of studies that enrich Heckman's original results for use with panel data have emerged (see for example Wooldridge, 1995; Kyriazidou, 1997; Dustmann and Rochina-Barrachina, 2007).
4 Immerzeel and Pickup (2015) examine the effects of supply side on voter turnout. They found that the emergence of successful PRR parties in Western Europe increases the propensity to go to the polls between specific groups of voters that are strongly opposed to the FR parties. This may reduce the FR vote share.
5 Political institutions have country-level variation and are typically invariant in the 14 years that this sample spans, but can correlate with the economic covariates as is argued below. To estimate consistently the effect of the contextual covariates on the FR vote share, panel data techniques are employed. While this ensures that the time-invariant political institutions do not bias the estimates of the effects of the contextual variables, the effects of the institutions themselves on the FR vote shares cannot be identified.
6 That is by including binary variables (one for each country), each taking the value 1 if the election took place in the country and 0 otherwise.
7 This is known as the incidental parameters problem (Neyman and Scott, 1948). Although the slope coefficients for the Tobit models are not affected, the standard errors cannot be consistently estimated (Greene, 2004). Standard errors in the Tobit model with region dummies are calculated by jackknife estimation.
8 Technically, these are missing observations, which are treated as zero values so that Tobit models might be employed.
9 We are indebted to Katerina Kyriazidou for suggesting this estimation approach.

References

Arzheimer, K. 2009. "Contextual Factors and the Extreme Right Vote in Western Europe, 1980–2002." *American Journal of Political Science*, 53(2), 259–275.

Arzheimer, K. 2018. "Explaining Electoral Support for the Radical Right." In *The Oxford Handbook of the Radical Right*, edited by J. Rydgren. Oxford: Oxford University Press.

Arzheimer, K. and E. Carter. 2006. "Political Opportunity Structures and Right-Wing Extremist Party Success." *European Journal of Political Research*, 45, 419–443.

Coffé H., B. Heyndels, and J. Vermeir. 2007. "Fertile Grounds for Extreme Right-Wing Parties: Explaining the Vlaams Blok's Electoral Success." *Electoral Studies*, 26, 142–155.

Dülmer, H. and M. Klein. 2005. "Extreme Right-Wing Voting in Germany in a Multilevel Perspective; A Rejoinder to Lubbers and Scheepers." *European Journal of Political Research*, 44(2), 243–263.

Dustmann, C. and M.E. Rochina-Barrachina. 2007. "Selection Correction in Panel Data Models: An Application to the Estimation of Females' Wage Equations." *The Econometrics Journal*, 10(2), 263–293.

Evans, G. and A. Need. 2002. "Explaining Ethnic Polarization Over Attitudes Towards Minority Rights in Eastern Europe: A Multilevel Analysis." *Social Science Research*, 31(4), 653–680.

Falk, A. and J. Zweimüller. 2005. "Unemployment and Right-Wing Extremist Crime." IZA DP No. 1540. Bonn: IZA Institute of Labor Economics.

Falk, A., A. Kuhn, and J. Zweimüller. 2011. "Unemployment Right-Wing Extremist Crime." *The Scandinavian Journal of Economics*, 113(2), 260–285.

Fennema, M. 1997. "Some Conceptual Issues and Problems in the Comparison of Anti-Immigrant Parties in Western Europe." *Party Politics*, 3, 473–492.

Funke, M., M. Schularick, and C. Trebesch. 2016. "Going to Extremes: Politics After Financial Crises, 1870–2014." *European Economic Review*, 88, 227–260.

Georgiadou V., L. Rori, and C. Roumanias. 2018. "Mapping the European Far Right in the 21st Century: A Meso-Level Analysis." *Electoral Studies*, 54, 103–115.

Golder, M. 2003. "Explaining Variation in the Success of Extreme Right Parties in Western Europe." *Comparative Political Studies*, 36(4), 432–466.

Greene, W. 2004. "The Behaviour of the Maximum Likelihood Estimator of Limited Dependent Variable Models in the Presence of Fixed Effects." *The Econometrics Journal*, 7(1), 98–119.

Heckman, J.J. 1979. "Sample Selection Bias as a Specification Error." *Econometrica*, 47(1), 153–161.

Honoré, B.E. 1992. "Trimmed LAD and Least Squares Estimation of Truncated and Censored Regression Models with Fixed Effects." *Econometrica*, 60(3), 533–565.

Husbands, C.T. 2002. "Combating the Extreme Right with the Instruments of the Constitutional State: Lessons from Experiences in Western Europe." *Journal of Conflict and Violence Research*, 4(1), 50–73.

Immerzeel, T. and M. Pickup. 2015. "Populist Radical Right Parties Mobilizing 'The People'? The Role of Populist Radical Right Success in Voter Turnout." *Electoral Studies*, 40, 347–360.

Inglehart, R. and P. Norris. 2016. *Trump, Brexit, and the Rise of Populism: Economic Have-Nots and Cultural Backlash*. Harvard Kennedy School, Working Paper Series No. RWP16-026. Cambridge, MA: Harvard University.

Jackman, R.W. and K. Volpert. 1996. "Conditions Favouring Parties of the Extreme Right in Western Europe." *British Journal of Political Science*, 26(4), 501–521.

Jesuit, D.K., P.R. Paradowski, and V.A. Mahler. 2009. "Electoral Support for Extreme Right-Wing Parties: A Sub-National Analysis of Western European Elections." *Electoral Studies*, 28, 279–290.

Knigge, P. 1998. "The Ecological Correlates of Right-Wing Extremism in Western Europe." *European Journal of Political Research*, 34(2), 249–279.

Koopmans, R. 1996. "Explaining the Rise of Racist and Extreme Right Violence in Western Europe: Grievances or Opportunities?" *European Journal of Political Research*, 30, 185–216.

Kyriazidou, E. 1997. "Estimation of a Panel Data Sample Selection Model." *Econometrica*, 65(6), 1335–1364.

Lubbers, M., M. Gijsberts, and P. Scheepers. 2002. "Extreme Right-Wing Voting in Western Europe." *European Journal of Political Research*, 41(3), 345–378.

Mondon, A. and J. Glynos. 2016. "The Political Logic of Populist Hype: The Case of Right Wing Populism's 'Meteoric Rise' and its Relation to the Status Quo." POPULISMUS Working Papers, vol. 4. Thessaloniki: POPULISMUS.

Mudde, C. 2007. *Populist Radical Right Parties in Europe*. Cambridge: Cambridge University Press.

Neyman, J. and E.L. Scott. 1948. "Consistent Estimates Based on Partially Consistent Observations." *Econometrica*, 16(1), 1–32.

Quillian, L. 1995. "Prejudice as a Response to Perceived Group Threat. Population Composition and Anti-Immigrant and Racial Prejudice in Europe." *American Sociological Review*, 60, 586–611.

Rydgren, J. 2007. "The Sociology of the Radical Right." *Annual Review of Sociology*, 33(1), 241–262.

Swank, D. and H.-G. Betz. 2003. "Globalization, the Welfare State and Right-Wing Populism in Western Europe." *Socio-Economic Review*, 1(2), 215–245.

van der Brug, W., M. Fennema, and J. Tillie. 2005. "Why Some Anti-Immigrant Parties Fail and Others Succeed. A Two-Step Model of Aggregate Electoral Support." *Comparative Political Studies*, 38, 537–573.

van Spanje, J. and N.D. de Graaf. 2018. "How Established Parties Reduce Other Parties' Electoral Support: The Strategy of Parroting the Pariah." *West European Politics*, 41(1), 1–27.

Veugelers, J.W.P. and R. Chiarini. 2002. "The Far Right in France and Italy: Nativist Politics and Anti-Fascism." In *Shadows Over Europe: The Development and Impact of the Extreme Right in Western Europe*, edited by M. Schain, A. Zolberg, and P. Hossay, 83–103. New York, NY: Palgrave.

Veugelers, J.W.P. and A. Magnan. 2005. "Conditions of Far-Right Strength in Contemporary Western Europe. An Application of Kitschelt's Theory." *European Journal of Political Research*, 44, 837–860.

Voigtlander, N. and H.J. Voth. 2012. "Persecution Perpetuated: The Medieval Origins of Anti-Semitic Violence in Nazi Germany." *The Quarterly Journal of Economics*, 127(3), 1339–1392.

Wooldridge, J.M. 1995. "Selection Corrections for Panel Data Models Under Conditional Mean Independence Assumptions." *Journal of Econometrics*, 68(1), 115–132.

Wooldridge, J.M. 2010. *Econometric Analysis of Cross Section and Panel Data*. Cambridge, MA: MIT Press.

8

METHODS FOR MAPPING FAR RIGHT VIOLENCE

Jacob Aasland Ravndal and Anders Ravik Jupskås

Far right ideology is often associated with violence in the sense that (extreme versions of) it motivates and justifies acts of violence (see e.g. Wilkinson, 1995; Taylor et al., 2013; Weinberg and Assoudeh, 2018). Indeed, several recent incidents reminds us that far right violence is far from a historically distant phenomenon in contemporary (Western) Europe. In 2016 were there at least seven deadly events whose target selection seems to have been determined by far right beliefs.[1] One high-profile event was the street murder of British Member of Parliament Jo Cox, committed by Thomas Mair, a 52-year-old man who bought material from the American national socialist group National Alliance (Cobain et al., 2016). Before repeatedly stabbing and shooting Cox – a politician well known for her pro-immigration viewpoints – Mair shouted: "this is for Britain. Britain will always come first". Another deadly event, which got significantly less press coverage, occurred in the small Italian town of Fermo. A man associated with the Italian far right used a traffic pole to beat a Nigerian migrant – Emmanuel Chidi Namdi – who tried to defend his wife from racial abuse. Chidi Namdi died a few days later form the injuries caused by the attack. The Nigerian couple were reportedly escaping the terror of Boko Haram (BBC News, 2016).

These events suggest that far right violence still exists in contemporary liberal democracies. However, we know surprisingly little about its prevalence, patterns and perpetrators. Is far right violence increasing or decreasing? Should we interpret seven deadly attacks in 2016 as a high or low number? Are some countries experiencing more violence than others? Are perpetrators like Thomas Mair typical of the far right? Who are the main victims of far right violence – politicians as in the case of Jo Cox, or immigrants as in the case of Chidi Namdi? Existing events datasets and chronologies are to a greater or lesser degree unable to answer such important questions due to a number of methodological shortcomings.

The aim of this chapter is twofold. First, and most importantly, we review existing datasets on far right violence showing that they largely fail to include all relevant incidents and to exclude all irrelevant incidents. More specifically, the datasets seem to suffer from one or several methodological pitfalls related to (1) availability, (2) representativity, (3) measurement validity, (4) replicability, and (5) comparability. Second, we propose and evaluate three strategies to remedy some of the methodological shortcomings and improve the quality of existing data, including crowdsourcing, international standardized police reporting, and victimization surveys. The combination of these three strategies will enable scholars to provide empirically grounded and theoretically sophisticated answers to pressing questions about the nature of far right violence.

Before delving into these shortcomings and strategies, however, we will first explain precisely what we mean by far right violence and how it relates to different but similar concepts such as terrorism and hate crime.

Concepts and definitions

While 'far right' remains a scholarly contested concept, there is a growing consensus in the literature (see e.g. Carter, 2018). In line with this consensus, we define 'far right' as the combination of anti-egalitarianism (Bobbio, 1996), nativism (Mudde, 2007) and authoritarianism (Stenner, 2005). These ideological constructs – and beliefs that are strongly associated with them, such as racism and conspiratorial thinking (see Mudde, 1995; Fennema, 1997) – produce a set of political and social groups that are considered to be enemies. Most notably, but not exclusively, this includes immigrants, minorities, and left-wing politicians. The justification for a rather *broad* definition of 'far right' – in which we include not only acts motivated by coherent far right ideology but also those committed due to for example racist beliefs – is simply the major challenge of distinguishing the two in practice. In most cases, it would be very difficult to determine whether the perpetrator subscribes to a coherent ideology.

Violence is probably less contested than 'far right', yet scholars do disagree whether violence is only physical acts or if one should also speak of symbolic forms for violence. In this chapter, we refer to violence exclusively as the intentional use of *physical* force with the potential for causing death, disability, injury, or harm. This does not mean that we consider threats, hate speech, or symbolic attacks against material targets as irrelevant or trivial. However, the justification for a rather *narrow* definition of violence is that the threshold for committing physical attacks against other human beings is considerably higher than for making threats or hateful remarks. By implication, such physical attacks require different explanations, and they should therefore be treated as an analytically distinct phenomenon.

All violent perpetrators are evidently not terrorists. One authoritative definition of terrorism argues that terrorists deliberately use or threaten violence to trigger far-reaching psychological repercussions beyond the immediate victim or target (Hoffman, 2006: 40). However, in the case of far right terrorists, such deliberate use of violence can be hard to document because far right perpetrators rarely issue demands or claim responsibility for the attacks they carry out. Most attacks are never claimed or explained, but they generally involve demonstrating hostility towards and installing fear in some target group represented by the victim. Thus, although specific demands may be lacking, these attacks do contain a clear political message about the target group being unwanted. As such, the target selection may be seen as a political message in and of itself, and the larger target group may be seen as the primary audience to be influenced by the attack. One could therefore consider an attack as far right terrorism if it was premeditated, and if the victim was targeted primarily because he or she belongs to a group predefined as an enemy or as unwanted by the far right. By contrast, far right violence does not require premeditation, and includes spontaneous attacks against perceived enemies or people regarded as unwanted by the far right

The types of actors involved in far right violence may thus range from strongly organized elite-sponsored groups, such as *l'Organisation de l'Armeé Secrete* in France or *Ordine Nero* in Italy, via more loosely organized subcultural groups such as *Combat 18* in the UK or *Nationalsozialistischer Untergrund* in Germany, to unorganized groups and individuals involved in less premeditated forms of violence that to some extent overlap with violent hate crime (Ravndal, 2015).

However, far right violence differs from hate crime in at least three important respects. First, not all hate crimes are motivated by far right beliefs. For example, Muslim fundamentalists seem to be responsible for a significant amount of anti-Semitic violence in contemporary Western Europe (Enstad, 2017). Second, hate crimes are not restricted to physical violence, but include also bullying, harassment, verbal abuse or insults. Third, violent attacks against left-wing politicians, government officials or law enforcement agents are normally not considered acts of hate crime since the victim is targeted due to political or professional rather than social or ethnic/racial belonging. In sum, this means that while most far right violence can be subsumed under the broader concept of hate crime, some acts of far right violence – that is, those that are directed towards *political* opponents and state representatives – would not, which means that the two concepts are only partially overlapping.

Five barriers to mapping far right violence[2]

If the subject of inquiry is far right violence, there are several existing databases and chronologies where relevant information might be available. This includes, most notably, a number of cross-national terrorism databases developed by scholars (e.g. Global Terrorism Database and Terrorism in Western Europe: Events Data (TWEED)) or supranational agencies (Europol's annual EU Terrorism Situation and Trend Report (TE-SAT)). It also includes several within-country chronologies on far right violent incidents (Koehler, 2014), national hate crime statistics and reports from anti-racist organizations (e.g. EXPO in Sweden and Southern Poverty Law Center in the USA). As discussed in the following section, however, existing data collected by scholars, agencies and organizations commonly suffer from one or several methodological pitfalls.

Availability

A first problem concerns *availability*, i.e. the simple yet surprising fact that it is difficult to come across systematic data on far right violence. Besides a general lack of documentation, existing terrorism datasets seem to suffer from one of two shortcomings: either they do not include far right violence as a separate category, or they are outdated.

For example, larger and well-known terrorism databases, such as the Global Terrorism Database (GTD) and the RAND Database of Terrorism Incidents (RDWTI), do not code for the political profile of the perpetrators. This lack of perpetrator coding makes it hard to distinguish far right attacks from others. And even if a handful of relevant events can be found using suitable search queries, these databases also suffer from problems of representativity (haphazard registration) and replicability (missing source references).

Among the top 20 terrorism databases reviewed by Routledge's *Handbook of Terrorism Research*, only 4 databases allow for isolating right-wing attacks in Western Europe from other attacks. Two of these – the Worldwide Incidents Tracking System (WITS) and the MIPT Terrorism Knowledge Base (TKB) – recently became unavailable, leaving us with Terrorism in Western Europe: Events Data (TWEED) and Europol's annual EU Terrorism Situation and Trend Report (TE-SAT).

While TE-SAT suffers from major underreporting (see below), the 648 far right terrorist attacks registered by TWEED are certainly useful for identifying major trends and key actors in post-WWII Western Europe. However, TWEED only covers the period 1950–2004, and is less helpful for capturing recent developments. Similarly, the Domestic Terrorism Victims Dataset (DTV – not included in the Routledge handbook) (DTV Codebook, 2009), includes two relevant perpetrator categories ("Extreme-right" and "Neo-Nazi"), but is limited to the period from 1965 to 2005 (De la Calle and Sanchez-Cuenca, 2011).

National hate crime statistics based on police reporting suffer from similar problems. Notably, many countries, e.g. the UK and Finland, do not distinguish racist hate crimes (some of which are committed between minority groups) from crimes committed by far right activists. Swedish hate crime statistics used to include far right violence, but this category has been left out since 2013.[3] In the Danish security service's (PET) reports on extremist hate crime, left- and right-wing crimes were lumped together in the same category. However, political violence has been left out entirely in the new hate crimes reports produced by the Danish police (rather than PET).[4] Finally, some West European countries such as Greece, Italy, and Spain, do not produce regular reports on hate crime or political violence at all.

Representativity

Our second theme is *representativity*, i.e. the extent to which existing datasets that do include far right violence correctly mirror the actual universe of far right violence. Europol's often-cited Terrorism Situation and Trend (TE-SAT) reports – based on annual accounts of terrorist events from EU member states – clearly fail to include many relevant events. Between 2006 (when Europol started reporting terrorist events systematically) and 2015, we find only nine far right events (four attacks, five plots) of which only two happened in Western Europe. By comparison, the Right-Wing Terrorism and Violence (RTV) dataset – recently developed to remedy some of the problems discussed in this chapter – registered 265 events during the same period in Western Europe, including 67 deadly events resulting in 126 deaths. Among these 265 events, 189 were premediated attacks, and in 46 of these premediated attacks, the perpetrator(s) used explosives or firearms.[5] The great disparity between TE-SAT and RTV is likely caused by the fact that TE-SAT mainly reports events that have been tried legally as a terrorist act, whereas RTV covers all violent events (of a certain severity) whose target selection was determined by far right beliefs.

Another problem with TE-SAT is that they only cover events from the previous year and do not backlog. As a result, major events discovered more than one year after they occurred, such as the NSU-murders, are not covered. Despite these shortcomings, however, TE-SAT reports extensively on other forms of terrorism. For example, Europol registered 2,111 "ethno-nationalist and separatist" terrorist events between 2006 and 2015. The discrepancy between far right and ethno-separatist events may reflect a true yet probably smaller difference in attack frequencies. However, it likely also reflects EU member states' interest in reporting certain types of terrorism and not others. Many far right attacks go under these governments' radars, either because they are registered as hate crimes rather than as terrorism, or because they are never registered at all.

A similar but smaller problem pertains to the TWEED and DTV datasets. TWEED relies entirely on a single news source: Keesing's Record of World Events (Engene, 2007). While a single source ensures (some kind of) data consistency, it also means that many events remain unreported. Considering that only the most spectacular events get media coverage, many never made it to the news headlines that Keesing's daily news digest relies upon. Moreover, the extent to which journalists are willing and capable of reporting about far right violence likely varies across countries and periods. By contrast, the DTV dataset uses more than one single source. However, by excluding non-lethal events and terrorist plots, DTV misses many relevant but non-deadly events.

National hate crime statistics also suffer from problems of underreporting. In fact, we may speak of a double underreporting: first, there are victims of hate crimes who decide not to report the incidents to the police and, second, there are police officers who fail to recognize violent acts as motivated by far right beliefs. The first problem is mentioned by Lambert (2013: 37) in his study of anti-Muslim violence in the UK. The second problem might be due to either unawareness or, as in known cases from Greece, politically motivated unwillingness. For example, there are extensive reports about police abuse of migrants in Greece, and many therefore fear reporting violent attacks to the police (Sunderland et al., 2012). In both cases, official police statistics end up misrepresenting the actual levels of far right motivated hate crime in society.

Measurement validity

A third problem concerns *measurement validity*, i.e. whether exiting datasets actually measure far right violence or something else. A recurrent problem, especially within events chronologies compiled by anti-racist activists, is that they include events that may have been committed by far right activists, but whose targeting was not political but personal. For example, the Swedish anti-racist organization Expo has created a fact sheet listing "persons killed by people with a background from the white power movement", suggesting a causal connection between the perpetrator's ideological background and their violent behaviour. However, several of the events included in the list are clearly personal and not political, such as when a 32-year-old man killed his girlfriend and stepdaughter, or when one 19-year-old killed his own nationalist friend at a party (Expo, 2008). By applying overly lax inclusion criteria, these actors may therefore end up exaggerating or distorting the far right threat.

The problem of including irrelevant events is also the case with supposedly more politically neutral statistics. For example, a re-examination of the events listed in the DTV dataset shows that some events should not have been included, either because the target selection was not based on far right beliefs or because their circumstances remain extremely vague (Ravndal, 2016: 4).

Replicability

Our fourth theme is *replicability*, i.e. whether existing datasets include source information enabling other scholars to re-examine the information used to code each event. Without such information, it is impossible to validate the interpretation and classification of the events included in a dataset. For example, in the case of TWEED, the dataset is available online as an SPSS file, but the information used to code each event is unavailable.

Some datasets do include source overviews, but do not explicitly link particular sources to particular events. For example, in his extensive chronology of terrorist events in America, Hewitt presents the main sources used in the study, but does not include source references in the actual events chronology (Hewitt, 2005). A more general problem is that reliable sources on far right violence are rare. For example, the coding book of the DTV dataset explicitly states that "it was much more difficult to find reliable information about the perpetrators of [extreme right and neo-Nazi] killings" and that "the information we have obtained about these killings is, in general, of worse quality than the one on nationalist and leftwing [sic] terrorism."

It is even more difficult to replicate chronologies developed by anti-racist organizations. Notwithstanding the detailed information provided by some of these chronologies, most events cannot be corroborated by external sources. For example, the Spanish anti-racist organization *Movimiento contra la intolerancia* has published an impressive amount of material on racist and far right violence.[6] However, most of this material is not backed by external sources and therefore difficult to validate. Similarly, the Southern Poverty Law Center in the United States has developed an extensive online dataset on hate crimes in the USA.[7] However, the sources used to register each event are not made available.

Yet the perhaps most common problem concerning replicability is that existing datasets on far right violence are not made publicly available at all. This is the case with the CTC dataset on far right violence in the United States (Perliger, 2012), the United States Extremist Crime Database (Freilich et al., 2014), and the GIRDS database on right-wing terrorism in Germany (Koehler, 2014). Although there might be several good reasons as to why they are unavailable (e.g. privacy concerns or academic advantage), it leads to a problem of replicability. Ideally, more databases should be publicly available as is the case with SOVA Center's database on xenophobic events in Russia. This database includes source links for all registered events, and one can easily distinguish violent from non-violent episodes.[8]

Comparability

A fifth and final problem is that of *comparability*, i.e. the difficulty of comparing data between countries. Although some countries provide extensive data on far right violence, they are of limited value in comparative research because they cannot be compared with similar data from other countries. Each country uses different definitions, different registration methods, and different inclusion criteria. Some countries also tend to change their methods and criteria from time to time, making time-series analysis difficult. For example, the Finnish, Danish and Swedish hate crime reporting systems have undergone substantial changes over the past 10 years, making both temporal and cross-country comparisons difficult.

Besides national hate crimes statistics, some scholars have developed datasets on far right violence (e.g. Arnold and Markowitz, 2017; Freilich et al., 2014; Hewitt, 2005; Karpantschof and Mikkelsen, 2016; Koehler, 2014; Kundnani, 2012; Perliger, 2012). However, most of these datasets cover only one country and are difficult to compare due to divergent data collection and registration methods. The only existing dataset that covers all West European countries is the RTV dataset. However, even this dataset, which is aimed at facilitating cross-country comparisons, is likely biased towards countries and periods that are better covered by available sources (Ravndal, 2016: 6). We might therefore benefit from considering some new and innovative strategies for mapping far right violence.

Strategies against methodological pitfalls

Many of the shortcomings described above are difficult to deal with because they stem from inherent political or practical deficits. Admittedly, no matter how you approach far right violence, it remains a clandestine phenomenon, which is hard to measure systematically. Methodological improvement therefore requires creative solutions. In this section, we propose three strategies that we believe could help overcome some of the most salient problems: (1) crowdsourcing, (2) international standardization of police reporting (3) and victimization surveys.

Crowdsourcing

To overcome the most pressing problem discussed above – *availability* – a new online-based method known as crowdsourcing could be part of the solution. Crowdsourcing is essentially about using the Internet to outsource a problem-solving task to an undefined public (Estellés-Arolas and González-Ladrón-de-Guevara, 2012). The perhaps most successful example of crowdsourcing to date is the online encyclopedia *Wikipedia*. To map far right violence, crowdsourcing is mainly useful for identifying events that otherwise would not have been reported and registered. One key advantage is that information can be shared anonymously, which lowers the threshold for people at risk to report a violent attack. In such cases, the reporting person must document the event by providing reliable sources, such as newspaper articles or police reports describing the event, and by demonstrating that the target selection was indeed determined by far right beliefs.

All crowdsourcing systems are confronted with four key challenges: (1) recruiting a crowd, (2) facilitating proper contributions, (3) synthesizing contributions in a way that solves the problem, and (4) evaluating users and contributions (Doan et al., 2011). To crowdsource far right violence, the first challenge may be more about public promotion than about recruiting a crowd. Important contributors will be those affected by an attack, either as a victim, as a victim's friend or relative, or as a witness. Anyone affected by far right violence should be aware of the opportunity and importance of reporting attacks to the crowdsourcing site. This can only be done through branding, promotion, and publicly demonstrating that the system is working. One example of such successful promotion is the UK-based Tell-MAMA project, which monitors anti-Muslim bigotry of all sorts, ranging from discrimination and public harassment to vandalism and violent attacks (e.g. Tell-MAMA, 2013, 2014). Within a few years, TellMAMA has become an authoritative voice in the UK on all concerns related to anti-Muslim bigotry.

The second challenge concerns how to facilitate proper contributions. As a first step, it would be necessary to establish a user-friendly and easily accessible system for online reporting. In addition, it is important to clearly define and communicate the types of events to be reported versus those belonging to other categories such as verbal abuse or violent attacks with personal rather than political motives. At the same time, one does not want to discourage people from reporting poorly documented events. One solution to this dilemma is to rank reported events according to the quality of available information. One example can be found at the crowdsourcing site "The City at a Time of Crisis" which documents racist violence in and around Athens, Greece, and where each event is labelled either as verified or unverified.[9]

The third challenge concerns how to combine contributions in a way that actually solves the problem. To map far right violence, combining contributions is simply about adding together events that have passed the registration criteria. The challenge may therefore lie more in *presenting* the combined contributions in a meaningful way. For example, "The City at a Time of Crisis" has produced an interactive online map visualizing the geographical distribution of all reported events, [10] while TellMAMA produces a number of relevant products, including online infographics and annual reports (e.g. TellMAMA, 2013, 2014).[11]

The fourth challenge concerns how to evaluate contributions and users as reliable sources. An important feature will in this case be anonymous reports, which make source evaluation more difficult. There is no quick fix to this challenge, and the only way to verify anonymous reports is to attach other reliable sources such as news articles, police reports, or non-anonymized testimonies.

In sum, crowdsourcing would score high on availability by generating otherwise unavailable information, provided that people are aware of the opportunity to report violent events. It would also do well on validity because the system managers are able to filter out irrelevant events, as well as on replicability, because all events and corresponding open sources could be made available online. Potential weaknesses thus lie in representativity and comparability. To develop a representative overview, a majority of events would have to be reported, which would require major promotional efforts and high public awareness. Furthermore, reporting frequencies and practices would likely vary over time and between places. A dataset based on crowdsourcing can therefore easily become biased towards certain regions or periods and would therefore not be appropriate for comparative analysis.

International standardized police reporting

As described above, existing hate crime statistics based on police reporting suffer from a number of shortcomings, such as being incomparable across countries or not distinguishing far right attacks from others. Ideally, all countries should register and report on hate crime and political violence in the same way. However, we realize that this is likely never going to happen due to different legal systems, norms, and traditions.

A second-best alternative would therefore be if all countries could contribute to a shared and standardized report on political violence. While some may consider this an unsurmountable task, international standardized reporting is already taking place across a wide range of domains, in particular among EU countries. For example, Eurostat offers annual statistics from all EU countries within areas such as health, migration, education, culture, sport, and crime, but not political violence.[12]

Moreover, some existing initiatives are already covering political violence, most notably Europol's terrorism trend reports (TE-SAT). However, as explained above, different countries use different criteria for categorizing terrorist events, and therefore end up reporting violence and terrorism differently.

Another relevant initiative is a project at the EU Agency for Fundamental Rights developing a shared methodology for recording and collecting data on hate crime.[13] But, considering the rather wide application of the hate crime concept, which includes both violent and non-violent events, and generally does not distinguish far right crimes from others, we suspect that this initiative will not generate comparable events data on far right violence specifically. Thus, in terms of documenting far right violence systematically, there is a gap between Europol's terrorism report covering "too little" on the one hand and existing hate crime reporting covering "too much" on the other.

Our proposition is to develop a shared reporting system on political violence using a set of imposed inclusion criteria that all countries must employ regardless of their particular jurisdictions. To uphold comparability between countries, this report would have to focus on the most severe types of events – events that are highly likely to have been registered by the police, such as murders, armed attacks, bombings or major terrorist plots. This dataset should include all kinds of extremism, including left-wing, right-wing, religious, separatist and possibly environmentalist and animal rights.

International standardized police reporting would primarily cater to the problem of comparability. If all countries follow the guidelines and submit their annual reports, this dataset could become an important source for comparing the extent of (severe) far right violence over time and between countries. However, it would still not include events not reported to the police, and therefore compromise on representativity. Furthermore, considering that all events are based on classified police reports, scholars will not be able to replicate the data to assess their validity.

Victimization surveys

While standardized police reporting is weak on representativity, crowdsourcing is weak on comparability. Victimization surveys represent a third method that is strong on both these areas (representativity and comparability). The basic idea is to survey a representative sample of a given target group and ask them about their experiences with a particular threat, in this case far right violence. However, since far right violence seems to be a rather marginal phenomenon in most Western countries, it makes little sense to survey the entire population – so-called national victimization surveys. Only a few respondents from a representative sample, if anyone at all, are likely to have experienced a violent attack motivated by far right ideology. Thus, instead of surveying the general population, we suggest – in line with the well-known FRA-surveys[14] (carried out by The European Union Agency for Fundamental Rights) – that one should survey particularly vulnerable groups. Previous research has demonstrated that far right activists in Europe are likely to target immigrants, religious minorities such as Muslims, Jews and Roma, sexual minorities, political opponents, government officials, police officers, homeless and disabled people (Ravndal, 2016). In other words, extreme right activists do not carry out violent attacks randomly. They target groups or people they perceive as enemies or as unwanted.

How can we survey hard-to-reach population groups? In most cases, there is (fortunately) no register from which to draw a representative sample of respondents. Only cases of government officials, police officers and left-wing politicians represent clearly defined populations. There are at least two ways to deal with the problem: Either the sample is so large that even small minorities amount to the several hundred respondents needed to carry out meaningful statistical analysis. For example, Herek's (2009) study of sexual minority adults in the USA relies on responses from a national probability sample consisting of 662 gay, lesbian and bisexual adults drawn from an existing panel of more than 40,000 US households. The other option is to use convenience sampling. The previously mentioned FRA agency has developed their own method to reach marginal and often socially stigmatized groups such as Roma and Jews.[15] Their 2012 study aimed at collecting data about the 'experiences of antisemitism' and 'feelings of safety' among self-identifying Jews in Europe, relied on a standardized online questionnaire which was made available to Jewish communities on the FRA website, via Jewish organizations (both international and national) and Jewish media outlets. To be sure, the sample suffers from problems of self-recruitment (i.e. it depended on individuals' willingness to participate) and inaccessibility (i.e. it depended on some level of computer skills), yet this approach seems to produce (more) representative samples than other methods (FRA,, 2013: 73).

To the extent that we can establish a representative sample, victimization surveys are particularly strong on representativity and comparability. They allow us to bypass some of the obvious limitations of having to rely upon media reporting or criminal complaints registered by the police. Instead, victims can report directly to the researchers. As such, these surveys may be the closest we can get to the "truth" about far right violence and thus the best point of departure for doing comparative analysis at the cross-national level.

Even so, there are some disadvantages to this method as well. Notably, the method allows the victim to determine the perpetrator's motive, resulting in possible validity problems. This may lead to events being classified as far right even they were not, but also to not reporting events because the victim did not realize they had a far right motive.

Despite the possible disadvantages of the three strategies, we argue that crowdsourcing, standardized police reports and victimization surveys would be of great value when assessing the prevalence and patterns of far right violence. The three strategies are particularly fruitful when used in combination given that they have distinct strengths and weaknesses, as illustrated by Table 8.1. Our preferred strategy

TABLE 8.1 Methodological strengths and weaknesses of selected strategies

	Availability	Representativity	Validity	Replicability	Comparability
Crowdsourcing	+	−	+	+	−
Standardized police reporting	+	−	+	−	+
Victimization survey	+	+	−	+	+

is thus similar to the one carried out by Lambert (2013) in his more limited case study of anti-Muslim violence in the UK. This study relies on incident data from media reports, police statistics (mainly from the Metropolitan Police) and survey data provided by Mosques, Islamic centres and Muslim organizations.

Conclusion

To develop precise explanations of far right violence, we need to match our theories with reliable empirical evidence documenting variation in violence across time and place. However, as this chapter shows, available evidence on far right violence suffers from problems of availability, representativity, validity, replicability and comparability. This is also the case for well-known databases available to scholars in the field, such as GDT, TE-SAT and national hate crime statistics. Consequently, it becomes very difficult, if not say impossible, to assess whether far right violence is increasing or decreasing, let alone explain under which social, political and economic circumstances this kind of violence is most likely to pose a security threat and democratic challenge (Koopmans, 1996; Ravndal, 2017).

To overcome some of the existing methodological problems, we have proposed three strategies that we believe will significantly improve available data on far right violence. Crowdsourcing is particularly strong on validity and replicability, but weaker on representativity and comparability. Standardized police reporting is strong on comparability, but it will most likely continue to suffer from under-reporting and problems of replicability. Victimization surveys are therefore necessary to gain a more accurate but far from perfect assessment of the scale of the phenomenon. To be sure, this method has its own problems of biases, sampling challenges and validity issues, but in combination with the other strategies, it will provide scholars with a far better foundation for analyzing the prevalence, patterns and characteristics of far right violence both within and between countries.

Notes

1 This number is derived from an updated version of the RTV dataset yet to be released publicly. For more details, see "Right-wing terrorism and violence in Western Europe: the RTV dataset." *C-REX - Center for Research on Extremism*: www.sv.uio.no/c-rex/rtv [accessed 5 April 2019].
2 This section draws heavily on a previous article by Ravndal (2016), originally published in *Perspectives on Terrorism*.
3 See 'Hate crime,' *Swedish National Council for Crime Prevention – Brottsförebyggande rådet (Brå)*https://www.bra.se/bra-in-english/home/crime-and-statistics/hate-crime.html [accessed 25 August 2018].
4 See Rigspolitiet Forebyggelsescenter (NFC), *Hadforbrydelser I 2015* (June 2016) https://www.politi.dk/NR/rdonlyres/C452577B-1EFE-4C73-8207-62B05E3E783E/0/%C3%85rsrapport_hadforbrydelser_2015.pdf [accessed 15 June 2017].
5 See "Right-wing terrorism and violence in Western Europe: the RTV dataset." *C-REX – Center for Research on Extremism*: www.sv.uio.no/c-rex/rtv [accessed 5 April 2019].
6 See Movimiento contra La Interancia (2019): http://www.movimientocontralaintolerancia.com/html/raxen/raxen.asp [accessed 5 April 2019].

7 See Southern Poverty Law Center (2019) "Hate incidents: Incidents of apparent hate crimes and hate group activities listed here are drawn primarily from media sources." Southern Poverty Law Center: https://www.splcenter.org/fighting-hate/hate incidents [accessed 5 April 2019].
8 See База Данных [Database] http://www.sova-center.ru/database/ [accessed 5 April 2019].
9 See The City at a Time of Crisis (2014) "Map of attacks on migrants in Athens." The City at a Time of Crisis: http://map.crisis-scape.net/ [accessed 5 April 2019].
10 See The City at a Time of Crisis (2014) "Map of attacks on migrants in Athens." The City at a Time of Crisis: http://map.crisis-scape.net/ [accessed 5 April 2019].
11 See also, TellMAMA (2019) "Islamophobia – Series of reports and resources." Tell-MAMA: https://tellmamauk.org/resources/ [accessed 5 April 2019].
12 See Eurostat (2019) "Your key European statistics." Eurostat: http://ec.europa.eu/euro stat [accessed 5 April 2019].
13 See European Union Agency for Fundamental Rights (2016) "Subgroup on methodologies for recording and collecting data on hate crime." European Union Agency for Fundamental Rights: http://fra.europa.eu/en/project/2017/subgroup-methodologies-re cording-and-collecting-data-hate-crime [accessed 5 April 2019].
14 See European Union Agency for Fundamental Rights (2016) "Research & projects." European Union Agency for Fundamental Rights: http://fra.europa.eu/en/research [accessed 5 April 2019].
15 See European Union Agency for Fundamental Rights (2013) "FRA survey of Jewish people's experiences and perceptions of discrimination and hate crime in European Union Member States." European Union Agency for Fundamental Rights: http:// fra.europa.eu/en/survey/2012/fra-survey-jewish-peoples-experiences-and-perceptions-discrimination-and-hate-crime [accessed 5 April 2019].

References

Arnold, R. and L.P. Markowitz. 2018. "The evolution of violence within far-right mobilization: Evidence from Russia." *Ethnic and Racial Studies*, 41(9), 1558–1573.
BBC News 2016, July 7. "Italy migrants: Nigerian killed in Fermo race attack." *BBC News*, July 7. Retrieved from http://www.bbc.com/news/world-europe-36733575
Bobbio, N. 1996. *Left and Right: The Significance of a Political Distinction* (A. Cameron, trans.). Chicago, IL: University of Chicago Press.
Carter, E. 2018. "Right-wing extremism/radicalism: Reconstructing the concept." *Journal of Political Ideologies*, 23(2), 157–182.
Cobain, I., N. Parveen, and M. Taylor. 2016. "The slow-burning hatred that led Thomas Mair to murder Jo Cox." November 23. *The Guardian*. Retrieved from https://www.theguardian.com/uk-news/2016/nov/23/thomas-mair-slow-burning-hatred-led-to-jo-cox-murder
De la Calle, L. and I. Sanchez-Cuenca. 2011. "The quantity and quality of terrorism: The DTV dataset." *Journal of Peace Research*, 48(1), 49–58.
Doan, A., R. Ramakrishnan, and A.Y. Halevy. 2011. "Crowdsourcing systems on the world-wide web." *Communications of the ACM*, 54(4), 86–96.
DTV Codebook. 2009. Centre for Advanced Study in the Social Sciences (Juan March Institute). Retrieved from http://recursos.march.es/web/ceacs/proyectos/dtv/datasets/DTV% 20Codebook.pdf
Engene, J.O. 2007. "Five decades of terrorism in Europe: The TWEED dataset." *Journal of Peace Research*, 44(1), 109–121.
Enstad, J.D. 2017. *Antisemitic Violence in Europe, 2005–2015: Exposure and Perpetrators in France, UK, Germany, Sweden, Norway, Denmark and Russia.* Report. Oslo: Center for Studies of the Holocaust and Religious Minorities and Center for Research on

Extremism (C-REX), University of Oslo. https://www.hlsenteret.no/publikasjoner/digitale-hefter/antisemittisk-vold-i-europa_engelsk_endelig-versjon.pdf

Estellés-Arolas, E. and F. González-Ladrón-de-Guevara. 2012. "Towards an integrated crowdsourcing definition." *Journal of Information Science*, 38(2), 189–200.

Expo2008. *Personer som dödats av människor med bakgrund i vit makt-rörelsen (4)*. Retrieved from http://expo.se/www/download/Expo_Intolerans_12.pdf

Fennema, M. 1997. "Some conceptual issues and problems in the comparison of anti-immigrant parties in Western Europe." *Party Politics*, 3(4), 473–492.

FRA2013. *Discrimination and Hate Crime Against Jews in EU Member States: Experiences and Perceptions of Antisemitism*. Vienna: European Union Agency for Fundamental Rights. http://fra.europa.eu/sites/default/files/fra-2013-discrimination-hate-crime-against-jews-eu-member-states-0_en.pdf

Freilich, J.D., S.M. Chermak, R. Belli, J. Gruenewald, and W.S. Parkin. 2014. "Introducing the United States Extremis Crime Database (ECDB)." *Terrorism and Political Violence*, 26(2), 372–384.

Herek, G.M. 2009. "Hate crimes and stigma-related experiences among sexual minority adults in the United States: Prevalence estimates from a national probability sample." *Journal of Interpersonal Violence*, 24(1), 54–74.

Hewitt, C. 2005. *Political Violence and Terrorism in Modern America: A Chronology*. Westport, CT: Praeger Security International.

Hoffman, B. 2006. *Inside Terrorism*. New York, NY: Columbia University Press.

Karpantschof, R. and F. Mikkelsen. 2016. "The rise and transformation of the radical right movement in Denmark, 1980–2015." *Studies in Conflict & Terrorism* [advance online publication].

Koehler, D. 2014. "German right-wing terrorism in historical perspective. A first quantitative overview of the 'Database on Terrorism in Germany (Right-Wing Extremism)' – DTGrwx Project." *Perspectives on Terrorism*, 8(5).

Kundnani, A. 2012. *Blind Spot? Security Narratives and Far-Right Violence in Europe*. The Hague: The International Centre for Counter-Terrorism (ICCT).

Lambert, R.A. 2013. "Anti-Muslim violence in the UK: Extremist nationalist involvement and influence." In *Extreme Right Wing Political Violence and Terrorism*, edited by M. Taylor, P.M. Currie, and D. Holbrook, 31–63. New York, NY and London: Bloomsbury Academic.

Mudde, C. 1995. "Right-wing extremism analyzed. A comparative analysis of the ideologies of three alleged right-wing extremist parties (NPD, N DP, CP'86)." *European Journal of Political Research*, 27(2), 203–224.

Mudde, C. 2007. *Populist Radical Right Parties in Europe*. Cambridge, UK and New York, NY: Cambridge University Press.

Perliger, A. 2012. *Challengers from the Sidelines*. West Point, NY: Combating Terrorism Center. Retrieved from https://www.ctc.usma.edu/wp-content/uploads/2013/01/ChallengersFromtheSidelines.pdf

Ravndal, J.A. 2015. "Thugs or terrorists? A typology of right-wing terrorism and violence in Western Europe." *Journal for Deradicalization*, 1(3), 1–38.

Ravndal, J.A. 2016. "Right-wing terrorism and violence in Western Europe: Introducing the RTV dataset." *Perspectives on Terrorism*, 10(3).

Ravndal, J.A. 2017. "Explaining right-wing terrorism and violence in Western Europe: Grievances, opportunities and polarization." *European Journal of Political Research*. doi:10.1111/1475-6765.12254.

Stenner, K. 2005. *The Authoritarian Dynamic*. New York, NY: Cambridge University Press.

Sunderland, J., E. Cossé, and B. Ward. 2012. *Hate on the Streets: Xenophobic Violence in Greece*. New York, NY: Human Rights Watch. Retrieved from https://www.hrw.org/sites/default/files/reports/greece0712ForUpload.pdf

Taylor, M., P.M. Currie, and D. Holbrook. 2013. *Extreme Right Wing Political Violence and Terrorism*. New York, NY and London: Bloomsbury Academic.

Tell MAMA2013. "Anti-Muslim hate crime." http://tellmamauk.org/

Tell MAMA2014. "Analyzing the lexicon of anti-Muslim prejudice." http://tellmamauk.org/analysingthe-lexicon-of-anti-muslim-prejudice/

Weinberg, L. and E. Assoudeh. 2018. "Political violence and the radical right." In *The Oxford Handbook of the Radical Right*, edited by J. Rydgren, 412–432. New York, NY: Oxford University Press.

Wilkinson, P. 1995. "Violence and terror and the extreme right." *Terrorism and Political Violence*, 7(4), 82–93.

9

CHALLENGES AND OPPORTUNITIES OF SOCIAL MEDIA RESEARCH

Using Twitter and Facebook to investigate far right discourses

Jasper Muis, Ofra Klein and Guido Dijkstra

The number of studies addressing social media has markedly increased during the past years. 'Digital footprints' from online platforms enable us to study social behaviour in novel ways (Golder and Macy, 2014; Mosca, 2014; Ruths and Pfeffer, 2014). The examination of online discussions is non-reactive. In contrast to traditional methods such as face-to-face interviewing, the data are 'given' and as such are not influenced by researchers (Bryman, 2015). Social media thus allow us to unobtrusively get an insight into real-life everyday discussions among far right supporters (Cleland, Anderson, and Aldridge-Deacon, 2018; Klein and Muis, 2018).

Far right groups were early adaptors of the Internet using forums and message boards such as Stormfront as early as the mid-1990s (De Koster and Houtman, 2008; Hawley, 2017). For far right groups the web serves "above all as a public space of debate where positions can be exchanged, where exponents of different parts of the sector can support each other, and where new contacts can be made" (Caiani and Wagemann, 2009: 68). It offers possibilities for reaching their followers, connecting with like-minded groups, and spreading their message (Caiani and Parenti, 2013).

They do that quite successfully. For instance, the Dutch Party for Freedom (*PVV*) leader Geert Wilders has more followers on Twitter than Prime Minister Mark Rutte, and the German *AfD* has more likes on Facebook than the Christian Democrats. Recently, far right groups have left sites that were specifically aimed at supporters and have joined discussions on social media and comment sections of major news outlets. By applying this strategy, the alt-right movement in the United States has gained mainstream attention (Hawley, 2017). In contrast to previous American far right movements, the alt-right exists predominantly on social media (Hawley, 2017).

Social media also provide far right leaders the opportunity to circumvent traditional news channels, making their voices heard without interference from gate-keepers and journalists (Stier, Posch, Bleier, and Strohmaier, 2017). In contrast, relying on traditional media coverage to investigate far right claims is prone to selection bias (Koopmans, Statham, Giugni, and Passy, 2005; Muis, 2015).

This chapter reviews the methodological opportunities and challenges of using social media as a source of data. We limit ourselves to the online discourses of the far right on Twitter and Facebook. To put flesh to the bones, we formulate two research questions. First, to what extent are there differences *between* and *within* far right parties and movements in the outgroups that their followers discuss? Second, to what extent do far right leaders moderate their ideological outlook once they become member of a government?

Using Facebook to compare far right followers

Far right orientations seem to have shifted over time: some scholars have argued that especially anti-Semitism has been replaced by Islamophobia (Zúquete, 2008). According to Williams (2010), Muslims increasingly feature as the 'other' in most far right party manifestos across Western Europe. This demonstrates that the specific enemies and targets of the far right and how they are portrayed could change over time and vary between different far right organizations. This raises the following question: To what extent are there differences *between* and *within* Western European far right parties and movements in the outgroups they discuss?

Using Facebook we conduct content analyses of both the posts of far right groups and the comments of their followers. We investigate the most prominent far right movements and parties in three West European countries: *Front National* and *Génération Identitaire* in France; National Democratic Party of Germany (*NPD)*, *Alternative für Deutschland* (*AfD*) and *Pegida* in Germany; and the English Defence League (EDL), British National Party (BNP) and United Kingdom Independence Party (UKIP) in the United Kingdom.

One of the primary challenges is defining the population of such a study. Analysing online comments implies sampling bias, comparable with using responses from an unrepresentative survey (Ruths and Pfeffer, 2014). Facebook pages mainly serve as a communication platform for sympathizers of these groups (Ben-David and Matamoros-Fernández, 2016). However, communication on social media represents only a partial picture of the stances of the sympathizers of these movements (Bartlett, Birdwell, and Littler, 2011; Puschmann, Ausserhofer, Maan, and Hametner, 2016).

A core question is thus how well the sample represents the members of the group or party who are not on Facebook. Interestingly, the opposite is also relevant. In their study based on an online survey of Facebook followers, Bartlett et al. (2011) note that a significant number of Facebook fans of far right parties – about one third – do not actually vote for the party. A related bias arises from 'trolling', as individuals who are opposed to the group in question may join the group in order to cause confusion (Bartlett et al., 2011). For instance, as a form of protest against right-wing radicalism, a German comedian infiltrated several far right groups, took over the role as moderator and changed their ideologies (De Haldevang, 2017).

The most straightforward solution to this methodological challenge is to simply avoid any claim that online samples of Facebook followers represent the offline supporter base of these movements and parties. For instance, Bartlett et al. (2011: 89) claim that they "take care not to claim, at any point in the text, that our sample represents or reflects the official views of the group, or indeed of its offline membership". All references in their study to "supporters" explicitly refer to the sample of "social media supporters".

Obviously, this is not necessarily a weakness, since the opinions and statements of Facebook members are interesting in themselves. In fact, in many cases the online membership of far right organizations outnumbers the offline membership. Indeed, the number of followers on Facebook is often larger than their formal membership, as people can show online support or become a 'member' of far right online communities with just a click of a mouse (Awan, 2016).

Just as offline groups and organizations can be opportunities for comparative case studies, so too can online groups (Golder and Macy, 2014). Both between-group and within-group comparisons are possible. The latter opportunity implies analysing Facebook in order to illuminate *internal* debates within certain online communities or movements. For instance, Arzheimer (2015) concluded that the German *AfD* leadership does not qualify as either nativist or populist, but statements of Facebook followers hint at more radical currents among *AfD* supporters. The topics that people devoted most attention to (Islam and immigration) were hardly mentioned in *AfD*'s own posts. This raises questions about the strength of affinity of online followers, and the relationship between online and offline involvement (Bartlett et al., 2011).

In any case, online hate speech and virtual xenophobia constitute a reality on their own. As Golder and Macy (2014: 143) put it: "The online world is not identical to the offline, but it is entirely real". Online radicalization could affect people's perceptions, and thereby people's behaviour offline, such as the party they vote for and their face-to-face contacts with ethnic minorities (Awan, 2016). Thus, studying far right groups online is a valuable addition to studying them offline. Most studies still focus on attitudes expressed in surveys and interviews, but people increasingly express their attitudes and acquire their beliefs and opinions on social media.

The main advantage of using social media is that it allows for large amounts of time-stamped data, such as posts and comments, as well as the activity of users around these posts (e.g. how often users like certain posts). The Internet is especially useful for studying prejudices and grievances of far right groups, which are often considered as difficult to reach using traditional research methods, such as surveys or interviews. Social media data are generally considered non-reactive: online behaviour is observed unobtrusively, limiting the potential for social desirability biases (Bryman, 2015). Consequently, the question arises what data can be used without ethical concerns (Cleland et al., 2018).

Facebook users have not given their explicit consent to use their data. At the same time, Facebook is a platform on which people present their views out in the

Section 2 30 ?

open. The more the setting is acknowledged to be public, the less a researcher is obliged to seek informed consent and to protect the confidentiality and anonymity of users (Bryman, 2015; Buchanan, 2011). Moreover, in practice it would also be difficult to achieve informed consent from everybody, since it involves so many people. When large datasets with anonymized data are used, ethical issues are less problematic (Buchanan, 2011).

The case is different if researchers decide to reproduce social media posts in an academic publication. These have to be handled with care, especially concerning posts or tweets related to sensitive topics, such as hate speech. A simple online search could expose the identity of specific individuals (Buchanan, 2011: 92). As Sveningsson (2004: 55) argues, "if ... the information shared is sensitive we might have to be more careful when making our decisions" about whether and how to use this material.

Much on Facebook is happening in closed groups of which you need to be a member in order to access them. Studying these groups poses a larger privacy dilemma, as the data of these groups are not publicly accessible. The nature of Facebook as a mostly private network thus limits what we can learn from it (Olmstead and Barthel, 2015).

Data collection and operationalization

For studying outgroups of far right followers, we selected publicly accessible Facebook pages. We gathered data from eight pages, covering three months (August, September and October 2015).[1] The number of posts and comments gathered per page, the number of users who posted comments, and overlap between users are shown in Table 9.1. It shows that about 800,000 comments were posted during the three-month period. The sheer volume of social media data also poses challenges, especially in terms of the computational power needed to gather, store and analyse data, and sorting useful data from 'noise' (for recommendations, see Quan-Haase and Sloan, 2017).

We used Netvizz to gather the data, which is a widely used application to extract data from Facebook (Rieder, 2013). There were several restrictions related

TABLE 9.1A Activity on far right Facebook pages in the UK, and the overlap between users (%).

UK	EDL	BNP	UKIP
English Defence League	–	9.95	6.95
British National Party	2.67	–	7.19
UKIP	3.34	12.87	–
Number of active users (N)	61,933	16,612	29,750
Number of likes (21-12-2015)	268,264	198,900	517,962
Comments (N)	164,366	54,135	116,857
Posts (N)	1,422	531	181

TABLE 9.1B Activity on far right Facebook pages in the France, and the overlap between users (%).

France	Génération Identitaire	Front National
Génération Identitaire	–	3.73
Front National	11.60	–
Number of active users (N)	4,388	13,635
Number of likes (17-01-2016)	91,872	343,667
Comments (N)	7,015	43,241
Posts (N)	115	380

TABLE 9.1C Activity on far right Facebook pages in the Germany, and the overlap between users (%).

Germany	NPD	AfD	Pegida
NPD	–	6.6	8.3
AfD	5.9	–	17.0
Pegida	6.1	13.9	–
Number of active users (N)	26,790	29,920	36,406
Number of likes (04-01-2016)	147,421	181,464	184,321
Comments (N)	90,964	114,299	195,841
Posts (N)	554	186	773

Note: Reading example: 9.95 per cent of those who posted comments on the BNP page also posted on the EDL page. In its turn, this group constitutes 2.67 per cent of all people who posted comments on the EDL page.

to using Facebook as a data source. First, data are "easiest to collect at the moment of their creation" (Bright, Margetts, Hale, and Yasseri, 2014: 24). Extracting data at a later point in time is problematic, as content that has been removed cannot be accessed at a later stage. This is especially the case for hate-related content, as large social media platforms are obliged by European governments to remove harmful content within 24 hours after reporting. Second, the amount of user profile information that we could extract was limited by the privacy settings of users and limitations set by Facebook (Rieder, 2013).

The Cambridge Analytica scandal has recently led social media companies to further restrict researchers from accessing data from their platforms. For example, Netvizz – the tool we used for this study – has been denied access to Facebook following the scandal (Rieder, 2018). Consequently, arguably the largest challenge when it comes to continuing researching social media in the future is access to data. As Rieder (2018) argues, restricting access to data from social media platforms makes carrying out independent research harder. Platforms now work towards forms of industry–academic partnerships through which researchers need to apply to gain access to data (King and Persily, 2018).

We first performed qualitative analyses, which consisted of manually reading random samples of 100 comments and posts from each page (cf. Atton, 2006). Subsequently, we performed automated content analyses. In line with Caiani and Della Porta (2011), we used keywords to count how often outgroups were referred to. The selection of keywords was based on the preceding qualitative analysis.

To analyse large amounts of textual data in an efficient way, text mining – turning text into data for analysis – is a useful method. For example, it can reveal valuable insights in relation to the topics discussed by people, their views and opinions. The statistical programming language R contains several packages such as the widely used text-mining package **tm** (Feinerer, 2017). We used the Natural Language Toolkit (NLTK) in Python (Bird et al., 2009). The NLTK makes it easy to pre-process textual data and analyse them by calculating the most frequently occurring words, common bigrams (two words that often occur next to each other) or trigrams (Bird et al., 2009). Open source tools, such as Mallet (McCallum, 2002) and SentiStrength (Thelwall et al., 2010), can also be used to carry out these analyses.

Results and conclusion

Tables 9.2 shows how often the two main outgroups –Muslims and immigrants –are discussed on the different Facebook pages. For brevity, we left out other groups that could be targeted as 'other' (Cleland et al., 2018). Our results reveal remarkable differences *between* and *within* far right movements and parties. Judging from the online discourses, the followers of both UKIP and *AfD* are much more concerned about Islam than its leadership. Islam/Muslims are only mentioned 0.15 and 0.20 times per each 1,000 words in the posts of UKIP and *AfD*, respectively The comments of followers suggest a slightly different picture, since this outgroup is mentioned 1.74 (UKIP supporters) and 1.20 (*AfD* supporters) times. Our analysis can also reveal interesting differences *between* groups. For example, both the EDL and BNP view Muslims as a more salient outgroup than immigrants. The opposite is the case for the three far right groups in Germany. Remarkably, even the anti-Islam movement *Pegida* emphasizes 'Muslims' (2.50 times) less often than 'immigrants' (3.87 times).

A frequency analysis can thus already provide valuable insights in how far right groups differ from one another in which groups they target, and whether moderators differ from commenters in what topics they deem important. A downside of this method is that we leave out posts in the form of images, videos and links. While comments are mostly textual in nature, posts often contain images. Results from frequency analyses might therefore not always accurately reflect all content posted on these pages.

Framing of outgroups could be further investigated through for instance visual representations – word clouds – of the most frequently used words (see Awan, 2016) or word co-occurrences (see Klein and Muis, 2018). However, these do not provide an in-depth view of sentiments (Ceron, Curini, Iacus, and Porro, 2014). It

TABLE 9.2A Outgroup salience on British far right Facebook pages, absolute and relative (per 1,000 words) amount of words.

| | English Defence League | | | | UKIP | | | | British National Party | | | |
| | Posts (n=1,422) | | Comments (n=164,366) | | Posts (n=181) | | Comments (n=116,857) | | Posts (n=531) | | Comments (n=54,135) | |
	abs	rel	abs	rel	abs	rel	abs	rel	abs	rel	abs	rel
Total Islam/Muslim	194	10.63	29,428	9.52	2	0.15	5,518	1.74	237	2.44	3,420	3.64
muslim(s), islam(ic)(s), islamism, islamification, islamised, islamisation, islamified, islamist(s), sharia (h)												
Total immigrants/foreigners	53	2.90	4,392	1.41	31	2.34	9,148	2.90	370	3.82	2,850	3.03
invader(s), foreign, foreigner(s), alien(s), immigration, migrant(s)												

TABLE 9.2B Outgroup salience on French far right Facebook pages, absolute and relative (per 1,000 words) amount of words.

	Front National				Génération Identitaire			
	Posts (n=380)		Comments (n=43,241)		Posts (n=115)		Comments (n=7,013)	
	abs	rel	abs	rel	abs	rel	abs	rel
Total Islam/Muslim	1	0.13	512	0.62	35	6.30	211	2.15
(L') Islam, islamique, islamiste(s), (l') Islamisation, (les) musulman(s), la charia								
Total immigrants/foreigners	31	3.96	2,131	2.52	39	7.02	217	2.22
Les étranger(s), migrant(s), les immigrant(s), les réfugiés, les clandestin(s)								

TABLE 9.2C Outgroup salience on German far right Facebook pages, absolute and relative (per 1,000 words) amount of words.

| | NPD | | | | AfD | | | | Pegida | | | |
| | Posts (n=554) | | Comments (n=90,964) | | Posts (n=186) | | Comments (n=114,299) | | Posts (n=773) | | Comments (n=195,841) | |
	abs	rel	abs	rel	abs	rel	abs	rel	abs	rel	abs	rel
Total Islam/Muslim	39	1.09	1594	0.85	4	0.20	3,757	1.20	172	2.50	10,046	1.95
Total immigrants/foreigners	143	3.98	7,515	3.99	52	2.62	9,897	3.12	265	3.87	14,327	2.79

islam(s), islamitisch(e/n), islamischer, islamist(en), islamis(t)ierung, islamic, sharia(h), scharia, Muslim(s), Muslime(n), Moslem(e), Moslems, muslimische(n/r), muslimin

ausländer(n), immigrant(s/en), migrant(en), zuwanderer, flüchtling(en) remains difficult to detect sentiments using automatic content analyses as words can be interpreted in different ways. Word counts show that *peaceful* and *happy* occur frequently on the Facebook page of EDL, but these terms are often used in a sarcastic way. Note for instance the difference between: "*Not all Muslims are terrorists just like not all Germans were Nazi. I'm sure the majority of Muslims are peaceful*", versus: "*Muslims fighting Muslims, such a peaceful religion or should I say cult?*" Obviously, a dictionary-based sentiment analysis – assign a text to a certain opinion category if some pre-determined words appear in the text – has difficulty to correctly classify the sentiment of the second sentence because of the expression 'such a peaceful religion'.

Other methods have been developed to better measure sentiment. Ceron et al. (2014), for example, use a two-stage method in which researchers manually code Tweets first on the basis of which an algorithm is trained to detect sentiment. Considerable progress has been made in automatic sentiment analysis (Giachanou and Crestani, 2016). It is possible to assess whether the tone of the text is negative, neutral or positive towards a certain topic. Accuracy of sentiment increases with length of the text, and when different texts are combined for the same user.

Another difficulty arises when comparing the discourses of far right groups in different countries. In comparative political research, language analysis becomes increasingly important (Lucas et al., 2015). Lucas et al. (2015) developed a package to directly translate texts into English before comparing them; but words might have different connotations in different contexts and across time periods. Koopmans et al. (2005) for example argue that the dominant vocabulary for the word 'foreigner' is characterized by specific constructions on the relation between migrants and the receiving country (e.g. immigrants in France, foreigners in Germany, and ethnic minorities or racial groups in the UK).

Using Twitter to assess far right party stances

Our second research question is under what conditions far right leaders radicalize or moderate their ideological outlook over time. The so-called inclusion-moderation thesis holds that far right parties moderate their stances after taking up government responsibility (Akkerman, De Lange, and Rooduijn, 2016). One of the difficulties of research on this issue is the lack of comprehensive time series on far right party stances. It is pivotal to reliably tap positions over time. Three different sources are often used: (expert) surveys, party manifestos, and media coverage. All three approaches have merits as well as deficiencies.

First, (expert) surveys have been criticized for the ambiguity about of the time period for which measurements are valid and about the precise understanding of parties as collective actors. What 'party' is exactly being judged: the voters, the party organization, or the party leader? The second method, coding political texts, has the advantage that the time series can be extended backwards as long as manifestos are available. However, coding party manifestos has also important weaknesses. Few people actually read manifestos. Most individuals perceive political parties' stances by what they read in the media instead. A second limitation is that manifestos are generally only delivered during election times. Finally, both expert surveys and manifestos tend to reflect the standpoint of leaders, concealing internal ideological and political differences.

These caveats are addressed by content analysis of media coverage (Kriesi, Grande, Lachat, Dolezal, and Bornschier, 2008). Even so, this method also has significant drawbacks. There might be bias concerning both the selection of topics and the accuracy of content that is reported (Helbling and Tresch, 2011). Far right parties sometimes hardly achieve media attention and at other times receive disproportionally large amounts of publicity (Muis, 2015). By relying on traditional media one overlooks persistent forms of far right activism that simmer underground.

For instance, the sudden rise of the alt-right is not surprising for those who closely study the far right. Long before Trump's election and their arrival on the national public stage, white supremacists withdrew from the public realm and "found sanctuary on the Internet, embracing concealment as a savvy survival strategy" (Futrell and Simi, 2007: 76).

Ideally, estimating ideological positions relies on a source that is directly and frequently produced by far right parties or movements themselves, and at the same time reaches a large audience (cf. Caiani and Della Porta, 2011). With the rise of social media, such sources are increasingly at hand. For example, Twitter has become an important platform for politicians (Spierings and Jacobs, 2014). Searching for quotes from politicians, traditional media have increasingly picked up messages posted on Twitter. Exploiting Twitter data can fruitfully complement other methods to assess where far parties stand.

To illustrate our argument, we investigate the Dutch Party for Freedom (*PVV*) headed by Geert Wilders. In the 2017 parliamentary elections, it became the second-largest party, receiving about 13 per cent of the vote. Wilders uses Twitter as his main source of communication. The party manifesto only consisted of a few bullet points on a single page.

The *PVV* is an interesting case to test the inclusion-moderation thesis because it was in a pact with a minority government consisting of the moderate right *VVD* and *CDA* from October 2010 until April 2012. Wilders typically pits the allegedly corrupt elite against the 'common Dutch'. After taking up government responsibility, this stance seems difficult to uphold since he became part of the political establishment.

Albertazzi and McDonnell (2015) dismiss the received wisdom that populist parties have inherent problems with assuming power. Likewise, Akkerman et al. (2016) conclude that there is no trend towards mainstreaming of far right parties on their core issues of immigration and integration, European integration and authoritarianism – they uphold their radical rhetoric.

Interestingly, however, the Dutch *PVV* seems to be an exception. According to Akkerman et al. (2016), providing support for the minority coalition had a moderating effect. This is a striking finding. It contradicts the *communis opinio* that Wilders' ideas about Islam and the EU became more extreme over time. In their study, radicalism was measured by coding pledges in two party manifestos at different points in time on a cosmopolitan-nativist dimension (i.e. restrict immigration and assimilationist integration policies versus open borders and cultural pluralism). We will cross-validate this finding of Wilders' moderation (Akkerman et al., 2016) with another data source: tweets.

Data collection and operationalization

We manually gathered and hand-coded all tweets posted by Wilders between 2010–2013.[2] Tweets had to be gathered manually as Twitter does not make archives of tweets available and restricts how far back researchers can gather existing Tweets (Bright et al., 2014). Retweets and replies to others were excluded from the analysis. Subsequently, we excluded tweets that have no link whatsoever with politics. This yielded in total 756 political tweets (N=756). Based on its status as opposition party or not, three periods can be distinguished: (1) 1 January 2010–13 October 2010: *PVV* in opposition; (2) 14 October 2010–22 April 2012: minority government supported by Wilders; (3) 23 April 2012–31 December 2012: the *PVV* in opposition again after the fall of the minority government.

To measure issue salience and issue positions, first, a list of 16 different issues was created. Of the total amount of 756 tweets, 550 mention at least one substantial political issue. Tweets sometimes also contain multiple issues. Second, in line with media coding procedures (Kriesi et al., 2008; Koopmans et al., 2005), we coded Wilders' issue position. For each issue, a positive (1), negative (−1), or neutral or ambiguous stand (0) can be taken. Using three categories indeed masks much of the nuance of party positioning, but tweets are less rich in detail as compared with manifestos, where more fine-grained scales are more common. However, note that we rely on average scores of many measurements (tweets).

Unfortunately, studies on the far right that analyse texts often lack information about the reliability (i.e. dependability) of coding procedures. Since an important goal of content analysis is "to identify and record relatively objective (or at least inter-subjective) characteristics of messages, reliability is paramount. Without the establishment of reliability, content analysis measures are useless" (Neuendorf, 2002, as cited by Lombard, Snyder-Duch, and Bracken, 2002). We recommend that researchers report a statistical measure of the amount of agreement among coders, such as the widely used Krippendorff's alpha (Hayes and Krippendorff, 2007). Our coding process proved reliable. A random selection of 50 tweets was coded independently by two authors. We calculated Krippendorff's alphas for each dummy variable indicating whether the tweet contained the respective issue or not. The alphas for these issue salience-dummies are 0.90 (for 'European Union') or higher. Concerning the agreement on issue positions, the alphas are 0.71 (for 'Finance') or higher.

Results and conclusion

Table 9.3 shows the development in issue positions and issue salience over time. We highlight the four most important issues. Our results clearly refute the claim

TABLE 9.3 Salience and position of four most important issues in Wilders' tweets 2010–2013 (number of tweets between parentheses).

	Period 1: Opposition		Period 2: Inclusion		Period 3: Opposition		Overall	
	%	Mean score	%	Mean score	%	Mean score	%	Mean score
Integration and Immigration	39.5 (17)	−1.00	30.1 (55)	−0.92	31.2 (101)	−1.00	31.5 (173)	−0.97
European Union	11.6 (5)	−1.00	26.2 (48)	−1.00	36.4 (118)	−1.00	31.1 (171)	−1.00
Finance and economy	9.3 (4)	−1.00	6.6 (12)	0.36	21.0 (68)	−0.41	15.3 (84)	−0.29
Public order, security and justice	25.6 (11)	0.86	13.1 (24)	0.90	9.3 (30)	0.96	11.8 (65)	0.92
Total number of issue tweets	43		183		324		550	

Note: Position scale: Integration/immigration: nativism (−1) vs. cosmopolitism (1). European Union: anti–EU (−1) vs. pro–EU (1). Finance and Economy: state regulation (1) vs. free market (−1). Public order: authoritarianism (1) vs. libertarian (−1).

that the *PVV* moderated its political stance when it supported the minority government. To the contrary, the outspoken nativist stance is remarkably consistent The overall average position on integration and immigration approximates −1.00, which indicates that the *PVV* is very consistent in its opposition to immigration and the view that minorities should assimilate into the dominant Dutch culture. In fact, all 173 tweets Wilders sent about these topics were scored nativist (−1), except one. The slightly less nativist score (−0.92) is due to one single tweet with an ambivalent position (0). In October 2010, after an attack on a mosque, Wilders tweeted: "the less mosques in the Netherlands, the better. But violence directed at existing mosques is unacceptable and should be severely punished".

The *PVV*'s anti-EU stance is also strikingly unequivocal: the mean position on issues concerning European integration is always −1.00. Furthermore, the *PVV* did not tone down its stance in favour of harsher punishments and stricter laws. The position concerning public order, security, and justice is again quite constant and approximates 1.00.

In addition to issue positions, we can also focus on issue salience (Helbling and Tresch, 2011). Moderation could imply that Wilders diversified his political agenda and became less focused solely on nativism. Table 9.3 shows that the most important issue for the *PVV* is immigration and integration: overall, about one third of Wilders' tweets mention this issue. The issue of European integration is a close second with 31.1 per cent. A closer analysis of the tweets reveals that immediately after the *PVV* withdrew its support from the minority coalition, this topic received much more attention than immigration and integration. During that period, almost 70 per cent of the tweets address the European Union. One could perhaps consider this stronger emphasis on the anti-EU stance (compared to anti-immigration statements) as moderation. If so, it again contradicts the inclusion-moderation thesis: this shift towards more tweets about the issue of European integration took place *after* Wilders withdrew his support for the minority government (see 'Period 3: Opposition' in Table 9.3). This proves the added value of relying on the time series of tweets: the timing of such shifts is much harder to discern when we rely on expert surveys or manifestos.

Concluding remarks

In this chapter we reflected on the use of social media to study the far right. More specifically, we discussed the investigation of Facebook and Twitter as means to explore far right discourses. All in all, it showed that social media are fruitful sources for analysing statements of both leaders and supporters of far right parties and movements. More generally, at stake is whether we experience "fundamental change in the nature of political life as a result of the disruptive influence of digital communication" (Chadwick, 2017: 3–4).

A possible avenue for future research is Marshall McLuhan's (1994) famous phrase that "the medium is the message": do tweets or Facebook posts of the same parties and movements yield similar positions as 'traditional' outlets, or do new social media imply more provocative and radical position-taking? People need to adapt to the requirements and restrictions of the medium. Thus, it may be necessary to untangle to what extent communication is actually platform-driven (Ruths and Pfeffer, 2014). Not only between old and new media, but also between different social media platforms, the medium influences the message. Marwick and Lewis (2017: 25) show that new platforms, such as Gab.ia, Voat and Discord, were designed specifically for "discussions that are banned on more mainstream social media". Whether they express themselves on popular platforms such as Facebook or Twitter, or whether they create their own social media platforms, the Internet will most likely remain a central space for far right activists to connect with each other and express their grievances.

Notes

1 More details on our study can be found in Klandermans et al. (2016).
2 For more details on our study, see Muis and Dijkstra (2014).

References

Akkerman, T., S.L. De Lange, and M. Rooduijn. 2016. *Radical Right-wing Populist Parties in Western Europe: Into the Mainstream?* Abingdon: Routledge.

Albertazzi, D. and D. McDonnell. 2015. *Populists in Power*. London: Routledge.

Arzheimer, K. 2015. *"The AfD's Facebook wall: A new hub for far-right mobilisation in Germany?"* Paper presented at the APSA Annual Meeting, San Francisco, 3–6 September.

Atton, C. 2006. "Far-right media on the internet: Culture, discourse and power." *New Media & Society*, 8(4), 573–587.

Awan, I. 2016. "Islamophobia on social media: A qualitative analysis of the Facebook's walls of hate." *International Journal of Cyber Criminology*, 10(1), 1–20.

Bartlett, J., J. Birdwell, and M. Littler. 2011. *The New Face of Digital Populism*. London: Demos.

Ben-David, A. and A.M. Matamoros-Fernández. 2016. "Hate speech and covert discrimination on social media: Monitoring the Facebook pages of extreme-right political parties in Spain." *International Journal of Communication*, 10, 1167–1193.

Bird, S., E. Klein, and E. Loper. 2009. *Natural Language Processing with Python*. Sebastopol, CA: O'Reilly Media Incorporation.

Bright, J., H. Margetts, S. Hale, and T. Yasseri. 2014. *The Use of Social Media for Research and Analysis: A Feasibility Study*. London: DWP.

Bryman, A. 2015. *Social Research Methods*. Oxford: Oxford University Press.

Buchanan, E.A. 2011. "Internet research ethics: Past, present, and future." In *The Handbook of Internet Studies*, edited by M. Consalvo and C. Ess, 83–108. Oxford: Blackwell Publishing.

Caiani, M. and D. Della Porta. 2011. "The elitist populism of the extreme right: A frame analysis of extreme right-wing discourses in Italy and Germany." *Acta Politica*, 46(2), 180–202.

Caiani, M. and L. Parenti. 2013. *European and American Extreme Right Groups and the Internet*. Farnham: Ashgate Publishing.

Caiani, M. and C. Wagemann. 2009. "Online networks of the Italian and German extreme right. An explorative study with social network analysis." *Information, Communication & Society*, 12(1), 66–109.

Ceron, A., L. Curini, S.M. Iacus, and G. Porro. 2014. "Every tweet counts? How sentiment analysis of social media can improve our knowledge of citizens' political preferences with an application to Italy and France." *New Media & Society*, 16(2), 340–358.

Chadwick, A. 2017. *The Hybrid Media System: Politics and Power* (second edition). Oxford: Oxford University Press.

Cleland, J., C. Anderson, and J. Aldridge-Deacon. 2018. "Islamophobia, war and non-Muslims as victims: An analysis of online discourse on an English Defence League message board." *Ethnic and Racial Studies*, 41(9), 1541–1557.

De Haldevang, M. 2017. "The comedian who hacked the German far right by seizing power from its Facebook bots." *Quartz* [online]. Available at: https://qz.com/1111678/shahak-shapira-an-israeli-german-comedian-hacked-far-right-facebook-bots-exposed-twitter-hate-speech-and-reclaimed-berlins-holocaust-memorial-from-instagrammers [accessed 1 September 2018].

De Koster, W. and D. Houtman. 2008. "'Stormfront is like a second home to me.' On virtual community formation by right-wing extremists." *Information, Communication & Society*, 11(8), 1155–1176.

Feinerer, I. 2017. "Introduction to the tm package. Text mining in R." Retrieved from: https://cran.r-project.org/web/packages/tm/vignettes/tm.pdf

Futrell, R. and P. Simi. 2017. "The [un]surprising alt-right." *Contexts*, 16(2), 76.

Giachanou, A. and F. Crestani. 2016. "Like it or not: A survey of Twitter sentiment analysis methods." *ACM Computing Surveys (CSUR)*, 49(2), 28.

Golder, S.A. and M.W. Macy. 2014. "Digital footprints: Opportunities and challenges for online social research." *Annual Review of Sociology*, 40, 129–152.

Hawley, G. 2017. *Making Sense of the Alt-Right*. New York, NY: Columbia University Press.

Hayes, A.F. and K. Krippendorff. 2007. "Answering the call for a standard reliability measure for coding data." *Communication Methods and Measures*, 1(1), 77–89.

Helbling, M. and A. Tresch. 2011. "Measuring party positions and issue salience from media coverage. Discussing and cross-validating new indicators." *Electoral Studies*, 30(1), 174–183.

King, G. and N. Persily. 2018. *A New Model for Industry-Academic Partnerships*. Working Paper. Available at: http://j.mp/2q1IQpH [accessed 22 September 2018].

Klandermans, B., J. Stekelenburg, C. Duijndam, A. Honari, J. Muis, M. Slootman, S. van Welschen, O. Klein, and G. Mahieu. 2016. *Bedreigde identiteiten: De wisselwerking tussen anti-islambewegingen en de radicale islam*. Amsterdam: Vrije Universiteit Amsterdam.

Klein, O. and J. Muis. 2018. "Online discontent: Comparing Western European far-right groups on Facebook." *European Societies* [online first publication]. Available at: https://doi.org/10.1080/14616696.2018.1494293

Koopmans, R., P. Statham, M. Giugni, and F. Passy. 2005. *Contested Citizenship: Immigration and Cultural Diversity in Europe*. Minneapolis, MN: University of Minnesota Press.

Kriesi, H., E. Grande, R. Lachat, M. Dolezal, and S. Bornschier. 2008. *West European Politics in the Age of Globalization*. Cambridge: Cambridge University Press.

Lombard, M., J. Snyder-Duch, and C.C. Bracken. 2002. "Content analysis in mass communication: Assessment and reporting of intercoder reliability." *Human Communication Research*, 28(4), 587–604.

Lucas, C., R.A. Nielsen, M.E. Roberts, B.M. Stewart, A. Storer, and D. Tingley. 2015. "Computer-assisted text analysis for comparative politics." *Political Analysis*, 23, 1–24.

Marwick, A. and R. Lewis. 2017. *Media Manipulation and Disinformation Online*. New York, NY: Data & Society.

McCallum, A.K. 2002. *MALLET: A Machine Learning for Language Toolkit*. Retrieved from: http://mallet.cs.umass.edu

McLuhan, M. 1994. *Understanding Media*. Cambridge, MA: MIT Press.

Mosca, L. 2014. "Methodological practices in social movement online research." In *Methodological Practices in Social Movement Research*, edited by D. Della Porta, 379–417. Oxford: Oxford University Press.

Muis, J. 2015. "The rise and demise of the Dutch extreme right: Discursive opportunities and support for the Center Democrats in the 1990s." *Mobilization: An International Quarterly*, 20(1), 41–60.

Muis, J. and G. Dijkstra. 2014. *"Government responsibility and the radicalness of the Dutch right-wing populist PVV. Using tweets to measure party positions."* Paper presented at Annual Conference of Dutch and Flemish Associations for Political Science, Maastricht, June 12–13.

Olmstead, K. and M. Barthel. 2015. *The Challenge of Using Facebook for Research*. Washington, DC: Pew Research Center.

Puschmann, C., J. Ausserhofer, N. Maan, and M. Hametner. (2016). *Information laundering, Counter-publics: The News Sources of Islamophobic Groups on Twitter*. Tenth International AAAI Conference on Web and Social Media. Social Media in the Newsroom: Technical Report WS-16–19.

Quan-Haase, A. and L. Sloan. 2017. "Introduction to the *Handbook of Social Media Research Methods*: Goals, challenges and innovations." In *The SAGE Handbook of Social Media Research Methods*, edited by A. Quan-Haase and L. Sloan, 1–10. London: Sage.

Rieder, B. 2013. "Studying Facebook via data extraction: The Netvizz application." *Proceedings of the 5th Annual ACM Web Science Conference*, 346–355.

Rieder, B. 2018. "Facebook's app review and how independent research just got a lot harder. The politics of systems." *The Politics of Systems* [online]. Available at: http://thep oliticsofsystems.net/2018/08/facebooks-app-review-and-how-independent-research-just-got-a-lot-harder/ [accessed 22 September 2018].

Ruths, D. and J. Pfeffer. 2014. "Social media for large studies of behavior." *Science*, 346(6213), 1063–1064.

Spierings, N. and K. Jacobs. 2014. "Getting personal? The impact of social media on preferential voting." *Political Behavior*, 36(1), 215–234.

Stier, S., L. Posch, A. Bleier, and M. Strohmaier. 2017. "When populists become popular: comparing Facebook use by the right-wing movement Pegida and German political parties." *Information, Communication & Society*, 20(9), 1365–1388.

Sveningsson, M. 2004. "Ethics in Internet ethnography." In *Readings in Virtual Research Ethics: Issues and Controversies*, edited by E.A. Buchanan, 45–61. Hershey, PA: Information Science Publishing.

Thelwall, M., K. Buckley, G. Paltoglou, D. Cai, and A. Kappas. 2010. "Sentiment strength detection in short informal text." *Journal of the Association for Information Science and Technology*, 61(12), 2544–2558.

Williams, M.H. 2010. "Can leopards change their spots? Between xenophobia and trans-ethnic populism among West European far right parties." *Nationalism and Ethnic Politics*, 16(1), 111–134.

Zúquete, J.P. 2008. "The European extreme-right and Islam: New directions?" *Journal of Political Ideologies*, 13(3), 321–344.

10

BIG DATA AND THE RESURGENCE OF THE FAR RIGHT WITHIN THE UNITED STATES OF AMERICA

Peita L. Richards

The internet has become a key source of data for research on criminal and extremist groups, with the far right proving the most experienced and adept at utilising its power to mobilize individuals within a principle of leaderless resistance. As the first known extremist group to use the internet through the launch of Stormfront, the White Supremacist movement within the United States has developed the capacity to articulate a narrative within the boundaries of the First Amendment, concurrent with facilitating the ideological incentives and non-physical group dynamics necessary for the facilitation of lone wolf operatives in defense of the movement's Fourteen Words mantra.

This chapter will demonstrate the role of big data analytics in presenting both quantitative data from, and sentiment analysis of, social media communications of the racially motivated far right within the context of the United States. With data sets anchored on key salient events – commencing with the verdict in the case of George Zimmerman and the shooting death of an unarmed black man in Florida under the stand your ground legal provisions to the emergence of the Black Lives Matters movement following the unrest in Ferguson, Missouri – the data will demonstrate a growing escalation in reactivity – both frequency and volatility – of individuals who present far right and extreme right attitudes. Supporting qualitative analysis of the representation of self-identity of high influencers within these data sets will lend depth to the discussion of how big data social media analytics can facilitate the application of social identity theory to our understanding of individuals involved in the advocation and perpetration of violent responses to racially based events and social movements.

The chapter will provide a new approach to the integration of social media in developing a deeper understanding of individuals affiliated with far right ideologies, beyond traditional network analysis; where to even commence research, a known identity and their network is required to have been identified. Network analysis also relies on metadata, such as patterns in phone calls or online interactions, as opposed to the content of those conversations. Social media, on the other hand, is information posited into the public sphere via the internet, that is not subject to subpoena, and provides opportunities for both qualitative and quantitative analysis of content and behaviors.

Trajectory of the "second life" concept

Since its inception, the Ku Klux Klan (KKK) provided two crucial aspects to the American white supremacist movement. In the first instance, it provided a sense of belonging. An organization where those aligned with, or interested in, a racially based right wing ideology, could find like-minded individuals. A community where those ideological attitudes and beliefs could be both expressed, and transitioned to action. And in this transition to action, it gifted the movement with the most important aspect to its existence: anonymity. A second life.

Emboldened by the perceived audacity of the civil rights movement, and inspired by global nationalist movements, they aligned with other far right organizations (Bjelopera, 2013; Johnson, 2012). The recently armed militia wings of the Christian Right became fast allies, with conjoint operations forging bonds (Adamczyk, Gruenewald, Chermak, and Freilich, 2014). If nothing else, the far right was adaptable.

Infiltrated by the FBI in the 1980s, individuals faced repercussions for the actions of their second, anonymous lives, in the courts of law. The veil was lifted, and their adaptability again tested. Amongst the individuals who were convicted of racially motivated hate crimes and acts of domestic terrorism was the influential Louis Beam. A theorist of the social movement and violent Klansman in his own right, Beam advocated the end of formal group dynamics as early as 1983. Whilst invoking the concept of a political wing – one in which constitutionally protected free speech could enact a political agenda; discuss issues; and enlighten individuals as to the concerns of the Aryan race – Beam further wrote the foundations of what was to become the new face of the underground wing: Leaderless Resistance. Based on the 1962 report of Colonel Ulius Amoss, a United States anti-communist Intelligence Officer, which stated an appreciation for the worsening of conditions in order to mobilize greater efforts, Beam wrote:

> As honest men who have banded together into groups or associations of a political or religious nature are falsely labeled domestic terrorists or cultists and suppressed, it will become necessary to consider other methods of organization: non-organization.
>
> *(Lenz, 2015: 11)*

Calling for the actions of lone wolves or small cells comprising of no more than four to six most trusted men; there would be no formal collaboration with others of similar mind. No directions would be given, nor taken; and initiative would fall to the individuals themselves.

Whilst no specific directive may be given under this format, the creed which had previously been issued by Klansman Lane, communicated from prison where he was serving a sentence of natural life without parole for murder, acts as guidance for individuals so inclined. A starting point and point of return to for clarity, Lane's Fourteen Words not only remain prevalent in the USA today, but has become the single most adopted statement for White Supremacists, neo-Nazis and Skin Head groups worldwide. He wrote:

> We must secure the existence of white people and a future for white children.
> *(Lane in Weinberg, 2013: 18)*

The far right white supremacist movement are the first known extremist group to present a coherent online presence through the forum Stormfront.org. Launched in 1996 by Don Black, who had developed the site and become proficient in computer mediated communications whilst imprisoned for an attempted coup in the Dominican Republic, the forum became both a portal to other means of propaganda; as well as a place where individuals could engage in discussion with likeminded individuals under the anonymity of a screen name (Banks, 2010; Burris, Smith, and Strahm, 2000; Perry and Olsson, 2009). The notion of anonymity meant that the internet, and eventually wider spread online communities and social media platforms, became a natural trajectory for the gathering of the far right. From its inception, Stormfront alone replicated the previous Sunday Town Meetings through live streamed talk back programs and regularly featured commentary from renowned figures said as David Duke (Bowman-Grieve, 2009). Moderated by senior organizers, the site maintained a sense of order and decorum, and provided guidance by prohibiting posts or material which did not live up to the family values, dignified forms of expression, and topics of importance which it deemed necessary to the cause (Bowman-Grieve, 2009; De Koster and Houtman, 2008). For the far right, the online communities became their second home, and the gateway to their second life (De Koster and Houtman, 2008). Indeed, research conducted by George Washington University in 2016 has evidenced that the far right is not only more active, but more successful in the process of radicalization via social media, than ISIS (Berger, 2016).

Social media as a research methodology

Social media networks are widely used by security and intelligence agencies for network analysis. However, emerging research into online expressions or personality and identity provide an opportunity for greater understanding of how salient events may trigger reactions in both individuals, ideological groups, and emerging social movements. Indeed, it was the events of Ferguson, Missouri, that would lead to the formalization of Black Lives Matter as a national social and political movement.

The selection of the social media platform is the first stage in utilizing content to build data frames, and it is here that we enter the emerging minefield of uncharted ethical territory, privacy settings, and access. Replicability of studies, and truly randomized samples which allow us to track movements, need to be factored into research design; and, as with all research in the social sciences, the context needs to be weighted. It is here that current tools such as NVivo's NCapture, Advanced Search portals and live Application Program Interface, commonly known as an API, presents limitations. In the first instance, you need to be ready to conduct research at the moment a salient event occurs. But more pressing to a comprehensive research study is the relevance of comparative salient triggers and access to data which on their own may have had little significance to a broader study.

The methodology presented herein focuses on developing an understanding of the strengths and limitations of Twitter as a data source, by evidencing archival data structures and the ability to build new data frames of random sample reactions to salient events. It was determined that when considering what prevalence racially motivated commentary has in reaction to salient events, it was necessary to present a representative sample of all commentary as selective parameters within a live data stream retrieval would artificially skew the results. Additionally, it allows for the quantitative analysis of a volume of related content in comparison to the overall usage of the medium and restrains the analysis to a set calendar month in each sample set. From here, the potential for data exploration is near endless, and opens potential research questions for those investigating the far right through a communications method now publicly most perceived as being affiliated with, or dominated by, Islamic Extremism (Berger, 2016).

Twitter: Platform and purpose

Launched in July 2006, Twitter was established as a micro-blogging site utilizing a similar format for communication as the initial cellular Short Message Service (SMS). Limiting posts, or Tweets, to 140 characters, the site had a mild impact on the social media landscape in its initial years. However, post 2009, usage of the site increased in excess of 100 per cent per annum and today boasts a total 974 million user accounts (Koh, 2015). Whilst online statistics services report that approximately 44 per cent of accounts in existence today have never sent a Tweet, it is the access to dialogue and content that Twitter affords which is unparalleled (Koh, 2015). This is represented through access to URLs embedded in Tweets which generate in excess of 1 billion unique views on a monthly basis (Twitter Inc, 2015).

With approximately 340 million active users generating content on a monthly basis, Twitter comprises an average of 500,000,000 Tweets per day (Internet Live Stats, 2015); equating to 200 billion contributions per annum. According to CEO and Co-Founder of Twitter, Jack Dorsey,

> Twitter stands for freedom of expression. We stand for speaking truth to power. And we stand for empowering dialogue.
>
> *(Dorsey, 2015a)*

Dorsey continues,

> Twitter is the most powerful communications tool of our time. It shows everything the world is saying right now … 10–15 minutes before anything else.
>
> *(Dorsey, 2015b)*

Hashtags, in particular, are a driving feature of Twitter interaction. Articulated as #keyword, hashtags are fluid and user driven, allowing individuals to connect by selecting a hashtag and finding other Tweets that have utilized the same expression. The applicability of hashtags is unlimited and applies to all spheres of social interaction. Whether it be searching for a specific known far right community (#stormfront); expressing social opinions on children of mixed race couples (#mudbloods) or using derogatory terms to connect with other likeminded individuals (#nigger, #nigga, #niggah), this user friendly feature requires minimal knowledge to search, and connects likeminded individuals with those they would likely not ever encounter in the physical realm.

The more prolific a hashtag in terms of usage, the greater salience the issue will have to the Twitter community as a whole. Embedded in the Twitter user algorithm is the link to Trending Topics; a list of the top events, issues or points of discussion, worldwide, in real time. This feature allows new users to easily identify the hashtags which may be of interest to them and engage with the related Twitter feeds without prior knowledge of events or experience in searching for key terms. It also provides news outlets a real time indication of new trending issues and breaking events globally; from which early publications and updates of stories are often pulled.

With polarity to the provisions of operation for Facebook, Twitter has no intention on directing the re-establishment of contact with past colleagues, high school friends, or those who inhabit your physical experience. Its intent is to generate new relationships, and build connections between individuals who would likely never meet, or even interact, in the real world, absent of the opportunity of introduction through Twitter (Faruqi, 2015).

Sources of Twitter data

Whilst current argument surrounds the financial future of Twitter – concurrent with public petitions to nationalize or internationalize the platform, in a fashion similar to the CB Radio mode of ownership – the corporation is engaged in the preservation of data for future research. In 2010, Twitter united with the United States Library of Congress to establish a server farm upon which every tweet ever generated would be archived (Raymond, 2010). Furthermore, Twitter hosts active mechanisms through which individuals, corporations and research institutions can access various levels of data.

In a hierarchy of depth of content and speed of access, Twitter offers four levels of access to live data streaming. At the most basic level, the Spritzer sample permits the retrieval of 1 per cent of data within set parameters. These parameters consist of restricting the sample retrieved to a set number of results within a set time frame. The number of results is speculated to be between 1000–1500 per 10 minutes – it is a constraint not publicly released – and consequently, coding for this needs to allow for the list to pause and restart when the threshold is reached. A step up in terms of volume at 5 per cent, the option of Garden Hose is provided, conditional on an application to Twitter and the issuance of an OAuth, or key,[1] to increase the retrieval volume. This specific mechanism is the most popular and is specifically marketed to App Developers and public relations or marketing firms (Morstatter, Pfeffer, Liu, and Carley, 2015). With access to 20 per cent of live data streaming is the option of Firehose, a commercially purchased mechanism with basic search parameters starting from $500 per day of use. These parameters will allow you to search for a restricted number of key terms, over a restricted time frame, with a greater quantity of results. Archived data, generally over 2 years old, are now deemed outside of the basic search parameters for Firehose users. Finally, as of 2014, Twitter has launched a full access program based on a formal research application process – not dissimilar to research grants – and to date has awarded 8 out of 412 applications, all to medical research projects (Twitter Data Grants, 2014).

Whether it be the Spritzer, Garden Hose or Firehose access level that is being utilized, live data streaming permits a user to set specific parameters for retrieving data. Be they key words, hashtags, user handles, dates or a combination, the return rate of relevance is naturally immediately enhanced as only the targeted information is obtained. This process allows a user to effectively filter and remove any "noise", including RTs,[2] and view only those Tweets with direct importance to the topic at hand. By contrast, a REST sample, defined below, involves accessing a previously archived data set, without the provision of refinement beyond its establishing parameters.

In partnership with the Library of Congress archiving of Twitter feeds for historical records, the non-profit institution Archive.org established a public access REST archive at the Spritzer level of content. Each archive comprises a randomized sample of 1 per cent of tweets over the course of one month, and is intended to provide a snapshot of society as expressed on Twitter, at any given point in time. It is these archives that have been selected as the base data sets for the development of this research methodology.

Salient events used for methodology development

The data sets retrieved in the development of this research method are those of July 2013, February 2014, and August 2014. This comprises two months with pre-determined active salient events and a third data set at a point in time where no active salient event of equal or comparable magnitude was reported. As this method of research was developed to track changes in expressed attitudes and online behaviors as a risk assessment tool, the third group served as the control data set to allow comparatives to be drawn.

The data set of July 2013 was selected due to the salient event of the verdict in the trial of George Zimmerman. Zimmerman faced charges of murder in the first degree, murder in the second degree and manslaughter for the 2012 shooting death of 18-year-old Trayvon Martin in Florida. A former member of neighborhood watch, and a resident of a largely white neighborhood, Zimmerman had called 911 after noticing a young black male in the area, declaring a sense of insecurity and suspicion. Arguing he acted in the prevention of a potential violent crime under the controversial "Stand Your Ground" laws in Florida, Zimmerman shot and killed Martin, who was later determined not only to be unarmed but also a new resident to the community. The verdict declared that malicious intent could not be determined and an acquittal was recorded (Linder, 2015).

In contrast to the Zimmerman Verdict, which may be seen as a victory or positive event for those who possess a racially motivated far right ideologically based identity, with the upholding of the controversial Stand Your Ground law that allows one to engage in acts of force if a threat is felt or perceived (Florida State Legislature Acts 776.012 and 776.013), the salient events within the data set of August 2014, would be viewed in a negative light. On August 9, in Ferguson, Missouri, 18-year-old Michael Brown – an African American male – was shot and killed by Darren Wilson – a white male who was serving in the Ferguson Police Force. The event sparked an immediate backlash for over two weeks, with civil unrest in the form of protests and riots in opposition to the racial profiling used in approaching People of Color, as well as the militarization of the policing sector (BBC News, 2015). Generating the hashtag #BlackLivesMatter and sparking a national dialogue on racial inequalities, the salient event sparked a display of a greater divide between primarily black and primarily white Americans, and national reports of an increase in activity by groups associated with a White Supremacy ideology were recorded.

The final data set, February 2014, was an opportune time coinciding the mid-point of these two salient events; thus, mitigating changes in methods, means and degrees of interactions through Twitter by controlling the parameter of time. However, despite extensive research, no national event or event of comparable reportage in relation to any issues of race is recorded. Therefore, this data set was selected to provide a base line for the quantitative analysis within the two data sets anchored to salient events.

Data analysis method

The retrieval of the archival data was relatively simple: each month of sample data is compressed into a layered tarball,[3] and linked to a URL for download. Each tarball is approximately 50GB in compressed state, and thus a sustained internet connection is necessary.

The archival process had nested the Spritzer samples gathered in what appeared to be a folder per day, however the data themselves were then further fractured into an archival structure of more than14,000 nested folders. As a result, the basics of R^4 as a coding language were exceeded and technical research assistance had to be employed to write the code which could loop through these folders, extracting the.bz2 files,[5] and building them into a single RData data frame[6] to commence analysis. Whilst time consuming in its first stage, the code that is constructed to create these data frames is then replicable to any future studies utilizing the archives. Thus, the initial time (and intimidation) of learning coding becomes a transferrable research skill, not only to other instances of activity within events pertaining to the far right but across disciplines, and individual subject timelines.

In the first instance, the newly created data frames needed to be separated using a strategic method – in this instance a lexicon of key terminology relevant to the subject matter at hand – in order to identify the tweets relevant to the study. This is as opposed to attempting to work with the full snapshot, which is archived by the Library of Congress. With the original samples exceeding 300 million tweets and their metadata,[7] separating the noise from the relevant content was the critical first step.

Existing research into racial expression on Twitter was identified as having utilized the Demos Project in order to identify linguistic features and patterns in social media pertinent to hate speech (Challenging Racism Project, Western Sydney University, 2016). Whilst providing a wealth of information on its own, it did not take into account the colloquial nature of language in context, and thus presented limitations to direct application on a sample of this size and nature. Further research through the databases available from the Southern Poverty Law Center led to the website *hatebase.org*. An online project funded by the United Nations, *hatebase.org* applies the work of the Sentinel Project, which retroactively tracked the use of language on issues of region, ethnicity, religion, and gender groups with contextual parameters, based on evidence gathered from communications in the lead up to internationally recognized genocides and acts of genocide. With the aim of identifying patterns for future prevention and intervention, the website allows you to enter a linguistic term or collection of terms and to assess the volatility of this within a specific geographical region. For the purpose of this research, all terms were anchored on the Continental United States. This determination to use terminology anchored on the Continental United States was linked to the original focus of the research, which was salient events within the United States; and the output of the research, which focused on implications for risk assessment by law enforcement and intelligence within the legal confines of the United States judicial system. These terms, however, can be modified based on the region in which you are undertaking research on the far right, in order to produce an immediately relevant data set for your research. Terms identified from both the Demos Project and the Southern Poverty Law Center as well as those identified through research as being codified within the White Supremacist movements were run through the online database for evaluation. Terms and phrases which returned a frequency of negative sentiment or aggressive intent higher than 75 per cent were added to the core lexicon,[8] as intent of the use of such language is largely consistent with hate speech intent whereas those that were recorded with a frequency rating of negative sentiment or aggressive intent lower than 75 per cent were excluded from the list.

The baseline lexicon which was applied to all three sets comprised a total of 90 key terms, including variations of spellings and phraseology. The data sets anchored in known salient events additionally included the hashtags pertinent to their discussion on Twitter.

The lexicons were then cross checked with the online tool *regex.com* for guidance on coding regular expression extraction, and coded in R for application to the data frames. The full lexicon was run on each data frame, with the additional hashtags applied as relevant, and the results sub-set to active data sets for analysis.

Approaches to data analysis

Whilst the initial hopes for the research methodology were to identify quantitative patterns in expressions of far right identity using linguistic based coding, it is the metadata within these archives that is of significant value to researchers in adopting this method for future research into the far right.

Behavior of data sets

Anchored in identity theory, social psychologists have demonstrated the relationship between salient events and increased expressions of relevant ideological belief systems (Burke, 1991; Stets and Burke, 2000; Taylor and Louis, 2004). However, how this is demonstrated in a virtual environment has yet to be documented in detail. Focusing on the key events, the metadata within each set allowed the tweets to be assessed in the context of behavioral acts. To this end, the data permits a researcher to identify the percentage of tweets which are new content, are retweets or repeat content, or are offered in reply to another tweet. These types of tweets constitute types of behaviors and allow researchers insight into how the users are engaging with the platform in reaction to, or absent of, a specific event or expressed attitude.

Sentiment analysis

Utilizing the software LIWC, the data sets in full were analyzed across the full spectrum of categories available. Due to their size, the files need to run individually and not as a comparative batch, however it is anticipated that as big data become more prevalent in academic research, these capacities will increase. Because of its focus on expressions of identity, the data used in the method's development established a comparative matrix across pronouns – both personal and collective –

and pure sentiment, notably aggression, anxiety and negative expressions. Interestingly, the initial comparative of Sentiment Analysis, combined with the comparative of behavioral acts as outlined above, showed little notable difference in the data set anchored around the Zimmerman verdict to that of the Baseline set with no notable salient event. In contrast, heightened degrees of both aggression and negative emotion and the use of pronouns, combined with a significant increase in the generating of original content, was evident in the data set anchored around the initial uprising in Ferguson, Missouri.

Information gateways

In the assessment of the behavior of the data sets, the metadata also permit a researcher to identify the purpose of the tweet itself, notably, is it commentary, or does it provide a gateway to further information? This is evident through the inclusion in the data frame of both any embedded URLs as well as the full extension, which permits further sampling for thematic analysis and evidence development in terms of recruitment, radicalization and propaganda.[9] Whilst some of these are recognizable on sight, and relatively easy to count in either R or NVivo coding methods, others offer an insight into group mentality and emerging influencers. A URL that includes *.insta* or *yo.utube* in its hyperlink will indicate visual content. Indeed, the notable behavioral variable in the Ferguson data set was the significant increase in YouTube links; a characteristic which was much lower in frequency when measured in the Zimmerman and Baseline data sets. From a sociological position this suggests that the increase in original content and heightened expression comes from the visual of the African American not maintaining their social place and status, and this being shared through social media to engage user attention to the behavior of protestors. As Cromwell Cox wrote:

> For the white supremacist, in contrast, the 'Negro' is just fine – in his/her place: as an exploitable supply of cheap, menial labour power.
>
> *(Fraser, 1995)*

In the instance of video footage of the Ferguson uprising, which would later evolve into the Black Lives Matter movement, the far right indeed viewed the African-American population as behaving in an inappropriate manner; and expressing views that contradicted, and therefore threatened, the ideology of the far right.

As physical movements of people in opposition to the far right increase, and as footage of retaliatory acts circulate expediently through social media, this tool alone offers a portal for the examination of commentary and visuals in one location.

However, further investigation into hyperlinks allows researchers to determine thematic schema, including the role of social media in expressions of ideology and propaganda more broadly; the role of mainstream and online news media in the propagation of far right ideology; and the other links – including, but not limited to, clearly expressed opportunities for engagement in criminal activities in the advancement of the far right ideological agenda.

Influencers

The metadata of the users' profiles also presents an opportunity for researchers to develop matrices for the examination of influence. Whilst the frequency of an actor within the set on its own can be a measure of influence and engagement, their potential reach presents an additional layer for examination. Whether based on modelling used by commercial entities to increase your social media influence (e.g. Klout.com), or those weighted to specific interests, the presentation of statistical data evidencing each account' followers, friends, tweets, replies, retweets, and favorites[10] at the time the content was generated, allows researchers to identify new modes of influence. Further, whilst the initial development can be time consuming and weightings adjusted to eliminate the inclusion of bots, sock puppets, or automated accounts,[11] the process allows researchers to identify potential new influencers, emerging actors, and individuals at risk of radicalization to a far right extremist ideology with consequential actions.

User timelines and network analysis

From the above method, further data can be retrieved via the Twitter API. Twitter will prevent access to any account if it has been closed at the time of request – both by the user themselves, or by Twitter in breach of its Terms and Conditions of usage; or if the account is set to private. Beyond this, classified as Secondary Public Data, the Twitter API enables the retrieval of the most recent 3200 lines of data of any identified timeline. For researchers of the far right, this provides an opportune source of information for both linguistic quantitative analysis designed with regional and subject specifications; as well as thematic analysis of both content and frequencies of behavioral acts within the platform.

It is anticipated that forthcoming research into identity expressions of the far right through social media, when layered with existing practices of network analysis, will assist in the risk assessment of individuals known to law enforcement as potential criminal actors – particularly in light of psychological evidence supporting a disinhibition in online mediums (Suler, 2016) – without incurring substantial increases in costs or resources. Within the United States, this key principle is notable for continual research development due to the dismantling and defunding of Homeland Security departments focused on "non-Islamic Terrorism" (Johnson, 2012.

Future research opportunities

As it stands, the method presented can appear laborious and time intensive. Most certainly, in its initial development it was both! However, the substantial replication of source code to a known and continuous public archive of data presents only opportunities for future research. Be they specific interest in key events, known groups, political movements or linguistic patterns, the embedded data present contextual information well beyond the visual tweet. With the mainstream media consistently shortening presentations of stories, and their lifespan reducing to keep pace with the need to constantly be generating new, short stories, big data archives from social media platforms allow a more comprehensive insight into the behaviors and reactions of groups. When coupled with an increasingly political environment which seems to normalize far right sentiment to an extent, it also allows researchers to go straight to those who are propelling the activities, attitudes and ideologies of the far right, and to analyze a vast range of information regarding the movements; be it from sentiment analysis, behavioral acts, portals to other platforms, or social movements and event planning. It also coincides with a time in academia, where universities have simultaneously become increasingly risk adverse to field research, whilst dealing with challenging budget cuts. By removing physical proximity, the researcher also has a benefit of safety; lower costs with components such as travel and accommodation often removed; and a larger data set with which to work and draw correlations.

At a time when internet access is continuing its global expansion and dominance, and when public attention is drawn to its capacity to recruit, radicalize and disseminate misinformation, the potential for researchers to reach subject material well beyond the depictions of those presented as threats by mainstream media is near endless. With over 42 per cent of the global population being active social media users as of January, 2018 (Hootsuite Commercial Social Media Reports, 2018), it is an audience and data source that one would be remiss to dismiss. It further opens the door for true interdisciplinary research endeavors, with development of only basic computer coding needing for all academics to contribute substantial new findings in this emerging method of scholarship.

Notes

1 OAuth is the term used by Twitter to assign an original authentication code, which identifies you as a researcher on their network. This is paired with a unique key, similar to a password. Both are required to work in concert in order to gain access to the API network.
2 RT as pertaining to Re-Tweet, to repost in full that of another user
3 A compression system for large, layered folders and data files
4 Now the most commonly used language for big data analysis, "R" is a language with similar purposes to earlier languages such as XML and Python; however, it is the most frequently used when working with social media platforms and data sets beyond 20,000 lines or data points.
5 .bz2 files are not dissimilar to a winzip or .zip compressed file but, are usually much larger in size and consist of a multitude of .zip files within the single compressed .bz2 file.
6 A working data frame comprising of all data retrieved. An RData data frame is not dissimilar to Excel or NVivo, however it allows much greater file sizes to be processed, and integrates the ability to run searches or extract subsets of data using R code within the one computer window.

7 The archived data sets include the metadata of a user in addition to the actual tweet that was sent. Examples of this metadata include a location, if one was set; the user's handle and name, if entered; links to a personal URL or biography, friends lists; and numerical data such as the numbers of tweets sent, RTs, likes, and comments.

8 The core lexicon refers to the list of key terms that were used to create a subset of relevant data out of each archived set, and was used across all three sets of data. An extended lexicon was added to the salient events to include event-specific hashtags.

9 Prior to commencing sampling, please check your institution's IT usage policy and ensure permissions are granted to avoid tripping any links to pages under legal surveillance, or breaching conditions of use in relation to violent or racist content being accessed on institutional property.

10 A tweet which was marked by the user as a particular post of interest, enabling them to either demonstrate support, or to quickly review at a later time.

11 Bots and automated accounts are user accounts set up by advanced coding to identify other users engaging with specific key words, accounts or hashtags. These accounts either follow or respond with pre-programmed, automated messages. Similarly, sock puppets are accounts which do not depict real users, but are run by real people working full time on the dissemination of propaganda, behind multiple, fictional identities.

References

Adamczyk, A., J. Gruenewald, S.M. Chermak, and J.D. Freilich. 2014. "The Relationship Between Hate Groups and Far-Right Ideological Violence." *Journal of Contemporary Criminal Justice*, 30(3).

Banks, J. 2010. "Regulating Hate Speech Online." *International Review of Law, Computers and Technology*, 23(3).

BBC News. 2015. "Ferguson Unrest: From Shooting to Nationwide Protests". 10 August. Accessed online http://www.bbc.com/news/world-us-canada-30193354

Berger, J.M. 2016. *Nazis vs. ISIS on Twitter: A Comparative Study of White Nationalist and ISIS Online Social Media Networks*. Washington, DC: George Washington University Program on Extremism.

Bjelopera, J.P. 2013. *The Domestic Terrorist Threat: Background and Issues for Congress*. Washington, DC: Congressional Research Service.

Bowman-Grieve, L. 2009. "Exploring 'Stormfront': A Virtual Community of the Radical Right." *Studies in Conflict and Terrorism*, 32(11), 989–1007.

Burke, P. 1991. "Identity Processes and Social Stress." *American Sociological Review*, 56(6), 836–849.

Burris, V., E. Smith, and A. Strahm. 2000. "White Supremacist Networks on the Internet." *Sociological Focus*, 33(2), 215–235.

Challenging Racism Project, Western Sydney University, 2016.

De Koster, W. and D. Houtman. 2008. "Stormfront is Like A Second Home to Me." *Information, Communication and Society*, 11(8), 1153–1175.

Dorsey, J. (2015a) Verified Tweet, October 5, 2015, 4.59am, http://twitter.com/jack

Dorsey, J. (2015b) Verified Tweet, October 5, 2015, 5.00am, http://twitter.com/jack

Faruqi, O. 2015. "The Hearts are the Final Straw: It's Time to Nationalize Twitter." *The Guardian*, November 4, 2015.

Florida Legislature Acts 776.012 and 776.013. "Stand Your Ground." Published online at Official Internet Site of the Florida Legislature http://www.leg.state.fl.us/Statutes/index.cfm?App_mode=Display_Statute&URL=0700-0799/0776/Sections/0776.012.html

Fraser, N. 1995. "From Redistribution to Recognition? Dilemmas of Justice in a 'Post-Socialist' Age." *New Left Review*, 312(July/August), 68–93.

Hootsuite Commercial Social Media Reports. 2018. Accessed online https://hootsuite.com/resources/barometer-2018-global

Internet Live Stats. 2015. "Twitter Facts." Published online http://internetlivestats.com/twitter-statistics/

Johnson, D. 2012. *Right-Wing Resurgence: How a Domestic Terrorist Threat is Being Ignored.* Lanham, MD: Rowman & Littlefield.

Koh, Y. 2015. "Report: 44% of Twitter Accounts Have Never Sent a Tweet." *Wall Street Journal*, April 14, 2015.

Lenz, R. 2015. *Age of the Wolf: A Study of the Rise of Lone Wolf and Leaderless Resistance Terrorism*, Montgomery, AL: Southern Poverty Law Center.

Linder, D.O. 2015. "The George Zimmerman Trial: An Account." Kansas City, MI: Faculty of Law, University of Missouri–Kansas City. Published online at http://www.bbc.com/news/world-us-canada-30193354 (accessed October 31, 2015).

Morstatter, F., J. Pfeffer, H. Liu, and K.M. Carley. 2015. "Is the Sample Good Enough? Comparing Data from Twitter's Streaming API with Twitter's Firehose." Tucson, AZ: Office of Naval Research, University of Arizona. http://www.public.asu.edu/~fmorstat/paperpdfs/icwsm2013.pdf (accessed November 2, 2015).

Perry, B. and P. Olsson. 2009. "Cyberhate: The Globalization of Hate." *Information and Communications Technology Law*, 18(2), 185–199.

Raymond, M. 2010. "How Tweet It Is! Library Acquires Entire Twitter Archive." Library of Congress Blog, April 14, 2010. http://blogs.loc.gov/loc/2010/04/how-tweet-it-is-library-acquires-entire-twitter-archive/ (accessed October 3, 2015).

Stets, J.E. and P.J. Burke. 2000. "Identity Theory and Social Identity Theory." *Social Psychology Quarterly*, 63(3), 224–237.

Suler, J.R. 2016. *Psychology of the Digital Age: Humans Become Electric.* New York, NY: Cambridge University Press.

Taylor, D.M. and W. Louis. 2004. "Terrorism and the Quest for Identity." In *Understanding Terrorism: Psychosocial Roots, Consequences, and Interventions*, edited by F.M. Moghaddam and A.J. Marsella. Washington, DC: American Psychological Association.

Twitter Data Grants. 2014. "Introducing Twitter Data Grants." https://blog.twitter.com/2014/introducing-twitter-data-grants (accessed October 31, 2015).

Twitter Inc. "Company". https://about.twitter.com/company (accessed September 30, 2015).

Weinberg, L. 2013. "Violence by the Far Right: The American Experience." In *Extreme Right Wing Political Violence and Terrorism*, edited by M. Taylor, P.M. Currie, and D. Holbrook. London: Bloomsbury.

11

RESEARCHING FAR-RIGHT HYPERMEDIA ENVIRONMENTS

A case-study of the German online platform einprozent.de

Andreas Önnerfors

One of the largest methodological challenges in studying contemporary far-right mobilization is a proper approach towards the dynamics between online and offline communication and socialization processes. The rapid rise and radicalization of the European New Right (ENR) has been propelled significantly by online tools of mobilization transgressing traditional presence on the World Wide Web and thus call for mixed methods in research combining qualitative and quantitative approaches as well as sensitivity towards the media logic of online communication itself (Bar-On, 2013: 22). Qualitative approaches have hitherto focused on content and for instance scrutinized the rhetorical and linguistic strategies of online media (Wodak, 2015: 125–35; Thielemann, 2016: 74–101). Using quantitative big data, researchers have been able to demonstrate how 'new' social media has contributed to shaping agendas in 'old' mainstream media (Šlerka and Šisler, 2018: 61–86; Hock and Lindenau, 2018). Big data analysis also allows the creation of linguistic corpora on the language of the far-right and thus provides insights into the re-semantization of political language (Scharloth, 2017: 1–13). 'Netnography' has enabled participatory or non-participatory fieldwork to be carried out online (Kozinets, 2010). Whereas the fruitful complementarity of such approaches is evident, this chapter proposes to take the specific hyper-medial fabric (in short: combining verbal, visual, textual and performative content and hyperlinking between different social media platforms and formats) of far-right online communication spaces into account, focusing on the dynamics between online and offline as a significant feature of meaning-making (Madisson, 2016).

The methodological proposals of this chapter draw from research into the German 'right-wing populist movement of indignation', PEGIDA, and its support environments (Vorländer et al., 2016, 2018). PEGIDA and its allies of the German far-right have contributed to a radicalization of political language and engaged in populist styles of politics through performance of 'the people' as the supposedly legitimate source of political agency. 'Retrotopian' longing has been exploited in the German electorate, leading to massive support for the far-right party *Alternative für Deutschland* (AfD), which in the autumn of 2018 entered the national parliament Bundestag with double-digit results (Önnerfors, 2018: 87–119; 2019: 173–200; 2020: 135–149; Bauman, 2017). The discursive strategies employed in order to bring about this conceptual shift are part of a conscious 'metapolitical' strategy to challenge existing prerogatives of interpretation and to conquer the public discourse at large (Bar-On, 2001: 333–351). The claims of representing the people are staged in a host of different 'discursive events' (Wodak, 2009: 1) both offline ('in-real-life', IRL) and online (virtually), added together to create the image of persistent popular endorsement over time.

In this chapter, I will elaborate how the far-right multi-platform einprozent.de, "the largest patriotic network of citizens ('Bürgernetzwerk') in Germany" ('Ein Prozent', website), constructs its popular support. In particular I will illustrate how discursive events are staged and recorded IRL with the deliberate purpose of online dissemination, appealing to both cognitive and behavioural dimensions of social activism. A particular type of content is represented by short 'activist videos', produced in the mode of a (highly edited and scripted) documentary of a symbolic action IRL – for instance raising a cross at a building site of a mosque – with the primary purpose of achieving maximum dissemination online. These activist video clips (a) communicate condensed expressions of meaning (thus resembling the inter-mediality of emblems, in which text and image reinforce the symbolic meaning of the message); (b) are characterized by the hybridity and dynamics of offline production and online dissemination; (c) are intentionally developed for impact within a hyper-medial environment; and (d) convey varieties of a greater strategic political narrative. The goal of these emblematic hybrid media narratives, gearing between online and offline realities as an "intertwined realm" of reality formation and identity-creation (Madisson, 2016: 12), is to enhance the impact of mobilization, generating meaning-making and positive identification with the political messages 'Ein Prozent' aims to advertise and to communicate the image of Germany in terminal decline and the immediate urgency of organized far-right resistance. Hence, the emblematic hybrid media narratives studied in this chapter can be understood as commodities on the larger market of strategic communication in complex contemporary political media economies. The methodological insights of this case study are thus applicable to a wide range of online sources explored within the wider research area. For instance, media scholar Michael Krona, who has extensively studied the media world of ISIS, has stated the need to approach the "significance of media propaganda and virtual interaction in the process of developing radical ideas and support for extremist ideologies" (Krona, 2017). In the same vein, Jesper Falkheimer has stressed the intersections between terrorism, propaganda and strategic communication and how media frames determine actions in real life (Falkheimer, 2013: 44–55, elaborating Breivik's Norwegian terrorist attacks as an example).

Another important implication of my study lies in its interconnections to social movement theories. Although this does not constitute the main methodological focus of this chapter, the hybridity of online and offline activism poses a particular challenge in methodologically determining and classifying social movements of the far-right and calls for significant re-conceptualizations (Hentges et al., 2014: 1–26). After defining the concept of hypermedia environments more closely, I will provide some background to the German context of far-right online presence and then turn to the emblematic hybrid media narratives of einprozent.de, outline how to approach them and conclude with some methodological considerations for future trajectories of research.

What are radical right hypermedia environments?

Following Mari-Liis Madisson who has extensively analyzed online communication in the Estonian far-right, hypermedia is characterized by a "nonhierarchical or network-like structure, internal multiplicity, the lack of a centre or a central axis of organization, fluidity, and temporariness, all of which are most often connected with the abstract textuality of the hypermedia environment" (Madisson, 2016 : 25). Moreover, "primary specifics of hypermedia texts reside in using hyperlinks which allow the connection of various kinds of text fragments, e.g. a hypertextual whole may incorporate verbal, visual, acoustic and inter-semiotic elements" and the informational sphere of the far-right "does not constitute a coherent textual system" (Madisson, 2016: 7–8).

Madisson's main focus is how semiotic processes of meaning-making can be discerned in the Estonian far-right and its hypermedia narratives and thus, ultimately, how identities are created online. In this process it is observable that "relatively homogeneous spheres of meaning" are formed, relative to individual choices, along the so-called confirmation bias leading to the establishment of 'echo chambers' through 'filter bubbles' or "polarizing hermetic auto-communication", reinforced by search engine algorithms and automated recommendation systems of social media (Madisson, 2016: 9–10, 21 and 24; Bauman, 2017: 151). As Roger Griffin has pointed out, it is a specific feature of the extreme right to organize in "minuscule and ephemeral formations" or "groupuscules", which are characterized by their 'rhizomic' communication patterns – non-hierarchical and creating tangled interconnections across (virtual) space, propelled by information and communication technology in an "asymmetrical pattern of growth and decay" (2003: 27–50). Whereas this to a certain extent applies to the case discussed below, einprozent.de was launched top-down as a coordinated effort to create a platform among various actors in the German New Right. It maintains and promotes the view of representing the vernacular voice of 'the people' engaged in a vast social movement of resistance against 'mainstream media', the elites and the existing political order of Germany in general. Madisson points out that informational spheres of the far-right (or "vernacular webs of sceptical knowledge") create appeal "because they reify complex and fluid issues, structures and identities and offer simplistic and eschatological explanations to the intangible complex problems" (2016: 10).

The German radical right online

In 2013, the German domestic secret service Verfassungsschutz released a report on "Right-wing extremism and its internet presence" (Verfassungsschutz, 2013). By then, different forms of internet presence included (a) individual websites (e.g. of organizations), (b) topic-related websites (e.g. created for particular events), (c) communication in social networks (e.g. on Facebook), (d) the use of video-platforms (such as YouTube), and (e) micro-blog platforms (such as Twitter). Already in 2013 it was stated that "disputed [and sometimes emotionally charged] topics of social interest" (such as migration politics or criminality) were increasingly being communicated in an ideologically cloaked fashion in the sense that the ideological origin of the sender was not "immediately obvious for everybody" – a form of communicative style Wodak has called "calculated ambivalence" (Verfassungsschutz, 2013: 8, 13; Wodak, 2015: 52–54; Madisson, 2016: 20). The report also noted that the far-right milieu is very adaptable to new ICT-applications, demonstrated by the use of PicBadges and QR-codes, cognitive codes constituting ideological positions and facilitating immediate and quick communication of far-right content. This has in recent years been expanded to include the development of memes and GIFs as well as certain iconic names and numbers as shorthand for far-right narratives (e.g. '300', referring to the Hollywood movie on the Battle of Thermopylia, 'Charles Martell' as the hero of the Reconquista or '1683' as the iconic year of the Battle of Vienna – all referring to the symbolical clash of civilizations between East and West).

All in all, far-right information spheres create hypermedial environments in which it is easy to "move and to gain and to exchange information in a virtual world which is almost exclusively used by politically like-minded people" (Verfassungsschutz, 2013: 12). The political purpose is to "gain approval in a certain subject area serving as an intersection between their own political agenda and that of civil society in order to be perceived as a real [and credible] political alternative in the long run" (Verfassungsschutz, 2013: 23). In this sense, far-right internet presence is a tool employed to move the socio-political mainstream in the desired direction. The increasing electoral support for far-right populist parties across the European political spectrum seems to indicate that this strategy is successful within the dynamics of only a few election cycles. Between 2013 and 2017, support for the far-right *Alternative für Deutschland* (AfD) almost tripled from 4.7 per cent to 12.6 per cent (Wahlrecht, 2018) and AfD is now represented in the parliaments of all German federal states as well as in the federal parliament *Bundestag*. Together with PEGIDA, representatives of the AfD were also active in the launch of the platform einprozent.de (on these constellations on the German far-right, see Salzborn, 2016: 49–51).

The dynamics developed between online presence and offline activism constitute one united realm of 'reality' and ontology, at least when it comes to performative (individual and collective) interpretative schemata of meaning-making and identity formation. They "condense the 'world out there' by selectively punctuating and encoding objects, situations, events, experiences, and sequences of actions within one's present or past environment" (Snow and Benford as quoted in Hentges et al., 2014: 14).

During recent years, along and across the thin border between virtual and real-life activism, the so-called 'Identitarian movement' has been particularly active (Zúquete, 2018; Dahl, 2018). Although there is an ideological hard core of Identitarianism with prolific ideologues such as Alexandr Dugin and Alain de Benoist, the Identitarians (almost a youth branch of the ENR) have been prolific in developing new forms of blended activism in which online presence is a constitutive and inseparable element of conventional offline activism on the streets (observable also in the recent French 'gilets jaunes' movement). The difficulties of treating the German branch of the Identitarians, *Identitäre Bewegung Deutschland* (IBD) as a hybrid object of research was highlighted by Hentges et al. (2014) who asked whether the IBD represents a 'real' social movement or a virtual phenomenon. Since the IBD to a huge extent mobilizes online (and for instance uses einprozent.de as one of its platforms), it is difficult to give a precise account of its dissemination and forms of organization. Hentges and her co-authors furthermore attempt to "dissolve the alleged contradiction between movement and virtual world". The example of the Identitarians serves as a case to study how "mobilization on the Internet can impact ideologization and design of young movements" and which dimensions can be regarded as "internet-specific" (Hentges et al., 2014: 1).

Researching online/offline socialization poses difficulties to conventional research into social protest movements since it blurs the scope and implications of what hitherto has been perceived as their constitutive factors: (1) protest; (2) network organization; (3) collective identity; (4) continuity; (5) claims for social-political change (from progressive to reactionary); (6) strategical political and cultural goals, frequently overlapping (Hentges et al., 2014: 5–6). These elements have conventionally been studied in offline environments, with little attention paid to online patterns of socialization and identity-formation. The virtuality of contemporary radical right mobilization asks thus for more sophisticated methodological approaches. This relates in particular to activism staged IRL with the intent to online dissemination, a (social) media strategy utilized frequently among Identitarians since at least 2012. Actions and events are filmed and uploaded to official websites and on Facebook or other social media, together with (links to) reports and explanatory texts. These posts are then in turn liked and linked further and transgress national/vernacular boundaries in a pan-European and even global network of interconnected sites. Virtual reports of activism create a large outreach and generate public interest which they without digital marketing and the phenomenon of virality never would have achieved.

"Forms of activism on the Internet and 'on the street'" enter into a "new constellation" and "because of the changed conditions of time and space it is necessary to arrive to new determinants of the unfolding and continuity of protests". With a much lower organizational investment it is possible to "simulate a continuous event of protest which is maintained" across time and space despite of the discrepancy to 'real' activism on the streets (frequently only engaging a handful of activists) and the "virtual echo these actions receive because of their viral dissemination on the internet" (Hentges et al., 2014: 9). Intentional styling of events in social media paired with deliberately open-ended, ambivalent and diffuse modes of interpretation shape enticing online spaces of experiences through which young people easily are attracted to the worldviews and attitudes of the Identitarians. For the case of einprozent.de and its emblematic hybrid media narratives it is relevant to study the merger of a consumer/user of online media who at the same time also acts as producer or co-producer through up-/downloading of hypermedial online content or disseminating and commenting social media content ('user generated content', UGC), a "politicised and ideologized prosumer" (Hentges et al., 2014: 10). What becomes evident is how UGC frequently mimics the style of mobile journalism ('MOJO') or radical citizen journalism (Madisson, 2016: 10, 21).

Overview over the analyzed source einprozent.de

'Ein Prozent' states on its website (2019, 'Über Uns') that its purpose is to provide a "professional platform of resistance for German interests", the "first serious lobby organization for responsible citizens loving their homeland [*heimatliebend*]" with the aim to finally give "a tacit majority of discontented democrats" a voice. According to their own assessment, 'Ein Prozent' (during 2017 alone, the latest figures) has 44,000 supporters, has raised €250,000 for "patriotic projects" has "enlightened the Germans" with 800,000 printed matters, and reached 400,000 people weekly through their website. Declaring their mission statement, two aims are stressed in particular: the "patriotic protest" against "the irresponsible politics of mass immigration" and the "growing abyss between the governing political cast and the true sovereign – the people". This protest is channelled by 'Ein Prozent' and thus brought to "the centre of society", helping the people "down there" to be taken seriously by those "up there". This requires tools of grass-roots activism: "Networking, funding and organization are the essential pillars of professional resistance" ('Ein Prozent' 2019, website).

Developing its activities further, 'Ein Prozent' claims to "offer resistance against a political class that no longer protects the interests of its own population and even claims there is no 'genuine' people". 'Ein Prozent' links individuals and "groups of citizens who dare to search for alternatives in times of no alternatives". Contacts and ideas for "courageous citizens" are mediated, front line activists are supported and relief brought to those in need. "Not everyone can be an activist and offer resistance", but everyone can contribute according to his/her own capacity. The object of resistance is exemplified as follows: "The refugee invasion [*Flüchtlingsinvasion*] is a catastrophe for Germany and Europe". Therefore, people are called to support legal and political actions and those geared towards the media with the aim to disseminate information that is not to be found elsewhere and to provide assistance to those in local communities who defend themselves "against the dissolution of our state". The goal is to recruit one per cent of all Germans, 800,000, to sign up behind the initiative that has three general aims: to protect German borders against unlawful entry, to register and extradite all illegal immigrants and to protect the property of the people [*Volkseigentum*] and individuals. Moreover, 'Ein Prozent' demands to be included in discussions about the future of Germany and more forcefully: "Those responsible for the dissolution of the constitutional state and our natural order of life [*Lebensordnung*] have to resign".

'Ein Prozent' invites its readers to support the initiative financially through micro-donations, by spreading the word, engaging locally or by contributing with specific (professional) skills. These four building blocks clearly represent different levels of interactive engagement, ranging from micro-donations of a few Euros to contributing with voluntary work to the resistance movement. Particularly interesting to notice are the different options combining traditional offline and online approaches.

Between 2015 and 2019, 'Ein Prozent' ran a Facebook page and Instagram-account: *Ein Prozent für unser Land* and *@einprozentfuerunserland*, followed by 90,000. Following a lawsuit, these accounts were closed down in November 2019, resting on the assessment that *einprozent.de* is a 'hate organization' according to the German law NetzDG (also called the 'Facebook-law'). The case moved up to a higher level of German jurisdiction in 2020, where the legal decision was confirmed. The Twitter-account (@ein_prozent) has 2,800 tweets followed by almost 15,000. The YouTube channel *Einprozent-Film* has over 10,000 subscribers, around 60 videos, and almost 1.8 million views. Furthermore, the website *einprozent.de* itself also includes a blog with more than 769 posts which has explored a host of subjects and events since November 2015. Although these social media outlets clearly deserve close attention (all figures as of May 2020), the main focus of this chapter will be to showcase how online and offline activism reference and reinforce each other and the methods that can be used to study that relationship.

Studying the double dynamics of reality and virtuality

Example 1: 'Resistance map of Germany' – creating imagined spaces of resistance

In the summer of 2016, an 'Ein Prozent' newsletter (2016/23) announced the launch of an interactive map of IBD-activism in Germany in which is it stated that as the "first patriotic NGO", 'Ein Prozent' not only supports civil resistance financially, logistically and legally, but also by cross-linking. More than 50 groups had interlinked with each other and it was time to launch a "digital interface" (*digitale Schnittstelle*). The newsletter linked to the map itself and to a tutorial. No less than 130 groups (together with their statements of purpose) were listed on the map, mostly in Germany and Austria, and many of them related to the IBD. Some of the groups have other revealing names such as 'Reconquista', *Völkerfreunde*

('Friends of the People'), Patriotic or Courageous Citizens, Patriotic Departure, the 'Shield', *Heimatliebe* ('Love of the homeland'), Resistance, Awakening, Counter-culture, Pro Patria and so on. It is impossible to assess the real existence or the size of these groups and initiatives, but they generate the impression that continuous resistance is organized across the country. And only by offering services "can our civilian protest grow into a serious antagonist of the establishment". Furthermore, supporters of 'Ein Prozent' are (still of January 2019) asked to contribute with their specific competences and thus to sign-up to the resistance: "We are looking for independents, organizers, places of resistance, master mechanics [sic!], hotel owners, policemen, lawyers etc". An ambitious online-form was created where personal data can be submitted for a "register of supporters". It is obvious that computer and social media literacy are part of the resistance evoked.

In a video message (1'19", seen by a modest 5,263 people) screened on You-Tube, Philip Stein of 'Ein Prozent' presented the initiative of the interactive map of Germany (Ein Prozent Film, 'Patriotische Netzwerke: die interaktive Deutschlandkarte', 30 June 2016). Caring about the citizens that have decided to resort to civilian resistance and in the absence of a well-organized NGO, 'Ein Prozent' has taken upon itself to provide key areas of support. But the aim is also to cross-link citizens and citizen groups, which is why it was necessary to create a central contact point "to see where resistance is exercised in Germany" (0' 44"–48").

When accessing the map ('Ein Prozent', website) pulsating orange spots created the image of vivid activity across Germany with offshoots in Austria and even in Paris. Most of the around 120 groups (active in May 2017) can be counted to the IBD. As an example, clicking the spot 'Greifswald' brought the viewer to the Hanseatic city at the Baltic shore with a short presentation of the local group of IBD and a link to its website (www.identitaere-mv.de). It was also possible to announce actions and events, but as of May 2017 no activities had been located on the map. Other links brought the viewers to the 'Ein Prozent' website and in particular to the video-page. A series of five videos titled 'Widerstandsnester' ('Pockets of resistance') were released between December 2017 and January 2018, covering particular spots on the German map of resistance more extensively. It is unclear why the map was taken offline during 2018, but perhaps, as one supporter expressed in a comment to the video, there were concerns that it would facilitate the organization of counter-activism and the work of law enforcement. In another video, posted 5 April 2018 and viewed about 18,500 times, 'Ein Prozent' again highlighted its ambition to coordinate and network resistance across Germany.

On the whole, the resistance map of Germany visualized local activities IRL on a quite advanced digital platform and thus generated the impression of vigorous and ongoing activities, "the simulation of a continuous protest occurrence" between the street and its "virtual echo" online (Hentges et al., 2014: 14) trans-locally and nationally. Many of the local links provided access to a host of local activities and actions that follow similar narrative patterns. Online-medialization made offline-activism visible and created an image of united resistance across German space.

Example 2: 'Homeland in blind flight' – symbolic blindfolding of statues across Germany

In June 2016, 'Ein Prozent' announced that a nationwide action had been staged, 'Homeland in blind flight'; "a call to all Germans to think through thoroughly in which danger our country, our people and our culture find themselves today, when the readiness to protest continues to be dominated by 'looking away'" (Newsletter 2016/21). On the website, the wording was even more vitriolic: "Thus and by other means day by day a fog of denial of reality cloaks our country and our people. … Massively looking away facilitates the daily breaking of the law of the government Merkel. The blindfold is the symbol of this self-imposed blindness". In each city, 'Ein Prozent' explained further, statues of poets, musicians, monarchs or politicians as well as Justitia symbolized "tradition, law, achievements and German identity". The aim of the action was to put a blindfold on these symbolical figures in order to ask the rhetorical question "Blind into the nemesis?", a motto that also was attached to the monuments ('Ein Prozent', website). The action in Dresden was filmed and posted on the YouTube channel of 'Ein Prozent' (Ein Prozent Film, 'Heimat im Blindflug', 6 June 2016). It is a 1'13"clip viewed 6,900 times through YouTube and 26,000 through Facebook and representative of the dramaturgy of 'Ein Prozent' activism. In the first sequence (0' – 0'16") we can witness how the activists climb the statue of Martin Luther in Dresden and attach a blindfold. This is then followed by a relatively long sequence in which the vibrant street life of Dresden is portrayed (0'16" – 0'44"). In the third and final sequence, the activists occupy the space in front of the monument, raise a ladder, blindfold Luther and attach a signpost with the motto around his neck.

In a sense, 'Ein Prozent' activism directly hacks into the carnivalesque atmosphere in downtown Dresden with street performers (a piano player and a woman posing as a golden statue of a fairy) and tourists in front of the re-built Frauenkirche (as such a disputed symbol of the far-right memory-culture and legacy of the so-called 'Feuersturm', the allied elimination of Dresden in February 1945). In several takes of the video, it zooms into a banner on the Frauenkirche; it reads (in German and English) "Blessed are the peace-makers" (Matthew 5:9). The question is whether the 'Ein Prozent' slogan "Blind into the nemesis" can be interpreted as a commentary against Christianity, since the German far-right in general attacks the so-called 'do-gooders' (*Gutmenschen*), who pretend to be kind and of high moral standards but naively undermine the existence of Germany. Judging from the number of views, this particular event engaged only a handful of activists for a relatively short amount of time, but created its main outreach through social media, particularly Facebook.

Example 3: 'Cross against half-moon' – anti-Islam activism

Since about 2015, the (non-conformist) Muslim Ahmadiyya-movement has attempted to build a mosque in a suburb of the east German city of Erfurt.

Although the movement clearly does not represent any 'mainstream' Sunni or Shia forms of Islam and many members have escaped from persecution in their home countries, the projected construction of a mosque evoked massive protest and was exploited heavily in anti-Islam rhetoric. A protest group, "Citizens for Erfurt" was established, which on its vitriolic Facebook page has about 1,500 followers (Bürger für Erfurt, Facebook). "Citizens for Erfurt" are linked to a Russian email address, through which the platform anonymousnews.ru can be accessed, which in March 2017 ran a story dedicated to the protest, viewed 14,000 and disseminated 1,500 times. Anonymous News, posing as an offshoot of the true Anonymous-movement, has been revealed as a prolific far-right fake news provider with a host of anti-Semitic, revisionist and pro-Putinist content (Gensing, 2017).

'Ein Prozent' described on its website how the protest was carried forward through an alliance with the right-wing populist party AfD. The Erfurt city council was blamed for not respecting the will of its inhabitants and instead supporting the needs of a "religious community alien to our culture [*kulturfremd*], whose radical shape in Europe is responsible for continuing and horrible terror". The Ahmadiyya-movement was portrayed as a "wolf in sheep's clothing" secretly promoting Islamization and terrorism ('Ein Prozent', website). In this situation, 'Ein Prozent' could not accept that the "legitimate interest of the citizens of Erfurt for order and security is ignored" and therefore the movement supported "more than ever – civilian resistance". In December 2016, 'Ein Prozent' claimed that the city council secretly had given away a building area and consciously deceived the public: "The responsible ... will understand that the people don't accept back room agreements with the immigration lobby [*Einwanderungslobby*]". 'Ein Prozent' also bemoaned the low degree of responsiveness, no "critical mass" had been formed yet, no "masses have been mobilized yet". However, it was necessary to remain defiant in order to "obstruct the perverse plans of the immigration lobby" and to defend "the legitimate interests of the citizens" ('Ein Prozent', website). A protest action was also filmed and posted online (Ein Prozent-Film, 'Protestaktion', 5 December 2016).

In January 2017, a petition (with thousands of signatories) from the 'Citizens for Erfurt', "Regulation of religious and cultural conflicts and dangers with sacral buildings", was received and discussed in the state parliament of Thuringia. This is not the place to analyze how blatant anti-Islamism was cloaked in vocabulary such as that "in the case of expected conflicts, the security of the citizens has to be placed above the plans of immigrated parallel societies" or that the legitimate interests of "autochthonic citizens urgently have to be considered in future development plans" ('Ein Prozent', website). 'Ein Prozent' made clear that it was important that the petition was treated by the parliamentary committee (in which the establishment 'block parties' were in a majority, a term that refers to the fake-parties of the GDR that were completely subordinated to the ruling communist party) because of the disadvantages that were to be expected arising from the construction of the mosque: "worsened security, rising levels of criminal activity, emerging no-go-areas and growing parallel societies" ('Ein Prozent', website).

It is against this backdrop the activism of 'Ein Prozent' must be understood. In the morning hours of 4 March 2017, "numerous citizens erected a massive, 10-meter-tall wooden cross as a symbol of our endangered Occident [*Abendland*]" adjacent to the mosque building area (Ein Prozent, Newsletter 2017/7). Since all legal protest against the construction of the mosque had been unsuccessful, it was now time to concentrate on "civil disobedience" (Ein Prozent, website). Subsequently the cross was overthrown but raised again. An additional 4-meter-tall cross was also erected by inhabitants of the suburb. Finally, both crosses were demolished and removed by the city authorities. The 1'19" video "Protest against the mosque: residents erect a cross" was viewed about 15,000 times on YouTube (Ein Prozent Film, 'Moscheeprotest', 5 March 2017) and 82,000 times on Facebook. It shows a group of men collaborating in the work on constructing and erecting a huge wooden cross, accompanied by heroic music. As sociological studies have pointed out, formal religious affiliation among sympathizers of the right-wing movement of indignation PEGIDA is low (Vorländer et al., 2016: 53, 57, 61, 63, 138). To the contrary, at the rallies of the PEGIDA, Christian symbols have been displayed at numerous occasions in order to protest against the presumed 'Islamization' of the Occident (the term used is the same as in the 'Ein Prozent' newsletter above, *Abendland*). It appears as if the action of 'Ein Prozent' in Erfurt followed the same rhetorical pattern. The "simple wooden cross, … a symbol of our culture" was not raised as a token of a particularly strong commitment to Christianity (and its inclusive values), but as an anti-Islamic signpost ('Ein Prozent', website). This impression is deepened when reading the comment fields (and additional blog posts) on the 'Ein Prozent' website and on Facebook as well as Anonymous News, which suggest that Christianity is intrinsically intertwined with German or European identity, defined in irreconcilable opposition to the Muslim world.

'Ein Prozent' activism in this video is expressed through raw virile determination and masculine teamwork, materiality, craftsmanship and community. As the axe notches the massive wooden pole, chipped wood flies through the crispy morning air, pegs are hammered down, screws are tightened and ropes are attached; finally, a quasi-phallic anti-Muslim monument is erected through the happy collaboration of male muscles, a band of brothers has raised a symbolic cross of resistance. Ten people appear to have been involved in the IRL action that was staged in early March 2017. With a digital outreach of almost 100,000 views, the virtual multiplicative factor is 10,000 and is not limited to one spot and one particular point in time.

Taken together, the cases discussed in this section demonstrate how offline and online activism are fused and support each other in their rhetorical and narrative functions. On a more abstract level, the resistance map of Germany – as all maps throughout history – is a semiotic abstraction of geographical data themselves, in this case a map of the prevalence of groups and initiatives, social activism across space symbolically placed on a representation of Germany. But this abstraction allowed also for the establishment of direct and virtual contacts and thus assumes a function of a directory IRL.

In the case of 'Homeland in blind fight' it appears as if the hacking of Dresden street life IRL was enacted not primarily to influence real life, but rather to produce a short and snappy clickable clip geared towards the narrative logics of online media. As compared to traditional street action that possibly would have been interrupted by the authorities within minutes, the online format allowed for a digital afterlife and dissemination far beyond the rather limited circle of (obviously confused) eyewitnesses to the action (see Hentges et al., 2014: 9 and 11).

The same logic applies in principle to the Erfurt video. Direct action on the ground (the collective male marking of territory with a phallic symbol – comparable to the iconic image of raising the flag on Iwo Jima), which too predictably not would last, was staged primarily to generate a message for wider dissemination in social media. 'Ein Prozent' even admitted ('Ein Prozent', Newsletter 2017/7) that they were surprised that citizens had re-erected the first cross and raised yet another. With other words: to promote activism IRL was not the ultimate aim of the IRL action itself.

Unlocking the media strategy of 'Ein Prozent' as a hypermedial multiplatform

'Ein Prozent' together with its social media offshoots (Facebook, Twitter, You-Tube) creates a hypermedial multiplatform where offline and online activism mutually enforce each other, assisting to magnify the distribution and outreach of its general message: the existential duty of 'patriotic' resistance against governmental politics (mainly in the area of immigration), against the elites of and media and politics combined with activism for the promotion of protectionism, nativist rights and security and the exclusive right of agenda-setting for the future. Blatant xenophobia in general and anti-Islamism in particular are cloaked in low-key creative activism and media messages focused on the ordinary citizen and his (distinctly male) concerns. Through the launch of 'Ein Prozent', an official channel is created that pools and produces messages of disparate activism along the entire German IBD spectrum, from 'concerned' citizen's groups to the more radical identitarian wing. As compared to shaky DIY-videos of PEGIDA-rallies randomly posted on Facebook, 'Ein Prozent' clearly works with visual scripts and an aesthetic concept. 'Ein Prozent' has managed to receive a remarkable outreach among its audience: to sympathizers, unaligned population, the media and ideological adversaries alike. By constantly repeating the image that the activism promoted constitutes 'resistance' and 'civil courage', audiences can feel as participants in and identify with the ongoing struggle against the allegedly oppressive state of affairs in Germany. Any form of participation is encouraged, from contributing a few Euros for a general or specific cause to placing yourself on the map of or even enrolling in the resistance movement. Thus, the media and what is mediatized are a tool and symbol of resistance as such; as a consequence, the border between real actions and simulacra (in the sense of Baudrillard) is blurred.

The multiplatform approach magnifies the multitude of links from where videos and other material can be downloaded, either you arrive at them from the newsletter to the website or through Facebook and Twitter and finally to the YouTube channel. It is obvious that some form of hijacking takes place, for instance that 'Ein Prozent' hacks into already prominent cases such as the case of Daniel H. in Chemnitz, the UN Migration Pact and more recently the 'Gilets Jaunes' protests in France. The news stories of 'Ein Prozent' convey an aura of citizen journalism and MOJO from below that is continuously opposed to the sanctioned 'system media' from above, thus cementing populist elite and media critique of the 'Liar press'. According to Hentges *et al.* the new media environment is crowded with 'ideological prosumers', a blend of consumers and producers who at the same time create and consume media content in order to generate media savvy affinity with right-wing ideas primarily among young consumers (2014: 10–11).

Ein Prozent's spin techniques and news cycles have become more refined over time; for instance, as demonstrated in the case of the protest against the construction of a mosque in Erfurt. 'Ein Prozent' persistently exploits the image that Germany is under attack from inside (staged by corrupt elites) and outside (through an orchestrated refugee 'deluge'). Against this, 'resistance' is evoked as a legitimate idea to promote political change.

Research into far-right hypermedia environments: Methodological conclusions

The production of media content within far-right hypermedia environments is embedded within the semiotic logic of hypermediality itself. To produce meaning, impact and dissemination demands particular strategic choices of communication. The short activist video clips analyzed in this chapter demonstrate how symbolic meaning is condensed into a visual plot combining text, image and sound. To decode their meaning implies to deconstruct these inter-medial building blocks. A second step is to analyze their hybridity, since whatever is staged IRL is primarily intended for dissemination and impact online. To engage with these dimensions requires study of the media environments (for instance social media platforms) within which they are disseminated and specifically take the specific conditions of their hypermedial setting into account. Last but not least, the short activist video clips convey variations of a greater strategic political narrative within which they are embedded (in the case of einprozent.de that of Germany's imminent breakdown and the necessity of organized far-right resistance). This interrelationship between the individual media product and the larger frame narrative deserves particular attention.

The far-right has been successful in capitalizing on the formation of a political ontology in which online presence is the key to reach, shape and sustain audiences and provide them with ideological messages, multiple offers of identification, community-formation and mobilization. If people understand the world through that political reality is expressed virtually, the logical consequence for far-right metapolitics is to conquer the virtual realm and to create hybrid-forms of activism online and IRL which reinforce each other. To research this political ontology does not imply to embrace it, but to engage with its epistemological foundations.

The first productive methodological approach is to understand the fabric of hypermedia environments as such. Their liquid, fractal, rhizomic, non-linear and inter-medial design poses a particular challenge to researchers who are used to conventional methods in researching 'solid' textual sources either diachronically or synchronically. Multiple medializations, hyperlinks, interactivity, and multiple platforms blur precise conceptualizations of time and space or of authorship and readership through the creation of the 'prosumer', who both is co-producer and consumer. The second approach following from studying hypermediality is to grasp the autotelic and self-referential nature of the sources studied: UGC- and MOJO-style content, content mimicking forms of conventional communication (such as quasi-documentaries) as well as content adapted to digital-born modes of expression (such as GIF:s, memes, pic-badges or QR-codes) are produced with the primary purpose to promote hypermedial meaning-making as such. Virality turns into the key component of strategic communication and marketing of the ideological message within an almost sealed sphere of information ('echo chambers'), contributing to the polarization of the public sphere and erosion of the authority of traditional knowledge-producing institutions. As illustrated by the examples from 'Ein Prozent', activism is staged IRL with the primary purpose of online dissemination, where outreach is multiplied potentially infinitely. A third approach is to acknowledge that a virtual political ontology impacts upon socialization patterns and social identification online and offline and that traditional modes of studying social activism need to be expanded to include the interplay between these levels. Community can be created online locally as much as trans-locally (and on a pan-European, even global level) around certain hot issues of the far-right (migration, 'cultural Marxism', 'femo-Nazism', postmodernism etc.), but as the establishment of IBD, PEGIDA or the Chemnitz riots of autumn 2018 forcefully demonstrate, online forms of socialization can also be powerfully translated into offline forms of traditional street mobilization and furthermore heavily influence electoral behaviour. Studying the emblematic hybrid media narratives of einprozent.de (and more broadly, the Identitarian movement) illuminates this relationship on the interface between online and offline activism.

References

Bar-On, T. 2013. *Rethinking the French New Right*. London: Routledge.

Bar-On, T. 2001. "The ambiguities of the *Nouvelle Droite*, 1968–1999". *The European Legacy*, 6(3), 333–351.

Bauman, Z. 2017. *Retrotopia*. London: Polity.

Dahl, G. 2018. *Folk och Identitet: Identitarismen och dess källor*. Korpen: Stockholm.

Falkheimer, J. 2013. "Terrorism, medier och propaganda." In *Vetenskapssocieten i Lund – Årsbok 2013*. Vetenskapssocieten: Lund.

Gensing, P. 2017. "Anonym hetzen via Russland." *Tagesschau*, 15 November 2017. fakten finder.tagesschau.de/inland/anonymous-russland-101.html (accessed 13 March 2019).

Hentges, G., G. Kökgiran, and K. Nottbohm. 2014. "Die Identitäre Bewegung Deutschland (IBD)—Bewegung oder virtuelles Phänomen?" *Forschungsjournal Soziale Bewegungen*, 27(3), S1–26.

Hock, A. and J. Lindenau. 2018. "Roboter mobilisieren gegen den Migrationspakt." *Die Welt*, 10 December.

Kozinets, R. 2010. *Netnography: Doing Ethnographic Research Online*. London: Sage.

Krona, M. 2017. "ISIS schools and indoctrination of children." 30 April. http://michaelkrona.com (accessed 12 March 2019).

Madisson, M.-L. 2016. *The Semiotic Construction of Identities in Hypermedia Environments: The Analysis of Online Communication of the Estonian Extreme Right*. Tartu: Tartu University.

Önnerfors, A. 2018. "Moving the mainstream radicalization of political language in the German PEGIDA movement." In *Expressions of Radicalization: Global Politics, Processes and Practices*, edited by A. Önnerfors and K. Steiner. London: Palgrave.

Önnerfors, A. 2019. "Performing 'the people'? The populist style of politics in the German PEGIDA-movement." In *Imagining the Peoples of Europe*, edited by R. Breeze and J. Zienkowski. Amsterdam: John Benjamins.

Önnerfors, A. 2020. "'Retrotopia' as a progressive force in the German PEGIDA-movement." In *Nostalgia and Hope at the Intersections of Welfare and Culture*, edited by O.C. Norocel, A. Hellström, and M.B. Jørgensen. Springer: London.

Salzborn, S. 2016. "Renaissance of the New Right in Germany? A discussion of New Right elements in German right-wing extremism today." *German Politics and Society*, 119(34), 36–63.

Scharloth, J. 2017. "Ist die AfD eine populistische Partei? – Eine Analyse am Beispiel des Landesverbands Rheinland-Pfalz." *Aptum*, 2, 1–13.

Šlerka, J. and V. Šisler. 2018. "Who is shaping your agenda? Social network analysis of anti-Islam and anti-immigration movement audiences on Czech Facebook." In *Expressions of Radicalization: Global Politics, Processes and Performances*, edited by A. Önnerfors and K. Steiner. Palgrave: London.

Thielemann, N. 2016. "Patriotyzm genetyczny, półka kulturowa and Palikotyzacja X-a –blends as catchwords in Polish political discourse." *Zeitschrift für Slawistik*, 61(1), 74–101.

Verfassungsschutz2013. "Right-wing extremists and their internet presence", *Bundesamt für Verfassungsschutz*. https://www.verfassungsschutz.de/embed/publication-2013-08-right-wing-extremists-and-their-internet-presence.pdf (accessed 22 May 2018).

Vorländer, H., M. Herold, and S. Schäller. 2018. *Pegida and Right-Wing Populism in Germany*. London: Palgrave.

Vorländer, H., M. Herold, and S. Schäller. 2016. *PEGIDA: Entwicklung, Zusammensetzung und Deutung einer Empörungsbewegung*. Berlin: Springer.

Wahlrecht. N.D. Results of the federal election. http://www.wahlrecht.de/ergebnisse/bundestag.htm (accessed 22 May 2018).

Wodak, R. 2015. *The Politics of Fear: What Right-Wing Populist Discourses Mean*. London: SAGE.

Wodak, R. 2009. "The semiotics of racism: A critical discourse-historical analysis." In *Discourse, of Course. An Overview of Research in Discourse Studies*, edited by J. Renkema. Amsterdam: John Benjamins.

Zúquete, J.P. 2018. *The Identitarians: The Movement Against Globalism and Islam in Europe*. NDP: Notre Dame.

Online sources

Ein Prozent für unser Land. September 2015. @einprozentfuerunserland Facebook. https://www.facebook.com/pg/einprozentfuerunserland/about/ (accessed 1 June 2017).

Bürger für Erfurt. No date. @buergerfuererfurt Facebook. https://www.facebook.com/buergerfuererfurt/ (accessed 1 June 2017).

References to the You Tube channel Ein Prozent Film. 7 November 2015. Youtube. https://www.youtube.com/channel/UCDVMut6Xd5duYCxBHHwwJTA (accessed 1 June 2017):

'Patriotische Netzwerke.' 30 June 2016. https://youtu.be/Jmh7Tj-3WX8 (accessed 1 June 2017).

'Heimat im Blindflug.' 6 June 2016. https://youtu.be/SsxHKDA46hc (accessed 1 June 2017).

'Protestaktion zum Moscheebau in Erfurt.' 5 December 2016. https://youtu.be/G_PFnd0J5_I (accessed 1 June 2017).

PART III

Interviewing the far right

12

METHODOLOGY MATTERS

Researching the far right

Amy Fisher Smith, Charles R. Sullivan, John D. Macready and Geoffrey Manzi

While participant interviews – either with active or former members of extremist far right groups – are generally highly valued within this research context as they provide a first-hand account of terrorist activities and processes both at the individual and organizational level, there have been few explicit discussions of the procedures of method utilized in the research (Harris, Simi, and Ligon, 2016). In our view, the general tenor of methodology in extremist far right studies (and indeed in terrorist studies in general) is more opaque than transparent.

This methodological opacity is problematic for several reasons. First, while the tools of qualitative methodology are often utilized in far right extremist studies, rarely are the particular qualitative approaches or orientations identified in an explicit way. Qualitative methodologies are diverse and complex, and the multiplicity of qualitative practices have different epistemological, ontological, and ideological pre-investigatory assumptions, all of which impact the researcher's interpretive stance toward the data and even the findings (Gergen, 2014). Additionally, different methods lead to different practical applications, given their epistemological commitments. Hence, it is imperative that such methodological approaches and procedures be made explicit especially because, in some cases, researchers in terrorism studies seem to be conflating quantitative methodological standards of prediction and control in research designs that incorporate epistemologically incompatible qualitative methodologies. Second, the lack of methodological clarity may sabotage efforts to advance reliable and valid research results. When the procedures or steps of data analysis are not described, other researchers in the field are ill-equipped to critique the current research and are unable to replicate the methods in order to advance the field.

This chapter outlines the methodological limitations that currently characterize some of the research in far right extremism. We also examine our own research methodology, thematic analysis (Braun and Clarke, 2006), which has its roots in the social sciences and psychology. After examining the epistemological and onto-logical assumptions of this method and how we utilize it in our research with "formers," we explore the tensions between the inescapable values of the researcher and their impact on the research findings and knowledge claims, the role of the research participant as a source of interpretive authority, and the ethical dilemmas that this creates for the research at large.

As scholarly interest in terrorism has grown, there has been a concomitant increase in the attention paid to research methodology. Indeed, several recent reviews of terrorism research and extremist literature concluded that terrorism research "lags behind" other disciplines with respect to data analysis and "sophisti-cated research methods" (Freilich and LaFree, 2016: 569; see also Feddes and Gallucci, 2015). Indeed, in what has become an often-cited statistic, Lum, Ken-nedy, and Sherley (2006: 492) described the bulk of terrorism research as "thought pieces, theoretical discussions, or opinions," with only 3–4 per cent of studies reviewed utilizing empirical analysis of data.[1] In another significant review, Silke (2001) suggested that in those studies which identified interviews as part of their methodology, interviews with actual terrorists contributed relatively little to the overall research, and in a large scale systematic review of 114 studies of disengage-ment from violent extremist groups – the bulk of which utilized qualitative methods – the reviewers noted methodological lapses such as the failure to report demographics and sampling methods (Windisch, Simi, Ligon, and McNeel, 2017). These challenges have encouraged more rigorous methodological reporting and publishing practices in terrorism research generally (Harris, Simi, and Ligon, 2016).

Of course, the recent attention to methodology may represent the literature's state of development. For instance, some scholars view terrorism research in general as "pre-theoretic" and "pre-paradigmatic," given its recent emergence as a field of inquiry (Bjørgo, 2009; Horgan, 2009). Research in far right extremism (FRE) may be similar. In the brief history of the literature on FRE, researchers have used a wide variety of methods – including case study, participant interviews, participant observation, government and police indexes, and analysis of archival material including newspaper stories or other media reports, legal documents, websites and other open source materials including terrorism event, offender, and organizational databases – with many of the more respected empirical studies utilizing some combination of these approaches. While the statistical analysis of both official government sources and open source materials has its own methodological limita-tions (cf., Freilich and LaFree, 2016), our concern in this chapter is primarily par-ticipant interviews as a source of empirical data in FRE research.

The problem, as the recent reviews of the literature suggest, is that, while par-ticipant interviews and other kinds of fieldwork or participant observation are highly valued, relatively few studies are conducting interviews with extremists, and among those studies that are using interviews as part of their methodology, few pay careful attention to what Harris, Simi, and Ligon (2016) describe as methodological transparency and consistency. That is, they tend to neglect specifying methodolo-gical procedures and standardized reporting practices. Additionally, scholars who conduct research with extremists must grapple with conceptual issues such as lack of agreement regarding how terrorism is defined, as well as the complexities that accompany a multidisciplinary approach including lack of methodological coherency across disciplines (Dalgaard-Nielsen, 2010; Harris, Simi, and Ligon, 2016; Horgan, 2011; Windisch, Simi, Ligon, and McNeel, 2017).

But, methodology matters. Accordingly, the goals of this chapter are twofold. First, we examine how this requirement for methodological transparency and consistency applies to research in FRE, particularly research that incorporates interviews with extremists. How can such research in FRE better clarify its methods and the methodological procedures utilized? We think that part of the answer resides in making more refined distinctions between the qualitative and quantitative research traditions. Second, we will examine our own research with former far right extremists using a particular qualitative method – thematic analysis (Braun and Clarke, 2006) – that meets the methodological demands of transparency and consistency. We also use this qualitative approach to explore some commonly discussed problems in the literature when conducting interviews with research participants. These problems include how the procedures for textual analysis address researcher bias, the role of researcher reflexivity, and implications for interpretive validity.

The case for methodological transparency

While recent critiques of methodology in FRE and terrorism research recognize the importance of interviewing, there continues to be some persistent confusion regarding what constitutes the qualitative research interview. Some contemporary reviewers have questioned what might be described as over-reliance on interview or self-report data and under-reliance on statistical methods (Feddes and Gallucci, 2015; Freilich and LaFree, 2016). Other methodological critiques view the interview and its place within terrorism research more positively and attempt to flesh out the interview as a valuable and rigorous data collection tool (Horgan, 2009).

What is a qualitative research interview?

From our perspective, it is helpful to differentiate between qualitatively driven forms of research interviewing and quantitatively driven forms of interviewing. In the former, the purpose of the interview is to elicit concrete descriptions of the research participant's lived experience with the goal of holistic understanding rather than analytic explanation (Josselson, 2013; Polkinghorne, 1989). In the latter, as in standardized survey interviewing, the structure and form of the question and response is pre-determined from the outset, with the goal of quantifying the research participant's response. While this quantification allows for statistical analysis, it does not allow for "meanings and interpretive frames" that might exist outside of the pre-determined structure itself to emerge (Brinkmann, 2018: 578).

Most qualitative research interviewing is unstructured or semi-structured, allowing research participants to describe their experience in their own terms. It is important to keep in mind that qualitative research interviewing is not conversation, which often lacks a strategic aim, nor is it journalism, which is typically not methodological or scientific. In the most rigorous sense, qualitatively driven interviews are conducted within the rubric of a qualitative research method that predetermines how textual analysis will be undertaken and qualitative results derived (whether those results be thematic analysis, grounded theory, narrative analysis, or phenomenological analysis to name a few). The point is that method is particularly salient with respect to interviewing, because method drives how the interview text is analyzed and differentiates it as a scientific procedure. This is why, in their recent review, Harris, Simi, and Ligon (2016) propose guidelines for reporting findings when interviewing current and former extremists which include explicit articulation of the sampling method, interview design, and procedures for data analysis.

Are we conflating quantitative and qualitative methodological standards?

While we support the proposed guidelines offered by Harris, Simi, and Ligon (2016) and view methodological transparency as a cornerstone of good scientific practice, we also believe that the conversation regarding method and methodological clarity often suffers from a fundamental conflation of standards that ultimately results in a kind of asymmetry between the approaches. For instance, when quantitative and qualitative differences in approach are recognized in research with extremists, the standards of one approach may be inappropriately applied to the other. Specifically, qualitative approaches are assessed either explicitly or tacitly by quantitative standards of validity and reliability. The result is that the potential contribution of qualitative studies to terrorism and FRE research tends to be diminished.

An example of this problem may be found in a special issue on measurement in the journal *Studies in Conflict and Terrorism*. Here Freilich and LaFree (2016: 572) recognize interviewing, particularly the flexibility and adaptability of this technique. However, the authors (following Silke, 2001) also note various limitations of the "method" including "interviewer bias, generalizability, opportunity sampling, and interviewer effects". Freilich and LaFree (2016) point to criminologists who collect such "self-report" data using both qualitative and quantitative methods, and they emphasize that the field of criminology has responded to the methodological challenges cited above in innovative ways, while terrorism researchers have not. The problem, in our view, is that Freilich and LaFree's (2016) assumptions about interviewing appear to be grounded in the standards of quantitative methodology exclusively. This is why the authors emphasize the "limitations" of "interviewer bias" and "interviewer effects." Only from a quantitative perspective that privileges objectivism and neutrality would the interviewer's potential impact on the data (i. e., "bias" and "effects") be construed as a limitation or a factor that should be mitigated and controlled methodologically. Indeed, such impacts are construed very differently from a qualitative perspective.

In the case of Freilich and LaFree (2016), then, there is a conflation of methodological standards, with the conventions of one approach being applied to the conventions of another. In other instances, there seems to be a clear preference for quantitative over qualitative approaches (rather than a conflation per se), as in the call for evidence-based research in terrorism studies which tends to emphasize quantitative approaches as a gold standard (see, for instance, Feddes and Gallucci, 2015). We view these general strategies as common ones, and as strategies that fail to recognize the important differences between the two methodological orientations.

The differences between quantitative and qualitative methods mean that standards for sample selection, reliability, and validity are different and often inappropriate when applied outside of their own methodological context. For instance, (quantitative) random sampling techniques are typically considered inappropriate for qualitative studies (Morse, 2018; Polkinghorne, 1989). While there are multiple reasons for this, Marshall (1996: 523) argues that "there is no evidence that the values, beliefs, and attitudes that form the core of qualitative investigation are normally distributed, making the probability approach inappropriate". For this reason, alternative types of sampling techniques, such as purposive or convenience sampling, are used in qualitative methods (Polkinghorne, 1989).

In qualitative research, sample size is typically defined by concerns regarding saturation rather than representation (Denzin and Lincoln, 2018). Hence, the questions that ultimately govern sample size in qualitative research focus more on whether the appropriate research participants have been selected and queried – that is – participants who are best suited and able to provide rich descriptions in relation to the research question being investigated. Saturation does not necessarily reflect the number of participants, but rather the quality of participants and how fully they describe the experience or phenomenon under investigation. In some ways, the validity or "trustworthiness" of qualitative results "may not come from conducting a comprehensive mapping of variation within the *population*, but rather from selecting experiences that map the variation within a *phenomenon*" (Levitt, Motulsky, Wertz, Morrow, and Ponterotto, 2017: 12, original emphasis). We address the problem of validity, particularly from a qualitative research perspective and how this differs from the way validity is conceptualized in quantitative contexts, in a later section.

While quantitative and qualitative approaches can be complementary (e.g., consider the increasing interest in mixed method approaches), the epistemological grounds and aims of the two approaches are divergent. This divergence is why it is inappropriate to apply the standards of one approach to the standards of the other. In highlighting the differences between the two, our aim is not to privilege one over the other, but rather to elaborate the parameters of a qualitative approach since it appears to be the less transparently practiced of the two approaches. To be clear, we support methodological pluralism. In maintaining an openness to both quantitative and qualitative methodological approaches, researchers are equipped with more tools to extract a fuller and deeper account of the research phenomenon under investigation and research validity increases (Creswell and Plano Clark,

2011). This fuller and deeper account through *plural methods* is why we view an exclusive preference for quantitative approaches in evidence-based research as problematic (for a broader view of evidence-based practices in terrorism research that also values methodological pluralism, see Lum and Kennedy, 2012).

Focusing on method: A thematic analysis with former far right extremists

There are several established qualitative orientations in the social sciences including phenomenology, discourse analysis, narrative study, autoethnography, and action research (Gergen, 2014). In our own research on the processes of disengagement and deradicalization among far right extremists, we have adopted Virginia Braun and Victoria Clarke's (2006) qualitative thematic analysis (TA), which in general falls under narrative study. TA grew out of the behavioral sciences, but Braun and Clarke (2006) elaborated and refined TA as a rigorous, six-phase, procedural approach for analyzing narrative data. To date, our research group has conducted nine semi-structured interviews with individuals formerly affiliated with white supremacist organizations. We have conducted face-to-face interviews, either in person, or by video link, and our participants include two women, seven men, and both European and North American subjects ranging in age from mid-30s to mid-50s. The periods during which our participants were active in extremist movements varied, but collectively included the span of time ranging from the late 1980s through the early 2000s. The in-depth interviews were variable in duration, lasting between 45 minutes and 120 minutes.

In order to prepare for the in-depth interviews, our group developed 11 semi-structured interview questions which served to guide the interviews with participants (see Table 12.1). Our understanding of the processes of disengagement and deradicalization was informed by the existing literature, and we have remained theoretically sensitive to these understandings throughout the data collection and analysis. Disengagement is typically defined as a change in a role or function of an individual in a violent extremist group, whereas deradicalization is defined as the process of reducing cognitive, affective, and behavioral commitments to extremist ideology and violent activity (Horgan, 2009). We valued the semi-structured interview format, because it allowed us both to guide the interview process and to query our participants according to our research questions. The interview format also allowed our participants to shape the process as well, since we were open to where the dialogue might take us. Hence, we viewed the semi-structured format as a collaborative process.[2]

In order to recruit appropriate participants, we used convenience and snowball sampling techniques. All of the interviews except one were conducted by the lead researcher and another member of our research team. Circumstances dictated that one of the interviews be conducted by a single member of our team rather than the usual dyad. Our success in recruiting appropriate research participants was facilitated by one of the members of our research team, who had already made contact with a high profile "former" extremist. This "former" had made a public

TABLE 12.1 A listing of semi-structured research questions used in our qualitative study with former far right extremists regarding the processes of disengagement and deradicalization

1. Describe your **first encounter** with members of the organization that you joined.

2. What were the **immediate benefits** of joining the organization? (How were these benefits important to you?)

3. Can you tell me about your **family?** (Characterize your home-life? Your relationship with your siblings? Relationship with parents? **Religiosity? Community?**)

4. Did you experience any **conflict with** the beliefs or values of the **organization** when you joined? If so, how did you overcome it?

5. What were the **reasons** that led you to leave the organization? How long did it take for you to **leave**; how did that process unfold?

6. Describe your **feelings** after you left.

7. Once you left the organization, how did your beliefs and **values change** over time?

8. Are you **still in contact** with members of the organization? Have you helped others leave the organization and how is that significant or meaningful for you?

9. Have you formed **new relationships** outside of the organization?

10. Do you **fear reprisals** from members of the organization?

11. Did leaving the organization give you a **different perspective** on issues (e.g., life, relationships, jobs, skills, others)?

exit from an extremist group primarily through the media. Our group member's contact with this high profile "former" served as legitimation for our group, and by way of snowballing techniques and introduction to other "former extremists" through this initial gatekeeper, our group established connections to other potential participants. The research is on-going.[3] In conducting in-depth interviews and in adopting the method of TA, our aim is to prioritize the experiences and meanings of the FRE-participants, but also to locate those experiences within the broader socio-historical and cultural context.

What is thematic analysis (TA)?

TA is a method for "identifying, analyzing, and reporting patterns (themes) within data" (Braun and Clarke, 2006: 79). The approach is inductive: codes and then themes emerge from an intensive engagement with the textual data. We tend to take a "semantic" approach to theme identification, in which themes are identified based on explicit meanings – that is, paying close attention to what the participant has actually said. However, we are also influenced by the phenomenological approach in qualitative research, which assumes that all participants co-constitute phenomena or experience. In our work, these assumptions suggest that we are not only attuned to explicit meanings in the participant's narrative, but also contradictions and reversals within the narrative that are often outside the participant's awareness. This kind of research attunement results in what Braun and Clarke (2006) describe as latent theme analysis.

The steps of TA include, first, familiarizing oneself with the data (this includes the transcribed interview texts) [4] Familiarizing oneself with the data is more than an intellectualized activity, but rather requires what Churchill, Lowery, McNally, and Rao (1998: 65) describe as "empathic dwelling" in which the "researcher enters into direct, personal contact with the psychological event being studied". Churchill et al. (1998: 66) argue that a researcher's job at this point in the analysis is to literally feel one's way into the other's experience. Hence, our job as researchers is not to dispute the participant's narrative against external "facts," but to understand it in its own terms.

For instance, a male participant in our sample described what our research group thematically analyzed later as a "catalytic moment," or tipping point for disengagement from the FRE group. The participant noted that the catalytic moment occurred when he was confronted by an African-American shopper in a grocery store, and the participant's child pointed to the shopper and identified the shopper by a racial slur. He stated,

> But my son was in the grocery store with me, and I was walking down the cookie aisle or something, and he saw, uh, a black guy. And he says, "Look, daddy, there's a big, black—" and he blurted out the 'N' word. No big deal, you know? He did it at home all the time, and that's what he was taught; he didn't know the difference between right and wrong. And people shamed me an—and told me how horrible a father I was and this sort of stuff. And I was used to that, you know? I—I'm pretty sure that it had happened prior to that, and I'm pretty sure [sic] probably happened afterwards as well, but, that day, I was receptive.

In the beginning stages of TA, our purpose is not to dispute the participant's narrative nor to explain it with reference to theory, but to empathically enter the participant's experience. For this participant, the occasion for disengagement arose when he experienced a catalyzing moment of parental shame. It is in this moment of "receptivity" that the participant focuses his awareness not only on his growing sense of shame as a potentially failed parent, but also on his increasing disillusionment with what he perceives as the extremist group's contradictions and inconsistencies. It is in the catalytic moment that the participant's lived dissonances at both the ideological and personal level come to a head. For instance, in the larger interview text, the same participant referenced his employment history and explained how he could not escape the dawning realization that people of color were as proficient as whites. At the same time, he expressed disappointment that "quantity" rather than "quality" was being emphasized in extremist group recruitment. In the participant's view, the extremist group was recruiting "dirtbags" and "dopers," rather than focusing on "saving the white race." These dissonances coalesce and converge onto the catalytic moment of parental shame, reorienting the participant toward disengagement and evocations of uncertainty and disillusionment toward the group.

The second step of TA requires a coding process. In our research group, we meet weekly to examine the interview transcripts and to code features of the data that stand out as meaningful. Codes are typically the "most basic segment, or element of the raw data ... that can be assessed in a meaningful way" (Braun and Clarke, 2006: 88). Codes form the basis of broader themes or repeated patterns in the larger data set. In our group, we code data items manually, by creating an electronic document with tabled columns for the coded extract, the extract (or chunk of textual data), and the code itself (see Table 12.2).

Coding, in our research group, is a collective process in which we discuss potential interpretive meanings together. There is always the challenge when coding, identifying extracts, and assigning themes of losing the context and therefore part of the situated meaning of the narrative itself. We are sensitive to this potential problem and we are committed to the phenomenological approach precisely because it helps focus the analysis on meanings (Wertz, Charmaz, McMullen, Josselson, Anderson, and McSpadden, 2011).

TABLE 12.2 Organization of coding/data set

Interview text 1: Extracts	Coding
P: the quality: <u>it went from being quality to quantity</u>... uh, for—as far as skinheads were concerned, it was like 'Oh, we need more people. We need more people.' An—an—an— I.2: It didn't matter— P: ... and— I.2: ... about the quality of the person; what mattered was— P: ... an—and they were— I.2: numbers.	Step 2: Initial codes 1. Lived dissonance 2. Disillusionment with the membership 3. Disillusionment with the ideology
P: ... <u>and they were dirtbags</u>. I.2: Yeah. P: <u>They were dopers</u>. They were— I.2: And that wasn't consistent with the thinking that— P: ... Right— I.2: [Name withheld] had— P: ... right, and when I first got— I.2: ... instilled in you initially.	More dissonance; growing dissatisfaction with the inconsistencies within the ideology and greater distance between the ideals of the ideology and the lived experience of the membership.
P: ... yeah. When I first got involved, it was, you know, 'We're gonna save the white race, and it's political, and it's,' you know, 'W—<u>we must secure the existence of our people and a future for white children, and—and it's a honorable thing, and you must conduct yourself in an honorable way</u>.'	Step 4: Review potential themes **Two levels of disillusionment: first disillusionment and disappointment with the membership and their failure to meet the ideals of the ideology; and second, disillusionment with the ideology itself.** **The two levels reinforce one another.**

In the third step of analysis, codes from all the interviews are collated, sorted, and analyzed into broader themes. During the fourth step of analysis, potential themes are reviewed and refined. Some themes may emerge as unwieldy and require further parsing. Other themes may upon examination collapse into one another. Yet other themes may require reworking to better capture the common features of the corresponding codes. In our research group, the process of coding, identifying themes, and reviewing themes is a recursive process, which requires constant movement from the part to the whole and back again. As themes are reviewed and refined, a broader picture of how the themes relate to each other as a whole begins to appear. The fifth step of TA includes organizing themes into an internally consistent account, indicating how each theme coheres with other themes, and identifying an overall narrative. Throughout these final phases of textual analysis and theme development, Braun and Clarke (2006) advocate use of a thematic map as a visual representation of the emergent themes. In our research group, such thematic maps are useful as they pictorially represent the recursive, embedded, and simultaneous relationship among themes of disengagement and de-radicalization among far right extremists (see Figure 12.1 for a preliminary thematic map as it relates to our on-going research and analysis). The final and sixth step requires full articulation of the analysis, which must provide "sufficient evidence of the themes within the data" (Braun and Clarke, 2006, p. 93).

The role of researcher reflexivity and the importance of preconceptions

There are four of us in our research group, and so from time to time, we find ourselves at odds regarding the meanings at stake in the interview text. Discrepancies in interpretation became particularly relevant during our analysis of an interview transcript of another of our research participants and his description of the "catalytic moment" described earlier. Recall that in our thematic analysis, the "catalytic moment" is the tipping point for disengagement from the far right extremist group. It is during this "moment" that the participant's background disillusionments with the extremist group become foregrounded, opening fissures in the participant's group-based identity. It is also at this point that the participant consciously employs disengagement and actively stops participating in his or her role in the group. This is a precarious period for the participant, as he or she typically described intense psychological vulnerability.

In the narrative that our group had difficulty interpreting, the participant described a catalytic moment that occurred after he was forced to confront his stepfather's terminal illness and death, as well as the murder of a close friend who had also allegedly been involved in extremist organizations. Both deaths occurred within weeks of each other, leaving the participant feeling emotionally distraught and disoriented, but also resolved to leave the extremist organization. He stated,

> Yeah. Lost, uh, two of the best people I've ever known within two weeks of each other, and then their funerals were within two weeks of each other. [pauses] Yup … Yeah, um, I had—I always knew my stepdad wanted me out of it. Um, and I kinda [sic] told him I was workin' [sic] my way out—and I was done.

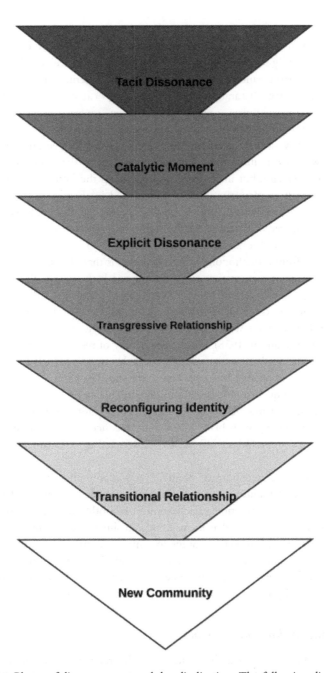

FIGURE 12.1 Phases of disengagement and deradicalization. The following diagram is the thematic map which has emerged in our research group's on-going thematic analysis of the processes of disengagement and deradicalization among former far right extremists. In the current chapter we have only discussed emergent themes regarding the Catalytic Moment.

Struggling to integrate his emotional loss in addition to the challenges of transi-
tioning away from the group, the participant decided to commit suicide. However,
his plan was abruptly stopped by "a little kitten sittin' [sic] there" on the steps to his
home. For the participant, the kitten saved him by offering him another life to
rescue. He elaborated, "I can't kill myself and let this cat starve. I can't let this cat
just die."

As we analyzed this extract, each member of our group gave it a different
interpretation. Several of our research members viewed the narrative, particularly
the kitten, with a certain degree of tentativeness, not in the sense of challenging
the narrative's veracity, but in terms of understanding the kitten as a symbolic foil
for the participant to maintain a self-view couched in themes of self-aggrandize-
ment and hyper-masculinity. One research member did not view the narrative
with the same degree of tentativeness, but rather interpreted the kitten narrative in
light of the participant's capacity for care.

The upshot, from a methodological perspective, is that *all* researchers – whether
using a qualitative or quantitative method – approach the data with their own set
of preconceptions, values, and beliefs, all of which invariably influence how the
research question is taken up (with respect to the data) and how the data are
interpreted. This is often why there are in principle multiple possible interpretations of the data (Hanson, 1958). This inescapability of researcher influence is often
referred to in the qualitative literature as researcher reflexivity. This suggests that
objectivity or a perspective-less perspective on the data is impossible, and even
undesirable from a qualitative orientation. Hence, qualitative researchers are not as
interested in minimizing bias, values, and preconceptions as much as they are
interested in identifying such bias, values, and preconceptions, because such biases
(preconceptions or prejudgments) *enable* understanding (Gadamer,1975; Levitt
et al., 2017).

The idea that preconceptions or prejudgments enable understanding comes out
of the hermeneutic tradition and the philosophy of Hans-Georg Gadamer, who
proposed that when interpreting a text, we must be both open and receptive to the
text's alterity or otherness so that its meaning can shine through, but also aware of
our preconceptions. However, in order for this to occur, we do not attempt to
hold our preconceptions in abeyance (as in one ideal of natural scientific "objectivity") but rather attune to our preconceptions or to what Gadamer (1975) referred to as "justified prejudices" that open us to experience from the outset.

Implications for interpretive validity

Given the influence of researcher reflexivity, divergence and variation in interpretive findings are likely to occur (as we saw in our own research group's work
with the data above). As Wertz et al. (2011: 280) note, "discrepancies" in qualitative analysis often originate from the individual researchers themselves, including
our "past experiences, our sensibilities, our analytic styles, and our background
stocks of knowledge". There is, consequently, always a horizon of potential

meanings surrounding any text. However, the inextricability of researcher reflexivity and the resultant interpretative variation does not mean that just any textual interpretation is acceptable. What is seen has to be plausible given the meaning constraints of the data themselves. As Ricoeur (1976: 79) argues, "if it is true that there is always more than one way of construing a text, it is not true that all interpretations are equal. The text presents a limited field of possible constructions". Hence, the key criteria of qualitative research are whether members of the research group can see what each other saw and whether readers of the text can then see what the researchers saw particularly given individuals' own stances (i.e., preconceptions and interpretive frame of reference) vis-à-vis the data.

The example of the "catalytic moment" discussed earlier in which a male participant struggled with suicidal ideation and later rescued a kitten illustrates how these criteria work. Our group struggled with the meanings in the data. One of our group members is a clinical psychologist, and her interpretations of the interview text could not help but be influenced by her background and training as a psychologist (e.g., viewing others in light of possibilities for change). The group challenged the psychologist's preconceptions and how these preconceptions might be influencing her interpretations of the data. This challenging was crucial because what ultimately unfolded was a more well-rounded and deeper analysis of the text in which the participant's lived experience of contradictory values emerged: violence, power, and intimidation on the one hand, and vulnerability and care on the other. The upshot is that each of the group members could see what the others saw (in the participant's catalytic moment with what was now considered to be a composite symbol of the kitten), but the analysis that evolved was more nuanced and less polarized.

This dialogical hashing out in order to refine the interpretive meanings in the polyvocal text or data has implications for understanding validity or what some scholars have discussed as the "trustworthiness" of the findings (Levitt et al., 2017). Validation in qualitative research contexts is best conceptualized as coherence rather than verification (Churchill et al., 1998). Hence, the question is not whether researchers have discovered the one "correct" interpretation in relation to the text and verified it against an empirical "reality." Rather, the question is whether there is coherence among the interpretation, researchers' question(s), and researchers' preconceptions, as well as among the contested narratives themselves. As Churchill et al. (1998: 81) rightly note, even when many narratives regarding one phenomenon fail to coincide, they often "cohere around a common nucleus of meaning". Ricoeur (1976: 79) has described this process of interpretive verification as a logic of "qualitative probability". By this, he means that an interpretation "must not only be probable, but must be more probable than another interpretation" (Ricoeur, 1976: 79). Hence, it is possible to argue for or against interpretations or to arbitrate among them. In many ways, our research group is like a friendly court, in which we listen to evidence, put interpretations regarding our data set to test, and make judgements. We think this process of co-generating research findings is in the service of fidelity to research validity.

Conclusion

Qualitative research and findings offer important access to the lived world of mean
ing as experienced by participants. Such methods should stand on their own as
legitimate forms of research and as reliable methods of attaining knowledge, while
also being critically examined from their own epistemological framework. In this
view, the researchers' preconceptions are not a liability or something that needs to be
bracketed by applying the procedures of method (as one might see in quantitative
procedures). Rather, the researchers' preconceptions and even biases are an asset,
because they help researchers understand their interpretive frames of reference in
regard to the data, and more radically, such preconceptions and biases facilitate the
very process of understanding itself. This is really the crux of the hermeneutic relationship that unfolds between researchers and the data and is the key to understanding validity as coherence. As we have emphasized throughout this chapter and
in our own research analysis, textual coherence recognizes the common nucleus of
meaning across researchers' interpretations of the data, while simultaneously respecting differences and recognizing the defined parameters of interpretive possibility set
by both the text and by the researchers' preconceptions. Hence, qualitative research
demands a rigorous examination of the intimate relationship between the lived
experience revealed in the data, the researchers' own assumptions and biases, and the
hermeneutic process of understanding that emerges between the two.

Notes

1 In their review, Lum et al. (2006) initially examined over 14,000 studies published
   between 1971 and 2003 with inclusion criteria including counter terrorism interventions.
   Studies were also selected using the Campbell Collaboration review process, a process
   that emphasizes an evidence-based approach.
2 Our preferences here are similar to the developing methodology of the oral history
   interview, on which see, Abrams (2016) and Oral History Association (2009) "Principles
   and Best Practices." Oral History Association webpage: http://www.oralhistory.org/a
   bout/principles-and-practice [accessed 5 April 2019].
3 In addition to semi-structured interviews, our research takes a multi-source approach that
   cross-references the semi-structured interview data with open source material and other
   publicly available information relevant to FRE and to our participants (e.g., websites,
   archived public videos, and newspaper stories).
4 For our purposes, we have found the Style Guide of the Baylor University Institute of
   Oral History (http://www.baylor.edu/oralhistory/doc.php/14142.pdf) useful.

References

Abrams, L. 2016. *Oral History Theory*. New York, NY: Routledge.
Bjørgo, T. 2009. "Processes of disengagement from violent groups of the extreme right." In
   Leaving Terrorism Behind: Individual and Collective Disengagement, edited by T. Bjørgo and J.
   Horgan, 30–48. New York, NY: Routledge.
Braun, V. and V. Clarke. 2006. "Using thematic analysis in psychology." *Qualitative Research
   in Psychology*, 3, 77–101.
Brinkmann, S. 2018. "The interview." In *The Sage Handbook of Qualitative Research*, edited
   by N.K. Denzin and Y.S. Lincoln. Thousand Oaks, CA: Sage.

Churchill, S.D., J.E. Lowery, O. McNally, and A. Rao. 1998. "The question of reliability in interpretative psychological research: A comparison of three phenomenologically-based protocol analyses." In *Phenomenological Inquiry in Psychology: Existential and Transpersonal Dimensions*, edited by R. Valle, 63–85. New York, NY: Plenum Press.

Creswell, J.W. and V.L. Plano Clark. 2011. *Designing and Conducting Mixed Methods Research* (2nd edition). Thousand Oaks, CA: Sage.

Dalgaard-Nielsen, A. 2010. "Violent radicalization in Europe: What we know and what we do not know." *Studies in Conflict and Terrorism*, 33, 797–814.

Denzin, N.K. and Y.S. Lincoln. 2018. *The Sage Handbook of Qualitative Research*. Thousand Oaks, CA: Sage.

Feddes, A.R. and M. Gallucci. 2015. "A literature review on methodology used in evaluating effects of preventive and de-radicalisation interventions." *Journal for Deradicalization*, 5, 1–27.

Freilich, J.D. and G. LaFree. 2016. "Measurement issues in the study of terrorism: Introducing the special issue." *Studies in Conflict and Terrorism*, 39(7–8), 569–579.

Gadamer, H.G. 1975. *Truth and Method* (J. Weinsheimer and D.G. Marshall, trans; 2nd revised edition). New York, NY: Continuum.

Gergen, K. 2014. "Pursuing excellence in qualitative inquiry." *Qualitative Psychology*, 1(1), 49–60.

Hanson, N.R. 1958. *Patterns of Discovery*. Cambridge: Cambridge University Press.

Harris, D.J., P. Simi, and G. Ligon. 2016. "Reporting practices of journal articles that include interviews with extremists." *Studies in Conflict and Terrorism*, 39(7–8), 602–616.

Horgan, J. 2011. "Interviewing the terrorists: reflections on fieldwork and implications for psychological research." *Behavioral Sciences of Terrorism and Political Aggression*, 4(3), 1–17.

Horgan, J. 2009. *Walking Away From Terrorism: Accounts of Disengagement From Radical and Extremist Movements*. New York, NY: Routledge.

Josselson, R. 2013. *Interviewing for Qualitative Inquiry: A Relational Approach*. New York, NY: Guilford Press.

Levitt, H.M., S.L. Motulsky, F.J. Wertz, S.L. Morrow, and J.G. Ponterotto. 2017. "Recommendations for designing and reviewing qualitative research in psychology: Promoting methodological integrity." *Qualitative Psychology*, 4(1), 2–22.

Lum, C. and L.W. Kennedy. 2012. "In support of evidence-based approaches: A rebuttal to Gloria Laycock." *Policing: A Journal of Policy and Practice*, 6(4), 317–323.

Lum, C., L.W. Kennedy, and A. Sherley. 2006. "Are counter-terrorism strategies effective? The results of the Campbell Systematic Review on counter-terrorism evaluation research." *Journal of Experimental Criminology*, 2, 489–516.

Marshall, M.N. 1996. "Sampling for qualitative research." *Family Practice*, 13(6), 522–525.

Morse, J. 2018. "Reframing rigor in qualitative inquiry." In *The Sage Handbook of Qualitative Research*, edited by N.K. Denzin and Y.S. Lincoln. Thousand Oaks, CA: Sage.

Polkinghorne, D.E. 1989. "Phenomenological research methods." In *Existential-Phenomenological Perspectives in Psychology*, edited by R.S. Valle and S. Halling, 41–60. New York, NY: Plenum Press.

Ricoeur, P. 1976. *Interpretation Theory: Discourse and the Surplus of Meaning*. Fort Worth, TX: Texas Christian University Press.

Silke, A. 2001. "The devil you know: Continuing problems with research on terrorism." *Terrorism and Political Violence*, 13, 1–14.

Wertz, F.J., K. Charmaz, L.M. McMullen, R. Josselson, R. Anderson, and E. McSpadden. 2011. *Five Ways of Doing Qualitative Analysis: Phenomenological Psychology, Grounded Theory, Discourse Analysis, Narrative Research, and Intuitive Inquiry*. New York, NY: Guilford Press.

Windisch, S., P. Simi, G.S. Ligon, and H. McNeel. 2017. "Disengagement from ideologically-based and violent organizations: A systematic review of the literature." *Journal for Deradicalization*, 9, 1–38.

13

INTERVIEWING MEMBERS OF THE WHITE POWER MOVEMENT IN THE UNITED STATES

Reflections on research strategies and challenges of right-wing extremists

Betty A. Dobratz and Lisa K. Waldner

In this chapter we explore selected methodological aspects and issues related to researching the white power movement in the United States during the last several decades. Typically, published articles and books are the final polished products of research emphasizing significant findings and do not provide much detail on the research process itself. As George succinctly concluded, 'A piece of research does not progress in the way it is "written up" for publication' (quoted in Merton, 1968: 157). After examining 41 articles including interviews with extremists, Harris, Simi, and Ligon (2016) recommended that researchers increasingly rely on interviewing and provide greater methodological transparency and consistency.

Given this increased focus on interviewing and transparency, we discuss our own work on right-wing extremism that used interviewing and observation of US white power rallies and other events starting May 29, 1992 with a rally of the Knights of the Ku Klux Klan in Dubuque Iowa and ending with the National Socialist Movement's rally in Kansas City Missouri November 8–9, 2013. These events typically occurred over a two-day period, although some took place for one day and others (for example, Aryan Nations' "World Congresses") for three days. Speeches by prominent supporters of white power ideology were often on the agenda. When it was possible, we contacted potential participants in advance to ask about interviews, but mainly we requested interviews during the events although we also did some telephone interviewing. We first review the work of three other authors on this topic and then we examine in depth our research on white power supporters in which we consider questionnaire development, gaining access to events, our emotions, use of rapport and empathy, and stigmatization of researchers on right-wing extremism.

Significant right-wing extremist white power research of three authors

First, we examine the work of three scholars who have interviewed white power activists between the 1990s and early 2000s and provided relatively contrasting yet rather extensive methodological information. Each author has numerous publications, but we highlight their methodology based on their books. Our major criterion was that they actually talked with white power supporters and used their discussions with them when reporting their findings. We know two of them personally and the third was quite helpful when contacted.

Jeffrey Kaplan, a scholar of religion on millenarian movements, right-wing extremism and terrorism, uses an interpretive perspective to 'translate the perceptions of the subject movement into a text that provides the academic audience with an insight into the group and lives of its members' (Kaplan, 2016: 46). The interpretive approach is not intended to 'explain away' or excuse violence that has originated from millenarian movements, although the much greater resources and power of the federal government indicates they have greater burden to avoid confrontation (Kaplan, 2016: 39, 44). Kaplan (2016: 39) suggests that a Weberian detachment is needed with the researcher placing his or her own preconceptions and biases in abeyance as much as possible in order to provide the adherent's view of the world 'regardless of how repugnant that view may be to a mainstream audience' (Kaplan, 2016: 48).

He believes research like his requires considerable interaction with both leaders and supporters and it could take years 'to earn even a qualified degree of trust' as one interacts with members and their families (Kaplan, 2016: 39–40). Developing rapport is not easy. If achieved, it influences both the scholar and the movement. Kaplan (2016: 31) defines empathy as 'the ability to "see through the eyes of the other."' The researcher must be careful not to become 'captured by the movement's worldview' (Kaplan, 2016: 39).

Kaplan (2016: 177) discovered those studied were 'considerably less threatening than their public image' although they did have repugnant political views and fantastically eccentric interpretations of sacred text. He described them as isolated and strange people who felt too much and understood too little and who 'In their words and deeds they harmed mainly themselves and their families' (Kaplan, 2016: 10). What is especially significant for Kaplan (2016: 11) is the following:

> the fact that the 'we' and 'they' are both human beings and have important commonalities ... by failing to recognize the humanity which binds us together, we lose the opportunity to do what anti-racism should be about: to try to bring the angry and the outcast back into our midst.

Kaplan (2016: 3) strongly believes demonization of the radical right does not facilitate our understanding of them. Participant/observer methodology and face-to-face interviewing, especially if conducted in the interviewee's home, are important since they provide nonverbal information and 'the aura of demonization ... fades away'.

Kathleen Blee (2002), a sociologist, engaged in in-depth, unstructured life-history interviews to study women in contemporary racist groups focusing on tensions created by their inclusion in the movement. Life histories provided unstructured presentations of women's life stories and personal narratives that have a beginning, middle, and end (Blee, 2002). Their material helps determine social identities and ideology as well as provide semantic context for their statements and can uncover possible patterns to peoples' political and personal lives. She acknowledges that respondent statements still need to be treated with caution and some events may be distorted by memory or omitted or downplayed so the results of narratives can be both 'revealing and concealing' (Blee, 2002: 203, 10).

Blee used her personal contacts, parole officers, correctional officials, journalists, newspaper reporters, former and current racial activists, attorneys, police and criminal investigators, etc. to help identify potential respondents. She told them upfront that she did not share their beliefs and was actually quite opposed to them but promised to portray them accurately. She maintains her method provided a more representative sample than snowballing or interviewees based on their accessibility to the researcher. She interviewed both leaders and rank-and-file members from a variety of age groups.

Blee believed standard interviews are less useful than life histories because the former were likely to provide little beyond slogans and propaganda and could lead to problems determining the causal relationship between racist attitudes and movement involvement. Other researchers have relied mainly on hate group literature to answer these questions but that typically does not reveal whether activists have read this literature or how they interpret such propaganda. She also cites the work of ethnographer Barrie Thorne who saw fieldwork as adventure: 'venturing into exciting, taboo, dangerous, perhaps enticing social circumstances; getting the flavor of participation, living out moments of high drama; but in some ultimate way having a cop-out, a built-in escape, a point of outside leverage that full participants lack' (Blee, 2002: 13).

As a woman Blee believed she was safer because she was less likely to be perceived as challenging or a threat. She became more afraid when she understood her white skin offered her less protection than she initially believed. Although researchers rarely discuss their emotions in publications, Blee (2002: 12) mentioned 'walking a tightrope' between keeping a distance that showed she rejected their views and developing enough rapport so women would share their life history. Standard methods of gaining rapport such as agreeing with their beliefs and sharing details of one's personal life weren't realistic so Blee (2002: 12) used indirect and fragile measures such as sharing concerns about one's body image once it was mentioned by the interviewee. She (2002: 13) felt relying on rapport was problematic but even more challenging was the 'prospect of developing empathy for a racist activist whose life is given meaning and purpose by the desire to annihilate you or others.' She identified mixed feelings regarding her work with respondents including fear yet intriguing, exciting yet horrifying. She became less afraid although 'not unafraid' (Blee, 2002: 18–19). As her fears declined, she felt so did her analytical edge (Blee, 2002: 19).

Sociologists Pete Simi and Robert Futrell used ethnography as their main methodology. Simi (Simi and Futrell, 2010; Simi, Futrell, and Bubolz, 2016) developed extensive contact with white power activists as he 'conducted unobtrusive nonconfrontational field observations as both a participant and observer ... and relied on an empathetic nonjudgmental interaction style to build rapport and gain insight' (Simi et al., 2016: 496). He used a snowball approach that ultimately allowed him contact with each of the major branches of the white power movement. He credits his ability to drink lots of beer and still control his faculties as means for gaining rapport. He describes himself 'As a relatively nondescript "white guy"', enabling him to blend into Aryan events.

Although he remained unharmed, Simi was occasionally accused of being an agent provocateur or allied with law enforcement and threatened with bodily harm. He (Simi and Futrell, 2010: 129) found participant observation 'requires compromise of one's beliefs and values to avoid conflicts.' For example, he outwardly portrayed himself as sympathetic to the Aryan cause despite his personal rejection of racist and anti-Semitic views. He found participant observations and interviews 'emotionally exhausting' (Simi and Futrell, 2010: 129). He argued that deception was necessary to build rapport in this risky environment including laughing at racist jokes and agreeing when Aryans discussed white genocide. He recognized that some researchers take the honest and direct approach making it clear they aren't open to recruitment and don't share the same beliefs, but he felt that such an approach would compromise

> the degree of intersubjectivity the ethnography can reach. I tried as much as possible to understand Aryans from that point of view... . I felt a tremendous amount of internal guilt and discomfort. The perversity and illogic of their world astounded me. Yet in many ways the form of Aryans' lives was far more ordinary than I expected.
>
> *(Simi and Futrell, 2010: 130)*

The authors faced methodological issues due to the secrecy in the movement and respondent engagement in illegal activities (Simi et al., 2016: 496).

Our research

We have worked together on white power research since the late 1990s but Betty first became involved in the early 1990s working with Stephanie Shanks-Meile and co-authoring *'White Power, White Pride!' The White Separatist Movement in the United States* (1997). Originally, our major source of data was going to be collecting white power newsletters, publications, etc., as well as examining newspaper and social science literature on this movement. However, in May 1992 Betty found out that the Knights of the Ku Klux Klan (KKKK) were holding a rally in Dubuque Iowa about 185 miles from Betty's university. Although Betty had not very seriously considered using face-to-face meetings or interviewing white power supporters, the proximity of the rally and the attention it was receiving sparked her interest.

Armed with a letter from Betty's department chair and her Iowa State University identification, Betty met Stephanie and they went to the rally. The Chief of Police and law enforcement in general were very helpful in providing temporary press credentials and allowing both inside the rally site. Without law enforcement permission, only KKKK supporters were allowed inside the site. The atmosphere surrounding the rally, talking with its leader and supporters, the speeches, and the crowd reactions inside and outside the park perimeter were factors that changed our methods and resulted in developing and administering a questionnaire that shaped the rest of Betty's research on this topic.

Kaplan, Blee, and Simi seemed committed to their data collection methods from the start. For us, it was serendipitous, 'the unanticipated, anomalous and strategic datum which exerts pressure upon the investigator for a new direction of inquiry' (Merton, 1968: 159). Our research strategy expanded to include attending numerous events and interviewing attendees. Ultimately, this led to much greater understanding of the diversity of views and conflicts within this movement. In retrospect, Betty has asked herself why she had not seriously considered interviewing earlier. One reason was certainly concern and fear about doing so based on the stereotypical portrayals of this movement that Kaplan noted. There were also practical considerations including how to find out about events, gain access, and fund traveling. By the time Lisa became involved, interviews were the primary means of collecting data.

Qualitative or quantitative research or both

Bryman (1988: 5) distinguished two major ways that quantitative and qualitative research is defined in the social sciences. The simpler view suggests that the two types represent different means of collecting data and that the type of social research selected is based partially on what kinds of research questions are being asked. The other is based on certain distinct philosophies and epistemological assumptions of what knowledge is. We tend to think that the philosophical divide between qualitative and quantitative research is quite deep and entrenched in the social sciences, but we don't think this is necessarily good for the discipline. The strengths of one approach can be seen as the weaknesses of the other so utilizing both potentially strengthens the findings or how the findings are perceived.

Questionnaire development

Unlike Kaplan, Blee or Simi, our set of questions was structured and composed of both closed and open-ended ones. We were especially interested in differing strategies and divisions in the movement. Ultimately, different versions of the questionnaire were formulated but a typical one contained about 55 questions covering topics on how interviewees labelled themselves (e.g., white power, white separatist, racialist), the meanings of those labels, organizational identification (if any), the process of becoming involved and length of movement participation, the influence of family, the roles of religion, violence, and women in the movement, links to other organizations (if any), and their reactions to being labelled by mainstream media as sexist, racist, anti-Semitic, and anti-gay. We queried about factions and social classes in the movement, whether activists should run for political office, and whether the movement was growing or declining in influence. Towards the end we asked for further comments to help us understand the movement and queried if and how one wanted to be identified in our work. About 40 per cent of the questions were open-ended. Interviews were transcribed by secretarial staff. Quantitative data were coded in SPSS while NVivo was utilized for qualitative material. We felt a combination of the two was appropriate – using interviewees' statements from open-ended questions and citing numbers based on responses to closed-ended questions.

One of our major modifications of the questionnaire involved adding questions on leaderless resistance. Ultimately, we (Dobratz and Waldner, 2012) published an article on the repertoires of contention or perceptions of interviewees regarding the appropriateness of violence and leaderless resistance versus leader led groups. Unstructured interviews are more flexible, but we were not completely passive interviewers. We probed and, if necessary, changed the question order or skipped questions. We also observed events and listened to numerous speeches, usually obtaining permission to tape them. We did not systematically take field notes as is typical of ethnographic research. Frankly, we both saw interviews as the primary way of obtaining data and did not consider ourselves ethnographers like Simi or spend extraordinary amounts of time with specific respondents and their families like Kaplan, or clearly disagree with the beliefs of movement supporters like Blee did. We spent a great deal of time and energy attending events and interviewing, found considerable diversity of beliefs, and did not believe most interviewees simply reiterated movement propaganda. The process involved a great deal of work and planning and seemed like Thorne's suggested adventure. We now turn to issues related to access to various events.

Gaining access

Attempting to gain access to an event was typically anxiety-producing as it required requesting permission to attend and attendance was key to achieving many of our interviews. Mostly though, access was allowed with no particular constraints. Betty contacted Aryan Nations (AN) for permission to attend as researchers for its annual 'World Congress.' That did not seem problematic until she received their registration material including a form to be signed and returned with one's registration fee. The form stated among other things:

> I am of the White Aryan Race. I understand that Aryan Nations is an organization comprised of Aryans of Angelo-Saxon, Germanic, Nordic, Basque,

> Lombardic, Celtic, and Slavic background. I further understand and agree with the Aryan Nations exclusion of *Jews, Mexicans, Orientals* and *Mongrels*.

Betty nervously called AN headquarters and informed them again that she was a sociologist, wanted to come to do research, but could not sign the form. To her relief, the AN representative said she could come anyhow.

The most negative experience regarding access occurred in the early years of data collection. Betty telephoned the leader in advance, explained the research, and arranged to come to an event. Once Betty and Stephanie arrived the night before and talked with the leader, he informed them they would need to receive permission before publishing anything about their event. This was shocking because he did not raise this in the earlier phone discussion. Given his demeanor and the context of this meeting, Betty and Stephanie simply listened and later discussed it. Both immediately realized they could not agree to his condition, but decided to stay for the event to observe and informally talk with attendees. Betty and Stephanie were carefully watched and never used any material from the event itself.

The first time Stephanie and Betty arrived at AN, they were immediately challenged about their presence. However, an attendee at the 'non-publishable' event approached them in a very friendly manner and started a conversation. After that, they never experienced problems with any AN staff. Sometimes a negative experience in one place can later lead to unanticipated benefits.

On the other hand, previous friendly interaction does not always mean continued acceptance. At a National Socialist event, we had spent most of the entire day with a group and had several informal exchanges with one individual in particular. However, in the evening after the group had been turned away from holding a skinhead concert, they met elsewhere. There without warning, that person challenged Lisa and asked who had allowed her to attend. Betty stepped in quickly reminding him that she had previously obtained permission for Lisa. Things were thus smoothed over rather quickly and we both were allowed to stay although a new venue was not found for the concert.

Public events should ideally mean easier access to groups, but part of the access to the actual group depends on how law enforcement treats a researcher. Some law enforcement officials were very helpful while others were not. Visiting in advance or making contact early did not necessarily make things easier. For one public event, law enforcement refused to provide Betty with temporary press credentials although they could have recognized her Georgia press credentials. She had requested permission earlier and made telephone calls to them. One particular officer told her she would 'never' get access. Irritated by the officers' handling of the request, she talked with the city's mayor, the ACLU, and the Klan leader about the right of association (not membership) that the police could not deny as long as the Klan group allowed it. Betty joined with the Klan group before they gathered with the police to be escorted to the courthouse where the event was held. After the rally she conducted an interview elsewhere and talked with others informally (see Dobratz and Shanks-Meile, 1997: 169–170 for more detail).

Conducting interviews

The questionnaire was used in various ways: face-to-face interviews mainly from contact at rallies, meetings, birthday celebrations, and two- or three-day events; mailed or distributed to people at events; and a small number of telephone interviews. The final sample was 159 questionnaires. Here we focus on interviewing which was the most frequently used method.

We told potential interviewees we wanted to learn more about the movement by finding out their views on various topics. The time we spent with respondents was normally limited to one interview although interviewees typically gave of their time very willingly with interviews lasting generally for at least an hour. We doubt the interview situation affected our respondents' actual views on race and the movement very much, although some intensification was possible because the location usually was either supportive of their views or neutral. Interviewing persons at an event likely meant getting those who were more committed to the movement in contrast to non-attendees or those limited to internet participation.

If event speakers were announced in advance, we contacted them about an interview. Otherwise, at the event we solicited some group leaders but also participants who were not known to be leaders. We consciously tried to interview women, but had no set geographical or age criteria. We understood variety was important. We emphasized interviewing over nonparticipant observation and for the large majority of interviews this ended our contact with the person although at times we exchanged pleasantries with a few at additional events or continued contact with them. This strategy was based in part on our comfort interacting with mainly male activists and our lack of resources including time, money, and training to carry out extensive observations or ethnography. We also wished to avoid possible negative types of interaction, possibly threats, that Simi reports experiencing. His research is extremely important and appropriate but was not a good fit for us.

Very few people turned us down for an interview. Although there tended to be minor concerns on both the interviewer and the interviewee parts when starting the interview (e.g., lack of complete anonymity for the interviewee, finding a quiet place without others, whether to record the interview, making sure the recorder worked), interviews tended to go well and almost all were recorded. Even if quiet, removing oneself and the interviewee from their normal activities for more than an hour sometimes generated suspicion. We encouraged the interviewee to select the place of the interview and this strategy seemed relatively successful.

Because interviewing became the main research focus, Betty found herself in some strange situations. She vividly remembers sitting in a skinhead's motel room conducting an interview with a person another movement member recommended. Betty watched him drink beer after beer seeming unaffected by it as he answered the questions. This was remarkable in itself (as was Pete Simi's ability) but troubling because Betty would never have put herself in such a situation except for the fact that she wanted this interview. Nothing negative happened and the interview was used in publications. On another occasion, we got into a car with almost complete strangers who were white power supporters we had arranged interviews with. They knew we had never been to Toronto before and wanted to give us a tour of their city. These two examples and others generated emotions and concerns that we now briefly elaborate upon.

Various emotions and concerns

Blee (2002: 13) used words like intriguing, exciting, and horrifying to describe the research and they were appropriate for us as well. We never firmly stated we were opposed to white power ideology and a few tried to recruit us, particularly to National Alliance, commonly regarded then as a more intellectual movement group. The attempts seemed half-hearted and were deflected by reminding people that we were sociologists doing research.

As Simi indicated, interviewing can be exhausting and stressful. At the end of our day (whenever that was), it was good to retreat to one's hotel room and/or decompress. Listening to the slogans such as Heil Hitlers and other stereotypical racist rhetoric was especially chilling. One general strategy that seemed somewhat helpful was separating our role as a researcher on the white power movement from other roles. Some (Bird and Bird, 1986; Settles and Sellers, 2002; Showers, 1992) suggest that the ability to compartmentalize or separate roles helps reduce role strain and stressful events. Once for Betty this role separation did not work very well. While talking with a few young men, she introduced herself by name and explained the research. Dobratz is not a common name and one person asked her a question about her brother. They were thousands of miles from where her brother lived and yet it turned out this person had been a student in one of his high school history classes. What were the odds of this happening? The discussion was pleasant, but she kept wondering what he really thought about her brother and her. She then interviewed him without any problems but felt like this unanticipated event 'hit a little too close to home.' She wanted her role as researcher to be strictly separated from her family but for that brief moment it wasn't.

Our research likely had possibilities for threats and danger as Blee and Simi suggest, but for us it was difficult to distinguish between what Aho (1990) labelled illusionary vs. real risks or dangers. Aho (1990) and Kaplan (2016) found some anti-racist groups over report the threats and potential violence from white power groups. Betty only once recalls hearing what could be interpreted as a possible threat and she ignored it. Some of our greatest safety concerns were when law enforcement interacted with movement members although we never witnessed a serious conflict. We were mindful of Gurr's (1989: 13) observation that 'authorities have substantial responsibility for violence, either by their own action or through inaction.' Our experiences may be different in part because we spent less time with white power supporters than did Kaplan or Simi and did not disagree with their views as Blee did. Also, Blee sometimes relied on contacts from parole officers, correctional officials, attorneys, and police and criminal investigators to identify respondents and we didn't. We possibly were interviewing people with less criminal history or we were less aware of such history. Most of our interviewing was done where movement members were in places where support of their views was readily available so they likely felt comfortable and secure enough to express their beliefs. Their feeling safe could have facilitated harmonious interaction with us. We feel interviewing people at rallies or get-togethers provided a very good sample of people who were actively involved in the movement and thus able and willing to answer our questions.

We, like Blee, believe that because we were women, we were less likely to be taken seriously, but we are not sure how strong that association was. With one group especially, being white women probably meant we benefitted from what Betty thought was a kind of old style "southern hospitality" and helpfulness extended by traditional older white men to older white women. For example, Betty was assisted in finding an appropriate place to stand and hear at a rally while males weren't. Another time she was encouraged to conduct interviews at a motel in between the time of the march/rally and the evening speeches and other activities. In this case, the evening events were cancelled due to heavy rain and cold; Betty knew of this in advance because of the interviews and thus did not go to the site. This triggered suspicions from reporters and other researchers wondering how Betty had advance notice about the cancellation. Suspiciousness is not limited to movement members.

Rapport and empathy

Developing rapport and empathy while interviewing was traditionally regarded as desirable, but more recently questioned when studying undesirable and/or far right groups. For example, Springwood and King (2001) challenged critical ethnographers to consider whether developing rapport was legitimate in 'uneasy field sites' (2001: 404) that included studying 'Whiteness.' They suggested critical ethnographers 'seriously ponder the suggestion that they must indeed "forget rapport"' (2001: 403) with 'repugnant' others (2001: 405) especially if they are 'using the words and actions of their informants against them' (2001: 404).

On the other hand, McQueeney and Lavelle (2017: 82) argued that although emotional labor 'often tested our empathy and threatened our critical edge, emotions need not be a barrier to critical analysis. What matters is that ethnographers use their emotional reflexivity to understand the meanings subjects attribute to their actions.' We suggest this can be applicable for other researchers as well.

During our interviews we nodded yes to their racist statements to suggest that we understood what the person was stating but realized some could have taken this to mean we agreed with them. Betty tried to find common ground with those who were critical of powerful economic elites or expressed concerns about earning a decent wage. She did not do this with racist statements but considered it important to be pleasant and friendly during the interview.

Some picture far right racists as enemies which could encourage questioning about why social scientists study them or try to develop rapport or empathy with them. Perlstein (1995) titled his article on researching the far right 'Sleeping with the Enemy: Academia Faces the Far Right', while Kleinman and Copp (1993) titled one of their subsections 'Making Friends with the Enemy.' Both sources raise some interesting and thoughtful points. Perlstein (1995: 81) calls it a 'scholarly imperative' to study 'ruthlessly antiliberal' social movements that have tended to be ignored by many social scientists. However, he is also concerned that researching their 'grotesque' ideas could legitimize them. Kleinman and Copp (1993: 38) are wary of developing cognitive empathy (defined as understanding why people think, feel and act as they do) because it could lead to sympathy for 'the enemy.' We recognize these as important concerns, but should it prevent or limit social scientific interviewing and other forms of research that try to understand how white power activists feel, think, and act and why they do so?

We believe that understanding why people think and act as they do is a worthy goal to research for any kind of movement. Kaplan's use of the interpretive framework, Simi's ethnographic approach, Blee's life histories, and our interviewing are important techniques to accomplish this. If as various authors have suggested that ordinariness often characterizes white power activists (Aho, 1990: 67; Simi and Futrell, 2010) or are 'simply people like ourselves' (Kaplan, 2016: 12), are they completely unworthy of researchers' cognitive empathy that could facilitate greater understanding of movement members? Isn't the enemy more appropriately defined as racism that we should remember is in the mainstream as well as this movement? Kaplan suggested attempts to bring people out of the movement could be based on their shared humanity with others. Betty recalls the wife of a former movement member who confided that her family life was much more peaceful after he left the movement.

Stigmatization of white power research

Movement members generally recognize they are stigmatized by many, but this stigma can be transferred to social scientists studying them. Blee (2002: 13) noted, 'I am not alone in worrying that the political stigma attached to these groups will sully those who study them.' It seems to us the more direct face-to-face contact the researcher has with white supremacists, the more likely the stigmatization. It may also be the more rapport and empathy the social scientist develops, the greater the stigma.

The stigma can exist in various ways. For example, Betty once walked down the hill at AN toward white supremacists debating with protesters who were standing on the public road. As she got closer, she heard protesters labelling her a 'Nazi Grandma.' Betty was not happy with either label and neither was true.

One can be stigmatized by law enforcement simply by being at a white power event. After one night's events at AN, Betty drove away in her rental car and immediately realized she was being followed by a police car. After she turned onto the paved highway, she was not sure of the speed limit and concluded it was safer to go 45 mph than 55. However, eventually Betty was pulled over by the officer for driving too slowly. Before the police officer got to her rental car, Betty remembered what Tom Metzger of White Aryan Resistance advised about protecting oneself so she turned the recorder on to capture the interaction with the officer. The officer quickly shined his flashlight into the car's back seat and told her she was driving too slowly. He took her driver's license and returned to his car for what seemed like an eternity. When he returned, he indicated how difficult it was to check with Iowa officials so late at night. He returned the license without giving her a ticket. She wondered how much information he now knew about her. While experiencing the drama of being pulled over, Betty considered using what Thorne referred to as the cop-out or built-in escape by identifying herself as a sociologist but did not.

We were at a National Socialist event when the police were called to evict this group from a building that had been rented under false pretenses. To exit the venue, we had to walk past, one at a time, a line of police officers and dogs. Lisa was embarrassed perceiving that the police believed her to be a neo-Nazi but she did nothing to correct those officers' perceptions. In this case using Thorne's 'cop out' would likely have created negative feelings from movement members who could have perceived her distancing herself from the group.

It is one thing for protesters or the police to label us incorrectly because of our presence in the field but another to experience negative evaluations by fellow sociologists because of our research topic. Kleinman and Copp (1993: 6–7) even suggest 'You are What you Study'. They believe that sometimes fieldworkers are unaware of potential topic stigma until their colleagues and friends react to it and wonder how the researcher could establish rapport with certain kinds of interviewees. Although some sociologists and others might think those who study far right groups are what they study, we challenge that stereotype even though we understand that one's employment role could be their master status. That kind of judgement could reduce the number of social scientists willing to do this research and/or limit what authors are willing to write or share about the research process. We agree with Kleinman and Copp (1993: 36) 'that avoiding these groups produces big gaps in our knowledge.'

Conclusion

In analyzing white power groups, we suggest a strong scholarly social science voice is needed that as much as feasible is independent of pressures from the groups themselves, those organizations who oppose the white power groups, law enforcement, various other political groups, or even some of our social science colleagues. Ultimately just as Kaplan, Blee, and Simi have done, we think that it is important to actually interview and observe movement supporters and publish our findings. We also support Harris et al. (2016) about their assessment of the value of interviews and the need for transparency. We point out though in the actual *process* of doing interviews, etc. each individual researcher needs to make their own methodological decisions about what kinds of information to ask and to share with activists, how to deal with their own feelings about their research, those who they study, the spontaneous decisions made in the field, how to handle stigmatization, and how to live within their own comfort zone. Finally, it is also important to recognize that interviewing and face-to-face contact are not the only ways to gain knowledge and understanding of right-wing extremist movements even though we consider it the most appropriate. Various types of social science research on the far right are necessary to advance and further knowledge on this very significant and complex topic.

References

Aho, J. 1990. *The Politics of Righteousness*. Seattle, WA: University of Washington Press.

Bird, G.W. and G. Bird. 1986. "Strategies for Reducing Role Strain Among Dual-Career Couples." *International Journal of Sociology of the Family*, 16, 83–94.

Blee, K. 2002. *Inside Organized Racism*. Berkeley, CA: University of California.

Bryman, A. 1988. *Quantity and Quality in Social Research*. London: Unwin Hyman.

Dobratz, B. and S. Shanks-Meile. 1997. *"White Power, White Pride!" The White Separatist Movement in the United States*. New York, NY: Twayne.

Dobratz, B. and L. Waldner. 2012. "Repertoires of Contention: White Separatist Views on the Use of Violence and Leaderless Resistance." *Mobilization*, 17, 49–66.

Gurr, T.R. 1989. "The History of Protest, Rebellion, and Reform in America." In *Violence in America: Protest, Rebellion, Reform* (vol. 2), edited by T.R. Gurr, 11–22. Newbury Park, CA: Sage.

Harris, D., P. Simi, and G. Ligon. 2016. "Reporting Practices of Journal Articles that Include Interviews with Extremists." *Studies in Conflict and Terrorism*, 39, 602–616.

Kaplan, J. 2016. *Radical Religion and Violence*. New York, NY: Routledge.

Kleinman, S. and M. Copp. 1993. *Emotions and Fieldwork*. Newbury Park, CA: Sage.

Merton, R. 1968. *Social Theory and Social Structure*. Enlarged edition. New York, NY: The Free Press Collier-MacMillan.

McQueeney, K. and K. Lavelle. 2017. "Emotional Labor in Critical Ethnographic Work." *Journal of Contemporary Ethnography*, 46, 81–107.

Perlstein, R. 1995. "Sleeping with the Enemy: Academia Faces the Far Right." *Lingua Franca*, 6(November/December), 79–83.

Settles, I. and R. Sellers. 2002, "One Role or Two? The Function of Psychological Separation in Role Conflict." *Journal of Applied Psychology*, 87, 574–582.

Showers, C. 1992. "Compartmentalization of Positive and Negative Self-Knowledge." *Journal of Personality and Social Psychology*, 62, 1038–1049.

Simi, P. and R. Futrell. 2010. *American Swastika: Inside the White Power Movement's Hidden Spaces of Hate*. Lanham, MD: Rowman & Littlefield.

Simi, P., R. Futrell, and B.F. Bubolz. 2016. "Parenting as Activism: Identity Alignment and Activist Persistence in the White Power Movement." *The Sociological Quarterly*, 57, 491–518.

Springwood, C.F. and C.R. King. 2001. "Unsettling Engagements: On the Ends of Rapport in Critical Ethnography." *Qualitative Inquiry*, 7(4), 403–416.

14

LIFE-HISTORY INTERVIEWS WITH RIGHTWING EXTREMISTS

Bert Klandermans

Why do people become actively involved in extreme-right activities? Life-history interviews are one way of finding answers to this question. The advantage of life-history interviews is that they do not ask 'why' questions, but 'what' questions. Such questions are less invasive and thus less threatening for the interviewee. I am deliberately using the plural, as more than one answer can be given. Not every activist has the same reasons to become involved in the movement. In this chapter I will develop four story-lines. Together they draw a fair picture of the rightwing extremists involved in this study. The first concerns membership: What are the individual life histories of active participants in rightwing organizations? When and how did they become involved in extreme-right organizations? Why do they stay involved? What does participation mean to their identity? And how does partici-pation, in turn, modify their identity? A second story-line concerns meaning: What is the rationale behind participation in a rightwing organization? What makes such participation a meaningful thing to do? More generally, this question concerns the collective action frame of the participants. Is there a specific injustice frame mobi-lizing extreme-rightwingers? A third story-line concerns continuity: Are today's rightwing organizations through personal or ideological links connected with rightwing organizations from the past? A final story-line concerns the context: Do the answers to these questions vary depending on the country we are in? In the following pages I will elaborate on these issues. In doing so, I also reflect on how to study movement activists and how life-history interviews are instrumental in that respect.

Interviewing rightwing extremists

In the introductory paragraph I set out the leading questions of a study of extreme-right activists Nonna Mayer and I (2006) conducted in five Western-European countries (Belgium, Germany, Italy, France, and the Netherlands). As we wanted to understand how people came to join the extreme-right (ER) movement and what happened after they entered, we chose to answer these questions through life-history interviews. This choice had both theoretical and methodological implications. *Theoretically*, because the employment of life-history interviews implies that one seeks to understand individual choices – in our case the choice to become and stay active in a movement labeled extreme right – as steps in a person's life course (Blee and Taylor, 2002). The reasons for this involvement in the extreme-right are sought in the individual's past. Indeed, much of what we try to understand is path-dependent. That is to say, the choices an individual has are determined by earlier decisions. The interviewer and the interviewee travel back into time to the point where the interviewee first encountered the movement and reconstruct the trajectory from then to their present activism. *Methodologically*, because a life-history interview is necessarily a qualitative form of data-collection that requires specific analytical tools (Rubin and Rubin, 1995). These interviews left us with some afterthoughts which I want to share with the reader before I move along.

At the time when we designed our study (cf. Klandermans and Mayer, 2006), we felt that the best way to find an answer to our research questions would be to conduct life-history interviews. We believed that activists of the extreme-right are as rational or irrational as any movement activist and wanted to understand the reasoning behind their activism. What does a world look like in which rightwing extremism is meaningful and how does someone come to see the world that way? As we thought that personal experiences play an important role in that respect (Teske, 1997; Andrews, 1991; Blee, 2002) life histories appeared to us a significant source of information. In the life of every activist there is a point in time where he or she makes the transition from non-active to active supporter of a movement. Such transitions seldom take place overnight, although conversions sometimes leave that impression. The final step to enter activism usually comes at the end of longer trajectories. It was these trajectories that we were interested in. Whether it was a conversion or a continuous track, we wanted to reconstruct it and understand its dynamics. Such a reconstruction is difficult to undertake within the framework of a structured questionnaire. Both the interviewer and the interviewee need the space to elaborate on the story to be told. Therefore, life-history interviews are necessarily in-depth interviews. It is difficult to imagine how otherwise one could explore someone's past. Events that took place a long time ago must be recollected, matters that are sensitive to the interviewee must be dealt with, and complicated stories must be told. We put a lot of effort into establishing the rapport needed for such interviews to work out and we believe that in most cases we succeeded.

This is not to say that we took everything the interviewees told us at face value. In fact, we put quite a lot of time and energy in acquiring independent information about the interviewees, the organizations, the events, and the people they were talking about. We scrutinized websites, written material from the organization, documentation available through the counter-movements and other sources.

Moreover, frequently our interviewees themselves provided unknowingly validation of the stories told by others. In this way we were basically able to check most
of the factual information given by the interviewees. Their interpretation of those
facts remains, of course, idiosyncratic and in a sense that was what we wanted to
explore. However, one must be careful to not take the reconstruction that results
from the interview as the real story. It remains a reconstruction (Blee and Taylor,
2002), but this was exactly what we were interested in.

We approached people via snowballing techniques. Interviewees were asked
whether they knew fellow-members who would agree to be interviewed. When
approaching activists to gain their co-operation, we were often treated with suspicion for understandable reasons. The extreme-right has been portrayed in the
media in a negative way. Their organizations have been infiltrated by undercover
journalists who fill the newspapers with stories about the life back-stage that the
people try to cover up at front-stage. In our efforts to counter these suspicions we
were, however, careful to not make the opposite mistake and suggest that we were
sympathetic to their objectives. In our team we spent quite some time on the
ethics of getting along with a movement and activists one does not sympathize
with. Every 'cookbook' on in-depth interviewing tells you that you have got to
establish rapport with your interviewees to be able to do good interviews. But,
how does one establish a relationship with people to whom one doesn't feel akin at
all? The usual recipe – show understanding and appreciate their viewpoints – was
not what we wanted. We certainly did not want to give the impression that we
agreed with what they were saying. Interestingly, our method – the life-history
interview – worked to our advantage.

We basically wanted our interviewees to tell us about their past and what it
meant to them to be actively involved in their organization. There was no need for
them to defend themselves, as we were genuinely interested in their views and
why these views motivated them to become an extreme-right activist. Evidence of
our ability to establish rapport came from the interviewees themselves who began
to call us back to give additional information or to invite us to meetings, social
events, gatherings, lectures, and the like. Such invitations we often accepted as we
felt that it would help us to deepen our understanding of their activism. In France
and the Netherlands such enduring relations could be fruitfully exploited to return
to some of the interviewees for a second round of interviews after significant
changes in the movement (a split within the *Front National* (FN) and devastating
elections in the Netherlands) had occurred.

We had expected that it would be difficult to persuade people to be interviewed, and indeed in Germany it appeared to be not easy to get access to organizations we wanted to include in our study, but on the whole the activists were
quite cooperative, especially after the first suspicion was evaporated. Indeed, on
quite a few occasions these were people who wanted to talk, who had a message to
convey. Once they figured that in fact the interviews remained confidential and
did not appear in a newspaper, they became more willing, sometimes even
anxious, to be interviewed.

Life histories: Joining and staying

There are three different steps to consider in becoming a rightwing extremist: the process begins with some susceptibility for extreme-right ideas which creates the potentiality for joining an ER movement organization. Then, usually some event triggers off the actual step of joining the organization. Finally, a separate question to be answered is why one stays involved.

Susceptibility

The factors that mold the potential activist, making a person susceptible for extreme-right ideas which facilitate membership of an extreme-right organization, could to a certain extent be the same as those for extreme-right voting. There are the personality explanations, such as the 'authoritarian personality' (Adorno et al., 1950) or the 'man of violence' (Billig, 1979), shaped since early childhood by family and education. Our interviews did not show that these activists are especially deviant or marginal or frustrated. To be sure, our interviewees formed quite a diverse group, but on the whole they appear with a few exceptions as perfectly normal people. This is in keeping with other research (cf. Roberts, 2018). Next to the personality explanations, there are the psycho-sociological explanations (Lipset and Raab, 1970; Kornhauser, 1959) linking extremism to job insecurity, inferior social status, social isolation, or the 'cognitive style' hypotheses developed by Rokeach (1960) in his works on dogmatism and rigidity, independent of political leaning, and the works on 'simplism', linking rightwing extremism to low education, seeing the world in black and white.

Yet another set of explanations concern ideological factors encompassing the weight of political socialization in youth and adolescence: family, school, friends, military training. In Italy, France and Belgium, most of our interviewees grew up in rightwing milieus. Orfali in her study of FN members (1990) confirms that most of them (43 out of 50) came from rightwing milieus, conservative by tradition, and more inclined to agree with Le Pen's ideas as expressed by one of them: 'My family was always right-wing, even if there are a few black sheep voting for the left, we traditionally are right-wing' (Orfali, 1990: 94). In France, sometimes these extreme-right ideological continuities in some families have existed for three generations. But as our interviews among the young activists revealed, what is transmitted is not necessarily an ideological leaning. It can well be the will to dedicate oneself to a cause, the 'activist' ethos, the need for general interest activities. One of the French interviewees in the FN felt closer to his working class and communist background than in a traditional right party, more 'bourgeois', while another felt closer to a communist union member, an activist like him, an opponent he respects, than with traditional rightwing members of parliament. Other vehicles of value transmission are school teachers and the army. Rossi (1995) stresses the influence on the young neo-fascists he studied of the time they spent in the army for their military service.

Precipitating events

These potentialities need some precipitating event to be converted into a push to become a member of the ER movement. This can be some personal drama as in the case of some Dutch activists, or an encounter with someone who already belongs to the movement, hearing a speech by a movement leader and being seduced, or, a traumatic event at a larger scale such as the independence of Algeria in 1962 obliging the 'pieds-noirs' settlers to abandon the former French colony. Ivaldi's study of the FN in the Department of Isère (2001), by questionnaire and by interviews, stresses the very high proportion of members and sympathizers who lived for some time in Algeria before 1962: up to a quarter of his sample ($N = 644$) of FN supporters. For Perdomo, one of the leaders of the FN in Marseille, the shock came earlier from seeing on television the Soviet Army invade Hungary in 1956. Ever since, he was on the side of the extreme-right because of his anticommunist stand. For some, the 1968 students' revolt and the sexual liberation that followed was the trigger. For some of the younger generation, it was the Gulf War.

Our interviews suggest that actual joining can be triggered by movement networks, something in the mass media (a television program, a book, a newspaper), friendship networks or partners and spouses. Hence, although the significance of social networks is reconfirmed, other transmitters appear to be important as well. Movement organizations are not passively waiting for potential participants to knock on their doors; they reach out, they mobilize. They actively seek contact with potential members. An example was provided by one of the Dutch interviewees explaining how he as a union member felt abandoned by his union when he got into a confrontation with his employer. He was then approached by members of the extreme-right party in his community who offered support.

Staying a member

Staying a member is a matter of affect and rationality. Declining commitment and satisfaction and again a precipitating event make people defect from the movement. Thus, in order to understand why one stays in the movement one has joined, a cost/benefit analysis is enlightening. Joining any organization and taking part in its activities comes with costs; it takes time, sometimes money, people might lose their job or their friends. Only a small proportion (between 1–5 per cent) of the adult population are members of a political party. The costs are higher in the case of an extreme-right party because of the moral reprobation attached to it and the memories of Nazism and the Holocaust. Rightwing activists experience significant levels of stigmatization, as Linden and Klandermans (2006) show for their Dutch interviewees. That is also expressed in the comment of one of the FN activists interviewed by Orfali (1990: 113): 'As far as the pals I could have are concerned many stopped talking to me, as if from one day to another one became racist, fascist; one had long teeth coming out, nails getting longer, hair growing all over'. It is even more costly with more radical extreme-right groups than the FN. In his study of young neo-fascist activists (N = 300), Eric Rossi (1995: 179) shows that two out of three have been in trouble with the police and one in five have been in prison. In order to overcome the stigma, activists become more closely attached to the movement. There they get the recognition society is withholding (Tristan, 1987).

Yet, there also are benefits attached to it. What can such movements offer? There are not many material benefits (jobs, offices, prestige positions, political career) offered by extreme-right groups. Yet the FN, though, as noted by Birenbaum (1992), has given to second-rate intellectuals the possibility to make a career in the party's structures, in its scientific council for instance, or in the party schools. And there are social benefits in joining: making friends, new relations, going to the ER movement events. That is what Anne Tristan (1987) shows in her study of the FN members in northern Marseille, for whom the party is like a second family, a substitute to the disappearance of social and associative life in the difficult neighborhoods where they live, deserted by the left associations. This is what activists in all five countries express; within the ER movement they get the respect that is denied them in the outside world.

Hence, there are important psychological benefits: practically all the activists we interviewed, say that it made them feel better to join, they were no more alone, other people were thinking like them, they felt demarginalized, recognized at last, finding their balance at last as witnessed in Orfali's study: 'It is feeling good for sure. I live in agreement with myself. That's something very important, it hadn't happened to me in a long time' (Orfali, 1990: 129). There are intellectual benefits too; the feeling that belonging to the group gives a meaning, (an 'interpretative frame' to speak in social movement theory terms) suddenly to the world they live in, that everything has become clear, a kind of revelation (Orfali, 1990: 126). Even the marginality of the party can be turned to their advantage, making them different, intriguing for the others, a non-conformist vanguard. Some go as far as to say that if the FN became a majority, it would deceive them: 'the day the FN will be a mass party, a large-scale party, with many members, I don't think I'll stay. I'll leave it, I think I will' (Orfali, 1990: 132). It is 'returning the stigma', to put it in the words of Goffman and the ethno-methodologists.

There are generational aspects to take into consideration, something that we did not theorize about thus far, but which seem to be important: The younger vs older generation of activists seem to tell different stories. Why is this so? Violence as rebellion against the established order has a specific appeal to the very young. The small radical neo-fascist groups have old leaders but young troops. After the age 22–25, they go to more intellectual and less radical movements (Rossi, 1995: 260). Skinhead groups also appeal to the very young, selling them a life style, a youth subculture with its symbols, its music, its hair and dress style. That is what we found among young activists in France, for whom the Algerian war belongs to a distant past.

Also, as factors keeping a person inside the organization, one must take into account the strategy of the organization itself – giving responsibilities to the new members, integrating them in the party networks, creating a party subculture, influencing their reading, their cultural activities, etc.

It is like a funnel of interpretation one should build, starting with early childhood socialization, then schooling, then military service, then occupation, immersion in different groups and networks, till the first encounter with the organization (s) and the present time, taking simultaneously into account personal factors, socioeconomic factors, political and ideological factors and contextual factors.

In some cases, there is no way back. Individuals have burned their bridges, have lost or been ousted from their previous social networks. They have become dependent on the organization for their friendships and their social relations. Especially to the activist, the movement is like a new family that helps them solve their identity problems. An activist identity is an all-inclusive identity. Moreover, organizations appear to apply strategies to keep participants in. For example, by creating structures which makes it possible for many people to take responsibilities upon themselves. But also by restricting contacts with the outside world. Extreme movements are 'greedy institutions' that demand unconditional loyalty.

The rationale of participation

Identity

From the very beginning identity was part of our theoretical framework. However, over the course of the project we have discussed and gradually developed our reasoning in this regard. We now acknowledge more clearly than before that participation and identity impact on each other. Identity has different aspects: (a) belongingness vs distinctiveness, (b) continuity vs breaks with the past or conversions, (c) esteem vs not deserving the esteem people feel they deserve, (d) action vs inaction. Belongingness vs distinctiveness are rooted in categorizations: in-group identification vs outgroup differentiation. If such identifications and differentiations acquire a political dimension identity rapidly politicizes (Simon and Klandermans, 2001; Simon, 2004).

Among our interviewees, identity seems to be related to such factors as consistency and standing up for your principles. Participants feel they are different, a non-conformist vanguard. Often, they disagree with the label of 'rightwing extremist' that society sticks upon them. They feel like good democrats or citizens, feel like they say what many people think but do not dare to say. In several settings our interviewees showed admiration for people who live for their principles, even if those people occupy opposite positions on the political spectrum. This suggests common elements between extremism and fundamentalism. Admiration for determination. On the other hand, we observed that participants in every country suffered from stigmatization, although the extent to which stigmatization occurred differed in the five countries.

There are many indicators in the interviews of the importance of the movement's culture in the creation and maintenance of a shared identity: books, music, etc. In each country this seems to be a deliberate strategy of the movement organization in order to attempt to inculcate the members.

An important matter is that of how identity politicizes? We define 'politicized identity' as an identity in opposition to some authority defined as unjust (Simon and Klandermans, 2001). Social movement literature suggests that politicization of collective identity presupposes collectively defined grievances which produce a 'we' feeling; causal attributions which denote a 'they' responsible for the grievances; and encounters with authorities perceived unjust. Social identity theory (SIT) does not state any explicit hypothesis of that kind but suggests that impermeability of group boundaries and illegitimacy of lower group status and in-group identification makes collective action more likely (Ellemers et al., 1988). SIT misses the dynamic aspect suggested by the element of encounters with authorities perceived to be unjust which is deemed important in social movement literature. Interestingly, it is precisely such encounters that some of our interviewees reference to explain their aversion to politics in general. Identity fosters participation in a movement organization and impregnates encounters with outgroups and authorities, while, on the other hand, participation and such encounters strengthen identity.

Ideology

As for the rationale of participation, we started to look into ideology, the role of nationalism, ethnocentrism and racism. The ideological dimensions that show up in the interviews are strikingly similar (Klandermans and Mayer, 2006): anti-establishment, opposition to parliamentarism, militarism, law and order, need for a strong leader, biologically founded racism and opposition to equalitarianism (Mudde, 1996). There are also conspiracy theories and the simplicity of a world in black and white.

Employing life-history interviews adds an intriguing dimension to the answers to this question. Interviewees do their best to make sense of why they do what they do. They reconstruct their past, express all kinds of justifications. This element of justification might be so important precisely because participation in an extreme-right organization is such a condemnable thing to do in the eyes of the wider social environment. Perhaps the interviewees are defending themselves in the interview. After all, the interviewer is part of the same hostile outside world. In any event, we paid special attention to these justifications because they reveal why the interviewees consider participation in a rightwing organization a meaningful thing to do.

In this context, it is of importance to note that many interviewees feel that they live in a hostile world, they feel besieged. Certainly, in some of the interviews a lot of resentment can be observed against what politics, the media, and in general the outside world did to them after they entered the movement. There are certainly important differences between the countries in this respect, but that makes it all the more interesting. In this context, the questions of how interviewees deal with the past and deal with fascism are also important. This theme brings us to the third question.

Links with the past

Another dimension for comparison might be the presence of an ongoing fascist and nationalist current in a country, which means that there is no clear organizational or ideological break with the past. This seems, for example, the case in Belgium and Italy at least more so than in the other countries. As for the third question, it turns out that there are all kinds of links with organizations and ideas from the past, but not necessarily pre-World War II. In France, for example, the Algerian war is more important; in Flanders, Flemish nationalism and its organizations; in Italy and Germany, the fascist history inevitably comes to mind. In Germany, in addition to Nazism and fascism, organizations of the so-called Heimatvertriebenen (Germans who fled from East European countries) play an important role. For the younger generation, however, such links with the past do not seem to exist. In any event, the picture is more complicated than the continuity-hypothesis suggests. This is not to say that no abeyance-structures are revealed. On the contrary, they are but of a greater variety than the literature thus far seems to recognize.

Indeed, in all five countries there is historical continuity, though rightwing extremism has laid in abeyance for some time after the World War II. But the structures that hosted the extreme-right in the various countries and shaped its trajectory are quite different. Links with the past appear to be an ambivalent asset. On the one side, abeyance structures provided contemporary rightwing extremism with connections to previous movements, with a reservoir of experienced activists, with ready-made action repertoires, and ideological interpretation frames to lean on. On the other hand, links with Nazism and fascism are essentially de-legitimizing. Rightwing extremist movements are better off when they can rely on a more diversified set of abeyance structures, as it was the case in Flanders, because of the pre-existing nationalist movement, or in France, with its two centuries old tradition of reactionary and revolutionary right. Italy is yet another case. *Alleanza Nazionale* (AN) is the direct heir of fascism and has built on the existing networks ever since World War II. But fascism was perceived as a lesser evil than Nazism, especially in the South where its traditional strongholds are. In Northern Italy, a bloody two-year long civil war (1943–1945), opposing partisans to the fascist Republic of Salo, strongly rooted anti-fascism in the region. While in the South, fascism had a better image, associated with public works and social integration, as compared to the former aristocracy. There was no civil war and the 'liberation war' ended two years earlier than in the North. Moreover, AN was offering the image of a democratic 'post-fascist' right party that marginalized the nostalgic fascism of the old *Movimento Sociale Italiano*.

Psychologically speaking, these are significant differences. The history of a group is an important element of its members' social identity. A heroic past is something to be proud of and to identify with, but a dark history makes one feel ashamed and guilty (Doosje, Branscombe, Spears, and Manstead, 1998; Klandermans, Werner, and Van Doorn, 2008; Lagrou, 2000). In France, Italy and Flanders the extreme right has a history that can be framed independently from German Nazism. Although in all three countries the extreme-right did collaborate with the Germans, it has more to refer to and take pride in. But in Germany and the Netherlands such a possibility did not exist. There, the extreme-right has nothing but a dark side.

Comparisons between countries

As we assumed the answers to the lead questions would differ depending on the national context, we designed the study (see Klandermans and Mayer, 2006 for details on the design of our study) in the five different countries mentioned in the introduction. It occurred to us that there might be differences between those countries with successful rightwing extremist organizations and the others. Success comes with professional management, providing organizations with a variety of opportunities to participate, whereas failure comes with a restriction of contacts with the outside world. A more or less repressive or hostile environment might be another explanation. These are, of course, only hypotheses, and below we propose some more, but we had the data to test them.

We chose these five countries because we thought they represented very different cases, with different levels of ER electoral strength, party size and embeddedness, different levels of acceptance of the extreme-right, and different historical pasts. Although we did not have much theory with regard to the comparison between the countries, we did try to relate what we were told in our interviews to the meaning of rightwing extremism in the individual countries. Several possible comparative dimensions have been mentioned in the course of our meetings.

The electoral system: On the one hand, Italy, Belgium and France are three countries where the extreme-right has been, electorally, relatively successful, whereas Germany and the Netherlands are two countries where the extreme-right has failed in that regard.[1] Why so? Part of the reason might be that in the latter two the climate has been more repressive. In France the electoral system limits the national representation of the extreme-right, despite the high proportion of votes it draws. At the regional and local level has the FN been able to secure more influence. The German system keeps the extreme-right out of power too, but basically because the extreme-right parties remain small and below the electoral threshold. Parties of the size of the FN, the AN or the *Vlaams Bloc* (VB) would have easily made it into the German *Bundestag*. In the Netherlands, even minor parties can enter the representative bodies at the various levels of government. For some time, the extreme-right was represented in the national parliament and in regional and local councils. But the parties remained too small and their representatives too incompetent to exert any influence. Belgium and Italy are the only two countries where rightwing extremist movements are well represented in the national political arena and in a position to have influence.

Antifascist mobilization: If, leaving the past aside, we concentrate on the time when we conducted our interviews, in those days, Italy seemed to be the only country where the multi-organizational field was not predominantly hostile, at least towards AN the new 'post fascist' party. In the remaining four countries, organizations of the extreme right were certainly not treated in a friendly manner. Under those circumstances, chances were high for anyone joining such movements or who was already a member to be stigmatized. Related to the previous dimension is that of how political parties in a country react to parties from the extreme-right. More generally, this and the previous factor concern the political opportunities for rightwing extremism in the five countries.

A large-scale comparative study on anti-rightwing extremist *cordon sanitaire* strategies and their efficiency in seven countries over a period of 10 years (1989–1999) corroborates our analysis (Van der Brug and Van Spanje, 2004). Expert judgments show clearly that, of our five countries, the Netherlands (for the *Centrumdemocraten*) and Germany (for the *Republikaner*) come first for the perceived strictness of the *cordon sanitaire*, measured on a 10-point scale, with a score of 9.4 on the scale (same level only in Wallonia, or the Belgian *Front National*). Then comes Flanders for the VB, with a score of 8.6. France is in the third position for the FN, with a score of 7.5. And last of all comes Italy for *Alleanza Nazionale*, with a score of 1.9, even below the *Lega Nord* (2.3). Italy was, at the time of our study, indeed the most favorable context for present or ex-rightwing extremist movements and Germany and the Netherlands the harshest.

Internal matters: Such differences in success in themselves create different situations for participants. It makes, of course, a difference whether you are participating in a relatively strong movement or a weak one. Especially if the movement is despised; the difference between ridiculed or feared. The presence or absence of charismatic leaders is yet another comparative dimension – a factor that might hold for France and Belgium. And finally, the extent to which activists are fighting among themselves, which was very much the case in the Netherlands.

Conclusion

In this chapter I reflected on investigating rightwing extremists. More specifically, I discussed the use of life-history interviews as a means of exploring the habitat of rightwing extremist activists. In a way, our research was meant to correct the picture of rightwing extremist activists as irrational, aggressive and violent men. We wanted to portray them as movement activists in their daily life. We have tried to picture the world of extreme-right activists. As through a magnifying glass we have focused on a small part of that world, approximately 150 activists in five different countries. They allowed us into their homes and into their movements, but more than anything else it's the stories they told us in sometimes lengthy interviews that gave us a unique look into their lives. Life-history interviews are like invasions on someone's private territory. By letting us in and showing us around our interviewees made it possible for us to put together a unique set of data. We do not know, certainly regarding the extreme-right, of any comparable compilation of interviews and additional information about the interviewees, their organizations, their position and their activities inside the movement.

Note

1 Meanwhile, both Germany and the Netherlands have successful ER parties. That does not mean that the observations reported here are invalid. This is what the ER was then.

References

Adorno, T.W., E. Frenkel-Brunswick, D. Levinson, and R.N. Sandford. 1950. *The Authoritarian Personality*. New York, NY: Harper Book.

Andrews, M. 1991. *Lifetimes of Commitment: Aging, Politics, Psychology*. Cambridge: Cambridge University Press.

Billig, M. 1979. *Fascists: A Social Psychological View of the National Front*. New York, NY and London: Harcourt Brace Jovanovich.

Birenbaum, G. 1992. *Le Front National en Politique*. Paris: Balland.

Blee, K.M. 2002. *Inside Organized Racism. Women in the Hate Movement*. Berkeley, CA: University of California Press.

Blee, K.M. and V. Taylor. 2002. "Semi-structured interviewing in social movement research." In *Social Movement Research*, edited by B. Klandermans and S. Staggenborg, 92–117. Minneapolis, MN: University of Minneapolis Press.

Doosje, B., N.R. Branscombe, R. Spears, and A.S.R. Manstead. 1998. "Guilty by association: when one's group has a negative history." *Journal of Personality and Social Psychology*, 75, 872–886.

Ellemers, N., A. Van Knippenberg, N. De Vries, and H. Wilke. 1988. "Social identification, and permeability of group boundaries." *European Journal of Social Psychology*, 18, 497–513.

Ivaldi, G. 2001. "L'analyse comparée des soutiens électoraux du national-populisme en" Europe occidentale. Apports et limites des grands programmes d'enquêtes transnationales." In *Les Cultures Politiques des Sympathisants et Adhérents du Front National, Enquête dans le Département de l'Isère*, PhD, IEP, Grenoble.

Klandermans, B. and N. Mayer 2006. *Extreme Right Activists in Europe. Through the Magnifying Glass*. London: Routledge.

Klandermans, B., M. Werner, and M. Van Doorn. 2008. "Redeeming Apartheid's legacy: Collective guilt, political ideology, and compensation." *Political Psychology*, 29, 331–350.

Kornhauser, W. 1959. *The Politics of Mass Society*. Glencoe, IL: The Free Press.

Lagrou, P. 2000. *The Legacy of Nazi Occupation. Patriotic Memory and National Recovery in Western Europe: 1945–1965*. Cambridge: Cambridge University Press.

Linden, A. and B. Klandermans. 2006. "Stigmatization and repression of extreme right the Netherlands." *Mobilization*, 11, 141–157.

Lipset, S.M. and E. Raab. 1970. *The Politics of Unreason*. New York, NY: Harper & Row.

Mudde, C. 1996. "The war of words defining the extreme right party family." *West European Politics*, 19(2), 225–248.

Orfali, B. 1990. *L'Adhésion au Front National. De la Minorité au Mouvement Social*, Paris: Kimé.

Roberts, K.M. 2018. "Populism, democracy, and resistance: The United States in comparative perspective." In *The Resistance: The Dawn of the Anti-Trump Opposition Movement*, edited by D.S. Meyer and S. Tarrow, 54–74. New York, NY: Oxford University Press.

Rokeach, M. 1960. *The Open and Closed Mind*. New York, NY: Basic Books.

Rossi, E. 1995. *Jeunesse Française des Années 80–90: La Tentation Néo-fasciste*. Paris: LGDJ.

Rubin, H.J. and S.R. Rubin. 1995. *Qualitative Interviewing: The Art of Hearing Data*. Thousand Oaks, CA: Sage.

Simon, B. 2004. *Identity in Modern Society. A Social Psychological Perspective*. Oxford: Blackwell.

Simon, B. and B. Klandermans. 2001. "Politicized collective identity. A social psychological analysis." *American Psychologist*, 56, 319–331.

Teske, N. 1997. *Political Activists America. The Identity Construction Model of Political Participation*, Cambridge: Cambridge University Press.

Tristan, A. 1987. *Au front*. Paris: Gallimard.

Van der Brug, W. and J. Van Spanje. 2004. "*Consequences of the strategy of a 'Cordon Sanitaire' Against anti-immigrant parties.*" Paper prepared for the ECPR joint sessions of workshops. Workshop 17: "Effects of incumbency on organisations of radical right-wing parties", Uppsala, 13–18 April.

PART IV

Ethnographic studies of the far right

15

AN OBSERVATIONAL STUDY OF THE NORWEGIAN FAR RIGHT

Some reflections

Katrine Fangen

Ethnographic studies of political activist groups that employ anti-democratic practices such as illegal demonstrations or violence can help us to understand why people join such groups and how their views and actions take form (Bessant, 1995; Hamm, 1993). However, much research on extremists has not involved speaking directly with the participants, but has relied heavily on internet data, diaries and secondary data, as noted by Mahmood (2001) and Harris, Simi, and Ligon (2016: 602). These authors also criticize the lack of transparency in the few studies that draw on direct contact with extremists.

By reflecting on my own study, and referring to other similar studies, in this chapter I share experiences of doing observational research on the far right in the hope of making it easier for other researchers in this field.[1] I discuss entrance, development of rapport and dilemmas from my ethnographic study of the Norwegian far right between 1993 and 1994. When conducting this study, I was concerned about the need for informed consent and confidentiality, and was open about the purpose of my research and my ideological and political difference from the participants. Informed consent and confidentially, and respecting participant integrity, are important with any group a researcher is studying. In my experience, it is possible to get access by being open, and that this can build rapport (see also, Ezekiel, 2002). By contrast, Simi and Futrell (2015) reports he needed to pretend to agree to some degree with activists' views in order to develop rapport with members of the American white supremacist group, Aryan Nations.

Background to the study

My study of far right activists dates back to 1993 when I received a 2-year grant from the Ministry of Children and Families for a fieldwork study on racism, nationalism and National Socialism among Norwegian youth, resulting in a research report (Fangen, 1995). A scholarship from the University of Oslo enabled me to expand the study into a doctoral thesis (Fangen, 1999). My study was analytically positioned within the broader tradition of youth subculture research, combined with various cultural sociological perspectives. This has been my analytical frame in several of my studies – of anarchist, communist, and neo-Nazi youths in East Germany (Fangen, 1992), young adult Somalis (Fangen, 2007), and young adult immigrants in Europe (Fangen et al., 2012).

According to the various paradigms of interpretative sociology, the social sciences should aim to arrive at a method built upon communicative experience as well as focusing on action (Habermas, 1984: 109). This makes it possible to study far right groups with an analytical gaze that extends people's common understanding of these groups. In my work this has involved analyzing the practices of far right activists in relation to the cultural contexts where they occur, and which they produce.

My aim has been to explore far right activists' own interpretations and justifications of their practices and utterances. I wanted to find out who these far right activists were – their worldviews, but also their personal narratives, especially the trajectories that led them into or out of the movement, and to grasp the communicative structures of their scene.

Participant observation was an obvious choice of method. As argued by Bessant (1995: 10), who has studied Australian neo-Nazis, ethnographic methods are necessary in order to find out in detail why some young people join such groups, and what is/is not 'possible to think, say or do for a young Nazi'.

Entering the scene

I started contacting far right activists during the summer of 1993. I had heard that they met at a pub in downtown Oslo on the first Saturday of each month. After wandering through the area for several hours one Saturday afternoon, I saw two skinheads enter a pub. I followed them in, and immediately noticed a group of skinheads sitting by the window. I went to the bar and ordered a drink, and realized that they were staring at me. Taking a sip of my drink, I walked over to them. I explained that I was writing a book about skinheads, and asked if I could join them. One of them smiled and said 'sure'. They were in a party mood, and were quite welcoming.

After a while, I told them 'I'm definitely not a racist'. One man, who had been friendly up to that point, looked displeased at that, and remained silent and disapproving for a while. I later learned how they felt about labels like 'racist' and 'Nazi': not that they did not have ideas that were racist or Nazi, but that views that they did not identify with were often attributed to them. Other marginalized groups often express similar frustrations, and may want the public to get a more complete picture of them, for better or for worse. This appeared to be the main reason why these far right activists decided to let me in.

Importantly, the leading figures welcomed me. They seemed able to view the movement also with a view from the outside, and could often confirm my interpretations of the underlying social mechanisms of the movement. The importance of leaders acting together with the researcher, providing new insights and confirming their own, is described by Whyte (1981: 301–302). Whyte's key informant/collaborator, 'Doc', explained that as long as he told the others that he was a friend of Doc's, nobody would bother him. I experienced the same thing: if the leading persons accepted my being there, nobody else objected.

On the first evening I spent with the far right activists, I met Egil (31), who, as I later learned, represented the most militant line. Asked for an interview the following week, he willingly agreed. During this interview, he told me about his life, the turbulent family situation, an absent father, and his own deep loyalty to his mother and grandparents. He had 'been in and out of school', attended a boarding school where he 'didn't fit in', and then encountered the militant scene when he was 15 years old. Before then, he had drifted in and out of many scenes, including various religious groups, squatters and drug addicts. Egil's views and previous actions were extreme. I could not excuse him: however, I also felt that he himself did not want that, but had an intense desire to be understood.

I met Sverre (29), a leading skinhead, the second time I met the far right activists. He came directly to me, shook hands and said, 'hello, my name is Sverre, I've heard you're going to write a book about us. Then you should visit my place for a real skinhead party, that's the only way to get to know how we really are. Phone me if you like, I'm in the telephone directory, and I live in …'. He added that I should simply spend time around them, rather than doing interviews: 'You'll get much more information that way'. This example further supports existing argument in favor of ethnographic observations more generally. By being there, listening to people talk, seeing how they interact, you learn much more than by asking questions. Whyte's informant Doc explained that asking too much about why, when, what, and where makes people suspicious: it is better to get the answers by just hanging around (Whyte, 1981: 302).

I also got to know three other leading activists (and after my fieldwork finished, two more as well) within this broad network of far right activists (which consisted of several groups of different degrees of extremeness). Audun became an important key informant: he read drafts of almost all of my publications, and now and then provided further information. For him, this relationship functioned as a channel for reflecting on his own participation in a marginal setting. I invited him to be involved in the interpretation work. This approach is similar to that proposed by, *inter alia*, Smith (1987: 13).

Many younger and less experienced activists appeared uncertain about the kind of information I should have access to. It was the older activists who spoke most openly about sensitive details (like their own previous offences, contacts among the leaders, or how the militant cells were organized). They felt more confident, probably because they also set the rules and did not have to fear reprimands from others. They also had much more experience in deciding how to present information without risking too much. Sometimes I was amazed at how freely they told me secret details. Why did so many of them tell me so much? Perhaps they wished to impress, to shock (and test my reactions), to put other activists in a bad light – or, as several explained, they wanted me to write the whole story, 'the truth' about the scene.

One younger activist was surprised that I had so much contact with the core activists, because they were usually the most sceptical. I myself think that those who approached me wanted to explain how things were. That desire may grow stronger among those who have participated for many years without much contact with outsiders. It takes a lot of effort to keep all the secret information within the group all the time.

Since leaders have a more independent role, they are in a sense also more marginal than the other activists. I often heard core activists express their dissatisfaction with the scene, and even their willingness to quit it. One said he was 'fed up' with the scene (because of all the negativity associated with it, the violence, the negative world views, the distrust between the members), and would leave it if he could find a girl to settle down with. However, years later, I learned that he had still not left the scene – and leaving certainly becomes more difficult after many years of involvement. This partly has to do with the stigma being attached to them. Many have been named in public several times, and experience problems getting jobs or having people trust them because of their earlier affiliation with this scene. This is also related to the slogan "one time Nazi always Nazi", which many of them have experienced being confronted with.

Another, younger, informant became less and less satisfied towards the end of my fieldwork, and repeatedly told me he was not 'that interested in politics anymore'. After I had left the scene, I spoke with him again, and heard that he was no longer very involved. He did not explain why, but I got the impression that our many talks together had led him to take a more distanced view than before. However, the effect was not permanent. During my fieldwork, he distanced himself from the militant parts of the scene, and from its Nazi content – but then, many years later, he joined one of the most ideologically extreme groups on the scene.

Developing rapport

For a scene which is supervised by the Special Branch of the police (PST, 2018), it was a real threat to let outsiders in and give them access to sensitive information. As one leading activist put it, 'even I have been suspected of being a traitor sometimes, and since you're going to write about us, it's not to be wondered that they sometimes suspect you'. Nevertheless, the activists wanted me to experience how their lifestyle was; some said they wanted me to write the 'true' story, both the positive and the negative parts. They seemed less worried about what I would write about the scene in general, and more about what I would write about them as individuals. Although there were exceptions, and some willingly let me conduct life-story interviews. For them, it was important to be understood as whole persons, not solely as activists affiliated with an extreme scene.

Although they knew that I was 'not one of them', the relationship between us functioned because the contradictions between them and me were rarely verbalized, and could remain unconscious to some degree. However, I had to listen to lengthy monologues on, for example, ZOG (the Zionist Occupation Government), a conspiracy theory about an alleged Zionist power elite dominating world policies. Usually I listened to such talk without interrupting since I wanted to be able to explain how these people think, and how, in turn, their thinking structures their way of acting and people's responses to their actions.

I followed these far right activists as a part-time observer for one year. I met individuals with differing views on ideology and practice. During that year of fieldwork, I spoke with most of those who regularly attended the gatherings for far right activists in southern and eastern Norway. They generally took the initiative to contact me, and I had many conversations with the leading and most militant individuals. They gave me their phone numbers so that I could learn where and when they would meet next.

As I was studying a field that in Norway had not been examined from the 'inside' before, the exploratory aspect of the study was important. The approach to such a study is not set in stone from the very beginning. How to write about the field and what issues are important will change during the course of the study. This flexibility, so central to qualitative research, also makes it impossible to give participants a clear idea of what to expect to read later on, when the results are published. In other words, obtaining fully informed consent is not possible.

At the beginning of my fieldwork, I conducted life-story interviews with some of the activists, and had follow-up interviews with them later. My questions concerned their general beliefs, their views of their adversaries, and of their own scene. I then asked detailed questions about their upbringing. Otherwise, almost everyone answered my questions about their background, how they had entered the scene, and similar topics when these points emerged in natural field settings. However, some were paranoid. For example, when I searched my pockets and handbag for money, they would ask, 'What are you doing? Are you turning on a tape recorder?' Moreover, when I gave a ride to some activists, and the one sitting beside me was unable to open my glove compartment, he thought I was hiding a tape recorder there. Because of their active scepticism, I never carried a notebook during my fieldwork sessions. I did not want any of them to rifle through my notes. Instead, I always jotted down my impressions after I had come home at night, and would then work on my notes the following day. This is a common strategy in fieldwork settings where taking notes openly can affect the participants. As argued by Mulhall (2003: 311), there are merits to writing field notes in situ, and at the end of the day. Both approaches ensure that memories are not lost. However, Mulhall also adds that both short-term and long-term reflection may provide more reflection on events. In much fieldwork (not only among violent groups), in situ field notes are not possible or advisable.

The far right activists were accustomed to outsiders trying to gain access to information about them in order to attack or break up the scene. To be able to relax, and gain access to information, I needed their trust. I needed them to relax around me, and not see me as an agent of the police, political opposition groups, or the tabloids. I have never been a good actor, so I spoke honestly when asked whether I was playing a double role. They had no problem with the fact that I worked for the Norwegian Youth Research Institute. I explained that the Institute financed research on youth drug abuse, leisure habits, awareness of environmental issues, and many other areas. This was fine because they saw these areas of research as neutral and therefore not part of what they considered 'the conspiracy' (i.e. Zionist occupation government) (see Fangen, 1998).

I did not have to say words of approval in response to their statements, or that I agreed with their actions. They appeared to accept me as long as I was honest about the differences between us. I think that they would have been more sceptical if I had tried to give the impression of being one of them. They explained that they took it for granted that I would never have received financing for such a project if I personally had attitudes like theirs. I never felt that they were trying to convince me, but rather that they wanted me to fully understand how they thought. Also, other researchers in similar scenes report that participants did not seem very interested in the researchers' political views (see e. g. Blee, 1998; Jansson, 2010). Of course, these activists might have been using their involvement with me to develop and rehearse their own justificatory narratives, or simply enjoy storytelling.

When discussing my fieldwork with friends or colleagues, I was surprised to find that it was generally assumed that I had infiltrated the scene. Apparently, many people think the only way to gain access to the far right is by lying about one's identity and purposes. In fact, being honest about who I was and what I believe in helped to gain trust and access to information. After all, this community consists of people who have good reason to fear informers and infiltrators; they were understandably sceptical towards people who pretended to be one of them.

I sometimes became insecure when one of the participants was brusque or evasive in contacts with me (see also Simi and Futrell, 2015). I asked the leading activists why they acted this way, and they told me that several of the group were sceptical about me. They added that this was self-evident, because everybody there was paranoid. One of them remarked, 'Even I have been accused of being a snitch.' This person said that he thought I could earn their trust if I joined them on trips outside Oslo and at private parties. This could enable them to test my reactions when I was unable simply to retreat. In addition, as noted, they felt it was important for me to join them on such occasions, to see how they 'really' were. The one time I attended a White Power rock concert in Sweden with them (see Fangen, 2003), clearly had such a function. On such fieldtrips, I felt a more profound sense of fear than with activists at their monthly pub gatherings, when other people, not related to the scene, also were present. Blee (1998) writes in detail about how fear was the dominant feeling when she conducted life-story interviews among US racist activists. I did not have constant feelings of fear: they would emerge and disappear, depending on how the situation evolved. Not being entirely alone with activists gave me stronger feelings of security than when I was alone with them in their homes or the White Power concert arenas.

Occasionally, participants would tell me things they would not tell each other. For example, it was easier for them to confide in me concerning their doubts about participating in such a scene. That they were more open towards me on such matters could indicate trust, but also that they did not fear censure or reprisals, as might be the case if they made such comments to fellow activists. Some participants contacted me frequently on a private basis, and wanted to chat over a beer. They were much more open with me during these conversations than when I met them together with other activists.

I sometimes encountered people who did not understand that I was not an activist, but a researcher. I tried to let people know as soon as possible, and rumors about my role spread quickly. However, once I attended a meeting held by a local group of the Norwegian Union, a group of elderly anti-immigration activists. The members of this union entered an agreement at this meeting concerning a transfer of IT equipment to far right youth activists. I later learned that leading figures within the Union were angry that I had written about this, as they did not want the public to know about their close relations with youth activists who had a pronounced anti-democratic profile. However, I had told the people present at the meeting that I was not an ordinary participant, and that I was writing a book about the activists, so they could have asked me to leave.

Following the far right activists for such a long time provided me with access to information about their private lives. Some of them worried that I would misuse the data. Such information was important to me, as I wanted to learn more about how the participants managed to balance an everyday life with an unsafe scene. To calm the activists' fears, I usually replied that yes, I did learn a great many intimate details about them, but that I would focus on treating such information confidentially and anonymize details that might allow anybody to recognize them. This is also what I did. With some informants, I used several different pseudonyms, so that information about them as private persons could not be linked to other information about them. Also, for those who had jobs, I changed their occupations to those similar in the labour hierarchy. It is often hard for a researcher to guess what details are problematic for an individual person to describe; for example, Doc, who was the key informant for Whyte in his study, felt it embarrassing even to have been described so positively, and felt as if he had promoted himself. It might be that I have hurt some participants or that they felt recognized by others in the scene or people outside, but I have never heard any of them complain of such things. What I heard is that they felt that I had managed to describe them correctly, and for good and for worse, they liked this, rather than being (intentionally) wrongly represented as they were used to.

When I was present at the monthly gatherings of the activists, I mostly spoke with those who approached me themselves. Often, so many came up to me that I simply went from one informant to the other without having to initiate contacts myself. However, sometimes when I started talking to an activist who otherwise usually enjoyed my company, he turned his back on me. Contact was probably not always equally convenient. Thus, I usually sat down beside one of the two or three who always wanted my company, and then let the others join in when they felt like it. This made it easier for me because I never had to 'plan' the evening: I could just be there and let things unfold.

Compared to other kinds of fieldwork on secretive and potentially dangerous groups (see overview in Lee, 1995: 49–51), I gained surprisingly good access. Lee reports of researchers having had to take a covert role or present themselves as potential sympathizers or members. Assuming a covert role when studying violent groups might lead the researcher into major ethical dilemmas. As reported by Mitchell (1991: 106), who studied a group of paramilitary survivalists by means of covert participant observation, researchers who take covert roles 'must do more than confirm the action, they must contribute to it'. As noted by Lee (1995: 196), if you are not to be excluded, one must talk and act in ways acceptable to those studied, even if they are at odds with your own personal values. Mitchell had to participate in a discussion where the participants were expected to propose violently homophobic measures.

As an acknowledged researcher, I could listen to such talks without having to express agreement. There were times when I could not leave it at that – but, knowing that I was not one of them, they did not seem to mind that I did not share their attitudes. From the start, I saw it as much safer for me to be open about the differences between myself and them, rather than trying to hide them. I would participate by drinking beer with them, chatting with them at the pub table. Sometimes I had to participate more actively: once, while I was driving the car, the activists sitting in the back started a fight and I had to ask them to calm down. Other times I had to fend off boys who wanted intimate contact with me.

In contrast to many male researchers who study such violent groups, there was no demand that I should relate to my informants as 'one of them', and I was not exposed to violent 'tests' to the same degree. Jankowski (1991: 75) reports that he was 'only seriously wounded twice' in the gangs he studied; his own gang background and karate abilities proved very useful during his fieldwork.

Rather than testing my physical strength or my openness to involving myself in militant actions, the activists tested what Lee (1995: 22) has termed the 'limits of humor and forbearance'. I was never forced to respond to racist jokes. My informants were pleased enough if I laughed at their everyday comic remarks. Some comments were in fact very funny, and I had many good laughs during my fieldwork. Yes, my sense of humor made access to the far right activists much easier – but implicit here is also acknowledging them as fellow human beings (see Mahmood's 2001 study of militant Sikhs).

Methodological and ethical challenges of fieldwork among the far right

Ethnographic studies of the far right face many of the same methodological challenges as studies of criminal groups or gangs. Many research projects on the far right have felt the need to discuss ethical dilemmas in detail (see for example Bailey, 2016).

The far right activists gave me information and allowed me to observe their activities. They would probably have reacted more strongly if I had turned them in to the authorities, than if it had been someone who had entered their ranks under false pretenses. I managed to build up trust with them even though I was open about my political and ideological differences with them, and they, on their hand, dared to open themselves up to me. They told me, 'No outsider has ever seen as much of our world as you.'

I often found myself in methodologically challenging situations. For instance, I witnessed street violence where one of the activists attacked an opponent. I got a clear idea of who controlled the groups that carried out militant acts, I received information about who published the militant magazines, and I eventually under-stood who were the key figures in planning acts of violence, meetings and trips. I witnessed the prelude to an act of collective violence, although I was not told about what was going to happen.

Because I conducted research on far right activists by spending time with them and talking with them, anti-racists in the 1990s saw my work as being in opposi-tion to the work they were doing. However, I feel that this type of fieldwork should never be viewed in such a reductionist manner that it becomes a simple question of 'whose side are we on' (Becker, 1971). While acting in accordance with the trust I had built up in relation to my informants, I never became one of them, nor did I present myself as a champion of their causes. Yes, it is possible to build rapport and at the same time retain a critical view. Cohen (1991) and Ezekiel (2002) have argued that it is more useful to give racists a human face than to create a demonology, turning them all into evil monsters. The best strategy, according to Cohen, is to construct a space where racist youths can give voice to other and more complicated accounts with a wider register.

My argument is very much in line with that of Cohen. I have criticized those anti-Fascists whose strategy is to scare far right activists away from the local com-munity (Fangen, 2001). Excluding people from the community might lead those who are excluded to become even more filled with hate, and to have their con-spiracy theories confirmed. It is better to counter-argue respectfully, and show acceptance of them as fellow human beings. Some activists who have managed to exit the scene have done so after meeting a person who did not stigmatize them, but who also gave them food for thought in another direction than that of the far right scene (see for example the story of Tom in Fangen and Eiternes, 2002).

In addition to some instances of street violence, there was one particular evening that proved problematic. After having asked me to leave, without further expla-nation, the activists then went on to throw Molotov cocktails and open fire against the anarchist Blitz House. This took place during the holidays between Christmas and New Year's Eve in 1993. I had an idea that something was going to happen, but did not know exactly what. The next day, I read in the papers that some 20 to 30 far right activists had thrown Molotov cocktails and one of them had fired a shotgun against the Blitz House. Soon after, the police entered the place and demanded the names of all those present. However, some of them had already managed to escape, taking the weapons with them. My description of this evening at a panel discussion arranged by anti-racists led the Blitz group to file a complaint about me to the Norwegian Ethical Committee for Social and Humanistic Sciences. The contrast between their description of the event (at which they were not present) and mine is that they reported it as an incident which I had full knowledge of, whereas in reality I had not known what was going to happen. The ethical committee gives advice, but does not act like a court. Their general response was that without certain knowledge of what will happen, the researcher cannot be expected to report, and the safety of the researcher as well as the need for knowledge about such a setting must be taken into account. Also, they held that the fact that the incident involved two scenes in violent conflict with each other was different from when a group attacks a non-violent target.

There is a difference between having concrete knowledge that a crime will be committed and overhearing comments which could simply be bragging. In fact, it is difficult to classify such statements as bragging or serious encouragement. In this type of scene, such statements always have serious undercurrents, even when they take the form of jokes. Researchers will normally not get access to information that a serious attack is to be committed on a particular evening. In conducting fieldwork among the far right, my standpoint was that if I had received concrete information about a person who was going to be killed or beaten up at a specific time, I would definitely have taken measures to prevent this from happening by contacting the police. On the other hand, I also knew that I would probably never hear such information. I touched on this topic with my informants, who pointed out that even participants in the scene will generally be told as little as possible about future serious acts of violence. Serious crimes were usually planned by the militant cells of the scene. This information was not passed on to anyone other than the people directly involved. I knew that I would never hear the names of people who were going to commit specific acts of violence and I would never learn when these crimes were going to be committed (see also Pilkington et al., 2010 on not being interested in gaining information about violent acts).

Conclusions

Long-term fieldwork in communities of criminal and violent scenes can provide useful data. Ethnographic research and being together with people for extended periods is important in addition to studies that employ only textual data, as is common in studies of the far right or other extreme groups. When I have disseminated the results of this study to youth-club workers, teachers and others who encounter far right activists in their work, they have stressed the importance of knowing how to contact the participants in such scenes to help minimize the danger of future occurrences of violence. I have received positive responses: the type of information I was able to provide was of great help to their work and was information that they have wanted for some time. For example, I have been able to give advice on how to get in touch with young far right activists, and their more tolerant repertoires could be encouraged by talking about music, subcultural effects or clothing, etc. For example, some activists were very interested in the history of skinhead culture. They were knowledgeable about the non-political versions of this scene in the very beginning, even the Caribbean inspiration of *ska* music in its earliest forms.

In this chapter, I have also discussed my entry and evolving relations to far right activists during my fieldwork a few decades ago. In Norway, I am still the only person to have conducted such an extensive study by participant observation among far right activists, except for a philosophy student who entered the scene after me (Winsnes, 1998). Internationally, there are some studies, not least Kathleen Blee's and Pete Simi's extensive studies of the American far right. I think that many, including researchers of the far right, operate with the stereotyped assumption that it is not possible, practically or ethically, to conduct a field study of the far right. That has not been my experience. When you get to know such people, you experience that they too are human beings, and it is possible to 'like' them even though you may not like their views or their actions. Furthermore, access can be possible even though you are open about the differences between your views and theirs: in practice, the participants themselves are often not very interested in the views of the researcher (Blee, 1998; Jansson, 2010).

There are of course many challenges involved in making observations of a scene which is extreme and where some practices are illegal. But these challenges are not necessarily different from those related to studies of other extreme, illegal or anti-democratic groups. I agree with Kathleen Blee, who argues that 'the pitfalls, problems, and dilemmas of fieldwork on hidden communities does not mean that such research should be avoided.' Rather, she underlines that 'such studies need to be done with respect for the integrity and privacy of those who are the subjects' (2009: 23). Research on such groups is important because it can provide deeper insights into recruitment, and how such group members think and act than studies that rely solely on second-hand data or interviews. Spending time with the activists and seeing the flow of events can provide rich, contextual data which give valuable insights into the kind of groups these are, and how they think and act regarding violence and other contentious issues.

Note

1 I have previously written about this in Norwegian books and articles, as well as in my PhD thesis, which is available in English.

References

Bailey, G. 2016. "Extremism, community, stigma: Researching the far right and radical Islam in their context." In *Researching Marginalized Groups*, edited by K. Bhopal and R. Deuchar, 22–35. New York, NY: Routledge.

Becker, H. 1971. "Whose side are we on?" In *Sociological Work: Method and Substance*, by H. Becker. London: Penguin Press.

Bessant, J. 1995. "Political crime and the case of young neo-Nazis: A question of methodology." *Terrorism & Political Violence*, 7(4), 94–116.

Blee, K. 1998. "White knuckle research: Emotional dynamics in fieldwork with racist activists." *Qualitative Sociology*, 21(4), 381–399.

Blee, K. 2009. "Access and methods in research on hidden communities: reflections on studying U.S. organized racism." *eSharp*, Special Issue: Critical Studies in Researching Hidden Communities, 10–29.

Cohen, P. 1991. *Monstrous Images, Perverse Reasons: Cultural Studies in Anti-racist Education*. London: University of London, Centre for multicultural education.

Ezekiel, R. 2002. "An ethnographer looks at neo-Nazi and Klan groups." *American Behavioral Scientist*, 46(1), 51–71.

Fangen, K. 1992. *Tysklands nye ungdom: DDR-ungdom i overgangen til det kapitalistiske samfunn*. Oslo: Institutt for sosiologi, Universitetet i Oslo.

Fangen, K. 1995. *Skinheads i rødt, hvitt og blått. En sosiologisk studie fra 'innsiden'*. Oslo: Program for ungdomsforsking.

Fangen, K. 1998. "Living out our ethnic instincts: Ideological beliefs among far right activists." In *Nation and Race: The Developing Euro-American Racist Subculture*, edited by T. Bjørgo and J. Kaplan. Boston, MA: Northeastern University Press.

Fangen, K. 1999. *Pride and Power: A Sociological Interpretation of the Norwegian Radical Nationalist Underground Movement*. Oslo: Department of Sociology and Human Geography, University of Oslo.

Fangen, K. 2001. "Demonisering eller ansvarliggjøring." *Tidsskrift for ungdomsforskning*, 1(1), 26–44.

Fangen, K. and T. Eiternes. 2002. *Bak nynazismen*, Oslo: Cappelen.

Fangen, K. 2003. "A death mask of masculinity. The brotherhood of Norwegian right-wing skinheads." In *Among Men. Moulding Masculinities* (vol. 1), edited by S. Ervø and T. Johansson. London: Ashgate.

Fangen, K. 2007. "Citizenship among young adult Somalis in Norway." *YOUNG*, 15(4), 413–434.

Fangen, K., T. Johansson, and N. Hammarén. 2012. *Young Migrants: Exclusion and Belonging in Europe*. London: Palgrave.

Habermas, J. 1984. *The Theory of Communicative Action: Reason and the Rationalization of Society*. Boston, MA: Beacon Press.

Hamm, M. 1993. *American Skinheads. The Criminology and Control of Hate Crime*. London: Praeger Publishers.

Harris, D.J., P. Simi, and G. Ligon. 2016. "Reporting practices of journal articles that include interviews with extremists." *Studies in Conflict & Terrorism*, 39(7–8), 602–616.

Jankowski, M.S. 1991. *Islands in the Street. Gangs and American Urban Society*. Berkeley, CA: University of California Press.

Jansson, D. 2010. "The head vs. the gut: Emotions, positionality, and the challenges of fieldwork with a Southern nationalist movement." *Geoforum*, 41, 19–22.

Lee, R. 1995. *Dangerous Fieldwork*. London: Sage.

Mahmood, C.K. 2001. "Terrorism, myth, and the power of ethnographic praxis." *Journal of Contemporary Ethnography*, 30(5), 520–545.

Mitchell, R. 1991. "Secrecy and disclosure in fieldwork." In *Experiencing Fieldwork: An Inside View of Qualitative Research*, edited by W.B. Shaffir and R.A. Stebbins. Thousand Oaks, CA: Sage.

Mulhall, A. 2003. "In the field: Notes on observation in qualitative research." *Journal of Advanced Nursing*, 41(3), 306–311.

Pilkington, H., E. Omel'chenko, and A. Garifzianova. 2010. *Russia's Skinheads: Exploring and Rethinking Subcultural Lives*. London: Routledge.

PST2018. *Threat Assessment 2018*, Oslo: The Norwegian Security Police. Available online at: https://www.pst.no/alle-artikler/trusselvurderinger/annual-threat-assessment-2018/

Simi, P. and R. Futrell. 2015[2010]. *American Swastika: Inside the White Power Movement's Hidden Spaces of Hate*. Lanham, MD: Rowman & Littlefield.

Smith, D. 1987. *The Everyday World as Problematic: A Feminist Sociology*. Boston, MA: Northeastern University Press.

Whyte, W.F. 1981. *Street Corner Society – The Social Structure of an Italian Slum*. Chicago, IL: University of Chicago Press.

Winsnes, A. 1998. *Terror eller dialog?*Oslo: Martins forlag.

16

OVERCOMING RACIALISATION IN THE FIELD

Practising ethnography on the far right as a researcher of colour

Vidhya Ramalingam

Introduction

It was the year the Sweden Democrats (SD) would mark its transition from a past tainted by neo-Nazism and white supremacy to a political party represented in the Parliament. It was the first time SD were permitted to campaign in schools, and activists from the SD chapter in Gothenburg are proudly standing by their table at a local school with a few SD lanyards, candies, pens and flyers. An SD activist carefully explains to two curious young women that they were not 'racists' and that swastikas were forbidden in the party.

Two students, both people of colour, approach the table as a joke and take pens, laughing to one another about using 'Nazi pens'. One of them notices me and pauses. He points at me and says in Swedish, laughing, 'You are also a Sweden Democrat? Ha!' My presence as a woman of colour sitting with far-right activists certainly was a strange sight.

A school director then approaches the table. Speaking angrily, he demands that I leave the premises. Despite carefully explaining my position as a researcher observing their campaign process and proposing that I sit farther away from their campaign station and observe from afar, I am told firmly that I must leave the building. The school director argues that SD are permitted to bring two representatives to campaign, and I am to be considered a third party representative. I am told that my presence will 'confuse the students'.

Anthropology has unique contributions to make to the study of far-right extremism, particularly as scholars have increasingly called for what Hainsworth (2008) describes as an 'internalist' examination of the radical right (Mudde 2007; Rydgren 2003). Such a research approach recognises that far-right movements and parties are 'neither bystanders, nor simply recipients' of opportunities that present themselves. Rather, they are agents in the narrative about their success or failure

(Hainsworth 2008: 128). Anthropological research methods are valuable in this regard, not only through their ethnographic approach and emphasis on fieldwork, but through, as Gingrich and Banks write, their 'ability to see the world as the neo-nationalists see it (while never seeking to endorse those perspectives) with scepticism towards their view of the world' (2006: 1).

Ethnographic fieldwork requires intensive and often immersive participation in the community that is the subject of research. This research method is fraught with challenges when the subjects of research are far-right movements, whether non-violent or violent. The exclusionary nature of far-right environments, as homogenous and often male-dominated and hyper-masculine communities, pose additional challenges for female researchers. A small number of researchers have pushed boundaries in this regard, including Kathleen Blee's pioneering contributions to the field based on life histories and fieldwork with Ku Klux Klan members (Blee 2002; 2007). However, understandably, much of this vanguard fieldwork has been carried out by researchers who share the same racial background as far-right research subjects.

For Researchers of Colour (ROCs), fieldwork on far-right movements may be deemed impossible given the unique challenges around access, safety, exposure to racism, and objectivity.[1] This chapter draws on my experiences as a female ROC carrying out fieldwork on the far right to reflect on the limitations and possibilities of ethnography under these circumstances. The school director's characterisation of my presence with the far right as 'confusing' aptly describes the experience of my ethnography not only from my subjects' and outside observers' perspective, but from my own perspective as a ROC. Both my gender and my race shape my positionality in my research, and this chapter reflects on my unique circumstances for ethnographic fieldwork with far-right activists, from neo-Nazis to radical right politicians, across Europe.

This chapter particularly draws on research I carried out between 2008 and 2011 on SD, a Swedish political party which transitioned from a white supremacy movement to a party today represented in Parliament (Ramalingam 2011; 2012).[2] Much of this research was conducted while based at the Centre on Migration, Policy and Society (COMPAS) at the University of Oxford. In 2011, I transitioned out of academia and ran a programme set up by the Swedish government in response to Anders Behring Breivik's far-right terror attack in Norway. With EU support, the Swedish Ministry of Justice launched a programme called *Preventing and Countering Far-Right Extremism and Radicalisation: European Cooperation*, publicly launched by the EU Commissioner for Home Affairs, then Swedish politician Cecilia Malmström (Ramalingam 2014). My transition from ethnographer into counter-extremism practitioner effectively curtailed future possibilities for fieldwork with the Swedish far right. However, my early research sought to understand far-right movements through the experiences and voices of movement activists themselves, and the findings from this fieldwork continue to inform my work to design responses and outreach efforts that recognise the agency and needs of individuals enmeshed in these movements (Ramalingam 2014; Ramalingam and Tuck 2014).

Taking my early fieldwork in Sweden as a point of departure, and drawing on my recent work as a practitioner responding to far-right violence and extremism, this chapter reflects not only on the limitations but also on the opportunities unique to ROCs carrying out fieldwork with far-right subjects. It addresses the need to adjust the framework of inquiry surrounding 'unsympathetic' research subjects, assess positionality of the ROC, manage the problematic identity of the ROC among far-right subjects, and navigate practical challenges such as negotiating access, safety, and the emotional impact of interviews and participant observation.

I argue that there are far more possibilities than limitations to ROC-led fieldwork on the far right. The continued absence of this fieldwork risks perpetuating a significant gap in the field. For reasons discussed below, it is imperative that more ROCs engage in fieldwork where safe, and with an appropriate methodology suitable for their research questions. However, these researchers must structure their approach and analyse their data in the context of their own racial identity and its implications.

Researching a stigmatised community

I began my fieldwork in the year before SD's first election to parliament. At this time, the party was struggling to shed its public image as a party of 'neo-Nazis' and 'racists', and was met with widespread hostility in Swedish society.

SD emerged into the political scene in 1988, born from the Bevara Sverige Svenskt (Keep Sweden Swedish) movement, heavily implicated in white supremacist and neo-Nazi subcultures. Several of the party's founders had been involved in openly Nazi and skinhead circuits, including the neo-Nazi party Nordiska Rikspartiet (Nordic National Party) and the fascist organisation Nysvenska Rörelsen (Neo-Swedish Movement), and many of the party's early events were attended by skinheads in uniforms touting Nazi flags. However, SD have over the years undergone a profound transformation to distance themselves from their unsavoury past, expelling party members with openly extremist connections, publicly denouncing neo-Nazism and mirroring the ideological frameworks of more successful radical right parties like the Danish People's Party and the French Front National. This transition helped SD achieve a landmark election result in 2010, when they received 5.7 per cent of the vote in the general election, finally passing the 4 per cent threshold required to gain representation in the Riksdag, the Swedish Parliament. Today SD have become even further mainstreamed, with 17.5 per cent of the vote in the latest general election.

Before its election to parliament, the marginalisation of SD was more far-reaching than the simple fact of political coalitions excluding the party; 'stigma' is a more appropriate term to encapsulate the nature of their exclusion. The stigmatisation of SD occurred on nearly every level of the party's existence. My research subjects recounted having lost their jobs, often numerous times, when their activities with SD were made public. The party regularly reported that they were unable to rent office space, book spaces for meetings or hold the same campaign activities as mainstream parties, both because they feared attacks or violence against them and because they were discriminated against and barred from doing so. Every Sweden Democrat interviewed in my study recalled fellow candidates who had had their windows smashed or recounted personal experiences of violent threats. The national headquarters of the party lay in a bunker in a parking garage in southern Stockholm with no signs or indications of their presence, the entrance an unmarked blue door with no doorknob. Local party leaders explained that this was partially for their own safety, but also because landlords would often refuse them.

Attempts at 'silencing' the party, though often founded on ideals of equality and tolerance, also had a history of revealing a darker face when manifested in violent suppression. In addition to unorganised activism, Antifascistisk Aktion (Anti-Fascist Action) had since the 1990s countered SD through violent and anti-democratic means, smashing candidates' windows and violently threatening local council members.

It is worth noting that SD have moved into a new era of political influence since this fieldwork was carried out. Some of my interviewees have achieved great political success as Members of Parliament. Others I interviewed were subsequently arrested on charges for racial assault. Others left SD believing it was too extreme and incapable of truly disentangling from its unsavoury past. The research experiences referred to in this chapter are reflective of a particular time and place, despite the individual stories of my interview subjects and the collective story of SD having evolved.

Sympathising with the 'unsympathetic'

Few scholars have produced research from the perspectives of far-right parties themselves (see Klandermans and Mayer 2006; Blee 2007). In Gingrich and Banks' anthropological contribution to the study of neo-nationalist parties, many of the authors employ traditional fieldwork methods; however, none of the authors conducted fieldwork with these politicians and activists (Gingrich and Banks 2006). Gingrich and Banks mention that anthropologists may make a conscious choice not to conduct fieldwork with far-right activists 'for the sake of moral hygiene' (Gingrich and Banks 2006: 7).

Anthropologists have, since the birth of the discipline, focused on marginalised and dispossessed populations; it is often assumed that anthropologists are inclined to 'take the side' of 'fragile, marginal and politically dispossessed populations' (Gingrich and Banks 2006: 24). However, the stories of most Western European or North American far-right activists in recent history are ultimately those of a struggle for power, in some cases not only by a stigmatised people but also by a stigmatised ideology. A number of moral dilemmas for the anthropologist arise when studying the far right, as these movements in some contexts could be described as 'fragile, marginal and politically dispossessed populations'. Gingrich and Banks state that neo-nationalists' rhetoric against 'the more fragile, more marginalised and more dispossessed minority migrant groups in Europe' deems them 'unsympathetic' to anthropologists (2006: 24). 'Empathy not sympathy' is thus the appropriate formula for fieldwork amongst people with whom one might not otherwise associate with or relate to. Sympathy in this case is deemed impossible because the premises of most far-right groups' ideological frameworks and their tenets of cultural exclusion and assimilation inherently contradict anthropology's endorsement – intellectual and moral – of cultural relativism.

However, my own work as a female ROC with far-right activists complicates this understanding of the anthropologist's relationship with an 'unsympathetic' subject. During my fieldwork and engagements with far-right activists, there have been numerous occasions when I felt 'sympathy' for these movements and its struggles, despite my personal attachments to race equality and anti-racism causes.

The sympathy I have felt during fieldwork emerged in two forms: sympathy for those who were socially stigmatised and met with a high level of hostility (as a 'fragile, marginal and politically dispossessed population' themselves) and sympathy for those enmeshed in a worldview filled with perceived terror and assault on their community, and fear and anger towards others. The emotional burden of an unconditional fear and mistrust of ethnic minorities, immigrants and political elites is immense. I found that as a detached ROC, even I was not immune to the emotional strain of repeatedly hearing of horrific abuses of power, rapes, violent abuse and other attacks my research subjects believed that ethnic minorities perpetrated. It is possible to sympathise with the 'unsympathetic,' and as an anthropologist immersing oneself in the world of one's subject, it is one's duty to depoliticise the framework of inquiry and deconstruct the social context which allows us to deem the subject 'unsympathetic'.

Bridging divides in cross-racial ethnography

The racialisation of the ethnographic research context has been explored by several scholars in recent years. These include numerous reflections on the intersectional identity of the researcher, particularly the experience of being both a ROC and a woman in contexts where the subjects are of a different racial background and gender (Mählck 2013; Egharevba 2010; Brown 2011). In a reflection on ethnography as a woman of colour, Brown (2011) notes that doing cross-racial research, particularly as a fieldworker of colour doing a 'racialised inquiry' with white participants, requires that one go into the field with an understanding of how racial dynamics might delimit engagement with key trademark characteristics of ethnographic research.

Ethnographic research traditionally requires bridging differences between the researcher and subjects, to allow for the researcher to more closely view the world from the point of view of their subjects. Egharevba (2010), reflecting on the experience of being a black woman researching South Asian women's lives, argues that whilst social characteristics such as gender, language, religion and culture are important in determining notions of commonality and difference between researchers and their subjects, other factors can foster this relationship in the absence of these traits. In her study, this factor is a shared experience of racism between the researched and the researcher.

The role of shared experience in bridging differences also features in descriptions of fieldwork by white researchers conducting ethnography on the far right. Pilkington (2016), a white female researcher of the English Defence League (EDL), describes how joint experience, in her case a particularly challenging experience of being arrested along with her research subjects, and shared feelings of nervousness, frustration, anger, and relief, was marked by one of her research subjects giving her a big hug and stating, 'You're one of the boys now'. Pilkington describes that the joint experience and shared emotions 'signalled the start of the ethnographic process'. Pilkington's reflections on fieldwork demonstrate the possibilities for researchers to find commonality with far-right interview subjects through shared experiences during fieldwork itself.

It is perhaps natural to question whether such commonalities can be established across racial boundaries, even when the researcher comes from a racial or ethnic background their research subjects are advocating against. My field experiences in Sweden demonstrate the possibilities for this; I was able to build relationships with my key informants, over time, through repeat engagement. This process was certainly bolstered through shared experiences of exclusion and stigma during fieldwork, but was more often developed through selective revelation of insights into my own history and past experiences. It was often the mundane details that inspired a sense of commonality between us – my experience learning how to drive a car as a teenager, or a detail about the neighbourhood I grew up in. I found that my interview subjects often pointed out our commonalities themselves, perhaps out of genuine surprise that such a commonality might exist, or perhaps to make themselves more at ease in what was an unusual and uncomfortable position for them, to be asked very personal questions by someone who embodies the 'enemy'. However, commonalities between my research subjects and I were acknowledged by my subjects in a distinct way. When criticising people of colour, research subjects with whom I had developed a strong rapport often spoke as if I were not a person of colour, or stated that the accusations were about immigrants who were "not like [me]." The overarching message 'you're not one of them,' referring to groups that were conceived of as the enemy, was repeated to me by key subjects, in a tone that indicated closeness or fondness. It was a conveyance of trust likely to be uniquely heard by an ROC in this environment, and notably different to the message 'you're one of us'. It is possible for an ROC to build mutual trust and find commonalities between the researcher and a far-right subject, though it is important to acknowledge the unique challenges and limitations in bridging racial boundaries in this context.

The positionality of an ROC

The experience of participant observation with the far right will, however, always be affected by the inherent discomfort of a person of colour situated in a space designed to exclude them. Data gathered under these conditions cannot thus be analysed as traditional participant observation, as the mere presence of ROCs can confuse and threaten the power structures traditionally imposed by these groups. However, in other contexts, scholars have argued that being an outsider is not a liability one necessarily needs to overcome. Bucerius (2013), drawing on experiences researching an all-male group of second-generation immigrants in Germany as a female researcher of different socioeconomic and ethnic background, challenges commonly held conventions within anthropology that ethnographers should strive for insider status. She suggests that being an outsider, and being a female in particular, need not necessarily pose a hurdle to research. Bucerius suggests that achieving status as an outsider trusted with 'inside knowledge' may provide the ethnographer with a different perspective and different data than that potentially afforded by insider status. Drawing inspiration from these challenges to the conventions of anthropology, ROCs can thus understand their ethnographic data to be reflective of the far right's *performative strategy* under these unique and rare conditions, rather than of their objective reality.

When engaging in fieldwork, any researcher is likely to serve as a springboard for subjects to express their *desired* social identity, rather than their actual social identity. Over the course of my fieldwork with the Sweden Democrats, I was, in effect, an audience for my subjects' performances and projections of their own social identity, particularly of how they seek to be perceived by people of colour and by the sections of society they believe disapprove of them. My identity as an ROC served as an opportunity for particular activists concerned about claims of 'racism' to manage and challenge this perception. Accepting and acknowledging this, I used the data collected to examine how the party aimed to position itself under these circumstances, and critically analysed the group's behaviour and performances of identity with a nuanced understanding of their factual history in mind.

The problematic identity of an ROC

Gingrich and Banks pose an important question for the anthropologist studying neo-nationalist movements: how is fieldwork best pursued under conditions which do not allow for any 'advocacy' by the anthropologist? (2006: 11). The moral dilemmas of fieldwork with and publishing data from radical right party activists leave the researcher knee-deep in quandaries: for example, how will this body of work ultimately affect the legitimisation of the groups one is studying? This question becomes more pertinent for ROCs, where one's presence with the research subjects themselves may constitute unintentional advocacy.

Though my early research has explored how the far right manage their 'problematic identity', I have been forced to manage and negotiate my own problematic identity as an ROC among anti-immigrant activists, racist movements, and violent far-right groups. The line between participant and observer is not as thin as the term 'participant observation' – a tradition in anthropology – suggests. ROCs can inevitably become an unwilling (yet ironically willing, as participation is the *aim* of fieldwork) actor in the far-right's performances of their social identity. An ROC's presence can influence the image of the far-right movement projected to onlookers as well as to its own members.

Over the course of my fieldwork with the far right, I was constantly aware of the potential that I might become an actor in their performances of their social identity. In 2010, my presence as a woman of colour at SD campaigning events inevitably drew attention from bystanders, reporters and other observers. I experienced responses ranging from interested curiosity – upon which I carefully explained my position as a researcher – to hostility. Many onlookers were confused over my own relationship with the party, and I was continually weighing up the implications of my presence at their events.

At party events in Stockholm, eggs were thrown by anti-racism activists in my direction while I was observing a street campaigning event by SD. On another occasion, as described in the epigraph to this chapter, I was expelled from an SD campaign event at a Gothenburg school by an angry school director who believed me to be part of their campaign.

After I was instructed to leave the school by the school director, the SD activists I had been with submitted a press release to local media titled, 'Oxford researcher expelled from local school for sitting with the Sweden Democrats.' While local media ultimately did not pick up the article, the act itself was essentially a performance by the party of the discrimination they face, in which I became an actor, sharing in the party's stigmatisation.

My frequent presence undoubtedly influenced the image projected by the party to onlookers and to fellow party members, many of whom were equally puzzled by my presence. My identity had a number of implications for my fieldwork; for example, I was explicitly told not to attend party meetings where there would be new members in attendance, as 'it might be confusing to them'. I was continually confronted by SD activists seeking my affirmation of their ideologies, or even casually glancing in my direction to observe my facial reactions at internal or public campaigning events.

ROCs must be aware of the unique implications of their presence with their subjects. Within the past five years alone, several seminal photographs of women of colour confronting far right activists have gone viral through sharing and dissemination by mainstream media and social media.[3] While white researchers bear emotional and physical risks, they have the benefit of being more capable of blending in and going unnoticed. ROCs, by the sheer difference of the colour of their skin, bear the burden of constant attention to how their presence is being monitored, documented and projected within the movement itself, but also to the wider world.

Negotiating access, safety, and emotional impact

Like any anthropologist inquiring about his/her subjects' identities for the purpose of publishing written work, the power of the researcher to shape their subjects' stories must constantly be acknowledged. For ROCs, fieldwork and interviews under these circumstances challenge normative power dynamics, as even white subjects of the research are aware that a person of colour holds the power to shape the public narrative on them.

Other aspects of normative power structures, including the positionality of women carrying out fieldwork in male-dominated environments, and the positionality of a person of colour in a racialised environment with individuals hostile to minorities, need to be acknowledged and managed carefully. However, these challenges can also present opportunities.

Unique access

Upon engaging in fieldwork with Swedish far-right activists, I was told by my research subjects that they often refused to meet with Swedish academics and journalists because they were 'biased,' 'distorted' their statements and 'used them against the movement.' Indeed, several academics and journalists I interacted with in the years I carried out fieldwork in Sweden expressed their shock that I was to be meeting directly with my research subjects, and referred to them as 'almost like a freak show' and joked that I would need a 'brainwash' after my fieldwork. White researchers who have conducted fieldwork with the far right in other contexts often describe 'suspicion of the researcher' as a barrier, to varying degrees and with different experiences overcoming this. In a British context, Busher (2016) explains that 'while some activists were initially suspicious of [him], during the 16 months [he] spent attending EDL events only one initially refused to speak to [him]'. Pilkington (2016) describes the long process of gaining trust of EDL members, and particularly demonstrating that she was 'not UAF' (Unite Against Fascism).

During the course of my research, I never directly experienced suspicion or faced vetting or accusations about my political leanings. My outsider status, both by race and citizenship, as neither white Swedish nor an immigrant to Sweden, afforded me some lenience here that white researchers or even ROCs who share the nationality of their subjects may not be granted. My access to the field was negotiated through two strategies: (1) sending emails to activists whose contact details were published online, and (2) attending demonstrations and rallies, standing in the back – neither part of the demonstration, nor with the counter-demonstrators – and approaching activists at the right moment to ask questions. The two strategies proved to go hand in hand, as I became known amongst activists as the "Indian woman who kept turning up" at demonstrations, and my emails were subsequently answered as a result of the questions and rumours about why I was there. The success of this strategy, according to my subjects themselves, relied on two interacting emotions: confusion and curiosity.

My research subjects acknowledged that their curiosity about why I, as a woman of colour, wanted to meet with them, was a key driver in accepting my requests to meet. I was repeatedly told that my research subjects had never been approached by a researcher or journalist who looked like me. My identity appeared to offer me unique access, as I was told that I was 'confusing', 'strange' and 'harmless'. These descriptions were of course coloured by both my gender and race. Gender inherently plays a role in shaping the research environment for anthropologists in any context; it also shapes the opportunities afforded to enter communities. In the context of researching SD, my interview subjects were predominantly white men. Though I informally interacted with several female activists doing administrative work, women were less visible or noticeably absent from most internal meetings and campaigning events.

Scholars have long assessed the unique research dynamics of female researchers in male-dominated settings, where some have argued women may trigger specific behaviours by their research subjects, including gender-related behaviours of 'sexual hustling' and 'sexist treatment' (Gurney, 1985). Female ethnographers, and particularly female ROCs, must adopt a reflexive approach and recognise the influence of their social position on interactions with their subject.

Beyond the context of my fieldwork with SD, I have interviewed numerous former far-right extremists in countries such as the United States, United Kingdom, Canada, Australia, Germany, and Sweden, who describe the development of complex relationships with women of colour as pivotal moments in their ideological transitions away from far-right movements. It is clear that female ROCs are likely to have unique opportunities engaging with far-right research subjects, but they must also be conscious of the role they may play in shaping the environment and worldview also for their subjects. Lumsden (2009) argues that an awareness of these interactions 'does not undermine the data but instead acknowledges that the researcher and the researched are embedded within the research. Hence, they shape the ethnography while also being shaped in turn'.

Of course, the positionality of an ROC will not always work in the researcher's favour. Even in the context of non-violent movements such as SD, not all those individuals I approached for meetings were open to speaking with me. My requests to meet were often met with scepticism, and on a few occasions hostility. I was informed in several instances that internal arguments had taken place over the access that was being provided to me by certain members, particularly given the concerns over how members would react to a person of colour in the room. There were however several key gatekeepers who accepted my requests to meet, and over the course of repeated meetings I gained their trust, and they eventually offered to introduce me to other members, take me along to group events, and ultimately introduce me to their families. Those gatekeepers put their own reputation on the line to bring a woman of colour to anti-immigrant meetings and events, and had to explain their decisions not only to other members, but to their leadership. Even without speaking a word, my presence as an ROC was disruptive and confusing, and my gatekeepers were ultimately responsible for the effect this had on the movement. It is critical to be aware of the impacts of participant observation by ROCs on gatekeepers in this context, and acknowledge that ROCs may not be aware of the exact explanation that has been used to justify their presence. Explanations given for the ROC's presence may vary based on the gatekeeper and their own personal reasons for assisting the research.

Safety

ROCs should consider the risks and do detailed risk and mitigation planning before engaging in fieldwork with the far right. Ethnography can occur in public and private settings, and there are of course limitations to the data that will be gathered through meeting far-right activists solely in public spaces or attending public events. The subjects I met with were for the most part extremely conscious of the way they were publicly regarded, and often times referred to their own public appearances as 'provocations'. One subject noted, "It's not just provoking to provoke. You must provoke for a reason, to start to get people talking". I began to see all public interactions with my research subjects as performative, intended to be viewed by the wider community around us, particularly given my position as an ROC and many of my subjects' ambitions to breakdown the 'racist' image of the party. This in itself is not problematic, and researchers can acknowledge the limitations of an ethnographic method focused on public events and interactions, and the impact it may have on their findings.

However, there are also significant benefits to doing ethnographic research with the far right in settings out of the public eye. Safety considerations are critical for ROCs in this context. When I first met the Sweden Democrats, I was told to arrive at a parking lot in south Stockholm, where their office was located in an unmarked bunker accessible only through the parking lot. In accepting offers to meet activists in their bunker office, I needed to take calculated risks that will be familiar to many female ethnographers. Given that the party was attempting to shed its neo-Nazi past, to mainstream and legitimise its image, and ultimately to rise to Parliament, the likelihood that I would be subject to violence by my interview subjects was low. However, as any female ethnographer carrying out interviews in male-dominated environments, I needed to constantly be aware of my surroundings. This was heightened by the fact that several of my interview subjects had violent pasts, including one party activist who lifted his sleeve during an interview to reveal a swastika tattoo, which he claimed was from his 'activist years.' Others I interviewed were arrested on assault charges in the months and years following my interviews, in some cases for racist attacks including the infamous 'Iron Pipe Scandal', in which three of my interviewees were filmed verbally assaulting a Swede of Kurdish descent with racist comments, assaulting several witnesses, and arming themselves with iron pipes. The subjects involved resigned from their positions with the party following this incident.

During my fieldwork, situations arose where I needed to negotiate a quick exit from the research context out of concern for my own well-being and safety. Some scholars have reflected on the everyday risks and professional dilemmas encountered when conducting participant-observation with participants who are inebriated (Palmer et al., 2010), and these challenges are particularly relevant for female

ROCs engaging in fieldwork with the far right, where social events play a key role in group membership. On one occasion, I was in a car with a group of male activists following a party social event outside of Stockholm, several of whom were inebriated on the drive back to Stockholm. During this drive, I became concerned about the nature of the conversation unfolding, including uncomfortable comments made about women. I also became uncertain about destination of the car, and cognisant of my inability to control the situation. I needed to negotiate a swift and early exit from the situation, preferring to find my way home from the highway than to remain with my research subjects.

During my fieldwork with SD, in many cases I needed to navigate complex power dynamics, be constantly aware of subtle signals and shifts in the research environment, and plan mitigation strategies. However, the data I obtained from interviews and participant observation in private spaces were far more insightful than those I obtained in public spaces. Private spaces were the most effective environment to obtain life histories of my subjects, uncover truths about their pasts, and unpeel the public performance element of many of my subjects' interactions with 'outsiders'. Indeed, it is unlikely that one of my research subjects would have unveiled a hidden swastika tattoo in a public space. In any context, the revelation of a swastika tattoo, by a white man to a woman of colour, may be intended to demonstrate power and inspire fear. In conducting interviews in this setting, my awareness of body language, tone of voice, and the sometimes tenuous nature of the researcher–subject relationship, was heightened. ROCs in general, and female ROCs in particular, should be vigilant and calculate risks when engaging in this kind of research, and crucially, know when to retreat to prioritise their own safety and emotional well-being.

Emotional toll

Ethnography necessarily involves management of personal boundaries, and negotiations of difference and commonality between the researcher and the subject in order to obtain personal information from subjects. Researchers may need to offer personal information and open up to their subjects to build trust and facilitate information gathering.

In my experiences as an ROC carrying out fieldwork with the Swedish far right, I managed a careful balancing act, providing personal details about my own life and managing how that information was used by my subjects. Given that my interviewees were political activists in the midst of a campaign, it was perhaps unsurprising that I often found my personal information, and my identities as an Indian-American, a Hindu, and a woman, manipulated by my subjects in attempts to pull me into their ideological worldview. I was often told horrific stories by my subjects about Muslims persecuting Hindus in India and raping Hindu women. These stories were likely intended by my subjects to bridge their perceived struggle and their perception of my identity.

Any researcher carrying out fieldwork with the far right should be prepared for the emotional toll of embedding oneself in a movement that propagates xenophobic and hateful ideologies. However, as an ROC, the experience of being subjected to hateful thinking and denigrating language was a deeply personal experience. I sat through numerous meetings and events where I was the only person of colour in the room, listening to my subjects discuss the need to rid their society of ethnic minorities, offering evidence about the genetic proclivity of Asian and Arab men to rape women, and speaking of immigrants as a 'disease.'

Particularly challenging was maintaining the integrity of the relationships with my subjects while also struggling with the emotional toll the experience had on me, including the constant suppression of anger or fear. There were moments when interview subjects who I had connected with through repeat interviews, would make racist jokes with their colleagues at events when they thought I was not looking. On other occasions, my interviewees would intentionally say something racist or offensive and would look in my direction to see how I would react. They would look my way at events when racist jokes had been made to observe my reactions. An excerpt from my fieldwork journal describes my experience navigating this environment:

> "What is so tough is to watch people I had built a relationship with, who I had come to feel were almost oddly becoming friends with me, to see them on stage making racist and insulting remarks about minorities. Or to see them sitting in the audience buying into everything that was said, nodding and knowingly smiling at incredibly horrific claims being made about the "fact" that "it's in Muslims' DNA to want to rape". Nodding along at photos of a Muslim's brain and how it differs from a Swede's. Laughing hard and clapping at incredibly offensive jokes about people who look like me. These are people who just a few days earlier had my sympathy, I had been beginning to feel for them! And now I felt a lump in my stomach. I felt like the kid in Roald Dahl's "The Witches" when he gets trapped in the conference room with all the witches who look like normal women, and then they all take off their wigs and are freaky bald witches.
>
> How do you conduct fieldwork with people whose values you are inherently opposed to, but whose trust you need to earn and keep? They are so paranoid, and have a reason to be, of "left-winger infiltrators" who are trying to prove they are racist and take them down ... and I don't exactly blend in. They stare at me in the meetings, and of course they do, why wouldn't they? I know they expect me to frown, expect me to be angry at what they say here, but I have to supress it. I keep catching myself nearly frowning or looking shocked and having to adjust my smile, keep having to force myself to clap at times. I don't want them to think I am "out to get them", as they have repeatedly told me most academics and journalists are, and they won't talk to them. But by not arguing against any of their points, by sitting here, they automatically assume I'm on their side."

Additionally challenging was navigating the performative element of fieldwork, particularly managing my relationships with subjects in public settings. An excerpt from my fieldwork journal describes the challenge:

> "It's easiest when I'm alone with them in party offices, or in their family homes. We make jokes, I even have some inside jokes with some of the members! But this gets

*incredibly uncomfortable when there are other people around not from the party …
journalists, Muslims, anti-racism activists, who are watching me interact with them, and
don't know my intentions. Some of them look at me with the same disgust as they do to
[the Sweden Democrats], but a particular kind of disgust, as if I've turned my back on
my own people. I want to break out of this act and yell 'Wait! I'm one of you! Trust
me, I think they are horrible too!'."*

Johansson (2015) argues that in modern anthropological methods, forging egalitar-
ian relationships with subjects involves responding to and fulfilling expectations of
reciprocity and 'giving back' where the researcher is able. However, in the context
of my research as an ROC engaging with the far right, 'giving back' and revealing
my personal beliefs may have closed off opportunities to engage in further interviews and fieldwork. Debates regarding the intersections between activism and
applied anthropology have been limited in their discussion of how to manage this
tension in a racialised research environment (Scheper-Hughes 1995; Stanford and
Angel-Ajani 2006).

Impacts and considerations

The many possibilities enabled by ROC-led fieldwork on the far right considerably outweigh the limitations of such work. We must encourage and enable
more ROCs to engage in fieldwork where safe, and with an appropriate methodology for their research questions. These researchers must structure their research
and analyse their data in the context of their own racial or ethnic identity and its
implications.

The long-term impacts of fieldwork on the ROC's careers and future research,
or transitions into government and activism, must also be acknowledged and
accepted. ROCs will need to consider the timing of this research within their
career tracks, as publicly available anti-racism or counter-extremism work, and
affiliations with institutions that deliver such work, can curtail opportunities for
research, as subjects are likely to close off opportunities to 'activist' researchers. The
'confusion' and 'curiosity' my interview subjects described feeling when they
accepted my meeting requests were bolstered by the fact that I had not yet published any work with anti-racism or counter-extremism organisations, and my
'digital footprint' appeared non-threatening. In the years that followed, this 'digital
footprint' grew to include public details on my work with the Swedish Ministry of
Justice to respond to far-right extremism across Sweden and Europe, and global
work to engage white nationalists in social work and offer a route out of these
movements. Through continued contact with several of my research subjects in the
years following my fieldwork, I am aware that my trajectory shifted the nature of
our relationship, as I became perceived as an 'activist' with a clear agenda, rather
than a curious 'observer'.

Though my personal transition into counter-extremism practice effectively curtailed future possibilities for fieldwork with the Swedish far right, my fieldwork

continues to inform my work to design both anti-racism and counter-extremism initiatives that recognise the agency and needs of individuals in these movements. This pioneering research method continues to be met with scepticism within some parts of the sector, typically those arguing that this method offers these groups a platform and amplifies their voices. Over the course of my career, I have continually had to defend my choices to engage directly with the far right within practitioner circles.

However, for far too long policy and practice responding to the far right have been designed and delivered without an understanding of the people behind these movements, without meeting them face to face and engaging with their stories. My experience carrying out fieldwork with SD challenges conventionally held perceptions of barriers to ROCs engaging in direct ethnography and participant observation with the far right. ROCs can bring unique perspectives to these research methods and should continue to push methodological boundaries in this field.

Notes

1 This chapter uses the term Researchers of Colour to describe researchers who self-identify as 'persons of colour', defined as persons who are not white or of European heritage, often sharing common experiences of individual, institutional, cultural, or systematic racism. While this is a commonly accepted term in 2020, the year this chapter is to be published, I acknowledge that the terminology and language used to describe racial designations is often limited in many ways, and may shift over time.

2 The results of this study are available in 'The Sweden Democrats: Anti-Immigration Politics under the Stigma of Racism,' Centre on Migration, Policy and Society (COMPAS), University of Oxford: Working Paper No. 97. The entire publication is accessible from the University of Oxford or the author upon request: Ramalingam, Vidhya (2011) *The Sweden Democrats: Anti-immigration Politics under the Stigma of Racism*. Dissertation in Anthropology, Migration Studies, University of Oxford, UK.

3 Images of women of colour confronting the far right include British woman Saffiyah Khan smiling defiantly at an English Defence League protester in Birmingham, United Kingdom. Information available from the *Guardian* [https://www.theguardian.com/uk-news/2017/apr/09/birmingham-woman-standing-in-defiance-of-edl-protester-goes-viral]. Another seminal photo was taken of Tess Aplund, an anti-racism activist in Sweden, standing defiantly with her fist raised at a Nordic Resistance Movement demonstration in Borlänge, Sweden. Information available from the *Independent* [http://www.independent.co.uk/news/world/europe/woman-sweden-tess-asplund-who-defied-neo-nazis-in-viral-photo-says-group-should-never-have-been-a7012421.html].

References

Blee, Kathleen M. 2002. *Inside Organized Racism: Women in the Hate Movement*. Berkeley, CA: University of California Press.

Blee, Kathleen M. 2007. Ethnographies of the far right. *Journal of Contemporary Ethnography*, 36(2): 119–128.

Brown, Keffrelyn. 2011. Elevating the role of race in ethnographic research: Navigating race relations in the field. *Ethnography and Education*, 6(1): 97–111.

Bucerius, Sandra. 2013. Becoming a "trusted outsider": Gender, ethnicity, and inequality in ethnographic research. *Journal of Contemporary Ethnography*, 42(6): 690–721.

Busher, Joel. 2016. *The Making of Anti-Muslim Protest, Grassroots Activism in the English Defence League*. New York, NY: Routledge.

Egharevba, Itohan. 2010. Researching an-'other' minority ethnic community: Reflections of a black female researcher on the intersections of race, gender and other power positions on the research process. *International Journal of Social Research Methodology: Theory & Practice*, 4(3): 225–241.

Gingrich, André and Marcus Banks. 2006. *Neo-Nationalism in Europe and Beyond: Perspectives from Social Anthropology*. Oxford, UK: Berghahn Books.

Gurney, Joan Neff. 1985. Not one of the guys: The female researcher in a male-dominated setting. *Qualitative Sociology*, 8(1): 42–60.

Hainsworth, Paul. 2008. *The Extreme Right in Western Europe*. New York, NY: Routledge.

Johansson, Leanne. 2015. Dangerous liaisons: Risk, positionality and power in women's anthropological fieldwork. *Journal of the Anthropological Society of Oxford*, 7(1): 55–63.

Klandermans, Bert and Nonna Mayer. 2006. "Right-wing extremism as a social movement." In Klandermans, Bert and Nonna Mayer (eds), *Extreme Right Activists in Europe: Through the Magnifying Glass*. London, UK: Routledge.

Lumsden, Karen. 2009. 'Don't ask a woman to do another woman's job': Gendered interactions and the emotional ethnographer. *Sociology*, 43(3): 497–513.

Mählck, Paula. 2013). Academic women with migrant background in the global knowledge economy: Bodies, hierarchies and resistance. *Women's Studies International Forum*, 36: 65–74.

Mudde, Cas. 2007. *Populist Radical Right Parties in Europe*. Cambridge, UK: Cambridge University Press.

Palmer, Catherine and Kirrilly Thompson. 2010. Everyday risks and professional dilemmas: fieldwork with alcohol-based (sporting) subcultures. *Qualitative Research*, 10(4): 421–440.

Pilkington, Hilary. 2016. *Loud and Proud: Passion and Politics in the English Defence League*. Manchester, UK: Manchester University Press.

Ramalingam, Vidhya. 2011. *The Sweden Democrats: Anti-immigration Politics under the Stigma of Racism*. Dissertation in Anthropology, Migration Studies, University of Oxford, UK.

Ramalingam, Vidhya. 2012. *The Sweden Democrats: Anti-immigration Politics under the Stigma of Racism*, Working Paper No. 97. Oxford, UK: Centre on Migration, Policy and Society (COMPAS), University of Oxford.

Ramalingam, Vidhya. 2014. *Old Threat, New Approach: Tackling the Far Right Across Europe*. London, UK: Institute for Strategic Dialogue & Swedish Ministry of Justice.

Ramalingam, Vidhya and Henry Tuck. 2014. *The Need for Exit Programmes: Why Deradicalisation and Disengagement Matters in the UK's Approach to Far-right Violence*. London, UK: Institute for Strategic Dialogue.

Rydgren, Jes. 2003. Meso-level reasons for racism and xenophobia. Some converging and diverging effects of radical right populism in France and Sweden. *European Journal of Social Theory*, 6(1): 45–68.

Scheper-Hughes, Nancy. 1995. The primacy of the ethical: Propositions for a militant anthropology. *Current Anthropology*, 36(3): 409–440.

Stanford, Victoria, and Asale Angel-Ajani. 2006. *Engaged Observer: Anthropology, Advocacy and Activism*. New Brunswick, NJ: Rutgers University Press.

17

NEGOTIATING ETHICAL DILEMMAS DURING AN ETHNOGRAPHIC STUDY OF ANTI-MINORITY ACTIVISM

A personal reflection on the adoption of a 'non-dehumanization' principle

Joel Busher

'Understanding people does not', as Hammersley (2006: 11) observes, 'require sharing their beliefs, or being obliged to offer them support; if it did, this would considerably reduce the range of people that could be studied'. Yet researchers that use ethnographic methods to understand and analyze the broadly conceived far right are likely at some point to find themselves having to work through what Blee describes as 'the tangled issues of balancing scholarly ethics of fairness to the subject with moral and political interests in exposing and helping to disable the very movements they are studying' (2007: 125).

In this chapter I discuss how I negotiated these 'tangled issues' during the course of an ethnographic study of activism in the English Defence League (EDL), ostensibly an anti-Muslim protest movement, carried out between early 2011 and mid 2012 (Busher, 2016). I discuss in particular how I navigated these issues using a basic principle. This was that as a researcher I would attempt to treat EDL activists in the same way as I would activists in a movement whose aims I broadly endorsed, so long as this did not entail me becoming complicit in what I considered the most fundamentally problematic aspect of their movement: their dehumanization of various Others – primarily Muslims, but sometimes also ethnic minority groups, left-wing activists and members of 'the establishment'. I would over time come to think of this as a 'non-dehumanization principle', using it as a rule of thumb to prompt me to repeatedly ask myself some basic questions: 'Is what I am doing somehow contributing to the EDL activists' dehumanization of others?' 'Am I treating the EDL activists differently to how I would treat activists in a movement with which I am more sympathetic?' 'If so, do I have a justification for doing so, and what is it?'

In what follows I first discuss how I arrived at this principle, before describing some of the ways it shaped my practice across three phases of the research: project design, fieldwork, and writing up. My intention is not to argue that others should adopt a similar approach, or that this approach is morally superior to others: it is simply to share some reflections about how I managed, more or less successfully, to pick my way through the thorny moral dilemmas that I encountered during the course of this research.

Arriving at a 'non-dehumanization' principle

I have often tried to trace how I arrived at the non-dehumanization principle. Part of the explanation, I am sure, lies in my route into this project. I did not have a background in researching the far right and, while I had long been concerned about issues of prejudice and discrimination, neither had I been involved in anti-racist or anti-fascist movements. Rather, for most of the preceding decade I had been steeped in the practice of and research into international and community development. Having worked for a few years with international NGOs, mostly in health and education, I completed a PhD in Development Studies – for which I undertook an ethnographic study of community-based responses to HIV/AIDS on the Namibia–Angola border. I had transitioned into researching groups such as the EDL through a rather unexpected chain of events. Post-PhD I had taken up a research role in the UK government, where I was put to work on a meta-analysis of research on the pathways into violent extremism, with a particular focus on far right-inspired violent extremism.[1] I became increasingly interested in the topic and subsequently jumped at a chance to take up a post-doc fellowship at the University of East London that would allow me to carry out some empirical research of my own, addressing what I considered some of the limitations in the literature at the time. As such, my academic *habitus* was one largely of a community development researcher. I suspect that to some extent I took it for granted that I had a duty of fairness towards my research subjects, whatever I thought of their views and aims, and that I needed a specific justification if I was to treat EDL activists differently than I would, say, somebody organizing voluntary counselling and testing programmes for HIV.

There were however other reasons – more consciously deliberated during my initial planning. Some of these were about my conception of 'good social science'. I believed, and still believe, that we comprehend people and groups better when we see them *as* people, capable of beauty, kindness, love, joy and creativity, just as they are capable of spite, unkindness, aggression and hate. If we fail to do this, we risk failing to grasp the full extent of their agency, and are therefore likely to overlook important insights into how and why people do what they do (Barrett-Fox, 2011).

I primarily wanted to understand two aspects of EDL activism. First, building on the meta-analysis work that I had carried out in government, I was interested in how people became involved in EDL activism. Recent research on extreme right activists indicated that there were several pathways into such groups (Linden and Klandermans, 2007). I wanted to find out whether similar pathways could be discerned in the case of the EDL, and what this could tell us about how the group built support. Second, I was interested in how the group maintained support and momentum despite widespread opposition and public condemnation. It is one thing to be sufficiently motivated to protest once or twice: it is another thing to do it month after month, in the wind and the rain, when there is scant possibility of achieving one's goals (Summers Effler, 2010). I believed that both of these research tasks would be best served by me getting as close as possible to the life-worlds of EDL activists.

My adoption of the non-dehumanization principle was also shaped by political or strategic reasons, and my understanding of my role within the political process. I, like many others, was keen to see the EDL lose traction. However, influenced by Harding's (1991: 393) argument that, as uncomfortable as it may be, we need to 'come up with more nuanced, complicated, partial, and local readings' of the 'repugnant cultural other' if we are to 'design more effective political strategies to oppose directly the specific positions and policies' that they advocate, I also believed, and still believe, that *I* could best contribute to reduce their traction and minimize their societal impacts by undertaking research that shed new light on their lived experience, without simply reproducing their arguments or glamourizing their endeavours.

I was particularly keen that my research should not produce a caricatured picture of EDL activists. This was because I believed that turning them into modern 'folk devils' (Cohen, 1972) was likely to lead us towards the wrong conclusions about how to effectively respond to such groups. I believed, for example, that doing so would likely encourage us to overestimate their ability to gain public support; generate a distorted and reductionist understanding of the genesis of their activism; and make it more likely that we fail to engage sufficiently with questions about how ideas and practices circulate between the 'extreme' and the political 'mainstream'. While activists in groups such as the EDL undoubtedly acquire interpretive frames that radically alter their perception of the world around them (Aho, 1994; Blee, 2003; Busher, 2016: 74–96; Simi and Futrell, 2010), it is disingenuous to believe that the ideas and practices that circulate within these groups are not intertwined with those that we can find in 'mainstream' society (Billig, 1995). While it might feel politically and emotionally expedient, we should resist the temptation to locate all that we consider undesirable or repugnant as pertaining to or seeping out of the 'extreme'.

Finally, my adoption of the non-dehumanization principle also stemmed from a belief that it enabled me to address some of my moral discomfort about this project – a consideration of some importance when embarking on more than a year of intensive fieldwork. As already mentioned, my underlying objection to the EDL was that they engaged in what I considered the willing dehumanization of various Others. I did not want my work to contribute to that process – for example, by appearing to justify their positions. At the same time, however, I also wanted to minimize the extent to which my work might dehumanize or 'infrahumanize' (Vaes et al., 2003) activists themselves – as to do so would imply a moral contradiction that, I believed, I would have struggled to resolve.[2] Dehumanization comes in many forms. While we might often think of it primarily in terms of the most severe examples with the most grotesque outcomes – such as those of genocidal killings (e.g. Staub, 1989) – dehumanization or infrahumanization also comes in more subtle forms, through which we more or less advertently deny people their human attributes. This might be done, for example, by implying that they have sub-human intelligence or failing to attribute to them the capacity for 'refined' or 'secondary' emotions (Haslam and Loughnan, 2014; Vaes et al., 2003). Of course, not all forms of dehumanization are morally equal. Nonetheless, I felt more morally comfortable when, as well as taking seriously the risk of contributing to the EDL's dehumanization of their various Others, I also took seriously the risk that my research could dehumanize or infrahumanize EDL activists.

Project design and set up

The non-dehumanization principle contributed to two significant decisions during the research design phase. The first of these was *the decision not to undertake covert research*. Of course, in the context of ethnographic research the line between overt and covert research is not as clear cut as some undergraduate methods manuals and ethics committee protocols might have us believe. As Bourgois observes:

> we are taught in our courses preparatory to fieldwork that the gifted researcher must break the boundaries between outsider and insider. We are supposed to 'build rapport' and develop such a level of trust and acceptance in our host societies that we do not distort social interaction. Anything less leads to the collection of skewed or superficial data. How can we reconcile effective par-ticipant/observation with truly informed consent? Is rapport building a covert way of saying 'encourage people to forget that you are constantly observing them and registering everything they are saying and doing?'
>
> *(2012: 327)*

Part of the reason I intended to spend more than a year with EDL activists was to build the kind of rapport that would enable observation of activists' social interac-tions largely undistorted by my presence. As a minimum, however, I wanted to ensure that would-be participants were informed, at least initially, that I was a researcher and about the broad focus of my research. I decided that I would seek permission from local organizers to undertake the research; that whenever I met somebody I had not previously met I would explain as soon as possible that I was a researcher; that I would seek their consent for me to include our interactions in my research; and that I would only mislead people about my identity if I believed that it was necessary for my own safety – something I never had to do.

There were a number of reasons for this. Most importantly, my preliminary enquiries indicated that such an approach was feasible. I was put in contact with a handful of people who had flirted with or been around the periphery of EDL events by Jamie Bartlett, another researcher undertaking work on the group at the time (see Bartlett and Littler, 2011), and by personal acquaintances who knew people on the fringes of the scene. All of these people believed that access would not be a problem. Indeed, I assessed that it would be more dangerous to go 'undercover' as, if discovered, they would be more likely to assume I was an anti-fascist infiltrator or a journalist – two groups who tended to arouse a combination of suspicion and ire among EDL activists.

My first direct encounters with EDL activists supported this view. After a brief email exchange, one of the local organizers came to meet me at the university. We had a lengthy conversation – a couple of hours or so. They asked me about my research plans and interests and eventually invited me to a forthcoming demonstration. They offered to introduce me to other activists, but made clear that it would be up to individuals whether they spoke with me or not. On the day of the march I was first introduced to one of the national leaders of the EDL. He broadly repeated the same message – I was welcome there, but it was up to individuals to decide whether to speak with me.

That day every conversation began with me explaining who I was and what I was doing there. Only one person said they did not wish to speak with me. Most seemed quite pleased to have me there – something that would give me much cause for thought over the coming months – and some thanked me for taking time to try to 'really understand' what their movement was about. Most, I believe, were flattered that an academic researcher was taking an interest them, as it gave them a sense that they were being taken seriously.

These preliminary conversations and initial observations also made me confident that I would be able to generate the required data without using covert methods. Some of the activists were initially wary around me, and one or two in particular played up to my ethnographic gaze – one activist would occasionally chastise fellow activists who made openly racist comments or advocated violence, before pointedly looking over at me, as if encouraging (willing?) me to take note. Most seemed to quickly assimilate my presence, however. Indeed, I was soon being invited to attend private functions, albeit a handful of activists – mainly those previously involved in established far right political formations – appeared cautious about that. Shortly after attending a second march I received multiple Facebook friend requests from activists. I accepted these and used Facebook to communicate with a number of activists, although I only used the private message function.[3]

Given this relative ease of access, the use of covert methods seemed difficult to justify. I was also concerned that, if I used covert methods and was subsequently discovered by activists, I would simply provide them with further evidence that academia and 'the establishment' are not to be trusted and are riddled with double standards.

The other significant choice I made was about *suspending, for the time-being, the decision about whether or not to frame this research as a study of the 'new far right'*. The EDL was widely seen to be breathing new life into the UK's far right street protest scene (Copsey, 2010; Jackson, 2011) – something that had largely disappeared during the previous decade, as the British National Party (BNP) had moved away from its 'march and grow' strategy and focused instead on electoral campaigning and community politics (Copsey, 2008). It was clear that there were, at the very least, some overlaps with established far right groups in terms of issue frames and 'membership'[4] (Bartlett and Littler, 2011). It was however also clear that movement leaders and a substantial portion of their supporters staunchly rejected the 'far right' label and actively sought to distance themselves from established far right organizations such as the BNP and the National Front (Busher, 2016: 97–122; Copsey, 2010; Pilkington, 2016: 92–124).

Ethnographers always face difficult decisions about how to strike a balance between adopting the language used by the people they are studying and imposing external conceptual frameworks and categories (Atkinson and Hammerlsey, 2007: 191–208). Here, these questions were particularly acute. I was well aware that one of the reasons why EDL activists resisted the 'far right' label was to avoid the deep stigma that it brings, thereby potentially removing a recruitment barrier. Yet I was also concerned about what I saw as the implications of studying them *as* a far right group. I believed that researching the EDL *as* a far right group when they explicitly rejected that label would make it difficult for me to trace the internal logics of activists' emergent worldviews and identities. I also felt uncomfortable about implying either that their positioning as a 'not-far-right' group was entirely strategic or intentionally mendacious, something I believed was unlikely given the seemingly genuine hostility and revulsion expressed by *some* activists towards established far right groups such as the National Front; or that it represented a form of false consciousness, which seemed to insinuate *a priori* a diminished capacity for intelligence.

On the other hand, I was unwilling to adopt their monikers of choice – e.g. that they were a 'patriotic movement' or that they were a movement that represented 'ordinary English people' or the 'working class'. While I did not doubt that some activists believed such labels accurately described their movement, they were clearly intended to enhance their public image. I also believed they were misleading. To my mind, EDL activists' claims to represent 'ordinary English people' or 'working class people' were akin to the claims of groups such as Al-Muhajiroun to represent Muslims more generally. I was reluctant to support such claims, tacitly or otherwise, not least because I believe such framings can, intentionally or otherwise, exacerbate the stigmatization of low income predominantly white communities as some kind of pool of latent support for groups such as the EDL, and in doing so obscure the racial and religious prejudice of the elites and middle classes. While it might be true that much of the support for the EDL came from low income predominantly white communities, this does not mean that they are somehow *representative* of such populations (see Beider, 2015; Thomas et al., 2018).

As such, I decided for the time-being to study the EDL as a movement in its own right, and that questions about what the EDL was 'a case of' could be addressed once I had completed the fieldwork. At the time this felt like 'kicking the can down the road', but I would later be glad that I had made this choice. It was certainly not, however, an easy route through this dilemma, not least because almost every conversation I had with academics, policymakers or journalists over the next two years would begin with them asking 'So, is the EDL a far right group?', to which I would proffer what seemed to me a fairly inarticulate response about issue complexity and the heterogeneity of activists' interests. For an early career researcher with no prior experience of working in this field and trying to make a good impression on their peers, this was often an uncomfortable experience.

Two years later, as I was writing up the research, I would eventually settle on referring to the EDL as an anti-Muslim protest movement. This choice of terminology was not intended as a statement about whether the EDL was or was not *objectively* a far right group (Busher, 2016, 20). Rather, it reflected the fact that 'anti-Muslim protest movement' seemed to me the terminology that best enabled me to accomplish the research task I had set for myself: of getting beyond caricature to provide insight into how the EDL operated as a social movement and how EDL activism shaped the lives and life-worlds of those who became activists. This was partly because it seemed to faithfully capture the core focus of political interest around which the movement coalesced. Conversations within the EDL activist community often comprised a rather eclectic pick 'n' mix of prejudice organized around assorted national, racial, ethnic, religious and other ideological and social categories, but it was their shared antipathy towards Muslims and Islam around which they mobilized. Indeed, differences across the activist community and over time in terms of how their anti-Muslim positions intersected with their use of other categories or frames would eventually contribute to the fragmentation and decline of the EDL (Busher, 2016: 123–156). In addition, this strategy of description also seemed to have the advantage of making it easier to capture how the EDL's emergent movement culture drew from across a variety of sub-cultural scenes (see also Quinn, 2015).

In 2016, I was interested to see that Hilary Pilkington, who undertook ethnographic research with EDL activists around the same time (Pilkington, 2016), had taken a similar approach, referring to the EDL as an anti-Islam movement.[5] In subsequent collaborations with Gareth Harris and Graham Macklin, we would use the term 'anti-minority activism' and 'anti-minority politics' to talk about a wider swathe of groups and practices with more diverse objects of loathing (Busher, Harris and Macklin, 2019). For me, one of the attractions of this terminology has been that it resists the binarization of talking about the 'extreme' and the 'mainstream', 'right' and 'left', making it easier therefore for us to talk about and analyze how anti-minority politics manifests across a range of different political formations.

Fieldwork

As expected, the fieldwork was emotionally and intellectually exhausting. In some ways the 'culture shock' I experienced on entering the field for this research was more profound than that which I had experienced while carrying out my doctoral research on the Namibia–Angola border. The activists looked and sounded in many ways familiar. We had multiple shared cultural reference points, especially on sports and music, and even sometimes during discussions about politics – I remember feelings of ambivalence during conversations with some activists in which I found us agreeing about what we saw as the folly of the invasion of Iraq in 2003, or the injustices implied by the UK government's politics of austerity. Yet at the same time their world was quite alien to me, with all aspects of their lives saturated with anxiety and fear about a supposed Islamic takeover of their town, England, Britain, or 'the West'.

One of the principal challenges during the initial phase of fieldwork was *identifying what I considered to be an appropriate mode of participation in EDL-related activities*: one that would get me close enough to EDL activists so that I would be able to understand and describe their lived experience, while not lending them support.

I decided that I would walk through marches with the EDL activists. Here there is an obvious dilemma: by walking through the march I would, at least to those outside the march, appear to be adding my support to their cause – an extra body in the politics of numbers. I believed however that walking through the marches would render important insight about the lived experiences of the activists and the internal dynamics of the movement. I walked through as an observer. I did not participate in any of the rituals except for walking though the march and observing the various minute silences, called usually in remembrance of people who had passed away (even if I had wanted to breach such silences, doing so would have seemed inappropriate and would, I suspect, have decimated any rapport that I had established).

I would still make the same decision today. Walking through the marches, I saw EDL activists' interactions with the police and counter-protestors first-hand and up close. This was often uncomfortable. I experienced being associated with the EDL by counter-protestors. On some occasions this entailed being threatened by anti-EDL activists, having 'scum!' shouted in my face and even having objects, including horse excrement, whistle past my ears. When this happened I experienced shame at my presumed association with the EDL and frustration at not being able to say 'I'm only a researcher!', but I also experienced fear and on some level anger, irritation and even resentment at the attempts of some of the anti-EDL protestors not just to oppose the EDL, but to jeer at and humiliate them. Such experiences, I believe, helped me to document and understand the choreography and the emotional rhythms of these events and of EDL activism more broadly.

I also had to work out how to interact with EDL activists on a day-to-day basis. To build rapport and gain insight into what it meant to be an EDL activist, I allowed myself to engage in 'banter', laughing and participating in conversations and jokes that did not overstep the boundaries of what I considered acceptable. This of course was something I had to define, revisit and redefine as the fieldwork progressed, but much of the time conversations among EDL activists revolved around sport, fairly innocuous comments about what people had seen on television last week, nostalgic recollections of earlier demonstrations, fairly light-hearted teasing of one another, and movement gossip. More challenging were the moments when the 'banter' and 'jokes' were about Muslims or other religious or ethnic minorities. These instances provided important data for me, so I was loathe to disrupt the flow of the conversation, but I would still try to signal – usually physically e.g. by remaining stone-faced – that at that point I was not part of their community of shared understanding. Similarly, when talking with activists, I would allow them space to tell me about their social and political views, but would also try to adopt active listening positions that would disrupt possible assumptions by activists that I was complicit in their views e.g. using questions such as 'what makes you think that' or 'when did you come to those conclusions' or offering alternative interpretations of events using phrases such as 'but could it be that...?'. When asked my views, I would give them as honestly and diplomatically as possible.

Another way in which my fieldwork practice was shaped by my attempts to apply the non-dehumanization principle was that *I tried to allow myself to be attuned to the full emotional repertoire of EDL activism*. As noted above, one of the ways in which we can make others less human is by denying, or overlooking, their capacity for 'complex' or 'secondary' emotions (Haslam and Loughnan, 2014; Vaes et al., 2003).

While popular, journalistic and even some academic accounts of the broadly-conceived far right tend to emphasize emotions such as anger, hate and, to a lesser extent, fear, ethnographic accounts of activism in such movements have increasingly highlighted the existence and role of other emotions, such as individual and collective pride, hope, amusement, self-confidence, sensuality, boredom, excitement, belonging and collective effervescence (Blee, 2007; Busher, Giurlando and Sullivan, 2018; Pilkington, 2016). Capturing more fully the emotional dynamics of these movements not only gives us a more complete picture of them, but also helps us understand key movement processes, such as identity formation and maintenance, and activist retention (see Latif et al., 2018).

As such, as well as documenting the anger and the rage, I also captured in my fieldnotes activists' shame when other activists went 'too far'; the feelings of betrayal when fewer people than expected attended a demonstration; the regret when they realized their own actions might have damaged the EDL's cause; the relief when they learned that a prosecution against them had collapsed; the exhaustion after yet another night of arguments on Facebook; the admiration for fellow activists who 'really know their stuff'; the indignation when they were called a racist while handing out EDL flyers on the high street; the gratitude when fellow activists supported them during a difficult period in their lives, and the humiliation when they wet themselves in police custody. This also helped me to avoid accidentally glamourizing EDL activism. Yes, activists spoke about the 'buzz' of and adrenaline of demonstrations, but EDL activism was also characterized by long periods of boredom, gnawing anxiety and general misery.

This often went hand in hand with *getting to know the activists as more than simply activists*. I sought to ensure that in my mind and in my writing, I did not reduce them to just this one aspect of their lives. This was not always easy, however. While most of the activists seemed quite happy to have me spend time with them at EDL marches and other events, it took much longer for activists to begin talking more openly in my presence about their personal lives.

Writing up

In some respects, this was the phase of the research in which it was most difficult to apply the non-dehumanization principle. As I waded through the transcripts and fieldnotes and began developing first drafts of outputs, it was easy to lose sight of the people behind the data and slip into convenient generalizations and simplifications.

Where the non-dehumanization principle perhaps had most influence was in my sustained efforts to *draw out the heterogeneity of the EDL activist community and the dynamic nature of EDL activism*. Even in the smallest grassroots organizations, there are likely to be a number of different routes into activism, and differences of opinion will emerge among activists about what 'the problem' is, what should be done about it, and who belongs in the group (Blee, 2012). While some activists already had a deep and articulated sense of grievance when they became part of the EDL, others had initially engaged socially with the EDL through family or friendship ties and only really became ideologically engaged once they were already part of the activist scene. While some of the activists were drawn into the EDL by the prospect of violent confrontations with opposition activists and the police, for others these confrontations were a cause of anxiety or irritation, and other activists still had initially been attracted by the violence and public disorder, but later came to see it as counter-productive, even if they still hankered for the buzz of confrontations. And while some activists argued that they should oppose the building of any new mosques, others insisted they should only oppose 'mega-mosques' or those associated with 'radical Islam'. I believed it was important to capture and describe the more repugnant aspects of EDL activism, such as the 'jokes' about gunning down Muslim women and the wilful desecration of religious symbols; but that it was also important to capture the aspects of EDL activism that were usually edited out of, or overlooked by, reports that framed EDL activists as a bunch of more or less racist thugs.

To my mind this was not about producing a sympathetic picture of EDL activists. Rather, I believed, and still believe, that by capturing and faithfully documenting the heterogeneity of groups such as the EDL we are better able to understand and effectively respond to them, while still protecting fundamental rights and freedoms. For example, exploring ideological, tactical and affective heterogeneity within movements such as the EDL can help us to identify and understand the fault lines that run through such movements and the opportunities that these offer in terms of interventions.[6]

Writing this heterogeneity was one of the most challenging aspects of this project. I only identified what seemed to me a satisfactory strategy for doing this several months after I began writing. This entailed a subtle shift in focus from writing about *the EDL* and *EDL activists* to writing about *EDL activism*, with EDL activism conceived of as comprising a series of social and psychological processes. At the individual level these processes were about activists' journeys into and through the EDL, such as joining the organization, becoming established as a member of the activist community, forging and developing their opinions and worldviews, constructing their activist identity, or becoming disillusioned with the movement. These corresponded with group-level or organizational processes, such as recruitment, acculturation, indoctrination, and fomenting movement cohesion. This subtle shift in focus meant that I began to foreground questions about *how* these people and this group got from point A to point B – how, for example, had people begun their journeys into EDL activism, and how had the EDL activists managed to foster in-group solidarity – instead of foregrounding questions such as 'what is the EDL', 'who are EDL activists', 'why do they join' and 'why do they do what they do'. This seemed to enable me to capture more effectively the dynamic and often inconsistent nature of EDL activism, and the emergent nature of activists' lived experience, social and political positionalities, worldviews and tactical tastes. Rather than trying to describe the ideology of the EDL as if it were a coherent and stable object for investigation, I begun to explore how these ideological structures worked, how they evolved over time and how individual activists engaged and disengaged with them during the course of their journey through the EDL.

During this phase I also adopted what I came to think of as my *'acid test'*. This comprised repeatedly asking myself whether I would feel able to say and defend what I was writing if I was reading it out in a room in which a significant minority of the audience were either a) people who have experienced fear or anxiety as a result of the actions of EDL activists, or b) the EDL activists that I had known. The second part of this proved more challenging. This was partly because the former required considerably less imagination on my part as I did, on several occasions, present my work to civil society and local authority networks promoting community cohesion, where a significant minority of the participants had experienced fear or anxiety as a result of the actions of EDL activists. It was also more difficult because when presenting to and writing for primarily academic audiences, I was aware that the vast majority, if not all, of those audiences were likely to find the EDL repugnant, and I knew from observing presentations about similar groups by other researchers that disparaging comments usually played fairly well, building a certain rapport of implied 'we-ness'. Meanwhile, comments that could be construed as 'favourable' or 'sympathetic' were likely to elicit mutterings that the researcher had 'gone native'.

Again, this was not to my mind about holding back from writing critically about the EDL as a movement, but about ensuring that I was fair and that I wasn't drawn into making convenient generalizations or flattening out the heterogeneity of the movement. When I eventually completed my book in 2015, I sent several copies to the activists who had given up their time to speak with me. Two of them called me to discuss the book, several others wrote to me via Facebook and one published a review of the book. While none was in full agreement with me about some of my conclusions, neither did they believe the book was unfair. In some ways this meant as much to me as the favourable academic comments and reviews that I was receiving at the time. Despite making clear that I found their beliefs and activities deeply problematic, I had managed to carry out the project in a way that the activists themselves still believed was fair and had, at the very least, not given them further cause to feel resentful towards and betrayed by academia and the 'liberal establishment'.

Concluding thoughts

Ethnography has considerable potential to advance our understanding of anti-minority politics, including but not limited to far right parties and movements. This is particularly the case when the research comprises extended periods of fieldwork and is undertaken by researchers willing to grapple with the messy realities of such movements and the activists who comprise those movements. It raises a number of challenges, however. In this chapter I have reflected on my experiences of navigating one of the foremost of these: how to balance the 'scholarly ethics of fairness to the subject with moral and political interests in exposing and helping to disable the very movements they are studying' (Blee, 2007: 125). I have described how I tried to do this using a basic principle: that I would attempt to treat activists in the EDL in the same way as I would activists in any other movement, so long as I did not consider that this entailed me becoming complicit in their dehumanization of others.

I would not expect everybody to agree with my use of this principle. I am also sure that other researchers would identify different thresholds in terms of, for example, what they saw as 'appropriate' involvement in EDL activities, or the point at which their research practice would contribute to the dehumanization wrought by the group under investigation. Indeed, I suspect that my interpretation of the principle would have been different had I undertaken the research with a different or more militant group, or if my fieldwork had primarily been either in an area of the country where, or at a point in time when, EDL activists appeared less committed to distancing themselves from established far right formations.

What I can say with some confidence is that I don't, at the time of writing, regret the approach I took. I believe that it enabled me to write about anti-minority politics in a way that has shed some new light on how such movements build and sustain support. In a context of increasing societal and political polarization, I believe that research that grapples with the nuance, complexity and basic humanity of the 'repugnant cultural other' is more important than ever.

Notes

1 A change of government in 2010 and the concomitant restructuring of research and investment priorities meant that this piece of meta-analysis was never completed.

2   This was partly about my position of relative power in comparison with the grassroots activists with whom my research was primarily concerned. While recognising the potential harm that groups such as the EDL can do – undermining community relations and spreading fear, distrust, anger and hatred – most of the activists I knew inhabited structurally marginal positions. My assessment might have been different had my research been primarily about the movement's leadership.

3   I did not contribute to discussions on Facebook pages or groups, and did not share information about or images from EDL events via Facebook. I was concerned that if I did, this might be perceived by activists, or by my friends and family, to indicate tacit support for the group.

4   The EDL was not a membership organization. Here I use 'member' referring to those who regularly attended EDL events.

5   I also considered using the term anti-Islam, but opted for anti-Muslim as it seemed to me that the activists I met were not only protesting against the religion in the abstract, but about the people who practiced or identified with that religion.

6   Morrison's (2014) work on 'splits' in dissident Irish republican groups provides a good illustration of this point in another context.

References

Aho, J.A. 1994. *This Thing of Darkness: A Sociology of the Enemy.* Seattle, WA: University of Washington Press.

Atkinson, P. and M. Hammerlsey. 2007. *Ethnography: Principles in Practice.* 3rd edition. Abingdon: Routledge.

Barrett-Fox, R. 2011. "Anger on the Picket Line: Ethnography and Emotion in the Study of Westboro Baptist Church." *Journal of Hate Studies*, 9(1), 11–32.

Bartlett, J. and M. Littler. 2011. *Inside the EDL: Populist Politics in a Digital Age.* London: Demos.

Beider, H. 2015. *White Working-Class Voices: Multiculturalism, Community-building and Change.* Bristol: Policy Press.

Billig, M. 1995. "Rhetorical Psychology, Ideological Thinking, and Imagining Nationhood." In *Social Movements and Culture*, edited by H. Johnston and B. Klandermans, 64–81. London: UCL Press.

Blee, K.M. 2003. *Inside Organized Racism: Women in the Hate Movement.* Berkeley, CA: University of California Press.

Blee, K.M. 2007. "Ethnographies of the Far Right." *Journal of Contemporary Ethnography*, 36(2), 119–128.

Blee, K.M. 2012. *Democracy in the Making: How Activist Groups Form.* Oxford: Oxford University Press.

Bourgois, P. 2012. "Confronting the Ethics of Ethnography: Lessons from Fieldwork in Central America." In *Ethnographic Fieldwork: An Anthropological Reader* (2nd edition), edited by A.C.G.M. Robben and J.A. Sluka, 318–330. Oxford: Blackwell.

Busher, J. 2016. *The Making of Anti-Muslim Protest: Grassroots Activism in the English Defence League.* Abingdon: Routledge.

Busher, J., P. Giurlando, and G. Sullivan. 2018. "Introduction: The Emotional Dynamics of Backlash Politics beyond Anger, Hate, Fear, Pride, and Loss." *Humanity & Society*, 42(4), 399–409.

Busher, J., G. Harris, and G. Macklin. 2019. "Chicken Suits and Other Aspects of Situated Credibility Contests: Explaining Local Trajectories of Anti-Minority Activism." *Social Movement Studies*, 19(2), 193–214.

Cohen, S. 1972. *Folk Devils and Moral Panics.* London: MacGibbon and Key.

Copsey, N. 2008. *Contemporary British Fascism: The British National Party and the Quest for Legitimacy*. 2nd edition. Basingstoke: Palgrave Macmillan.

Copsey, N. 2010. *The English Defence League: Challenging Our Country and Our Values of Social Inclusion, Fairness and Equality*. London: Faith Matters.

Hammersley, M. 2006. "Ethnography: Problems and Prospects." *Ethnography and Education*, 1(1), 3–14.

Harding, S. 1991. "Representing Fundamentalism: The Problem of the Repugnant Cultural Other." *Social Research*, 58(2), 373–393.

Haslam, N. and S. Loughnan. 2014. "Dehumanization and Infrahumanization." *Annual Review of Psychology*, 65, 399–423.

Jackson, P. 2011. *The EDL: Britain's New 'Far-Right' Social Movement*. Northampton: Radicalism and New Media Group Publications.

Latif, M., K.M. Blee, M. DeMichele, and P. Simi. 2018. "How Emotional Dynamics Maintain and Destroy White Supremacist Groups." *Humanity & Society*, 42(4), 480–501.

Linden, A. and B. Klandermans. 2007. "Revolutionaries, Wanderers, Converts, and Compliants: Life Histories of Extreme Right Activists." *Journal of Contemporary Ethnography*, 36(2), 184–201.

Morrison, J.F. 2014. *The Origins and Rise of Dissident Irish Republicanism: The Role and Impact of Organizational Splits*. London: Bloomsbury.

Pilkington, H. 2016. *Loud and Proud: Passion and Politics in the English Defence League*. Manchester: Manchester University Press.

Quinn, C.M. 2015. *Tainted Love: A Critical Analysis of Participation in Contemporary English Patriot and Loyalist Movement, as Exemplified by the English Defence League*. PhD Thesis, University of Leeds, Leeds.

Simi, P. and R. Futrell. 2010. *American Swastika: Inside the White Power Movement's Hidden Spaces of Hate*. Plymouth: Rowman & Littlefield.

Staub, E. 1989. *The Roots of Evil: The Origins of Genocide and Other Group Violence*. New York, NY: St. Martin's.

Summers Effler, E. 2010. *Laughing Saints and Righteous Heroes: Emotional Rhythms in Social Movement Groups*. London: University of Chicago Press.

Thomas, P., J. Busher, G. Macklin, M. Rogerson, and K. Christmann. 2018. "Hopes and Fears: Community Cohesion and the 'White Working Class' in One of the 'Failed Spaces' of Multiculturalism." *Sociology*, 52(2), 262–281.

Vaes, J., M.P. Paladino, L. Castelli, J.-P. Leyens, and A. Giovanazzi. 2003. "On the Behavioral Consequences of Infrahumanization: The Implicit Role of Uniquely Human Emotions in Intergroup Relations." *Journal of Personality and Social Psychology*, 85(6), 1016–1034.

18

WHITENESS, CLASS AND THE 'COMMUNICATIVE COMMUNITY'

A doctoral researcher's journey to a local political ethnography

Stephen D. Ashe

In this chapter I provide a reflective account of my doctoral research on the electoral rise and fall of the British National Party (BNP) – a party with its ideological and organizational origins in neo-Nazism and neo-fascism. In doing so, I will offer an account of the dialectical interplay of theory, method and data. Moreover, I will throw light on the way in which my research design evolved during the course of this study, thus demonstrating the ways in which it, and the decisions taken once in 'the field', were shaped by my personal biography and sociological training, as well as a range of other institutional, political, cultural and ethical factors. In doing so, I will draw attention to the significance of whiteness and class when negotiating the contours of the local 'communicative community' (Hewitt, 2005) through three overlapping periods of data collection on my journey towards a political ethnographic study of the BNP in the outer-East London Borough of Barking and Dagenham. I then conclude with a discussion which addresses a criticism that I (and others) have faced while presenting their work in this area: namely, that there is no place for ethnographic academic research involving the far right. Drawing on Back's (2002) concept of 'active listening', I will suggest that there is an important role for anti-racist, anti-fascist activist-scholarship in a field largely dominated by white people, and often susceptible to the pitfalls of 'white logic' and 'white methods' (see Zuberi and Bonilla-Silva, 2008).

Archival, documentary and online research (2008)

An immersion in historical and political sociology during my sociological training, especially theories and applications of hegemony (e.g. Connell, 2005; Hall et al., 2013[1978]; Williams, 1977), had a profound impact on my research design. I was especially cognizant of the emphasis Gramsci (1971) placed on offering a 'concrete analysis' of the 'concrete situation'. This chimed with the importance James

Rhodes (2006; see also Veugeler this volume) attaches to the significance of place[*] in his research on the BNP in the North-West town of Burnley. For me, such local case studies added much needed 'thick description' and nuance to national level analyses (e.g. Goodwin, 2011). Furthermore, Raymond Williams' theorization of hegemony and 'residual cultures' appeared to complement Nigel Copsey's (2008) historical-archival research on the BNP. For Williams, residual cultures consist of experiences, meanings and values not expressed or legitimized by the 'dominant' culture. Indeed, 'the past is not just dead, inert and confining, it carries signs and evidences' (Thompson, 1981[1968]: 407–408).[1] Taking these theoretical insights on board, I was mindful that the BNP's local electoral breakthroughs had not emerged as if from nowhere. Rather, part of the explanation for the BNP's electoral inroads lay within in local history and the contours of place. Alongside theories of hegemony, social movement theory would also shape my research design. In terms of exploring questions of 'supply', social movement theory provided me with a conceptual vocabulary through which to explore and break down the significance of political and ideological discourses, the role of political networks and alliances and action repertoires. Not only this, Gramsci's (1971) theorization of the state–civil society nexus, especially his contention that building support and consent within civil society was a central feature of parliamentary democracy in Western Europe, led me to consider the following question: what was the relationship between the dominant local Labour Parties and civil society both prior to and after the emergence of the BNP? Acquiring a grasp of the local state–civil society nexus would add depth to Eatwell's (2010) rather list-like overview of 'responses to the extreme right' in Britain, which, while useful, had not adequately grasped the importance of the networks and alliances forged between different political actors in an attempt to thwart the BNP's electoral advance (for a more sophisticated account, see Copsey, 2012). Indeed, as I note below, the relationship between local government and civil society would be an important explanatory factor in the BNP's electoral rise and fall in outer-East London.

Data collection began in earnest in early-to-mid 2008. At this point I was planning to conduct an international comparative study of the BNP and the One Nation Party in Australia. Having received ethical approval to carry out archival, documentary and online research, the first few months of research were spent in various archives across England, collecting material from BNP publications, campaign leaflets, circulars, memoranda and internal bulletins. Following Copsey's (2008) historical-archival approach, these materials provided detailed insights into the development and rationale underpinning the BNP's 'modernization' strategy. Whilst in the archives, I also amassed a collection of material from various anti-fascist publications which offered rich insights into the nature of anti-fascist alliances forged and campaigns mounted to oppose the BNP. I also spent several months in the Barking Learning Centre (BLC) reading through local newspapers in order to acquire a detailed understanding of the specificities of the local context.

As well as being a rich source of information, the above sources had several limitations. First, these sources tended to over-represent the voices of powerful leading figures in political party and civil society organizations. Furthermore, leading figures and their organizations were usually portrayed in a favourable light, while also having 'axes to grind, scores to settle, or excuses to make' (see Hammersley and Atkinson, 1995). When collecting this material, I was also aware that I would only be able to provide a limited account of both what was happening inside the BNP and the nature of the relationship between the BNP and the electorate. Indeed, as Blee (2007) explains, an overreliance on publicly available data limits research to exploring the 'front-stage' image that the far right wishes to project, while also being of limited use when it comes to exploring the relationship between leaders and activists, as well as activists' motivations and perceptions. In hindsight, I can see that information gleaned from monthly editions of *International Searchlight* provided several insights in this regard. Nevertheless, I repeatedly sought ethical approval to interview BNP members, observe BNP activists campaigning and also interview local residents about their voting behaviour.

While making the case to adopt a more political ethnographic approach, I also carried out almost daily online research. This included gathering data from BNP, anti-fascist, political party, trade union, civil society and media websites. In carrying out this research, I assembled an extensive collection of articles, blogs, discussion forum debates, podcasts, radio and television broadcasts, speeches and videos. These data offered rich insights into both the BNP's private meetings and public campaign activities, as well as internal debates, tensions and decision-making processes.[2] Bearing in mind that the motives and actions of far right actors are often very different from what has been previously assumed by 'following the activities and ideas of leaders or the rhetoric of [...] newspapers and recruiting pamphlets' (Moore, 1996: 560), the sort of 'anthropological sensitivity' that can be brought to the aforementioned types of data – namely, questions of kinship and agency – can be a useful substitute for ethnographic methods (see Banks, 2006).

It was also during this first stage that I began analyzing published local histories (e.g. Curtis, 2000; 2006; Howson, 1990; Tames, 2002) and seminal sociological studies that had been carried out in Barking and Dagenham (i.e. Beynon, 1973; Willmott, 1963). While these histories and studies provided important historical contextual insights, they were underpinned by 'white logic' and 'white methods' (see Zuberi and Bonilla-Silva, 2008; Bhambra, 2017). That is, Barking and Dagenham, and its 'people', were routinely constituted and represented as being both 'white' *and* working class. More recently, such narratives have been reproduced by Ford and Goodwin (2010) in their quantitative individual-level analysis of the BNP's electoral base and in Gest's (2018) research on the 'white working class' both in Barking and Dagenham and in other places. It was also around this time that I collected data from the Office for National Statistics, as well as local Census data, and London Borough of Barking and Dagenham local authority statistics.

I then set about contextualizing the data collected up until thus point by exploring the local impact of wider structural and political-economic processes such as Fordism and post-war welfare capitalism, deindustrialization and neoliberalism. This enabled me to provide insights into the nature of poverty, racial inequality and local demographics, thus challenging some of the core features of Ford and Goodwin's (2010) 'angry white man' and 'left behind' (2014; see also Ferber, 2000), both of which overlook the fact that the working class in Britain has been both multi-racial and multi-ethnic since its very formation (see also Rhodes, Ashe and Valluvan, 2019; see also Bhambra, 2017; Khan and Shaheen, 2017; Mondon and Winter, 2019; Shilliam, 2018; Tilley, 2017).[3] Moreover, such accounts gloss over the fact that neoliberalism, deindustrialization and austerity have had a profound impact on the lives of *all working class people*; while often having a disproportionate impact on working class people racialized as non-white British. For example, when deindustrialization took hold in Barking and Dagenham, a multi-racial, multi-ethnic working class was 'left behind' (see Ashe, 2013).

The long hours spent reading local newspapers in the BLC enabled me to develop an appreciation of the extent to which the BNP had established roots in specific areas of local civil society which had either been neglected or abandoned by Labour councillors who refused to share a platform with the BNP. Maintaining a visible and sustained presence in local residents' forums, which tended to be covered uncritically in local newspapers on a near weekly basis, was integral to the BNP being able to establish a 'reputational shield' (Ivarsflaten, 2006) against the stigma of the 'racist-hooligan couplet' with which the party had long been associated (see Rhodes, 2009).[4] What is more, the letters pages in local newspapers also allowed the BNP a platform to position the party as dedicated local community activists in touch with and responding to the concerns of 'local people' who were racialized as white. In short, local newspapers – a constituent feature of local civil society – played an integral role in both challenging the hegemony of the local Labour parties through its hostility towards the local Council, while also legitimizing the BNP's' 'modernization' strategy and mainstreaming racism. Whilst gaining a number of important insights, I was conscious that this material told me little about how local residents understood these developments or how these developments shaped residents' voting behaviour. However, little did I know at the time, the decision to spend months wading through copies of local newspapers dating back to the 1970s would be the single most important decision that I would make during my research.

Over the course of several months, I would be the only person sitting at the large communal tables in the BLC getting my fingers (and even my face) covered in newspaper ink. This attracted the attention of both staff and library users. The latter were usually either young college students or older residents. Almost every day someone would ask me what I was doing. When I explained my research to them, I opened the door to rich, detailed ethnographic conversations. However, this created a dilemma – I did not yet have ethical approval from my institution to conduct these conversations. But what was I supposed to do? Say 'sorry I can't talk to you; I don't have ethical approval'? I addressed this dilemma by providing an overview of my research before securing oral consent in much the same way as I would later do when conducting qualitative interviews. So, whenever the opportunity arose, I proceeded to hold conversations guided by the following questions:

1. 'How would you describe Barking and Dagenham?'
2. 'How would you describe local politics?'
3. 'Who did you vote for and why?'
4. 'Why did you not vote for any of the other candidates or parties?'

The first of the above questions was originally intended as an 'ice-breaker'. However, this turned out to be the single most important question that I would ask during all three phases of research. In the space of just a few weeks I had held no fewer than 25 conversations which lasted between 5 minutes to over 1 hour. Truth be told, I was particularly lonely during this first phase of research. I had moved to London and away from my hometown, family and friends for the first time. Indeed, I was often just as pleased to have someone to talk as the older residents for whom the BLC was an important site of community and interpersonal contact. That is, until I was confronted with explicit forms of racism and support for the BNP's more extreme political standpoints. In these instances, the discussion was often brought to an abrupt halt when residents got even the slightest hint that I did not share their point of view. I will return to the nature of these encounters when reflecting on the third phase of research that I undertook in 2010.

Even after the first few conversations, it became apparent that there was a clear disjuncture between the insights gained from these conversations and academic, media and political understandings of support for the BNP. What is more, older residents provided in-depth insights into their experiences of the post-war welfare capitalism, deindustrialization and the activities of the National Front and the BNP in the area during the 1970s and 1980s, as well as local traditions of anti-fascist activism dating back to the 'Battle of Cable Street' in the 1930s (see Kushner and Valman, 2000). Local anti-fascist resistance is something that is often overlooked by far right scholars, who tend to whiten local populations when portraying such areas as either inherently racist or susceptible to the far right (e.g. Goodwin, 2008; Ford and Goodwin, 2010). In fact, Goodwin's work has contributed to broader narratives caricaturing, if not stigmatizing, places like Barking and Dagenham.[5]

In contrast to my conversations with older residents, younger people aged approximately 17–25 years tended to focus on the lack of affordable housing and relatively secure, well-paid local employment. Moreover, conversations with local college students racialized as non-white often focused on their everyday experiences of racism, including institutional racism, the impact that the presence of the BNP had had on their everyday lives, as well as voting for the Labour Party under duress after the local parties had legitimized and mainstreamed white victimhood, anti-immigrant sentiment and opposition to multiculturalism.

In short, these ethnographic conversations would strengthen my conviction that I had to adopt a more political ethnographic approach capable of capturing the dynamic, relational and interactive nature of politics between different political parties, local civil society and the anti-fascist movement. Drawing on Charles Tilly (2007), I was convinced that political ethnography would bring me into closer contact with local political processes and create opportunities to generate unique insights into the causes and motivations behind different forms of political action when I returned to Barking and Dagenham in 2009.

First steps towards a political ethnography (2009)

After completing the first tranche of data collection, I started presenting my findings at various academic events. At these events I was routinely asked why I was not interviewing BNP members. In fact, this was the very first question I was asked during the defence of my doctoral thesis. More often than not these questions came from experienced ethnographers and established scholars in far right studies that I very much respected. Repeatedly facing this question created considerable anxiety. Indeed, I felt that if my research was to be taken seriously then I had to follow the 'ethnographic turn' that had recently been initiated by leading far right scholars (e.g. Klandermans and Mayer, 2005; Blee, 2007). This further strengthened my belief that I had to apply for ethical approval to conduct participant observation, as well as interview BNP members and local residents.

During the early months of 2009, I continued to make the case for adopting a more political ethnographic approach based around observing local political campaigns (including door-to-door canvassing and public meetings), key actor interviews and postal surveys similar to the those carried out by Rhodes (2006) in an attempt to recruit local residents to take part in in-depth interviews. There was a number of reasons why I placed considerable emphasis on participant observation and key actor interviews. First, participant observation would allow me to build on the ethnographic conversations that I had already conducted in the BLC, thus allowing me to gain further detailed insights into interactions between local residents, political parties and anti-fascist campaigners among a larger, more diverse section of local constituents. Second, existing accounts of the BNP's local electoral breakthroughs (e.g. Goodwin, 2008; Wilks-Heeg, 2009: Rhodes, 2009) had paid little, if indeed any, attention to anti-fascist campaigns organized by Hope not Hate (HnH) and Unite Against Fascism (UAF), particularly when it came to considering the relationship between local party politics and civil society. Third, as I mentioned earlier, Goodwin's (2008) account of the BNP's local electoral breakthroughs overlooked both historical and contemporary multi-racial and multi-ethnic working class traditions of anti-fascist and anti-racist resistance.

In response to my desire to change approach, my doctoral supervisors rightly expressed concern about both the feasibility and practicalities of changing research strategy at this stage. Looking back, I can now also accept that it may have seemed that I was looking to revise my research design every time I encountered criticism from seasoned academics in the field rather than accepting that I could not do everything within the parameters of my doctorate and also recognizing that all research designs will ultimately have their own intrinsic limitations. Perhaps what I also did not fully appreciate at the time was that doctoral supervisors are coming under increasing pressure from their institutions to ensure that their supervisees successfully submit their theses within the allotted funding periods. Therefore, I decided to abandon the international comparative approach and shift the focus to a comparative study of the BNP in Barking and Dagenham and in Burnley. Whereas Rhodes had focused on the BNP's electoral breakthrough in Burnley, this new comparative approach would enable me to explore similarities and differences in the BNP's electoral fortunes in different localities after the Party's initial electoral breakthroughs.

In addition to the concerns of my supervisors, my institution also suggested that I should complete my research using the design already approved and then look to adopt a political ethnographic approach once I had graduated. At the time, I could not accept these arguments for two reasons: (1) I was not sure at this point that I wanted to pursue an academic career; and (2) I was of the view that the chances of securing access to conduct such research would only diminish once I started publishing, and the likes of the BNP became aware of both my doctoral research and my left-wing anti-racist politics. It was also around this time that my institution made it clear that they would not, under any circumstances, grant ethical approval to conduct either participant observation or interviews involving BNP members. This decision was based on a heightened sense of risk which can emerge when looking to interview actors commonly characterized as being racist, violent thugs. In fairness, such concerns cannot be readily dismissed. As I discuss below, the white researchers' experiences of engaging with the likes of the BNP can be very different from that of people racialized as non-white. Indeed, many of the contributors to this collection have also reported encountering threats of violence and intimidation.

In the end, I was granted ethical approval to conduct ethnographic conversations with local residents and participant observation with local political actors, just not with the BNP. Although disappointed, I resigned myself to trying to bring a sociological and 'anthropological sensitivity' to my sources, thus exploring questions of agency, kinship and the symbolism inherent in 'websites, surveys, autobiographical accounts, interviews, newspaper articles and political manifestos' (Gingrich and Banks, 2006: 7). However, as I would later discover, being given a green light to observe other local actors campaigning would mean that I would encounter the BNP in a number of unanticipated ways.

When I returned to the Borough in March, the 2009 European election campaign had just gone into full swing. By this point, the BNP had amassed over 50 local councillors across England. Not only this, 2 years after being elected as a councillor in Barking and Dagenham, the BNP's Richard Barnbrook won a seat on the Greater London Assembly. In addition to participant observation, key actor interviews and ethnographic conversations with local residents, I continued collecting archival, documentary and online data when I returned to Barking and Dagenham for a second round of fieldwork.

As I mentioned above, participant observation regularly brought me into close contact with the BNP. In fact, I often found myself standing just yards away from BNP activists campaigning on the very next doorstep. Not only this, just being present in Barking town centre and in the main public thoroughfares in Dagenham afforded me an abundance of opportunities to observe the BNP's various staged public performances and campaign activities which would testify to the effectiveness of the BNP's 'modernization' strategy. In most instances, where stalls, placards, flags and party logos and symbols were absent, it could be difficult to tell the difference between BNP and non-BNP activists until I either saw the leaflets being distributed or heard the arguments being articulated. On the surface, these encounters were a far cry from the sort of popular representations of violent fascists and Nazis. That said, there were occasions where it was clear that such encounters where predicated on the privileges of whiteness which meant that I was not perceived as being a political opponent a priori. That is to say, BNP campaigners were not always as civil during their interactions with people racialized as non-White, or when their politics were challenged, especially by anti-fascist campaigners. Thus, the threat of violence and intimidation was never totally absent. In addition to this, I often heard local Labour, Conservative and United Kingdom Independence Party activists make relatively similar arguments to the BNP in terms of opposing immigration and multiculturalism. Racism was not only pervasive, it was being legitimized by mainstream party politics, both locally and nationally, often under the guise of nationalism and patriotism. So much so, that in the context of entrenched mainstream racism, you could be forgiven for thinking that the BNP were somewhat unremarkable, had you not been aware of the fundamentally violent, racist and anti-democratic ideologies which lurked behind such 'front-stage' performances seeking to deliver the party's messages to the public in a more palatable form.

Participant observation also enabled me to establish a strong rapport with key local actors of an anti-racist and anti-fascist persuasion. In fact, I attended the majority of HnH and UAF events and campaign days at which I observed activists, including members of local political parties, distributing leaflets and engaging with local residents and BNP campaigners. On more than one occasion, Labour Party and anti-fascist activists told me that I had proven my 'anti-fascist credentials'.[6] This was integral to securing interviews with key actors whom up until that point had proven to be somewhat elusive. Participant observation also created seemingly never-ending opportunities to hold more ethnographic conversations with local residents.

Between March and August 2009, I conducted 16 key actor interviews across a range of political parties, as well as with anti-fascist activists, trade unionists and representatives from residents' groups. When doing so, I was particularly interested in the 'specialized knowledge' these actors held in relation to particular events or time periods. These interviews presented alternative residual narratives to those found in existing local histories and seminal sociological studies (i.e. Beynon, 1973; Willmott, 1963), as well as key far right studies (Ford and Goodwin, 2010; Goodwin, 2008), particularly in relation to the Borough's industrial-culture heritage and local labour movement politics. The knock-on effect of which often resulted in further local archival research that would challenge the nostalgic representations of post-war welfare capitalism found in such accounts. For example, a combination of key actor interviews and local archival research shed light on the forms of racism that blighted the everyday working lives of Black and Asian workers at the Ford Dagenham plant during the 1960s and 1970s, including Inder Singh Jamu, the first Sikh Mayor of Barking and Dagenham, outbreaks of racist violence on local housing estates, as well as forms of multi-racial and multi-ethnic anti-fascist and anti-racist resistance; thus, revealing a more nuanced local history than those underpinning the 'angry white man' and 'left behind' theses.

Key actor interviews also allowed me to acquire a more sophisticated under-standing of the internal dynamics within various organizations, as well as the con-tradictions, tensions and struggles between those political parties and civil society groups that would form 'united' and 'popular fronts' to oppose the BNP.[7] In contrast to Copsey's (2012) account of these campaigns, I was able to show that not only were the HnH and UAF campaigns in 2009 and 2010 shaped by local anti-fascist traditions, they were also shaped by fraught debates in relation to whiteness, 'progressive patriotism', antisemitism and anti-Zionism. Thus, I was able to draw out nuances that were absent in the 'official accounts' presented in archi-val, documentary and online sources, particularly in relation to the depth of decay of local party politics, the deep-seated complacency that had seeped into both the Barking and the Dagenham branches of the Labour Party following decades of facing no real political opposition, and the extent to which local BNP actors had been able to embed themselves in local residents groups.[8] In doing so, I was pie-cing together a picture of the way in which local party politics was being rebuilt, as well as how the local Labour Parties were re-establishing their hegemony by rebuilding the party's relationships with local residents' groups and local churches, mosques and gurdwaras. These findings would enable me to engage in more of a critical dialogue with residents during my third and final period of fieldwork.

More political ethnography (2010)

Following a break from fieldwork due to knee surgery in late 2009, I returned to Barking and Dagenham in February 2010. Political ethnography in 2010 was a completely different kettle of fish. The political stakes were now much higher following the announcement that BNP Chairman Nick Griffin, rather than the well-established Leader of the BNP group on the local Council, would contest the seat of Barking at the forthcoming national general election. Not only this, the 2010 general and local elections were to be held on the very same day, at which all 51 of the Borough's council seats would be contested. The BNP set their stall, boasting that they were looking to take control of the council.

Alongside further archival, documentary and online data collection material and continuing to conduct participant observation and key actor interviews, the pri-mary aim of what would be my third and final phase of data collection was con-ducting semi-structured interviews with local residents in relation to their voting behaviour. By the end of this third phase of data collection, I had conducted 31 in-depth interviews, as well as 163 ethnographic conversations, with local residents. What is more, by August 2010, I had carried out 35 key actor interviews in total, while participant observation during 2009 and 2010 helped me to collect 156 separate pieces of campaign literature.

Reflecting on the ethnographic conversations conducted during 2008 and 2009, it was evident that I had used this approach to capture how residents made 'sense and articulated their placement in the social order of things' (Anthias, 2005: 43). Exploring residents' 'locational narratives' (Anthias, 2002) would turn out to be a useful way of apprehending the different ways that residents placed themselves in particular social categories (i.e. class, ethnicity and gender) as they talked their way back and forth across time and space. Thus, I was able to gain detailed insights into who and what residents identified with socially, culturally and politically. As Anthias notes, such narratives are often unequivocal statements about what 'one is not, rather than a clear and unambiguous formulation of what one is' (Anthias, 2005: 42). Perhaps more importantly, data generated by the ethnographic conversations conducted in 2008/2009 revealed that support for the BNP was not always consistent across different types of elections. It was for this very reason that I would make the case to carry out in-depth interviews with local residents, as well as design a short voting behaviour survey tailored to the specificities of parties and candidates standing for election in each local ward. These surveys would be used during both interviews and ethnographic conversations with residents during my 2010 fieldwork, thus tracking their voting behaviour across the different types of elections held between 2006 and 2010.[9]

The central aim of my doctoral research had also shifted at this point. My research was no longer just a political ethnographic study of the BNP. After the 2010 local election results were announced on 5 May, I was now just as interested in how the BNP had lost all 12 of the seats that they had won in 2006 despite the total number of votes going to the BNP actually increasing. I was also now very much interested in how it came to be that the Labour Party now occupied all 51 seats on the Council. Moreover, my research was now a broader study of the changing dynamics of local political hegemony. In order to change tact yet again, something had to give. Alas, to include interviews with residents I now had to abandon my plan to conduct similar comparative research in Burnley.

A variety of methods were used to recruit a sample of residents willing to take part in qualitative interviews. I initially wanted to devise a self-completion postal questionnaire similar to that used by Rhodes (2006). Not only would the questionnaire have been used to recruit participants, it would have contained a series of closed and open-ended questions that would have also generated data on the views and opinions of a larger number of residents, including those who may not have wanted to take part in an interview or ethnographic conversation. Following advice from my supervisors, I accepted that I did not have either the time or the resources required to undertake such an approach. I was also advised that such an approach was unlikely to generate the sort of sample size required to produce 'statistically meaningful results'. Therefore, I opted for a cheaper option.

Using the local electoral register, I hand-delivered postcards to some 4,800 homes across 6 of the Borough's 17 local electoral wards. This consisted of an initial invitation postcard and a reminder postcard delivered 2 week later. The postcards were delivered across three wards that had exhibited the highest average levels of electoral support for the BNP across the various local, Greater London, national and European elections held between 2006 and 2010, as well as the Borough's two most affluent wards and the area's two most ethnically and racially diverse wards. The primary aim of doing so was to try and recruit an interview sample that was diverse along ethnic, racial and class lines, as opposed to a sample that would centre just the voices of 'white working class' constituents.

In addition to the postcards, I submitted letters to the Borough's newspapers, as well as the Local Council's free fortnightly newspaper, which at the time was being distributed to some 70,000 homes.[10] My ethnographic experiences in 2008 and 2009 also made me aware that meeting people in person was the most effective way of recruiting interview participants and sparking opportunities to have ethnographic conversations; hence the decision to hand-deliver the aforementioned postcards. With this in mind, I tried to recruit interview participants by attending local councillors' surgeries and local residents' meetings. Each of the approaches outlined above also enabled me to recruit participants via snowball sampling. And, although each of these approaches on their own may not have yielded the desired number of interview participants (see Figure 18.1 below), they proved to be effective in terms of generating further opportunities to hold ethnographic conversations. By the end of 2010, I had carried out 163 ethnographic conversations in total, 86 of which were held during this third tranche of fieldwork. And like the 31 interviews with local residents, the conversations were markedly shaped by

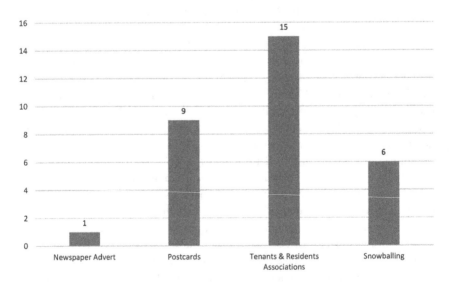

FIGURE 18.1 Interview participants by recruitment method

whiteness, class and a socially constructed local 'communicative community' that was both white and working class, which residents often referred to as the 'traditional working class' – a term commonly found in wider academic, political and media discourses in Britain.

The 'insider–outsider' debate has been a matter of considerable academic discussion. Central to these discussions has been the suggestion that

> researchers who share membership in the same social categories as their respondents (the most common being race, gender, and class) were best suited to uncover ideas, arguments, and opinions about issues and concerns related to those people or to those social categories... . A corollary presumption was that those researchers who do not share such membership either had to work especially hard to acquire the trust and confidence of respondents, or else accept that their scholarly analysis and interpretation may not reflect the veracity, depth, or subtlety that emerges from so-called 'insider' research.
>
> *(Young, Jr., 2004: 187)*

Such assumptions have underpinned numerous conversations that I have had with academics over the course of my research career to date, particularly in relation to this area of study. Indeed, it has regularly been suggested that as a white person other white people would talk to me about racism in ways that they would not if the researcher was non-white.[11] Similarly, it has been suggested that people who have experienced racism would not talk to a white researcher about their experiences of racism in quite the same way as they would to a researcher racialized as non-white.[12] The dynamics of race, class and the significance of place were very much prevalent during my encounters with local residents.

Many of the ethnographic conversations and interviews conducted between 2008 and 2010 were marked by the 'hidden injuries of class' (Sennett and Cobb, 1966), communicated as feelings of inadequacy and/or a lack self-worth and value. For example, while in the BLC I would notice users looking over at me somewhat shyly, lacking the confidence to ask me what I was doing with the piles of newspapers. Noticing this, I would look over and say, 'How you doing?' For many residents, this was a sign that it was okay to come over and talk to me. When they did so, I gave them an overview of what I was doing before asking if it was okay to ask them a few questions. This request was often met with awkwardness and shyness, with some residents stating that they were not sure whether they had 'anything worth saying'. As residents became more at ease and more confident talking to me, many remarked that I did not look or talk 'like a researcher'. I tended to respond to this by light-heartedly asking, 'what does an academic look and talk like?' I also encountered similar feelings of inadequacy and low self-worth while hand-delivering the aforementioned postcards. Not only this, upon hearing my Scottish/ Glaswegian accent or seeing my institution's logo on the postcards, some residents became quite suspicious. More specifically, they wanted to know why someone all the way from a University in Glasgow was interested in what they had to say.

Such feelings of unease, suspicion and inadequacy were also triggered by standard academic approaches to securing informed consent. For example, when I pulled out participant information sheets and consent forms many residents were clearly uncomfortable, if not visibly intimidated by the idea of signing a form which appeared to them as being a formal written contract. Some residents were also clearly uncomfortable, if not intimidated when, I asked them if I could audio record our conversations. In these situations, I put the information sheet, consent form and Dictaphone away, opting instead to negotiate consent verbally and write up detailed notes of the discussion as soon as the conversation had finished. Once at ease, many residents were more than willing to engage and were also very generous with their time. In fact, as their confidence grew, most residents were happy to let me use the aforementioned voting behaviour survey. The ethnographic conversations conducted at public residents' meetings were slightly different to those held on residents' door steps and in the BLC. For many residents this was an opportunity to 'set the record straight'. In fact, many residents were aware of the way in which the working class people in places like Barking and Dagenham had been represented as both 'white' and racist in the broader media and political narratives outlined earlier. At the same time, many residents did not shy away from the fact that racism was both heard and challenged during these meetings.

As I have also mentioned above, many local residents were willing to speak to me about their personal experiences of racism. However, on several occasions it was suggested that I 'wouldn't get it' because I am white. At the same time, other non-white participants seemed keen to talk to me in order to challenge some of the white locational narratives outlined above, thus providing local insights in relation to matters which they felt might not be immediately obvious to a white researcher from Glasgow. It also seemed to me that trust and confidence was built by showing empathy with regard to people's feelings and experiences, especially when I could bring insights from the archival, documentary and online data that I had already collected into the conversation, as well as articulate my own anti-racist politics. In different ways, these instances not only highlight the role of whiteness, they also draw attention to the significance of place.

When talking to white residents, my status as an 'outsider' was again apparent as participants positioned themselves as part of a 'communicative community' made up of experiences, 'ideas, opinions, narratives, gossip, jokes etc.', which also served as a 'final court of appeal and legitimator of social opinion and action' (Hewitt, 2005: 65–66). In fact, in those moments when I openly questioned racist viewpoints using the voices of non-white residents, as well as archival, documentary and online data, the discussion was often quickly shut down and I was reminded that I was an 'outsider', despite the similarities of whiteness and class background and, as such, I was not qualified to pass judgement on the way that participants saw the world.[13] Picking up on my Scottish accent, some residents and key actors sought to downplay, or even justify racism, by comparing the situation in Barking and Dagenham to Glasgow, which was considered to be 'worse' and 'less tolerant'. Residents, and key actors for that matter, also sought to justify racist points of view by referring to other local people who were said to think the same way.[14] Aware that challenging residents' views too early in the discussion could shut down the conversation completely, I learned to wait until the end of conversations and interviews, until after all other questions had been asked, to problematize racist aspects of residents' locational narratives. In doing so, I would empathize with residents' material situation in terms of the lack of affordable housing and relatively secure, well-paid local employment without sympathizing with racist explanations as to how they had found themselves in such circumstances.

While such exchanges may be of limited value in terms of being an anti-racist intervention that changes people minds, I will conclude by suggesting that engaging in this type of critical dialogue outlined here is but one step that white far right scholars can take in order to avoid complicity in the reproduction of whiteness. Not only this, such encounters can provide insights that can inform the kind of anti-racist, anti-fascist education work required to challenge both the far right and mainstream racism.

Conclusion

This chapter has narrated my journey towards a local political ethnography of the BNP in outer-East London. In concluding, I want to address a criticism that I and other far right scholars have faced when presenting their research. That is, when attending academic, left-wing, anti-fascist and trade union events, I have witnessed and contributed to what are often tense and heated exchanges regarding the ethics and politics of conducting ethnographic research engaging far right activists and supporters. On more than one occasion I have heard academics suggests that there is no place for ethnographic academic research involving the far right, which was often articulated as part of a broader 'no platform' argument and, in anti-fascist circles, calls to 'unite and fight, smash the [the far right]'.[15]

I also want to reflect on my interactions with white scholars in the field of far right studies, particularly in terms of the role of whiteness and how this relates to questions of methodological whiteness highlighted throughout this chapter, particularly in terms of who and what becomes the far right scholars' focus of study. Here I will reflect on a series of sustained and on-going discussions I have had with scholars, when teaching students interested in the field, as well as when working with anti-fascists and trade unionists, not to mention a prolonged engagement with published academic and non-academic writings dating back to 2006. In addressing these issues, I want to suggest that white far right scholars must consider the type of white identity they are enacting and reproducing through their research, as well as call for a turn to an 'active listening' (Back, 2002) approach and a greater attentiveness to the deleterious effects of whiteness in this field of study.

In response to the suggestion that there is no place for academic research that engages the far right, I want to draw attention to the writings of Phil Piratin, a Jewish Communist Party MP in East London, who played an important role in the Stepney Tenants Defence League in the 1930s. In alliance with others, the Stepney

Tenants Defence League took a variety of measures to thwart the efforts of Oswald Mosley's British Union of Fascists (BUF) to mobilize in areas of East London where Jewish people lived. In *Our Flag Stays Red*, Piratin notes that he and his allies responded to those who said 'Bash the fascists wherever you see them', by asking:

> How was Mosley able to recruit Stepney workers? This, in spite of our pro-paganda exposing the fascists. If they saw in the fascists the answer to their problems, why? What were the problems? Did we, in our propaganda, offer a solution? Was propaganda itself sufficient? Was there more that ought to be done?
>
> *(2006[1978]: 18)*

As I wrestled with the ethical and political dilemmas discussed throughout this chapter, I often returned to this passage, asking myself, 'How would anti-fascists such as Piratin know the answers to these questions if they did not listen to what those people drawn to what the BUF had to say?' When thinking about this question, I also was persuaded by Les Back's reflexive sociological account of interviewing BNP leader Nick Griffin in the 1990s, especially his call for the adoption of,

> a form of active listening that challenges the listener's preconceptions and position while at the same time it engages critically with the content of what is being said and heard. It also means entering into difficult and challenging cri-tical dialogues with one's enemies as well as one's allies.
>
> *(2002: 23)*

By engaging in a form of 'active listening', the research discussed throughout this chapter drew attention to a number of issues which I felt had to be addressed through local anti-racist, anti-fascist work. What is more, while conducting parti-cipant observation, I routinely fed the following insights back to those I was observing, including local anti-fascist organizers.

First, during exchanges with key party political and anti-fascist gatekeepers, I highlighted the way in which the BNP had developed strong roots in key areas of local civil society, as well as strategically employing non-white members and sup-porters to deflect accusations of racism,[16] and how this had a considerable impact on the voting choices of many local residents. Second, I used my research to note that while anti-fascist attempts to label Nick Griffin a Nazi and fascist were partly successful, such efforts were not as effective when it came to BNP actors firmly embedded in local civil society, especially among younger constituents. By listening to residents, I heard BNP supporters, as well as constituents who could not bring themselves to vote for the BNP using terms such as 'dedicated' 'community activist (s)', 'nice', 'normal', 'approachable', 'very respectful', 'polite' and 'pleasant' to describe their encounters with locally embedded BNP actors. This is a marked contrast to the anti-fascist campaign narratives, especially those articulated by more militant groups employing counter-demonstration tactics, which often described the BNP as 'aggressive', 'threatening', 'undemocratic' and 'violent' 'outsiders'. Thus, I soon developed the view that the anti-fascist campaigners had to do more to counteract the different 'reputational shields' that the BNP had developed. Not only this, I also argued that while anti-fascist campaigners might clearly understand the rationale and traditions underpinning their democratic right to mobilize counter-demonstrations, this is not always clear to sections of the public. Drawing on my research, I pointed out that local residents often failed to make a distinction between HnH and UAF, including those who did not even vote for the BNP. In fact, many constituents also claimed that the BNP and anti-fascist campaigners were 'just as bad as each other' or 'two sides of the same coin'. I also pointed out that anti-fascist campaigners often had little political legitimacy amongst sections of the local electorate precisely because they were considered to be 'outsiders'. Here I noted Copsey's (2012) research on the way that anti-fascist campaigners are often guilty of 'parachuting' into local areas and failing to meaningfully engage or build support within the local community beyond one or two key civil society groups, usually trade unions and local places of worship, and then leaving the scene. Moreover, local anti-fascist campaigns also tended to use generic campaign materials which did not engage with the particularities of the local context or offer anti-racist political responses to broader far right and mainstream political discourses underpinned by nativism and anti-immigrant sentiment. When listening to residents, it was clear that such far right and mainstream discourses fed into and were shaped by the very real ontological insecurities experienced by local residents (for example, in relation to housing, employment and access to local schools).

Third, just listening to local residents talk their way backwards and forwards across time and space provided valuable insights into their common-sense understandings of racism and everyday forms of 'race talk'. In fact, doing so revealed that there was still much to be done in terms of challenging popular common-sense understandings of racism which reduced the focus of conversation to notions of hatred, malice and intent, and/or 'extremism', 'irrationality' and 'violence'. Such conceptions were integral to the obfuscation of both institutional and structural racism at the local level, as well as claims of 'reverse racism' and notions of white victimhood, which had been popularized by the far right and legitimized by mainstream politicians. These are just some of the insights that can be gained by adopting an 'active listening' approach. However, in making a case for 'active listening', my engagements with some far right scholars, as well as recent academic debates in Britain, lead me to think that any turn to such an approach, on its own, would not be sufficient.

With the exception of scholars with a background in critical race theory and those simultaneously studying the far right and anti-racism/ anti-fascism, my engagements with far right scholars (mostly in Britain) have often engendered feelings of unease. I often find myself in rooms where the conversation is dominated by established white academics (usually men) demonstrating little, if indeed any, interest in racism and racial inequality. Relatedly, there is often little concern with regard to the impact that far right activities have on people racialized outside of the dominant white group; whether that be the effect of the far right emerging as an electoral threat, shoving their leaflets through letter boxes or taking to the streets in the places where people on the receiving end of far right racism have made their homes. There have also been too many occasions where people racialized as non-white only appear in the conversation as passive objects of racism and study, rather than as scholars contributing to the field or actors expressing political agency in opposition to the far right. Not only this, my engagements in this field of study have often left me feeling that scholarly interest in the far right has been driven by white (and middle class) voyeurism, if not titillation. Similarly, my conversations with white students have often left me feeling that they are drawn to the field by a desire to study that which is 'exciting' and 'edgy' rather than intellectual engagement with critical race theory and/ or a commitment to anti-fascism and opposing mainstream racism.

In 2019, my feelings of unease have deepened considerably. In the past, far right scholars have used 'ethnic competition theory' (e.g. Goodwin, 2008) rather than critical race theory to explore support for the far right. In more recent times, Goodwin and Eatwell (2018) have articulated arguments similar to Eric Kaufman's (2018) contention that 'white racial self-interest' is not a form of racism, as well as supporting Kaufman's application of 'ethnic replacement theory' – a theory which shares similarities with the 'great replacement' conspiracy theory advanced by white supremacists. What is more, Goodwin helped organize a seminar, titled 'Is ethnic diversity a threat to the West?' This prompted over 200 academics, including myself and some of the contributors to this collection, to sign an open letter opposing the 'debate' because it was provocatively framed 'within the terms of white supremacist discourse' and 'with no concern for the public implications and effect of this framing' (Open Democracy, 2018; see also Hampshire, 2018; Trilling, 2019).

It is for these reasons, as well as issues of methodological whiteness highlighted throughout this chapter, especially in terms of the racialization of the working class as white, not to mention the lack of attention paid to critical race theory, postcolonial and decolonial theory and methodologies, anti-racist and anti-fascist scholarship and the political agency of people racialized as non-white, that I want to argue that far right studies, a field largely dominated by white people, must critically reflect on its role in the reproduction of whiteness (for example, see Zuberi and Bonilla-Silva, 2008; Bhambra, 2017). As well as undertaking the kind of 'active listening' approach outlined above, it is my encounters in the field of far right studies that lead me to suggest that some white far right scholars need to reflect on the form(s) of racialized identity they are enacting in and through their research. Thus, I want to encourage white far right scholars to seriously consider their privilege, and whether they are complicit in the reproduction of white hegemony – for example, by producing white accounts of place, by reducing the discussion of racism to something that is carried out by individuals, thus silencing the nature, scale and impact of structural and institutional racism, or by whitening the working class. In making this call, I am mindful of Malcolm X's views on the role of the 'sincere white people'. For Malcolm X, the role of the 'sincere' white ally should be to work in conjunction with people subjugated to white supremacy and teach 'non-violence to white people', while also 'trying to convert' white people to anti-racist politics.[17] In light of this, are white far right scholars willing to commit to exposing and undermining white supremacy, which is all too often inextricably linked to hetero-patriarchy, classism and ableism (see Joseph-Salisbury, 2018), in both far right and mainstream politics?

Notes

1 While the work of Gramsci, Williams and Thompson had a profound impact on my sociological imagination, I was mindful of key silences and the limitations in each of their writings, especially when it comes to matters of race and racism (see Gilroy, 1987; Matthews, 2013; Wilderson III, 2003).

2 The letters pages in the BNP's monthly magazine demonstrated considerable levels of debate and disagreement between the party hierarchy and its members. For example, see the letters pages of the May and June 2006 editions of *Identity* for an insight into the depth of debate that emerged from Nick Griffin's decision to try to tap into what he considered to be a growing sense of 'Englishness' characterised by feelings of cultural, economic and political inequity.

3 The 'angry white man' thesis has recently been reconceptualised as the 'left behind' thesis in an attempt to explain electoral support for the United Kingdom Independence Party, as well as the outcome of the 2016 EU referendum. Both the 'angry white man' and the 'left behind' theses echo many of the core elements of the 'losers of modernization' thesis which dominated this field study in the 1990s (see Betz, 1994; Betz and Immerfall, 1998).

4 For an overview of the way in which the structures and editing of local newspapers, including letters pages, can influence both the politics of racism and the types of newspaper coverage that political parties receive, see Richardson, 2001; Richardson and Franklin, 2003; 2004).

5 For example, when 12 BNP councillors were elected in Barking and Dagenham in 2006, the *Guardian* – a leading broadsheet newspaper in Britain – ran the following headline: 'Welcome to Barking – new far right capital of Britain: As the BNP celebrates, local people face up to the area's new notoriety' (Muir, 2006). The British Broadcasting Corporation (BBC) also got in on the act, producing a provocatively titled documentary called *All White in Barking*, which while noting the activities of the BNP, failed to cover the localized forms of anti-racist and anti-fascist opposition that had also emerged at this time (for a critique of the BBC *White Season*, see Ware, 2008; see also, *Last Whites of the East End,* a documentary aired by the BBC on 24 May 2016). Similarly contentious academic articles would soon follow, such as Goodwin's (2008) 'Backlash in the "hood"' (see Rhodes, 2011 for critique of Goodwin's article).

6 That said, there were other occasions whereby other key actors were more suspicious of me after having seen me observing other political parties campaigning.

7 United and popular fronts are typically conceptualised in terms of class. The former is basically an attempt to forge an alliance led by the working class in the interests of the working class, while the later seeks to unite 'working class organisations with middle class, liberal, and bourgeois parties' to 'form a people's front rather than a workers' front' (Rees, 2011: 46).

8 The depth of complacency is captured in the following quote from the incumbent Labour Member of Parliament for Barking, Margaret Hodge, during a BBC radio interview in 2009:

'Until the BNP really emerged, come elections you might deliver a few leaflets, you might have a presence at the polling station. Nobody really knocked on doors, nobody asked people what was the thing that mattered to them in their local communities. Nobody really listened … . And there we were, us politicians, being voted in year on year and we were simply not listening …'.

9 Interestingly, this short questionnaire revealed that even though the 2010 general and local elections were held on the same day, many residents had voted for local BNP candidates but not Party Chairman Nick Griffin. Similarly, some residents also informed me that while they had voted for local BNP candidates at local elections in 2006 and 2010, they had also voted for Labour and Conservative candidates because each ward was able to elect three councillors to represent them. Residents also explained that they did not vote for the BNP in the GLA, national and European elections because they did not think that the BNP had a realistic chance of winning. This highlights a limitation in the way that knowledge on the electoral support for the far right is generated using opinion polls, which although examining previous support for other candidates and parties, tend not track voting behaviour across different types of elections. Not only this, surveys such as the one deployed during my research also have the potential to offer new insights in terms of temporal dimensions and strength of far right electoral support.

10 Launched in late 2009, the local Labour-run council began printing *The News* as a response to the negative coverage it was receiving in the area's two local newspapers. Therefore, *The News* was not simply a 'community newspaper'. It was also, at least in part, an attempt to bolster the hegemony of both the Barking and the Dagenham branches of the Labour Party.

11 Although, as Ramalingam's contribution to this collection shows, far right activists expressed their racist views to a 'female Researcher of Colour' (see also Ezekiel, 1995).

12 I was born in the town of Paisley in the West of Scotland. Both my parents were factory workers for almost two decades before deindustrialization hit the town. Prior to redundancy both my parents were 'affluent workers'; that is, 'unskilled' working class people who experienced relatively well-paid and secure employment. I lived in the neighbourhood into which I was born for more than three decades – a neighbourhood which in 2016 was classified as the most deprived in Scotland. Other than periods of doctoral fieldwork, I had never lived anywhere else. My family consists of a mix of white Scottish, Irish, Catholic and Protestant backgrounds. From a very early age, I was aware of both anti-Catholic racism and sectarianism, most of which is centred around the rivalry between Glasgow's two main football clubs and the political situation in the North of Ireland. I was also introduced to anti-racism, anti-fascism, family histories of left-wing activism and trade unionism at a relatively young age. I draw attention to the above, not to play working class hero, but because my background was often a key feature in my interactions with local people in Barking and Dagenham. I also draw attention to this because amid recent academic discussion in and around Brexit and the far right in Britain, where some have sought to lay claim to a sense of working class authenticity (for an overview, see Shilliam, 2018; and Tilley, 2017). Often presented as a radical response to liberal and right-wing academic, political and media discourses which stigmatize the 'traditional working class' or 'left behind', these narratives serve as proxies for 'white working class', and obfuscate both middle class racism and the structural and institutional racism enacted by Britain's political and economic elites. In many ways, such claims of working class authenticity are not authentic to me. Such claims are both politically and intellectually unhelpful, not to mention exclusionary, if not nativistic. Reinforcing the very kind of identity politics they purport to oppose (see Valluvan, 2019), cruder claims to authenticity demand recognition for a homogenized, and whitened, working class, while also feeding into, if not reinforcing, notions of 'deserving' and 'undeserving poor' (see Shilliam, 2018). Such accounts, to my mind at least, obscure the fact that the working class in Britain has been multi-racial, multi-ethnic and politically heterogeneous from its very inception (see Virdee, 2014), while also failing to take appropriate account of the fact that neoliberalism, globalization, deindustrialization and austerity have had a

disproportionate impact on working class people racialized as non-White British, especially women (see Hall et al., 2017). For me, such claims to authenticity are the residue of a strain of socialist nationalism long advocated by sections of left in Britain (see Virdee, 2014).

13 For example,

Quote one: You don't live here. You can't tell us how to think [long pause]. There were people coming over here that genuinely needed to be here and they need a job. But now I'm changing again because our people can't get jobs. Our families are suffering and everybody else's families are suffering. Our families are suffering badly.

Quote two: I mean you must see it in Glasgow, because I don't think you're quite as tolerant of multicultural, race as we are, or you weren't at one time. I mean I'm not being, I've got a, one of my relations is from Glasgow.

14 Indeed, while watching anti-fascist campaigners knocking on residents' doors I heard similar arguments when racism was challenged. For example,

Out observing in Becontree tonight. Several heated exchanges between HnH [campaigners] and local people. Objection taken to the BNP being called 'fascists', 'Nazis' and 'racists' ... Two young white men, aged 18–25 years confronted me and the Green Party activist from Islington [a borough in Central London]. One shouted 'Who the f**k do you think you are? Come to my door with those 'f**king leaflets!' The other guy shouted 'f**k off back to Islington' several times as we walked away (Field diary extract – Wednesday 28th April 2010).

The catalyst for some of the more fiery exchanges stemmed from the way in which some anti-fascist campaigners were too quick to reach for terms like 'fascists', 'Nazis' and 'racists' rather than listening to what local residents had to say. From an anti-fascist perspective, this is not to say that the use of such terms was not justifiable on many occasions but rather these exchanges demonstrated that sustained anti-racist, anti-fascist work that engages with local residents' experiences, opinions and anxieties was required.

15 For a further discussion on the origins of 'no platform' politics, see Smith, E. (2015) " 'By whatever means necessary': The origins of the 'no platform' policy." *New Historical Express*, 3 November 2015. https://hatfulofhistory.wordpress.com/2015/11/03/by-whatever-means-necessary-the-origins-of-the-no-platform-policy/ [accessed 24 July 2019].

16 It is important to note that such individuals usually shared the BNP's hostility towards a particular racialized group (see Copsey, 2008).

17 Osmundson, J. (2013) "Love letter to white people". *The Feminist Wire*, 3 September 2013. https://thefeministwire.com/2013/09/love-letter-to-white-people/ [accessed 24 July 2019].

References

Anthias, F. 2002. "Where do I belong? Narrating collective identity and translocational positionality." *Ethnicities*, 2(4), 491–514.

Anthias, F. 2005. "Social stratification and social inequality: Models of intersectionality and identity." In *Rethinking Class: Culture, Identities and Lifestyle*, edited by F. Devine, M. Savage, J. Scott, and R. Crompton. Basingstoke: Palgrave Macmillan.

Ashe, S.D. 2013. *The Electoral Rise and 'Fall' of the British National Party in Barking and Dagenham.* Unpublished PhD thesis, University of Glasgow.

Back, L. 2002. "Guess who's coming to dinner? The political morality of investigating whiteness in the gray zone." In *Out of Whiteness: Color, Politics and Culture*, edited by V. Ware and L. Back. Chicago, IL: University of Chicago Press.

Back, L. 2007. *The Art of Listening.* London: Bloomsbury.

Banks, M. 2006. "Performing 'neo-nationalism': Some methodological notes." In *Neo-Nationalism in Europe & Beyond: Perspectives from Social Anthropology*, edited by A. Gingrich and M. Banks. New York, NY and Oxford: Berghahn Books.

Betz, H-G. 1994. *Radical Right-Wing Populism in Western Europe*. New York, NY: St. Martin's Press

Betz, H-G. and Immerfall, S. (eds). 1998. *The New Politics of the Right: Neo-Populist Parties and Movements in Established Democracies*. New York, NY: St. Martin's.

Beynon, H. 1973. *Working for Ford*. London: Penguin Books.

Bhambra, G. 2017. "Brexit, Trump, and 'methodological whiteness': On the misrecognition of race and class." *British Journal of Sociology*, 68(1), S214–S232.

Blee, K. 2007. "Ethnographies of the Far Right." *Journal of Contemporary Ethnography*, 36(2), 119–128.

Connell, R.W. 2005. *Masculinities*. Cambridge: Polity Press.

Copsey, N. 2008. *Contemporary British Fascism: The British National Party and the Quest for Legitimacy*. New York, NY: Palgrave Macmillan.

Copsey, N. 2012 "Sustaining a mortal blow? The British National Party and the 2010 general and local elections." *Patterns of Prejudice*, 46(1), 16–29.

Curtis, S. 2000. *Dagenham & Rainham Past*. London: Phillimore.

Curtis, S. 2006. *Barking: A History*. London: Phillimore.

Eatwell, R. 2010. "Responses to the extreme right in Britain." In *The New Extremism in 21st Century Britain*, edited by R. Eatwell and M.J. Goodwin. London: Routledge.

Ezekiel, R.S. 1995. *The Racist Mind: Portraits of American Neo-Nazis And Klansmen*. New York, NY: Viking Penguin.

Ferber, A.L. 2000. "Racial warriors and weekend warriors: The construction of masculinity in mythopoetic and white supremacist discourse." *Men and Masculinities*, 3(1), 30–56.

Ford, R. and M.J. Goodwin. 2010. "Angry white men: Individual and contextual predictors of support for the British National Party." *Political Studies*, 58(1), 1–25.

Gest, J. 2018. *The White Working Class: What Everyone Needs to Know*. Oxford: Oxford University Press.

Gilroy, P. 1987. *There Ain't No Black in the Union Jack: The Cultural Politics of Race and Nation*. London: Hutchinson.

Gingrich, A. and M. Banks. (eds). 2006. *Neo-Nationalism in Europe & Beyond: Perspectives from Social Anthropology*. New York, NY and Oxford: Berghahn Books.

Goodwin, M.J. 2008. "Backlash in the 'hood': Determinants of support for the British National Party (BNP) at the local level." *Journal of Contemporary European Studies*, 16(3), 347–361.

Goodwin, M.J. 2011. *The New British Fascism: Rise of the British National Party*. Oxford: Routledge.

Goodwin, M.J. and R. Eatwell. 2018. *National Populism: The Revolt Against Liberal Democracy*. London: Pelican.

Gramsci, A. 1971. *Selections from the Prison Notebooks*. eds and trans Quintin Hoare and Geoffrey Nowell-Smith. London: Lawrence and Wishart Ltd.

Hall, S., C. Critcher, T. Jefferson, J. Clarke, and B. Roberts. 2013. *Policing the Crisis: Mugging the State and Law & Order*. 35th Anniversary Edition. Basingstoke: Palgrave Macmillan.

Hall, S.-M., K. McIntosh, E. Neitzert, L. Pottinger, K. Sandhu, M-A. Stephenson, H. Reed, and L. Taylor. 2017. *Intersecting Inequalities: The Impact of Austerity on Black and Minority Women in the UK*. A report by the Women's Budget Group and Runnymede Trust.

Hammersley, M. and P. Atkinson. 1995. *Ethnography: Principles in Practice*. 2nd edition. London: Routledge.

Hampshire, J. 2018. "The legitimation of racial resentment." *Discover Society*, 63. Available at: https://discoversociety.org/2018/12/04/the-legitimation-of-racial-resentment/

Hewitt, R. 2005. *White Backlash and the Politics of Multiculturalism*. Cambridge: Cambridge University Press.

Howson, J. 1990. *A Brief History of Barking and Dagenham*. Barking & Dagenham: Libraries Department.

Ivarsflaten, E. 2006. *"Reputational shields: Why anti-immigrant parties fail."* Paper presented to the annual conference of the American Political Science Association, Philadelphia, 30 August – 3 September.

Joseph-Salisbury, R. 2018. "Confronting my duty as an academic: We should all be activists." In *The Fire Now: Anti-Racist Scholarship in Times of Explicit Racial Violence*, edited by A. Johnson, R. Joseph-Salisbury, and B. Kamunge. London: Zed Books.

Kaufman, E. 2018. *Whiteshift: Populism, Immigration and the Future of White Majorities*. London: Allen Lane.

Khan, O. and F. Shaheen. 2017. *Minority Report: Race and Class in Post-Brexit Britain*. Runnymede Trust and CLASS.

Klandermans, B. and N. Mayer (eds). 2005. *Extreme Right Activists in Europe: Through the Magnifying Glass*. London: Routledge.

Kushner, T. and N. Valman. 2000. *Remembering Cable Street: Fascism and Anti-Fascism in British Society*. London: Vallentine Mitchell.

Matthews, W. 2013. *The New Left: National Identity, and the Break-Up of Britain*. Chicago, IL: Haymarket Books.

Mondon, A. and A. Winter. 2019. "Whiteness, populism and the racialization of the working-class in the United Kingdom and the United States." *Identities: Global Studies in Culture and Power*. 26(5); 510–528, DOI: 10.1080/1070289X.2018.1552440.

Moore, L.G. 1996. "Good old fashioned new social history and the twentieth century American right." *Reviews in American History*, 24(4), 555–573.

Muir, H. 2006. "Welcome to Barking – new far right capital of Britain." *The Guardian*, https://www.theguardian.com/politics/2006/may/06/uk.localgovernment2

Open Democracy. 2018. "Framing ethnic diversity as a 'threat' will normalise far-right hate, say academics." Available at: https://www.opendemocracy.net/en/opendemocracyuk/framing-ethnic-diversity-debate-as-about-threat-legitimises-hat-0/

Piratin, P. 2006. *Our Flag Stays Red*. Lawrence and Wishart.

Rees, J. 2011. *Strategy and Tactics: How the Left Can Organize to Transform Society*. London: Counterfire.

Rhodes, J. 2006. *Far Right Breakthrough: Support for the BNP in Burnley*. Unpublished PhD thesis, University of Manchester.

Rhodes, J. 2009. "The Banal National Party: the routine nature of legitimacy." *Patterns of Prejudice*, 43(2), 142–160.

Rhodes, J. 2011. "'It's not ust them, it's whites as well': Whiteness, class and BNP Support." *Sociology*, 45(1), 102–117.

Rhodes, J., S. Ashe, and S. Valluvan. 2019. *Reframing the 'Left Behind': Race and Class in Post-Brexit Oldham*. Manchester: University of Manchester, British Academy & The Leverhulme Trust. http://hummedia.manchester.ac.uk/institutes/code/research/projects/left-behind/oldham-report-2-september-2019.pdf

Richardson, J.E. 2001. "'Now is the time to put an end to all this': Argumentative discourse theory and 'letters to the editor." *Discourse and Society*, 12(3), 143–168.

Richardson, J. and B. Franklin. 2003 "'Dear Editor': Race, readers' letters and the local press," *Political Quarterly*, 74(2), 184–192.

Richardson, J. and B. Franklin. 2004. "Letters of intent: election campaigning and orchestrated public debate in local newspapers' Letters to the Editor." *Political Communications*, 21, 459–478.

Sennett, R. and J. Cobb. 1966. *The Hidden Injuries of Class*. New York, NY: Vintage Books.

Shilliam, R. 2018. *Race and the Undeserving Poor: From Abolition to Brexit*, London: Agenda.

Tames, R. 2002. *Barking Past*. London: Historical Publications.

Tilly, C. 2007. "Afterword: Political ethnography as art and science." *Qualitative Sociology*, 29, 409–412.

Tilley, L. 2017. "The making of the 'white working class': Where fascist resurgence meets leftist white anxiety." *Wildcat Dispatches*. Available at: http://wildcatdispatches.org/2016/11/28/lisa-tilley-the-making-of-the-white-working-class-where-fascist-resurgence-meet s-leftist-white-anxiety/

Trilling, D. 2019. "'I'm not racist, but …'." *London Review of Books*, 41(8), 19–22.

Thompson, E.P. 1968. *The Making of The English Working Class*. Harmondsworth: Penguin.

Valluvan, S. 2019. *The Clamour of Nationalism: Race and Nation in Twenty-first-century Britain*. Manchester: Manchester University Press.

Virdee, S. 2014. *Racism, Class and the Racialized Outsider*. Basingstoke: Palgrave.

Ware, V. 2008. "Towards a sociology of resentment: A debate on class and whiteness." *Sociological Research Online*, 13(5), 9.

WildersonIII, F. 2003. "Gramsci's Black Marx: Whither the slave in civil society?" *Social Identities*, 9(2), 225–240.

Wilks-Heeg, S. 2009. "The canary in a coalmine? Explaining the emergence of the British National Party in English local politics." *Parliamentary Affairs*, 62(2), 377–398.

Williams, R. 1977. *Marxism and Literature*. Oxford: Oxford University Press.

Willmott, P. 1963. *The Evolution of a Community: A Study of Dagenham After Forty Years*. London: Routledge and Kegan Paul.

YoungJr, A.A. 2004. "Experiences in ethnographic interviewing about race: The inside and outside of it." In *Researching Race and Racism*, edited by M. Bulmer and J. Solomos. London: Routledge.

Zuberi, T. and E. Bonilla-Silva. 2008. *White Logic, White Methods: Racism and Methodology*. Plymouth: Rowman & Littlefield Publishers, Inc.

PART V

The significance of place, culture and performance when researching the far right

19

STUDYING LOCAL CONTEXT TO FATHOM FAR-RIGHT SUCCESS

John W.P. Veugelers

'Place matters': once upon a time this would have sounded banal. Today – when travel and communication erase distance ever more easily, and material cultures and built environments issue ever more repetitively from the same moulds – whether place still matters is less obvious.[1] On this score, research on the far right has shown a certain insouciance. Since the 1980s, scholars of European politics have published more studies on the far right than on all other party families put together (Mudde, 2017: 2). Whether they examine socio-demographic, attitudinal, contextual, or institutional effects, many of these studies rely on national data. Yet between-country differences in far-right support can be significantly smaller than the differences within countries (Golder, 2016: 491). This sets limits on research that takes the country as its unit of analysis:

> Social, political and economic conditions vary massively at the sub-national, e. g., across provinces, districts, towns and even neighborhoods. It stands to reason that citizens rely on these local conditions, which have a massive impact on their everyday lives, to evaluate politicians, parties and policies at the national level.
>
> *(Arzheimer, 2012: 46)*

Neither isolated from external influences nor a direct reflection of them, each locality harbors a complex of formal and informal institutions that are sedimentations of past practices, belief patterns, and power relations. Across institutional spheres (politics, economics, religion, associations, families, communications, and so on), growth, adaptation, and rupture can play out at different tempos. The specificity of a locale arises from its institutions, the relations between these, and the relations between its institutions and the outside world. The premise for this chapter is that local research on the far right offers insights missed by analysis that ignores the multiple paths of sub-national development (Van Gent and Musterd, 2012).

The locality can serve as the unit of analysis for a range of research designs: from large *n* studies of comparable sub-national units (e.g., municipalities, counties, or departments) down to studies of a single case (e.g., neighborhood, town, or city), with comparative case studies in between. All of these can contribute to knowledge – but not necessarily in the same way. To see why, this chapter distinguishes between five contributions to causal analysis, empirical verification, and theory making. The possible contribution of local research, I propose, will depend significantly on the sample size.

To explore these ideas in more detail, this chapter concentrates on single-case studies. After reviewing past research on localities in Britain, France, and Italy, the middle section of this chapter examines the challenges and opportunities of a study of the *Front national* (FN) that the author conducted in the French city of Toulon. The discussion extracts lessons about the strengths and weaknesses of a single-case, local study of the far right that relies on mixed methods. This chapter concludes with the problem of disciplinary boundaries. Local studies can make a unique contribution to our understanding of the far right. Scrutiny of single-case studies, however, emphasizes the need to bridge social scientific and historical methods. Otherwise, researchers will be ill equipped to trace processes or identify mechanisms that link antecedent and contextual conditions to far right outcomes.

Five rationales for local studies of the far right

Local studies justify themselves in at least five ways. First, when far right action or success is noteworthy but confined to a locality, a well-constructed study will try to isolate the relevant conditions that set this locality apart. Second, local analysis can reveal mechanisms or events that link causal conditions to far right outcomes. Third, local analysis can enhance causal explanation by showing how multiple paths might lead to a common outcome. Fourth, it can demonstrate that correlations at higher levels of analysis do not hold at the local level. Fifth, the discovery of anomalous findings can inspire new theory.

Isolating specificities that explain unusual local success, activity, or failure

Despite the electoral rise of the far right since the 1980s, rarely does it win elections. Sometimes it governs, but then only as a partner. By default, other forms of strength or influence command attention. As these tend to be concentrated spatially, well-constructed explanations will explain why the far right has succeeded, exhibited more activity, or suffered setbacks, in some localities but not others (Goodwin, 2012). Social scientists agree with historians that statistical estimates of average effects can have few, or even no, empirical referents; average effects (as captured by regression lines in statistical analysis) thus may provide a poor fit with cases of substantive importance that are outliers (Lieberman, 2005). Local studies contribute by identifying conditions unimportant at the national level (such as political corruption or a broken *cordon sanitaire*) that have turned a far-right potential into actual support.

Enhancing the plausibility of explanation by entering the black box of causation

Causal explanation gains in plausibility when it specifies a mechanism, process, or event sequence that connects a cause or prior condition to the outcome of interest. This does not imply the superiority of positivistic over interpretive approaches. Although embedded in rival epistemologies (Mahoney, 2008), both the specification of causal mechanisms (Elster, 1989; Hedström and Swedberg, 1998; Gross, 2018) and the elaboration of historical narrative (Aminzade, 1992; Somers, 1992; Sewell, 1996; Rast, 2012) enter into the black box between cause and effect. Local study gives researchers an opportunity to develop explanations of far-right success that are more convincing because they are explicit and detailed about causal linkages.

Showing different paths to a shared outcome

Local studies can contribute to causal explanation in another way. Assume no aspect of far-right success, persistence, or failure has a single cause; and causes of each of these outcomes do not operate in isolation from each other (Veugelers and Magnan, 2005). Establishing which causes are necessary or sufficient requires a comparison of different combinations of preconditions and outcomes. If properly designed, comparison of the far right across localities can meet this requirement. This may reveal that diverse paths can lead to a similar outcome (Ragin, 1987). It also provides a corrective to idiographic accounts that could connect with each other, but do not, because they assume that local trajectories are unique and incommensurable.

Identifying reversals in correlation across levels of analysis

Not just the strength but also the direction of the effect (positive or negative) of independent variables can vary between national and local levels. No far-right research examines this possibility explicitly or systematically, to my knowledge, so consider instead a comparative study of identity politics in 30 localities of the United States (DeLeon and Naff, 2004). Analysis of liberal orientation, political activity, and protest activity reveals that only one of four variables (class) has consistent effects across localities. The other variables (race, gender, religion) vary not only in their strength but also, significantly, in whether their effect is positive or negative. Place thus matters for far-right studies because the relations between independent and dependent variables at the local level may contradict the corresponding relations at a higher level of analysis.

Stimulating theorizing

Scholars commonly assign the factors that explain far-right success into two categories: those affecting voter demand and those affecting the supply of parties meeting this demand (Kitschelt and McGann 1997; Eatwell, 2003; Golder, 2016). Demand-side attributes – notably nativism, authoritarianism, and anti-elitism – pervade society. This raises a provocative question: if the demand for them is so widespread, why are far right parties so unsuccessful (Mudde, 2010)? Giving equal weight to the two categories of factors would appear to inflate the importance of demand, at best a necessary but not a sufficient condition (Rydgren, 2007). This, in turn, implies that research should concentrate on variation in the supply. Attention to what is relatively immediate, however, risks missing aspects of society that change more slowly (Rast, 2012). For some analytical purposes, it may well be useful to take demand as a given. For other purposes, however, demand itself requires explanation. Local studies can make a distinctive contribution by explaining the nature, origins, and transmission of demand – a neglected area of research.

Strengths and weaknesses of local studies

The preceding rationales make a strong case but taken together they promise too much. Apart from stimulating theorizing, these rationales cannot apply with equal force to all local studies. Studying a single case can provide only a partial understanding of multiple causal paths or reversals in correlation. For these purposes, comparative case studies seem more appropriate. A comparative case study or a large *n* study seems a better choice for explaining an unusual example of far-right success. Large *n* studies are less suitable for process tracing.

Rather than presenting a complete inventory of how sample size might affect the strengths and weaknesses of local studies, we can deepen the analysis by focusing on studies of a single case. Consider these examples:

1. To explain the surge in support for the National Front in Britain during the 1970s, Husbands (1982; 1983) singles out East London. Long immune to recruiting and organising by the Labour and the Conservative Parties, this locality harboured a tradition of working-class nativism already exploited during the interwar years by the British Union of Fascists.
2. To explain a deadly bomb that neo-fascists planted at a 1974 labour rally in the northern Italian city of Brescia, Chiarini and Corsini (1983) probe the local legacy of the 1943–1945 Italian Social Republic. Personal networks and political organizations in this industrial city preserved a potential for violence that erupted when neo-fascist activists reacted to a surge in worker mobilization by applying the so-called strategy of tension.
3. To explain the first local breakthrough of the FN in France, Roy (1993) points to unusual activism in fertile territory. The leader of the far right in Dreux used this town to test a grassroots campaign of anti-immigrant

activism. Local leaders of the moderate right, in turn, decided that defeating the left justified an opportunistic alliance with the FN.

These studies converge in highlighting local specificities that explain noteworthy examples of far-right activity or success.

They diverge, though, when it comes to a core problem for historical research: the issue of continuity versus change. Husbands (1982; 1983) highlights the uniqueness of Hoxton, Shoreditch, and Bethnal Green, parts of East London that already in the late nineteenth century were islands of poor natives surrounded by neighborhoods of immigrants, many of them Jews from Russia and Russian Poland. An enduring racial exclusionism with roots in anti-Semitism and defense of territory explains the locality's receptivity toward the 1970s far right. In his study of Dreux, by contrast, Roy (1993) emphasizes change. This town run by the Socialist Party became a laboratory for the FN, a testing-ground for new tactics (in the Centre region of France, not Dreux but an area south of the Loire River harbored continuity with anti-Republican traditions of royalism and catholic traditionalism). For their part, Chiarini and Corsini (1983) find a mix of continuity and change in the interaction between enduring local neo-fascist activism on one hand, class strife and national neo-fascist strategy on the other.

Notwithstanding their contrasts, these studies bring out the importance of conditions, forces, or processes often overlooked in the general literature on the far right: territorial defense and conflict; far right grassroots organization; and interaction between the tactics and strategies of the left, the moderate right, and the far right. Among these, only interaction between the different political blocs receives serious attention in research at the national level. Territorial defense or conflict as well as grassroots organization fall through the cracks. Scrutiny of these examples thus confirms that even studies of single localities can provide a stimulus to theorizing.

A mixed-method study

The foregoing rationales and examples suggest that local studies can do more than draw attention to factors or processes that elude higher levels of analysis. They can also contribute to causal explanation and theoretical refinement. Realizing this potential raises various challenges, however. This became evident when I carried out research in Toulon, which in 1995 became the largest city of any post-war, multi-party democracy in Europe to fall under the far right. Apart from material resources (for extended fieldwork, archival research, electoral surveys, and statistical analysis), conducting this research raised the challenge of building and maintaining rapport with informants. Another challenge was conceptual, for this research required a willingness to adjust the analytical framework and data collection in light of new findings, puzzles, and implications. The project also required a deeper immersion in history than expected.

The far right was well into its 6-year term when I made my first research visit to Toulon. Instead of arriving with no hunches (as advocated by Glaser and Strauss

(1967)), whose empiricist method is naïve epistemologically because it relies on letting the data speak for themselves, a trick they cannot perform), I came with a provisional hypothesis – a baseline against which to compare the evidence, and a preliminary idea against which to build a better explanation. In parts of France like the Red Belt around Paris, previously the Communist Party had created a segmented milieu that isolated its supporters from cross-pressures. Reasoning by analogy, I hypothesized that the FN had triumphed in Toulon by filling a void: the established parties had lost partisan loyalty because they lacked proximity to voters. The far right could not have spread its effort of societal segmentation equally, however. Significant variation in FN support across neighborhoods would constitute evidence of grassroots organization.

A visit to the Prefecture for the Var department disabused me. The Prefect's amiable Chief of Staff let me scrutinize the results of the latest parliamentary elections for the city's polling stations. Instead of the hypothesized heterogeneity in far-right support, inspection of tables with fine-grained data from the Ministry of the Interior revealed homogeneity across neighborhoods. Sensing my puzzlement, the Chief of Staff offered a leading question: Was I aware of the city's influential population of *pieds-noirs* (European settlers from French North Africa)? He then put me in touch with the president of that community's main association, Georges Boutigny.

Meeting this man born in Algiers when it still belonged to French Algeria would change the course of my research. It would also spur my evolution from a North American sociologist who worked at the intersection with European political science into a practitioner of a historical social science. Boutigny felt closer to the left (in the 2002 presidential election, he would vote for a Socialist). Yet he recognized the strength of anti-Communism and anti-Gaullism within his community, as well as its underlying affinity with the far right. His late father, a leader of the *pieds-noirs* in this part of Provence for almost four decades, had bequeathed primary and secondary documents pertaining to the associational and political life of this community. Putting this collection to use was Boutigny's initial motivation for helping me. It gave meaning to his father's hoarding, since the 1960s, of enough material to fill dozens of cardboard boxes.

Entering the world of France's ex-colonials brought to mind a distinction between *cultura politica* and *ideologia politica* that Chiarini and Corsini (1983) apply in their study of Brescia. Although they do not make this distinction explicit, their handling of these terms is suggestive enough. *Cultura politica* refers to a shared outlook (such as social conservatism) that may lack internal consistency, clear boundaries, self-awareness, or organizational referents (e.g., movements or parties). *Ideologia politica* refers to a more consistent, self-aware, or unified program of ideas, a weapon in the struggle for power. For Chiarini and Corsini, after 1945 the carriers of the conservative *cultura politica* in Brescia had favored the Christian Democratic Party while retaining a latent affinity toward the *Movimento sociale italiano* (MSI), whose *ideologia politica* was neo-fascist. During the labour strife and student activism of the 1960s and 1970s, the neo-fascist outlook surfaced.

In Toulon, by analogy, the ex-colonials belonged to a *cultura politica* opposed to Communism and usually favoring the non-Gaullist moderate right, but receptive to the far right. Which option prevailed depended on party system dynamics. Accordingly, my research would trace the history of the *cultura politica* of the Algerian ex-colonials; but also identify the circumstances under which they (and their city) had switched from the moderate to the far right. Given these tasks, a mix of methods guided my research project: (1) archival research; (2) survey research (3) semi-structured interviews; (4) secondary research; (5) field observation.

Archival research

The far right exploits collective memories, emotions, and mentalities kept alive by what social capital theory calls bonding groups (e.g., associations of military veterans, religious militants, urban vigilantes, or soccer fans; see Veugelers and Menard, 2018). A key source of association funding in France is municipal government. Who gets what depends on a mix of factors: perceptions of an association's contribution to the public good; a municipal council's desire to spread resources across the community; an association's partisan proximity to councillors; and patron--client relations that tie politicians to special interests or constituents.

Pied-noir associations had cultivated the patronage of politicians. The Municipal Archives of the City of Toulon contained city budgets with lists of associations receiving grants and the amounts awarded. The Boutigny papers included the minutes of political meetings as well as personal correspondence with the Mayor, city councillors, and the departmental Prefect. Archival research confirmed that local political institutions had upheld a *cultura politica* with the Communists and the Gaullists its main enemies, and the non-Gaullist conservative right and the far right its main allies.

Expenditures of time and energy do not guarantee the success of archival research. Consultation of on-line catalogues may help the researcher, but not all archives have them. A visit to the Departmental Archives for the Var turned up little relevant information. A private archive like the Boutigny papers may prove more fruitful, but it lacked order (no archivist had arranged its contents by source, date, or subject). As every historian learns from experience, an archivist who knows a collection well can provide valuable leads. At the Municipal Archives of the City of Toulon, though, the chief archivist refused my request to view documents about association funding by the current city council (perhaps because the subject was too sensitive politically).

Survey research

Immediately after the French national elections of 2002, 2007, and 2012, I conducted mail surveys of *pieds-noirs* living in the Toulon area (Veugelers et al., 2015). My goal was to confirm that, net of other factors, patterns of association membership affected the likelihood of far-right support. Perhaps so I could make better use of his father's papers, Boutigny acted as my broker with the *pied-noir* community. To launch the first survey, he gave me a list of his association's members as well as a signed cover letter urging them to participate. To enlarge the sample, the questionnaire asked respondents for the name and address of other *pieds-noirs* who might participate.

Knowing how others judge them, some supporters of the far right avoid electoral surveys or refuse to reveal how they voted. Compounding these challenges, a local priest who saw himself as a leader of the *pied-noir* community issued a statement that expressed suspicion about my research. I countered by enlisting the public endorsement of another *pied-noir*, a medical professional and senior administrator. How all this affected the response rate remains unknown. The advanced age of the target population presented one other challenge: between 2002 and 2012, the sample size fell due to decreased capacity and high mortality among the original respondents.

Interviews

For local research on the far right, methodological skill may count for little unless the researcher gets access to key informants, cooperating subjects, and information gatekeepers. Being an outsider with no apparent stake in local politics probably does no harm. For this kind of research, it may even help. Gaining trust can require a significant investment of time and patience, though. It also requires that a researcher appear unmoved yet still curious if an informant's words offend their sensibilities.

For field-testing of the first survey, I interviewed 24 *pieds-noirs* (mostly FN supporters, with men and women in equal numbers). I am fluent in French, but not from France. This may have enhanced my rapport: as a French-Canadian academic, what stake could I have in their answers? As the interview unfolded in their home, ex-colonials would elaborate on matters they maybe thought would be lost on a foreigner. I listened without criticizing, and this seemed to release pent-up needs for recognition and self-justification. Like everyone else, FN supporters are multidimensional: they are not reducible to their political positions, themselves complex and situational. Few had always supported the far right, and some still voted for other parties. Remembering all this made it easier for me to sit and listen quietly when utterances defied my personal convictions.

Many interviewees believed in a racial hierarchy. They blamed 'the Arabs' for their past and present troubles. Supporters of Jean-Marie Le Pen called him a man of honor. During the 1950s, they emphasized, he put his skin on the line by fighting to keep Algeria in France. He had not compromised with parties and politicians eager to forget the sacrifices – in blood even – so many had made for France. Often my interviewees complained that France treats its immigrants today better than it has treated those who fled Algeria as French citizens in 1962.

Surprisingly, the interviews enabled catharsis. Some wept as they described the horrors of the Algerian war or the pain of abandoning their colonial homeland at the time of independence. The interviews gave entry into a *cultura politica* that attributed moral slights to loss of empire. These the *pieds-noirs* would personalize in a manner that disregarded the structural forces behind their predominance in Algeria as settlers, later difficulties during the war of decolonization, and ensuing resettlement in the metropole. A window opened onto the emotional side of far-right support.

Secondary research

Studies by colonial historians helped to piece together the making of a far-right affinity in French Algeria. The local newspaper of record (on microfilm in the Municipal Library of Toulon) helped to reconstruct the recent history of the Var department. Articles in French political science journals helped to contextualize local political developments and electoral results. Unpublished M.A. theses and Ph.D. dissertations provided further insight into politics and society in Provence. Although this material was rich and helped me to understand the historical context, it was silent about the social background of far-right supporters and hence related only indirectly to the main findings from my interviews and surveys.

Field observation of ritual and territoriality

Sociologists define ritual as expressive interaction that symbolizes social relations. More formal than instrumental interaction, ritual enacts or dramatizes values, thereby re-affirming the bonds that unite a community and the differences that separate it from others (Wuthnow, 1987). Field observation of ritual can provide insight into collective imaginaries. It also offers a means of grasping the forms of social interaction that sustain these imaginaries over time.

Every year, the *pieds-noirs* of Toulon gather for two ceremonies: on March 26, the anniversary of the 1962 Rue d'Isly Massacre (when French soldiers in Algiers fired on Europeans, with dozens wounded or killed); and on July 5, the anniversary of the Oran Massacre (a carnage on the day of Algerian independence that left hundreds of Europeans dead, wounded, or missing). These ceremonies attract mostly elderly participants, with many men wearing their military beret and war medals. The French flag flies, but instead of singing the national anthem the participants sing *Le Chant des Africains* (a Second World War song of French colonial troops, during the Algerian War it became a *pied-noir* anthem – a symbol of resistance to Algerian independence and the Gaullist regime). The presence or absence of local politicians signals their friendship, indifference, or rejection. At one commemoration of the Rue d'Isly Massacre, participants listened to speeches that mourned the dead, followed by a ghastly audio recording of guns firing and people screaming. Through these ceremonies, the *pieds-noirs* reaffirm their collective identity as patriots made victims by the Fifth Republic and Algerian self-determination.

Research on French far-right voting emphasizes the centrality of ethnocentrism (Mayer, 2018). Field observation can reveal its expression in territoriality, an abiding concern in far-right activism and rhetoric. Seeking the roots of support for the National Front in East London, Husbands (1982: 6) writes that during the nineteenth century the inhabitants of Shoreditch and North Bethnal Green 'developed a *laager* mentality about their neighborhood, seeing it ... in confrontation with the ethnic diversity that for a hundred years has marked Spitalfields and Whitechapel immediately to the south or south-east'. Chiarini and Corsini (1983) observe that when neo-fascists planted a bomb in Brescia, their fatal act was symbolic: it answered a transgression, the workers' occupation of a main square in the very heart of the *polis*. Defence of territory also motivated the FN's first activists in the Var:

> The Algerian war, their war, had given them an education in political engagement. They had learned a conception of political engagement both personal and vigorous, one with plenty of references to their trajectory 'on the other side of the sea'. Their speech code was suggestive. Their vocabulary referred to clearing or occupying the zone, to rat hunting, to sweeping the territory.
>
> *(Delmonte, 1999: 74)*

Before the FN in Toulon lost power in 2001, likewise, one of its last decisions was to rename a traffic roundabout after General Salan (who in 1961 had led a failed coup against the Gaullist regime).

The *pieds-noirs* hold their ceremonies in the chained-off section of a public square near the city walls. This space backs onto a stone bas-relief they commissioned for the 150th anniversary of the conquest of Algeria. Baptized the Monument to the Martyrs for French Algeria, it depicts a firing squad executing a soldier: Roger Degueldre, leader of die-hards from the *Organisation Armée Secrète* (OAS) who launched a campaign of terror and destruction as the independence of Algeria approached. Whereas occupation of the *Piazza della Loggia* by demonstrating workers provoked the neo-fascists in Brescia, construction of the Monument to the Martyrs for French Algeria provoked an anonymous bombing that shattered the original bas-relief before its inauguration. In both cases, then, the use of civic space became a pretext for contention.

Entering into the symbolic world of far-right supporters puts field observation at a distance from structural analyses of political opportunity. Before he or she can read the codes peculiar to such milieus, the above examples suggest, a researcher may need to invest considerable time and patience. The payoff can be a better grasp of non-mainstream conceptions of history, morality, and identity that feed the demand for the far right. Exploiting this payoff requires supplementary evidence, however, through types of research that provide contextual data (such as archival research, field observation, or subject interviews).

Discussion

The research described above suggests that study of a single locality can enhance the plausibility of explanation not only by tracing causal processes but also by unveiling cultural framings behind far-right demand. Further, it suggests a claim posited early in this chapter requires qualification – the claim that studies of a single case are unsuited for: (1) identification of local differences that explain unusual far-right outcomes; (2) demonstration of different paths to a shared outcome; and (3) identification of reversals of correlation across levels of analysis. Meeting these aims still seems more likely for studies of multiple cases embedded in a research design that samples appropriately, given the question at hand. Still, background knowledge of other localities can broaden the lessons from a single case: the decisive combination of a corruption scandal and a broken *cordon sanitaire* set Toulon apart from other municipalities also with a significant far-right demand, but no FN victory (Gombin, 2015; Ivaldi and Pina, 2016; Fourquet and Lebourg, 2017). Studies of single cases can also achieve wider significance by selecting crucial cases (a crucial case would be a locality where a far-right outcome should have happened, given theory or experience, but did not; or a locality where a far-right outcome should not have happened, but did). Current hypotheses about support for the far right among the so-called losers of globalization seem ripe for local research that selects crucial cases.

Conclusion

Where did the fears, prejudices, and hopes associated with voting for the far right originate?

Partly they came from top-down, elite discourse (Mondon, 2015). In complementary fashion, local research can set the agenda for research that instead traces the bottom-up origins, milieus, and carriers of ethnocentrism, stigmatization, and populism. Local research can also uncover mechanisms or processes – such as territorial defense or collective ritual – that sustain a group with a far-right potential. By addressing these questions, local studies can round out and even challenge the supply-and-demand paradigm now dominant in far-right research.

Connecting social capital research with analysis of the far right, another innovative strand of scholarship is examining the effect of voluntary associations (Coffé, Heydels and Vermeir, 2007; Rydgren, 2009; Jesuit, Paradowski and Mahler, 2009; Rydgren, 2011; Poznyak, Abts and Swyngedouw, 2011). National data tend to amalgamate association types, however, thereby obscuring the distinction between bonding and bridging. Without fine-grained information about the permeability of ethnic boundaries, moreover, research that relies on aggregate data cannot properly test the contact hypothesis (Rydgren, 2008). By addressing these problems, local studies can make a valuable contribution to social capital analysis of the far right.

This chapter began with the assertion that place matters; it concludes that history matters too. Although sociology and political science contain rich traditions of historically informed research, these depart from prevailing approaches, often ahistorical whether behaviorist, attitudinal, or ethnographic. Problems with stitching together historical and social scientific approaches arise in part from differences in their mode of explication. Strong causal explanation requires a specification of conditions under which the posited relations hold. Using a vocabulary less comfortable to historians, social scientists examine the effects of variables. Less acceptable to social scientists, in turn, would be the historian's alternative: examination of context. Researchers engaged in local studies of the far right will cross this divide only by mixing their methods.

Note

1 The author gratefully acknowledges the support provided by a grant from the Social Sciences and Humanities Research Council of Canada. Parts of this chapter were written while the author was Visiting Professor, Department of Political Science and School of Government, LUISS Guido Carli, Rome, Italy. Thanks also to Milos Brocic, Roberto Chiarini, Gabriel Menard, Sébastien Parker, and the chapter reviewers for their comments, questions, and suggestions.

References

Aminzade, R. 1992. "Historical Sociology and Time." *Sociological Methods & Research*, 20(4), 456–480.

Arzheimer, K. 2012. "Electoral Sociology – Who Votes for the Extreme Right and Why – and When?" In *The Extreme Right in Europe: Current Trends and Perspectives*, edited by U. Backes and P. Moreau, 35–50. Göttingen: Vandenhoeck and Ruprecht.

Chiarini, R. and P. Corsini. 1983. *Da Salò a Piazza della Loggia: Blocco d'ordine, neofascismo, radicalismo di destra a Brescia (1945–1974)*. Milan: Franco Angeli.

Coffé, H., B. Heyndels and J. Vermeir. 2007. "Fertile Grounds for Extreme Right-Wing Parties: Explaining the Vlaam Blok's Electoral Success." *Electoral Studies*, 26(1), 142–155.

DeLeon, R.E., and K. Naff. 2004. "Identity Politics and Local Political Culture: Some Comparative Results from the Social Capital Benchmark Survey." *Urban Affairs Review*, 39(6), 689–719.

Delmonte, F. 1999. "Le Front national à Toulon: De la sous-société des débuts à la contre société de juin 1995." *Recherches Régionales – Alpes-Maritimes et contrées limitrophes*, 148, 51–83.

Eatwell, R. 2003. "Ten Theories of the Extreme Right." In *Right-Wing Extremism in the Twenty-First Century*, edited by P.H. Merkl and L. Weinberg, 47–73. London: Frank Cass.

Elster, J. 1989. *Nuts and Bolts for the Social Sciences*. Cambridge: Cambridge University Press.

Fourquet, J. and N. Lebourg. 2017. *La Nouvelle Guerre d'Algérie n'aura pas lieu*. Paris: Fondation Jean Jaurès.

Glaser, B. and A.L. Strauss. 1967. *The Discovery of Grounded Theory: Strategies for Qualitative Research*. Chicago, IL: Aldine.

Golder, M. 2016. "Far Right Parties in Europe." *Annual Review of Political Science*, 19, 477–497.

Gombin, J. 2015. "Le changement dans la continuité: Géographies électorales du Front national depuis 1992." In *Les faux-semblants du Front national: Sociologie d'un parti politique*, edited by S. Crépon, A. Dézé, and N. Mayer, 395–416. Paris: Presses de la Fondation nationale des sciences politiques.

Goodwin, M. 2012. "Backlash in the 'Hood': Exploring Support for the British National Party (BNP) at the Local Level." In *Mapping the Far Right in Contemporary Europe: From*

Local to Transnational, edited by A. Mammone, E. Godin, and B. Jenkins, 17–32. Abingdon: Routledge.

Gross, N. 2018. "The Structure of Causal Chains." *Sociological Theory*, 36(4), 343–367.

Hedström, P. and R. Swedberg. 1998. "Social Mechanisms: An Introductory Essay." In *Social Mechanisms: An Analytical Approach to Social Theory*, edited by P. Hedström and R. Swedberg, 1–31. Cambridge: Cambridge University Press.

Husbands, C.T. 1982. "East End Racism 1900–1980: Geographical Continuities in Vigilantist and Extreme Right-Wing Political Behaviour." *London Journal*, 8(1), 3–26.

Husbands, C.T. 1983. *Racial Exclusionism and the City: The Urban Support of the National Front*. London: Allen & Unwin.

Ivaldi, G. and C. Pina. 2016. "PACA, une victoire à la Pyrrhus pour la droite?" *Revue Politique et Parlementaire*, 1078, 139–150.

Jesuit, D.K., P.R. Paradowski, and V.A. Mahler. 2009. "Electoral Support for Extreme Right-Wing Parties: A Sub-National Analysis of Western European Elections." *Electoral Studies*, 28(2), 279–290.

Kitschelt, H. with A. McGann. 1997. *The Radical Right in Western Europe: A Comparative Analysis*. Ann Arbor, MI: University of Michigan Press.

Lieberman, E.S. 2005. "Nested Analysis as a Mixed-Method Strategy for Comparative Research." *American Political Science Review*, 99(3), 435–452.

Mahoney, J. 2008. "Toward a Unified Theory of Causality." *Comparative Political Studies*, 41(4–5), 412–436.

Mayer, N. 2018. "The Radical Right in France." In *The Oxford Handbook of the Radical Right*, edited by J. Rydgren, 433–451. New York, NY: Oxford University Press.

Mondon, A. 2015. "The French Secular Hypocrisy: The Extreme Right, the Republic and the Battle for Hegemony." *Patterns of Prejudice*, 49(4), 392–413.

Mudde, C. 2010. "The Populist Radical Right: A Pathological Normalcy." *West European Politics*, 33(6), 1167–1186.

Mudde, C. 2017. "Introduction." In *The Populist Radical Right: A Reader*, edited by C. Mudde, 1–10. London: Routledge.

Poznyak, D., K. Abts, and M. Swyngedouw. 2011. "The Dynamics of the Extreme Right Support: A Growth Curve Model of the Populist Vote in Flanders-Belgium in 1987–2007." *Electoral Studies*, 30(4), 672–688.

Ragin, C.C. 1987. *The Comparative Method: Moving Beyond Qualitative and Quantitative Strategies*. Berkeley, CA and Los Angeles, CA: University of California Press.

Rast, J. 2012. "Why History (Still) Matters: Time and Temporality in Urban Political Analysis." *Urban Affairs Review*, 48(1), 3–36.

Roy, J.P. 1993. *Le Front national en région centre (1984–1992)*. Paris: L'Harmattan.

Rydgren, J. 2007. "The Sociology of the Radical Right." *Annual Review of Sociology*, 33, 241–262.

Rydgren, J. 2008. "Immigration Sceptics, Xenophobes or Racists? Radical Right-Wing Voting in Six West European Countries." *European Journal of Political Research*, 47(6), 737–765.

Rydgren, J. 2009. "Social Isolation? Social Capital and Radical Right-Wing Voting in Western Europe." *Journal of Civil Society*, 5(2), 129–150.

Rydgren, J. 2011. "A Legacy of 'Uncivicness'? Social Capital and Radical Right-Wing Populist Voting Eastern Europe." *Acta Politica*, 46(2), 132–157.

Sewell, W.H. 1996. "Historical Events as Transformations of Structures: Inventing Revolution at the Bastille." *Theory and Society*, 25(6), 841–881.

Somers, M.R. 1992. "Narrativity, Narrative Identity, and Social Action: Rethinking English Working-Class Formation." *Social Science History*, 16(4), 591–630.

Van Gent, W. and S. Musterd. 2012. "Les transformations urbaines et l'émergence des partis populistes de la droite radicale en Europe: Le cas de la ville de La Haye." *Hérodote*, 144, 99–112.

Veugelers, J. and A. Magnan. 2005. "Conditions of Far-Right Strength in Contemporary Western Europe: An Application of Kitschelt's Theory." *European Journal of Political Research*, 44(6), 837–860.

Veugelers, J. and G. Menard. 2018. "The Non-Party Sector of the Radical Right." In *The Oxford Handbook of the Radical Right*, edited by J. Rydgren, 285–304. New York, NY: Oxford University Press.

Veugelers, J., G. Menard, and P. Permingeat. 2015. "Colonial Past, Voluntary Association and Far Right Voting in France." *Ethnic and Racial Studies*, 38(5), 775–791.

Wuthnow, R. 1987. *Meaning and Moral Order: Explorations in Cultural Analysis*. Berkeley, CA and Los Angeles, CA: University of California Press.

20

STUDYING THE PERIPHERIES

Iconography and embodiment in far right youth subcultures

Cynthia Miller-Idriss and Annett Graefe-Geusch

Prevailing methodological approaches to studying the far right tend to speak of the 'far right' or the 'right-wing' as a fixed and definable category, regardless of whether the data sources in question rely on quantitative survey research, qualitative interviewing, or ethnographic fieldwork. Quantitative research typically uses defined measures for far right attitudes and engagements through analyses of voter behaviour data or survey research assessing political preferences and attitudes about immigration, xenophobia, religious affiliation, or diversity (Arzheimer, 2009; Bacher, 2001; Boehnke, Hagan, and Merkens, 1998; Heitmeyer, 1988; Heitmeyer et al., 1992). On the qualitative side, anthropologists, sociologists and journalists have immersed themselves in studying identified groups of right-wing youth at festivals, music concerts, and in broader subcultural scenes (Rommelspacher, 2006; Shoshan, 2016), or have conducted interviews with youth who have exited or dropped out of right-wing scenes (Simi, Bubolz and Hardman, 2013). In both cases, scholars tend to fix the categories of 'far right' or 'right-wing' as clearly-defined and bounded entities into which individuals can be neatly classified, often based on direct self-reports from youth (especially through surveys, interviews, and observations).

In this chapter, we make two methodological arguments, drawing on a long-term research project on the commercialization of far right youth culture in Germany. The multi-methods research project combined the creation and analysis of a digital archive of thousands of images of symbols and commercial far right products with 62 interviews conducted in two vocational schools for construction trades in Berlin in 2013–14. Our arguments both focus on methodological implications for youth populations in particular. We argue, first, that focusing on fixed categories of far right membership both obscures an important source of information about the far right and mistakenly identifies youth as having static identifications with political and ideological scenes. Second, we suggest that direct reports from youth about their relationship with the far right can be significantly aided by integrating elements of material culture into focused interviews. In the empirical study we discuss here, we found that asking youth to examine images, iconography, symbols, or objects and offer interpretations of their meanings during the course of conversations about the far right was not only useful for the iconographic interpretations we sought, but also helped us tease out multiple layers of youth affiliation and understandings of the far right across the interview sample, shifting our understandings of what it means to be associated with or exposed to far right scenes and subcultures.

Data and methods

The research project upon which this chapter is based was a multi-year, multi-method project focused on the commercialization of far right iconography, symbols, and codes in Germany and included both extensive image and symbol analysis and interviews with young people to help determine whether and how they understood coded symbols and iconography. The data collection for this project, conceived and directed by the first author, took place in two major phases: the assembly and analysis of an image archive in 2011–12 and qualitative fieldwork in two vocational schools in 2013–14.

The initial archive was continually added to over the years, but at the time of its initial assembly and coding, was comprised of nearly 3,000 images drawn from a variety of contemporary and historical sources (see Miller-Idriss, 2018, for a fuller explanation). Images were selected for inclusion in the digital archive if they depicted the use of commercial brands, symbols, messaging, or iconography popular with the far right. These included historical images from the 1930s and 1940s, drawn from the special collections of prints, photographs, and Nazi propaganda at the John W. Kluge Center at the U.S. Library of Congress in Washington, DC, the digitized collections housed at the U.S. Holocaust Memorial Museum in Washington, DC, and the digitized historical images at the Granger Archive, a historical picture archive in New York City (www.granger.com). For example, several images in the archive were drawn from still slides of Hitler Youth Propaganda Films which show Nordic and Viking symbols, iconography and messages, which are drawn on by the far right as a way of suggesting that Germanic tribes descended from Nordic ones. More recent historical images from the 1980s and 1990s, along with contemporary images, came from the collections at the Anti-Fascist Press Archive and Educational Center (apabiz) in Berlin. The largest group of images came from the digitized collections of three professional German photographers who specialize in photographing far right youth, right-wing extremists and neo-Nazi groups. Finally, the digital archive also includes screen shots of the websites of several commercial brands that sell far right extremist clothing and products, and digital images captured on the street in Berlin and other German cities. Such images included stickers, posters, graffiti, buttons, patches, banners, flags, clothing, and other products observed in places like an anti-fascist rally, subways, bus stops, train stations, bathroom stall doors, sidewalks, stairwells, and commercial stores. The digital archive of images was coded in Atlas.ti both inductively and deductively, with the first author (a non-native German speaker) and a native German research assistant using a pre-determined codebook but adding new codes as they emerged.[1]

The codebook for the digital archive was comprised of a set of broad, categorical codes that helped sort individual images into groups by tagging portions of the images or the entire image with a code, thereby breaking up the large database of images into analyzable clusters. The clusters themselves were informative in terms of the quantitative frequency with which particular kinds of iconographic tropes and codes were deployed (see the fuller discussion in Miller-Idriss, 2017), but they also enabled groups of images to be studied together according to their thematic cluster – such as all images relating to Nordic myths or which used historical Nazi codes. Further analysis focused on understanding how these categories of images worked in terms of appeal to far right youth. While these clusters were meaningful on their own – ultimately contributing to several chapters in the first author's recent book (Miller-Idriss, 2018) such as topics like death symbols, Nordic myths and transnational nationalism – the analysis of individual images was also critical. Studying individual photographs of how a particular symbol was deployed at a far right demonstration or march, for example – including studying the larger scene, the crowd or surrounding individuals, posters and signs, and facial expressions – enabled deeper understanding of how the context and setting in which any given symbol is deployed contributes to the meaning of particular far right symbols and codes that are marketed to youth. A background setting in a catalog photo which depicts Nordic architecture or landscapes while marketing a t-shirt with far right messaging, for example, has evocative power for far right narratives about Nordic and Aryan origins (Miller-Idriss, 2018), in addition to what the iconographic message of the depicted t-shirt conveys.

Following the research phase in which the digital archive was constructed and analyzed, that primarily took place in 2011–12, the project expanded to include the study of two vocational schools for construction trades in 2013–14, where we interviewed youth to see whether and how they understood the symbols and iconography deployed in the commercialized products. The lead author selected the two schools because one school has implemented a comprehensive policy banning the display of all right-wing extremist symbols, brands, and codes. At the second school, there is no banning policy; students can freely display brands and symbols unless they are legally banned, like the swastika. The schools' student populations are quite similar, drawing largely from the same region and youth backgrounds, and students do not directly choose the schools – they are assigned based on their selection of occupation. The similarities in the student bodies and the variation in policy decisions thus set up a naturally-occurring, quasi-experimental design, providing the opportunity to examine whether and how the bans affect the use of coded symbols among youth and the participation of youth in the right-wing more generally (Miller-Idriss, 2018). From her previous research in vocational schools in

Germany (Miller-Idriss, 2009), the first author knew she would be able to gain access to a population of youth who were high-risk for far right and extremist participation, or who had spent much of their lives around youth in those scenes, at these two schools.

After securing local School Senate (*Schulsenat*) approvals in Berlin, the support of the teacher faculty at each school, and the approval of the required human subject study review panel in the USA, data collection began at the two schools. There were no formal selection criteria for interview participants, but we over-sampled from occupations which have historically had higher numbers of far right youth, such as scaffold-building. Participants were recruited through classroom announcements asking for volunteers to participate. Between January 2013 and March 2014, we conducted interviews with 51 youth aged 16–39, with an average age of 21, and with 11 teachers and principals at two schools. All but two of the youth interviewed were born in Germany, though the two born elsewhere (in Poland and in Kazakhstan) grew up in Berlin. Four of the youth (who were born in Germany) had names that are traditionally Turkish in origin, indicating at least partial Turkish heritage. Two of the 51 youth were female, which is consistent with male-dominated fields in construction. Youth interviews aimed to understand whether young people own or wear any of the banned clothing, how they define their own sense of style and its meaning to them, how they feel about school bans of symbols or clothing brands, and how they interpret a series of images depicting far right symbols in clothing.

Using a semi-structured interview instrument, we asked youth to describe their own personal style and its evolution over time, to talk about brands of clothing, school bans of clothing, and specific brands of clothing known within the far right scene. But the most important data to emerge from the interviews came from the portion of the interview when we showed them a notebook with 34 images of clothing, tattoos, and other subcultural styles and asked them to tell us what they saw in the images. They interpreted various symbols, iconography, and styles, told us what they thought about the clothing, and what kinds of messages, if any, they thought the symbols or styles sent to observers. The use of a notebook with images – which youth examined at their own pace – proved to be an extraordinarily helpful tool in ways we couldn't have anticipated. In addition to helping abstract discussions become more concrete, having a physical object to look seemed to help young people relax and open up. It was often during this portion of the interview that we learned the most about their far right affiliations and relationships with others who were close to the scene.

The second author joined the research project as a graduate research assistant post data collection to help with transcriptions and data coding. All interviews were fully transcribed and initially coded in Atlas.ti with a set of categorical codes, and then further analyzed by the lead author for patterns and themes within each code. The challenge of developing a classification system for interviewees' degrees of closeness to the far right became a significant discussion point between the first and second author during the analysis phase, ultimately leading to a new, second level of analysis. In this second phase of coding, we re-read each transcript in its entirety and applied a new set of codes that aimed to tease out degrees of closeness, knowledge, and exposure to the far right. It was this second round of coding that ultimately led to this co-authored chapter.

Studying youth who are 'in and around' far right scenes and subcultures

Although we don't wish to detract from the importance of conducting research with actively-engaged or formerly active far right youth, we suggest there is much to be learned about the varied pathways in and out of extremism from studying youth who are not only in the 'core' of extremist and radical right-wing movements but also those who are on the 'periphery' or in interstitial spaces (Miller-Idriss, 2018; Miller-Idriss and Pilkington, 2017). For many – perhaps even most – far right youth, we argue, extremist engagement is characterized by a process of moving in and out of far right scenes throughout their adolescence and young adulthood in ways that scholars have yet to fully understand. Policymakers and scholars appear to have at least casual awareness of the fluid nature of youth engagement in extremism; some scholars, for example have implied that youth participation in the far right is a phase of adolescence – one that youth would presumably 'grow out of' as they age.[2]

We did find some support for the notion that some youth will simply age out of their participation in far right subcultures or radical and extremist groups. In our interviews with youth in vocational schools, who were in their late teens and early 20s, youth sometimes referred to engagement in far right subcultures or music scenes as something they had done in early adolescence, from about ages 12–15. Of the 51 young people we interviewed, the only current self-identified right-wing extremist was also the youngest interviewee, at age 16. One youth even used language about 'growing away from' his right-wing peer group as he described becoming more distant from their activities while still remaining friends. Others describe entering the scene because they grew up around it:

> Georg: Well, I all of my friends ... we have known each other forever, right? Since we were really young, and we just grew up with it [right wing extremism] ... and so, of course, you sort of slide into such a scene, yes? Sort of looked around what is going on [in right-wing extremism], but also distanced yourself from it again, yes? [...] but as I said, you also quickly abandoned it, when you realized yourself that it was not worth it.[3]

Georg says he was actively engaged from age 12 to 15 and then realized the scene was nothing for him because of a relationship his uncle had with a 'foreign girl-friend'. While not feeling as part of the right wing, Georg, however, continued to engage with violent, xenophobic, and misogynistic ideas through the consumption of clothing brands. The complexity of Georg's case – his early adolescent phase of more active engagement with the far right scene, followed by intentional distancing from the scene and a current enthusiasm for violent, xenophobic and misogynistic iconography and clothing – shows why it is hard to clearly categorize some youth as 'far right' per se.

Our findings showed, moreover, that flexible engagements with far right subcultures and ideologies are not only a question of age and development. Rather, our interviewees showed that engagement in the far right can also be malleable over the course of a single evening or weekend. Individuals might attend a far right festival or concert at one point during their week but spend the rest of the time with classmates, colleagues, friends or family members who are not far right. Youth we interviewed also described having far right friends as well as friends with migrant backgrounds, indicating that they sometimes attended a demo or listened to far right music, for example, but also had 'a lot of foreign friends.' Young people thus move across peer groups and subcultures and into and out of the mainstream on a regular basis. They may engage in racist talk or actions while maintaining friendships with youth of migrant backgrounds.

Studying youth who are in and around the far right scene created challenges in how we classified their closeness to the scene. We spent hours experimenting with various ways of categorizing and classifying the 51 youth interviewees in terms of their relationship to the far right scene. In the end, we devised a classification system with 13 categories of 'degrees of belonging and familiarity with the far right,' some of which had multiple sub-categories. We then re-read and re-coded each interview transcript to assign one or more of the categories to each individual (see Table 20.1).

What is perhaps most important about this classification system methodologically is that in traditional studies of far right youth, only young people who fell into category 1a and 1b would typically be studied. We found, instead, that there was a wide range of 'closeness' and 'belonging' to the scene as well as knowledge and understandings of the scene across our informants (see Table 20.2). While only two young people fell into categories 1a or 1b (by directly volunteering or self-identifying as a current or former member of the far right wing), we classified 48 of 51 youth as having what we call "intimate knowledge" of the far right scene. Such knowledge emerged, for example, through current or former ownership of a brand associated with the far right; family, friends or classmates who owned such clothing; or family, friends, or classmates who are in the far right scene or used to be. Across the interviews, only three youth were classified as having "no exposure" based on what they volunteered during the interviews, but even these three youth were attending schools where far right youth are a steady presence (Miller-Idriss, 2018).

We also found that the classification of 'exposure' was particularly useful. We applied this category mainly to instances where youth described being in contact with right-wing ideologies by listening to right-wing bands, growing up in environments that are or were dominated by the right wing (even if participants actively distanced themselves from this scene), or when they were exposed to or in fear of

TABLE 20.1 Categories of belonging and familiarity with the far right

Category	Description
1a and 1b	Self-identifies as a current (a) or past (b) member of the right wing Note: Voluntary statements only (not directly asked)
2	Owns/owned clothing brands directly associated with the right wing (such as Thor Steinar, Ansgar Aryan, Erik and Sons, Consdaple) Note: Reviewed list of banned brands and logos
3a, 3b, 3c	Expresses views consistent with right-wing ideology as follows: (a) xeno-phobia, islamophobia, anti-Semitism, anti-immigration; (b) against the estab-lishment, anti-established parties, antigovernment, "something has to change in Germany or the country will be destroyed" attitude; (c) fear of losing German culture, norms, heritage – "Überfremdung"
4a and 4b	Has/had friends or family that are identified as current (a) or past (b) mem-bers of the right wing
5a, 5b, 5c	Has/had acquaintances (neighbors, classmates, colleagues, friends of friends) that are part of the right wing or suspected to be part of the right wing: (a) may be indifferent to them; (b) may be sympathetic to them; (c) may actively distance themselves from them
6	Own(ed)/wear(wore) clothing brands associated with the right wing but may also have other meanings (such as Lonsdale, New Balance, Fred Perry, Alpha Industries, Pit Bull)
7	Distances themselves from the right wing: (a) by saying so; (b) by emphasiz-ing "foreign"/"Turkish"/"Black" friends; (c) claims no knowledge of the right wing
8	Self-identifies as belonging to a different youth subculture (metal, goth, hip hop etc.) or ethnicities other than German Note: Other subculture experience related to strong views/knowledge of far right; youth identifying with 'non-German' ethnicities often experienced with far right prejudice
9	Has/had friends or family who own or wear (owned or wore) clothing brands directly associated with the right wing (Thor Steinar, Ansgar Aryan, Erik and Sons, Consdaple, etc.)
10	Has/had friends or family who own or wear (owned or wore) clothing brands associated with the right wing but may also have other meanings (Lonsdale, New Balance, Fred Perry, Alpha Industries, Pit Bull, etc.)
11	Has/had acquaintances (neighbors, classmates, colleagues, friends of friends) who own or wear (owned or wore) clothing brands directly associated with the right wing (Thor Steinar, Ansgar Aryan, Erik and Sons, Consdaple, etc.)
12	Has/had acquaintances (neighbors, classmates, colleagues, friends of friends) who own or wear (owned or wore) clothing brands associated with the right wing but may also have other meanings (Lonsdale, New Balance, Fred Perry, Alpha Industries, etc.)
Exposure	Other exposure to the far right scene – e.g., through experiences of dis-crimination or racism, consumption of music, or other sources of knowledge

discrimination from right-wing classmates, colleagues or acquaintances. Some youth who were classified with the "exposure" code had intimate knowledge of right-wing ideologies and subcultural codes and behavior through observation from

TABLE 20.2 Youth association with far right scene*

	Self	Family/ friends	Classmates/neighbor/ acquaintance	Totals as unique individuals
Part of far right scene (current or former)	2	7	17	21 youth who are, were, or have family/friends in far right
Owns/wears clothing associated with far right	25	25	30	43 youth who own, owned or know someone who owns/owned brands
Volunteered views consistent with far right ideology	9	N/A	N/A	9 youth
Other exposure	35	N/A	N/A	35 youth

*This table is duplicated from Miller-Idriss (2018).

a distance. Others were unknowing consumers of right-wing ideologies without actively engaging in the subculture themselves.

The addition of this code to our coding schema helped reveal just how prevalent seeing or being around right-wing youth or ideologies was for our interview participants. We found that youth were extraordinarily informative about the far right scene and the meaning of subcultural elements – such as symbols, codes and iconography on clothing brands – even when they had no direct relationship with the far right, because knowledge about the far right came about through exposure to the scene through experiences of shared classroom discussion with colleagues, and even the experience of class bullying or victimhood. The 'exposure' code also enabled us to capture instances where youth were not aware of the right-wing ideologies they consumed, for example, by listening to certain bands or buying certain brands of clothing. Furthermore, this code showed where certain youth subcultures overlapped with the right wing, complicating our understanding of what indicators capture belonging to this subcultural scene. One youth, for example, expressed significant anti-left wing sentiments and defended music bands who "represent a certain loyalty to the homeland,"[4] but did not volunteer any self-identification as far right or describe active engagement in far right youth scenes. Thus, he was hard to officially categorize as a 'far right' youth, even though ideologically and behaviorally his interview comments indicated we might consider him as such. We suggest that the idea of "exposure" would benefit from more research in the future to parse out and further investigate what kinds of exposure are crucial for youth and their engagement with the far right, and under what conditions 'exposure' to the far right contributes to radicalization or engagement in violence.

Table 20.2 shows how the classification we devised for understanding youths' degree of closeness to and knowledge of far right scenes worked when we applied it to the 51 youth we interviewed, as evidenced through our coding of the voluntary remarks youth made in interviews. We did not ask youth directly if they were currently or formerly engaged in the far right – the two youth classified here as "part of the far right scene" volunteered this information. Others hinted at prior involvement but were not included in this cell because we found their remarks too suggestive to officially classify them as "currently" or "formerly" actively engaged in the far right scene.

Using the classification system detailed in Table 20.1, across the interviews, 21 of the 51 youth mentioned friends, family, classmates, neighbors or acquaintances who they identified as currently or formerly part of the far right scene. Forty-three of 51 were either consumers of brands known to be part of the far right or had family, friends, classmates, neighbors or acquaintances who consumed such products. Forty-eight of the 51 youth had what we considered to be "intimate knowledge" of the scene through one or more markers of closeness or knowledge, or through significant exposure to the far right. Even the remaining three youth were attending schools with significant populations of far right youth, but because they did not volunteer information in the interview that suggested knowledge, closeness or exposure, we classified them as having no intimate knowledge or exposure of the far right.

In the final part of this chapter, we turn to a brief discussion of the use of material and visual data in interviews with youth in and around far right scenes. We learned that using elements of material culture or visual data can be a significant resource in helping uncover degrees of closeness to or knowledge of far right scenes among interview participants.

Combining material and visual data with interviews

The use of material and visual data, in combination with interviews, adds a new layer of depth to understandings of the embodiment of extremist and nationalist beliefs. Political ideologies are not only held intellectually, particularly for youth; they are inscribed on bodies in youth choices about clothing, hair style, tattoos, musculature, body image, and violence enacted against other bodies (see Nayak, 2005). Visual and material culture – captured in historical and contemporary photographs, artifacts, posters, banners, stickers, license plates and more – proved to be a critical empirical domain for understanding the appeal of extremist thinking (Miller-Idriss, 2018).

Not only the visual data themselves, but especially the combination of visual data and qualitative interviews proved most critical for this project. Without the digital archive, the project would have overlooked dozens of coded symbols, key images, and right-wing clothing and products that youth display and wear. The archive on its own would also have been inadequate, however, because the images alone cannot tell us why youth are utilizing these symbols or whether and how public policy decisions – like school bans – have an impact on their consumption of those symbols. The qualitative interviews with youth in and around the far right scene was invaluable to our understanding of the brands, symbols, and their meanings. In particular, youth's analysis of the selection of 34 images was especially critical to developing a fuller understanding of how the symbols and codes are received and interpreted (Miller-Idriss, 2018).

In addition, the discussion of these images by youth revealed information that they may not otherwise have produced by taking the focus off of the individual interview and providing a concrete focal point for mutual discussion and conversation. Often youth would discuss their connections to or knowledge of the right-wing during this phase of the interview using the images as reference, noting that they owned a t-shirt pictured in an image, or that a classmate was wearing it. They also related their experiences with varied dress codes and bans at their current and previous schools, clubs, and stadiums, sometimes making reference to particular images but often broadening their discussion from these specific images to brands of clothing more generally or other specific items of clothing they owned. As they perused the images, some youth talked about the ways in which clothing styles or brands acted as an 'entry-point' to the scene, enabling connections with other far right youth at stadiums or parties, for example. The one youth who volunteered his current identity as a "right-wing nationalist" explained that the use of far right clothing brands and styles was critical in gaining access to subcultural scene events like unadvertised or underground music concerts, particularly if one arrived at such events unaccompanied by a known member of the local scene. Across the interviews, in other words, the images provided both a concrete context for conversations as well as an entry point into discussions about broader aspects of the far right subcultural scene.

The discussion of these various codes also revealed how deeply engaged youth actually were with right-wing ideologies. While the one self-identified active member in the sample was not able to correctly decode many of the 34 images, others (often those who expressed their opposition to the right-wing) revealed intimate knowledge of the meaning of codes, symbols and images. This again shows how complex and varied engagement with and the participation in subcultures for youth can be. Providing youth with images to discuss during the interviews also revealed their interpretations of which ideological statements were acceptable to wear or not wear in public. One youth, in reaction to an image showing someone with a side hair parting and mustache, explained that it was perfectly acceptable now to dress up as Hitler for carnival as everyone would understand that it was just a joke. Discussions such as this complicated our understanding of what it means to be part of the far right in Germany today and made it crucial for us to devise a more complicated scheme to describe youths' closeness to the far right as discussed above.

Conclusion

Studying youth who are in and around far right scenes helps to avoid one of the key methodological problems in research on the far right – namely, that researchers tend to sample on the dependent variable.[5] On the contrary, we argue that youth on the periphery of the far right proved to be just as – and in some ways, more – informative compared to youth who were or are actively engaged in the far right.

While there may be some far right youth who have strong ideological commitments that are consistent across the varied spaces in their lives, we argue that for many other youth, far right engagements are often characterized by contradictions, uncertainty, and spontaneity rather than firm or fixed ideological positions and commitments. We need research agendas that can capture youth engagements in far right activities as part of the broader spectrum of ideological or subcultural participation in their lives. This is especially important because we know little about the depth of those engagements during early adolescence or under what conditions periodic or episodic far right activity leads to further radicalization toward extremist terrorism or violence. More importantly, we argue that it is reckless to dismiss flexible or fleeting engagements with the far right as unimportant because youth may "age out" of their engagements. Such approaches overlook the damage even fleeting engagements with far right or racist movements can cause, such as through violence directed toward ethnic minorities, the potentially long-term effects of the socialization that takes place within such groups toward valorization of violence, dehumanization of victims and celebration of race-based nationalism, or the life consequences of criminal activity.

There are, of course, aspects of the far right that are more difficult to investigate by focusing on youth who move in and out of far right scenes. Research samples like the ones we utilized are unlikely to produce sufficient numbers of hard-core, ideologically-committed youth or large numbers of youth who participate in organized violence through far right terrorist movements. But we argue that a more expansive sampling frame could be useful in the study of other subcultures associated with youth violence. Urban gangs in the USA could be studied by focusing on all young people within a particular neighborhood and developing a richer understanding of the pathways in and out of gang violence. The study of ISIL (Islamic State of Iraq and the Levant) foreign fighter recruitment might similarly benefit from studying not only youth who are former fighters or who are actively engaged with online recruiters, but also broader groups of youth who are at risk for radicalization or are particularly vulnerable to becoming recruited. While this chapter does not permit sufficient space to discuss this at greater length, it is worth emphasizing that it is critical to engage with at-risk youth in a way that does not stigmatize wider populations. Such engagement requires partnership and joint participation with local religious and neighborhood councils, youth centers, and other educators in the search for settings where at-risk youth might be found, in order to consider appropriate sites for outreach. A recent collaboration between the German Institute on Radicalization and Deradicalization Studies with martial arts schools, for example, is one such model. Because both far right and Islamist extremists have encouraged recruits and followers to train in martial arts, the new German Association of Martial Arts Schools against Violent Extremism has now incorporated counter-radicalization "into the daily training school routine."[6] Searching for non-traditional settings and partnerships like this might help scholars, practitioners and policymakers develop richer understandings of how youth in various milieus encounter extremist, radical or violent ideologies, whether and how they engage with those ideologies, how they cycle in and out of varied engagements, and what opportunities might exist for intervention.

Notes

1   The digital image archive did not ever become a finite entity; over the years, additional screenshots and photographs were added and new symbols and codes analyzed. Moreover, some of the original set of nearly 3,000 images were essentially duplicate images retained because clothing items or catalog pages were photographed from multiple angles in order to show the larger context of the catalog page or frame. Some individual products could thus be associated with as many as 3–4 single images, as separate codes, iconography, symbols or text on a shirt sleeve, front, back, pocket were digitized or due to "zooming in" on particular symbols in order to make text legible or parts of a symbol more visible. For this reason, quantitative descriptors for the archive turn out not to be very useful except to illustrate its scale and scope. See Miller-Idriss (2018), especially the Methodological Appendix, for further discussion.
2   As communicated by an external reviewer for an early grant proposal for Miller-Idriss (2018)'s research, for example – but published scholarship has offered similar framings. Hagan, Merkens and Boehnke (1995: 1034) describe "adolescent inclinations to drift into subterranean traditions of right-wing extremism as well as juvenile delinquency," indicating that there is a liminal phase during which risk of participation in the far right is highest, after which it presumably declines. Notably, there is also some research indicating a life-cycle trajectory for both left- and right-wing youth activists, in which 'postactivist adult lives' are characterized by continuity in political orientations but 'less radical style' (Braungart and Braungart, 1990: 243 and 279)
3   319: Naja, ick hab eigentlich alle Kumpels… wir kennen uns ja auch schon ewig lange, ja? Schon seit unserer Jugend und wir sind einfach damit aufgewachsen. Wir haben halt unsere Sachen da mitgemacht und ehm ja… kam der erste mit 'ner Alpha Jacke, dann kam der zweite mit 'ner Alpha Jacke, so fing das allet mal an. Ja, dann ist man natürlich damals auch mal in so'n Szenen mit ringerutscht, ja? Hat mal geguckt, wat da los ist, aber sich davon auch wieder distanziert, ja?
    Interviewer: Welche Szene meinst du damit?
    319: Ja, natürlich eh die rechts-extreme, ja? Aber wie gesagt, da ist man denn eh sehr schnell auch wieder von abgekommen, wenn man selber gemerkt hat, dass nischt bringt.
4   114: "denen man eine gewisse Heimattreue unterstellen kann."
5   As argued by Mabel Berezin in a presentation during a seminar in Athens, Greece as part of the Economic and Social Research Council-funded research network "Right-Wing Extremism in Contemporary Europe," September 2014.
6   For more information, see http://girds.org/projects, accessed January 30, 2018.

References

Arzheimer, K. 2009. "Contextual Factors and the Extreme Right Vote in Western Europe, 1980–2002." *American Journal of Political Science*, 53(2), 259–275.

Bacher, J. 2001. "In welchen Lebensbereichen lernen Jugendliche Ausländerfeindlichkeit? Ergebnisse einer Befragung bei Berufsschülerinnen und Berufsschülern." *Kölner Zeitschrift für Soziologie und Sozialpsychologie*, 53, 334–349.

Boehnke, K., J. Hagan, and H. Merkens. 1998. "Right-Wing Extremism Among German Adolescents: Risk Factors and Protective Factors." *Applied Psychology: An International Review/Psychologie Appliquee: Revue Internationale*, 47(1), 109–126.

Braungart, M. and R. Braungart. 1990. "The Life-Course Development of Left- and Right-Wing Youth Activist Leaders from the 1960s." *Political Psychology*, 11(2), 243–282.

Hagan, J., H. Merkens, and K. Boehnke. 1995. "Delinquency and Disdain: Social Capital and the Control of Right-Wing Extremism among East and West Berlin Youth." *American Journal of Sociology*, 100(4), 1028–1052.

Heitmeyer, W. 1988. *Rechtsextremistische Orientierungen bei Jugendlichen* (2nd edition). Weinheim: Juventa.

Heitmeyer, W., H. Buhse, J. Liebe-Freund, K. Möller, J. Müller, H. Ritz, G. Siller, and J. Vossen. 1992. *Die Bielefelder Rechtsextremismus-Studie: Erste Langzeituntersuchung zur Politischen. Sozialisation männlicher Jugendlicher.* Munich: Juventa Verlag.

Miller-Idriss, C. 2009. *Blood and Culture: Youth, Right-Wing Extremism, and National Belonging in Contemporary Germany.* Durham, NC: Duke University Press.

Miller-Idriss, C. 2017. "Soldier, Sailor, Rebel, Rule-breaker: Masculinity and the Body in the German Far Right." *Gender and Education*, 29(2), 199–215.

Miller-Idriss, C. 2018. *The Extreme Gone Mainstream: Commercialization and Far Right Youth Subculture in Germany.* Cultural Sociology Series. Princeton, NJ: Princeton University Press.

Miller-Idriss, C. and H. Pilkington. 2017. "In Search of the Missing Link: Gender, Education and the Radical Right." *Gender and Education*, 29(2), 133–146.

Nayak, A. 2005. "White Lives." In *Racialization: Studies in Theory and Practice*, edited by K. Murji and J. Solomos, 141–162. Oxford: Oxford University Press.

Rommelspacher, B. 2006. "*'Der Hass hat uns geeint': Junge Rechtsextreme und ihr Ausstieg aus der Szene.*" Frankfurt: Campus Verlag.

Shoshan, N. 2016. *The Management of Hate: Nation, Affect, and the Governance of Right-Wing Extremism in Germany.* Princeton, NJ: Princeton University Press.

Simi, P., B.F. Bubolz, and A. Hardman. 2013. "Military Experience, Identity Discrepancies, and Far Right Terrorism: An Exploratory Analysis." *Studies in Conflict & Terrorism*, 36(8), 654–671.

21

NORMALIZATION TO THE RIGHT

Analyzing the micro-politics of the far-right[1]

Ruth Wodak

In my chapter, I discuss adequate qualitative and quantitative methodologies to systematically analyze the – ever more acceptable – exclusionary rhetoric of far-right populist parties while focussing – as a case study – on the Austrian Freedom Party (FPÖ) and a TV-interview with the FPÖ's former leader HC Strache. The critical discourse-analysis requires a careful context-dependent, multi-methodical, multimodal, and critical interdisciplinary investigation of the 'micro-politics' of the far-right, their texts and talk (and images). The dynamics of everyday performances frequently transcend careful analytic categorizations; boundaries between categories are becoming blurred and flexible, open to change and ever new socio-economic developments.

Defining the far-right

In this chapter I am concerned with the *micro-politics* of far-right[2] political parties – *how they produce and reproduce their ideologies and exclusionary politics in everyday politics, in the media, in campaigning, in posters, slogans and speeches.* Ultimately, I am concerned with how *they succeed (or fail) in sustaining their electoral success and why their messages resonate so well with specific audiences.* Indeed, what becomes apparent is what I would like to label as the *normalization* of formerly tabooed expressions, prejudices, and policies (e.g., Wodak, 2015b, 2020), a process which should be carefully deconstructed.

Much research in the social sciences provides ample evidence for the current rise of the far-right and related political parties in most European Union (EU) member states and beyond.[3] On the one hand, we observe neo-Nazi movements in the form of extreme-right parties and horrific hate crimes such as those committed by Anders Breivik in July 2011 in Norway, from which all far-right and right-wing populist parties immediately distanced themselves publicly;[4] on the other hand, two salient shifts are occurring in the forms and styles of political rhetoric of far-right parties which could be labelled, firstly, as 'the *Haiderization* of politics' – a label relating to the former leader of the Austrian Freedom Party (FPÖ; *Freiheitliche Partei Österreich*), Jörg Haider – and, secondly, what journalists and experts call '*Post-Truth politics*', following Donald Trump's election as President of the United States on 7 November 2016.[5]

Haider's performance, style, rhetoric and ideologies have become the metonymic symbol of such parties' success across Europe. Indeed, the Austrian FPÖ has certainly paved the way for the dissemination of a new, though frequently *coded*, xenophobic, racist and antisemitic, exclusionary and anti-elitist politics since 1989 and the fall of the so-called Iron Curtain.[6] Moreover, the significant increase of distrust towards the EU and its institutions (Standard Eurobarometer 86, 2016), due to the major global and European crises since 2008 (such as the economic crisis, the Euro-zone crisis, the so-called refugee crisis, and ever more terrorist attacks) has brought the problems of the political systems within the European Union (EU) member states and the EU's institutions to the surface and manifested the frustrations of the public towards it (Angouri and Wodak, 2014; Hay, 2007; Rizakis, 2016). This erosion of trust in politics is necessarily a far more serious threat than the loss of trust towards a specific political party or an individual. The loss of trust in the political system implies a search for alternatives – which is where right-wing populist, far-right, and extreme-right political parties enter the scene: we encounter new and self-defined saviours of 'the people' dominating the political stage, presenting themselves as authentic and trustworthy.

The new far-right populist politicians work to create an image of themselves as the 'true representatives of the people' in contrast to 'the untrustworthy political classes', perceived by them as having failed (Hochschild, 2016; Pelinka, 2013; Wodak, 2015a). In these parties' efforts to substantiate their claims, their discourse becomes 'magically non-falsifiable, as only factual statements could be verified or falsified. Far-right populist communication style creates its own '"genre" as a mix of scandal, provocation, transgression, and passion' (Sauer, Krasteva and Saarinen, 2017: 28). In other words, they strategically create their own visions, beliefs, threat scenarios, and nationalistic/nativist identities which they claim to represent in a 'post-truth' world.[7]

It is thus not surprising that in 2016/2017, political rhetoric increasingly relies on the construction of a distinct dichotomy which aims to divide the people living in a country into two quasi homogenous blocs: '*the people*' are juxtaposed with '*the establishment*' within a specific narrative of threat and betrayal, accusing the so-called 'establishment' of having intentionally or subconsciously neglected the so-called 'people', having instead pursued only their own interests, failing to protect the people and to voice their interests, and having ignored the obvious anxieties of the people. Indeed, this narrative arbitrarily constructs two groups via text and image in manifold ways. Such a Manichean[8] opposition portrays these two groups as vehemently opposed to each other, two epistemic communities, one defined as powerless, the other as powerful; one described as good, innocent, and hard-working, the latter as bad, corrupt, criminal, lazy and unjustly privileged, and so forth.

Accordingly, the mechanism of 'scapegoating' (singling out a group for negative treatment on the basis of collective responsibility) constitutes an important feature of far-right populist parties' discourse. Sometimes, the scapegoats are Jews, sometimes Muslims, sometimes Roma or other minorities, sometimes capitalists, socialists, career women, NGOs, the European Union (EU), the United Nations, the USA or Communists, the governing parties, the élites, the media, and so forth. 'They' are foreigners, defined by 'race', religion or language. 'They' are élites not only within the respective country but also on the European stage ('Brussels') or at the global level ('Financial Capital'). Important fissures and divides within a society, such as class, caste, religion, gender and so forth, may be neglected in focusing on such internal or external 'others', when expedient, and are interpreted as the result of 'elitist conspiracies'.

This dichotomous view of society (a merger of anti-elitism with a nativist nationalistic anti-pluralism) is part and parcel of far-right ideology, alongside other salient dimensions which I have elaborated elsewhere (see Wodak, 2015a: 66–67). Accordingly, protecting the fatherland (or heartland, homeland) implies belief in a common narrative of the past, where 'we' were either heroes or victims of evil. Revisionist histories thus blend all past woes into success stories of the Volk or stories of treachery and betrayal by others.

Moreover, conspiracies are part and parcel of the discursive construction of fear which frequently draws on traditional antisemitic and anti-elitist tropes. Furthermore, such parties endorse traditional, conservative values and morals (family values, traditional gender roles) and, most importantly, support common sense simplistic explanations and solutions (anti-intellectualism). Usually, a 'saviour' is appealed to, the (more or less) charismatic leader of the respective party who oscillates between the roles of Robin Hood and 'strict father' (for example, see Donald Trump's promise to "make America great again"; Wodak, 2017). *Certainly*, not all far-right populist parties endorse all the above-mentioned positions. Moreover, even if they do, the level of support for any of these typical stances depends on the specific context of a given country or even situation of speaking.

In the following, I first discuss and then present approaches from Critical Discourse Studies (CDS), specifically the Discourse-Historical Approach (DHA) which allows analyzing political rhetoric (in various genres and across social fields) in much detail. I then focus on a case study which deconstructs the patterns of a 'politics of denial' frequently occurring in the so-called 'blame-game' in political debates and controversies, especially related to accusations of racism and antisemitism (Wodak, 2018). In this case, an intentionally distorted, antisemitic caricature on HC Strache's Facebook account (Strache was the former leader of the Austrian Freedom Party (FPÖ) and Vice-Chancellor in the Austrian far-right/national-conservative coalition government from December 2017 until May 2019) caused a huge media and political scandal. Finally, I discuss the causes and consequences of such scandals as well as the pros and cons of the specific qualitative DHA employed in the analysis.

The dynamics of *everyday performances* frequently transcend careful analytic categorizations; boundaries between categories are blurred and flexible, open to change and ever new socio-economic developments. Thus, when analyzing far-right (or any other political) movements and their rhetoric, it is essential to recognize that their propaganda – realized as it is in many genres across relevant social domains – always *combines and integrates form and content*, targets specific audiences and adapts to specific contexts. Only by doing so, are we able to deconstruct, understand and explain their messages, the resonance of their messages and their electoral success.

Analyzing far-right text and talk

Studying various dimensions of far-right populism from a discursive point of view implies making explicit decisions on what kind of complex social phenomenon/ problem one would like to understand and explain, i.e. the clearly defined research questions which then focus on specific aspects of that phenomenon, and depending on these decisions and related selection procedures, the kind of data that will be used to operationalize the research questions and will be analyzed (see Wodak and Meyer, 2015).

Far-right politics can be studied both from an *inside perspective*, i.e., by interviewing politicians, experts, party-followers, through conducting focus groups before elections, analyzing politicians' speeches in various contexts as well as their programs, brochures and websites, or by participant observation at election campaign rallies, or by any combination of such methods and genres); or from an *out-side perspective*, by studying media reports about, and the mediatization of, far-right populism, their staged 'spectacles', their policy papers, legislation, manifestoes and programs of political parties, election campaign materials, and so forth. All these *genres* necessarily consist of *text and talk* – written, spoken or visual communication.[9]

Indeed, an interview for example has to be regarded as a dialogue and analyzed accordingly. Frequently, however, social scientists only reproduce snippets of interview material in a paper or book which are supposed to illustrate some claims or findings. They seem thereby to forget that every text is dialogical; that is, every text acquires its meaning in context and in dialogue with the specific audience, reader, listener or viewer who is part of that context. This is why analyses and interpretations have to be *retroductable*,[10] systematic and explicit, deconstructing the texts via linguistic (rhetorical, argumentative, pragmatic, and semantic) means.

The *discourse-historical approach* (DHA) presented in this chapter and widely applied in research on identity politics, populism and far-right politics, discriminatory rhetoric, and so forth, allows the systematic relating of macro- and mezzo-levels of contextualization to the micro-level analyses of texts. Such analyses consist primarily of *two levels*, the 'entry-level analysis' focusing on the thematic dimension of texts, and the 'in-depth analysis' which deconstructs coherence and cohesion of texts in detail. The general aim of the *entry-level* thematic analysis is to map out the contents of analyzed texts and through that mapping to assign them to particular discourses. The key analytical categories of thematic analyses are *discourse topics*, which, "conceptually, summarize the text, and specify its most important information" (van Dijk, 1991: 113). The *in-depth analysis*, on the other hand, is

informed by the research questions. The in-depth analysis consists of the identification of the genre (e.g., TV interview, policy paper, election poster, political
speech or homepage), analysis of the macro-structure of the respective text, the
strategies of identity construction (self-and other presentation) and of the argumentation schemes, as well as of other means of linguistic realization it uses.

The discourse-historical approach

The DHA views *discourse* as a set of 'context-dependent semiotic practices' which
are 'socially constituted and socially constitutive,' 'related to a macro-topic' and
characterized by a 'pluri-perspective,' i.e., linked to argumentation (Reisigl and
Wodak, 2009: 89). The approach focuses on *texts* – be they audio, spoken, visual
and/or written – as they relate to structured knowledge (*discourses*), are realized in
specific *genres*, and must be viewed in terms of their *situatedness*. That is, many texts
cannot be fully understood without considering different layers of *context*.

Here, I follow a *four-level model* of context that includes the historical development
of far-right populism in a specific nation state (the *socio-political/historical context*), discussions which dominated a specific debate/event (*the current context*), a specific text
(*text-internal co-text*, i.e. the detailed micro-context of each utterance in a text), and
intertextual and interdiscursive relations (Reisigl and Wodak, 2001: 40 ff.). The pair of
terms 'interdiscursivity/intertextuality' denotes the linkage between discourses and
texts across time and space – established via explicit or implicit references. If text
elements are taken out of their original context (de-contextualization) and inserted
into another (re-contextualization), they (partly) acquire new meaning(s) as meanings
are never context-independent and thus always constituted in context.

Taking such a perspective, the media incident analyzed below can be understood
as texts which draw on existing opinions and collective memories about Austrian or
indeed European history, while also *mobilizing* and *radicalizing* these discourses. Positive self- and negative other-presentation is realized via *discursive strategies* (Reisigl and
Wodak, 2001: 45–90). Here, I primarily focus on *nomination* (how events/objects/
persons are referred to) and *predication* (what characteristics are attributed to them).
Finally, *argumentation strategies* concern the justification and legitimation of specific
claims, in our case related to certain traditional antisemitic stereotypes.

Within the DHA (Reisigl and Wodak, 2001: 74f), the notion of *topos* designates
both formal and content-related "conclusion rule[s] that connect[s] the argument
or arguments with the conclusion, the claim". Here, the DHA draws on Wengeler's (2003) and Kienpointner's (1996) context-specific notion of *topos*, defined as
semiotically manifested "figures of thought in approaching a political issue"
(Wengeler, 2003: 67). Kienpointner (quoted in Wengeler, 2003: 65), similarly,
views *topoi* "as being typical of arguments by speakers of a speech-community or at
least bigger groups of not especially trained speakers". These conclusion rules are
either sound or fallacious, enabling or preventing the *more or less* undistorted
exchange of standpoints through particular ways of representing events, objects or
persons.[11]

In sum, the DHA focuses on the ways in which power-dependent semiotic means are used to construct positive self- and negative other-presentations (US and THEM, in our case the pro and contra being US and the (rich) Jewish bankers, respectively). This also captures the ability to select specific events in the flow of a narrative as well as increased opportunities to convey messages by opening up space for '*calculated ambivalence*' (Engel and Wodak, 2009; 2013). The latter is defined as a phenomenon whereby one utterance carries at least two more-or-less contradictory meanings, oriented towards at least two different audiences. This not only increases the audience, but also enables the speaker/ writer to deny any responsibility: after all, 'it wasn't meant that way'. Finally, the power of discourse creates regimes of quasi 'normality', i.e. what is deemed 'normal', e.g. with regard to the political messages circulating during heated debates (Wodak, 2019).

A thorough DHA ideally follows an eight-stage program. Typically, the eight steps are implemented recursively (see Reisigl and Wodak, 2015 for more details):

1. Activation and consultation of preceding theoretical knowledge (i.e., recollection, reading and critical discussion/overview of previous research).
2. Systematic collection of data and context information (depending on the research questions, various discourses and discursive events, social fields as well as actors, semiotic media, genres and texts are focussed on).
3. Selection and preparation of data for the specific analyses (selection and downsizing of data according to relevant criteria, transcription of tape recordings, etc.).
4. Specification of the research question/s and formulation of assumptions (on the basis of a literature review and a first skimming of the data).
5. Qualitative pilot analysis, including a context analysis, macro-analysis and micro-analysis (allows testing categories and first assumptions as well as the further specification of assumptions; see example below).
6. Detailed case studies (of a whole range of data, primarily qualitatively, but in part also quantitatively).
7. Formulation of critique (interpretation of results, in respect to the specific knowledge of the relevant context and referring to the three dimensions of 'critique' [Reisigl and Wodak, 2001: 40*ff.*]).
8. Practical application of analytical results (if possible, the results might be proposed for practical application aiming at having social impact and challenging/ changing, for instance, [exclusionary] rhetoric).

The politics of denial

Blaming and denying

Clearly linked to positive self-presentation and the construction of positive group and collective identities is – what Teun van Dijk (1992) famously labelled – 'the denial of racism'. He described the strategies of denying racism in great detail and claims that

> [o]ne of the crucial properties of contemporary racism is its denial, typically illustrated in such well-known disclaimers as 'I have nothing against blacks, but… ' [. …] The guiding idea behind this research is that ethnic and racial prejudices are prominently acquired and shared within the white dominant group through everyday conversation and institutional text and talk. Such discourse serves to express, convey, legitimate or indeed conceal or deny such negative ethnic attitudes.
>
> *(van Dijk, 1992: 87–88)*

Moreover, van Dijk (1922: 92) provides a useful typology of the speech act of denial as part of a general defense/justification strategy when a person is accused or blamed of having uttered a racist remark or of being racist. These types are:

1. act-denial ('I did not do/say that at all')
2. control-denial ('I did not do/say that on purpose', 'It was an accident')
3. intention-denial ('I did not mean that', 'You got me wrong')
4. goal-denial ('I did not do/say that, to…')
5. mitigations, down-toning, minimizing or using euphemisms when describing one's negative actions

Apart from 'denial proper', van Dijk claims that there are also cognitive and social strategies which can be regarded as 'stronger forms of denial': blaming the victim and victim–perpetrator reversal (see also Hansson, 2015). Moreover, he mentions the use of *disclaimers*: recall the well-known examples of justification discourses, such as 'I have nothing against …, but', 'My best friends are …, but', 'We are tolerant, but …', 'We would like to help, but the boat is full', etc.

All these discursive utterances, labelled as *disclaimers*, manifest the *denial of racism or exclusion* and emphasize *positive self-presentation*. Usually, such speakers seek to justify the practice of exclusion without employing related overt rhetoric. Overt denials of prejudice basically involve two presuppositions. First, they presuppose the existence of 'real' prejudice. In this regard, the existence of extreme, outwardly fascist groups enables defenders of mainstream racism, exclusion or discrimination to present their own rhetoric as being unprejudiced – by comparison, thus also constructing an implicit *straw man* fallacy. Second, speakers, in denying prejudice, will claim that their criticisms of minority group members are 'factual', 'objective' and 'reasonable', rather than based upon irrational feelings, and will accordingly employ a range of discursive strategies of legitimization. Speakers can, of course, use similar denials of prejudice and arguments of reasonableness when invoking different forms of discrimination, such as sexism, racism, antisemitism or religious discrimination. Additionally, each type of exclusionary practice will integrate particular themes, stereotypes and argumentative devices (*topoi*), all contributing to the *syncretic nature of mainstream discriminatory discourse*.

In the extracts of the TV interview between the anchor-man of the Austrian public broadcasting service ORF (*Österreichischer Rundfunk*) and the then FPÖ leader HC Strache, several disclaimers and discursive strategies of denial could be observed: Strache insisted that because he had 'some Israeli friends' nobody could possibly accuse him of being antisemitic – a typical disclaimer in antisemitic discourse (a goal-denial). Secondly, he claimed that not he but somebody else had distorted the previous US-American caricature, thus fallaciously shifting the blame, a good example of control-denial. Thirdly, he denied recognizing the Star of David on the cufflinks of the banker, portrayed as a Jew via traditional and stereotypical antisemitic characteristics such as the hooked nose, although the Star of David was recognizable to everybody else, thus performing an act-denial (and in this way, constructing so-called 'alternative facts'; see Wodak, 2017, 2019). Denying the obvious and evading all rules of cooperativeness are part and parcel of far-right populist rhetoric. At this point, HC Strache argued with the *topos of definition*: "If I, HC Strache, define this as X, then this is X (and not Y)". And, finally, he claimed that a conspiracy of political opponents existed, launching false accusations against him and 'hunting' him down; accordingly, he constructed himself as the victim of such a dangerous conspiracy, another typical justificatory strategy of far-right populist rhetoric. The *politics of denial* seem to have worked well in this particular case: HC Strache was declared innocent from having explicitly contributed to hate incitement by the then Minister of Justice, Beatrix Karl. She claimed that the employed stereotypes were not antisemitic as they did not target all Jews – a noteworthy and peculiar *topos of definition* in itself.

Analyzing a TV interview

On August 18, 2012, the leader of the Austrian far right populist party FPÖ, HC Strache, posted a caricature on Facebook (Figure 21.1) which recontextualized a US-American caricature from 1962 (Figure 21.2) into a caricature which alludes to antisemitic caricatures from Nazi times that were published daily in the 1930s in the infamous German newspaper *Der Stürmer*. After the – predictable – scandal had erupted over the explicit antisemitic features of the caricature, most newspapers in Austria and Germany published editorials and news reports about this incident; Strache was interviewed on television August 20, 2012[12]; he first denied having altered the original caricature; he then denied that the stars visible on the cufflinks of the banker were Stars of David; and, finally, he categorically denied any resemblances with antisemitic caricatures:

The explicit differences between Figures 21.1 and 21.2 are easy to detect: The nose of the sweating and greedily eating banker had been changed to a crooked, so-called 'Jewish nose' and the cufflinks had each been decorated with a Star of David. These two changes both insinuate, and resonate with, images of the Nazi past: with the stereotypical image of 'the ugly and greedy Jewish banker' who exploits the poor (metonymically embodied by the image of a poor worker from the 1960s) and patronizes the government which tries to ingratiate itself with the

FIGURE 21.1 Caricature posted by HC Strache on Facebook 18 August 2012[13]

FIGURE 21.2 American caricature 1962 (DerStandard.at 2012)[14]

powerful and rich Jew by serving him an opulent meal and pouring wine. In Figure 21.3, the relevant segments have been enlarged.

By making these changes and posting the altered caricature with an extended comment (see Figure 21.1), Strache utilized the theme of the virulent financial crisis (2008/9) in at least three ways: firstly to accuse the government of wrong policies and of submitting to the EU; secondly to create a scapegoat that could be blamed for current woes by triggering traditional antisemitic stereotypes of world conspiracy and powerful Jewish bankers and capitalists; and thirdly to provoke a scandal and thus attract media attention and set the news agenda. The caricature is accompanied by a textbox on the right that explains the caricature in some detail and accuses the government of selling out to EU policies and foreign punters. This substantiates the above mentioned anti-Jewish stereotypes: the world conspiracy and the so-called 'Jewish capitalist'. I will come back to this text and its role in the entire scandal below.

FIGURE 21.3 Details of the 'greedy banker' (DerStandard.at 2012)

Text 1 below, taken from the beginning of a TV interview from August 22, 2012 (i.e., 4 days after the caricature was posted) on ORF II (ZIB 2 [*Zeit im Bild* II]; Austrian Broadcasting Company, daily news programme at 10pm), illustrates the politics of denial propagated by HC Strache well (AW is Armin Wolf, anchor-man on the main Austrian news programme ZIB 2, HCS is Strache):[15]

After asking HC Strache whether he is now 'proud' of being discussed in so many serious newspapers and radio stations across Europe (*Die Zeit, Der Spiegel, BBC*), Strache utters his first denial (lines 7–8, an act-denial):[16] "No. This is absolute nonsense! I got this caricature shared by a user". Anchor-man Armin Wolf immediately falsifies this claim and shows that Strache actually posted this caricature himself by pointing to a print-out of the relevant Facebook page. Strache then concedes that he first said something wrong and starts – by way of justification – to explain the caricature as illustrating the unfair and unjust redistribution of money taken away from the Austrian people. Here, Wolf interrupts in line 16 and qualifies the bankers as Jews ("who are Jews in your caricature"). At this point, the second round of denials starts.

Via a well-known disclaimer ("I have many Israeli, but also Jewish friends"; lines 17–19), Strache denies that the caricature should or even could be read as anti-semitic, a typical intention-denial: the fallacious argument (*post hoc, ergo propter hoc* fallacy) is obvious – if his many Jewish friends do not classify the caricature as antisemitic, it cannot be antisemitic. Such disclaimers are widely used to prove that an utterance *cannot* be categorized as racist, sexist or antisemitic because 'Turkish, Arabic, female or Jewish friends' share the speaker's or writer's opinions. Moreover, the justification implies that if one has Jewish friends, then one is incapable of

TABLE 21.1A Text 1

[1]	**AW** Now, last week you managed once again to make it into international
[2]	**AW** headlines, and you did it by using this caricature, which you posted **HCS** Hmhm
[3]	**AW** on your Facebook page. The Zeit, **HCS** Hmhm
[4]	**AW** a respected German weekly newspaper, refers to this as "antisemitic
[5]	**AW** provocation", the Spiegel refers to it as "a picture, just as in times of NS-
[6]	**AW** propaganda", and even the BBC reported on it. Are you
[7]	**AW** proud of that? **HCS** No. This is absolute nonsense! I got
[8]	**AW** You did **HCS** this, um, caricature, um, shared by a user

TABLE 21.1B Text 2

[16]	**HCS** No, no, they are not, **AW** What then?
[17]	**HCS** Mister Wolf. And, um, with all due respect, I have
[18]	**HCS** many Israeli, but also Jewish friends, who
[19]	**HCS** have, um, seen this caricature, and not one of them can recognize antisemitism

saying something antisemitic (see Wodak et al., 1990; Wodak, 2018 for the detailed analysis of similar fallacious argumentative schemes and moves).

After this unsuccessful denial, Wolf points to the Stars of David on the cufflinks and asks who might have put them there if not Strache himself. In his third attempt to deny wrong-doing and reinforcement of antisemitic stereotypes, Strache refuses to recognize Stars of David on the cufflinks (lines 23, 24) and starts a counter-attack with an *ad-hominem argument*: He claims that Wolf obviously cannot see well, his glasses are probably not strong enough; even if one would magnify the cufflinks, Strache further claims, no Stars of David would be visible. Wolf then shows a Star of David he has brought with him to the studio and asks Strache if he can spot any similarity (line 32); Strache denies again and states that the picture on the cufflinks is blurred and that there is no star but actually something like a diamond. After this fifth (act) denial, he refers to his 'Jewish friends' again who, Strache claims, believe that somebody is intentionally conspiring against him. In this way, Strache accuses the media and the public of conspiring against him, via quoting his 'Jewish friends' – another typical justification strategy: claiming victimhood via victim–perpetrator reversal. Wolf continues his line of questioning and asks Strache why he apparently finds it impossible to simply apologize for posting such a caricature and why he would rather use a strategy of victim–perpetrator reversal instead of an apology. Strache answers by repeating his denials: There are no Stars of David; the caricature is not antisemitic (this staccato-like question–answering sequence continues for several minutes).

In line 74 below, Wolf shifts to the meta-level and frames the entire discussion as a provocation strategy intentionally triggered by Strache to attract media attention. This interpretation is – not surprisingly – again denied by Strache (a goal-denial). The interview continues with other questions about Strache's program for the autumn of 2012.

After the interview, many commentators accused Armin Wolf of having been too 'strict' on Strache; some newspapers like the *Neue Kronenzeitung* (a tabloid similar to the *Daily Mail*) wrote that the line of questioning had been unfair and not acceptable for this kind of interview genre; others equated the interview-style with a tribunal or an interrogation.[17] These media comments show that Strache had obviously been quite successful in constructing himself as a victim, on the one hand, and as the saviour of the Austrian people, on the other, by telling the Austrians the 'truth' about the economic crisis, by uncovering the causes of the crisis

TABLE 21.1C Text 3

[20]	**AW** Mister Strache… **HCS** in this. If you see something else in this,
[21]	**HCS** um, then, um, you have to ask yourself the question, why do you want to see
[22]	**AW** Because you have three Stars of David here. Because you put three **HCS** something else in this, because there is no anti-Semitism
[23]	**AW** Stars of David here, or someone put them there… **HCS** That is incorrect, Mister Wolf.
[24]	**AW** No? You do not see three Stars of David here. **HCS** Well… No, maybe you should have the
[25]	**AW** Yes **HCS** strength of your glasses checked, if you magnify this picture,
[26]	**AW** Yes Really? Okay. We did **HCS** you can see no Stars of David. Yeah.
[27]	**AW** magnify the picture, Mister Strache. We did **HCS** I can show you, too, yes.
[28]	**AW** magnify the picture and you cannot see any Stars of David here? **HCS** Exactly. Yes. Yes. No,
[29]	**AW** Mister Strache, you don't see any Stars of David? **HCS** there are no Stars of David to be seen, because…
[30]	**AW** Mister Strache, I also brought you **HCS** No! There are no Stars of David to be seen here.
[31]	**AW** a Star of David for comparison. And **HCS** Yes…. and this picture… That is one! Yeah? No, that is
[32]	**AW** there are not three Stars of David here? **HCS** one. No, that's a star with continuous
[33]	**AW** Good. **HCS** lines, there is no way you can see that with that blurry picture.

TABLE 21.1D Text 4

[70]	**HCS** regarding that nose, I have already seen worse caricatures of my own
[71]	**HCS** there we, I can only think of Mister Sinowatz or as a
[72]	**HCS** neighbour, as a political neighbour, um, Mister Kohl or possibly
[73]	**HCS** Mister Konrad as a comparison, but certainly not what you
[74]	**AW** Well. Mister Strache, is it possible that you are **HCS** are trying to create here.
[75]	**AW** in reality quite pleased with the situation? Well, **HCS** No, I am not pleased at all!
[76]	**AW** well, you have once again created a lapse to provoke, the **HCS** Quite the contrary. Yes, yes.
[77]	**AW** outrage is enormous, um, not only in Austria, but also internationally,
[78]	**AW** and you can once again present yourself as the poor and the persecuted, now
[79]	**AW** you are the victim, suddenly, and can enjoy the headlines. **HCS** Yes, yes.

(allegedly, the 'Jewish banker') and by thus providing a scapegoat which everybody could blame for the crisis. However, simultaneously, the state prosecutor started to investigate if the Facebook incident could be prosecuted as hate incitement. In April 2013, the court decided that Strache's posting could not be regarded as a case of hate incitement. In fact, it is quite typical of the ways in which courts of law deal with far-right populist discriminatory and exclusionary rhetoric. In short: the lack of legal consequences seems to confirm that 'anything goes'.

Conclusion: Afterthoughts

By systematically employing genres such as caricatures and comic books to convey xenophobic and antisemitic messages, far-right parties cleverly play with the *fictionalization of politics* and argue that no discriminatory message was intended as such genres play with humour and are inherently ironic or even sarcastic (Wodak and Forchtner, 2014). The blurring of boundaries between fiction and reality, caricature and image, or between comic book plot and historical narrative is one of many ways of staging the strategy of *calculated ambivalence*, i.e., simultaneously addressing multiple audiences with – frequently contradictory – messages. Facebook potentially adds to this strategy at least in one way: denying having posted the incriminatory content oneself and using the (seeming) anonymity of the Internet.

This incident illustrates the typical rhetorical strategies of *provocation, calculated ambivalence* and *denial*; it emphasizes the power of digital media in their mediated use of traditional genres and the rapid spiral of scandalization; moreover, this example illustrates the importance of an in-depth and context-sensitive, multi-layered analysis when trying to understand and explain the dynamics of far-right populist propaganda and manipulation.

Notes

1 Research for this chapter was conducted in July 2018 prior to the collapse of the Austrian government in May 2019, after the publication of the scandalous "Ibiza-Video", May 17, 2019 (see Wodak 2020).

2 In this chapter (and book) the term 'far right' is used for many parties which are also labeled 'populist', 'right-wing populist', or indeed, 'extreme-right' parties. I distinguish here between far-right (also right-wing populist as defined in Wodak 2015a), and extreme-right parties (as defined in Wodak and Richardson, 2013) See also Wodak (2020) for an extensive discussion of these terms.

3 See, for example, Harrison and Bruter (2011); Feldman and Jackson (2013); Mudde and Kaltwasser (2012); Sir Peter Ustinov Institut et al. (2013); Wodak, KhosraviNik and Mral (2013); Wodak (2013a, 2013b; 2015a; 2015b; 2016; 2017a); Müller (2017); Krasteva 2017.

4 E.g., http://www.news.at/a/anschlaege-norwegen-fpoe-hetzt-302711 (accessed 20 April 2017).

5 See Montgomery (2017).

6 See, for example, Krzyżanowski and Wodak (2009); Matouschek et al. (1995); Pelinka and Wodak (2002); Reisigl (2013); Wodak and Pelinka (2002) for more details. It is important to emphasize at this point that far-right populist/national-conservative parties have now won majorities in the former Eastern Bloc countries such as Hungary and Poland. Unlike their counterparts in 'the West', they obviously find it less difficult to promote explicit xenophobic, antisemitic and antiziganist messages. They also draw on traditional antisemitic beliefs shared widely across the population which differ in their quality and explicitness from similar resentments in the UK or France, for example, where hegemonic Israeli politics are usually integrated into debates about Jews (thus sometimes also insinuating world-conspiracy themes, of course) (see Kovács, 2013; Wodak, 2018).

7 Belam, M. (2017) "Fact-checking isn't enough. To fight the far right, the media must spread the truth." *The Guardian*, 7 February 2017:
   https://www.theguardian.com/commentisfree/2017/feb/07/fact-checking-far-right-media-truth-donald-trump-terrorist?CMP=Share_iOSApp_Other [accessed 5 April 2019].

8 The term *Manichean* stems from a religious belief system of late antiquity and the early Middle Ages. In this sect, every phenomenon was divided into two opposing sides: light and darkness, good and evil, and so forth. Nowadays, this term has been recontextualized to label ideologies which structure the world into dualities, without any overtones (see Klein, 1991).

9 See for example, Richardson (2004); Wodak and Krzyżanowski (2008); Wodak (2011); Wodak and Meyer (2015) for more information on specificities of discourse and genre analysis.

10 "Retroductable" [in German: *nachvollziehbar*] implies that text analyses should be transparent so that any reader can trace and understand the detailed in-depth textual analysis.

11 For this normative distinction, see Boukala (2019); Forchtner (2011); Forchtner and Tominc (2012); Reisigl (2014); Wodak (2020); Wodak and Forchtner (2014).

12 See 'Streit um antisemitisches Bild auf Strache-Seite,' *Der Standard*, 19 August 2012: http://derstandard.at/1345164507078/Streit-um-antisemitisches-Bild-auf-Strache-Seite [accessed 9 September 2019]; http://www.sosmitmensch.at/search?q=Strache+Facebook&x=23&y=10; and 'Strache-Karikatur: SPÖ empört über ÖVP,' *ORF*, 5 March 2013: http://oe1.orf.at/artikel/336348/ [accessed 9 September 2019], for more details.

13 See http://derstandard.at/1345164507078/Streit-um-antisemitisches-Bild-auf-Strache-Seite (accessed March 12, 2015).

14 See http://derstandard.at/1345164507078/Streit-um-antisemitisches-Bild-auf-Strache-Seite (accessed March 12, 2015). Der Standard reproduced the US-American caricature, allegedly taken from hangthebankers.com. Other newspapers (https://kurier.at/politik/

klage-wegencartoon-auf-straches-facebook-seite/808.802 and https://www.bz-berlin.
de/artikel-archiv/antisemitismus-vorwurf-gegen-fpoe-chef-strache (both accessed May
12, 2020)) maintain that the original caricature was published by the Canadian Jude
Potvin (http://www.michaeljournal. org/juvdm/caricatures.html) (accessed May 12,
2020). Obviously, it is difficult to trace the relevant sources as the Facebook page of HC
Strache has been closed down by the FPÖ after the so-called 'Ibiza-Scandal' in
November 2019 and thus, HC Strache's original postings cannot be accessed anymore.
15 The transcription here follows rudimentary transcription rules developed for conversations. Such a transcription allows following the dynamic of the conversation and presents
all voices as they interact, overlap and interrupt each other. This is a simplified presentation of the full transcript, which follows the HIAT rules for transcriptions.
16 See Wodak (2015a) for an extensive discussion of denials, justification strategies and
disclaimers.
17 See Günter Traxler, 'Strache-Interview "im Weichspülmodus",' *Der Standard*, 27 August
2012 http://derstandard.at/1345165340089/Strache-Interview-im-Weichspuelmodus. The
Kleine Zeitung commented on how Strache had succeeded in presenting himself as victim:
http://www.kleinezeitung.at/nachrichten/politik/2936602/opferumkehr-des-h-c-strache.
story; other politicians were angry about Strache's attacks on his former mentor Jörg Haider,
and so forth: http://www.heute.at/news/politik/art23660,763710. In any case, the interview (and the provocation via the Facebook incident) proved to be agenda-setting [all links
accessed 20 April 2017].

References

Angouri, J. and R. Wodak. 2014. "'They became big in the shadow of the crisis': The
Greek success story and the rise of the far right." *Discourse & Society*, 25(4), 540–565.
Bauman, Z. 2017. *Retrotopia*. Cambridge: Polity.
Boukala, S. 2019. *European Identity and the Representation of Islam in the Mainstream Press*.
Berlin: Palgrave Macmillan/Springer.
Engel, J. and R. Wodak. 2009. "Kalkulierte Ambivalenz, 'Störungen' und das 'Gedanken-
jahr': Die Causen Siegfried Kampl und John Gudenus." In *Gedenken im 'Gedankenjahr':
zur diskursiven Konstruktion österreichischer Identitäten im Jubiläumsjahr 2005*, edited by R. De
Cillia and R. Wodak, 79–100. Innsbruck: Studienverlag.
Engel, J. and R. Wodak. 2013. "'Calculated ambivalence' and Holocaust denial in Austria."
In *Analysing Fascist Discourse: European Fascism in Text and Talk*, edited by R. Wodak and
J.E. Richardson, 73–96. London: Routledge.
European Commission2016. *Standard Eurobarometer 86: Public Opinion in the European Union*.
http://ec.europa.eu/COMMFrontOffice/publicopinion/index.cfm/Survey/getSurvey
Detail/instruments/STANDARD/surveyKy/2098
Feldman, M. and P. Jackson. (eds). 2013. *Doublespeak: The Rhetoric of the Far-Right since 1945*.
Frankfurt/M: Ibidem.
Forchtner, B. 2011. "Critique, the discourse-historical approach and the Frankfurt School."
Critical Discourse Studies, 8(1), 1–14.
Forchtner, B. and A. Tominc. 2012. "Critique and argumentation: on the relation between
the discourse-historical approach and pragma-dialectics." *Journal of Language and Politics*,
11(1), 31–50.
Hansson, S. 2015. "Discursive strategies of blame avoidance in government: A framework
for analysis." *Discourse & Society*, 26(3), 297–323.
Harrison, S. and M. Bruter. 2011. *Mapping Extreme Right Ideology*. Basingstoke: Palgrave.
Hay, C. 2007. *Why We Hate Politics*. Cambridge: Polity.
Hochschild, A. 2016. *Strangers in Their Own Land. Anger and Mourning on the American Right*.
New York, NY: The New Press.

Kienpointner, M. 1996. *Vernünftig argumentieren. Regeln und Techniken der Argumenta-tion*Hamburg: Rowohlt.

Klein, W. 1991. *Die Argumentation in den griechisch-christlichen Antimanichaica*. Studies in Oriental Religions 19. Wiesbaden: Harrassowitz.

Kovács, A. 2013. "The post-Communist extreme right: The Jobbik Party in Hungary." In *Right-Wing Populism in Europe: Politics and Discourse*, edited by R. Wodak, M. Khosravi-Nik, and B. Mral, 223–234. London: Bloomsbury.

Krasteva, A. 2017. "Re/de/constructing the far-right youth: Between the lost generation and the contestatory citizenship." In *Understanding the Populist Shift: Othering in a Europe in Crisis*, edited by G. Lazaridis, and G. Campani, 150–178. London: Routledge.

Krzyżanowski, M. and R. Wodak. 2009. *The Politics of Exclusion. Debating Migration in Austria*. New Brunswick, NJ: Transaction Publishers.

Matouschek, B., R. Wodak, and F. Januschek. 1995. *Notwendige Maßnahmen gegen Fremde?* Vienna: Passagen.

Montgomery, M. 2017. "Post-truth politics? Authenticity, populism and the electoral discourses of Donald Trump." *Journal of Language and Politics*, 16(4) (special issue, eds R. Wodak and M. Krzyżanowski).

Mudde, C. and C.R. Kaltwasser. 2012. *Populism in Europe and the Americas. Threat or Corrective for Democracy?*Cambridge: Cambridge University Press.

Müller, J.-W. 2017. "Donald Trump's use of the term 'the people' is a warning sign." *The Guardian*, https://www.theguardian.com/commentisfree/2017/jan/24/donald-trumps-warning-sign-populism-authoritarianism-inauguration

Pelinka, A. 2013. "Right-wing populism: Concept and typology." In *Right-Wing Populism in Europe. Politics and discourse*, edited by R. Wodak, M. KhosraviNik, and B. Mral, 3–22. London: Bloomsbury.

Pelinka, A. and R. Wodak. (eds). 2002. *"Dreck am Stecken"– Politik der Ausgrenzung*. Vienna: Czernin.

Reisigl, M. 2013. "Zur kommunikativen Dimension des Rechtspopulismuss". In *Populismus. Herausforderung oder Gefahr für eine Demokratie?*, edited by Sir Peter Ustinov Institut, A. Pelinka, and B. Haller, 141–162. Vienna: New Academic Press.

Reisigl, M. 2014. "Argumentation analysis and the discourse-historical approach: A methodological framework." In *Contemporary Critical Discourse Studies*, edited by C. Hart and P. Cap, 67–96. London: Bloomsbury.

Reisigl, M. and R. Wodak. 2001. *Discourse and Discrimination. Rhetorics of Racism and Antisemitism*. London: Routledge.

Reisigl, M. and R. Wodak. 2009. "The Discourse-Historical Approach (DHA)." In *Methods of Critical Discourse Analysis* (2nd edition), edited by R. Wodak and M. Meyer, 87–121. London: Sage.

Reisigl, M. and R. Wodak. 2015. "The Discourse-Historical Approach (DHA)." In *Methods of Critical Discourse Analysis* (3rd edition), edited by R. Wodak and M. Meyer, 23–61. London: Sage.

Rheindorf, M. and R. Wodak. 2018. "'Borders, fences and limits' – protecting Austria fromrefugees: Metadiscursive negotiations of meaning in the current refugee crisis." *Journal of Immigrant & Refugee Studies*, 16(1–2), 15–38.

Richardson, J.E. 2004. *(Mis)representing Islam*. Amsterdam: Benjamins.

Rizakis, M. 2016. *The Rise of the Far Right in Greece and France*. Unpublished PhD Thesis, Glasgow University.

Sauer, B., A. Krasteva, and P. Saarinen. 2017. "Post-democracy, party politics and right-wing populist communication." In *Populism and the Web: Communicative Practices of Parties and Movements in Europe*, edited by M. Pajnik and B. Sauer. London: Ashgate.

Sir Peter Ustinov Institut, A. Pelinka, and B. Haller. (eds). 2013. *Populismus. Herausforderung oder Gefahr für eine Demokratie?*Vienna: New Academic Press.

Van Dijk, Teun A. 1991. *News as Discourse.* New York, NY: Erlbaum.

Van Dijk, Teun A. 1992. "Discourse and the denial of racism." *Discourse & Society*, 3(1), 87–118.

Wengeler, M. 2003. *Topos und Diskurs. Begründung einer argumentationsanalytischen Methode und ihrer Anwendung auf den Migrationsdiskurs (1960–1985).* Tübingen: Niemeyer.

Wodak, R. 2011. *The Discourse of Politics in Action. Politics as Usual* (2nd revised edition). Basingstoke: Palgrave.

Wodak, R. 2013a. "'Anything goes!' The Haiderization of Europe." In *Right-Wing Populism in Europe. Politics and Discourse*, edited by R. Wodak et al., 23–38. London: Bloomsbury.

Wodak, R. 2013b. "The strategy of discursive provocation – a discourse-historical analysis of the FPÖ's discriminatory rhetoric." In *Doublespeak: The Rhetoric of the Far-Rights Since 1945*, edited by M. Feldman and P. Jackson, 101–122. Frankfurt/M: Ibidem.

Wodak, R. 2015a. *The Politics of Fear. What Right-wing Populist Discourses Mean.* London: Sage.

Wodak, R. 2015b. "Normalisierung nach rechts: Politischer Diskurs im Spannungsfeld von Neoliberalismus, Populismus und Kritischer Öffentlichkeit." *Linguistik Online*, 73(4), 27–44.

Wodak, R. 2016. *Politik mit der Angst. Zur Wirkung rechtspopulistischer Diskurse.* Wien: Konturen.

Wodak, R. 2017. "The 'Establishment', the 'Élites', and the 'People': Who's who?" *Journal of Language and Politics, 16(4).* doi:10.1075/jlp.17030.wod

Wodak, R. 2018. "The radical right and antisemitism." In *The Oxford Handbook of the Radical Right*, edited by J. Rydgren, 61–85. Oxford: Oxford University Press.

Wodak, R. 2019. "Entering the 'post-shame era' – the rise of illiberal democracy, populism and neo-authoritarianism in EU-rope: The case of the turquoise-blue government in Austria 2017/2018." *Global Discourse.* doi:10.1332/204378919X15470487645420

Wodak, R. 2020. *The Politics of Fear. The Shameless Normalization of Far-right Populist Discourses* (2nd extended and revised edition). London: Sage.

Wodak, R. and B. Forchtner. 2014. "Embattled Vienna 1683/2010: Right wing Populism, collective memory and the fictionalization of politics." *Visual Communication*, 13(2), 231–255.

Wodak, R. and M. Krzyżanowski. (eds). 2008. *Qualitative Discourse Analysis in the Social Sciences.* Basingstoke: Palgrave.

Wodak, R. and M. Krzyżanowski. (eds). 2017. "Right-wing populism in Europe and USA: Contesting politics and discourse beyond 'Orbánism' and 'Trumpism'", Special Issue, *Journal of Language and Politics*, 16(4).

Wodak, R. and M. Meyer. 2015. "Critical Discourse Studies: History, agenda, theory, and methodology." In *Methods of CDS* (3rd edition), edited by R. Wodak and M. Meyer, 1–22. London: Sage.

Wodak, R. and A. Pelinka (eds). 2002. *The Haider Phenomenon in Austria.* New Brunswick, NJ: Transaction Press.

Wodak, R. and J.E. Richardson (eds). 2013. *Analyzing Fascist Discourse. European Fascism in Text and Talk.* London: Routledge.

Wodak, R., M. KhosraviNik, and B. Mral (eds). 2013. *Rightwing Populism in Europe: Politics and Discourse.* London: Bloomsbury.

Wodak, R., P. Nowak, J. Pelikan, H. Gruber, R. de Cillia, and R. Mitten. 1990. *"Wir sind alle unschuldige Täter!" Diskurshistorische Studien zum Nachkriegsantisemitismus.* Frankfurt/M: Suhrkamp.

PART VI

The intersection of academic and activist positionalities and disseminating far right research

22

GETTING INSIGHTS AND INSIDE FAR RIGHT GROUPS

Chip Berlet

How have I kept the activist, journalist, and scholar separate and ethical when researching the far right for the past 40 years? As a coherent persona they are a mind meld. Let's say I go bowling, however, and I have three favorite individual lanes. I can start bowling in any lane, but I can't shift lanes during the game. Yet the target pins that I knock over still fall down.

I had no plans to become an expert on right-wing social and political movements when I arrived on the campus of the University of Denver in the autumn of 1968. I identified myself as a conservative, had passed out flyers for Republican Presidential candidate Barry Goldwater, and touted the wisdom of *National Review* and its publisher, William F. Buckley, Jr. My goal was to work at the *New York Times* as a photo-journalist covering the tumultuous societal unrest. My major was sociology, an interest sparked by my participation in the Civil Rights Movement through my very-White Presbyterian Church in suburban New Jersey.

The Public Eye Network

My monitoring of right-wing groups with the Public Eye Network began in the mid-1970s. I learned that several leftist groups with which I was active had been infiltrated by a network of right-wing ideologues posing as our allies. The infiltrators were loosely affiliated with the John Birch Society (JBS). The two spies I had worked with, John Rees and Sheila O'Connor, passed the information they surreptitiously collected to right-wing Congressman Larry McDonald (a leader of the JBS) who entered information into the Congressional Record. From there the information was secretly entered into the file system of the Federal Bureau of Investigation. Legal investigators Sheila O'Donnell and Eda Gordon interviewed me about Rees and O'Connor for a National Lawyers Guild lawsuit. I worked with their Guild Investigative Group researching a national right-wing spy network cooperating with government intelligence agencies. Some of us were trained to do undercover work, visiting right-wing offices and attending meetings incognito, and conducting surreptitious photographic surveillance.

Studying neo-fascists and neo-Nazis

My focus on fascism and Nazism was sparked by the uniformed members of the National Socialist White Peoples Party who periodically held rallies in the DC Capital area. Before one rally Sheila O'Donnell and I visited their offices in suburban Virginia for what we called a 'site visit.' Our demeanor was part of our 'undercover' trainings that emphasized skeptical curiosity and wads of $10 bills to purchase literature and various artifacts such as the swastika armband I still have in a drawer.

Eda Gordon and Harvey Kahn, two progressive researchers were using the *CounterSpy* offices to produce 'Brownshirts of the '70s' (Terrorist Information Project, 1976) The study was about Left turned Right former socialist Lyndon H. LaRouche. His 'LaRouchies' had been assaulting Leftists in several cities, most notably in a New York City street battle that resulted in serious injuries.

Would calling the LaRouchies the 'Brownshirts' be libelous? I was the local presumed 'expert' on journalistic ethics and libel laws, having been sued for defamation while editor of the *Clarion*. To determine the validity of the text I turned to a colleague and friend Gabrielle Edgcomb, a leftist poet and activist who had escaped the Nazi genocide by coming to the USA in 1936 with her mother (Flora, 2016). Gabrielle's apartment near DuPont Circle was packed with books; and she tutored me over several weeks with books and readings on Nazism and Fascism. I learned enough to believe the term 'Brownshirts' was accurate and fair, and there were actual experts (other than me!) who could be called to testify in case of a defamation lawsuit by the LaRouche organization.

The Public Eye Network was formed in 1978 by a group of progressive investigative reporters, licensed investigators, paralegal investigators, attorneys, and activists who shared information about political repression and right-wing movements that undermine civil liberties and civil rights. The network was drawn from the National Lawyers Guild, Guild Investigative Group, Repression Information Project, and people who had worked on *CounterSpy* Magazine and the Coalition to Stop Government Spying ('The Public Eye Network,' n.d.; 'CounterSpies,' n.d.).

The Public Eye Network was probing the relationships among government intelligence abuse and repression with various right-wing organizations and private and corporate spy networks. We knew the FBI had worked with the John Birch Society as well as the Church League of America; and suspected the CIA or FBI worked with the far-right religious organization, the Unification Church, led by the Rev. Sun Myung Moon. It was unclear at the time whether any government agency had an information-sharing relationship with groups like the Christian Anti-Communist Crusade (CACC) or the World Anti-Communist League (WACL). The Moon network was later shown to have cooperated with elements of the CIA through the World Anti-Communist League, a network implicated in the Iran-Contra hearings and death squads in Latin America (Anderson and Anderson, 1986). Time seems to erase memories of investigative journalism. A disturbingly positive obituary of Moon later appeared in the *New York Times* in 2012 (Wakin).

The exposure in 1974 of the FBI's secret and illegal Counterintelligence Program (COINTELPRO) provided thousands of pages of documentation (Donner, 1980; Glick, 1989). The documentation of the spying came from a break-in by antiwar activists at the FBI office in Media, Pennsylvania (Medsger, 2014). Some 20,000 pages were then pried out of the FBI by NBC News through a federal Freedom of Information Act request by NBC reporter Carl Stern (Columbia Journalism Review Centennial, 2014).

The bulk of the documentation – literally millions of pages – was revealed over several years in lawsuits against illegal government surveillance. I worked on several such lawsuits as a paralegal investigator along with attorneys and researchers from the Public Eye Network, the National Lawyers Guild, and American Civil Liberties Union (ACLU) in cities across the USA.

Anti-racist research and organizing

In the late 1970s I married Washington, DC activist Karen Moyer and we moved to the Southwest side of Chicago. There she could do union organizing and I could study the protests and violence against Black people moving into the previously all-White neighborhoods surrounding Marquette Park. She found a job building battery chargers in an industrial plant. I continued freelance writing. I remained active in the Public Eye Network and eventually assumed the editorship of the *Public Eye* magazine.

Karen and I had been active in various union struggles, anti-imperialist actions, and anti-racism demonstrations in Washington, DC. When we moved to Chicago, we became active in an umbrella civil rights group, The Southwest Community Congress, composed of White and Black residents straddling the racial divide down Western Avenue. The neighborhood was being block-busted and there was violence against Black people, including the fire-bombings of the homes of Black families. When I first arrived, I thought the neo-Nazis perpetrated the actual violence, but that turned out not to be true. It was more complicated.

My LaRouche research began appearing in the *Chicago Reader, Chicago Lawyer, Chicago Sun-Times*, and *Des Moines Register* newspapers. To collect information, I spent several months attending meetings and visiting the Chicago offices of the LaRouche movement, using a false name. As proof of potential loyalty, I was asked to hand out flyers on State Street in downtown Chicago. One day I handed out flyers attacking an article on LaRouche by 'Chip Berlet.' One of the lawyers I worked for just took the leaflet and rolled his eyes.

Alternative journalists Dennis King in New York and Russ Bellant in Detroit were also researching and writing about the LaRouchites. We covertly helped members of the LaRouche movement members escape from what they characterized as a 'cult.' They brought out dozens of boxes of internal files that helped our research. When the LaRouche downtown Chicago office skipped out on its rent, I dressed up in work clothes and posing as a scrap and paper recycler, I bought the contents of the many file cabinets left behind, including financial records.

Bellant, King, and I eventually combined our research and on December 16, 1981 issued documentation that the LaRouche movement was engaged in at least $10 million per year in tax fraud and other illegal practices. According to the LaRouchites our 'seven-page press release would show up almost verbatim years later, in opening statements of various prosecutorial teams assembled' to take down LaRouche, who with several top aides were convicted of financial crimes. Dennis and I took the train south to watch LaRouche being led out of the Alexandria, Virginia courthouse in handcuffs. Yes, we felt really great. No qualms.

Investigative journalist

In this identity, I specialize in writing about government repression and right-wing movements that defend systems of oppression based on race, gender, and class. Journalism schools teach ethics, as do several non-academic centers and groups, including Investigative Reporters and Editors, to which I belong. Even within journalism there are debates about the ethical boundaries of investigative reporting especially concerning the appropriateness of using fictitious identities. Over the years I have had discussions with other investigative reporters about the stress and ethical boundary issues involved in pretext identity or 'undercover' site visits.

Another disagreement involves surreptitious audio or video taping – which some states allow with limits and some ban altogether. Is it acceptable for a journalist to arrange a meeting across a nearby state line to be inside a state that allows surreptitious audio or video taping? Do some reporters illegally tape record conversations just in case they feel they need proof and would rather face a judge for illegal taping than have their credibility undermined? All of this is done all the time by reporters, but it is controversial. I confess I have done both.

When reporting on intelligence agencies or using information supplied 'not for attribution' or 'on background' a journalist needs to assess whether they are being used for a nefarious purpose. 'Big Stories, Spooky Sources' was an article I wrote for the *Columbia Journalism Review* (1993) after I saw several colleagues watch their careers implode by being insufficiently skeptical of sources. The ethics here involve the Two Source rule; now often ignored even in corporate or 'mainstream' journalism (Berlet, 2014a). The growth of the Internet as an information source and the shrinkage of the news cycle from days to minutes have exacerbated this problem. I acknowledge the irony of being a former denizen of the underground press now teaching journalistic ethics to progressive reporters.

Movement journalist

Left movement journalistic ethics should be based on the quote by Amilcar Cabral: 'Hide nothing from the masses of our people. Tell no lies. Expose lies whenever they are told. Mask no difficulties, mistakes, failures. Claim no easy victories' (Cabral, 1970).

Journalists working as part of a social or political movement are often expected to adjust or abandon some of the customary ethical standards of corporate journalism. There are sets of standards for being an 'alternative journalist' *covering* Left movements, and there are often a different set of expectations for alternative journalists *working inside* Left movements. There was a panel of alternative journalists discussing these issues at the 2012 Left Forum conference in New York City (Gupta, 2012). It can get very messy, and it is important to raise the subject of ethics on a regular basis.

In 1994, radical journalists Michael Albert and Lydia Sargent, cofounders of Z Magazine and South End Press, established the Z Media Institute (ZMI) 'to teach radical politics, media, and organizing skills; the principles and practice of creating non-hierarchical institutions and projects; and a special emphasis on vision and strategy for social change.' Hundreds of progressive media activists have attended ZMI and learned not only the tools of movement activism, but also responsibilities and ethics. Holly Sklar developed a media curriculum to teach young alternative journalists the basics of journalism as a craft, including the norms and ethics. Sklar brought me in to team teach, and after several years I taught the class with sociologist and journalist Abby Scher (Sklar, Berlet, and Scher, 2013). Sociologist Charlotte Ryan also taught media classes, as did alternative radio guru David Barsamian. Other ZMI instructors have included Michael Bronski, Leslie Cagan, Noam Chomsky, Rosa Clemente, Ron Daniels, Barbara Ehrenreich, Amy Goodman, bell hooks, and Danny Schecter.

Movement journalists are sometimes asked to do things that are clearly unethical in terms of corporate journalism. In 1991 then federal judge Clarence Thomas, a Black man with intensely conservative views, was facing nomination hearings for appointment as a Supreme Court Justice. Some left-leaning Black leaders wanted to know if Thomas while in college had spied on campus civil rights or antiwar activists. A member of the Congressional Black Caucus contacted me with this rumor and a request. Senator Teddy Kennedy was willing to ask the FBI to produce any evidence in their possession, but only if an article discussing the possibility appeared in print. I struggled with the ethics of this request, but eventually – knowing it was unethical – I wrote a short article for the radical *Guardian* newspaper in New York City. I suggested the possibility without revealing the role of the Black activists in generating the article. Senator Kennedy requested and received the FBI information. There was no evidence that Thomas had ever spied on activists for the government. After tumultuous hearings, Thomas took his seat on the Supreme Court. I was castigated publicly for having written a shabby article. I took it in silence.

Paralegal investigator

A paralegal investigator works under the direct supervision of an attorney, while a licensed private investigator can work for an attorney or directly with a client. I was trained as a paralegal investigator by Eda Gordon and Sheila O'Donnell (a licensed private investigator) of the original Public Eye Network; and attorney Matthew J. Piers, for whom I worked on a lawsuit against illegal government spying in Chicago. In the 1980s I worked on several other lawsuits against government surveillance abuses, or in defense of movement activists enmeshed in legal troubles or harassment.

Working for attorney Piers I did document analysis and deposition preparation on cases against the Federal Bureau of Investigation (FBI), the Central Intelligence Agency (CIA), Military Intelligence, and the Chicago Police 'Red Squad' intelligence unit. In this role there are strict legal ethics. For example, I had to sign a legal document swearing under oath I would not divulge to the public the contents of any government documents covered by court protective orders. And I didn't. Yet having read over 100,000 pages of these documents, my writing on government repression is based on solid information that cannot be revealed. So, this nevertheless shapes and supports my reporting. I believe I walk this ethical tightrope successfully.

Legal ethics can conflict with movement ethics. In 1988 I was asked to review the evidence in a court case filed by the Christic Institute against alleged US government misconduct involving the Contra rebels seeking to overthrow the leftist government of Nicaragua. The plaintiffs were two American journalists involved with progressive movements. My supervisor at Christic was a licensed private investigator. We both agreed there were serious and substantial deficiencies in both the evidence and legal work in the case. Our first impulse was to go directly to the plaintiffs. Being unsure of the ethics, we contacted an attorney to advise us. He told us that the only ethical conduct would be for us to inform the lead attorneys in the case, and if they chose to do nothing, we had to remain silent.

Political Research Associates

In the late 1970s a small discussion group was established by women from the Chicago-based Reproductive Rights National Network (R2N2) to discuss the growth of right-wing groups ranging from the neo-Nazis to the Christian Right. Sorting out the ideas and actions of these groups was in its infancy. In this group, I met a lesbian feminist research names Jean Hardisty, a political scientist who left academia to study anti-feminist woman's movement for the ACLU of Illinois. Her special focus was Phyllis Schlafly and the Stop ERA movement run from Schlafly's home in Alton, Illinois across the river from St. Louis.

At one meeting a librarian in the group suggested I read a book on social movements by sociologists McCarthy and Zald (1973). She thought it might help me understand how the neo-Nazis were mobilizing the youth around Marquette Park and how we in the Southwest Community Congress could refine our tactics and strategies. Sociology had grown up, and the book's analysis changed the way we organized (Berlet, 2001). During one meeting of the study group we broke out laughing when we realized how many of us subscribed to Schlafly's *Stop ERA* newsletter. Hardisty wondered if maybe we should start a central collection for periodicals and other documents for the serious study of right-wing movements.

Hardisty opened Midwest Research as a think tank and document repository in 1981. Along with staffer Peggy Shinner we collected information on right-wing movements and organizations, but also on government intelligence abuse. Our analysis of the interactions linking these two domains grew far more sophisticated over the over 30 years I worked for Hardisty.

Several reporters found a reference to me and my knowledge of the Posse Comitatus in a pre-Internet news database. The NBC television network morning news program, the Today Show, invited me to New York to discuss the Posse Comitatus in a live interview. This was following the shooting death of Posse Comitatus leader Gordon Kahl after Kahl was involved in a shootout with police. Jean Hardisty and I discussed our obligations as movement activists to highlight the collapsed economy of the farm belt. We were working with progressive farm organizers such as Merle Hansen of the North American Farm Alliance who were competing with the Posse Comitatus for recruits among beleaguered farm families struggling with harsh economic realities and structural 'adjustments'.

We decided that I would agree to the interview only if I could bring a farmer. It was as if I was asking to bring a talking turnip. The Today Show producers were flabbergasted. I held out. The producers relented. The farmer who appeared was terrific. This is an example of leveraging relative privilege to give voice to constituencies seldom consulted by the mainstream media.

The next year, in 1984, when civil rights activist Jesse Jackson toured the farm belt for his Presidential campaign, some of the people who organized on his behalf were affiliated with the Posse Comitatus and similar anti-regime right-wing groups. Those of us on the Left knew who they were, and they knew who we were – we all kept our mouths shut. This was not ethical in terms of journalism. But it was ethical in terms of the movement idea of principles of unity for tactical rather than strategic coalitions (Berlet, 2014b).

An early project for me was writing a report for some Chicago City Council members concerned about the race riots occurring around Marquette Park. They passed me on to local NBC News reporters who began to broadcast stories sometimes featuring me as an 'expert.' Using the micro-frame analysis of Hank Johnston, I wrote about the different ideologies involved in the racial struggles in Chicago (Berlet, 2001). The volume editors (Dobratz, Walder, and Buzzell, 2001) then included thoughtful critiques of my work by James Aho, Kathleen Blee, Abby L. Ferber, Jack Levin, and Stephanie Shanks-Meile. I was really getting to like sociology.

As an activist scholar I was using sociological studies of right-wing movements to reverse engineer their strategies and tactics to help activists in left-wing movements develop more effective counter-movement measures. Over time I discovered that some of my counterparts on the right were doing the same thing. For this study I picked up the phone and called one of my adversaries, Ron Arnold, founder of the 'Wise Use' movement. Arnold considers himself an environmentalist – while I consider him an anti-environmentalist. According to Arnold, to build the Wise

Use movement he first studied scholarly social movement theories based on leftwing movements and converted them to create a counter-movement on the right. Arnold says he tried to tamp down calls for armed confrontations, which he says he also opposes in current rural movements on the Right (author interview with Arnold, January, 2018).

Our office at Midwest Research was computerized from day one. In my basement at home I hooked up a computer to the existing Internet online gateway. As I went online, anarchist hackers told us that racists and neo-Nazis were posting messages online on bulletin board systems (BBS). They decided to try to hack the racists sites, and suggested I help set up an anti-racist BBS. Encouraged by a public call from the Rev. Jesse Jackson to confront online racism, a small group of us established AMNET, the first BBS that targeted racism and antisemitism; and it also promoted civil liberties and the use of the Federal Freedom of Information Act (AMNET BBS, n.d.). AMNET BBS was housed in our basement in the Southwest Side of Chicago, home to the uniformed neo-Nazis.

Hardisty moved Midwest Research from Chicago to Boston for personal reasons, and I was hired full-time at the renamed Political Research Associates. Hardisty developed a set of organizational practices and ethics for our work:

- Dress appropriate to the event to be inconspicuous.
- No disruption
- No active participation
- Men: shortish and groomed haircuts
- Women: shaved legs, stockings, and bras
- No taking materials without permission or purchase – No 'garbology.'

I did, however, once fix a broken film stuck in a 16mm projector at a meeting packed with members of the John Birch Society, Conservative Republicans, and participants in the Patriot movement. I had always wanted to see the classic anticommunist film 'Operation Abolition' tarring the Berkeley Free Speech Movement as a subversive plot. Was I conflicted? Sure. Someone eventually was going to figure out how to fix the projector. I did, however, briefly think of the ethical quandary in Pierre Boulle's book *The Photograph*, in which the photographer has to choose between stopping an assassination or getting the quintessential photo of the murder taking place. It is, however, a quandary on a different order of magnitude.

The Christian right and gay rights

As my status as a progressive researcher and writer grew (albeit it in a small pond), I was asked by Urvashi Vaid of the National Gay and Lesbian Task Force (NGLTF) to be a resource for the group. When Colorado passed the homophobic initiative Amendment 2 in 1992, I was asked to attend a major meeting of leaders of gay rights groups formulating strategy and tactics to push back the looming legal battles pushed by the right-wing antigay movement.

My role was to answer factual questions if they arose, yet I intervened when the group decided to make the slogan for resisting the initiative 'Colorado: The Hate State.' I raised my hand and asked this question. 'OK, imagine I am an organizer in Pueblo, Colorado and I knock on a door and say 'Colorado: The Hate State! … What's my next line?' The assembly brushed that aside, but a small white-haired older woman was striding toward me. Then she hugged me from behind and said into my ear 'We have to talk later.' That was how I met legendary Arkansas organizer Suzanne Pharr.

After the meeting, Pharr and I joined activist Robert Bray, nationally-known as skilled at media relations. We discussed strategic messaging aimed at conversations about basic rights instead of pompous slam-dunk slogans. And we discussed the ethical issues of mounting an aggressive grassroots campaign. Near the end of our conversation I said quietly that social science tells us that activists sometimes die in social movement struggles for liberation. There was a brief silence. Then we agreed we needed to accept our ethical responsibility for encouraging gay rights activists in rural areas and states dominated by the Christian Right to come out and push back. Our decision was emotionally painful. Clearly Pharr, Bray, and I were only playing a tiny role in the expanding gay rights movement (now the LGBTQ movement). Yet every organizer seeking liberation for any group of oppressed people needs to be cognizant that others inevitably will pay a price for their activism.

PRA was asked to collect documentation for the lawsuit seeking to block implementation. Jean Hardisty mobilized the staff to review tens of thousands of pages in our files for homophobic statements by members and leaders of the Christian Right. We all agreed it was an ethical extension of our work. Hardisty wrote a report that was sent to the legal team in Colorado, and she and I were asked to attend the trial. Jean testified in court, and I sat in the courtroom with boxes of documentation in case anything she said was challenged. Using one of the documents, an attorney was able to show that an article written prior to the case contradicted the witness defending Amendment 2 in his sworn testimony in court.

Back in Massachusetts, Jean Hardisty worked with a small group of gay rights activists and people of color activists to pull together a national strategic convening. Suzanne Pharr, Loretta Ross and I were asked to serve as the co-coordinators. The meeting was convened to find a way to counter the national wave of homophobic initiatives. This was also tied to the need to find a way for predominantly White gay rights activists to reach people of color using an approach that recognized the longstanding struggle for racial justice in communities of color. This conflict was dramatized in the 2017 television series 'When We Rise' (Black, 2017).

Invitees had to agree to attend the entire meeting, held at the Blue Mountain Center, which furnished meals and housing. No phone calls during the meeting. The discussion was to remain in the room. We were concerned that frayed emotions would lead to the meeting falling apart in rancor. I rented extra vans to bring factional groupings separately back from the Adirondacks to the Albany airport. In fact, we all came to grips with our many errors and plunged into three days of intense discussions on developing a plan to teach organizers to spend time when strategizing to 'do no harm' to other progressive groups or members of oppressed communities. Over several months after the meeting I drafted and then edited a collective statement on the basis of comments and criticisms made by the conference participants over a period of several months. Some participants chose to remain anonymous (Blue Mountain Working Group, 1994).

Another result of the meeting was that Matthew N. Lyons and I were asked to set aside our work researching and writing our book *Right-Wing Populism in America* (2000) which we had started as a collaborative research project 1991 and did not finish until 1999. Under the auspices of PRA, I rushed into print an edited volume on right-wing challenges undermining democracy and human rights in the United States. The contents were designed to elevate the voices of progressive writers too often overlooked even in the progressive media. Titled *Eyes Right: Challenging the Right-Wing Backlash*, it was published by South End Press (Berlet, 1992).

The Oklahoma City bombing

In late 1994, the armed citizen militia movement was growing, as was the militancy in some sectors of the Christian Right opposing reproductive rights for women – in part because many felt aborting a fetus should be prosecuted as murder. Devin Burghart at the Coalition for Human Dignity based in Oregon had started sending around messages to other researchers seeking information. In New York City, a group of researchers working with Planned Parenthood were seeing similar signs of militancy. At PRA I started an e-mail message list, while at the American Jewish Committee Ken Stern began collecting information. The Southern Poverty Law Center also was working with researchers, as was the Northwest Coalition Against Malicious Harassment where staff networked with authors Leonard Zeskind and Daniel Levitas.

The result was that a national emergency meeting was held outside Seattle under the auspices of the Northwest Coalition. All the named organizations and researchers attended as did other experts. There were formal presentations, and the mood was grim. Ken Stern offered to prepare a detailed memorandum warning of impending anti-government violence. It was sent to US government officials. We waited.

On April 19, 1995, the Federal Building in Oklahoma City (OKC) was destroyed by a powerful truck bomb killing 168 people. Those arrested for the bombing were Timothy McVeigh, a neo-Nazi, and Terry Nichols, a member of the Militia Movement. I became CNN's on-air expert on the bombing because I had attended militia gatherings and interviewed militia members, as well as had experience with neo-Nazi groups. Also, because all of CNN's early experts on the bombing had wrongly blamed the blast on Middle Eastern terrorists.

Much later I was subpoenaed to be an expert document analyst of right-wing literature by the defense team representing OKC bombing co-conspirator Terry Nichols. The government was alleging that both McVeigh and Nichols shared the same White supremacist ideology. I had said that their ideologies differed. I was asked to review all the material set to be introduced in court. I stuck with my analysis that Nichols was not a neo-Nazi, and the government withdrew that claim. McVeigh was sentenced to death. Nichols is spending the rest of his life in prison rather than receiving the death penalty – in part due to my research. Ethically, I could have taken payment for the work, but I couldn't stomach the idea since 168 people had died in the blast. It was a decision based on personal morals rather than ethics.

Sociological samplings

In 1997, the Marxist Section of the ASA invited me to present a paper at the Annual Meeting of the American Sociological Association in Toronto. My paper was 'Fascism's Franchises: Stating the Differences from Movement to Totalitarian Government.' This eventually brought me into a small group of people in the Marxist Section, and the Collective Behavior and Social Movements Section, of the ASA who took the study of right-wing movements seriously and expanded my horizons exponentially.

The ASA has a set of strict rules about the ethical studying of individuals and obtaining consent. So, I started asking individual people if they were OK with me interviewing them for both journalistic and scholarly purposes – although sometimes offering to do so without identifying them by name. These and other ethical issues are struggled over and discussed by other sociologists and journalists who study right-wing movements – from Republicans out to the armed extreme right such as the Ku Klux Klan and neo-Nazi movements.

There was even a discussion held at the 1998 ASA annual meeting that drew over 20 scholars including Jerome L. Himmelstein (1992; 1998) and Kathleen Blee (1991); both of whom along with other sociologists basically tutored me on social movement research skills. At that meeting several sociologists wondered if there was an ethical problem of interviewing neo-Nazis but not revealing oneself as Jewish or gay or a leftist.

Another topic was the difficulty of gathering accurate information from right-wing groups that routinely misrepresent their views and activities, unless the researcher uses some pretense. Sociologists, including Kathleen Blee (2002), Jerome Himmelstein (1998), and Betty Dobratz and Stephanie Shanks-Miele (1997), are among the scholars who have written about the fine line they dance around when studying right-wing groups that are racist, antisemitic, sexist, or homophobic. One ASA conference paper by Himmelstein was titled 'All but Sleeping with the Enemy' (1998).

When working on scholarly projects, I try to abide by the ethical mandates of the academy in general and the American Sociological Association in particular. I am acutely aware of this when I am engaged in subject research. But I nevertheless incorporate into my research and writing some material collected by others not bound by these ethical considerations. I try not to use material I gathered while wearing a different hat unless the information has been published by someone other than just me. Is that sufficient? I hope so. It's thin ice. I worry about it. I try very hard to start a project in one lane, and not shift lanes: || Activist || Journalist || Scholar ||.

Terminology itself raises questions regarding principles and ethics for both scholars and movement intellectuals. Language is loaded with social and political baggage, and an ethical scholar should consider this when writing or speaking. Himmelstein, for example, argues the term 'extremism' is at best a characterization that 'tells us nothing substantive about the people it labels', and at worst the term 'paints a false picture' (Himmelstein, 1998: 7). Lyons and I have been critical of the term 'extremism' because we argue it implicitly valorizes the political center which defends the status quo in US society while oppressive systems based on race, gender, and class are allowed to function with little attention (Berlet and Lyons, 1998). A term clearly contentious among both scholars and activists is 'hate crime' (Altschiller, 1993; Berlet, 2004; Dyer, 2001; Herek and Berril, 1992; Jacobs and Potter, 1998; Jakobsen, 1999; Jenness and Broad, 1997; Jenness, Ferber, Grattet, and Short, 1999; Levin and McDevitt, 1996). Kay Whitlock and Michael Bronski are among a growing number of activists for LGBTQ rights who now are opposing the use of the term "hate crime" (Whitlock and Bronski, 2015; Beyerstein, 2015).

Conclusions

Left movement activism, journalism, and scholarly research for me are tools to defend civil society and democracy itself (Berlet, 2016). Paul Bookbinder writes about the 'Fragility of Democracy' (n.d.) and discusses this in the context of a time when civil society and civil liberties are being ravaged by right-wing movements and the current President, Donald J. Trump (Berlet, 2015; 2019). Francesca Polletta (2002) points out in terms of progressive social movements 'Freedom is an Endless Meeting'; and God knows I spent many days at the Highlander Center when Suzanne Pharr was director discussing strategy and ethics – always linked in the minds of us who know that democracy itself is an endless struggle. Most of the people in these right-wing movements are "otherwise" average people with beliefs that do not represent some aberrant flaw in their character. They are no more "stupid" or "crazy" or "irrational" than their neighbors in their own zip code. That part of Richard Hofstadter's analysis was just wrong.

I am asked "what works?" Two thoughts:

- If sociology and journalism have taught me anything, it is that if I treat with respect the grassroots people I interview who hold right-wing views ... nine times out of ten they will calmly tell me their thoughts and move my research forward.
- As my friend, colleague, and renowned labor organizer Bill Fletcher, Jr. reminds me with a smile each time we meet: "Resistance is not Futile – Resistance is Essential."

Notes

Much of the material on ethics in this article first appeared as Chip Berlet 2014b, 'Public Intellectuals, Scholars, Journalists, and Activism: Wearing Different Hats and Juggling Different Ethical Mandates' in *RIMCIS: The International and Multidisciplinary Journal of Social Sciences*, 3 (1), http://www.hipatiapress.com/hpjournals/index.php/rimcis/article/view/954

In that study I also discuss ethical movement building for progressives, including these sections:

- Develop Principles of Unity
- Be Agile and Responsive
- Don't Stab Your Existing or Potential Allies in the Back
- Practice Participatory Democracy
- Work Across Boundaries
- Leverage Privilege and Celebrity

See also: Berlet, C., H. Sklar, and A. Scher. 2012. "Ethics for Citizen Journalists." I am assisting the compilation of resources for studying right-wing movements at: https://figshare.com/account/home#/projects/59039

References

Altschiller, D. 1993. *The United Nations' Role in World Affairs.* New York, NY: H.W. Wilson.

Anderson, S. and J.L. Anderson. 1986. *Inside the League: The Shocking Exposé of how Terrorists, Nazis, and Latin American Death Squads Have Infiltrated the World Anti-Communist League.* New York, NY: Dodd, Mead.

Berlet, C. n.d. "AMNET BBS 1985–1988." http://www.researchforprogress.us/topic/amnet-1985-1998/

Berlet, C. 1992. *Right Woos Left: Populist Party, La Rouchian, and Other Neo-fascist Overtures to Progressives, and Why They Must be Rejected.* Cambridge, MA: Political Research Associates.

Berlet, C. 1993. "Big stories, spooky sources." *Columbia Journalism Review*, 32(1), 67.

Berlet, C. 2001. "Hate groups, racial tension and ethnoviolence in an integrating Chicago neighborhood 1976–1988." In *The Politics of Social Inequality*, edited by B.A. Dobratz, L. K. Walder, and T. Buzzell. Amsterdam: Jai/Elsevier.

Berlet, C. 2004. "Christian identity: The apocalyptic style, political religion, palingenesis and neo-fascism." Totalitarian Movements and Political Religions, 5, 469–506.

Berlet, C. 2014a. "An introduction to power structure research." Research for Progress http://www.researchforprogress.us/research/power/structure.html (last accessed on 20 July 2020).

Berlet, C. 2014b. "Public intellectuals, scholars, journalists, and activism: Wearing different hats and juggling different ethical mandates." *RIMCIS: The International and Multidisciplinary Journal of Social Sciences*, 3(1), http://www.hipatiapress.com/hpjournals/index.php/rimcis/article/view/954

Berlet, C. 2015. "'Trumping' democracy: Right-wing populism, fascism, and the case for action." *The Public Eye.* Political Research Associates. https://www.politicalresearch.org/2015/12/12/trumping-democracy-right-wing-populism-fascism-and-the-case-for-action/

Berlet, C. 2016. "What is democracy?" http://www.progressivemovements.us/now/a rchives/concept/what-is-democracy/

Berlet, C. 2019. *Trumping Democracy in the United States: From Reagan to Alt-Right*. Abingdon: Routledge.

Berlet, C. and M.N. Lyons. 2000. *Right-wing Populism in America: Too Close for Comfort*. New York, NY: Guilford Press.

Berlet, C., H. Sklar, and A. Scher. 2012. "Ethics for journalists." Progressive citizen journalism training, Progressive movement commons. http://www.progressivemovements.us/now/743/progressive-citizen-journalism-training/

Beyerstein, L. 2015. "Beyond the hate frame: An interview with Kay Whitlock and Michael Bronski." *The Public Eye Magazine*, July 27. https://www.politicalresearch.org/2015/07/27/beyond-the-hate-frame-an-interview-with-kay-whitlock-michael-bronski/

Black, D.L. 2017. "When we rise." Television series; see review at https://www.nytimes.com/2017/02/16/arts/television/when-we-rise-abc-dustin-lance-black.html

Blee, K.M. 1991. *Women of the Klan: Racism and Gender in the 1920s*. Berkeley, CA: University of California press.

Blee, K. 2002. *Inside Organized Racism: Women in the Hate Movement*. Berkeley, CA: University of California Press.

Blue Mountain Working Group1994. "A call to defend democracy and pluralism." http://www.politicalresearch.org/1994/11/17/a-call-to-defend-democracy-and-pluralism/

Bookbinder, P. n.d. "The Weimar Republic: The fragility of democracy." Facing History and Ourselves. https://www.facinghistory.org/weimar-republic-fragility-democracy

Cabral, A. 1970. *Revolution in Guinea: Selected Texts*. New York, NY: Monthly Review Press.

Columbia Journalism Review. 2012. *Centennial collection, '1973: Exposing COINTELPRO, Carl Stern.'*http://centennial.journalism.columbia.edu/1973-exposing-cointelpro/

Dobratz, B.A. and S.L. Shanks-Meile. 1997. *"White Power, White Pride!" The White Separatist Movement in the United States*. New York, NY: Twayne Publishers.

Donner, F. 1980. *The Age of Surveillance: The Aims and Methods of America's Political Intelligence System*. New York, NY: Alfred Knopf.

Dyer, J. 1997. *Harvest of Rage: Why Oklahoma City is Only the Beginning*. Boulder, CO. Westview.

Federal Bureau of Investigation. n.d. "COINTELPRO: New Left." FBI records: The vault, https://vault.fbi.gov/cointel-pro; https://vault.fbi.gov/cointel-pro/new-left (accessed April 3, 2017).

Ferber, A., R. Grattet, V. Jenness, and J.F. Short. 1999. "Hate in America." Press briefing at the annual meeting of the American Sociological Association.

Flora, B. 2016. "50 Years/50 Collections: Gabrielle Simon Edgcomb and the Refugee Scholars of the HBCUs." Amistad Research Center, June 13. http://www.amistadresea rchcenter.org/single-post/2016/06/13/50-Years50-Collections-Gabrielle-Simon-Edg comb-and-the-Refugee-Scholars-of-the-HBCUs

Glick, B. 1989. *War at Home: Covert Action Against U.S. Activists and What We Can Do About It*. Boston, MA: South End Press.

Gupta, A. 2012. Making media, making trouble: The role of journalists in social movements. Panel. Left Forum 2012 Conference, New York, NY. http://www.buildingdemocracy.us/media/training/left-forum.html

Herek, G.M. and K.T. Berrill. 1990. *Violence Against Lesbians and Gay Men: Issues for Research, Practice, and Policy*. Newbury Park, CA: Sage.

Herek, G.M. and K. Berrill. 1992. *Hate Crimes: Understanding and Responding to Violence Against Lesbians and Gay Men*. Newbury Park, CA: Sage.

Himmelstein, J.L. 1992. *To the Right: The Transformation of American Conservatism.* Berkeley, CA: University of California Press.

Himmelstein, J.L. 1998. *"All but sleeping with the enemy: Studying the Radical Right up close."* Paper presented at the Annual Meeting of the American Sociological Association, San Francisco, August, https://www.academia.edu/17749280/

Jacobs, J.B. and K. Potter. 1998. *Hate Crimes: Criminal Law and Identity Politics.* Oxford: Oxford University Press.

Jakobsen, J.R. 1999. "Tolerating hate? Or hating tolerance? Why hate crimes legislation won't work." *Sojourner,* August, 9–11.

Jenness, V. and K. Broad. 1997. *Hate Crimes: New Social Movements and the Politics of Violence.* New York, NY: Aldine de Gruyter.

Jenness, V., A. Ferber, and R. Grattet. 2000. *"Hate in America: What do we know?"* Paper presented at the annual meeting of the American Sociological Association, Washington, DC.

Levin, J. and J. McDevitt. 1996. *Hate Crimes: The Rising Tide of Bigotry and Bloodshed.* New York, NY: Plenum Press.

McCarthy, J.D. and M.N. Zald. 1973. *The Trend of Social Movements in America: Professionalization and Resource Mobilization.* Morristown, NJ: General Learning Press,

Medsger, B. 2014. *The Burglary: The Discovery of J. Edgar Hoover's Secret FBI.* New York, NY: Alfred A. Knopf.

Polletta, F. 2002. *Freedom is an Endless Meeting: Democracy in American Social Movements.* Chicago IL: University of Chicago Press.

Public Eye Network. n.d. "The Public Eye Network." http://www.publiceyenetwork.us/

Public Eye Network. n.d. "Counterspies." http://www.publiceyenetwork.us/counterspies/

Right-Web. 1991. "Christian anti-communism crusade." http://rightweb.irc-online.org/christian_anti-communism_crusade/

Schlafly P. 1986. "A short history of E.R.A." Eagle Forum: Phyllis Schlafly Report, September, http://eagleforum.org/psr/1986/sept86/psrsep86.html

Sklar, H., C. Berlet, and A. Scher. 2013. *The Basics of Journalism as a Craft.*

Stern, K.S. 1996. *A Force upon the Plain: The American Militia Movement and the Politics of Hate.* New York, NY: Simon and Schuster.

Stern, K.S. 1996. "Militias and the Religious Right." *Freedom Writer,* Institute for First Amendment Studies, October 3–7.

Terrorist Information Project1976. *NCLC (National Caucus of Labor Committees): Brownshirts of the Seventies.* Arlington, VA: TIP.

Thomas, C.A. n.d. *Blood of Isaac,* Chapter 7: "The harvest." http://www.library.kent.edu/special-collections-and-archives/chapter-seven-harvest#_ftnref59

Wakin, D.J. 2012. "Rev. Sun Myung Moon, self-proclaimed Messiah who built religious movement, dies at 92." *New York Times,* September 12, http://www.nytimes.com/2012/09/03/world/asia/rev-sun-myung-moon-founder-of-unification-church-dies-at-92.html

Whitlock, K. and M. Bronski. 2015. *Considering Hate: Violence, Goodness, and Justice in American Culture and Politics.* Boston, MA: Beacon Press.

23

FROM DEMONIZATION TO NORMALIZATION

Reflecting on far right research

Aurelien Mondon and Aaron Winter

As much of the west is witnessing a resurgence of the far right and its mainstreaming (how once marginalized ideas creep, or are ushered, back into public discourse), the role played by researchers in the field is ever more vital to understand the phenomenon and inform wider society. Researching the far right and its performance and impact is essential as its resurgence has had very real consequences for the lives of millions, particularly those at the sharp end of their racism. However, while academic research goes on (or should) regardless of the status of such movements, it attracts greater attention and urgency when it is in the headlines and spotlight. This is made evident by the proliferation of media and academic publications on the far right that have come out in recent years. While these publications satisfy demand and a genuine urgency to address the phenomenon, they also participate, willingly or not, in shining a powerful light on the very issue: this creates both a degree of responsibility and risk.

In this context, researchers of the far right are often faced with two familiar criticisms. The first is that by focusing on and warning of the threat of extreme political movements and forces to society and democracy, researchers may be amplifying or 'hyping' their presence and significance and thereby ignoring, distracting from or legitimizing the more structural, institutional or mainstream forms of hate, inequality and scapegoating. The second, is that by focusing on such movements, researchers are giving them a platform through which these actors can express, explain and even legitimize and normalize their ideas. These are challenges which we have encountered and had to grapple with numerous times in our own research on the far right. Our work focuses primarily on far right and elite discourse (media, politicians and academics) and how racist ideas travel from the margins to the mainstream (having previously been marginalized) at particular historical junctures and through specific discursive processes and practices. This includes the ways in which the far right distances itself from or aligns with the

mainstream, and vice versa, as well as how academic, political and media discou...
facilitate these processes of mainstreaming and radicalization.

It is with this in mind that this chapter reflects on the challenges which arise from researching the far right. Our first section turns to the current media landscape which we believe has become an unavoidable part of research on such a polemical and extensively covered topic. To ensure that, as researchers, we avoid the many traps which come with such context, we then explore four interlinked areas which we believe are essential to consider before undertaking reflective and critical research on the far right. As way of concluding, we ask a series of questions, informed by our own experience and critique, for researchers to reflect on. Our intention is not to undertake an exhaustive study of the problems identified or negate different approaches, but think through and critically reflect on the politics of engaging with and analyzing the far right in research, the media and general public discourse.

Before we move to our analysis, it is worth noting that, while we use the term far right here, we do not claim that it is perfect, or that other terms could not be used to describe similar movements, parties and politics (for terminological discussions and debates see Mudde, 1997; 2007; Hainsworth, 2008; Mondon and Winter, 2020). Attempting to group different actors under a same name is a difficult and problematic exercise if it is not based on a clear and precise explanation as to what exactly these actors have in common. Yet, it is something we commonly see in the scholarship and even more so in the media, where terms are used interchangeably, regardless of the impact they may have. For the purpose of this chapter, we use 'far right' as it is broader and less loaded a term than 'extreme', 'radical' or 'populist' to cite but a few possibilities. Occasionally, we refer to the more violent and extreme sections of the broader movement and ideology as 'extreme right'. Our use of the terms encompasses both movements and parties, as well as ideas, found on the right of the mainstream right, something which we believe is well suited for the task at hand. It is also worth noting here that we do not consider the mainstream and far right as tangible and definite categories, and instead see them as contingent, evolving and with fuzzy borders: Today's mainstream could be tomorrow's far right and vice versa.

Researching the far right in the current media context

The current media landscape and the clickbait nature of news related to the far right have made it an inescapable element to any research in the field, whether as an object of study, an unavoidable actor or an external tool for dissemination of findings. It provides greater opportunities for researchers whose work may attract attention, but its uneven access can also shape the political agenda, both legitimizing and marginalizing certain ideas. Unsurprisingly, most of the coverage of the far right tends to be negative. The more extreme right groups such as the white supremacists in the USA or the EDL (English Defence League) in the UK receive almost unanimous condemnation across platforms. However, this does not prevent their figureheads such as Richard Spencer, Andrew Anglin or Tommy Robinson from receiving media attention and, in some cases, platforms. Similarly, and even though the attitude has changed over recent years and the more right-wing media have become increasingly less cautious, savvier far right politicians who have cultivated a more moderate image such as Nigel Farage or Marine Le Pen remain treated with a degree of suspicion or scorn by some sections of the media, despite again being given countless platforms and having their positions and ideas legitimized. This allows the media to use the far right for various purposes: appeal to a constituency or market the media believe shares or supports these ideas, appear politically balanced, and use them as foils and figures of mockery for the assertion of the rationality of the moderate, establishment parties.

While this coverage can provide an opportunity to expose both actors to criticism, scrutiny and even ridicule, it also lends them an incredibly powerful way to publicize their ideas, which until recently had been relegated to the margins of public discourse. In the US for example, it can be argued that the media platforming of the 'alt-right' played a role in their prominence and emboldening leading up to the Unite the Right rally in Charlottesville, which led to the murder of anti-fascist Heather Hoyer, and injuries to many more counter-protesters. Despite potential media blowbacks, it is also well known on the far right that any coverage is better than no coverage at all. For example, Jean-Marie Le Pen, the former leader of the French Front National, used to rely on damaging polemics about the Holocaust to stay prominent in the media between elections. While these revisionist comments led to prosecution and widespread condemnation even within the ranks of his party, they allowed him to appear in the media and provided him with a platform to share his broader politics. In the UK, the demise of the BNP (British National Party) and its clear association with the most extreme right opened the door to more polished far right politicians and facilitated the disproportionate presence of someone like Nigel Farage on the BBC and in the media in general as he was able to navigate the milieu better. As a result, and regardless of their treatment, it has become increasingly common for far right figures to occupy a prominent place on mainstream TV, and the media in general.

To cite but a few examples, Marine Le Pen was the first guest on the key political show on French television in the run-up to the 2017 presidential election. She was also given the possibility to write opinion pieces for the *New York Times* twice, something no other candidates were able to do. In recent years, Farage was one of the most invited guests on BBC's flagship political programme Question Time in recent years (Bennett, 2018), despite no longer being the leader of UKIP and failing to win a seat in the general election. He has since been given a radio show on LBC, as well as countless possibilities to access the print media through interviews or columns. Tommy Robinson was given a platform by various news outlets, including GMTV and Sky, following the Finsbury Park attack by fan Darren Osborne and the London Bridge attack by alleged IS terrorists (Mondon and Winter, 2017). Despite his role in stirring up and leading anti-Muslim hate and racism, he has become commonly referred to, euphemistically, as an 'anti-Islam activist' in *The Guardian*, as if it is a religion as opposed to people and communities, he and his followers target.

In the USA, one of the most frequent targets of such a criticism has been the *New York Times*. For Blake Seitz, the fact that the paper published two dozen articles on the alt-right and wider white nationalist movement between the November 2016 election and December 2016 gave 'an invaluable signal boost for the tiny coalition of racists' (Seitz, 2016). The newspaper also came in for a great deal of criticism for a profile of Tony Hovater, a white nationalist and Nazi sympathizer (Fausset, 2017). Many were critical of the focus on Hovater as a sympathetic figure, the guy next door, pictured doing his shopping like any other American. The NYT's defence of the charge of normalization was that it had become normal: 'The point of the story was not to normalise anything but to describe the degree to which hate and extremism have become far more normal in American life than many of us want to think' (Lacey, 2017). While we are not denying that these ideas deserve coverage, we are criticizing here the lack of reflection on the part of the NYT and their refusal to acknowledge their role in the process and responsibility in setting the agenda.

There has been a great deal of criticism about the media (including social media platforms), as well as politicians, providing a platform and 'normalizing' and legitimizing white nationalism, the far right and fascism, including by other journalists, representatives of monitoring organisations and academics (e.g. Dejene, 2018; Mondon and Winter, 2017; 2018; Liddle, 2018; Mudde, 2018; Pitcavage, 2017; Winter, 2019). Beyond issues of platforming described above, many have also denounced a type of analysis which legitimizes far right ideas about white victimization, nativism, the alleged threat from immigration and Muslims. In some cases, the latter also legitimizes the more mainstream far right, even when it is critical of the more extreme right seen as too illiberal and racist. Criticism is also directed at the construction of an 'objective' and 'balanced' two-sides argument or false equivalence (fascists vs anti-fascists and racists vs anti-racists) as if both are equal in their legitimacy, power and threat posed.

It is in this context of media hype around the far right, that the growing role of academics and representatives of monitoring groups in feeding the media expert analysis should make us reflect on how the far right is represented, researched, engaged with and analyzed by those seeking not just opinions and representation in news and editorial items, but wider research, knowledge and understanding.

The need for a critical appraisal of our standpoint as researchers of the far right

Publications on the far right (and related fields) have always been far more numerous than those on other parties or movements, and this, even before the recent resurgence. It is not surprising that they have increased dramatically in recent years, with many academics also switching their research interests to this fashionable hot topic. It is for this reason, we believe we must engage in serious reflective practice: despite the self-deprecation common amongst academics, our work matters and can have an impact, both good and bad.

We are not the first to engage in such a process and there have already been a number of reflective academic accounts of researching the far right, most notably James Aho's *This Thing of Darkness: A Sociology of the Enemy* (1994), Abby Ferber's *White Man Falling: Race, Gender, and White Supremacy* (1998), and more recently, contributor Kathleen Blee's *Understanding Racist Activism: Theory, Methods, and Research* (2018), as well as this book and its various contributions. Usually, this also occurs in introductions to studies and methodologies, and focuses on the rationale for the study and method chosen, and issues of access, ethics, power, trust, objectivity and politics when engaging with 'the enemy'. It has also appeared in work on methods in terms of politics and reflexivity (Lumsden and Winter, 2014). Responding and building on this, we think it is important to highlight and challenge researchers in terms of traps that are as much political as they are methodological and analytical, and beg the question, why are we researching this topic and how can we best avoid the pitfalls and risks associated with it?

To help navigate these issues, we outline below four interlinked areas which we believe are essential to consider before undertaking reflective and critical research on the far right: amplification, hype and legitimization; distraction and deflection; access, risk and representation; and bandwaggoning.

Amplification, hype and legitimization

Historically, there has been a good deal of criticisms of work on the far right for demonizing and pathologizing them, representing them as deviants and monsters (Berlet, 1996; Diamond, 1995; Ribuffo, 1983). The effect of which has been to distract from their overlap with the mainstream right, the existence of racism throughout society, and the wider structural factors for far right recruitment, mobilization and support. We argue against demonization and pathologizing of the far right that serves to separate them (and analysis) from the mainstream and wider structures and institutions of power, particularly in term of race and racism. However, we must also be aware that the representation of the far right in a legitimate analytical research context (i.e. journalistic or academic) can also serve to legitimize and normalize them and their ideas as part of the social-political discussion and worthy of mainstream representation as well as empathy or sympathy.

The issue of legitimization cannot be separated from that of amplification and hype, both fed by the current media and political landscape. These are issues that everyone researching the far right faces, and yet can be easily ignored under claims of objectivity and the belief, whether conscious or cynical that a researcher in social sciences stands above and beyond their topic of study. The very focus on the far right requires one to set out a particular category of the extreme and exceptional, which separates it from the mainstream and 'normal' and marks it out as an issue of specific concern. Increased focus on the far right is often a natural response to wider developments and concern such as electoral performance, but careless study in terms of framing and failure to consider the implications can amplify or hype its significance as a social phenomenon and threat beyond its real and practical impact. It can make them part of the social and political dialogue, or present them as a force, alternative and constituency whose prominence in public discourse can surpass its actual strength and reach. Such amplification can lead to better scrutiny of the far right due to a heightened sense of threat and to potential state repression of their activism. However, it may also facilitate the appropriation of their ideas by mainstream politicians and act as a distraction from problems elsewhere such as the limits or failures of liberal democracy, economic inequalities and institutional racism. An exaggerated focus on the far right in opposition to a rational and righteous centre may also lead to assuming that the centre is politically neutral and tangible, rather than its own form of politics and ideology, constructed and contingent, both historically and in comparison, to the 'extremes'. One of the other implications of this is that researchers may fail to account for their own standpoint and ideologically-loaded approach as their position is simply seen as objective rather than based in a hegemonic and thus contingent understanding of politics. This problem has been particularly well explored by Yannis Stavrakakis in the field of populism, where anti-populism has become a default position despite its clear ideological grounding (Stavrakakis, 2018).

Therefore, it is essential that the way the far right is researched, presented and understood addresses these issues, starting from the positionality of the researcher themselves, to how movements are represented, compared to what, under which hegemonic assumptions and for what impact. We argue that we must therefore always question our own approach and position, remain reflexive about our research and keep in mind that there is no such thing as pure objectivity in social sciences and that impartiality requires us to both acknowledge and challenge our own ideological pre-dispositions. In this sense, we are aligned with those proposing critical, reflexive and standpoint analysis in various fields and disciplines. Some questions can act as a useful starting point: Where do we stand regarding the far right? What do we think is the political centre or norm? What are the numbers we use in terms of vote or opinion data and how are they selected, what is omitted or obscured? What is the threat we discuss? Does the phenomenon deserve such attention? How does it relate to the mainstream? What is its function in discourse? How does the framing and analysis support or challenge representations and myths about the phenomenon?

In the field of political science in particular, the increased focus on psephology and the over- or mis-use of opinion polling to understand politics and society has played a key part in the misunderstanding and potential hyping of the far right in recent years. While most of the research conducted in the field is essential to provide us with a more fine-grained understanding of this crucial issue, we argue that some of the less critical kind has in fact contributed, whether consciously or not, to the legitimization of the far right. We have argued in our research that the reification of electoral and opinion data has obscured or ignored key parameters to understanding the current state of play in our political landscape (Mondon and Winter, 2019; 2020; Mondon 2015; 2017; Glynos and Mondon, 2016). The uncritical use of survey data provides only a limited and potentially biased under-standing of the situation if it often ignores issues of agenda-setting and wider pro-blems with sampling, accuracy and whether in fact there is such a thing as public opinion, and, if there is such a thing, how much it is shaped by the elite rather than the other way around. In recent years, we have also witnessed a tendency to rely overly on surveys at the expense of context, be it historical or political, and thus failing to account for structural and systemic issues. It is in this setting that dis-illusionment with liberal democracy, politicians, the media and experts has often been advertised as fueling the rise of the far right – the so-called revolt of the left-behind. However, a more careful analysis taking into account the role of abstention in particular, as well as the situation of other parties and the state of liberal democracy more generally, demonstrates that the rise of the far right is only a symptom of the crisis of our democracies.

This can be explored with even more precision with the oft-assumed role played by the working class in the rise of the far right (Mondon and Winter, 2019). While there is no denying that reconstructed far right parties have managed to appeal to a portion of this particular social category, we have argued that the inclusion of abstention, extremely widespread within lower social categories, the size of this section of the population and the oft-ignored diversity of the working class point again to a more complicated picture. Let's illustrate this with an example built loosely from existing data: imagine a headline stating uncritically that 30 per cent of the working class vote for a particular far right party. This claim may not be incorrect in terms of vote, and certainly worthy of note. However, should it be left at that, it would suggest to most readers/viewers/listeners that a third of the working class supports the far right. This would not only be incorrect, but in fact misleading. In our hypothetical case, if, as is can indeed be the case, two thirds of the working class abstain, then this would mean that 'only' 10 per cent of the working class actually voted for the far right – a very different headline. Of course, this is not to say that abstainers would not vote for the far right if they were forced to, but the simple fact is they did not.

These narratives, and their reflection in the media, also often ignore the size of the working class and the difficulties in defining it properly and precisely. For example, research has shown that in the case of the FN, UKIP and Trump, it is not the poorest sections of the working class which turn to the far right, but rather the wealthier ones, which could be seen as closer to the lower middle class typically attracted to fascism in the interwar period. Furthermore, even if in terms of pro-portions, the working class that votes provides a high percentage of far right voters, the size of this section of the population compared to others often leads to a much more nuanced picture where the actual number of voters comes predominantly from better-off classes (for more detail, see Mondon and Winter, 2019; 2020).

Such careless misreading of data, often added to a lack of historical knowledge of the topic, has led to a dual process where the far right has seen itself legitimized as the voice of the downtrodden, representing the symbolic working class, while the working class, and by extension the people, has become demonized and racialized in the process. This racialization took place on the assumption that the working class is essentially white despite being far more diverse than other classes.

Distraction and deflection

As scholars in the social sciences, our main duty is to research, analyze and explain social phenomena. While our research can focus on more precise fields such as the far right and racism, it is essential to remember that these develop, thrive and/or recede in a wider context and that their popularity or ignominy is dictated as much by their proponents than by their opponents, and perhaps more importantly by the social, economic and political contexts in which they exist. Power relationships and hegemony are thus essential aspects to take into account. Looking at the far right in a vacuum, out of historical and political context, or through a post-race lens that sees them as a historical monstrosity, fringe phenomenon and the sole site of racism, can deflect from mainstream, structural and institutional racisms (Mondon and Winter, 2020; Winter, 2018). This is not always intentional, and can be an effect or product of defining the boundaries of one's topic or research focus. It is also implicit in the label, construction or recognition of the 'extreme' or 'far' as distant or distinct, out of place and a threat to the mainstream in post war liberal democracies. By acknowledging the wider context, systemic trends appear and the far right becomes only one cog in a vast system of oppression, discrimination and insecurities, a symptom rather than the disease (or cure) itself.

As already discussed, much work has been dedicated recently to the so-called 'left behind' and 'white working class' turning to the far right (see Mondon and Winter, 2019). This has not only allowed some scholars to find an easy explanation for the resurgence of the far right, but it has also served as a reassuring mechanism to middle and upper-class liberals, inasmuch as they were not to blame for the rise of racism since the poor were (Glynos and Mondon, 2016; Mondon and Winter, 2020). This has ignored the reality of the far right vote which is spread across socio-economic boundaries contrary to what prominent narratives would suggest. It has also allowed for the issue to become about skewed socio-economic and class concerns as opposed to racism, which is not only limited to the far right, but also rendered a symptom as opposed to a part of the structuring of society intersecting with class. Related to this false race–class divide, it has ignored that the 'white working class' is a social construct which has largely served this analytical and political purpose, and that, if anything, the working class should be seen as the most diverse section of our society. Yet, these simplistic narratives have thrown blame upon less privileged, and less audible, sections of our population or rendered them invisible (ethnic and racial minority working class), while legitimizing the far right as the voice of 'the people' qua downtrodden rather than the defenders of the elite-run, anti-egalitarian and reactionary order it is. It is thus essential that researchers of the far right remain conscious of what is at play beyond the far right itself, and do not fail to see the forest for the trees. While the far right is certainly worthy of study, it must be placed into a context, taking into account social, economic and historical elements.

Focus on and amplification of the far right can help distract our attention from the mainstream, be it political parties, ideologies and more insidious structural and institutional racisms that can fuel the far right or be rendered more acceptable, legitimate or invisible by being opposed to them. In terms of party politics, the far right can be useful to deflect attention away from the racism and xenophobia present within mainstream parties as they are able to point to a more extreme version. Coupled with the amplification of the far right, this can also force the mainstream right (and sometimes left) to address this 'rise' as an electoral threat to contend with and popular demands to respond to (Brown, Mondon, and Winter, forthcoming). This in turn may lead to a rightward turn and the legitimization of certain discourses and policies by mainstream politicians, leading in turn to the normalization of the far right (see Mondon, 2013).

There is also the question of whether journalists and scholars working on the far right may themselves feed into this hegemonic frame that amplifies and exposes the far right to affirm the hegemony of liberal democracy by demonizing those outside the system as 'extremists', as exemplified by the work of Lipset (1955) and Lipset and Raab (1970; see critiques by Berlet, 1996; Glynos and Mondon, 2016; Mondon and Winter, 2020; Ribuffo, 1983). In Lipset's (1955) original work on the 'radical right', where he coined the term, the very conceptualization, definition and positioning of the phenomenon or 'problem' serves by intention or effect as a reification and defence of the rational centre or moderates against the 'radicals' on the right who are defined as such and pose a threat not because of their ideas, which they may share with the mainstream (e.g. racism), but adherence to established democratic procedures (see Berlet, 1996; Mondon and Winter, 2020).

A further distraction can be found regarding the place of racism in research on the far right. On the one hand, work on the far right can treat racism as a characteristic in a taxonomy and see liberal democracy, as opposed to racialized people, as the main target and threat. On the other hand, work on the far right can too easily feed the so-called 'post-racial' narrative (Goldberg, 2016; Lentin, 2012; Mondon and Winter, 2020; Winter, 2018) that constructs such movements as the primary site of racism that can be denounced as marginal and unacceptable and rejected from polite, tolerant, mainstream society and politics. An effect of this is both a false separation between the far right and the mainstream, and a distraction from less overt, structural and institutionalized racisms, what Eduardo Bonilla-Silva (2006) refers to as 'racism without racists'. Moreover, by making extremists the issue, it can be seen to sit too comfortably with terrorism and countering violent extremism (CVE) studies, which have played a role in exacerbating Islamophobia or anti-Muslim racism (Winter, 2015; 2018).

Access, risk and representation

It is unavoidable that research and analysis on the far right presents their words, ideas and stories, as well as explanations, justifications and defences. However, this necessitates researchers to face some difficult questions: What are the potential risks of giving such ideas air? When should individuals be given a platform? And how are these framed and who will they be read by?

It is often assumed that the reader will be another researcher who may, at worst, be offended by the ideas and politics, which may lead to ignoring that it might in fact reach potential or actual targets. This has been exacerbated in recent years with the increased emphasis on engagement and empathetic work in ethnography as well as quantitative and more theoretical research. In some cases, it is a response to demonization by the mainstream and calls for them to be heard. It may also be because it is assumed that such movements are not only marginalized as a movement, but made up of marginalized peoples (the so-called 'left behind') who are socio-economically disenfranchised or cut off from the mainstream, but speak to issues and phenomena we need to hear, thus framing and representing far right ideas as politically and sociologically legitimate, even if only as a symptom, and/or enabling that reception or use by the media and the political class by effect. It is also important to note how this may affect researchers and readers, as well as wider communities on the sharp end. To be clear, many of such studies have shed essential light on the ideas and practices of the far right. However, there remains a real risk that unreflective practice may not only amplify and distract, but obscure the harm done to those targeted by the far right as a personalized focus is placed on the actors rather than their victims or actions as part of structural issues. There is an added dimension to consider when dealing with ethnographic research and its representation: researchers who belong to target groups and do not share a privileged identity with the activists may not get the same access and, if they do, may experience added risk. It is thus essential to carefully consider how much space voices of hate are given, what the purpose is and what the impact may be.

Bandwaggonism

With the neoliberalization of higher education and research, fads have played an increasingly important role in academia as researchers battle for citations, impact and research funding. Most recently, Kaltwasser et al. (2017) have shown in their *Oxford Handbook of Populism* how much research has grown in this particular subfield. Researching the far right has always been a popular field, particularly when considering that their electoral standing remained marginal until recently. Obviously, we are not arguing here that it should not be researched or that colleagues and prospective PhD candidates should be put off from studying it. We simply warn against falling for buzzwords without proper engagement with the wider field and clear intent to advance knowledge. Any reviewer in the field will have come across articles submitted whereby the authors demonstrate a very limited knowledge of the field, despite the wealth of literature on the topic. In the most egregious cases, buzzwords such as 'populism' are added to the title of articles to generate attention, while the concept is hardly discussed or even nowhere to be found in the entire body of the article.

Again, we are not arguing against newcomers, but against poor academic practice, often undertaken by senior colleagues, which not only does no due diligence to the field but also crowds it with poor research, risking obscuring better research by junior scholars as gatekeeping mechanisms make it easier for bad research from senior academics to be published, cited and shared. Building on a previous point, this has been somewhat reinforced by the advent of psephology and the multiplication of articles based on surveys with little to no regard for context, discourse and politics. To be clear and to reiterate, we are certainly not against newcomers to the field or deny that psephology has a place in providing different ways to understand the phenomenon and sharpen our analysis. However, we argue that this must be done thoroughly, through a careful literature review and in-depth engagement with the field and issues, including racism, across disciplines and methods and with real intent to advance knowledge.

Concluding reflections: Going forward

This chapter is very much based on our own subjective practice and experience of our field and it may not match that of colleagues. However, we believe that our demands for a critical and scholarly approach to the field are hardly radical and in fact in line with much of the literature on methods in the field, and on reflective practice in particular. We believe that these have helped us throughout our careers, and while we are certainly not immune from traps, careful consideration of power relationships and the impact of our research has led us to weigh more carefully not only our methods and findings but also the way we go about doing research more generally. Therefore, we hope that academic researchers, monitoring groups and journalists will be motivated to reflect upon their practice, weigh the impact of their research and carefully engage with the dangers of mainstreaming, legitimizing and normalizing the far right. As such, the following considerations should be core to any prospective research in the field: Does our research take into account the historical, geographical and political context? Does it examine the far right and mainstream as contingent categories/phenomena, whose meaning, strategies and political positioning are fluid and adaptable to context and circumstances? Does our research promote or platform the far right, and if so, does it legitimize or mainstream racist discourses and parties rather than illuminate the situation and help combat these politics? And finally, does our research focus on individuals without dealing with issues, on racists without engaging with racism, and can this be at the expense of more structural, systemic analysis?

References

Aho, J. 1994. *This Thing of Darkness: A Sociology of the Enemy*. Seattle, WA: University of Washington Press.

Bennett, O. 2018. "UKIP appeared on a quarter of all Question Time shows since May 2010, Huff Post UK Reveals." *Huffington Post*, 16 February.https://www.huffingtonpost.co.uk/entry/question-time-ukip-nigel-farage_uk_58d95295e4b03787d35ae186 [accessed 4 June 2019].

Berlet, C. 1996. "Three models for analyzing conspiracist mass movements of the right." In *Conspiracies: Real Grievances, Paranoia, and Mass Movements*, edited by E. Ward. Seattle, WA: Peanut Butter Publishing.

Blee, K. 2018. *Understanding Racist Activism: Theory, Methods, Research*. Abingdon: Routledge.

Bonilla-Silva, E. 2006. *Racism Without Racists: Color-Blind Racism and the Persistence of Racial Inequality in the United States* (2nd edition). Oxford: Rowman & Littlefield. (

Brown, K., A. Mondon, and A. Winter. Forthcoming. "The far right, the mainstream and mainstreaming: Towards a heuristic framework."

Dejene, D. 2018. "Covering the new hate." *Ryerson Review of Journalism*, 20 June.http://rrj.ca/covering-the-new-hate/ [accessed 4 June 2019].

Diamond, S. 1995. *Roads to Dominion: Right-Wing Movements and Political Power in the United States*. New York, NY: Guilford.

Fausset, R. 2017. "A voice of hate in America's Heartland." *New York Times*, 25 November. https://www.nytimes.com/2017/11/25/us/ohio-hovater-white-nationalist.html [accessed 4 June 2019].

Ferber, A.L. 1998. *White Man Falling: Race, Gender, and White Supremacy*. Oxford: Rowman & Littlefield.

Glynos, J. and A. Mondon. 2016. "The political logic of populist hype: The case of right wing populism's 'meteoric rise' and its relation to the status quo." *Populismus Working Paper Series No. 4*.

Goldberg, D.T. 2016. *Are We All Postracial Yet?*Oxford: Polity Press.

Kaltwasser, C., Taggart, P., Espejo, P. O., and P. Ostiguy. (eds). 2017. *The Oxford Handbook of Populism*. Oxford: Oxford University Press.

Lacey, M. 2017. "Readers accuse us of normalizing a Nazi Sympathizer; we respond." *New York Times*, 26 November 2017. https://www.nytimes.com/2017/11/26/reader-center/readers-accuse-us-of-normalizing-a-nazi-sympathizer-we-respond.html [accessed 4 June 2019].

Lentin, A. 2012. "Post-race, post politics: The paradoxical rise of culture after multiculturalism." *Ethnic and Racial Studies*, 37(8): 1268–1285.

Liddle, C. 2018. "Media complicit in normalizing fascism." *Eureka Street*, 12 August.https://www.eurekastreet.com.au/article.aspx?aeid=56166 [accessed 4 June 2019].

Lipset, S.M. 1955. "The sources of the radical right". In *The New American Right*, edited by D. Bell. New York, NY: Criterion.

Lipset, S.M. and E. Raab. 1970. *The Politics of Unreason: Right-Wing Extremism in America, 1790–1970*. New York, NY: Harper and Row.

Lumsden, K. and A. Winter. (eds). 2014. *Reflexivity in Criminological Research: Experiences with the Powerful and the Powerless*. London: Palgrave.

Mondon, A. 2013. *A Populist Hegemony? Mainstreaming the Extreme Right in France and Australia*. Farnham: Ashgate.

Mondon, A. 2015. "Populism, the people and the illusion of democracy: The Front National and UKIP in a comparative context." *French Politics*, 13(2): 141–156.

Mondon, A. 2017. "Limiting democratic horizons to a nationalist reaction: populism, the radical right and the working class." *Javnost/The Public: Journal of the European Institute for Communication and Culture*, 24(3): 355–374.

Mondon, A. and A. Winter. 2017. "Normalized hate." *Jacobin*. https://jacobinmag.com/2017/08/islamophobia-racism-uk-far-right [accessed 4 June 2019].

Mondon, A. and A. Winter. 2019. "Whiteness, Populism and the racialization of the working-class in the United Kingdom and the United States." *Identities Global Studies in Culture and Power*, 26(5); 510–528.

Mondon, A. and A. Winter. 2020. *Reactionary Democracy: How Racism and the Populist Far Right Became Mainstream*. London: Verso.

Mudde, C. 1997. *The Extreme Right Party Family: An Ideological Approach*. PhD Thesis, Department of Politics, Leiden University.

Mudde, C. 2007. *Populist Radical Right Parties in Europe*. Cambridge: Cambridge University Press.

Mudde, C. 2018. "The far right hails 'Unite the Right' a success. Its legacy says otherwise." *The Guardian*, 10 August 2018. https://www.theguardian.com/commentisfree/2018/aug/10/unite-the-right-rally-alt-right-demise?CMP=share_btn_tw [accessed 4 June 2019].

Pitcavage, M. 2017. "10 tips for journalists newly covering extremists." *Anti-Defamation League*, 27 November 2017. https://www.adl.org/blog/10-tips-for-journalists-newly-covering-extremists [accessed 4 June 2019].

Ribuffo, L. 1983. *The Old Christian Right: The Protestant Far Right from the Great Depression to the Cold War*. Philadelphia, PA: Temple University Press.

Seitz, B. 2016. "New York Times gives valuable publicity to white nationalism." *Washington Free Beacon*, 21 December 2016. https://freebeacon.com/culture/new-york-times-gives-valuable-publicity-white-nationalism/ [accessed 4 June 2019].

Stavrakakis, Y. 2018. "Populism, anti-Populism and democracy", *Political Insight*, 9(3), 33–35.

Winter, A. 2015. "White terror and the racialization of violence." *Open Democracy*, 8 December 2015. https://www.opendemocracy.net/aaron-winter/white-terror-racism-and-racialization-of-violence [accessed 4 June 2019].

Winter, A. 2018. "The Klan is history: A historical perspective on the revival of the far-right in 'post-racial' America". In *Historical Perspectives on Organized Crime and Terrorism*, edited by J. Morrison, A. Silke, J. Windle, and A. Winter. Abingdon: Routledge.

Winter, A. 2019. "Online hate: From the far-right to the 'alt-right', and from the margins to the mainstream". In *Online Othering: Exploring Violence and Discrimination on the Web*, edited by E. Harmer and K. Lumsden. London: Palgrave.

INDEX